Les saints et leur culte
en Europe centrale au Moyen Âge

HAGIOLOGIA

Études sur la sainteté et l'hagiographie – Studies on Sanctity and Hagiography

Volume 13

Comité de Rédaction – Editorial Board

HAGIOLOGIA

Gordon Blennemann   Jeroen Deploige   Stefanos Efthymiadis
Stéphane Gioanni   Anne-Marie Helvétius

BREPOLS PUBLISHERS

2017

Les saints et leur culte
en Europe centrale au Moyen Âge
(XIe-début du XVIe siècle)

Études réunies par
Marie-Madeleine de Cevins et Olivier Marin

BREPOLS

©2017, Brepols Publishers n.v., Turnhout, Belgium

All rights reserved. No part of this publication may be reproduced, stored in a retrieval system, or transmitted, in any form or by any means, electronic, mechanical, photocopying, recording, or otherwise, without the prior permission of the publisher.

D/2017/0095/176
ISBN 978-2-503-57548-3
DOI 10.1484/M.HAG-EB.5.113207

Printed in the EU on acid-free paper.

Introduction

Olivier MARIN
(*Paris*)

Semper nova et vetera. Pour apprécier équitablement les articles de ce volume, il convient tout d'abord de les situer dans une perspective historiographique. Notre réflexion, en effet, n'est pas partie de rien. Elle a pris pour pierre de touche la thèse pionnière d'André Vauchez, intitulée *La sainteté en Occident aux derniers siècles du Moyen Âge d'après les procès de canonisation et les documents hagiographiques.* Publié pour la première fois il y a trente-cinq ans, ce grand livre a sonné le réveil des études hagiologiques dans le monde francophone et au-delà. L'un de ses principaux mérites a été d'esquisser une modélisation de la sainteté à l'échelle de toute la Chrétienté latine, sous la forme d'une géographie différentielle des cultes. L'historien français y oppose deux Europe. La première, qui regroupe l'Italie et l'Angleterre, mais à laquelle se rattachent aussi, quoique dans une moindre mesure, la France, l'Allemagne du Sud et la Scandinavie, donne le ton. Une ouverture résolue aux saints « modernes », comprenons aux saints proches dans le temps, voire contemporains, la caractérise. Conséquence de cette « effervescence créatrice » par laquelle les dévots préfèrent s'adresser à des personnages morts récemment en odeur de sainteté, fussent-ils de simples laïcs, le sanctoral ne cesse dans ces contrées de s'enrichir et de se renouveler. S'en distinguent des régions où la stabilité l'emporte. Là, les saints anciens, généralement les confesseurs des premiers temps de la christianisation, demeurent des valeurs sûres, à l'ombre desquelles leurs cadets ne parviennent que très difficilement à se tailler une place. Eu égard à sa faible perméabilité au changement, cette seconde aire reçoit le qualificatif de « régions froides » de la sainteté. Y voisinent les zones intérieures et atlantiques de la péninsule Ibérique, l'Allemagne du Nord et l'Europe centrale, qu'André Vauchez appelle, dans le langage de l'époque qui était encore celui de la Guerre froide, « Europe de l'Est »[1].

---

[1] Les références données correspondent à la première édition, publiée en 1981 dans la Bibliothèque des Écoles françaises d'Athènes et de Rome, t. 141, ici p. 153-158.

*Les saints et leur culte en Europe centrale au Moyen Âge (XI*ᵉ*-début du XVI*ᵉ *siècle)*, éd. par Marie-Madeleine de CEVINS et Olivier MARIN, Turnhout, 2017 (*Hagiologia*, 13), p. 1-28.

Cette appréciation qualitative trouve une confirmation statistique dans la mise en série des procès de canonisation ouverts par la Curie entre 1198 et 1431. Durant cette période, l'Europe centrale n'est entrée que pour 5,6 % du total, soit très loin derrière le trio de tête que forment l'Italie (31 %), la France (23,9 %) et l'Angleterre (19,7 %). Comment interpréter cette sous-représentation ? On pourrait être tenté d'incriminer l'indifférence de la papauté à l'égard de contrées qu'elle aurait perçues, à tort ou à raison, comme périphériques. Pour le savoir, André Vauchez confronte ces chiffres avec ceux des demandes d'instruction de procès demeurées sans suite. Or, la part de l'Europe centrale y demeure faible, de l'ordre de 6 % à nouveau, comme si ces Églises n'avaient pas éprouvé le besoin d'étoffer leur sanctoral primitif. Cette moyenne, il est vrai, dissimule une évolution notable. Alors que Rome avait, au XIIIe siècle, honoré la plupart des demandes émanant des royaumes polonais, hongrois et tchèque, passé 1304, elle leur opposa une fin de non-recevoir systématique. Mais André Vauchez montre, chiffres à l'appui, que cette réaction de fermeture fut générale et affecta l'ensemble de la Chrétienté, y compris l'Italie[2]. Même si la distance, d'ordre à la fois géographique et politique, entre le centre romain (ou avignonnais) et les Églises particulières d'Europe centrale a pu jouer en y induisant un réflexe d'autocensure, elle ne semble donc pas avoir été déterminante. Et l'historien français d'en conclure que les disparités relevées au sein de la Chrétienté latine révèlent moins une inégalité de traitement de la part de la papauté qu'une pression variable des clergés et des fidèles locaux en faveur du renouvellement des cultes.

Restait à expliquer cet attachement persistant des « régions froides » à des saints anciens et éprouvés. André Vauchez se risque à formuler quelques hypothèses : il allègue en priorité le faible degré d'urbanisation et le relatif enclavement qui seraient, selon lui, le lot commun à tous ces espaces ; dans le domaine ecclésiastique, il invoque la moindre influence qu'y auraient exercée les ordres mendiants, que l'on sait grands pourvoyeurs de saints nouveaux. Conscient cependant que ces facteurs explicatifs demeurent insuffisants, il confie *mezza voce* : « Seule une étude régionale très fine, prenant en considération les structures économiques et sociales, mais aussi l'histoire des institutions ecclésiastiques et les rapports de force entre les différents éléments du clergé, pourrait permettre d'expliquer la carte du culte des saints médiévaux[3]. »

---

[2] *Ibid.*, p. 318-323, notamment les tableaux XXIV et XXVI.
[3] *Ibid.*, p. 157.

INTRODUCTION

Il nous a semblé que cette piste entrouverte méritait qu'on la poursuive, maintenant que la chute du rideau de fer a permis à l'hagiologie centre-européenne de sortir de la léthargie forcée qui était la sienne au temps où écrivait André Vauchez[4]. À cet effet, Marie-Madeleine de Cevins et moi-même avons réuni, au cours de trois journées d'étude qui se sont tenues successivement dans les universités de Rennes 2 (1er février 2013 et 7 février 2014) et de Paris Nord-Sorbonne Cité (14 novembre 2014), une quinzaine d'artisans de ce renouveau, pour la plupart issus de ces pays mêmes. Ces manifestations n'auraient pas vu le jour sans le soutien financier, logistique et humain des institutions suivantes : l'Institut Universitaire de France, l'Université Rennes 2 et le Centre de Recherches Historiques de l'Ouest (CNRS UMR 6258) devenu entretemps l'EA TEMPORA, de même que l'Université de Paris Nord-Sorbonne Cité et le Laboratoire Pléiade (EA 7338). Les éditeurs de ce livre leur en sont reconnaissants.

Dans notre esprit, il ne s'agissait pas de livrer une synthèse parfaitement lisse et cohérente, mais plutôt de proposer un état des lieux de la recherche, en traduisant les interrogations qui nous taraudent et qui n'ont pas encore trouvé de réponse commune. Trois principaux problèmes ont retenu notre attention.

La première partie, consacrée aux saints anciens et modernes, revisite la distinction opérée par André Vauchez, afin de la mettre à l'épreuve. Nous sommes partis du constat statistique de sa thèse, qui demeure un acquis irremplaçable. Tout au plus regrettera-t-on que l'historien ait clos son enquête à la date de 1431, la fin du pontificat de Martin V et la mort de Jeanne d'Arc n'ayant qu'une pertinence très relative pour notre objet. Mais mener l'analyse jusqu'à la Réformation ne changerait guère la donne. Jusqu'à plus ample informé, les demandes d'ouverture de procès en canonisation émanant au cours de cette période de la Pologne-Lituanie ou de la Hongrie demeurèrent rares et n'aboutirent que plus exceptionnellement encore[5]. Il est même très

---

[4] Comme le prouve la publication des bilans dus à G. KLANICZAY et E. MADAS, « La Hongrie », dans *Corpus christianorum. Hagiographies*, II, éd. G. PHILIPPART, Turnhout, 1996, p. 103-160, et à T. DUNIN-WĄSOWICZ, « L'hagiographie polonaise entre XIe et XVIe siècles », *ibid.*, III, 2001, p. 179-202. Sur la Bohême, voir la synthèse : P. KUBÍN, *Sedm přemyslovských kultů*, Prague, 2011. On trouvera une récente mise en perspective de ces renouvellements sous la plume de G. KLANICZAY, « The Cult of the Saints in recent historiographies of Central Europe », *Rivista di storia del cristianesimo*, 9 (2012), p. 461-484.
[5] La Bohême constitue un cas à part, car la révolution hussite ayant provoqué la vacance du siège archiépiscopal et ruiné les ordres religieux, les institutions susceptibles de promouvoir efficacement la mémoire des saints locaux y faisaient défaut. Des prélats et des barons tchèques purent malgré tout s'associer à la demande de canonisation de l'évêque de Meissen saint Benno. Voir Ch. VOLKMAR, *Die Heiligenerhebung Bennos von Meissen (1523/4)*.

improbable que le procès en canonisation de saint Casimir ait abouti dès 1521, comme on l'a répété jusqu'à une date récente[6]. Si significatives soient-elles, ces démarches ne semblent pas témoigner, à elles seules, d'un véritable retournement en faveur des saints modernes.

En revanche, il est loisible de discuter l'appareil conceptuel mobilisé pour rendre compte des éventuelles spécificités centre-européennes. « Régions froides » de la sainteté : l'expression employée par André Vauchez porte l'empreinte de l'anthropologie structurale de Claude Lévi-Strauss, dont elle rappelle la fameuse distinction entre « sociétés froides » et « sociétés chaudes ». C'est suggérer que, comme celles-là, les zones réputées réfractaires à la sainteté moderne, tout en étant soumises à l'histoire, auraient été portées à résister aux modifications de leur structure et de leurs équilibres internes. Le recours à un tel modèle a, entre autres avantages, celui d'attirer l'attention sur les effets déstabilisateurs que recèle toute introduction de nouveaux cultes. Il présente néanmoins le risque de durcir l'opposition entre deux systèmes autorégulateurs prétendument étrangers l'un à l'autre et de sous-estimer les capacités de mise à jour et de recomposition des sociétés dites froides[7].

De manière plus concrète, on objectera que vénérer des saints anciens ne constitue pas nécessairement un indice d'archaïsme. Loin de se figer dans des formes pérennes, un culte ancestral n'est pas à l'abri de réajustements plus ou moins drastiques, qui visent à l'accorder aux nouvelles sensibilités du temps. Les innombrables réécritures hagiographiques que le Moyen Âge, en Europe centrale comme ailleurs, s'est plu à composer sont un terrain privilégié pour observer ce genre de réactualisations. Qu'il suffise ici de citer le cas de saint Venceslas : comme l'a bien montré Zdeněk Uhlíř, la légende *Oriente iam sole* fut retouchée autour de 1370 à Roudnice et réinterprétée dans le sens de la nouvelle piété eucharistique qui venait d'éclore en Bohême[8]. À quoi bon alors recourir à de nouveaux intercesseurs, si les anciens avaient, comme le disait plaisamment Alain de Lille des autorités textuelles, un « nez de cire » assez

---

Spätmittelalterliche Frömmigkeit, landesherrliche Kirchenpolitik und reformatorische Kritik im albertinischen Sachsen in der frühen Reformationszeit, Münster, 2002, notamment p. 96.

[6] La bulle de canonisation aurait, avancèrent ensuite les Lituaniens, disparu lors du sac de Rome. L'argument porta, puisque Rome confirma cette pseudo-canonisation en 1602. Voir H. D. WOJTYSKA, « Początki kultu i procesy kanonizacyjne św. Kazimierza », *Analecta Cracoviensia*, 16 (1984), p. 187-231.

[7] Cl. LÉVI-STRAUSS, *Anthropologie structurale*, Paris, 1971, p. 40 et suiv., et sa critique par G. BALANDIER, « Tradition, conformité, historicité », dans *L'Autre et l'Ailleurs. Hommages à Roger Bastide*, Paris, 1976, p. 15-38.

[8] Zd. UHLÍŘ, *Literární prameny svatováclavského kultu a úcty v vrcholném a pozdním středověku*, Prague, 1996, p. 29-30.

malléable pour pouvoir être tourné en divers sens ? À ce titre, même une dévotion en apparence la plus immobile est, elle aussi, susceptible de devenir le témoin ou le vecteur d'une discrète, mais réelle, modernisation des sensibilités religieuses.

Il faut donc éviter de s'enfermer dans une opposition binaire entre les deux pôles de l'ancien et du moderne. Comme le laisse entendre le sous-titre « Permanences, réinventions, concurrences » que nous avons retenu pour cette partie, les cas de figure sont variés, tant l'imbrication et la superposition priment. Il est en réalité rarissime qu'un nouveau saint remplace purement et simplement un ancien. À une substitution potentiellement sacrilège, le Moyen Âge préférait une logique cumulative, qui associait les intercesseurs de manière hiérarchisée. C'est ainsi que des saints reconnus depuis longtemps étaient appelés à la rescousse pour en patronner un nouveau, avec lequel ils partageaient un même nom, une même affiliation religieuse, un même charisme. Typique est la vision rapportée par la *Vita* de saint Hyacinthe, selon laquelle la Vierge Marie en personne lui aurait confirmé que ses prières seraient toutes exaucées : en ce début du XIVe siècle, le culte du dominicain cracovien était encore balbutiant, et il ne fallait pas moins que l'intervention de la Mère de Dieu pour balayer les possibles résistances[9]. D'où de constants effets de duplication et de mimétisme entre les différentes générations de saints, mais aussi de complémentarité, dans un sens comme dans l'autre. Car il se rencontre aussi des cultes anciens réinventés ou, à tout le moins, réactivés au contact de figures hagiographiques plus récentes. À l'automne du Moyen Âge, saint Jean l'Aumônier avait tout d'un culte démodé. Pourtant, au tournant des XVe et XVIe siècles, il connut un coup de jeune inattendu à Cracovie, à la faveur de la translation de ses reliques. La figure de l'antique patriarche d'Alexandrie en vint alors à satisfaire tant les goûts orientalisants des élites humanistes que l'attirance des rois Jagellons pour un modèle d'action charitable de type mendiant[10].

Ces nuances mises à part, revenons à la question du phénomène constaté par André Vauchez. Pour le dire en bref, l'indifférence de l'Europe centrale à l'égard de la sainteté moderne n'est-elle pas, au moins pour partie, un effet de sources ? Car se focaliser sur les procès de canonisation laisse de côté les innombrables cultes locaux qui n'ont jamais fait l'objet au Moyen Âge de la

---

[9] *De vita et miraculis sancti Iacchonis (Hyacinthi) Ordinis Fratrum Praedicatorum auctore Stanislao lectore Cracoviensi eiusdem ordinis*, éd. L. ĆWIKLIŃSKI, Lwów, 1884, repr. Varsovie, 1961 (Monumenta Poloniae Historica, 4), cap. 5 « Quomodo beata Virgo apparuit sancto Iazechoni in oracione vigilanti », p. 849-850.
[10] J. KUBIENEC, « The Office of St John the Almsgiver in Cracow », *Musica Iagellonica*, 4 (2007), p. 5-18.

moindre enquête officielle, comme André Vauchez en est lui-même le premier conscient[11]. Il est vrai que les traces (une légende, un recueil de miracles, quelques images, éventuellement une mention plus ou moins fugace dans les chroniques) en sont le plus souvent ténues. On connaît bien, cependant, le cas des Hussites et la manière dont ils procédèrent à la canonisation « sauvage » de leurs héros. Le 6 juillet, jour anniversaire de la mort de Jean Hus sur le bûcher à Constance, en 1415, devint rapidement la fête du héros éponyme de la révolution, ainsi que de tous les martyrs de la cause du calice ; le ciel bohémien se peupla ainsi d'une nuée de nouveaux venus, qui côtoyèrent, voire supplantèrent, les saints des Xe et XIe siècles. De ce point de vue, la Bohême hussite est tout le contraire d'une « région froide » de la sainteté et n'a rien à envier à la créativité de l'Italie dans ce domaine, même si les critères de la sanctification y demeurèrent plus cléricaux et plus masculins, donc plus traditionnels en un sens, que ceux retenus par la piété méditerranéenne[12].

Cas limite, dira-t-on, qui ne concerne que des « hérétiques » mis au ban de la Chrétienté. Soit. Certains indices laissent à penser néanmoins que des milieux parfaitement orthodoxes n'étaient pas restés insensibles à cette exigence de mise à jour du sanctoral. Une gerbe de *Vitae* composées à la fin du XIVe siècle dans les pays tchèques en l'honneur d'évêques (Ernest de Pardubice, Jean de Jenštejn) et de prédicateurs (Milíč de Kroměříž) morts en odeur de sainteté le suggère. Le plus remarquable ici n'est pas seulement que la piété ait mis en avant des personnages contemporains, mais qu'elle l'ait revendiqué haut et fort. Les hagiographes déployèrent alors un véritable plaidoyer en faveur d'une plus grande proximité des saints, celle-ci étant vue comme la condition *sine qua non* pour que les fidèles se sentent appelés à les imiter. Cette double requête de familiarité et d'exemplarité, qui prend parfois, comme chez Matthias de Janov, des accents polémiques[13], est ainsi traduite sous la plume du biographe de Jean de Jenštejn, le chanoine régulier Pierre Clarificator :

---

[11] *La sainteté en Occident, op. cit.*, p. 152.
[12] A. T. Hack, « Heiligenkult im frühen Hussitismus. Eine Skizze », dans *Patriotische Heilige. Beiträge zur Rekonstruktion religiöser und politischer Identitäten in der Vormoderne*, éd. R. R. Bauer, K. Herbers et G. Signori, Stuttgart, 2007, p. 123-156. Sur le cas du culte rendu à Hus, on se reportera désormais à Ph. N. Haberkern, *Patron saint and Prophet: Jan Hus in the Bohemian and German Reformations*, Oxford, 2016.
[13] Sur le thème des *sancti conviventes* chez Janov et sur son application à la figure de Milíč de Kroměříž, voir O. Marin, « Fin des temps et sainteté moderne : la *Narracio de Milicio* par Matthias de Janov », dans *Église et État, Église ou État ? Les clercs et la genèse de l'État moderne*, éd. Ch. Barralis *et al.*, Paris, 2014, p. 433-456.

INTRODUCTION

Jésus Christ, qui est 'le même hier, aujourd'hui et pour les siècles des siècles' (Hebr. 13, 8), ne cesse pas dans sa sollicitude de renouveler ses élus par des paroles et des exemples de vie. Prenant donc dans chaque génération, chaque époque et chaque état des ouvriers pour sa vigne, fût-ce à la onzième heure (cf. Mt. 20, 6 et suiv.), lorsque le soleil de la sainteté ne brille plus qu'à grand-peine, qu'abonde l'iniquité et que refroidit la charité (cf. Mt. 24, 12), il fait jaillir des étincelles du foyer de sa charité, afin que les cœurs tièdes se réchauffent et s'engagent sur le chemin de la vertu, sans se voiler la face sous prétexte que la fragilité de la chair et la décadence actuelle rendraient désormais impossible l'imitation des hauts faits des saints ; c'est ainsi que, de nos jours, Il a daigné offrir des exemples de pénitence aux prélats de notre sainte Mère l'Église, ainsi qu'à tous les fidèles du Christ, à travers le très révérend père et seigneur en Christ Jean, qui fut le troisième archevêque de Prague avant de devenir patriarche d'Alexandrie[14].

De tels témoignages suggèrent que Prague a été le premier point centre-européen touché par la vogue des saints récents. Le cosmopolitisme de la capitale tchèque, ainsi que le « polycentrisme religieux » qui la caractérisait et en faisait un intense bouillon de culture, expliquent sans doute cette avance[15].

Mais la Silésie et la Petite Pologne voisines ne sont pas restées longtemps à la traîne. Sur la foi de cinq recueils de miracles conservés pour les années 1430-1520, Aleksandra Witkowska a montré l'intensité de la vénération qui, à Cracovie, entourait de simple *beati* locaux comme Jean de Kęty († 1473), Simon de Lipnica († 1482) ou encore Stanislas Kazimierczyk († 1489). Orchestrée par les archevêques autant que par les Frères mendiants, leur popularité attira des pèlerins venus de loin et concurrença les grandes figures officielles, au point de faire du XVe siècle l'une des périodes les plus fastes de la sainteté

---

[14] « Vita domini Iohannis, Pragensis archiepiscopi tercii », éd. H. KRMÍČKOVÁ, dans *Querite primum regnum Dei. Sborník příspěvků k poctě J. Nechutové*, Brno, 2006, p. 444 : *'Iesus Cristus heri et hodie ipse et in saecula suorum' curam agens electorum eos non desinit innovare verbis vitalibus et exemplis. Unde singulis quibusque etatibus, temporibus et statibus sue cultores vinee instituens eciam circa horam undecimam iam vix sole sanctitatis utcunque apparente, habundante inquitate et refrigescente caritate adhuc prebet igniculum de suo camino caritatis, quo et tepencia cordia incalescant et ad iter virtutum accedant abiecto excusacionis velamine, quo iam corporum allegata fragilitate deficiente temporum etate ardua sanctorum facta ad imitandum impossibilia reputantur; ut temporibus nostris penitencie exemple alme matris ecclesie presulibus et eciam Cristi fidelibus premonstrare dignatus est in reverendissimo in Cristo patre et domino, domino Iohanne, Pragensi archiepiscopo tercio, post patriarcha Alexandrino.*
[15] Sur la notion, voir J. CHIFFOLEAU, « Note sur le polycentrisme religieux urbain à la fin du Moyen Âge », dans *Religion et société urbaine au Moyen Âge. Études offertes à Jean-Louis Biget par ses anciens élèves*, Paris, 2000, p. 227-252.

polonaise[16]. L'enquête mériterait d'être transposée ailleurs. Sous bénéfice d'inventaire, il semble probable qu'au moins dans les grandes villes, les fidèles n'aient plus été nécessairement voués au culte des souffre-passion ancestraux. Le fossé est alors allé se creusant entre le panthéon des *sancti*, qui est demeuré à peu près clos, et celui, bourgeonnant tous azimuts, des *beati*. Avec un décalage d'un siècle et demi par rapport à l'Europe méditerranéenne, Dieu et ses saints n'étaient-ils pas, pour paraphraser le titre d'un livre célèbre, en train de changer en Europe centrale[17] ?

La deuxième partie, intitulée « L'emprise des ordres mendiants », s'attache à cerner les agents de ce réchauffement cultuel. L'historiographie présentant les Frères comme les principaux moteurs du changement religieux à l'œuvre durant les trois derniers siècles du Moyen Âge, toutes régions confondues, il fallait en effet mesurer leur participation à l'élargissement du sanctoral centre-européen.

Rappelons pour mémoire la forte présence, institutionnelle, sociale, humaine, des Mendiants en Europe centrale. Nous ne sommes certes pas en Italie, où les *Frati* se sont rapidement taillé une place hégémonique. Les régions centre-européennes ressemblent davantage au type anglais d'Église décrit par Robert James Brentano : les diocèses y sont moins nombreux, plus vastes et plus riches que dans la péninsule, l'épiscopat y est puissant et contrôle plus efficacement son clergé[18]. Sur place, les ordres mendiants ont pu toutefois exploiter deux atouts dont ils étaient privés en Angleterre. C'est d'abord qu'à leur arrivée dans les années 1220-1230, ils ont trouvé un réseau paroissial encore lâche et incomplet. Ils se sont donc logés beaucoup plus facilement qu'à l'Ouest dans ses interstices. *Secundo*, la proximité de populations non romaines, ou même non chrétiennes, a fait de l'Europe centrale une terre de mission idéale pour ces nouveaux ordres épris de martyre. Qu'il suffise de mentionner à cet égard l'intérêt que les premiers dominicains ont porté à la conversion des Coumans, ou les Franciscains à celle des Bogomiles. Puis, au XVe siècle, l'union de la Pologne et de la Lituanie a ouvert de nouveaux espaces à l'apostolat mendiant, en direction des populations aussi bien orthodoxes que païennes. Ces deux raisons ont par conséquent convergé pour attirer les Frères en grand nombre dans nos contrées. Le caractère massif de

---

[16] A. Witkowska, *Kulty pątnicze piętnastowiecznego Krakowa*, Lublin, 1984, notamment p. 94-106.
[17] Y. Lambert, *Dieu change en Bretagne. La religion à Limerzel de 1900 à nos jours*, Paris, 1985.
[18] R. J. Brentano, *Two Churches : England and Italy in the Thirteenth Century*, Princeton, 1968.

leur implantation se mesure en valeurs absolues : Jerzy Kłoczowski dénombrait pas moins de 380 établissements mendiants fondés entre la Baltique et l'Adriatique[19], un total que des enquêtes collectives ont récemment porté à plus de 430[20]. Mais il est évident aussi et surtout en valeurs relatives, autrement dit rapportées à la population locale : si l'on en juge par le cas hongrois, la proportion de religieux mendiants tournait autour d'un pour 300 citadins, soit une proportion sensiblement supérieure à la moyenne française[21].

Ceci posé, l'emprise des Mendiants sur l'hagiographie centre-européenne a-t-elle été à la mesure de leur poids numérique ? Question difficile ! Une première manière d'y répondre serait de prendre le problème à rebours, en chaussant les lunettes de leurs adversaires. La querelle entre mendiants et séculiers, qui a fait rage en Europe centrale après avoir déchiré Paris et la France du Nord, livre de ce point de vue quelques éléments éclairants. Les détracteurs des nouveaux ordres, tout en privilégiant d'autres enjeux d'ordre juridictionnel ou ecclésiologique, n'ont pas épargné l'abus que les Frères faisaient, selon eux, du culte des saints. Les Mendiants prêcheraient trop souvent et sans discrétion au sujet des saints. En particulier, et là réside le principal chef d'accusation, ils porteraient aux nues leurs saints fondateurs, avec un zèle attentatoire au culte divin. Les stigmates de saint François d'Assise, et plus généralement les pouvoirs spectaculaires attribués à certains Frères et Sœurs charismatiques, ont cristallisé les critiques[22]. Si les auteurs anti-mendiants s'y montrèrent à ce point réfractaires, c'est qu'ils y voyaient surtout une manœuvre intéressée de la part de leurs disciples, qui n'auraient pas eu d'autre but que de capitaliser sur les mérites de leur patron. Un Conrad de Waldhausen († 1369), entre autres, se déchaîna contre cette conception corporative de la sainteté, selon laquelle les bonnes œuvres du fondateur assuraient le salut de tous ceux qui s'affiliaient à sa règle[23]. Des « hagiolâtres » bouti-

---

[19] « The Mendicant Orders between the Baltic and Adriatic Seas in the Middle Ages », *La Pologne au XVe siècle. Étude sur l'histoire de la culture de l'Europe centre-orientale*, Wrocław, 1980, p. 95-110.

[20] Voir en particulier les inventaires établis dans le cadre du programme soutenu par l'Agence Nationale de la Recherche « MARGEC », dont on trouvera un état actualisé sur l'URL margec.univ-bpclermont.fr.

[21] M.-M. de CEVINS, « Les religieux et la ville au bas Moyen Âge : moines et frères mendiants dans les villes du royaume de Hongrie des années 1320 aux années 1490 », *Revue Mabillon*, 9 (1998), p. 97-126, ici p. 108.

[22] A. VAUCHEZ, « Les stigmates de saint François et leurs détracteurs dans les derniers siècles du Moyen Âge », *Mélanges d'archéologie et d'histoire*, 80 (1968), p. 595-625.

[23] *Apologia* (1364), éd. K. HÖFLER, *Die Geschichtsschreiber der hussitischen Bewegung in Böhmen*, t. 2, Vienne, 1865, ici p. 27 : *Sexto scripserunt me dixisse, quod monachi erant fatui ex eo quod, quia habuerunt unum sanctum qui instituisset ordinem eorum, crederent se sanctos et tamen adhuc sub cappa eorum laterent grossi locutores. Respondeo quod imponunt mihi falsum,*

quiers et tendancieux, voilà en somme l'image qu'entendaient donner des Frères leurs opposants.

Ce genre de réquisitoire a le mérite de traduire l'effet de rupture qu'a provoqué l'irruption d'un nouveau modèle hagiographique, appuyé sur des méthodes pastorales également inédites. Mais il ne faudrait certainement pas y souscrire en bloc. Remarquons aussitôt que les saints mendiants ne constituent qu'une part minime des saints honorés dans la prédication des Frères – ils pèsent moins de 4 % chez Pérégrin d'Opole[24]. Il est vrai que les prédicateurs étaient liés par les contraintes du calendrier liturgique. Mais l'enseignement des dédicaces des églises conventuelles, où régnait une plus grande liberté de choix, va dans le même sens. Parmi les 28 couvents franciscains que comptaient la Bohême, la Moravie et la Silésie aux alentours de 1500, seuls 6 étaient consacrés aux saints patrons de l'ordre, Bernardin et François; dans la moitié des cas, ceux-ci devaient d'ailleurs voisiner avec la Vierge Marie ou un autre dédicataire principal[25]. Ils se font encore plus discrets chez les Franciscains hongrois[26]. À ce propos, il y aurait lieu de se demander dans quelle mesure les Frères ne se sont pas contentés de se soumettre aux traditions hagiographiques, mais ont lancé de nouvelles modes. Petr Hlaváček a ainsi pu soutenir que l'idée de réunir en une même gerbe quatorze saints auxiliateurs traditionnels – des martyrs, pour l'essentiel – avait éclos à la fin du XIIIe siècle dans les couvents mendiants des rives du Danube, alors engagés dans une lutte difficile contre l'hérésie vaudoise[27]. On sait aussi que les Frères n'ont pas répugné à encourager le culte des saints évêques indigènes. Saint Stanislas, par exemple, doit beaucoup aux dominicains polonais. En tout cas, retenons que, contrairement aux assertions de leurs adversaires, les saints des Mendiants étaient très loin d'être tous des saints mendiants.

Ainsi ramenée à sa juste place, la dévotion des Frères à leurs saints patrons n'en mérite pas moins une attention spéciale, car c'est bien là que s'expriment

---

sed bene verum est, quod dixi in quodam sermone tractans illud quod dixit Johannes Baptista phariseis, i.e. falsi religiososi Judeorum, qui gloriabantur de patre suo Abraham credentes se posse per hunc beari, nolentes tamen ipsum imitari in bona vita Marc. III° Genimina viperarum – Nullus religiosus debet sperare quod propterea salvetur quia institutor ordinis sui fuerit vir sanctus.

[24] *Peregrini de Opole, Sermones de tempore et de sanctis*, éd. R. Tatarzyński, Varsovie, 1997.
[25] P. Hlaváček, *Die böhmischen Franziskaner im ausgehenden Mittelalter*, Stuttgart, 2011, tableaux p. 173-174.
[26] En attendant l'achèvement de la base de données du programme « MARGEC » évoqué plus haut, voir M.-M. de Cevins, *L'Église dans les villes hongroises à la fin du Moyen Âge*, Paris-Budapest-Szeged, 2003, p. 229.
[27] P. Hlaváček, « Vierzehn Nothelfer : Ein Kulturkode des mitteleuropäischen Spätmittelalters ? », dans *La Cour céleste. La commémoration collective des saints au Moyen Âge et à l'époque moderne*, éd. O. Marin et C. Vincent-Cassy, Turnhout, 2015, p. 261-267.

le plus immédiatement leurs valeurs et leurs attentes. Deux cas de figure sont à distinguer. Il y a d'abord les saints mendiants universels. De saint François d'Assise à saint Bernardin de Sienne, de saint Dominique à saint Thomas d'Aquin en passant par sainte Élisabeth et saint Louis de Toulouse : tous sans exception sont à l'origine des figures exogènes, qui ont été importées en Europe centrale. Celle-ci n'a cependant pas été un simple réceptacle passif. À l'amont de leur canonisation, elle a pu participer à la « fabrique » de la sainteté mendiante. C'est ainsi que les provinces dominicaines de Hongrie et de Bohême ont transmis à l'ensemble de l'ordre les miracles opérés sur place respectivement par Dominique et Pierre de Vérone. Mais l'exemple le plus éloquent est ici celui de Jean Capistran, pour la simple et bonne raison que son inhumation à Újlak (Ilok, en Croatie actuelle) a fait de la Hongrie l'un des principaux foyers de son culte naissant ; en témoigne le riche recueil de miracles qui y fut composé (*BHL* 4368)[28]. À l'aval, les fidèles d'Europe centrale se sont appropriés ces nouveaux cultes, non sans leur faire subir des altérations pour mieux les naturaliser. En tant que fille du cru, sainte Élisabeth s'y prêtait mieux que d'autres et elle est rapidement devenue en Hongrie une patronne à la fois dynastique et nationale. C'est toute la question des usages politiques et identitaires des cultes mendiants qui se trouve ainsi posée.

Il est ensuite des saints mendiants locaux, qui forment un contingent beaucoup plus flou et volatil, mais non moins intéressant que le précédent. Dressons-en un recensement provisoire. Pour cela, nous avons sélectionné les saints en fonction des quatre critères suivants :

(1) qu'ils soient membres à part entière des ordres mendiants (ainsi l'enrégimentement dans les rangs franciscains d'Élisabeth de Hongrie, qui ne fut jamais Clarisse, relève-t-il d'une récupération intéressante, mais trompeuse) ;

(2) qu'ils soient natifs de l'Europe centrale et y aient exercé l'essentiel de leurs activités religieuses, ce qui exclut une Hongroise expatriée comme la dominicaine suisse Élisabeth de Töss († 1338) ;

(3) qu'ils aient vécu (ou soient censés avoir vécu[29]) au cours des XIIIe-XVe siècles ;

(4) et qu'ils aient bénéficié localement d'une réputation de sainteté dès le Moyen Âge. Insistons sur ce dernier critère : il est décisif si l'on veut éviter

---

[28] St. ANDRIĆ, *The Miracles of St John Capistran*, Budapest, 2000.
[29] Nous n'entrons pas ici dans le débat de leur existence historique. Seule compte pour nous la réalité de leur culte. Sur le problème que pose par exemple Hélène de Hongrie, voir déjà R. FAWTIER, « La vie de la bienheureuse Hélène de Hongrie », *Mélanges d'archéologie et d'histoire*, 33 (1913), p. 3-23.

de verser dans l'anachronisme en rétro-projetant des cultes inventés de toutes pièces à l'époque de la Contre-Réforme.

Voici la moisson ainsi récoltée :

Liste des *beati* mendiants d'Europe centrale

	Pologne	*Bohême*	*Hongrie*
XIIIe s.	Ceslas † 1242 (OP) Hyacinthe † 1257 (OP) Martyrs de Sandomierz † v. 1260 (OP) Salomé de Halicz † 1268 (OCl) Kinga / Cunégonde de Cracovie † 1292 (OCl)	Agnès † 1282 (OCl)	90 martyrs † 1259 (OP) Marguerite de Hongrie † 1270 (OP) Gallus d'Esztergom † v. 1280 (OM) Hélène de Hongrie ? (OP ?)
XIVe s.	Jean de Schwenkenfeld † 1341 (OP) Jacques de Strepa † 1409 (OM)		Maurice de Csák † 1336 (OP) Gilles d'Esztergom † v. 1350 (OM)
XVe s.	3 martyrs (OP) de Ząbkowice Śląskie † 1428 Isaïe Boner † 1471 (OESA) Simon de Lipnica † 1482 (OM) Jean de Dukla † 1484 (OM) Ladislas de Gielniów † 1505 (OM) Raphaël de Proszowice † 1534 (OM)		

Ce tableau appellerait plusieurs commentaires. Il est d'abord frappant de constater qu'aucun de ces personnages n'a été porté à la gloire des autels au Moyen Âge, puisque nous en avons exclu sainte Élisabeth (canonisée dès 1235), qui constitue à tous égards une exception. Tous les autres ont dû attendre bien davantage : la plupart ont vu leur sainteté reconnue à l'époque de la Réforme catholique, à un moment où il était urgent pour la papauté de proposer de nouveaux modèles de perfection à des populations tentées de se rallier en masse au protestantisme (Hyacinthe, canonisé en 1597, Salomé de Pologne, béatifiée en 1672, Simon de Lipnica, béatifié en 1685, Cunégonde de Pologne, béatifiée en 1690, Ceslas, béatifié en 1712, Jacques de Strepa, béatifié en 1790). D'autres sont redevables de leur promotion tardive aux largesses du premier pape slave de l'histoire, Jean-Paul II. Enfin, certains cultes n'ont pas résisté à l'épreuve du temps ; ainsi la mémoire de Jean de Schwenkenfeld, sorte de doublet silésien de saint Pierre de Vérone[30], s'est-elle évanouie.

La distribution chronologique de ces personnages met ensuite en évidence d'intéressantes inflexions, tant quantitatives que qualitatives. Le XIIIe siècle correspond à un premier apogée, celui du temps glorieux des fondateurs, qui est aussi celui des martyrs des Tatars. Le XIVe siècle apparaît par contraste beaucoup plus terne. Sans soute faut-il incriminer un certain essoufflement institutionnel, joint au discrédit jeté sur l'idéal mendiant par la controverse de l'*usus pauper*. Les rares Frères de cette époque qui suscitèrent un culte le durent aux fonctions qu'ils exercèrent en dehors de leurs ordres respectifs – épiscopale dans le cas de Jacques de Strepa, inquisitoriale dans celui de Jean de Schwenkenfeld. Nuançons tout de même cette première impression en rappelant que c'est précisément à cette époque que certains cultes nés au XIIIe siècle, mais restés jusque là confidentiels, sont relancés, voire réinventés. Toujours est-il que le dernier siècle du Moyen Âge voit une nette remontée des eaux de la sainteté mendiante, sous l'influence de deux facteurs principaux qui se sont succédé et, parfois, additionnés : la réapparition du type du martyr lors des persécutions causées par la révolution hussite ; le dynamisme pastoral de l'Observance.

D'un point de vue typologique, les critères de la sainteté mendiante ont, eux aussi, sensiblement évolué au cours de ces trois siècles. Au début de la période prévaut le modèle évangélique, centré sur le service caritatif, hospitalier ou non, des pauvres et des malades. Il cède ensuite la place à des intellectuels et à des ascètes. Dans une large mesure, l'Observance a pour ainsi dire « monachisé » la sainteté mendiante. Rien là que de très banal. Une spécificité centre-européenne se dégage toutefois : la valeur persistante du modèle martyrial, ce qui n'étonnera guère étant donné la géopolitique propre à ces « boulevards de la Chrétienté ».

Un mot s'impose ensuite sur la ventilation des saints par ordre et par pays. On ne peut manquer de souligner la prédominance des Frères Prêcheurs tout au long du XIIIe et du début du XIVe siècle. Comment l'expliquer ? Ils étaient pourtant à cette date moins nombreux que leurs homologues franciscains.

---

[30] J. Szymański, « Johannes Swenkenfeldt – inquisitor et martyr », *Śląski Kwartalnik Historyczny Sobótka*, 58 (2003), p. 1-17.

Peut-être leur atout fut-il de s'être installés en Europe centrale avant les Mineurs et d'en avoir très tôt compris l'importance stratégique, ainsi que le suggèrent l'élection en 1241 comme maître général de Jean le Teutonique, un ancien provincial de Hongrie, ou encore la tenue du chapitre général à Buda, en 1254. Ajoutons-y le très lourd tribut qu'ils payèrent aux invasions mongoles. Les marges orientales de la Chrétienté latine, Pologne et Hongrie en tête, devinrent alors une terre d'élection de l'héroïsme dominicain, remplaçant l'Albigeois dans cette fonction[31]. Les Frères mineurs brillent en revanche par leur discrétion, au point de laisser longtemps les figures de saintes Clarisses capter seules les faveurs des fidèles. Ce n'est qu'à la toute fin du Moyen Âge qu'ils réalisent une percée. Quant aux autres ordres mendiants, ils sont représentés par un unique spécimen en la personne de l'Ermite de saint Augustin Isaïe Boner, un cas isolé certes, mais le rapide engouement que suscita le pèlerinage sur sa tombe atteste qu'à l'aube de l'époque moderne, dominicains et franciscains ne pouvaient plus prétendre au monopole qui avait été auparavant le leur.

Il est plus hasardeux de tirer des enseignements de la répartition de ces *beati* par pays. Vouloir dresser entre eux des barrières nationales étanches n'a guère de sens du fait de la fréquence des intermariages (Cunégonde de Cracovie naquit en Hongrie, et Salomé de Halicz s'y maria). La géographie ecclésiastique du temps recèle d'autres pièges : où classer une zone de transition comme la Silésie, qui, selon les ordres et les moments, fut rattachée à la Pologne ou à la Bohême[32] ? Il n'en reste pas moins que la lecture du tableau fait apparaître la Pologne comme le plus gros « réservoir » de saints mendiants. Ce déséquilibre est patent dès le XIIIe siècle et s'accentue encore à la fin de la période. Jusqu'à plus ample informé, il ne peut être imputé ni une densité plus grande des établissements mendiants dans ce royaume, ni à un soutien plus marqué de la part des dynasties régnantes. Cela intrigue d'autant plus que la Hongrie, qui fut elle aussi le berceau d'une branche dynamique de l'observance franciscaine, semblait *a priori* bénéficier de chances comparables, sinon supérieures[33]. Pourquoi toutefois aucun culte de saint mendiant autochtone n'y vit-il le jour au XVe siècle ? Il y a là une énigme.

---

[31] Comme l'a montré A. RELTGEN-TALLON dans « Vers un autre Sud ? Les marges orientales de la chrétienté comme nouvelle terre de mission dans l'imaginaire dominicain du Moyen Âge », dans *Tous azimuts. Mélanges Georges Jehel. Histoire médiévale et archéologie*, 13 (2002), p. 411-422.
[32] Nous avons ici pris le parti de l'intégrer à l'ensemble polonais, au motif que la région relevait de la province dominicaine de Pologne.
[33] M.-M. de CEVINS, *Les franciscains observants hongrois de l'expansion à la débâcle (v. 1450-v. 1540)*, Rome, 2008.

Last but non least, la part de la sainteté féminine dans ce tableau présente un contraste très accusé. Le XIIIe siècle se distingue en concentrant la totalité des religieuses mendiantes mortes en odeur de sainteté, au nombre de cinq. On sait que celles-ci étaient étroitement apparentées les unes avec les autres et qu'elles aidèrent les familles royales ou princières à reconvertir leur ancien prestige sacré dans les nouvelles valeurs de pauvreté et de chasteté[34]. Mais cette promotion de la sainteté mendiante féminine demeura sans lendemain. Alors qu'en Italie comme en France, les observances dominicaines et franciscaines s'appuyèrent largement sur les femmes, rien de tel ne s'observe en Pologne et en Hongrie. L'Europe centrale n'a certes pas, contrairement à une idée reçue, ignoré la mystique féminine, mais les visionnaires et les prophétesses qui l'illustrèrent ne s'y recrutèrent pas parmi les ordres mendiants[35].

Cette dernière remarque amène à poser à nouveaux frais la question clé de l'attractivité des cultes mendiants en Europe centrale. Notre hypothèse de travail est qu'il ne faudrait pas en surestimer l'impact, faute de mise en contexte. Il est par exemple significatif que le culte d'Agnès de Prague ne se soit guère propagé hors des couvents des Franciscains et des Chevaliers de l'Étoile rouge. En irait-il autrement des grandes figures universelles de la sainteté mendiante? À coup sûr, Élisabeth et Capistran ont beaucoup plus facilement rayonné. Pourtant, même en Hongrie, ni l'un ni l'autre ne semblent pénétrer en masse l'onomastique; leur emprise sur les vocables des églises s'avère également plus discrète qu'attendu[36]. Autant d'indices menus qu'il conviendrait de tester à plus vaste échelle.

Si ce diagnostic de demi-échec se vérifiait, il faudrait en chercher les causes moins dans l'archaïsme supposé des « mentalités centre-européennes », comme on disait naguère, que dans la situation hautement concurrentielle à laquelle étaient confrontés les Frères dans ces contrées. Sans doute peut-on parler, pour le XIIIe siècle, de quasi monopole mendiant sur la sainteté centre-européenne. Mais dès le début du siècle suivant, Franciscains

---

[34] G. KLANICZAY, *Holy Rulers and Blessed Princesses. Dynastic Cults in Medieval Central Europe*, Cambridge, 2002.
[35] P. T. DOBROWOLSKI, « La mistica femminile nella Polonia del tardo Medioevo: genesi i ricezione », dans *L'Église et le peuple chrétien dans les pays de l'Europe du centre-est et du nord XIVe-XVe siècles)*, Rome, 1990, p. 213-220. L'échec du culte de sainte Catherine de Sienne en Bohême est illustré par T. HERZIG, « Italian Holy Women against Bohemian Heretics: Catherine of Siena and the 'second Catherines' in the Kingdom of Bohemia », dans *Catherine of Siena. The Creation of a Cult*, éd. J. HAMBURGER et G. SIGNORI, Turnhout, 2013, p. 315-338.
[36] À la différence de ce que Ch.-M. de la Roncière a constaté en Toscane dans un article célèbre: « L'influence des Franciscains dans la campagne de Florence au XIVe siècle (1280-1360) », *Mélanges de l'École française de Rome. Moyen Âge – Temps modernes*, 87 (1975), p. 27-103.

et Dominicains furent rejoints, et parfois débordés, par diverses congrégations canoniales ou monastiques plus récentes, porteuses de leurs propres figures hagiographiques : chanoines réguliers, Chartreux, Ermites de saint Paul, Brigittines, Célestins, etc.[37]. Les clercs séculiers, dont la conscience identitaire s'aiguisa au cours de la période, n'étaient pas non plus en reste de modèles alternatifs de sainteté. Tous n'allèrent certes pas jusqu'à « déboulonner » les saints mendiants, comme le firent les Hussites, qui supprimèrent du calendrier liturgique la fête de saint Dominique. Mais ne faut-il pas nuancer l'idée couramment admise selon laquelle les Mendiants auraient été partout le principal agent du renouvellement des canons hagiographiques ?

Nous avons jusqu'ici parlé d'hagiographie centre-européenne sans autre forme de procès. Il faut cependant garder présent à l'esprit le fait que le sanctoral d'une région ne se réduit pas, tant s'en faut, à ses seuls saints autochtones. Par suite d'un processus de délocalisation du culte amorcé dès la fin de l'Antiquité chrétienne, les saints voyagent, par l'intermédiaire de leurs reliques, de leurs offices, de leurs images. C'est ainsi que l'Europe centrale a été exposée à plusieurs afflux de cultes importés, qui ne sont pas allés sans brouiller la « frontière invisible » censée séparer les deux Europe. Notre troisième partie porte précisément sur ce thème des saints d'implantation et des saints de souche. L'expression n'est pas de nous. Nous l'avons empruntée à l'historien polonais Aleksander Gieysztor, qui y consacra l'une des communications les plus marquantes d'un fameux colloque nanterrois[38]. Son propos était alors de distinguer, parmi les vocables des églises polonaises remontant aux Xe-XIIe siècles, deux strates d'inégale importance : les cultes greffés en même temps que le christianisme, de loin les plus nombreux, et les quelques cultes autochtones auxquels cette jeune Église a peu à peu donné le jour.

Si l'on essaie de voir comment opère la distinction, les difficultés s'accumulent aussitôt. Dans quelle catégorie, par exemple, verser Günther/Vintíř, cet ermite d'origine thuringienne, qui passa la fin de sa vie aux confins de la Bavière et de la Bohême, et dont le monastère bénédictin de Břevnov acquit la dépouille à sa mort, en 1045 ? L'hagiographie bohémienne en fit vite un saint tchèque et inventa un parrainage fictif pour le rattacher à la famille ducale du

---

[37] Un bon exemple est ici la part que prit l'Europe centrale, et singulièrement la Bohême, à la canonisation de sainte Brigitte de Suède : P. RYCHTEROVÁ, *Die Offenbarungen der heiligen Birgitta von Schweden. Eine Untersuchung zur alttschechischen Übersetzung des Thomas von Štítné*, Cologne, 2004.
[38] « Saints d'implantation, saints de souche dans les pays évangélisés de l'Europe du Centre-Est », dans *Hagiographies, cultures et sociétés, IVe-XIIe siècles*, Paris, 1981, p. 573-582.

cru, celle des Přemyslides[39]. Les cas-limites de ce genre sont légion. Dira-t-on, par exemple, que sainte Élisabeth était hongroise ou allemande ? Elle naquit certes à Buda, mais elle passa le plus clair de son temps en Thuringe. Du coup, son culte mit du temps à démarrer dans sa patrie : ce n'est que par un effet de choc en retour que la Hongrie en reçut les premières légendes. Par commodité, nous entendrons ici par saints de souche, *lato sensu*, tous ceux qui, sans y être nécessairement nés, ont connu dès leur vivant l'une ou l'autre des contrées d'Europe centrale – le fait nous paraît décisif, puisqu'il a permis à ces régions de participer à l'essor de leur culte et de le revendiquer immédiatement comme leur. En revanche, les saints d'implantation seront pour nous ceux dont la réputation de sainteté s'est fait connaître en Europe centrale seulement *post mortem*, avec un retard qui fut parfois de plusieurs siècles. Dans ce cas, les Églises de Pologne, de Bohême ou de Hongrie ont certes pu jouer un rôle actif en relayant, multipliant, remodelant même ces cultes préexistants. Mais la différence tient au fait qu'elles n'en ont pas été les foyers initiaux.

Se pose ensuite la question de savoir si la distinction ainsi comprise a une quelconque pertinence chronologique. Il serait assez tentant, au premier abord, de considérer qu'elle correspond à deux phases successives : au cours de la première, les jeunes Églises assimileraient des figures et des modèles hagiographiques étrangers ; puis la seconde phase les verrait, une fois devenues en quelque sorte adultes dans la foi, promouvoir leurs propres saints locaux. Ce modèle ne tient pourtant guère, car ces séquences se chevauchent largement. C'est d'abord que les cultes autochtones font partout très tôt leur apparition. En Bohême, la vénération pour sainte Ludmila, assassinée en 921, est attestée dès le règne de son petit-fils Venceslas, qui fit transférer sa dépouille de Tetín au château de Prague. On pourrait certes objecter que le culte de la princesse přemyslide a fait long feu, victime de l'obstruction de l'évêque de Ratisbonne, qui y voyait, non sans raison, un instrument de l'émancipation de la chrétienté tchèque[40]. Le cas de saint Étienne est plus probant. On sait que les reliques du souverain hongrois firent l'objet d'une élévation, synonyme de canonisation, en 1083, soit moins d'un demi-siècle après sa mort. Mieux : en portant ainsi à la gloire des autels un roi confesseur certes, mais qui n'était point mort martyr, la Hongrie a inventé un nouveau type hagiographique et ouvert le bal des saints rois qui allait battre son plein au siècle suivant (saint

---

[39] P. KUBÍN, *Sedm přemyslovských kultů, op. cit.*, p. 195-218. Le même auteur en a récemment édité à nouveaux frais la légende : *Legenda o sv. Vintířovi. Vita s. Guntheri*, Prague, 2014.
[40] P. SOMMER, « Der beginnende böhmische Staat und seine Heiligen », *Quaestiones Medii Aevi Novae*, 14 (2009), p. 41-54.

Édouard le Confesseur, etc.). À cet égard, l'Europe centrale a donc anticipé plutôt que suivi les transformations religieuses du monde latin[41].

En sens inverse, la floraison de saints de souche n'a pas rendu caduc le recours à des saints d'implantation. Voyez le paysage hagiographique polonais aux XIe et XIIe siècles. Bolesław le Vaillant fit de saint Adalbert, mort en 997 chez les Prussiens, et des cinq frères martyrs, les patrons du nouveau royaume. Mais voilà que leurs reliques sont dérobées en 1039 par le duc tchèque Břetislav Ier. Ainsi brutalement privée de saints locaux, la Pologne doit alors se tourner vers des saints étrangers: elle trouve son salut en saint Florian, modèle de chevalier martyr. Celui-ci fait l'affaire jusqu'en 1253, date de la canonisation du saint polonais Stanislas, qui prend désormais l'ascendant[42]. Encore Stanislas a-t-il, dans ce cas, peu ou prou éclipsé Florian, saint bien obscur, presque sans biographie. Mais, le plus souvent, saints de souche et saints d'implantation coexistent. Il leur arrive même de se conforter, comme en témoigne la place donnée à saint Sigismond dans le ciel tchèque. Charles IV, une fois couronné roi à Arles, rapporta en 1365 le chef du roi burgonde d'Agaune à Prague. L'empereur cherchait ainsi à manifester sa domination sur le royaume de Bourgogne. Mais, comme l'a suggéré David Mengel, il voulait aussi revitaliser le culte de son ancêtre saint Venceslas, qui battait de l'aile en ces années et qui ne pouvait que bénéficier de son association avec ce glorieux compagnon. Le fait que la date choisie pour la translation des reliques de Sigismond ait été précisément la vigile de la Saint-Venceslas accrédite l'hypothèse[43]. Le Luxembourg avait bien compris que les saints d'implantation n'avaient pas épuisé leurs vertus et que leur patronage pouvait contribuer à rehausser le culte des saints de souche.

Dans ces conditions, force est de constater que l'étrangeté et l'autochtonie ne sont, pas plus que l'ancien et le moderne, des essences stables, mais les pôles d'une interaction dynamique. Saints d'implantation et saints de souche subissent au cours des siècles des altérations à la fois symétriques et complémentaires: processus de naturalisation des premiers, mouvement d'universalisation des seconds. Prenons un cas extrême de l'un et l'autre phénomènes. Saint Guy, en Bohême, est un saint importé. Il y est introduit depuis Corvey au Xe siècle, quand le roi saxon Henri Ier l'Oiseleur offre à son allié Venceslas une relique de son épaule. Or, le saint s'y acclimate d'autant plus aisément que les premiers évêques pragois provenaient eux-mêmes de Saxe. La

---

[41] M.-M. de CEVINS, *Saint Étienne de Hongrie*, Paris, 2004.
[42] T. DUNIN-WĄSOWICZ, « Die neuen Heiligenkulte in Mitteleuropa um das Jahr 1000 », dans *Europas Mitte um 1000. Beiträge zur Geschichte, Kunst und Archäologie*, Stuttgart, 2000, p. 834-838.
[43] D. C. MENGEL, « A Holy and Faithful Fellowship: Royal Saints in Fourteenth-Century Prague », dans *Evropa a Čechy na konci středověku*, Prague, 2004, p. 145-158.

nouvelle cathédrale lui fut dédiée, sa fête le 15 juin se mit à accueillir les événements importants de Bohême, tels que les diètes, les couronnements, puis les synodes. Son intégration parmi les quatorze *Nothelfer* à la fin du Moyen Âge acheva d'en consacrer la popularité. Saint Guy a donc cessé d'être perçu comme étranger et est devenu un saint local, au point de figurer, aux côtés de saint Venceslas, de saint Adalbert et de saint Procope, parmi le quadrille des saints patrons du royaume[44].

Inversement, il est des saints de souche centre-européenne, que ce soient des saints dûment canonisés ou de simples *beati*, qui se propagent plus ou moins vite à l'extérieur des frontières. Paradoxalement, certains d'entre eux y connaissent même une carrière plus brillante que dans leur pays natal. Ainsi est-ce en Italie que se forgea la légende, à la fois textuelle et iconographique, de la stigmatisation de la dominicaine Marguerite de Hongrie, sans que l'écho en parvienne sur les rives du Danube. Nul n'est prophète en son pays. Le culte de sainte Marguerite a été largement un produit d'exportation[45].

Naturellement, ces processus ne se produisent pas par autogénération, mais relèvent de constructions concertées et sont fonction des intentions de leurs promoteurs, de la nature de leurs supports, des moments de leur réalisation.

Parmi les acteurs, une place de choix est évidemment revenue aux souverains, dont on sait qu'ils ont eu à cœur d'élever à la gloire des autels leurs proches parents. Les évêques, toujours soucieux d'augmenter le lustre de leur diocèse par l'enrichissement du sanctoral, y ont eu eux aussi leur part, ainsi que les ordres religieux, forts de leurs connexions internationales et de leur rôle de médiateurs culturels. Ainsi l'évêque de Litomyšl Albert de Šternberk profita-t-il de son bref passage sur le prestigieux siège de Magdebourg (1368-1371) pour rapporter les reliques du martyr saint Victorin dans son diocèse tchéco-morave[46]. Mais il ne faudrait pas non plus oublier, à la base, le relais que constituaient les simples prêtres. Sans son curé de paroisse, le petit chevalier de Bohême méridionale Thomas Štítný n'aurait jamais entendu parler, dès 1367, de saint Sigismond[47].

---

[44] K. H. Krüger et E. Doležalová, « Veit », dans *Die Landespatrone der böhmischen Länder : Geschichte, Verehrung, Gegenwart*, éd. S. Samerski, Paderborn, 2009, p. 231-242.
[45] V. H. Deák, *La légende de sainte Marguerite de Hongrie et l'hagiographie dominicaine*, Paris, 2013 (trad. française).
[46] V. Večeře, *Litomyšl Alberta ze Šternberka*, master de l'Université Charles de Prague, 2014, disponible en ligne à l'adresse *https://is.cuni.cz/webapps/zzp/download/130128245*, ici p. 81 et suiv.
[47] M. Studničková, « Kult des heiligen Sigismund (Sigmund) in Böhmen », dans *Die Heiligen und ihr Kult im Mittelalter*, Colloquia mediaevalia Pragensia, 11, éd. E. Doležalová, Prague, 2010, p. 299-339, ici p. 308.

Les vecteurs des cultes offrent une palette plus vaste encore. Un cas d'école aujourd'hui fort bien connu et analysé est celui de la mitre reliquaire de saint Éloi et des quatre manuscrits de sa légende et de son office conservés en Bohême : les uns comme les autres furent offerts à la guilde des orfèvres par Charles IV, de retour de sa visite en France (1378)[48]. Mais les reliques et les manuscrits liturgiques ne sont pas les seuls à circuler. Tel est le cas également des images saintes et des enseignes de pèlerinage. C'est bien par les routes de pèlerinage que la réputation de thaumaturge de saint Gilles s'est fait connaître à la fin du XIe siècle en Pologne, au point de décider le duc Ladislas Ier Hermann et sa femme Judith de Bohême, dont l'union était stérile, d'envoyer des présents au sanctuaire rhodanien[49]. Quant à l'hagiotoponymie et à l'anthroponymie, elles fournissent un bon baromètre des effets de mode hagiographique sur les moyen et long termes[50].

Enfin, si l'on observe de près la chronologie des cultes, se dégagent deux conjonctures particulièrement propices à l'invention de nouveaux saints en Europe centrale. D'une part, l'arrivée au pouvoir d'une nouvelle dynastie, qui apporte généralement dans ses bagages ses cultes familiaux propres et cherche aussitôt à les implanter sur place ; ainsi les Angevins importèrent-ils en Hongrie le culte de saint Louis de Toulouse et bien d'autres[51]. D'autre part, les fondations de nouveaux diocèses ou de nouvelles provinces ecclésiastiques entraînent immanquablement la recherche de nouveaux saints destinés à en soutenir le statut. Le vol des reliques d'Adalbert par Břetislav, par exemple, ne se comprend qu'à la lumière de sa – vaine – tentative d'ériger Prague en métropole, aux dépens de Gniezno[52].

Toujours est-il qu'il y aurait lieu de prendre le problème à rebours, en étudiant des situations où ces processus se grippent, soit que la conjoncture politique se retourne, soit que les nouveaux cultes se heurtent à des concurrences locales trop vives. Si saint Procope, par exemple, s'exporte mal en Thuringe, c'est que sa fête tombe le même jour que la Saint-Ulrich. Quant à saint

---

[48] *Z Noyonu do Prahy : kult svatého Eligia ve středověkých Čechách. De Noyon à Prague : le culte de saint Eloi en Bohême médiévale*, éd. H. PÁTKOVÁ, Prague, 2006.
[49] T. DUNIN-WĄSOWICZ, « Saint Gilles a Polska w wczesnym średniowieczu », *Archeologia Polski*, 16 (1971), p. 651-665. Un autre cas éloquent est le culte de saint Jacques, sur lequel on verra *Der Jakobuskult in Ostmitteleuropa*, éd. Kl. HERBERS et D. R. BAUER, Tübingen, 2003.
[50] Voir les recherches d'Eva Doležalová, menées à partir des registres pragois d'ordination : « Der Name Hroznata im spätmittelalterlichen Böhmen », dans *Die Heiligen und ihr Kult*, *op. cit.*, p. 29-36 ; « Stopy svatého Jeronýma v Čechách na konci 14. století », dans *Evropa a Čechy, op. cit.*, p. 209-220.
[51] P. MOLNÁR, « Idéologies monarchiques en Hongrie (XIIIe-XIVe siècles) », dans *Identités hongroises, identités européennes du Moyen Âge à nos jours*, éd. P. NAGY, Mont-Saint-Aignan, 2006, p. 23-50.
[52] J. ŽEMLIČKA, *Čechy v době knížecí (1034-1198)*, Prague, 1997, p. 55-59.

Gothard, son culte en Bohême ne survécut guère à l'alliance de circonstance entre l'empereur Lothaire III et le duc Soběslav I[er53]. On pourrait multiplier les exemples. Pourquoi, par exemple, saint Aignan ne « prend »-il pas vraiment en Hongrie ? Les échecs ont, eux aussi, une histoire.

Nous voilà ainsi conduits tout droit à l'interrogation, fondamentale pour notre propos, de l'existence d'un paysage hagiographique centre-européen[54]. L'alchimie qui s'y est opérée entre saints d'implantation et saints de souche permet-elle de repérer des traits communs aux trois royaumes qui nous intéressent ? La tentation est grande de considérer que l'unité de l'Europe centrale, en matière hagiographique comme dans beaucoup d'autres domaines, serait une création habsbourgeoise. De fait, quand aujourd'hui nous évoquons les dévotions centre-européennes, surgissent spontanément à l'esprit les images de la colonne de la Vierge ou de la Trinité plantée au centre de la grand-place, de la statue de saint Jean Népomucène sur les ponts, etc., autant de lieux de mémoire qui datent seulement de l'époque moderne et correspondent au modèle de piété promu et diffusé aux quatre coins de l'Empire austro-hongrois[55].

S'agissant de l'hagiographie médiévale, il vaut pourtant la peine de dépasser le cadre de référence des États et de faire apparaître, à l'échelle régionale, des phénomènes transnationaux d'intégration, d'échanges et de différenciation des cultes. Sans prétendre à l'exhaustivité, essayons de lancer la réflexion en soumettant quelques propositions liminaires[56].

D'abord, si l'on fait le bilan des saints importés et des saints exportés, nul ne niera que le solde soit massivement négatif. Le caractère tardif de la

---

[53] P. KUBÍN, « Die böhmischen Heiligen in den mittelalterlichen Handschriften Thüringens », *Zeitschrift des Vereins für Thüringische Geschichte*, 52 (1998), p. 271-281 ; J. ŽEMLIČKA, « Die Verehrung des heiligen Gotthard (Godehard) im přemyslidischen Böhmen », dans *Die Heiligen und ihr Kult, op. cit.*, p. 363-368.
[54] Nous rejoignons ici, sous l'angle particulier des pratiques cultuelles, la question de la mise en région de l'Europe centrale. Parmi une bibliographie pléthorique, retenons : M. TODOROVA, « Spacing Europe : What is a Historical Region ? », *East Central Europe*, 32 (2005), p. 59-78 ; St.TROEBST, « What's in a Historical Region ? A Teutonic perspective », *European Review of History*, 10 (2003), p. 173-188 ; P. GRADWOHL, « Réflexion sur la mise en région(s) de l'histoire de l'Europe centrale et médiane », dans *L'Europe médiane au XXᵉ siècle. Fractures, décompositions – recompositions – surcompositions*, éd. P. GRADWOHL, Prague, 2011, p. 239-268.
[55] Sur le sujet, voir l'étude classique d'A. CORETH, *Pietas austriaca. Österreichische Frömmigkeit in Barock*, Vienne, 1982, et les contributions réunies dans *Religiöse Erinnerungsorte in Ostmitteleuropa*, éd. J. BAHLICKE et T. WÜNSCH, Berlin, 2013.
[56] Nous laissons ici délibérément de côté la typologie des saints centre-européens, qui a fait l'objet d'une magistrale mise au point : G. KLANICZAY, « North and East European Cults in comparison with East-Central Europe », dans *Saints and their Lives on the Periphery. Veneration of Saints in Scandinavia and Eastern Europe (c. 1000-1200)*, éd. H. ANTONSSON et I. H. GARIPZANOV, Turnhout, 2010, p. 283-304.

christianisation y est bien sûr pour beaucoup. En quelques siècles, la *junge Europa* (Peter Moraw) n'a pas pu combler le retard initial qu'elle avait sur les chrétientés plus anciennes, riches d'un patrimoine hagiographique déjà millénaire. La réserve pontificale des canonisations a fait le reste : ancrée dans les esprits avant même d'être sanctionnée par le droit canon au XIIIe siècle[57], elle a filtré avec une sévérité toujours croissante les demandes issues de ces pays. Au total, les saints centre-européens canonisés avant 1520 se comptent sur les doigts des deux mains. Il est difficile de ne pas voir là une forme de dépendance de cette Europe que l'on dit centrale, mais qui est restée tout de même assez périphérique par rapport aux organes de décision de l'Église latine.

Deuxièmement, du point de vue de la structure du sanctoral centre-européen, s'observe presque partout une tendance à la concentration. Au lieu de se disperser entre une multitude d'intercesseurs comme en Allemagne, la dévotion centre-européenne tend à se focaliser sur un saint patron principal, saint Stanislas en Pologne, saint Venceslas en Bohême, ainsi que (mais à un moindre degré, puisqu'il fut rapidement escorté de Ladislas et d'Émeric) saint Étienne en Hongrie. Sans doute les différences dans la géographie et la culture politiques expliquent-elles en partie ce contraste. Alors que l'Allemagne n'a longtemps pas eu de capitale et se trouvait partagée entre six provinces ecclésiastiques concurrentes, les trois royaumes d'Europe centrale se distinguèrent précocement par leur relative centralisation politique et religieuse[58].

Troisièmement, l'éventail des saints implantés en Europe centrale trahit une forte empreinte germanique. À leurs débuts, les nouvelles Églises polonaise, tchèque et hongroise ont été créées dans le prolongement de l'Église impériale ottonienne. Les traces en sont multiples, à commencer par le succès remporté par la figure de saint Maurice : son culte, rayonnant à partir de Magdebourg, prit pied au XIe siècle à la fois chez les évêques d'Europe centrale et parmi la noblesse alors en voie de constitution[59]. Puis l'*Ostbewegung* a encore accentué la germanisation du paysage hagiographique. Certes, les colons n'y ont que rarement introduit *ex nihilo* de nouveaux cultes (tel saint

---

[57] Très révélatrice est l'attitude de Cosmas de Prague († 1125), qui, ayant été abordé par un pèlerin venu vénérer « saint Radim », lui opposa : *Quem tu dicis sanctum, adhuc non est per apostolicum incanonizatus, adhuc missam eius ut pro defunctis celebramus* (*Chronica Boemorum*, éd. J. EMLER, *Fontes Rerum Bohemicarum*, tome 2, Prague, 1874, p. 110-111). Radim, qui n'était autre que le demi-frère de saint Adalbert, fut le premier archevêque de Gniezno.

[58] Sur les concurrences structurelles entre saints impériaux, voir E.-D. HEHL, « Die heiligen Mauritius, Laurentius, Ulrich und Veit », dans *Europas Mitte um 1000, op. cit.*, p. 895-898.

[59] P. KUBÍN, « Le culte de saint Maurice en Bohême et en Moravie au Moyen Âge », à paraître dans *Honneur à saint Maurice ! 1500 ans de culte. Actes du colloque international organisé par la Fondation des Archives historiques de l'abbaye de Saint-Maurice (2-4 avril 2014)*. Je remercie l'auteur de m'en avoir procuré un exemplaire avant la publication.

Blaise), mais ont plutôt contribué à développer des dévotions préexistantes[60]. Il n'en reste pas moins que l'Europe centrale dans son ensemble a dès lors évolué au sein d'une vaste et dynamique *Germania slavica*.

Quatrièmement, cette influence a beau avoir été déterminante, elle n'en a pas exclu d'autres, plus lointaines, liées à l'intensification des échanges à grande distance, mais probablement aussi à la volonté des élites centre-européennes de contrebalancer la pression exercée par leurs puissants voisins. Dans ce grand jeu, quelles étaient donc les sources alternatives de légitimité ? On aimerait appliquer à l'hagiographie ce que Krzysztof Pomian disait de l'Europe centrale comme espace de confrontation et de transaction entre les deux Empires germanique et byzantin[61]. Il est certes avéré que les cultes de saint Alexis et de saint Démétrios ont été importés en Hongrie depuis Constantinople, directement ou *via* la Bulgarie ; l'onomastique princière en a longtemps porté la marque[62]. Mais ces emprunts sont somme toute modestes et se raréfient encore au fil du temps. À partir du XIIe siècle, l'Europe centrale s'arrime définitivement à la Chrétienté latine et tourne de plus en plus le dos au christianisme oriental[63]. Les tentatives ultérieures pour ressusciter par exemple un culte cyrillo-méthodien en Bohême furent le fait de quelques lettrés isolés et se soldèrent par un échec. La mémoire des deux évangélisateurs y fut occultée par un Père latin, dont les origines illyriennes firent croire que le mérite de la traduction de la Bible en slave lui revenait : saint Jérôme[64].

En réalité, c'est bien davantage vers Rome que les pouvoirs centre-européens se sont tournés. Cela est évident en Pologne, où se remarquent d'abondantes et précoces dédicaces à saint Pierre, parfois associé à saint Paul. Mais la Bohême, en dépit d'une orientation politique longtemps plus « gibeline », n'y a pas non plus échappé. Kateřina Kubínová a ainsi montré comment l'empereur Charles IV avait méthodiquement importé de la Ville éternelle des reliques des apôtres, des copies de la Véronique et de la Madone de l'*Ara cœli*,

---

[60] T. Wünsch, « Kultbeziehungen zwischen dem Reich und Polen im Mittelalter », dans *Das Reich und Polen. Parallelen, Interaktionen und Formen der Akkulturation im hohen und späten Mittelalter*, éd. A. Patschovsky et T. Wünsch, Ostfildern, 2003, p. 357-400.
[61] « Les particularités historiques de l'Europe centrale et orientale », *Le Débat*, 63 (1991), p. 23-35.
[62] M. Slíz, « Byzantine Influence on the Name-giving Practices of the Hungarian Árpád Dynasty », dans *Byzance et l'Occident*, II, éd. Z. Farkas, L. Horváth et T. Mészáros, Budapest, 2015, p. 171-179.
[63] G. Klaniczay, « Von Ostmitteleuropa zu Westmitteleuropa : Eine Umwandlung im Hochmittelalter », dans *Böhmen und seine Nachbarn in der Premysliderzeit*, éd. I. Hlaváček et A. Patschovsky, Stuttgart, 2011, p. 17-48.
[64] Fr. Graus, « Die Entwicklung der Legenden der sogennanten Slavenapostel Konstantin und Method in Böhmen und Mähren », *Jahrbuch für Geschichte Osteuropas*, 19 (1971), p. 161-211 ; J. Verkholantsev, « St Jerome as a Slavic Apostle in Luxemburg Bohemia », *Viator*, 44 (2013), p. 251-286.

afin de faire de sa capitale une nouvelle Rome[65]. Au moins deux raisons ont joué en faveur de ce tropisme romain. La première tient à un phénomène de compensation : en faisant appel au capital sacré de Rome, les pays d'Europe centrale ont sans doute voulu combler leur propre déficit d'ancienneté. D'un point de vue ecclésiologique, ensuite, la référence récurrente au prince des apôtres et aux autres saints romains a servi à sceller l'autonomie des Églises locales, qui ne voulaient reconnaître comme supérieur que le Siège suprême de l'Église. Il n'est pas innocent, à cet égard, qu'un fragment de la chaîne de saint Pierre ait été placé dans l'anneau de l'archevêque de Prague[66].

Voilà quelques tendances à l'œuvre dans l'hagiographie centre-européenne du temps. Il resterait s'entendre sur le sens de l'évolution entre 1000 et 1500, dates rondes. Le paysage hagiographique paraît avoir été, au seuil de l'époque moderne, plus disparate qu'il ne l'était cinq siècles plus tôt. Autour de l'an mil, un culte comme celui de saint Adalbert était de nature à cimenter les jeunes Églises naissantes, non seulement celles de Bohême et de Pologne, mais encore celle de Hongrie, puisque l'archevêché d'Esztergom lui fut consacré et que même le baptême de saint Étienne lui fut, par la suite (quoique à tort), attribué. Pourtant, la construction des États nationaux, dressés les uns contre les autres par des rivalités chroniques, leur a bientôt fait suivre des destins sensiblement divergents. Saint Venceslas est ainsi devenu trop tchèque pour que son culte puisse prospérer de manière durable en Pologne[67]. Au XVe siècle, le hussitisme a encore davantage différencié le sanctoral centre-européen. S'est alors créé une sorte d'isolat bohémien : le pays s'est doté, avec Jean Hus et ses compagnons, de saints martyrs par définition inexportables, tout en rejetant les nouveaux cultes qui faisaient florès en terre catholique, comme ceux de saint Antonin ou de sainte Anne[68]. Malgré l'influence unificatrice de la papauté, des ordres mendiants, de la colonisation allemande et des unions dynastiques, les particularismes ne se sont-ils pas, sur le long terme, renforcés ?

L'Europe centrale n'est pas une aire, c'est un monde. Puissent les contributions de ce volume aider à en prendre la mesure et stimuler le désir de relever les défis que sa compréhension lance à l'historien du Moyen Âge.

---

[65] K. KUBÍNOVÁ, *Imitatio Romae. Karel IV. a Řím*, Prague, 2006.
[66] La référence à des saints romains a aussi pu étayer la prétention de certains chapitres à l'exemption, tel celui de Vyšehrad, au sud de Prague : P. KUBÍN, « Svatý Pankrác – strážce vstupu na Vyšehrad. Řimský světec v Praze », dans *Evropa a Čechy, op. cit.*, p. 113-123.
[67] J. KUTHAN, « K šíření kultu svatého Václava za hranice Čech a Moravy v době Přemyslovců a Lucemburků », dans *Svatý Václav. Na památku 1100. výročí narození knížete Václava svatého*, éd. P. KUBÍN, Prague, 2010, p. 221-233, ici p. 222.
[68] O. HALAMA, *Otázka svatých v české reformaci*, Brno, 2002.

I
SAINTS ANCIENS ET SAINTS MODERNES : PERMANENCES, RÉINVENTIONS, CONCURRENCES

Saints fondateurs et saints modernes dans la Bohême médiévale

Petr KUBÍN
(*Prague*)

Pourquoi l'Europe centrale a-t-elle donné la priorité aux saints fondateurs plutôt qu'à ceux issus des rangs des ordres mendiants ? Faut-il, pour cette raison, la classer parmi les « régions froides » qui n'auraient guère été intéressées par ces nouveaux modèles hagiographiques à l'époque du Moyen Âge tardif ? Telle est la question que pose Olivier Marin en introduction et à laquelle je tenterai de répondre, à tout le moins dans le cas du royaume de Bohême.

Les débuts de l'État chrétien en Bohême sont – sur le modèle des fondateurs de l'empire chrétien, saint Constantin et sainte Hélène – liés au culte des premiers Přemyslides : la princesse Ludmila († 921) et son petit-fils Venceslas († 935)[1]. Tous deux sont des personnages difficiles à saisir historiquement, car les seules sources, ou à peu près, sur leur vie sont des légendes[2]. Ludmila et Venceslas sont morts en martyrs pour s'être, toujours selon la légende, réclamés de la foi chrétienne, en réalité sans doute bien plus probablement en raison de luttes de pouvoir. Ludmila fut tuée à Tetín, sur ordre de sa belle-fille Drahomíra, non pas parce que celle-ci aurait été païenne, mais tout simplement parce qu'elle voulait exercer la régence à sa place. Venceslas fut, quant

---

[1] À propos de la construction du culte de sainte Ludmila sur le modèle de sainte Hélène, voir M. HOMZA, *Mulieres suadentes. Presviedčajúce ženy. Štúdie z dejín ženskej panovníckej svätosti v strednej a východnej Európe v 10.-13. storočí*, Bratislava, 2002, p. 46-79.

[2] La plus ancienne légende en latin de sainte Ludmila conservée est intitulée *Fuit in provincia Bohemorum* (*BHL* 5026), celle sur saint Venceslas *Crescente fide* (*BHL* 8823). Toutes deux remontent approximativement aux années 970. Seule la *První staroslověnská legenda* (La première légende slave ancienne) sur saint Venceslas est plus ancienne. Elle fut rédigée dans les années 960. Sur la généalogie de ces légendes, voir P. KUBÍN, *Sedm přemyslovských kultů*, Prague, 2011, p. 81-150.

Les saints et leur culte en Europe centrale au Moyen Âge (XIᵉ-début du XVIᵉ siècle), éd. par Marie-Madeleine de CEVINS et Olivier MARIN, Turnhout, 2017 (*Hagiologia*, 13), p. 31-38.

à lui, assassiné par son frère cadet, Boleslas Ier, et ses comparses, hostiles à la diplomatie pro-saxonne du duc[3].

Bien que, quinze ans après cet assassinat, Boleslas Ier se soit publiquement repenti et ait fait transférer la dépouille de son frère de Stará Boleslav au château de Prague, Venceslas ne fut canonisé, pour des raisons évidentes, qu'après la mort de Boleslas, au tout début du règne de son fils Boleslas II (972-999). Décisive à cet égard fut la création de l'évêché de Prague (973), car la sanctification (c'est-à-dire la canonisation épiscopale) était alors encore entièrement dépendante des évêques diocésains et devenait effective par le simple acte liturgique de dépôt de la dépouille du saint dans un autel. Le culte dut être officialisé peu après 976, date de la consécration du premier évêque de Prague, Thietmar. C'est également à cette époque que remonte la légende *Crescente fide*, dont l'auteur, un moine anonyme de Ratisbonne, est le premier à qualifier sans équivoque Venceslas de saint[4].

Au cours des deux siècles suivants, le culte de saint Venceslas se transforma en un symbole institutionnel, le prince remplaçant *de facto* la notion abstraite d'État. Désormais, saint Venceslas serait l'éternel souverain des pays tchèques, qui déléguait de manière temporaire son pouvoir au roi ou au prince régnant[5]. C'est pourquoi, à partir du règne de Charles IV, la couronne royale fut déposée de manière permanente sur le crâne de saint Venceslas. Le roi de Bohême n'avait le droit de l'emprunter que le jour de son couronnement ou bien lors de célébrations exceptionnelles. La couronne devait en outre être replacée sur la tête du saint le jour même[6].

Le culte de Ludmila, la grand-mère de Venceslas et co-fondatrice de l'État chrétien, est né plus ou moins au moment de la sanctification de saint Venceslas, mais il fut circonscrit à une seule et unique, quoique prestigieuse, institution. Il s'agissait du chapitre de chanoinesses, devenu plus tard abbaye de bénédictines, de l'église Saint-Georges au château de Prague, fondé à la fin des années 960 par Mlada/Marie († après 983), l'arrière-petite-fille de Ludmila. C'est là que fut composée sa première légende : connue par son incipit *Fuit in provincia Bohemorum*, elle eut sans doute elle aussi pour auteur

---

[3] Parmi l'important corpus d'études dédiées à sainte Ludmila, on retiendra : Fr. STEJSKAL, *Svatá Ludmila. Její doba a úcta*, Prague, 1918 ; Id., *Svatý Václav. Jeho život a úcta*, Prague, 1925 ; Z. KALANDRA, *České pohanství*, Prague, 1947 ; D. TŘEŠTÍK, *Počátky Přemyslovců. Vstup Čechů do dějin (530-935)*, Prague, 1997.

[4] P. KUBÍN, *Sedm přemyslovských kultů, op. cit.*, p. 125-150.

[5] J. ŽEMLIČKA, « Svatý Václav jako věčný kníže 'Čechů' », dans *Svatý Václav*, éd. P. KUBÍN, Prague, 2010, p. 211-220 ; Zd. HLEDÍKOVÁ, « Postava svatého Václava ve 14. a 15. století », *ibid.*, p. 239-252 ; Fr. ŠMAHEL, « Úcta ke svatému Václavu v husitských Čechách », *ibid.*, p. 281-300.

[6] K. OTAVSKÝ, « Svatováclavská koruna a její funkce », *ibid.*, p. 253-266.

l'un des moines venus de Ratisbonne desservir la jeune communauté. En témoigne, entre autres, le fait qu'elle s'inspire directement de la Vie de saint Emmeran. Ludmila n'y est pas encore qualifiée de sainte, mais seulement de servante de Dieu (*famula Dei*), et aucun miracle n'est attribué à son intercession. D'après le premier continuateur de Cosmas de Prague, sa sainteté n'était toujours pas unanimement reconnue en 1142. J'ai expliqué ailleurs la raison de cette résistance au culte de Ludmila : les évêques de Prague (probablement pour des raisons de concurrence) souhaitaient empêcher son expansion dans tout le diocèse. Ce n'est qu'avec l'évêque de Prague Daniel, au milieu du XIIe siècle, que le culte fut reconnu au niveau diocésain. Des églises et des autels lui furent dédiés. Mais il fallut attendre encore cent-cinquante ans pour que sainte Ludmila soit considérée comme sainte patronne du royaume. Son culte n'atteignit du reste jamais l'importance de celui qui était rendu à saint Venceslas[7].

Le second évêque de Prague, Adalbert, mort en martyr parmi les païens de Prusse où il faisait œuvre d'évangélisation (avril 997), est un saint d'un tout autre genre que les légendaires Ludmila et Venceslas[8]. Sa vie est historiquement bien documentée dans deux biographies contemporaines, rédigées juste après sa mort. Adalbert avait la chance d'être un proche de l'empereur Otton III et de bien d'autres hommes importants de son temps. L'empereur, qui pleura amèrement la perte de son ami, décida de faire d'Adalbert un des saints principaux de son empire, sur le modèle de Charlemagne. Mais la prétendue canonisation d'Adalbert, sur décision de Sylvestre II en l'an 999, n'est que pure fiction, même si elle est soutenue jusqu'à aujourd'hui par une partie de l'historiographie polonaise. Il est en revanche établi que, suite à la décision de l'empereur, cinq églises consacrées à Adalbert furent construites dans les cinq années suivant sa mort, et ce, en des hauts lieux de l'empire : à Aix-la-Chapelle, à Liège, à Rome, à Afille près de Subiaco, à Reichenau et à Pereo, près de Ravenne. Malheureusement, le décès prématuré d'Otton III eut pour conséquence qu'il ne resta bientôt plus grand-chose du culte impérial d'Adalbert. En revanche, en Pologne et en Hongrie, fut créée autour de l'an mil, à partir du culte de saint Adalbert, une organisation ecclésiastique indépendante (archevêchés de Gniezno et d'Esztergom) et c'est là – ou des mains de leur archevêque (dans le cas hongrois) – que les souverains de ces deux

---

[7] P. Kubín, *Sedm přemyslovských kultů*, op. cit., p. 81-123.
[8] La bibliographie consacrée à saint Adalbert est immense. Les références indispensables sont : H. G. Voigt, *Adalbert von Prag. Ein Beitrag zur Geschichte der Kirche und Mönchtums im zehnten Jahrhundert*, Weltend-Berlin, 1898 ; G. Labuda, *Święty Wojciech, biskup-męczennik, patron Polski, Czech i Węgier*, Wrocław, 2000. Pour plus de détails, voir la contribution de Geneviève Bührer-Thierry dans ce volume.

contrées furent couronnés rois. En Bohême, où Adalbert avait échoué deux fois en tant qu'évêque avant d'être rejeté la troisième fois, il ne devint saint patron que quarante ans plus tard, après l'arrivée au pouvoir d'une nouvelle génération de Přemyslides, incarnée par le duc Břetislav Ier. Celui-ci déroba en 1039 la dépouille d'Adalbert à Gniezno et la rapporta dans la cathédrale de Prague. À partir de ce moment, Adalbert devint le deuxième saint patron de l'État přemyslide, aux côtés de saint Venceslas[9].

Parmi les saints anciens des débuts de l'État tchèque, on compte en général également l'abbé Procope († 1053), fondateur d'un monastère bénédictin dans la région de la Sázava[10]. Après une étude approfondie des sources, je suis toutefois parvenu à la conclusion que la figure de saint Procope avait été artificiellement créée vers le milieu du XIIe siècle, afin de protéger la communauté de tentatives d'expulsion et de remplacement par les nouveaux ordres, chanoines prémontrés et moines cisterciens en tête. La plus ancienne source qui concerne Procope, l'*Exordium Zazavensis*, appartient au genre bien connu des *historiae fundationum monasteriorum*. Il supplée l'absence de titres de propriété en énumérant les possessions que le monastère était censé avoir acquis au temps de Procope. C'est ce texte de combat qui servit de substrat à toutes les Vies ultérieures : la *Vita minor* (début du XIIIe siècle), la *Vita antiqua* (vers 1300), la *Vita maior* (début du XIVe siècle) et ses adaptations en tchèque.

De même, la canonisation de Procope par Innocent III, en 1204, est une pure fiction, même si jusqu'à récemment, personne ne doutait de sa véracité. En réalité, la seule mention de cet acte se trouve dans une addition de la seconde moitié du XIVe siècle à la *Vita maior* et elle n'est confirmée par aucune autre source. Selon moi, Procope a certes été canonisé en 1204, mais uniquement sous la forme d'un dépôt de sa dépouille dans un autel, son culte n'étant au départ qu'une affaire locale[11]. Ce n'est qu'au cours de la seconde moitié du XIIIe siècle que son culte commença à se diffuser dans tout le royaume de Bohême et qu'il en devint le troisième saint patron, après Venceslas et Adalbert. Cette promotion fut facilitée par le fait qu'on vit rétrospectivement en Procope le père spirituel du duc de Bohême Oldřich.

---

[9] P. Kubín, « Die Bemühungen Otto III. um die Einsetzung eines Heiligenkultes für Bischof Adalbert von Prag († 997) », dans *Böhmen und seine Nachbarn in der Přemyslidenzeit* (Vorträge und Forschungen, 74), vol. I, éd. Hlaváček et A. Patschovsky, Ostfildern, 2011, p. 317-340.

[10] Une fois de plus, je ne signale que les monographies principales : Fr. Krásl, *Sv. Prokop, jeho klášter a památka u lidu*, Prague, 1895 ; J. Kadlec, *Svatý Prokop, český strážce odkazu cyrilometodějského*, Prague, 2000 ; P. Sommer, *Svatý Prokop. Z počátků českého státu a církve*, Prague, 2007.

[11] P. Kubín, *Sedm přemyslovských kultů*, op. cit., p. 219-255 ; Id., « Saint Procopius of Sázava between Reality and Fiction », *Revue Mabillon*, 27 (2016), p. 46-82.

À la même époque que Procope vécut saint Gunther († 1045), un ermite du massif de la Šumava, originaire de Thuringe, enterré dans le monastère bénédictin de Břevnov, aux portes de Prague, sous l'abbatiat de Menhart (1035-1089)[12]. Contrairement à Procope, Gunther est un personnage bien réel, dont ses contemporains parlent abondamment. Son culte se développa d'abord entre les murs du monastère, sans éveiller ailleurs le moindre écho. Ainsi le chroniqueur Cosmas de Prague († 1125), qui est pourtant ordinairement très bien informé, n'en parle-t-il pas. Ce n'est que vers le milieu du XIIIe siècle, alors que Břevnov aspirait à occuper la première place parmi les monastères bénédictins de Bohême, que l'abbaye se résolut, avec l'appui du roi Ottokar II, à se lancer dans une action ambitieuse en demandant au pape Innocent IV de canoniser Gunther. À cet effet, une *Vita Guntheri* fut mise en chantier, qui insista sur les liens supposés entre Gunther et le duc de Bohême Břetislav I[er13]. Cette canonisation permettrait, espérait-on, de diffuser son culte à travers la Bohême et même toute la Chrétienté. Innocent IV (1243-1254) entama en effet le procès en canonisation, mais il mourut avant de pouvoir l'achever, et ses successeurs n'éprouvèrent que peu d'intérêt pour la démarche. Malgré une nouvelle tentative dans les années 1260, l'affaire resta au point mort. La tombe de Gunther continua d'attirer des pèlerins à Břevnov, sans faire l'objet d'un culte officiel avant l'époque baroque.

Le culte du bienheureux Hroznata, fondateur et prévôt du monastère prémontré de Teplá, en Bohême occidentale, n'a, à la différence des précédents, rien de dynastique. C'est sa mort violente en prison, le 14 juillet 1217, qui lui valut sa réputation de sainteté. Quarante ans après, l'abbé du lieu commanda une Vie en son honneur. Mais le culte ne dépassa jamais les frontières de l'abbaye de Teplá. Le prouvent le faible nombre de miracles que la *Vita* lui attribue et l'indigence de sa tradition manuscrite[14]. Il faut dire qu'au Moyen Âge, les chanoines prémontrés – au contraire des Bénédictins et des ordres mendiants – n'essayèrent jamais de faire canoniser l'un des leurs, pas même leur fondateur Norbert de Xanten[15]. Ainsi en est-il allé de Hroznata, dont la

---

[12] G. LANG, « Gunther, der Eremit, in Geschichte, Sage und Kult », *Studien und Mitteilungen zur Geschichte des Benediktiner-Ordens und seiner Zweige*, 59 (1941), p. 3-83 ; P. KUBÍN, *Der heiliger Gunther, Einsiedler, Kolonisator und Diplomat*, Prague, 2016.

[13] *Legenda o sv. Vintířovi. Vita s. Guntheri*, éd. P. Kubín, Prague, 2014 (Fontes Bohemiae Hagiographici, 1).

[14] P. KUBÍN, *Blahoslavený Hroznata. Kritický životopis*, Prague, 2000 ; *Legenda o beatru Hrozratovi. Vita fratris Hroznatae*, éd. P. Kubín, Prague, 2017 (*Fontes Bohemiae Hagiographici*, 2).

[15] I. EHLERS-KISSELER, « Heiligenverehrung bei den Prämonstratensern. Die Seligen und Heiligen des Prämonstratenserordens im deutschen Sprachraum », *Rottenburger Jahrbuch für Kirchengeschichte*, 22 (2003), p. 64-94.

Vita fut plus conçue pour alimenter la piété des chanoines que pour servir de pièce pour un éventuel procès en canonisation.

Viennent ensuite les saints liés aux ordres mendiants. Au XIIIe siècle, dans le royaume de Bohême, il s'agit de deux femmes : Agnès[16], une princesse přemyslide († 1282), et Zdislava[17], une femme noble de Bohême du Nord († 1252). Sainte Agnès fonda dans la Vieille Ville de Prague un couvent de Clarisses dont elle fut l'abbesse. À côté, elle fit construire un grand hôpital destiné aux malades pauvres, dirigé par une fraternité hospitalière particulière, les futurs Chevaliers à l'étoile rouge. Elle fut vénérée comme sainte dès son vivant. Aussi, juste après sa mort, le provincial des Frères mineurs de Bohême, Nicolas *Moravus*, tenta-t-il de déposer la première demande de canonisation d'Agnès. Pour des raisons inconnues, elle ne fut jamais remise. Ce n'est qu'en 1328 que l'arrière-petite-nièce d'Agnès, la reine Élisabeth de Bohême, s'adressa au pape Jean XXII avec la même demande. Mais le pape, qui était alors en conflit avec les Frères mineurs sur la question de la pauvreté et de l'obéissance, y opposa une fin de non-recevoir. Agnès continua néanmoins d'être vénérée par les Clarisses, les Frères mineurs et les Chevaliers à l'étoile rouge[18].

De même, sainte Zdislava était elle aussi vénérée pour ses soins apportés aux pauvres et aux malades. Sa mémoire fut essentiellement entretenue par les Dominicains, qui la considéraient comme l'une de leurs tertiaires. Au Moyen Âge, ce culte, si tant est qu'il ait existé, demeura totalement marginal.

Ce n'est que sous le règne de Charles IV que s'agrandit le groupe des saints patrons des pays tchèques : les quatre saints existants, soit Venceslas, Adalbert, Procope et Ludmila, furent complétés par deux autres saints, Guy et Sigismond[19]. Mais ces saints nouveaux n'avaient rien de saints modernes. Guy, le martyr des premiers temps chrétiens († v. 304), devint un saint patron tchèque car il était le patron primitif de la cathédrale de Prague ; quant à Sigismond, roi des Burgondes († 524), Charles IV avait fait l'acquisition de

---

[16] Monographies principales : J. K. Vyskočil, *Blahoslavená Anežka Česká. Kulturní obraz světice 13. století*, Prague, 1933 ; J. V. Polc, *Agnes von Böhmen 1211-1282. Königstochter – Äbtissin – Heilige*, Munich, 1989 ; A. Marini, *Agnese di Boemia*, Rome, 1991 ; V. Kybal, *Svatá Anežka Česká*, Brno, 2001 ; Chr.-Fr. Felskau, *Agnes von Böhmen und die Klosteranlage der Klarissen und Franziskaner in Prag. Leben und Institution, Legende und Verehrung* I-II, Nordhausen, 2008 ; H. Soukupová, *Anežský klášter v Praze*, Prague, 2011. Voir également la contribution de Christian-Frederik Felskau dans le présent volume.

[17] Zd. Kalista, *Blahoslavená Zdislava z Lemberka. Listy z dějin české gotiky*, Prague, 1991.

[18] P. Kubín, « Počátky anežské hagiografie », dans *Svatá Anežka a velké ženy její doby*, éd. M. Šmied et F. Záruba, Prague, 2013, p. 80-99 ; *Id.*, « The Earliest Hagiography of St Agnes of Bohemia († 1282) », *Hagiographica*, 22 (2015), p. 265-290.

[19] V. Ryneš, « Ochránci pražského kostela a české země », dans *Tisíc let pražského biskupství 973-1973*, Prague, 1973, p. 79-124, ici p. 97-106.

sa dépouille en 1365, à l'occasion de son couronnement comme roi de Bourgogne, à Arles[20].

À côté de ces six saints patrons tchèques, très populaires dans toute la société, trois cultes virent timidement le jour au cours de la seconde moitié du XIVe siècle et au début du XVe siècle. Il s'agissait d'une part de deux évêques, Ernest de Pardubice, le tout premier archevêque de Prague († 1364)[21], et Jean de Jenštejn, l'archevêque réformiste qui avait fini par devoir résigner sa charge († 1400)[22] ; d'autre part, du prédicateur à succès Milíč de Kroměříž, que l'historiographie traditionnelle dépeint, à tort ou à raison, comme le précurseur de Hus († 1374)[23]. Aucun de ces cultes ne parvint toutefois à s'imposer. Dans le cas de Jenštejn, ses démêlés avec le roi Venceslas IV en entamèrent durablement le crédit à la cour. La situation de Milíč était pire encore : mort en Avignon, alors que son procès pour hérésie était en cours, il devint le porte-drapeau du milieu béguinal pragois. Il était de ce fait « incanonisable ». Des trois, seul Ernest de Pardubice fut donc vénéré à partir de la deuxième moitié du XVe siècle, non pas en Bohême même, mais à Kłodzko (en Silésie, aujourd'hui en Pologne), où il était enterré[24].

En 1419, la Bohême connut un changement fondamental. La révolution hussite éclata et, pendant deux longs siècles, la Bohême s'éloigna de l'Église catholique au profit de l'utraquisme. Les nouveaux saints de cette époque furent les réformateurs brûlés à Constance, Jean Hus († 1415)[25] et Jérôme de Prague († 1416)[26]. Ils furent immédiatement intégrés au cercle des anciens

---

[20] M. STUDNIČKOVÁ, « Der Kult des heiligen Sigismund (Sigmund) in Böhmen », dans *Die Heiligen und ihr Kult* im Mittelalter, éd. E. DOLEŽALOVÁ, Prague, 2010, p. 299-339.

[21] On dispose à son sujet de deux monographies : V. CHALOUPECKÝ, *Arnošt z Pardubic, první arcibiskup pražský*, Prague, 1941 ; J. K. VYSKOČIL, *Arnošt z Pardubic a jeho doba*, Prague, 1947 ; Zd. HLEDÍKOVÁ, *Arnošt z Pardubic. Arcibiskup, zakladatel, rádce*, Prague, 2008.

[22] Il existe sur lui le livre de R. E. WELTSCH, *Archbishop John of Jenstein (1348-1400). Papalism, Humanism and Reform in Pre-Hussite Prague*, La Haye, 1968.

[23] Voir les présentations contrastées de M. KAŇÁK, *Milíč aus Kremsier. Der Vater der böhmischen Reformation*, Berlin, 1981 et de P. C. A. MORÉE, *Preaching in fourteenth-century Bohemia. The Life and Ideas of Milicius de Chremsir († 1374) and his significance in the historiography of Bohemia*, Heršpice, 1999. La question de l'authenticité des sources hagiographiques qui le concernent est débattue par D. MENGEL, « A Monk, a Preacher and a Jesuit : Making the Life of Milič », dans *The Bohemian Reformation and Religious Practice*, éd. Zd. DAVID et D. HOLETON, vol. 5/1, Prague, 2005, p. 33-47.

[24] P. KUBÍN, « Otázka Arnoštova svatořečení », dans *Arnošt z Pardubic (1297-1364), Osobnost-okruh-dědictví*, éd. L. BOBKOVÁ, R. GLADKIEWICZ et P. VOREL, Wrocław-Prague-Pardubice, 2005, p. 93-106.

[25] Je ne signale que les quatre dernières monographies, qui font référence à des travaux plus anciens : P. HILSCH, *Johannes Hus (um 1370-1415). Prediger Gottes und Ketzer*, Ratisbonne, 1999 ; J. KEJŘ, *Jan Hus známý i neznámý*, Prague, 2009 ; Fr. ŠMAHEL, *Jan Hus. Život a dílo*, Prague, 2013 ; P. SOUKUP, *Jan Hus*, Stuttgart, 2014.

[26] Fr. ŠMAHEL, *Život a dílo Jeronýma Pražského*, Prague, 2010.

saints patrons, sans avoir besoin d'être approuvés par Rome. D'autres martyrs de la cause hussite leur emboîtèrent bientôt le pas. Ils en vinrent parfois à susciter, comme dans le cas des martyrs de Kutná Hora, de véritables ostensions de reliques[27].

Revenons pour finir à la question de savoir si, en Bohême, les saints anciens ont éclipsé les saints modernes. Le duo de base des saints patrons – Venceslas et Adalbert – avait une importance primordiale, d'ordre symbolique, pour l'État tchèque. Ils étaient à ce titre irremplaçables. Il devenait difficile par conséquent de leur substituer qui que ce fût d'autre. Plus tard, saint Procope et sainte Ludmila vinrent se rajouter. Il faut souligner que tous ces saints commencèrent à être vénérés à une époque où la simple approbation de l'évêque suffisait à la sanctification. Or, le nouveau code de droit canon de 1234, le *Liber extra*, ne tarda pas à réserver le droit de canonisation au seul pape[28]. Désormais, les candidats à la sainteté devaient subir un procès en canonisation long et complexe, qui n'avait que peu de chances d'aboutir. Le jeu en valait-il la chandelle ? Certes, la canonisation pontificale valait ensuite pour toute la Chrétienté. Mais ni saint Gunther, ni sainte Agnès ne parvinrent à obtenir cet honneur, de sorte que leur culte resta circonscrit à certaines communautés régulières. D'autres cultes – ceux de Hroznata, Zdislava, Milíč et Jenštejn – ne bénéficièrent même pas de la moindre tentative d'introduction en cour de Rome. Et c'est à peine si, dans le cas d'Ernest de Pardubice, on consigna sa vie et ses miracles au début du XVIe siècle – trop tard : la Réformation protestante qui secoua alors la Silésie lui enleva aussitôt toute chance d'accéder à la gloire des autels. Dans ces conditions, à la fin du Moyen Âge, le « ciel bohémien » ne put s'enrichir que de saints anciens venus d'ailleurs, comme saint Guy et saint Sigismond.

Cependant, tout changea avec la montée du hussitisme. Les Hussites faisant fi de l'aval du pape, de nouveaux saints contemporains trouvèrent leur place tout naturellement aux côtés des traditionnels saints patrons de la Bohême. La domination constante des anciens cultes en Bohême doit donc beaucoup plus à des contraintes extérieures qu'à un prétendu immobilisme du christianisme local[29].

Traduit du tchèque par Anna Kubišta

---

[27] O. HALAMA, « Die utraquistische Verehrung der böhmischen Heiligen », dans *Die Heiligen und ihr Kult, op. cit.*, p. 203-213.
[28] S. KUTTNER, « La réserve papale du droit de canonisation », *Revue historique de droit français et étranger*, 18 (1938), p. 172-228.
[29] Cet article a été écrit avec le soutien du programme NAKI n° DF 11P010V V007 [Culture et art de l'ordre bénédictin en Europe centrale, 800-1300] (2011-2015).

The Universal Cult of the Virgin Martyrs in Late Medieval Transylvania

Carmen FLOREA
(Cluj)

In the year 1431 George Lépes, Bishop of the diocese of Transylvania from the kingdom of Hungary, requested from the Holy See approval for the foundation of two altars in his cathedral church from Alba Iulia (Gyulafehérvár, Weissenburg).[1] One of the altars was to be dedicated to St Michael, the patron saint of the Episcopate and the other to the Virgin Martyr Barbara.[2] When taking into account the patron saints of the altars existing at that time in Alba Iulia cathedral, one is compelled to notice the prevalence of the traditional saints (such as the Apostles and the martyrs).[3] Furthermore, with the exception of the Virgin Mary, no other female saint seems to have been popular among the cathedral clergy since the end of the thirteenth century when the altar *patrocinia* are recorded by our sources and the first decades of the

---

[1] This work was supported by a grant of the Romanian National Authority for Scientific Research, CNCS – UEFISCDI, project number PN-II-ID-PCE-2011-3-0359, code 225/2011. At the first mentioning of a place name its historical names would be given in brackets, afterwards the present-day name will be used.

[2] *XV. századi pápák oklevelei*, ed. P. LUKCSICS, Budapest, 1931, vol. II, no. 21, p. 44.

[3] The Bishopric of Transylvania was founded in the eleventh century as part of the church organization initiated by King Stephen of Hungary (1000-1038). Information about its first bishop came from 1111, whilst the activity of the cathedral chapter is attested by the surviving sources only from the thirteenth century. See Gy. KRISTÓ, "The Bishoprics of Saint Stephen, King of Hungary", in *In honorem Paul Cernovodeanu*, ed. V. BARBU, București, 1998, p. 56-76; J. TEMESVÁRI, *Erdély középkori püspökei*, Cluj-Koloszvár, 1922, p. 4-5; G. GYÖRFFY, "Gyulafehérvár kezdetei, neve és káptalanjának registruma", *Századok*, 5 (1983), p. 1103-1117. In his monograph of the cathedral church of Alba Iulia, Géza Entz has compiled a list with the altarpieces that once decorated St Michael's cathedral. Thus, the altars dedicated to The Virgin Mary, St John the Baptist and St Peter are mentioned in 1291, whilst in the fourteenth century are mentioned those dedicated to St Michael (1363), to the Holy Cross (1357), to St Andrew (1366), to St Lawrence (1370), to Corpus Christi (1374), to Sts. Cosmas and Damian (1381), to All Saints (1391), and to the 10,000 Martyrs (1400), G. ENTZ, *A gyulafehérvári székesegyház*, Budapest, 1958, p. 200-205.

Les saints et leur culte en Europe centrale au Moyen Âge (XIe-début du XVIe siècle), éd. par Marie-Madeleine de CEVINS et Olivier MARIN, Turnhout, 2017 (*Hagiologia*, 13), p. 39-56.
© BREPOLS PUBLISHERS DOI 10.1484/M.HAG-EB.5.113966

fifteenth century when two other Virgin Martyrs, Dorothy and Catherine, have altars dedicated to them in the cathedral of St Michael (mentioned in 1411 and 1431 respectively).[4] Whilst the surviving sources do not spell out clearly who were the founders of these two altars, their establishment can be connected with the activity of George Lépes, who has been provost of the cathedral chapter between 1403 and 1427 and afterwards filled the office of Bishop until his death in 1442.[5] A similar involvement of the high ecclesiastics in the promotion of the Virgin Martyrs' cult in the Episcopal Sees of the medieval kingdom of Hungary is disclosed by another example concerning the cathedral church of Oradea (Nagyvárad, Grosswerdein) where Bishop Demeter Mezesi (1345-1372) founded the altar of St Catherine and lavishly endowed that of St Dorothy.[6]

Additional information, such as that provided by church dedications, mural and panel paintings, suggests that devotion for the Virgin Martyrs became popular in Transylvania, particularly from the fifteenth century onwards. Thus, it should be observed that in the light of church *patrocinia* it was St Catherine to whom churches and chapels were dedicated, their mentioning occurring primarily in the course of fifteenth and sixteenth century.[7] On the other hand, St Dorothy was the patron of two chapels and one charitable establishment, the spread of her cult following the same chronological sequence as the dedications to Catherine.[8] In as much as St Barbara is concerned, one should notice a peculiar feature of this cult, as I have been able to gather information concerning a sole chapel dedicated to her, that of

---

[4] G. ENTZ, *A gyulafehérvári, op. cit.*, p. 203; Z. JAKÓ, *A kolozsmonostori konvent jegyzőkönyvei (1289-1556)*, Budapest, 1990, vol. I, no. 71, p. 209.
[5] J. TEMESVÁRI, *Erdély, op. cit.*, p. 327-353.
[6] V. BUNYITAY, *A váradi püspökség története alapításától a jelenkorig*, vol. I, Nagyvárad, 1883, p. 186.
[7] According to the list compiled by G. GÜNDISCH, "Die Patrozinien der sächsischen Pfarrkirchen Siebenbürgens", in *Forschungen über Siebenbürgen und seine Nachbarn. Festschrift für Zsigmond Jakó und Attila T. Szabó*, ed. B. KÁLMÁN *et al.*, vol. I, München, 1987, p. 94-103, the following parish churches from the Saxon ecclesiastical units were dedicated to St Catherine: Șeica Mică (Salschelk, Kisselyk) – 1414, Șercaia (Schirkanyen, Sárkany) – 1429, Toarcla (Tarteln, Prázsmár) – ?, Beriu (Lammdorf, Berény) – ?, and Vulcan (Wolkendorf, Szászvolkány) – 1549. Other church dedications of this Virgin Martyr, such as those from Hermannsdorf – 1401, Siciu (Somlyószécs) – 1465, Cojocna (Kolozs, Salzburg) – 1508 and Petrindu (Nagypetri) – 1509 were gathered by G. ENTZ, *Erdély építészete a 14.-16 században*, Kolozsvár, 1996, p. 113, 134, 305, 463.
[8] A chapel dedicated to St Dorothy was attested in the town of Bistrița (Bistriz, Beszterce), whereas the hospital of Sighișoara (Schässburg, Segesvár) also had a chapel devoted to this Virgin Martyr, see O. DAHINTEN, "Beiträge zur Baugeschichte der Stadt Bistritz", *Archiv des Vereins für Siebenbürgische Landeskunde*, 50 (1944), p. 210 and G. ENTZ, *Erdély, op. cit.*, p. 438.

the *leprosarium* from Braşov.[9] Therefore, it could be observed that based on church *patrocinia* we are indeed dealing with a late medieval development of the long-established cults of the Virgin Martyrs. It is perhaps this late medieval flourishing that prevented these universal saints to be more consistently reflected in church dedications, as the parochial network was largely established by the fourteenth century.[10] Yet, if one takes into account only St Catherine, the nine churches and chapels that were dedicated to her seem to suggest a growth of this cult in the ecclesiastical units subordinated to the Transylvanian Bishops and to confirm her almost unmatched popularity by any other Virgin Martyr in the kingdom of Hungary.[11]

Previous research has convincingly argued that an analysis of the panel paintings representing the Virgin Martyrs can be carried on only in what concerns images survived from polyptych altarpieces dedicated to other saints, as most likely none of the altars that had a Virgin Martyr as a titular saint has come down to us.[12] Thus, one has to take into account solely the iconic representations of the Virgin Martyrs that decorate the panels of the surviving altarpieces. However, given that these artifacts' were largely produced in the course of the fifteenth and the first half of the sixteenth century,[13] inves-

---

[9] E. JEKELIUS, "Die Spitäler", in *Das Burzenland*, vol. III, Kronstadt, 1928, p. 249.

[10] The ecclesiastical structure of Transylvania was composed of thirteen archdeaneries which together with several chapters (the so-called Landkapitels) organized in the areas inhabited by a Saxon population were subjected to the Transylvanian Bishops from Alba Iulia. Two chapters, those of Sibiu (Hermannstadt, Nagyszeben) and Braşov (Kronstadt, Brassó) were placed under the jurisdiction of the Archbishopric of Esztergom. A. BEKE, "Erdélyi egyházmegye képe a XIV. század elején", *Magyar Sion*, 52 (1894), p. 533-609, 609-620, 621-623, 624-625, 683-693, 759, 761-768; 768-773 and 848-855, 921-937, 938-942, 945-950, 951-955, 956-958; F. TEUTSCH, *Geschichte der evangelischen Kirche in Siebenbürgen*, vol. I (1150-1699), Hermannstadt, 1921.

[11] S. BÁLINT, *Ünnepi kalendárium. A Mária-ünnepek és jelesebb napok hazai és közép-európai hagyományvilágából*, Budapest, 1977, vol. II, p. 231-234.

[12] M. CRĂCIUN, "Narativ şi iconic. Rolul educativ şi devoţional al iconografiei referitoare la sfinţi în altarele poliptice din sudul Transilvaniei", in *Tentaţia istoriei. In memoria profesorului Pompiliu Teodor*, ed. N. BOCŞAN, O. GHITTA, D. RADOSAV, Cluj-Napoca, 2003, p. 37-82. The representations of the life of St Ursula on the interior of the mobile wings of the altarpiece from Beia (Meerburg, Homoródbene) have been considered as indicating that the altarpiece might have been dedicated to this Virgin Martyr. See particularly *ibid.*, p. 47 and 53.

[13] The Virgin Martyrs Barbara, Catherine, Dorothy, Agnes and Margaret were represented on the polyptich of Biertan; Barbara, Catherine, Dorothy and Margaret were depicted on the altarpiece from Tătârlaua (Seiden/Taterloch, Felsőtatárlaka); St Catherine was represented in the shrine of the polyptich from Băgaciu (Bogeschdorf, Szászbogács); Catherine, Barbara, and Appolonia were depicted on the coronamentum of the retable from Şaeş; Catherine and Barbara were represented on the predella of the polyptich from Moşna; Barbara, Catherine, Margaret and Agnes were depicted on the intermediate panels of the altarpiece from Mălâncrav (Malmkrog, Almakerék); Catherine and Margaret can be found on the exterior of the panels

tigating the way the Virgin Martyrs were depicted could provide interesting insights related to the manifestations of their cults.

A similar timeframe, that of the fifteenth and the first half of the sixteenth century, can be established when scrutinizing the mural paintings that have survived. From the large cohort of the Virgin Martyrs, Barbara, Dorothy, Catherine, Margaret and Ursula were represented more frequently, whilst episodes from the legends of Catherine, Margaret and Ursula were also preserved by Transylvanian mural paintings.[14] Let me suggest at this point, that based on church *patrocinia* and visual representations, the long-established cults of the Virgin Martyrs, particularly those of Sts. Catherine, Barbara, Margaret and Dorothy flourished in late medieval Transylvania.

The purpose of this investigation, therefore, would be that of examining in great detail the growing popularity of the cults of the Virgin Martyrs in the last centuries of the Middle Ages. Whilst the first part of the analysis will explore the agency of these long-established cults, particularly the clerical

---

from Proștea Mare [Târnava] (Grossprobstdorf, Nagyekemező); groups of Virgin Martyrs being also represented on the exterior of the panels from the altarpiece of Boian (Bonnesdorf, Alsóbajon) and on the interior of the wings at Leliceni (Csíkszentlélek), whereas statues depicting them were placed in the niches of the polyptich from Jimbor (Sommerburg, Székelyzsombor). G. and O. RICHTER, *Siebenbürgische Flügelaltäre*, Thaur bei Innsbruck, p. 59, 154, 194, 249; E. SARKADI NAGY, *Local Workshops – Foreign Connections. Late Medieval Altarpieces from Transylvania*, Ostfildern, 2011 (Studia Jagellonica Lipsiensia, 9), p. 51, 118, 125, 128, 131, 137, 141, 149, 173, 188, 199, 201, 204; M. CRĂCIUN, "'Moartea cea bună:' intercesori și protectori în pragul marii treceri. Între discursul clerical și pietatea populară", in *Discursuri despre moarte în Transilvania secolelor XVI-XX*, ed. M. GRANCEA, Cluj-Napoca, 2006, p. 236-237.

[14] Dorothy was depicted in the mural paintings of the churches from Mălâncrav (the end of the fourteenth century), Nemșa (the beginning of the fifteenth century), Mugeni/Bügöz (beginning of the fifteenth century) and Cluj (mid-fifteenth century); visual representations of St Catherine can be found in the churches of Drăușeni (end of the fourteenth century), Mălâncrav (end of the fourteenth century), Nemșa (beginning of the fifteenth century), Sușeni (fifteenth century), Sâncraiul de Mureș (fifteenth century), Cluj (mid-fifteenth century); representations of St Margaret of Antioch survived from the churches of Ghelința/Gelence (mid-fourteenth century), Mugeni (mid-fourteenth century), Mărtiniș/Homoródszentmarton (fourteenth century), Sic (end of the fourteenth century), Cluj (mid-fifteenth century), Daia/Szászdálya (sixteenth century). Images of St Ursula are depicted in the mural paintings of the churches from Sic/Szék (fourteenth century), Mălâncrav (end of the fourteenth century), Cluj (mid-fifteenth century), Biertan (first quarter of the sixteenth century). See V. DRĂGUȚ, "Iconografia picturilor murale gotice din Transilvania. Considerații generale și repertoriu de teme", *Pagini de veche artă românească*, vol. II, București, 1972, p. 65 and 76-77. Recent restoration work has also brought to light frescoes representing the Virgin Martyrs, such as those from Badești/Bádok (St Catherine), Sântimbru/Csíkszentimre (St Margaret), Imper / Kászonimpér (St Margaret or St Catherine), Sușeni (St Catherine and St Barbara), Chilieni/Kilyen (most likely St Dorothy). Z. JÉKELY and L. KISS, *Középkori falképek Erdélyben. Értékmentés a Teleki László Alapítvány támogatásával*, Budapest, 2008, p. 8-13, 50, 134-137, 190-194, 206-207 and 278-279.

one, the second part will try to decipher the way devotion for the Virgin Martyrs reverberated from the Episcopal See of Alba Iulia into the Transylvanian diocese. This detailed scrutiny of the modalities with which the cult of traditional saints was revived in the late Middle Ages could help gaining a more nuanced understanding of the nature of sanctity at the periphery of Latin Christendom.

Dorothy, Catherine and Barbara belonged to the group of *Virgines Capitales* and were included in late medieval times among the Fourteen Holy Helpers. Furthermore, as we are informed by medieval gender studies, the Virgin Martyrs, particularly St Catherine and St Barbara, became powerful cultural symbols, their cults being mostly supported and to a certain extent transformed to suit the needs of male ecclesiastical elite.[15] The mentioning of the altars of Dorothy, Barbara and Catherine at the time when George Lépes filled the offices of provost and Bishop in Alba Iulia undoubtedly proves his support of these cults. Further information in this regard concerns the architectural changes Bishop George initiated during his episcopate, changes that included a re-arrangement of the liturgical space of the cathedral through the building of several altars, which would disclose the Bishop's preference for certain saints. It should also be mentioned that in order to secure the financial means needed for such work, George Lépes sent envoys to the Metropolitan See of Esztergom to acquire the important amount of 1000 Golden Florins the former Transylvanian Bishop George Pállócz left in his testament for the cathedral of St Michael from Alba Iulia.[16]

If Sts. Barbara, Dorothy and Catherine appealed to the ecclesiastics because through their examples difference of status and knowledge could be re-enforced, then our Bishop could have been the perfect candidate for the initiation of such cults. He held the clerical offices which enabled him to efficiently propagate the cults of the Virgin Martyrs and was the commissioner of the re-building work of several parts of the cathedral church where his devotional choices could be materialized. There was much more. Bishop George was of aristocratic origin, studied at the University of Vienna and was the royal chaplain of King Sigismund.[17] The academic formation of Bishop George at the University of Vienna where St Catherine was held in great esteem, his ecclesiastical career, his social status and to be sure not lastly his

---

[15] A. SIMON, *The Cult of Saint Katherine of Alexandria in Late Medieval Nuremberg: Saint and the City*, Farnham, 2012; *St Katherine of Alexandria: Texts and Contexts*, ed. J. JENKINS and K. J. LEWIS, Turnhout, 2003; S. SALIH, *Versions of Virginity in Late Medieval England*, Cambridge, 2001.
[16] G. ENTZ, *A gyulafehérvári, op. cit.*, p. 115-116 and 184.
[17] TEMESVÁRY, *Erdély, op. cit.*, p. 329-333.

explicit preference for one of the Virgin Martyrs, might explain the emergence of these cults in Alba Iulia cathedral during his episcopate.

In what follows I would like to further suggest that the cults of the Virgin Martyrs were clerically driven cults in the Transylvanian Episcopal milieu not only because it was thanks to the high clergy's initiatives that Dorothy, Catherine and Barbara started to be venerated in the cathedral of St Michael beginning with the first half of the fifteenth century. It seems equally important to me, that these cults have been transformed as a result of this clerical support, since the men of religion could strengthen through the adoption of this particular model of sainthood their own authority and prestige.

For example, the only extant version of the legend of St Catherine depicted in the Transylvanian mural paintings that have come down to us is that from the church of Drăuşeni (Drass, Daróc) (see Figure 1, outside the text). In this pictorial narrative both the authority and intellectual abilities of the Virgin Martyr are strongly emphasized, as Catherine is represented wearing the crown and holding a book, symbols which could be considered as enforcing the public figure of the saint.[18] Furthermore, as it has already been observed, the philosophers are depicted in a manner that seems to ridicule them, as the one who appears to be the saint's main opponent is depicted as having six fingers.[19]

The popularity of the Virgin Martyrs' cult in the late Middle Ages has been regarded as reflecting its multifaceted nature, these young and faithful women being revered not only for their sacrifice when shedding their blood for the love of Christ, but also for their intellectual abilities, for their knowledge and exemplary way of life.[20] The dynamism of the cult for the Virgin Martyrs is evidence for the way ancient saintly figures were transformed in order to illustrate not only the expectations, but also the merits of their supporters. This can particularly be seen in the promotion of their cults by the male ecclesiastical elite and the subsequent transformation of the Virgin Martyrs' cult as a result of this promotion.

Recent research focusing on the way Sts. Barbara and Catherine were depicted in the late Middle Ages has revealed that emphasis was laid on those features which brought them closer to the clerical status. For example, for

---

[18] About the way Catherine's scholarship and preaching are reflected and transformed in the hagiographic tradition see S. L. KATZ, "To Speak of Silence: Clemence of Barking's Life of St Catherine and Her Vision of Female Wisdom", *Magistra: A Journal of Women's Spirituality in History* (Fall/Winter 2010), p. 1-19.
[19] V. DRĂGUŢ, "Însemnări despre pictura murală a bisericii fortificate din Drăuşeni", *Studii şi cercetări de istoria artei*, 1 (1962), p. 180-188.
[20] J. JENKINS and K. J. LEWIS, "Introduction", in *St Katherine of Alexandria, op. cit.*, p. 1-18.

late medieval Transylvania it has been observed that in the panel paintings, particularly those survived from the Saxon areas, Barbara tended to be represented with her usual symbol the tower, but also, with the chalice and host.[21] This kind of representation emerged in the German lands and was, in fact, a recent development in the cult of St Barbara, reflecting and underlining the Virgin's ability to provide a good death through the dispensing of Sacrament.[22] It was precisely this quality which transformed Barbara in one of the Fourteen Helpers, as a saint able to provide specialized help. At the same time, it should be remembered that dispensing the Sacrament was a clerical function, and hence Barbara performed one of the duties that defined the male clerical status and responded to the universal need of a "good death". But, as the surviving Transylvanian panel paintings testify, trends visible elsewhere in medieval Europe, pointing to the identification of the ecclesiastical elite with the Virgin Martyrs, seem to be reverberating to the margins of the Latin Christendom.

Similar developments are noticeable in the case of the cult of St Catherine. One could learn from the detailed analysis of the English Breviaries that Catherine was used as a model for the clergy, as those characteristics of the saint which bear close resemblance to those of an educated cleric were highlighted in these writings.[23] Such a tendency is detectable in the sermons produced in the medieval kingdom of Hungary. In the work of Pelbartus of *Themeswar*, renowned Observant Franciscan preacher, dedicated to the saints of the liturgical calendar, the four sermons for St Catherine highlight the merits of the Virgin's life and justify the veneration the Bride of Christ deserves.[24] Recently, attention has also been drawn to the changes occurring in the legend of Catherine. Among them were also those illustrating the intellectual abilities of St Catherine. Thus, she was learned not only in the seven liberal arts but, as we are instructed by the Observant Franciscan preacher, also in economy, ethics and politics, *scientiae* which were favoured

---

[21] M. Crăciun, "The Cult of St Barbara and the Saxon Community of Late Medieval Transylvania", in *Identity and Alterity in Hagiography and the Cult of Saints*, ed. A. Marinković and T. Vedriš, Zagreb, 2010, p. 138-63.

[22] M. Crăciun, *Moartea cea bună*, op. cit., p. 235-259.

[23] S. L. Reams, "St Katherine and the Late Medieval Clergy: Evidence from English Breviaries", in *St Katherine of Alexandria*, op. cit., p. 201-220.

[24] Among the most popular collections of sermons the Observant Franciscan friar compiled, one can mention *Sermones Pomerii de Sanctis Hyemales et Estivales, Sermones Quadragesimales, Stellarium Coronae benedicte Marie Virginis* works which were published again and again by different European *officina* such as those from Haguenau and Augsburg. See Á. Szilády, *Temesvári Pelbárt élete és munkái*, Budapest, 1880, p. 365-472.

by the humanists.[25] Therefore, it can be concluded that the model of Catherine construed by the ecclesiastics was a dynamic one, reflecting recent achievements in academic education.

This way of adopting and adapting the cult of this Virgin Martyr is also detectable in visual representations. In the Middle Ages, hair was a marker of identity, as it distinguished clergy from laity, virgins from married women or widows.[26] Catherine with short-hair or with it stopping at the shoulder is quite frequently found in the images of the Books of Hours produced in late fifteenth and early sixteenth century in North-Western Europe and it has been argued that it reassembles the way the hair of young male clerics was depicted.[27] Interestingly enough, a short-haired Catherine is represented in several Transylvanian panel paintings, such as the altarpiece of the church in Biertan (Birthälm, Berethalom), the Coronamentum of the retable from Şaeş (Schass, Segesd) and the predella of the retable from Moşna (Meschen, Muzsna).[28]

These examples further prove that latest trends associated to the Virgin Martyr's cult reached the most eastern corner of the Latin Christendom, finding their way in other visual media than that of book illustrations.[29] According to a detailed analysis, from a stylistical and compositional point of view of the polyptich of Biertan, it has been demonstrated that this work of art can be linked with the Viennese Schotten-workshop, emphasizing similarities with the Behaim predella and pointing out that this influence is clearly detectable in the depiction of the Virgin Martyr's hair (see cover illustration).[30] Another example is that of the retable from Moşna, where

---

[25] Fl. RAJHONA, *Alexandriai Szent Katalin legendája Temesvári Pelbárt feldologozásában*, online version http://sermones.elte.hu/?az= 312tan_plaus_flora (latest access 30 March 2016). Illustrative in this regard is the following fragment from the second sermon Pelbartus devoted to St Catherine: *Notandum ergo, quod sapientia est triplex, prima infima, secunda media, tertia summa... Secunda est sapientia media, quae est in scientia humana. Et ista quaedam est physica, ut sunt septem artes liberales, quas Catharina perfecte scivit. Quaedam est ethica, quae docet morum honestatem. Catherina omnibus virtutibus fuit decorata. Quaedam est oeconomica, quae docet domum et familiam regere. Ipsa palatium et familiam sapienter gubernavit. Quaedam autem est politica, quae docet urbes et regna pacifice gubernare. Catherina ut regina regnum optime rexit, ergo ista sapientia plena fuit.*
[26] R. BARTLETT, "Symbolic Meanings of Hair in the Middle Ages", in *Transactions of the Royal Historical Society*, Sixth Series, 4 (1994), p. 43-60.
[27] K. WINSTEAD, "St Katherine's Hair", in *St Katherine of Alexandria, op. cit.*, p. 172-186.
[28] G. and O. RICHTER, *Siebenbürgische, op. cit.*, p. 59 and 249.
[29] K. WINSTEAD, "St Katherine's Hair", in *St Katherine of Alexandria, op. cit.*, p. 183, argued that in North-Western Europe a short hair Catherine was frequently represented in the book illuminations, but not in other visual media.
[30] E. SARKADI NAGY, *Local Workshops, op. cit.*, p. 51 and 128-131 identified a first phase for the production of the altarpiece of Biertan in the year 1483 when the panels of the central part

St Catherine and St Barbara are depicted among the Fourteen Holy Helpers. Catherine is represented with her hair cut short, whilst Barbara, placed next to her, holds the chalice. The interesting idea that Barbara with the chalice and the Sacrament mirrored priestly function, thus suggesting the ecclesiastical support of her cult,[31] is worth following in the case of the representations of St Catherine as well.

The nuanced observations drawn by detailed studies dedicated to the significance of hair in the Middle Ages and its uses in order to masculinise a Virgin Martyr famous for her intellectual abilities could thus be employed in order to reveal the priestly status of Catherine. Somehow similar to Barbara who seems to undertake clerical function when dispensing the Sacrament is Catherine with her short-hair and the book she holds in her hands. Let me return once more to the predella of Moşna-retable. This work of art was produced in 1521, in the Transylvanian workshop of Vincentius *Cibiniensis*, being commissioned by the parish priest Alexander de *Muschna*. The commissioner was an educated cleric who studied at the University of Vienna, earning the title of doctor in canonical and Roman law.[32] It cannot be established with certainty if representing the Virgin Martyr in a manner that alluded to clerical abilities was the choice of the parish priest, who has wished to display devotion to the patroness of the students and of Vienna University. Apart from these academic and theological motivations, it might have been very well the choice of perhaps the most famous Transylvanian painter of that time, Vincentius. Whatever it might have been the justification, it could be observed that this type of pictorial representations depicts Catherine and Barbara as embodying a clerical ideal.

In late medieval Transylvania the cults of the Virgin Martyrs, particularly those of Barbara and Catherine, appear to have been popular with the clergymen to such an extent that they have been transformed in order to emphasize the clerical status. Such a change reflected by both hagiographic writings and visual representations beyond doubt contributed to the growing popularity of the cult of the Virgin Martyrs in Transylvania, as elsewhere in the Latin Christendom. This universal trend can also be regarded as revealing not only the multifaceted nature of long-established cults, but also their dynamism. It is precisely the rhythm of the spread of the cults of the Virgin

---

were painted, whereas the altarpiece was completed only in the first quarter of the sixteenth century. The arrangement of the saints' hair resembles closely that of St Catherine's from the predella of the Behaim retable from Nuremberg, produced by Hans Siebenbürger sometimes in the timeframe between 1460 and 1465.

[31] M. CRĂCIUN, *The Cult of St Barbara, op. cit.*, p. 147-152.
[32] E. SARKADI NAGY, *Local Workshops, op. cit.*, p. 127-129.

Martyrs in the Transylvanian ecclesiastical units that will be explored in the remaining part of this analysis.

Starting from the premise that devotion for the Virgin Martyrs was strongly supported by the ecclesiastical elite, the contribution the Transylvanian Episcopate made in the distribution of these cults should be scrutinized. It has previously been mentioned that in what concerns St Barbara, Bishop Lépes decisively contributed through his foundation to the regular veneration of this saint in the cathedral and most likely prompted devotion to other Virgin Martyrs, such as Dorothy and Catherine. Therefore, I would like to suggest that the model of saintliness the Virgin Martyrs embodied was adopted by other ecclesiastics who most likely further disseminated it within the Transylvanian ecclesiastical units.[33]

Highly illustrative in this regard is the example provided by the parochial functioning of the cults of the Virgin Martyrs. In the fourth decade of the fifteenth century, an agreement was concluded between the city council of Sibiu and the parish priest of the town, that among the Masses the local clergy would have to perform one would be dedicated to St Catherine.[34] It is also interesting that in the timeframe between 1432 and 1448 one is able to trace in Sibiu the emergence of the cult of another Virgin Martyr, that of St Barbara. Most likely the altar founded by Bishop Lépes contributed to the growth of the veneration for Barbara within the Episcopal milieu from Alba Iulia, as this is suggested by the altarists that were responsible for this altar in the following decades.[35] At the same time, it should be observed that among the cathedral clergy there was also a certain Anthony, doctor in canon law, whose career in this ecclesiastical structure can be followed in the timeframe between 1442 and 1457 and can be considered a successful one, since in 1450 the churchman became the vicar of the Transylvanian Bishop. But Anthony was not only an important member of the cathedral chapter, he also filled the office of parish priest of Sibiu for several years in mid-fifteenth century.[36]

It was precisely during this time that the parish church of Sibiu was enlarged by the construction of a new chapel. As our sources indicate, this

---

[33] For example, Dominic, parish priest in *Zeek* was the founder of the chapel dedicated to St Catherine in Cojocna. Zs. JAKÓ, *A kolozsmonostori, op. cit.*, no. 3462, p. 279-280.
[34] G. GÜNDISCH, "Hermmanstädter Messestiftungen im 15. Jahrhundert", *Siebenbürgische Vierteljahrschrift*, 64 (1941), p. 28-37: according to the settlement of 1432, the divine service devoted to St Catherine was to be celebrated daily and on Saturday at the altar of the Virgin Martyr.
[35] G. ENTZ, *A gyulafehérvári, op. cit.*, p. 203.
[36] G. SEIVERT, "Chronologische Tafel der hermannstädter Plebane, Oberbeamten und Notare (1309-1499)", *Archiv des Vereins für Siebenbürgische Landeskunde*, Neue Folge 12-13 (1874/1875), p. 530.

Figure 1: St Catherine's disputes with the philosophers.
Fresco from the church of Drăuşeni.

(photo : Bogdan Danielescu)

project was most likely initiated and supported by the parish priest and his parishioners. The indulgences they managed to procure in 1448 refer to the chapel as being dedicated to the patron saint of their parish church, the Virgin Mary and as many as other fourteen saints.[37] This could be considered an improvised group of fourteen holy helpers that included not the traditional figures one would expect, but saints who were popular among the German population, such as Wolfgang or Florian, saints who became highly revered as a result of Mendicant propaganda, such as Francis, Elizabeth or Claire, or those who benefited from a strong local reputation, such as the saints of the Arpadian dynasty, Stephen, Emeric and Ladislas.

Another sub-group of these fourteen holy helpers from Sibiu consisted of no less than four Virgin Martyrs, Catherine, Barbara, Dorothy and Cecily. We have seen that St Catherine seems to have been already popular in 1448 as the agreement with the parish priest concluded in 1432 enforced her celebration in the church of Sibiu. It cannot be excluded that the inclusion of the other Virgin Martyrs may have reflected their growing popularity. However, it could be ascertained that Anthony, parish priest of Sibiu and canon of the cathedral chapter from Alba Iulia in 1448, may have decided that the chapel to be built should be dedicated to St Barbara, as well. Not only because similarly to other cults of the Virgins, her cult too flourished at that time. St Barbara was constantly venerated in the cathedral of St Michael since 1431 when Bishop Lépes decided to found an altar dedicated to her. The Episcopal support of the cult of St Barbara might have inspired Anthony, one of the cathedral's canons, to introduce this cult in the parish church he was responsible for. The inclusion of St Barbara among the other fourteen patrons of the Sibiu chapel could thus be integrated within the general growth of the cult of the Virgin Martyrs in late medieval Transylvania. Even more importantly, this inclusion may have been connected with the emerging cult of St Barbara in the Episcopal milieu that determined its adoption and dissemination within the parochial environment from Sibiu.

Although the parish church of Sibiu was placed under the jurisdiction of the Archbishops from Esztergom and not subordinated to the Transylvanian Episcopate, the common affiliation of Anthony to the cathedral clergy of Alba Iulia and to the church of the town may have contributed to the propagation of the cult of St Barbara. The functioning of the cults of the Virgin Martyrs within the parochial milieu of Sibiu thus complements their clerical promotion in late medieval Transylvania. It would be

---

[37] *Urkundenbuch zur Geschichte der Deutschen in Siebenbürgen*, ed. F. ZIMMERMANN and G. GÜNDISCH, București, 1975, vol. V, no. 2634, p. 242-243.

therefore interesting to analyze the shaping of the cults of Sts. Barbara and Catherine within the parish churches of another two free royal towns, Bistrița and Cluj. As the parish churches of both of these towns were under the jurisdiction of the Bishops from Alba Iulia, one could assess the extent to which the cults of the Virgin Martyrs may have benefited from Episcopal support.

According to a testament drafted in 1513, no less than three confraternities of the Virgin Martyrs were endowed by a certain Anthony Heem.[38] Two of these devotional associations were dedicated to St Catherine, one functioning in the parish church of Bistrița and the other in the parish church of a nearby village, Dumitra (Mettersdorf). The third confraternity that was the object of devotion in the testament of Anthony Heem was patronized by St Barbara and most likely was organized in the parish church of Bistrița. Unfortunately, not much can be said about these fraternities, as neither the date of their founding, nor details regarding their functioning have survived up to our days.[39] Despite this lack of information, it can be considered that the cults of the Virgin Martyrs were popular in the town at the turn of the fifteenth to sixteenth century. I would like to emphasize that this popularity is suggested by the fact that Sts. Catherine and Barbara were the patron saints of devotional associations and it is precisely this institutionalization which demonstrates both the broader dissemination of these cults and the specific forms of worship usually assumed by the members of confraternities.[40] But how did these cults emerge in the town of Bistrița and to what extent were they the result of clerical impulses?

In 1504 the magistracy of Bistrița established the duties the parish curia would have to be responsible for, among them one which aimed at endorsing the cult of St Catherine at whose altar a Mass would be performed on a regular basis.[41] Since this regulation was included among several other articles which detailed the functioning of the local curia, one may notice the importance of the cult of the Bride of Christ in this town. This could be

---

[38] No. 487, Fund 44 of the Collection of the Medieval Town of Bistrița, National Archives of Romania, Cluj branch: *Ad confraternitatem Sancte Katherine Virginis et Martiris – 1 fl* and *ad fraternitatem sanctae Barbare virginis et martiris florenum unum.*

[39] L. GROSS, *Confreriile medievale în Transilvania (secolele XIV-XVI)*, Cluj-Napoca, 2004, p. 245-246 and 257-258.

[40] Devotion to the patron saints of fraternities was particularly shown through the altars the fellows founded and maintained in order to honour their protector, altars where Masses were held and the saint's feast was celebrated with great solemnity. See C. VINCENT, *Les confréries médiévales dans le royaume de France (XIIIe-XVe siècles)*, Paris, 1994, especially p. 85-106.

[41] F. TEUTSCH, *Geschichte, op. cit.*, p. 150: ... *quod in beatarum Annae et Katherinae altaribus singulis diebus festivis et feriatis (!) annuatim unam missam legibilem fieri faciat...*

inferred from the fact that the other cults which the city council requested to be celebrated by the parish priest were those of St Anne, Corpus Christi and that of the patron saint of the church, Nicholas. It is difficult to establish whether these were the preferences of the patriciate involved in the governing of the town or whether they were popular devotions at that time in Bistrița, embraced by the townspeople as a consequence of clerical promotion.

Interestingly enough, the cult of St Catherine seems to have been indeed favoured there, because as we have seen in the church of St Nicholas a confraternity dedicated to this Virgin Martyr was organized. It cannot be assessed whether this devotional association was established after the agreement of 1504 or whether it was already functioning at that time. However, it can be concluded that by the beginning of the sixteenth century the cult of St Catherine was important in the town, an importance which the urban magistrate sanctioned by requesting the solemn celebration of the Mass of St Catherine.

At this point, it is worth remembering that, according to the testament issued in 1513, another confraternity dedicated to this Virgin Martyr functioned in the nearby village of Dumitra. It has been observed that this is the only devotional association we are informed about which functioned in rural areas in medieval Transylvania and its emergence could be linked with the right of patronage the town of Bistrița received in 1472 from King Mathias over several churches, among which was also the church of Dumitra.[42] Although we lack details in regard with this rural church, still it can be observed that the magistracy of Bistrița did make use of its right of patronage over the church of Dumitra.[43] This example illustrates the way a particular form of devotion could have been propagated from one parish church to the other, in the case of the confraternity of St Catherine from Dumitra not by Episcopal mediation, but most likely as a result of the collaboration between the urban magistracy of Bistrița and the parish curia.

In what concerns the cult of St Barbara, to whom as I mentioned earlier a fraternity was dedicated in Bistrița, it is even harder to identify the channels through which it was propagated in this town. Was the local parish curia subordinated to the Transylvanian Episcopate emulating the support the Bishops provided to this cult? As our sources remain silent about the way this devotional association was founded and functioned, no undisputable answer can be given. On the other hand, it has been suggested that since Bistrița's

---

[42] L. Gross, *Confreriile, op. cit.*, p. 251-252; *Urkundenbuch zur Geschichte der Deutschen in Siebenbürgen*, ed. G. Gündisch, G. Nussbächer, București, 1991, vol. VII, no. 3930, p. 543-545.
[43] *Ibid.*, vol. VII, no. 4197, p. 145.

economic life was strongly impacted on by the mines from nearby Rodna, Barbara was a suitable protector for the local population.[44] As Barbara was one of the Fourteen Holy Helpers being able to provide a good death, the development of her cult in Bistriţa could also be connected to the economic profile of this town.[45]

Furthermore, I would like to suggest that the cult of St Barbara may have taken shape in Bistriţa at the beginning of the sixteenth century. The 1504 agreement concluded between the city council and the parish curia did not refer to any kind of divine service to be performed in order to honour this Virgin Martyr. This would suggest that, at that time, the cult of Barbara was not yet important enough or not even known in the town to the extent that its liturgical celebration deserved to be included among the responsibilities the parish curia would have to fulfill. A fraternity dedicated to this saint was mentioned in a testament drafted a decade later, in 1513, allowing one to consider that in the meantime the cult became popular in the town and Barbara had found her devotees. Thus, the confraternities dedicated to the Virgin Martyrs represent the institutional channel for the dissemination of their cults within the parochial milieu. Most likely by clerical mediation the cults of St Catherine and St Barbara were organized in order to meet the religious expectations of the laity.

The understanding of the propagation of the cults of the Virgin Martyrs has brought to light the complicated process through which these cults were favoured not only by the clergy, but also by the laity. In this regard, the case of the St Catherine fraternity from St Michael parish church of another Transylvanian town, that of Cluj, could provide us with a more detailed view. In the year 1408, the Transylvanian Bishop Stephen confirmed the donation made by Jacobus Bulkescher, Nicholas Mün and Christian Baumann to the fraternity of St Catherine. Whilst approving the endowment, the Bishop also endorsed the religious practices assumed by this devotional association. These practices included a solemn celebration each Monday of the Mass for the deceased souls at St Catherine's altar from the parish church and the processions the fraternity organized when undertaking the burials of those considered exiled.[46]

I would like to suggest in what follows that the emergence of this confraternity could be linked with the development of the cult of St Catherine

---

[44] L. Gross, *Confreriile, op. cit.*, p. 258.
[45] S. Bálint, *Ünnepi kalendárium, op. cit.*, vol. I, p. 17-27.
[46] E. Jakab, *Oklevéltár Kolozsvár története első kötetéhez*, Buda, 1870, no. LXXXV, p. 147-148.

in the parish church of the town. According to a testament drafted in 1368, referred to in the clauses of a charter issued by the vicar of the Transylvanian Bishop in 1509, bequests were made to no less than three altars, each of them dedicated to St Catherine.[47] These were placed in the church of St Michael, in the hospital of St Elizabeth from Cluj, and in the nearby Benedictine monastery from Cluj-Mănăştur. It could be observed therefore that already in the second half of the fourteenth century the cult of St Catherine was firmly established in Cluj and its environs, being supported not only by clerics, but also by the laity who provided for its further development.

Impulses for the emergence and subsequent development of St Catherine's cult in the parish church of Cluj could be detected in an indulgence issued in 1349. According to this, the visitors of St Michael's parish church were prompted to follow certain devotional practices aimed at displaying love for one's neighbor through processions organized on the occasion of burials and when carrying the Host to the sick people.[48] Among the feast days when these good deeds would be accomplished was also the feast of St Catherine. As the indulgence was re-confirmed several times by the Transylvanian Bishops (Andrew reconfirmed it in 1356, Emeric Zudar in 1387 and Maternus in 1400), additional penitential time was added and more importantly the continuity of the initial devotional practices was ensured.

The charter of 1408 referring to the Episcopal authorization of St Catherine's fraternity reveals an interesting feature of its functioning. We learn from this charter that it was a *fraternitas exulum*, a particular type of association dedicated to the care of the sick, the poor, prisoners or those strangers who happened to die far away from home.[49] It cannot be excluded that the assistance the 1349 indulgence recommended to be provided by the believers may have eased or even triggered the adoption of St Catherine as the patron

---

[47] E. JAKAB, *Oklevéltár, op. cit.*, no. XXXV, p. 62-63.
[48] E. JAKAB, *Oklevéltár, op. cit.*, no. LXVI, p. 104-106: *Aut earum cimiteria pie deum exorantes circumuierint... Aut qui Corpus Christi uel oleum sacrum cum infirmis portentur.*
[49] L. PÁSZTOR, *A magyarság vallásos élete a Jagellók korában*, Budapest, 1940, p. 59 and J. SZŰCS, *Városok és kézművesség a XV. századi Magyarországon*, Budapest, 1955, p. 328, pointed out that these fraternities were also called guilds of the dead or guilds of the poor and were usually dedicated to the Holy Spirit or to the Virgin Mary. M.-M. de CEVINS, *L'Église dans les villes hongroises à la fin du Moyen Âge (vers 1320-vers 1490)*, Budapest-Paris-Szeged, 2003, p. 196-198 discusses the Episcopal supervision of the functioning of this particular type of devotional association, the case of St Catherine fraternity from Cluj being used as an example in this regard. Adoption of a Virgin Martyr as patron of those being in a vulnerable state is also demonstrated by the St Barbara chapel from Braşov, which functioned as the chapel of the *leprosarium. Das Burzenland, op. cit.*, p. 43; M. PHILIPPI, "Die Unterschichten der Siebenbürgischen Stadt Braşov (Kronstadt) im 14. und 15. Jahrhundert", *Revue roumaine d'histoire*, 16 (1977), p. 683-684.

of those engaged in the distribution of charity. After all, she was the protector of the dying and the one whose precious mediation lay in her special status as the Bride of Christ.

Other local impulses for choosing this Virgin Martyr as the protector of the confraternity from Cluj could be identified in the development of the town. At the turn of the fourteenth to fifteenth century, Cluj grew in size and economic importance, achieving the status of a free royal town in 1405.[50] These key urban liberties were procured by representatives of the urban elite, the most important ones being the judge of the town Nicholas Mün, one of the jurors, Jacob Bulkescher and the parish priest Christian Baumann. It has been suggested that the three founded a fraternity of the exiles while they were forced to leave the town in 1403 in the turmoil which followed the attempt of replacing in the governing of Cluj the so-called old-type patriciate with members of patrician families involved in finance and trade.[51]

This assumption seems to be confirmed by similar examples from other urban communities, where the loyalties forged through common affiliation to a religious association were sometimes employed to serve political ends as well.[52] In the parish church of Cluj there is a fresco, dated to mid-fifteenth century, that depicts the Virgin Mary with the Child and a group of *Virgines Capitales*. Among them is represented St Catherine with a sword and the broken wheel at her feet, symbols considered to illustrate her political abilities.[53] This cult indices makes one suggesting that there was a strong connection between the political elite of Cluj who chose Catherine as its protector and her representation as an earthly potentate.

For two of those lobbying for Cluj's urban privileges, Jacob Bulkescher and Christian Baumann, St Catherine may have become a favoured saint while they studied at the University of Vienna, as both of them were enrolled there in 1392.[54] It is interesting therefore to observe that this acquaintance

---

[50] E. JAKAB, *Oklevéltár, op. cit.*, no. LXXVI.

[51] K. GÜNDISCH, *Das Patriziat siebenbürgischer Städte im Mittelalter*, Köln-Weimar-Wien, 1993, p. 275-280.

[52] S. REYNOLDS, *Kingdoms and Communities in Western Europe 900-1300*, Oxford, 1997², p. 67-75, suggested that religious associations lobbied for the procurement of urban liberties usually at times of economic and demographic growth. This feature is easily detectable in the case of Cluj too, where at the turn of the fourteenth to fifteenth century significant economic development enabled the town to become engaged in long distance trade and new social groups to make their way into the urban government.

[53] L. DARKÓ, "A kolozsvári Szent-Mihály templom 1956-57. évi helyreálítása során feltárt falfestmények", in *Emlékkönyv Kelemen Lajos születésének nyolcvanadik évfordulójára*, Bucarest, 1957, p. 213-215 and K. WINSTEAD, *St Katherine's Hair, op. cit.*, p. 196.

[54] S. TONK, *Erdélyiek egyetemjárása a középkorban*, Bucarest, 1979, p. 219-220 and 242; M. PALMER, "A Tendentious Plan. Towards an Understanding of St Michael's Kolozsvár

with St Catherine could be used in order to foster cohesion among members of an association whose purpose seems to reflect the transfer of personal dramatic experience, that of political exile, into the devotional sphere by providing assistance to those in need. This transfer may have been made possible by the charitable endeavours those visiting the parish church of Cluj were encouraged to follow since mid-fourteenth century as we can learn from the Episcopal indulgences. Furthermore, the origins and the functioning of the confraternity of St Catherine reflect accurately the multifaceted nature of the cult of this Virgin Martyr, as political and devotional motivations on the part of lay people and ecclesiastics could be identified in the model of saintliness she embodied.

The development of the cult of St Catherine within St Michael's parish church received additional impulses in the course of the fifteenth century. Episcopal regulations concerning the liturgical obligations of the local curia specified that each Monday the Mass for the deceased souls would be performed at the altar of St Catherine, thus acknowledging the devotional goals the confraternity of St Catherine assumed.[55] The cult of the Bride of Christ grew in the parish church of Cluj and the support ecclesiastical and urban elites provided led to a ramification of the cult itself. This is exemplified by a testament issued in 1492 by Anne, widow of a certain Jacob Goldschmidt.[56] The pious woman lavishly endowed the altar of St Catherine's confraternity and firmly linked the hope for the salvation of her soul and that of her husband with the religious responsibilities the members of this devotional association would have to undertake in this regard.[57]

On the one hand, this choice may have been the result of the prestige this confraternity acquired, being actively involved in the religious life of the town, as this is proven by a liturgical banner discovered on one of the keystones of the vault, most likely used in the processions the fraternity of St Catherine organized.[58] On the other, it can be argued that the particu-

---

(Cluj-Napoca)", *Acta Historica Artium Hungariae*, 40 (1998), p. 25-30 drew the attention to the architectural similarities between the chapel of St Catherine in Vienna and the church of St Michael from Cluj that could also be explained by the relatively numerous Transylvanian students attending this university.

[55] E. Jakab, *Oklevéltár, op. cit.*, no. LXXXIX, p. 152-154.
[56] L. Gross, *Confreriile, op. cit.*, p. 247 observed that the greatest majority of the last wills included bequests for several confraternities and that the testament issued by our widow Anne is the only such source which clauses consider only one devotional association. These findings would thus additionally prove the great importance the cult of St Catherine achieved within the devotional world of the citizens of Cluj.
[57] E. Jakab, *Oklevéltár, op. cit.*, no. CLXXXIV, p. 300-302.
[58] M. S. Salontai, "Arhitectura frontului apusean al bisericii Sf. Mihail din Cluj", *Ars Transsilvaniae*, 19 (2009), p. 23.

lar efficacious mediation the Bride of Christ could provide to her devotees stimulated the widow Anne to choose Catherine as her and her husband's intercessor and the devout fellows of the Virgin Martyr as vehicles through which this intercession could be sought.[59]

The parochial functioning of the cults of the Virgin Martyrs in the towns of Sibiu, Bistriţa and Cluj revealed on the one hand the role played by the Transylvanian Episcopal milieu in the propagation of these cults. At the same time, one should also emphasize the parochial support that contributed to the further growth of Sts. Catherine and Barbara' cults, a support evidenced by the liturgical celebrations and the pious goals assumed by devotional associations. The dissemination of these cults among the laity also meant the appropriation of the Virgin Martyrs as valuable protectors for those regarding them not as reflecting clerical ideals, but as the Brides of Christ who could ease the way to salvation.

The close scrutiny of the emergence and development of the cults of the Virgin Martyrs in late medieval Transylvania has brought to light several nuances worth mentioning in regard with the acknowledged popularity of these cults Europe wide. Clerically driven cults and transformed to suit the aspirations of the male ecclesiastical elite, the image of the Virgin Martyrs as disclosed by literary and visual evidence was that of cultural symbols. When disseminated at parish level, largely by the mediation and orchestration of the clergy, Sts. Catherine and Barbara came to be perceived as valuable protectors at moments of severe need. The Virgin Martyrs were the protagonists of long-established cults and the object of universal veneration. Yet, the model of sainthood they embodied was not static and unchanged. On the contrary, at the center of the Latin Christendom, as well as at one of its margins such as Transylvania, the cult for the Virgin Martyrs was persuasively revived in the last centuries of the Middle Ages.

---

[59] Similar devotional attempts focusing on the protection St Catherine could offer are documented in other Transylvanian places. For example in 1523 a couple made a donation *ad missam Beate Katherine Virginis et Martiris* to be celebrated in the parish church of Turda (Torda). *Monumenta Ecclesiastica tempora innovatae in Hungaria religionis. Egyháztörténelmi emlékek a Magyarországi hitujitás korából*, ed. V. BUNYITAY, R. RAPAICS, J. KARÁCSONYI, vol. I (1520-1529), Budapest, 1902, no. 102.

Bohemia's Treasury of Saints:
Relics and Indulgences in Emperor Charles IV's Prague

David C. MENGEL

(Cincinnati, USA)

Since late antiquity, the bodies of saints have anchored the practice of Christianity in Europe to the places where they lay.[1] Indeed, one way to map the process of Christianization is to plot the increasingly extensive and dense network of Christian holy places. The more prominent the saint's relic (or collection of saints' relics), the more important was the node within that network. The relic's prominence did not depend primarily on the place's historical or ecclesiastical significance, or even on the saint's renown during his or her life – although the association with apostles and martyrs certainly did confer a special status on Rome and a few other locations. Nor can political or economic grounds fully explain the standing of particular shrines. The great pilgrimage sites of high- and late-medieval Europe included not just Rome and Jerusalem, but also places such as Santiago de Compostela, Canterbury, and St Foy.[2] Such sites all possessed the bones of saints, but what especially distinguished them from the thousands of other relic-possessing sites were their associations with miracles.

Miracles – stories that people tell to explain the inexplicable and the wonderful – increased the status of relic-possessing places within the network of Christian holy sites.[3] Some pilgrims traveled long distances at great

---
[1] P. R. L. BROWN, *The Cult of the Saints: Its Rise and Function in Latin Christianity*, Chicago, 1981. Now see also R. BARTLETT, *Why Can the Dead Do Such Great Things?: Saints and Worshippers from the Martyrs to the Reformation*, Princeton, 2013, p. 239-332.
[2] See, e.g., the inquisitor Bernard Gui's thirteenth century list of major and minor pilgrimage sites, which reflects a geographical focus appropriate to his location in Toulouse. R. BARTLETT, *Why Can the Dead Do Such Great Things?, op. cit.*, p. 428.
[3] For a discussion of miracle stories in terms of personal narratives, see R. KOOPMANS, *Wonderful to Relate: Miracle Stories and Miracle Collecting in High Medieval England*, Philadelphia, 2011, p. 9-27. See also R. BARTLETT, *Why Can the Dead Do Such Great Things?, op. cit.*, p. 333-409.

Les saints et leur culte en Europe centrale au Moyen Âge (xɪᵉ-début du xvɪᵉ siècle), éd. par Marie-Madeleine de CEVINS et Olivier MARIN, Turnhout, 2017 (*Hagiologia*, 13), p. 57-76.
© BREPOLS PUBLISHERS   DOI 10.1484/M.HAG-EB.5.113967

expense to seek miracles and to thank saints for previous miracles, wherever the supernatural intervention had been experienced. Pilgrims journeyed, as Chaucer memorably wrote, "The hooly blisful martir for to seke / That hem hath holpen whan that they were seeke". Chaucer's motley pilgrims also remind us that the motives and goals of individual pilgrims might be complex, various and even little connected with piety. Still, there is no question that stories about miracles contributed to the reputations of shrines – and that these reputations in turn drew visitors for many different reasons. Similarly, not all modern visitors to the grotto at Lourdes come in faith to seek the favor of the Blessed Virgin, but its attraction for tourists of all kinds is undeniably rooted in the nineteenth-century stories of Marian apparitions there. For most of the Middle Ages, miracle stories proved the most effective way to establish and reinforce a reputation that would attract visitors to holy places – visitors whose presence, money, and own subsequent stories reinforced the status of a place and its saints.

Beginning in the eleventh century, another attractive force came to augment the role of miracles in bolstering the reputation of saints' shrines: indulgences. Historians have long noted the growth of indulgences in these centuries. They have especially focused on the sale of indulgences, a practice which already in the sixteenth century became a fixture in the narratives of Reformation. However, very few more extensive studies of medieval indulgences have appeared.[4] Even the revisionist histories that over the past few decades have provided an increasingly rich and complicated picture of late medieval religious practice have not fully incorporated indulgences into their depictions. Only recently have a few scholars begun to remedy this.[5] Robert N. Swanson has compared indulgences to "the 'dark matter' of the universe of medieval Catholicism" – ubiquitous and critically important to understand, but easy to overlook and difficult to study.[6]

The city of Prague during the reign of Emperor Charles IV (1346-78) offers a chance to study the growth of a particular sort of indulgence – one connected with a relic and available only at a certain location – in the immediate context of a new miracle-producing cult. Prague in these years witnessed the

---

[4] E. g., H. C. LEA, *A History of Auricular Confession and Indulgences in the Latin Church*, vol. 3, *Indulgences*, Philadelphia, 1896; N. PAULUS, *Geschichte des Ablasses im Mittelalter*, 3 vols., 1922-1923 (2^d ed. T. LENTES, Darmstadt, 2000).

[5] R. N. SWANSON, *Indulgences in Late Medieval England: Passports to Paradise?*, Cambridge, 2007, p. 2-3. See also, *Promissory Notes on the Treasury of Merits: Indulgences in Late Medieval Europe*, ed. R. N. SWANSON, Leiden, 2006 and R. W. SHAFFERN, *The Penitents' Treasury: Indulgences in Latin Christendom, 1175-1375*, Scranton, 2007.

[6] R. N. SWANSON, *Indulgences in Late Medieval England, op. cit.*, p. 522.

establishment of multiple new cults around saints' relics. One of them was prominently associated with miracles; the rest were supported instead by indulgences that the emperor assiduously sought.[7] Both miracles and indulgences brought honor to the saints whose bones rested in Prague and brought visitors to their shrines. Charles IV gladly leveraged miracles and indulgences alike to elevate the stature of Prague, his capital city as King of Bohemia. Yet the relative prominence of indulgences stands out. Charles IV seems to have understood unusually well the power that indulgences offered to rulers and authorities seeking to increase the prominence of their favored sites. Indulgences proved an ideal mechanism to magnify the impact of the collection of saints' relics he laboriously gathered from across Europe. Charles IV's sustained efforts resulted in an impressive treasury of indulgences in Prague. A better understanding of his actions and their effects can contribute to a growing understanding of the roles that indulgences played in late medieval European devotion.

Saints, Bohemia and Charles IV

The kingdom of Bohemia belonged to what Peter Moraw called "younger Europe".[8] Christianity reached this region – north and east of the old Roman borders – well after the first waves of late antique relic distribution from the Italian peninsula had already established some of Christianity's most sacred places. Prague nevertheless slowly accumulated its own modest relic collection. In the tenth century, Emperor Henry I gave to Duke Wenceslas (*c.* 907-929) the arm of St Vitus, the late antique Italian saint to whom the rotunda (and later the cathedral) within Prague castle came to be dedicated.[9] The gift of this and other relics – a practice for which Louis IX of France became particularly renowned – helped to strengthen the region's religious and political ties to "older Europe".[10] Some subsequent relics were home-grown, one might

---

[7] I first began exploring this topic for my unpublished 2003 doctoral dissertation at the Medieval Institute of the University of Notre Dame in the USA, and am returning to the subject in a chapter of my current book project.
[8] P. Moraw, "Über Entwicklungsunterschiede und Entwicklungsausgleich im deutschen und europäischen Mittelalter: Ein Versuch", in *Hochfinanz, Wirtschaftsräume, Innovation: Festschrift für Wolfgang von Stromer*, ed. U. Bestmann, F. Irsigler, and J. Schneider, vol. 2, Trier, 1987, p. 583-622.
[9] F. V. Mareš, "Svatý Vít", in *Bohemia Sancta: Životopisy českých světců a přátel Božích*, ed. J. Kadlec, Prague, 1989, p. 73.
[10] A. Podlaha and E. Šittler, *Chrámový poklad u sv. Víta v Praze: jeho dějiny a popis*, Prague, 1903, p. 3-17. On Louis IX's reputation for giving away portions of the prized Passion relics, see W. C. Jordan, *Louis IX and the Challenge of the Crusade: A Study in Rulership*, Princeton, 1979, p. 193-195.

say: Wenceslas's own murder in 929 led to the establishment of a chapel for his relics within the same rotunda.[11] Then in the eleventh century, Duke Břetislav I brought relics of St Adalbert back to Prague, four decades after the bishop's death in Prussia.[12] Prague's relic collection continued to grow slowly over the next three centuries as bishops, dukes and visiting dignitaries periodically brought relics from Italy, Asia minor, Poland, Hungary and elsewhere. But despite the acquisition of small bits of a handful of apostles and (like everyone else) a piece of the skull of John the Baptist, there remained in Bohemia's great city only a small collection of saints' remains well into the fourteenth century.[13]

This situation changed dramatically during the long reign of Charles V, the Luxemburg who was elected King of the Romans in 1346 and anointed King of Bohemia a year later. A deep, personal devotion to saints seems to have been nurtured during his youth at the court of his uncle, Charles IV of France.[14] His favorite saints included especially his two namesakes: Wenceslas, his own baptismal name, as well as the saint after whom he took the name Charles at his Paris confirmation – Charlemagne. The emperor fostered the cults of both these saints throughout his reign, well-aware of the dynastic and political significance.[15] He was an extremely well-informed collector of relics; he knew or learned many saints' stories and attended to the cultural resonances of their relics.[16] But that is not to say that he was particularly selective in his acquisitions. Charles IV venerated apostles and martyrs, royal saints and common ones, saints with celebrated cults and those whose cults had been relatively neglected. And he liked to acquire relics from each of them.

---

[11] L. WOLVERTON, *Hastening toward Prague: Power and Society in the Medieval Czech Lands*, Philadelphia, 2001, p. 147-161.
[12] L. WOLVERTON, *Hastening toward Prague, op. cit.*, p. 115; Cosmas of Prague, *Die Chronik der Böhmen des Cosmas von Prag*, ed. B. BRETHOLZ, Berlin, 1923 (*Monumenta Germaniae Historica*, Scriptores rerum Germanicarum, NS 2), p. 89-90. See also Geneviève Bührer-Thierry's contribution in this volume.
[13] These examples are drawn from my study of the inventories cited below, n. 18.
[14] A good starting place on this remains F. MACHILEK, "Privatfrömmigkeit und Staatsfrömmigkeit", in *Kaiser Karl IV: Staatsmann und Mäzen*, ed. F. SEIBT, Munich, 1978, p. 87-101.
[15] D. C. MENGEL, "A Holy and Faithful Fellowship: Royal Saints in Fourteenth-Century Prague", in *Evropa a Čechy na konci středověku. Sborník příspěvků věnovaných Františku Šmahelovi*, Prague, 2004, p. 148.
[16] R. SCHNEIDER, "Karls IV. Auffassung vom Herrscheramt, in *Beiträge zur Geschichte des mittelalterlichen deutschen Königtums*", ed. T. SCHIEDER, Munich, 1973 (Historische Zeitschrift, Beiheft 2, NF), p. 131.

The emperor had plenty of opportunities to do exactly that. Winfried Eberhard estimates that between 1330 and 1378, Charles made 1227 visits to 438 different places.[17] He obtained relics from many of these places and many relics from a few of them. A glance at records of the relics he donated to Prague's St Vitus cathedral provides a good sense of the scale of this activity. More than 450 relics were catalogued there in the seventeenth century, of which more than sixty percent were certainly brought to Prague by Charles IV. In fact, just over seven percent were known to have been brought to Prague by someone other than Charles IV.[18] This one ruler, in other words, was likely responsible for bringing at least three hundred relics to the church of St Vitus. That is not to mention those kept at Karlstein castle outside of Prague or those given by him to other churches in Prague or elsewhere. Charles IV was undoubtedly one of the greatest medieval collectors of relics.[19]

One of his journeys was particularly notable for the number of relics it produced and can serve here to illustrate the emperor's practice. Over the course of eleven months – August 1353 through July 1354 – Charles IV travelled from Prague through southern German lands and the middle Rhine before returning to Prague. The journey has rightly been described as a "raid for holy relics".[20] A chronicler hints at the affront caused by the emperor's actions: while traveling near Strasbourg in early November, he visited the shrine of Saint Florentius, the sixth-century Bishop of Strasbourg whose relics had been translated from that city to the abbey church at Haslach in 1143. Charles IV ordered for the tomb to be opened – a tomb, according to the chronicler, that had been "sealed with gold and silver for three hundred years". In fact, it had only been a little more than two hundred years since the saint's translation, but the chronicler's point remains: the tomb's caretakers were not in the habit of opening the shrine. Further stops in the next few days at the nearby abbeys of Andlau and Erstein followed the same

---

[17] W. EBERHARD, "Herrschaft und Raum: Zum Itinerar Karls IV.", in *Kaiser Karl IV, op. cit.*, p. 102.
[18] Tomáš Jan Pešina z Čechorodu, *Phosphorus septicornis, stella alias matutina*, Prague, 1673, p. 501-524. This inventory is reprinted under the title: "SS. Reliquiarum, quae in S. Metrop. Prag. D. Viti Ecclesia pie asservantur, Diarium" by A. PODLAHA in his *Catalogi SS. Reliquiarum quae in sacra metropolitana ecclesia Pragensi asservantur, annis 1673, 1691 et 1721 typis editi*, Prague, 1931. This seventeenth-century inventory was based on earlier inventories dating back to 1354, which A. PODLAHA and E. ŠITTLER printed in *Chrámový poklad*, p. iii-cii.
[19] R. BARTLETT, *Why Can the Dead Do Such Great Things?, op. cit.*, p. 281-282.
[20] J. ŠUSTA, *Karel IV*, vol. 2, *Za císařkou korunou*, Prague, 1948 (České dějiny 2.4), p. 349, cited by K. STEJSKAL, "Karel jako sběratel", in *Karolus Quartus: Piae memoriae fundatoris sui universitas Carolina*, ed. V. VANĚČEK, Prague, 1984, p. 458. On the itinerary, see J. PAVEL, "Studie k itinerary Karla IV.", *Historická Geografie*, 2 (1969), p. 38-78.

pattern: the long-sealed shrines of Lazarus and of Pope Urban I were likewise opened to reveal their holy relics to the emperor. All the more shocking was the emperor's intent to carry away some of each saint's relics. In one location after another he got exactly what he wanted – results that can be attributed to the emperor's public displays of personal piety, his powerful entourages of bishops and dukes, his generosity in granting coveted privileges, and perhaps especially his stubborn unwillingness to be refused.[21] As far as relics are concerned, this particular excursion reached its climax at Trier in February 1354, where the recent deaths of Archbishop Baldwin and of the abbess of St Irmina provided the emperor with an exceptional chance to accumulate saintly treasures without resistance from local prelates.[22]

Relics, Processions, Reliquaries – and Miracles

Charles IV by no means hoarded all of the relics he collected on this and other journeys. Nor should his collection be understood as a Renaissance-style assemblage of rarities, with contents prized more for their singularity than their sanctity.[23] Although he did eventually gather a select group at Karlstein castle, Charles IV – like Louis IX – also donated relics with an attention to detail that demonstrated his considerable knowledge of many different saints' cults. Relics went to Eichstätt and Aachen, to Luckau in Lower

---

[21] *Ascendens quoque rex visitat Bertholdum episcopum Argentinensem in Mollesheim decumbentem, et crastino casu in die beati Florencii veniens Haselahe aperit tumbam sancti Florencii CCCtis annis auro et argento reclusam et invenit caput et corpus eius. Et faciens ibi tabelliones instrumenta ibi dari iussit de invencione huiusmodi, quia canonici sancti Thome Argentinensis ubi sepultus fuit, asserunt se caput et corporis maiorem partem habere. Et aderant ibi Moguntinus et plures episcopi. Visitat eciam rex monasterium in Andelahe, ubi est corpus beati Lazari, et monasterium in Erstheim, ubi est corpus beati Urbani tunc et ante nunquam apertum. Et de hiis omnibus et aliis multis ibi et alibi reliquiis partes accepit animo Bohemiam traducendi.* Matthias of Neuenburg, *Chronica Mathiae de Nuwenburg*, ed. A. HOFMEISTER, Berlin, 1924 (*Monumenta Germaniae Historica*, Scriptores rerum Germanicarum, NS 4), p. 469-470.

[22] Charles IV provided an account in his letter of 17 February 1354: A. PODLAHA and E. ŠITTLER, *Chrámový poklad*, p. 31 no. 2. It may be that Charles IV's relationship and alliances with his great-uncle contributed to a sense that he had a particular right to the relics at Trier; on their relationship, see A. HAVERKAMP, "Studien zu den Beziehungen zwischen Erzbishof Balduin von Trier und König Karl IV.", in *Verfassung, Kultur, Lebensform: Beiträge zur italienischen, deutschen und jüdischen Geschichte im europäischen Mittelalter: dem Autor zur Vollendung des 60. Lebensjahres*, ed. F. BURGARD, A. HEIT, and M. MATHEUS, Mainz, 1997, p. 81-125.

[23] The opposite argument is made by K. STEJSKAL, "Karel jako sběratel", p. 466; K. STEJSKAL, *Umění na dvoře Karla IV*, Prague, 1978, p. 8-100; and V. BIRNBAUM, "Karel IV. jako sběratel a Praha", in V. BIRNBAUM, *Listy z dějin umění*, Prague, 1947, p. 146-147.

Lusatia and Herrieden in Bavaria.[24] Nuremberg received many.[25] Such gifts show the emperor's understanding of the power of relics to build and cement relationship with communities and their authorities, and to expand the geographical spread of cults that were particularly significant to him. The great majority of his new relics, however, went to Prague's cathedral. The emperor explained his motivation in a letter that accompanied some of the relics from this trip that he sent ahead of his own return to Prague.

> The zeal of devotion and love with which we are consumed for the holy church of Prague, our venerable mother, and for the blessed martyrs Vitus, Wenceslas, and Adalbert, our glorious patron saints, stirs our passion, so that when we, by our devout generosity, acquire something outstanding, an extraordinary jewel from among the treasures of the holy relics somewhere in the holy empire, in our royal benevolence we use it to adorn that church.[26]

In this and other such letters, Charles IV repeatedly refers to the saints' relics as "precious gems" and "treasures". They were indeed rarities, but rarities valued first of all for their religious significance. They were intended to become centerpieces of devotion, as Charles IV's instructions in this and other such letters confirm. Two strategies for honoring and publicizing the new relics stand out. First, several groups of relics and a number of especially significant relics were welcomed with elaborate processions of clergy and laity through the city. The emperor had, for example, insisted upon removing from Aquileia several leaves of a treasured copy of St Mark's gospel – written, it was believed, by St Mark himself (in Latin).[27] For the arrival of this relic in Prague, the emperor arranged for the archbishop and cathedral chapter, all the clergy of the city and suburbs of Prague, plus the deacons in their diaconal vestments together to usher the gospel leaves to the church of Prague

---

[24] F. MACHILEK, "Privatfrömmigkeit und Staatsfrömmigkeit", p. 91; M.-L. FAVREAU-LILIE, "Von Lucca nach Luckau: Kaiser Karl IV. und das Haupt des heiligen Paulinus", in *Vita Religiosa im Mittelalter: Festschrift für Kaspar Elm zum 70. Geburtstag*, ed. F. FELTEN and N. JASPERT, Berlin, 1999, p. 899-915; K. STEJSKAL, *Umění na dvoře Karla IV*, p. 258-259, fig. XVII.

[25] For the context of this gift, see D. C. MENGEL, "Emperor Charles IV, Jews, and Urban Space", in *Christianity and Culture in the Middle Ages: Essays to Honor John Van Engen*, ed. D. C. MENGEL and L. WOLVERTON, Notre Dame (Indiana), 2014.

[26] *Zelus devotionis et amoris, quo circa sanctam Pragensem ecclesiam, venerandam matrem nostram, et beatissimos martyres Vitum, Wenczlaum et Adalbertum, gloriosos patronos nostros incessanter afficimur, animum nostrum sollicitat, ut dum de sacrarum reliquiarum thezauris per loca sacri imperii egregium aliquid et insigne clenodium devotorum nostrorum largitione consequamur, per illud eandem ecclesiam benignitate regia decoremus.* A. PODLAHA and E. ŠITTLER, *Chrámový poklad*, op. cit., p. 36 no. 3.

[27] A. PODLAHA and E. ŠITTLER, *Chrámový poklad*, op. cit., p. 38 no. 4.

"with spiritual delight and joy", singing along the way in the most humble and honorable way possible.[28]

Second, the emperor arranged for new and elaborate reliquaries for the relics; remember that he had acquired most of them by removing them from original shrines and reliquaries.[29] Crystal monstrances, jewel-encrusted boxes, and even gilded sculptures of body parts paid honor to the saints while enhancing the visual power of the relics – just as they did at shrines across Europe.[30] For St Mark's gospel, the emperor ordered a case (*apparatum*) of gold and pearls worth 2000 florins.[31]

By arranging elaborate processions and supplying beautiful reliquaries, the emperor endeavored to honor the saints and make their presence in Prague better known. But that alone was not sufficient to transform this urban center of younger Europe into a pilgrimage center – and this, I believe, was one of Charles IV's intentions for his rapidly growing collection of relics. Arguably the single most successful of the new Prague-based cults was that of St Sigismund, the sixth-century Burgundian martyr king, about which I have written elsewhere.[32] More than ten years after his astoundingly productive "raid for relics", in June of 1365 Charles IV went out of his way on a return journey from Avignon to visit the monastery of St Maurice in Agaune. Just two weeks earlier, he had been crowned King of Burgundy at Arles and thereby became a successor of Sigismund. The early medieval Burgundian now joined Wenceslaus and Charlemagne as royal saints whose crowns had passed to Charles IV.[33] So the visit to Sigismund's burial place to acquire a relic – his second relic of Sigismund, in fact – fits into a recognizable pattern.

---

[28] A. Podlaha and E. Šittler, *Chrámový poklad, op. cit.*, p. 41 no. 1; A. Huber, *Die Regesten des Kaiserreiches unter Kaiser Karl IV*, Innsbruck, 1877 (Regesta Imperii, 8), p. 155 no. 1939.

[29] K. Stejskal, "Karel jako sběratel", *art. cit.*, p. 458; K. Stejskal, *Umění na dvoře Karla IV, op. cit.*, p. 80-81. Many of these appear in the 1354, 1355 or later inventories of the Prague cathedral treasury, printed in A. Podlaha and E. Šittler, *Chrámový poklad, op. cit.*, p. iii-cii. Those that still survive are described in the same volume, esp. p. 204-249, as well as in A. Podlaha and E. Šittler, *Der Domschatz und die Bibliothek des Metropolitancapitels*, Prague, 1903.

[30] R. Bartlett, *Why Can the Dead Do Such Great Things?, op. cit.*, p. 263-275.

[31] A. Podlaha and E. Šittler, *Chrámový poklad, op. cit.*, p. 39 no. 3; A. Huber, *Die Regesten des Kaiserreichs unter Kaiser Karl IV., op. cit.*, p. 155, no. 1938.

[32] D. C. Mengel, "A Holy and Faithful Fellowship", *art. cit.*, p. 145-158; D. C. Mengel, "Remembering Bohemia's Forgotten Patron Saint", in *The Bohemian Reformation and Religious Practice*, vol. 6, ed. Z. V. David and D. R. Holeton, Prague, 2007, p. 17-32.

[33] P. Hilsch, "Die Krönungen Karls IV", in *Kaiser Karl IV., op. cit.*, p. 111. On the wider significance of the coronation, see H. Stoob, *Kaiser Karl IV. und seine Zeit*, Graz, 1990, p. 207-213.

The introduction of St Sigismund to Prague was well suited to developing a new, location-based cult of a saint who was previously nearly unknown in Bohemia. A ceremonial translation brought Sigismund's head to its prominent new chapel within the gothic cathedral (which was still under construction) on the vigil of Saint Wenceslas in late September 1365 – the feast day of the kingdom's most important saint. The city would have been full of visitors at that time, for the feast as well as the annual market that coincided with it. When, the next morning, a great light shone down upon the city, it was hailed as a miracle.

These careful preparations of the new cult yielded results. Quickly a series of lay people claimed that they had been the beneficiaries of the new saint's miracles. Their stories were eagerly heard and provided critical impetus for the establishment of a miracle-producing cult. Next, after further investigation in some cases, their testimonies began to be recorded in a little book kept at the cathedral. This book survives in a single, incomplete copy, and there is no evidence that copies of the miracle collection were intentionally deployed to spread the cult.[34] Instead, news of the miracles was spread in different ways. Within weeks, the archbishop ordered the cult's announcement and promotion throughout the archdiocese.[35] Within months, the archbishop proclaimed himself to have been healed of fever by the new saint and added the feast of St Sigismund to the list of mandatory holy days within the

---

[34] The surviving copy seems to have found its way back to Agaune before eventually coming into the collection of the Bibliothèque Nationale: Paris, Bibl. Nat., Codex Nouv. acquis. Latin 1510. Also now see M. STUDNIČKOVÁ, "Kult Svatého Zikmunda v Čechách", in *Světci a jejich kult ve středověku*, Prague, 2006, p. 283-323. For a discussion of the reasons for creating miracle collections, see R. KOOPMANS, *Wonderful to Relate, op. cit.*, p. 97, 109, 201-210.

[35] *Cum autem gloriosus et mirabilis in sanctis suis nunccietur a fidelibus deus et tanto sanctorum merita et ipsorum miracula devocioni populi sint necessario intimanda, quanto per ipsorum suffragia humane necessitati consulitur et de remedio supernaturaliter a postulantibus gloriose providetur, nuper siquidem serenissimus et dominus noster dominus imperator predictus inter cetera bonorum actuum suorum insignia cupiens desiderio exaltari nostram Pragensem ecclesiam ac totam nostram provinciam omnesque incolas regni Bohemie speciali anthidote gracia consolari, sanctissimi martiris Sygismundi, regis Burgundiorum, corpus pia devocione ductus ad ecclesiam nostram predictam Pragensem, quod a monasterio sancti Mauricii in civitate Aganencium precibus obtentum reverenter transtulit et in dicta nostra Pragensi ecclesia sollempniter collocari ordinavit, ubi ad ipsius tumbam devote accedentibus multa beneficiorum gesta eius meritis circa debiles et infirmos miraculose actenus sunt ostensa et cottidie ostenduntur. Nolentes igitur ingrati esse beneficiis supradictis, in virtute sancte obediencie et sub interminacione maledictionis eterne precipiendo mandamus, ut cum ad vestras ecclesias accesseritis, populo vobis subiecto convocato predictam sancti corporis allacionem et ipsius beneficia fideliter nuncciare curetis seriose iniungentes, quatenus ipse deus sic in sanctis suis honoretur et dignis ipse laudibus a nobis preconizetur, ut in presenti vita consolacionem, in futura autem cum ipsis sanctis consequi mereamur vitam eternam.* J. POLC, "Councils and Synods of Prague and Their Statutes 1362-1395", *Apollinaris*, 52 (1979), p. 504.

diocese.[36] Within the year (or perhaps soon after), Sigismund even came to be considered one of the patron saints of the Bohemian kingdom.[37] Charles IV remained an active supporter of the cult: in 1368, he had his third son christened Sigismund, and in 1371 the emperor reported that he too had been healed of an illness by Sigismund. The empress expressed her thankfulness for this miracle by donating twenty-three marks' worth of gold, from which a new head reliquary for the saint was crafted.[38]

Carefully planted and cultivated by the emperor and the archbishop, the new, Prague-based cult of St Sigismund sprouted quickly and grew to be an astounding success. Sigismund joined the ranks of Bohemia's patron saints – and was depicted in their company repeatedly, most memorably in the mosaic of the Last Judgment installed in the early 1370s over the cathedral's south porch.[39] There his image greeted pilgrims to the cathedral, some of whom came to seek or announce miracles at his tomb. We know of more than thirty visitors from across and beyond Bohemia who proclaimed miracles within the first four months after Sigismund's arrival. After that, the text of the incomplete miracle collection breaks off – but there is good, indirect evidence that the cult grew in popularity and geographical extent in the following years.[40]

Sigismund's relic was only one of more than two hundred that Charles IV brought to Prague. It seems to have been the only one that became the center of a miracle-producing cult, the kind of cult that had for centuries defined the European geography of pilgrimage. But Sigismund's was not the only relic to draw pilgrims to the city. The other cults relied more heavily on a different kind of incentive – not the possibility of inducing a saint's supernatural

---

[36] Some manuscript copies of Arnošt of Pardubice's 1349 statutes add St Sigismund's feast to the original list of obligatory feasts in the archdiocese: R. ZELENÝ, "Councils and Synods of Prague and Their Statutes (1343-1361)", *Apollinaris*, 45 (1972), p. 529.

[37] *propter preclara et grandia miracula annotatus est cum aliis patronis ecclesie Pragensis et Regni Boemie... Huius festi fit specialis in dyocesi Pragensi tam in officio quam in celebracione memoria die sequenti post Philippi et Jacobi quia cum per miraculorum magnitudinem sit factus patronus Boemie decens fuit ut specialem pro sua festiuitate habeat diem.* PRAGUE, Knihovna metropolitní kapituly, Cod. C 5, fol. 64v and Cod. N 30, fol. 7v.

[38] Beneš Krabice of Weitmil, *Cronica ecclesie Pragensis*, ed. J. EMLER, Prague, 1884 (Fontes rerum bohemicarum, 4), p. 543-544; cf. A. HUBER, *Die Regesten des Kaiserreichs unter Kaiser Karl IV.*, p. 412 no. 4972a; A. PODLAHA and E. ŠITTLER, *Chrámový poklad, op. cit.*, p. xxxi, no. 21.

[39] Z. VŠETEČKOVÁ, "Monumentální středověká malba", in *Katedrála sv. Víta v Praze: k 650 výročí založení*, ed. A. MERHAUTOVÁ, Prague, 1994, p. 96-104; J. PEŠINA, *České umění gotické 1350-1450*, Prague, 1970, p. 198, no. 279.

[40] M. STUDNIČKOVÁ, "Kult Svatého Zikmunda v Čechách", *art. cit.*, p. 283-323.

intervention (or the obligation of proclaiming such an intervention), but rather the guarantee of increasingly large indulgences.

Relics, Indulgences and Visitors

The later Middle Ages were an age of indulgences in Europe, as more and longer indulgences became attached to the places and practices of religious life. The plenary indulgences offered by the 1300 and 1350 Roman Jubilee years stand out, but only as two peaks of an expansive mountain range.[41] Popes and bishops had begun issuing indulgences during the eleventh century. From the start, practice ran ahead of theory.[42] Eventually thirteenth-century theologians explained indulgences as fruit of the *thesaurus ecclesiae* – the treasury of the overflowing merits of Christ and the saints. The pope and, through him, all bishops were the caretakers and disposers of this treasury. Indulgences issued by them offered recipients release from a portion of the penance (*pena*) required of a repentant sinner, but certainly not remission of the guilt (*culpa*) of the sin itself. Moreover, true repentance was a prerequisite to benefitting from indulgences.[43] Of course, the laity did not always grasp such theological distinctions, as some preachers complained.[44] Indulgences came in several forms. One of the most common types offered release from a particular number of days' worth of penance in exchange for visiting a certain church or participating in a particular devotional act – acts that might include giving money for alms or church-building. The length of penance remitted ranged from a standard "lent" of forty days to a combination of several years and several lents; efforts to resist inflationary pressures were for the most part unsuccessful.[45]

---

[41] In addition to R. N. SWANSON, *Indulgences in late medieval England* and R. SHAFFERN, *The Penitents' Treasury*, see G. A. BENRATH, "Ablaß", *Theologische Realenzyklopädie*, ed. G. KRAUSE and G. MÜLLER, vol. 1, Berlin, 1977, p. 347-364; E. VODOLA, "Indulgences", in *Dictionary of the Middle Ages*, ed. J. R. STRAYER, vol. 6, New York, 1985, p. 446-450.

[42] N. VINCENT, "Some Pardoners' Tales: The Earliest English Indulgences", *Transactions of the Royal Historical Society*, 12 (2002), p. 27-28.

[43] G. A. BENRATH, "Ablaß", *art. cit.*, p. 349; on the theology of indulgences according to thirteenth- and fourteenth-century theologians and canon lawyers, see N. PAULUS, *Geschichte des Ablasses*, *op. cit.*, vol. 1, p. 188-291.

[44] R. N. SWANSON, *Indulgences in late medieval England*, *op. cit.*, p. 353.

[45] The Fourth Lateran Council (1215) had set limits on the rapidly inflating indulgences; the power of bishops in particular was capped at forty-day indulgences: X. 5.38.14, from chapter 62 of the Fourth Lateran Council. Not all bishops abided by this, and periodically the longer indulgences established by them were challenged or annulled: N. PAULUS, *Geschichte des Ablasses*, *op. cit.*, vol. 2, p. 47-55.

Prague's bishops and archbishops issued indulgences only sparingly in the later thirteenth and fourteenth centuries.[46] Charles IV, on the other hand, barraged a succession of popes with his requests for lengthy indulgences. Not all of his appeals were granted.[47] However, over the course of his reign the emperor secured many important papal indulgences for Prague churches, especially for Prague cathedral. These Prague indulgences have occasionally drawn the attention of historians, usually within the context of one of two historical narratives. First, the new indulgences contribute to the backdrop for late fourteenth- and early fifteenth-century Bohemian religious reforms. Critics targeted both the theology and practice of indulgences, especially in the several decades after Charles IV's death in 1378.[48] Such criticism of course preceded Luther's sixteenth-century condemnation of indulgences and thus supports the argument that late-medieval Bohemian religious reform deserves recognition as a distinct and precocious Bohemian Reformation. Secondly, these indulgences sometimes feature within discussions of the architecture and decoration that supported Charles IV's political and dynastic programs. Prague cathedral and Karlstein castle in particular have been well studied. Indulgences were associated with some of the elaborate presentations of special relics at both cathedral and castle, including those relics most closely associated with Charles IV's royal and imperial reigns. Such studies have often been marked by painstaking distinctions between the emperor's rule as (Czech) king and as (German) emperor – reflecting, inevitably, modern historians' own assumptions and convictions about national identity in Central Europe.[49] Now a new generation of historical and art historical research is providing a deepening understanding of what Paul Crossley has called the emperor's "politics of presentation".[50] Indulgences

---

[46] This changed with Archbishop John of Jenstein (1378-1395), who took office in the year of Charles IV's death. See now E. DOLEŽALOVÁ et al., "Reception and Criticism of Indulgences in the Late Medieval Czech Lands", in *Promissory Notes on the Treasury of Merits, op. cit.*, p. 101-145.

[47] The emperor requested, e.g., an indulgence of seven years and seven lents for those contributing to the renovation of a church in Litoměřice over the following decade. Clement VI, who gave precisely such an indulgence for those donating to St Peter's in Rome, instead offered one year and one lent: *Acta Clementis VI. pontificis Romani 1342-1352*, ed. L. KLICMAN, Prague, 1903 (Monumenta Vaticana res gestas Bohemicas illustrantia, 1), p. 672-674, no. 1263, 1265; N. PAULUS, *Geschichte des Ablasses, op. cit.*, vol. 2., p. 17.

[48] E. DOLEŽALOVÁ et al., "Reception and Criticism of Indulgences", *art. cit.*, p. 120-141.

[49] For a reliable introduction to this literature, see F. KAVKA, "The Role and Function of Karlštejn Castle as Documented in Records from the Reign of Charles IV", in *Magister Theodoricus: Court Painter to Emperor Charles IV*, ed. J. FAJT, Prague, 1998, p. 15-28.

[50] P. CROSSLEY, "The Politics of Presentation: The Architecture of Charles IV of Bohemia", in *Courts and Regions in Medieval Europe*, ed. S. R. JONES, R. MARKS, and A. J. MINNIS,

undoubtedly played a supportive role in these politics, yet not one that has left behind vaults, towers or even images to be studied. Whether or not they qualify as the "dark matter" of the emperor's religious agenda, indulgences have undoubtedly lurked within the shadows of Charles IV's well-studied reign.

An intentional search for indulgences among imperial and papal documents can bring them partly into the light. At the least, it provides clear traces of the emperor's use of indulgences to bring greater attention and more visitors to Prague. Indulgences served as capstones for the relics that Charles IV venerated and carefully deployed in his capital. He began soliciting indulgences even before his coronation as king or emperor. In 1344, Charles secured from Pope Clement VI (1342-1352) an indulgence of one year and one lent for all who visited the new chapel of All Saints within Prague Castle on All Saints' Day, plus one hundred days for those who visited within the octave of the feast day. This was an indulgence for visiting a church, and likely carried at least an implicit expectation that pious visitors would leave behind a gift of money.[51] Such indulgences had from the twelfth century been closely associated with the presence of specific relics within a church.[52] The same was true in this case. The rhetoric of papal letters suggests that this connection was nearly axiomatic: of course the treasury of saints' merits should be especially associated with the physical remains of the same saints – "holy treasures" in their own right. For visitors to the chapel of All Saints, the indulgence was granted because of the presence there of a thorn from the crown of thorns and "many other great relics".[53] This early indulgence sets a pattern that Charles IV, partnering with a succession of popes, was to follow for the remainder of his reign.

Two years later, for example, Clement VI granted indulgences for the new cathedral church of St Vitus on the basis of the presence of relics of saints Vitus, Wenceslas, George, Adalbert, Giles, Ludmila, Stanislaus, and others. As with other concessions of indulgences, the pope used standard language to identify his dual purpose: to honor worthy saints and to attract to their shrines a greater number of devout visitors. These would be available only to

---

York, 2000, p. 99-172. Other examples include, e.g., multiple essays in *Prag und die Grossen Kulturzentren Europas in der Zeit der Luxemburger (1310-1437): Internationale Konferenz aus Anlaß des 660. Jubiläums der Gründung der Karlsuniversität in Prag, 31. März – 5. April 2008*, ed. M. JAROSOVÁ, J. KUTHAN and S. SCHOLZ, Prague, 2008.

[51] R. N. SWANSON, *Indulgences in Late Medieval England, op. cit.*, p. 354-356.

[52] N. VINCENT, "Some Pardoners' Tales", *art. cit.*, p. 38.

[53] *Acta Clementis VI., op. cit.*, p. 239-240, no. 372-373. On the foundation of the royal chapel of All Saints, see Francis of Prague, *Chronicon Francisci Pragensis*, Prague, 1997 (Fontes rerum Bohemicarum, Series nova 1), p. 181.

penitent and confessed visitors, and only on specific feast days – including those of the saints named in the grant.[54] For an archiepiscopal church, this indulgence's provision of one year and one lent was not particularly impressive.[55] More unusual, but still by no means unique, was its availability to pious visitors on as many as fifteen different feast days spread out over the calendar year.[56]

With most of these early indulgences, Charles IV and Clement VI together supported the cults and promoted the honor of relics already in the possession of Prague churches. Pope and emperor concurred that these particular relics deserved new indulgences and also that the indulgences would attract more visitors. As Charles IV began to introduce new relics to Prague, he sought indulgences for many of them as well – although never, so far as I can tell, for the miracle-producing cult of St Sigismund. For example, a relic from St Peter's staff obtained in Trier in 1354 soon occasioned an indulgence of one year and forty days for all those hearing mass in Prague cathedral on any of the sixteen annual occasions when the archbishop was authorized to celebrate with a staff containing the new relic.[57]

Such papal indulgences were predicated on the presence of a relic, but also nearly always attached to a place, usually a church. Unlike relics, indulgences were not usually portable. So the relics that Charles IV obtained from across Europe arrived in Prague not only without their reliquaries, but also without any of the indulgences previously associated with them. The well-informed emperor thus used previous indulgences to justify his requests for new ones. He obtained, for example, a new indulgence for people who attended special masses at the Vyšehrad church in Prague before a stone tablet from an altar built by St Peter; the relic's original indulgence had remained associated with the church near Pisa from which Charles IV had taken the tablet.[58] Without such indulgences, the papal and imperial documents imply,

---

[54] *Acta Clementis VI., op. cit.*, p. 384-385, no. 648, dated 6 May 1346. A. Podlaha and E. Šittler attribute the document to 1345: A. PODLAHA and E. ŠITTLER, *Chrámový poklad, op. cit.*, p. 18, no. 1.

[55] Cf. an indulgence for the parish church of Dubenec, in *Acta Clementis VI., op. cit.*, p. 159, no. 261.

[56] Cf. the fourteen occasions on which an indulgence of one year and forty days granted in 1359 was available at the recently founded house of Poor Clares at Český Krumlov; the parish churches in Miličín and Malšice, as well as a chapel in Bošilec, received the same indulgence at the same time – all at the request of the powerful lord, Peter of Rosenberg: *Acta Innocentii VI. Pontificis Romani: 1352-1362*, ed. J. F. NOVÁK, Prague, 1907 (Monumenta Vaticana res gestas Bohemicas illustrantia, 2), p. 350-353, no. 880, 881, 887, 889, and p. 517-518, no. 1298.

[57] *Acta Innocentii VI., op. cit.*, p. 105-106, no. 249-250.

[58] *Acta Innocentii VI., op. cit.*, p. 139-140, no. 342-343. Cf. multiple English examples of what Robert. N. Swanson calls "branded pardons", namely the extension of a well-known

the relics gathered from distant lands would not receive fitting veneration in Prague.

Indulgences for individual Prague relics were eventually dwarfed by the establishment of two new relic-centered and indulgence-laden feast days in the city, plus a new jubilee every seventh year. The first commemorated the extraordinary haul of relics from the same 1353-1354 "raid for holy relics". In a letter from Mainz, the emperor had instructed the archbishop not only to welcome the relics with a one-time procession but also to establish a new, mandatory, kingdom-wide celebration to be repeated annually.[59] Charles IV then immediately petitioned the pope for this new feast day to be outfitted with indulgences for people who visited Prague cathedral.[60] His request was granted.[61]

Even more impressive than this feast of the Advent of the Relics was another new feast instituted in 1354: the feast of the Holy Lance and Nail, which later was also called the feast of the Display of Relics (*ostensio reliquiarum*).[62] This holy day developed over several years out of a series of papal indulgences secured by the emperor. Each year, many of the most valuable and significant relics from St Vitus cathedral and Karlstein castle were brought out for public veneration. They were revealed one by one to the crowds who gathered on the massive market square – today's Charles Square – that lay at the center of the Charles IV's greatly expanded city. The multiple meanings (and multiple names) of this April feast point to the layers of meaning and devotional practice it comprised: it was a portable, imperial feast based upon the presence of the imperial relics; a Bohemian feast of the kingdom's Christological relics; and a Prague feast glorifying the city's new saints within its newly built spaces.

The emperor's repeated requests for indulgences related to this feast and its many relics also suggest that his vision for it changed over time – and that he or the archbishop intentionally expanded the sanctioned feast of the Holy

---

indulgence – such as the Portiuncula indulgence in Assisi – to one or more specific churches elsewhere: *Indulgences in Late Medieval England*, op. cit., p. 54-56.
[59] [...] *atque sanctos eosdem reverenter suscipite*, [...] *diem celebritatis allationis reliquiarum hujusmodi sub certo anni tempore, sicut tibi archepiscopo visum fuerit, ob amorem nostri, et ut nostris satisfiat affectibus, statuendo, quem totus regni populus teneatur sub poenis debitis, quoties annali revolutione redierit, cum solemnitate debita venerari; ut ipsi nos in coelis dignentur suscipere, et diem extremi examinis, apud districtum illum judicem, gratis orationibus misericorditer praevenire.* Tomáš Jan Pešina z Čechorodu, *Phosphorus septicornis*, op. cit., p. 437.
[60] *Acta Innocentii VI. Pontificis Romani: 1352-1362*, ed. J. F. Novák, p. 83-84, no. 196.
[61] The new Feast of the Advent of the Relics received one year and forty days of indulgence: *Acta Innocentii VI.*, op. cit., p. 84, no. 197. The full text of the papal letter is printed from the extant original by A. Podlaha and E. Šittler, *Chrámový poklad*, op. cit., p. 27 no. 4.
[62] R. Zelený, "Councils and Synods of Prague", art. cit., p. 476.

Lance and Nail into something much broader. The chronicler Beneš Krabice of Weitmil's account (*c.* 1372-1374) provides a good witness of its fully developed practice:

> Thus Charles, inspired by a special devotion, obtained from the papacy the institution of a particular day for the veneration of the imperial *sanctuaria* in Bohemian and German lands, to be celebrated each year for all time on the Friday after Quasimodo Sunday with a special office composed by Charles along with theologians. At the request of the king, the pope conceded great indulgences, contained clearly in his bulls, to everyone coming to Prague for this celebration and the display of these relics.[63]

The Feast of the Holy Lance and Nail thus came to be celebrated in Prague as a general display of the most treasured relics from the cathedral and Karlstein castle. Two surviving texts list the many relics that were shown, in order.[64] Pious visitors could expect to receive a general indulgence of three years and three lents, plus further indulgences which Charles IV had separately secured for some of the other relics on display. The new feast day, according to the same chronicler, was an unmitigated success. The relics that the emperor had gathered throughout the empire and adorned with precious reliquaries now in fact brought crowds to Prague to witness the city's glory. As the chronicler also notes, Charles IV attended to the occasion's financial potential as well; he added a second annual market in New Town to coincide with the feast.[65] Visitors of all sorts might find this an event worth the journey to Prague.

Still Charles IV sought more. After acquiring one third of the veil of the Blessed Virgin from the monastery of St Maximin in Trier, he petitioned for a new Prague indulgence modeled on its original indulgence in Trier where

---

[63] *Unde dictus Karolus, accensus speciali devocione, obtinuit a sede apostolica, ut specialis dies pro veneracione illarum in Boemie et Almanie partibus deputaretur, et solempniter sub speciali officio, quod idem dominus Karolus cum aliis theologis exposuit, celebraretur singulis annis perpetuis temporibus VI feria post dominicam Quasimodo geniti proxima. Et dominus papa ad instanciam domini regis predicti omnibus Pragam ad dictam solempnitatem et earundem reliquiarum ostensionem venientibus largitus est magnas indulgencias, que in bullis ipsius evidencius continentur.* Beneš Krabice of Weitmil, *Cronica ecclesie Pragensis, op. cit.*, p. 519.

[64] The lance and nail are included, as well as the crown and sword of Charlemagne and the other imperial relics. Also listed are relics from some of Bohemia's patron saints, as well as evangelists, apostles and holy popes. Assorted articles of clothing from Christ and the Blessed Virgin, together with the tablecloth from the Last Supper and further passion implements were likewise to be displayed in an established order. A. Podlaha and E. Šittler printed a Czech translation of the text and some of the original Latin from a manuscript in Prague, Knihovna metropolitní kapituly, Cod. IX, in *Chrámový poklad, op. cit.*, p. 56-58.

[65] This new market was the third that Prague's Old Town and New Town together held each year; each likely lasted for a week or two, according to V. V. TOMEK, *Dějepis města Prahy*, vol. 2, Prague, 1892², p. 413.

it was available during the veil's public veneration every seventh year.[66] At Charles IV's request, Pope Innocent VI granted a similar indulgence of "three years and three lents every seventh year when it is displayed" in Prague.[67] As with the feast of the Holy Lance and Nail, the subsequent practice that developed in Prague seems to have outstripped the pope's intention and led to an entire "year of indulgences" (*annus gracie sive indulgenciarum*).[68] Every seventh year in Prague was pronounced a "jubilee year", beginning on the feast of the Assumption of the Virgin (15 August) with the display of the Virgin's veil.[69] Jubilee years were likely proclaimed in August 1354 and 1361, although the first direct evidence of the practice refers to the 1368-1369 jubilee.[70] Technically, the original indulgence was valid only for pious visitors to St Vitus cathedral on the day of the veil's presentation. According to the Beneš Krabice of Weitmil, however, the crowds streamed to Prague throughout the entire year.[71] The same veil was also woven into the program for the annual feast of the Holy Lance and Nail (or the Display of Relics). The chronicler attests to its success at filling the space of Charles Square: "there was such an assembly of people from foreign lands that the great square in New Town near Zderaz seemed to be utterly full of people. Everyone was saying that no one had ever seen so many people gathered together.[72]"

---

[66] A. PODLAHA and E. ŠITTLER, *Chrámový poklad, op. cit.*, p. 31, no. 2. On the surviving relic, see A. PODLAHA and E. ŠITTLER, *Chrámový poklad, op. cit.*, p. 184-186 and A. PODLAHA and E. ŠITTLER, *Der Domschatz in Prag, op. cit.*, p. 68-71.

[67] *Acta Innocentii VI.*, *op. cit.*, p. 108, no. 259.

[68] Beneš Krabice of Weitmil, *Cronica ecclesie Pragensis, op. cit.*, p. 538.

[69] The shorter of the two orders for the Feast of the Holy Lance and Nail was apparently intended for one of these jubilee years, as it ends with the following line: "Hic pronuncietur annus jubileus, qui hoc anno inchoabitur in festo Assumptionis sanctae Mariae, ubi ostendetur peplum beatae Virginis". A. PODLAHA and E. ŠITTLER, *Chrámový poklad, op. cit.*, p. 56, no. 3.

[70] A. PODLAHA and E. ŠITTLER, *Chrámový poklad, op. cit.*, p. 58, no. 2; V. V. TOMEK, *Dějepis města Prahy, op. cit.*, vol. 2, p. 60.

[71] *[...] et qui die, quo huiusmodi peplum ostenditur, ecclesiam ob devocionem ingressi fuerint, habeant de indulgenciis a sede apostolica tres annos et tres karenas. [...] Unde factus est ad ecclesiam Pragensem maximus concursus populorum per totum hunc annum, eciam de alienis partibus.* Beneš Krabice of Weitmil, *Cronica ecclesie Pragensis, op. cit.*, p. 538.

[72] *Eodem anno in festo Ostensionis reliquiarum tantus fuit concursus hominum de alienis partibus, ut illa placza magna in Nova civitate prope Zderazium videretur undique repleta hominibus. Talem populum in unum congregatum nullus unquam vidit hominum, ut communiter referebatur ab omnibus.* Beneš Krabice of Weitmil, *Cronica ecclesie Pragensis, op. cit.*, p. 539. Another massive crowd, this time at the cathedral, was reported for the days leading up to the Feast of the Assumption of the Virgin in 1369, at the end of the same jubilee year. *Eodem anno octo diebus ante festum Assumpcionis beate Virginis et in ipso festo iam exspirante anno gracie seu indulgenciarum tantus fuit concursus hominum ad ecclesiam Pragensem, qualem nulla meminit etas.* Beneš Krabice of Weitmil, *Cronica ecclesie Pragensis, op. cit.*, p. 539.

Conclusion

How effective were Charles IV's new indulgences at attracting crowds to Prague? Popular reception of indulgences proves extraordinarily difficult for historians to evaluate. Quantitative evidence in particular is elusive.[73] For fourteenth-century Prague, the most direct evidence of indulgences' drawing power comes from Beneš Krabice of Weitmil's claims that throngs of visitors – including foreign pilgrims – crammed into the city's unusually expansive market square for the new indulgence-rich feast days, especially during a jubilee year. Other evidence comes indirectly. For example, a few surviving examples of pilgrim badges for the Feast of the Holy Lance and Nail certainly imply a population – admittedly unquantified – of pilgrims interested in carrying home evidence of their Prague journeys.[74]

Consider as well the emperor's own sustained and repeated efforts to secure more and longer indulgences for Prague; such petitions to a succession of popes figured into complex power relationships in which boons were granted and requested by both parties. That Charles IV included so many indulgences among his own petitions suggests not only (or even necessarily) a personal belief in their real spiritual benefits; rather, it proves that he considered indulgences valuable. Their value came primarily as effective tools to achieve what he and the popes regularly cited in their documents: greater honor to the saints through drawing more visitors to their shrines. The emperor, in other words, believed that indulgences were attractive incentives likely to strengthen a place's gravitational pull on pious lay people. R. N. Swanson makes similar arguments for late-medieval England: first, that both supplicants and grantors of indulgences used them to establish or bolster pilgrimage destinations precisely because both believed that indulgences would attract visitors; and second, that prelates' granting of increasing numerous and lengthy indulgences offers strong, indirect evidence of lay demand and lay pressures for them.[75]

That is not to say that new indulgences could guarantee the success of a new or flagging cult, nor that large crowds responded to all of Charles IV's new indulgences. Neither indulgences nor efforts to tout miraculous powers was enough, it seems, for King Henry II's cult of the Holy Blood at Westminster

---

[73] R. N. SWANSON, *Indulgences in Late Medieval England*, op. cit., p. 349-418.
[74] K. STEJSKAL, *Umění na dvoře Karla IV.*, op. cit., p. 81 and 230.
[75] R. N. SWANSON, *Indulgences in Late Medieval England*, op. cit., p. 355 and 416. N. VINCENT describes indulgences as "an early form of rent-a-crowd" in N. VINCENT, "Some Pardoners' Tales", art. cit., p. 38.

to gain popularity in the thirteenth century.[76] Furthermore, Nicholas Vincent rightly warns historians not to measure a cult's drawing power by the size and number of its indulgences: "On the contrary, the greater the number of indulgences, the more anxious a church must have been to attract pilgrims to a particular relic or enterprise, and hence, we may assume, the less appeal such a relic or enterprise might have commanded on its merits alone.[77]" Located near the eastern edge of Latin Christendom, with a very limited tradition as a pilgrimage destination, Charles IV's Prague certainly needed as much additional incentive for pilgrims as the emperor could provide. The most successful of the new Prague cults were those that relied on more than indulgences, such as the feast of the Holy Lance and Nail. For that feast, numerous indulgences combined with an elaborate, open-air display of relics and even an annual market day to draw visitors. Whether the indulgences in themselves provided sufficient incentives to visit or instead supplied ancillary rewards for more or less pious market-goers cannot be determined – and must have varied by individual in any case.[78]

The attractive power of particular indulgences will remain difficult to evaluate, even as the great expansion of indulgences across Europe clearly establishes their importance within late medieval devotional practice. Charles IV's Prague provides a clear and focused example of a larger phenomenon. Even more, Charles IV's use of indulgences illustrate one final and critical attribute of indulgences. Here the comparison with miracle-based cults is particularly instructive. Indulgences offered rulers and popes a greater power to establish a successful cult than miracles ever did. When Charles IV asked and Innocent VI agreed, for example, a new indulgence simply came into existence. Their judgments, and even their negotiation, alone determined the size and rarity of the resulting spiritual benefit on offer. The development of a miracle-producing cult such as that of St Sigismund, on the other hand, depended not only on the decision of powerful lay and church officials to establish its conditions, but also on the decisions of numerous relatively powerless people to embrace the cult – and even to experience its power deeply. Without the spark created by a few local lay people who proclaimed themselves healed by the new saint, Sigismund's cult as a source of miracles would never have existed in Prague, let alone flourished.

---

[76] N. VINCENT, *The Holy Blood: King Henry III and the Westminster Blood Relic*, Cambridge, 2001, p. 155-156, 185.
[77] N. VINCENT, *The Holy Blood, op. cit.*, p. 160.
[78] R. N. SWANSON, *Indulgences in Late Medieval England, op. cit.*, p. 355, 417, 522.

The system of indulgences, on the other hand, privileged the roles of powerful church and lay officials. Distributing riches from the treasury of saints' merits required the intervention of a pope or bishop; an individual could not directly pray to a saint for such a favor. As Nicholas Vincent argues, in this respect indulgences were part of broader efforts by church authorities in these centuries to increase their own control over the relationships between saints and lay people.[79] Lay rulers too exercised an unusual degree of power in establishing indulgences. Dukes, kings, emperors and the like possessed the power and wealth that allowed them to make compelling petitions to popes and bishops, including through the building of new shrines or the commissioning of new reliquaries. Individual pilgrims of course chose for themselves which shrines to visit; collectively, this gave even lowly pilgrims the power to distinguish between more and less successful cults. Yet the initial establishment of a rich indulgence did not require pilgrims' early adoption of a cult, as did the launch of a cult based predominately on a reputation for miracles. Indulgences offered Charles IV a welcome tool – one of numerous he employed – to bring glory and visitors to the city that he hoped to transform into one of Christendom's greatest. However difficult to quantify, the impact of indulgences on the emperor's Prague was both real and illustrative of wider experience. Together rulers and bishops, popes and pilgrims, combined to embrace indulgences as vital elements of the rich and complex religious culture of the later Middle Ages.

---

[79] N. VINCENT, *The Holy Blood, op. cit.*, p. 156.

Intercession and Specialization

St Sebastian and St Roche as Plague Saints and their Cult in Medieval Hungary*

Ottó GECSER
(*Budapest*)

Saints in the Middle Ages and beyond were credited with offering special favors to specific groups of believers, including residents of cities and towns, members of religious orders, aristocratic clans and ethnic groups, as well as practitioners of various trades and professions. A further category of believers whom saints were assumed to distinguish by their special attention were those in need of a particular kind of help to survive a calamity, recover from an illness or resolve a more mundane problem like finding lost objects.[1]

The present study looks at the way and the extent that two saints, St Sebastian and St Roche, came to be trusted with supernatural help of a particular kind, focusing on (without being restricted to) one region of medieval Europe. In contrast to Italy, from where the veneration of both saints originated, Hungary was poor in autochthonous cults. In addition, the most important indigenous cults in Hungary were dynastic rather than regional or urban, even if these categories overlapped in some cases, particularly that of

---

* This article is based on research I made in the Herzog August Bibliothek in Wolfenbüttel, with a grant by the Federal State of Lower Saxony, and at the Institute for Advanced Study in Princeton, with the support of the Herodotus Fund. I am grateful to Gábor Klaniczay, Emese Sarkadi Nagy, and Edward Schoolman for having read previous versions of it and helped to make it better. If not indicated otherwise, all translations and emendations of the quoted sources are mine.

[1] For a typology of patron saints, see R. BARTLETT, *Why Can the Dead Do Such Great Things? Saints and Worshippers from the Martyrs to the Reformation*, Princeton, 2013, p. 221-238. For a discussion of venerating saints for the special kinds of help they were believed to offer, see O. GECSER, "Holy Helpers and the Transformation of Saintly Patronage at the End of the Middle Ages", *Annual of Medieval Studies at CEU*, 22 (2016), p. 174-201.

Les saints et leur culte en Europe centrale au Moyen Âge (XIe-début du XVIe siècle), éd. par Marie-Madeleine de CEVINS et Olivier MARIN, Turnhout, 2017 (*Hagiologia*, 13), p. 77-108.

the burial place of King St Ladislas at Oradea (Nagyvárad).[2] In such a situation, few saints could be perceived by their local worshippers as belonging explicitly to them and, thus, willing to ward off all dangers that threaten their community. Therefore, holy helpers expected to provide a particular kind of assistance would be most welcome, especially against such a general, grave and recurrent problem as the plague.

In the first two sections below I briefly sketch how St Sebastian came to be seen as a protector against the plague, as well as how, when and why St Roche appeared in the same guise. It is against this background that I discuss the cult of the two saints in Hungary in the remaining two sections, in terms of liturgical observance, name-giving, dating legal documents, dedications of ecclesiastical institutions, hagiographic texts, and visual representations. The mere presence of a saint in specific types of sources produced in a given area, however, is not a good indicator of the intensity or the character of his cult there. His images or the practice of naming children after him may have been widespread without much liturgical observance of his feast; or several vitae or liturgical texts may have survived about him without many visual representations. Thus, apart from assessing the role of the plague in the veneration of Sebastian and Roche, and reconstructing their fate in one medieval kingdom, a further goal of the paper is to contribute to the more general problem of to what extent different manifestations of a cult (like dating charters, naming persons, or venerating images) are interrelated or develop in tandem.

St Sebastian and the plague

According to his fifth-century *Passio*, Sebastian was a high ranking officer and a clandestine Christian in third-century Rome under Diocletian and Maximian. After his faith had been revealed through a series of conversions and miraculous healings in which he played an active role, Diocletian ordered his archers to kill him. Although "the arrow shots made him as bristly as a hedgehog" (*ut quasi hericius ita esset hirsutus ictibus sagittarum*), he miraculously recovered from his injuries to be subsequently beaten to death and thus gain the crown of martyrdom.[3] In spite of creating a strong visual

---

[2] For the dynastic cults, see G. KLANICZAY, *Holy Rulers and Blessed Princesses: Dynastic Cults in Medieval Central Europe*, Cambridge, 2002; for Oradea / Nagyvárad, see K. SZENDE, "*Civitas opulentissima Varadiensis:* Püspöki székhely és városfejlődés a középkori Váradon", in *Nagyvárad és Bihar a korai középkorban*, ed. A. ZSOLDOS, Oradea, 2014, p. 101-128.

[3] The *Passio* – ed. in *Acta Sanctorum*, 67 vols., Brussels-Leuven, 1643-1940 (hereinafter: *AASS*), here Ian. II, p. 265-278 and *Patrologiae cursus completus. Series Latina*, ed. J.-P. MIGNE, 221 vols., Paris, 1841-1864 (hereinafter: *PL*), here vol. 17, col. 1021-1058 (the quotation is from ch. 23, *PL* 17, col. 1056) – was written in the 430s and it has recently been

metaphor with the hedgehog simile that must have influenced the iconography of the saint, the *Passio* does not make any connection between the arrows and the plague as later commentators do. In fact, there is no reference to Sebastian's protection from the plague in the sources before Paul the Deacon. According to the latter a "very severe pestilence" was decimating the city of Pavia in 680, until

> it was said to a certain man by revelation that the pestilence itself would not cease before an altar of St Sebastian the martyr was placed in the church of the blessed Peter which is called "Ad Vincula". And it was done, and after the remains [*reliquiae*] of St Sebastian the martyr had been carried from the city of Rome, presently the altar was set up in the aforesaid church and the pestilence itself ceased.[4]

That Sebastian would have previously been known as a plague saint is not mentioned here; there is no allusion to arrows either. The reason for choosing precisely his relics and not those of another saint must have lain elsewhere. Relying on a tradition of humanist historiography in early modern Italy, Maria Teresa Mazzilli Savini connects the translation to a politico-religious alliance between the Lombards and the Papacy forged in 679-680. Depositing his relics in an altar in the San Pietro in Vincoli in Pavia – that is, in a church dedicated to another cult of Roman origin, spread, for its part, through the papal distribution of fragments from the holy chains kept in the homonymous Roman church – point in the same direction.[5]

By the end of the seventh century Sebastian was widely known outside Rome as it is attested by the earliest pilgrim itineraries which never failed to mention his grave. The *De locis sanctis martyrum quae sunt foris civitatis Romae*, written in the early 640s, already calls the church on the Via Appia – the predecessor of the present-day San Sebastiano fuori le mura initially

---

attributed to Arnobius the Younger, an ecclesiastical writer of presumably African origin who was active in Rome under popes Sixtus III (432-440) and Leo the Great (440-461). See (with references to the earlier literature) C. LANÉRY, "Arnobe le Jeune et la Passion de Sébastien (*BHL* 7543)", *Revue des études augustiniennes et patristiques*, 53 (2007), p. 267-293. The text has survived (in full or abbreviated form) in some five hundred manuscripts. C. LANÉRY, "La tradition manuscrite de la *Passio Sebastiani* (Arnobe le Jeune, *BHL* 7543)", *Revue d'histoire des textes*, n. s., 7 (2012), p. 37-116.
[4] Paul the Deacon, *History of the Lombards*, trans. W. D. FOULKE, 2nd ed., Philadelphia, 1974, bk. 6, ch. 5, p. 255; for the Latin original, see Historia Langobardicarum ed. G. WAITZ, Hannover, 1878 (*Monumenta Germaniae Historica*, Scriptores rerum Langobardicarum, 1), p. 166 or *PL* 95, col. 627-628.
[5] G. BARTOLOZZI CASTI – M. T. MAZZILLI SAVINI, "Il culto parallelo a S. Sebastiano nelle chiese di S. Pietro in Vincoli di Roma e Pavia", *Rendiconti della Pontificia Accademia Romana di Archeologia*, 76 (2003-2004), p. 345-448, on p. 406-424 (for the chain fragments, see p. 347-364).

known as *basilica Apostolorum – ecclesia sancti Sebastiani martyris*, and the pilgrims visiting Rome at the time could see him depicted in the crypt of St Cecilia or could pray at his altar in the Sant'Agata dei Goti as well.[6] His fame must have been one of the reasons why his relics were selected to be translated – with the permission of Pope Eugene II – from Rome to Saint-Médard in Soissons in 826.

In contrast to his reputation as a great Roman martyr, however, his ability to protect from the plague had apparently remained local knowledge in Pavia; it is never mentioned in the accounts of his translation over the Alps or in the collections of miracles linked to his relics.[7] When Soissons is said to have witnessed an outbreak of *pestis inguinaria* in 1126, just like the nearby village of Septmonts at an unspecified date, the miraculous end of the epidemics was attributed not to the intercession of St Sebastian but to that of Gregory the Great whose relics were reportedly stolen from Rome and brought to Saint-Médard together with those of the martyr.[8] The choice of Gregory as an in-

---

[6] B. PESCI, "Il culto di San Sebastiano a Roma nell'antichità e nel medioevo", *Antonianum*, 20 (1945), p. 177-200, on p. 189 and 191.

[7] See, first of all, the *Annales Regni Francorum*, ed. F. KURZE, Hannover, 1895 (*Monumenta Germaniae Historica*, Scriptores rerum Germanicarum, 6), a. 826, p. 171-172; the anonymous ninth-century poem in Città del Vaticano, Bibliotheca Apostolica Vaticana, Vat. Lat. 5777, ed. in C. LANÉRY, "La tradition manuscrite", *art. cit.*, p. 98-100; and Odilo of Saint-Médard, *Liber de translatione reliquiarum s. Sebastiani martyris et Gregorii papae in Suessionense sancti Medardi monasterium* (*BHL* 7545), in *AASS*, Ian. II, p. 278-295 or *PL* 132, col. 579-622. According to Odilo (chapter 5-6, *PL* 132, col. 585-587), it was originally the relics of Pope Sylvester I that Louis the Pious and his archchaplain, Hilduin, considered to obtain, but on their way to Rome, Sebastian let the envoys of Hilduin know (through a dream vision of a severely ill man) that they had to choose him. Cécile Lanéry interprets this miraculous intervention as masking a compromise: the politically charged Sylvester (the alleged recipient of the *Donatio Constantini*) was replaced by the politically neutral but more famous Sebastian. See C. LANÉRY, "La tradition manuscrite", *art. cit.*, p. 95. On Carolingian relic translations from Rome in general (with further literature), see J. M. H. SMITH, "Old Saints, New Cults: Roman Relics in Carolingian Francia", in *Early Medieval Rome and the Christian West: Essays in Honour of Donald A. Bullough*, ed. J. M. H. SMITH, Leiden, 2000, p. 317-339. For the miracle collections, see footnote 8.

[8] K. FUCHS, *Zeichen und Wunder bei Guibert de Nogent: Kommunikation, Deutungen und Funktionalisierungen von Wundererzählungen im 12. Jahrhundert*, Munich, 2008, p. 206-226, has organized the textually rather unstable, eleventh- and twelfth-century collections of miracles attributed to St Sebastian and Gregory the Great in Soissons in three groups. Two of these contain the plague miracles. One is edited in *Catalogus codicum hagiographicorum bibliothecae regiae Bruxellensis, Pars I: Codices Latini membranei*, 2 vols., Brussels, 1886-1889, vol. 2, p. 238-248 (plague miracles: p. 245-248); the other is published in K. FUCHS, *Zeichen und Wunder*, p. 255-269 (plague miracles: p. 265-267). For the alleged theft of Gregory's relics, see Odilo, *Liber de translatione*, chapter 15, *PL* 132, col. 594; and F. H. DUDDEN, *Gregory the Great: His Place in History and Thought*, 2 vols., London, 1905, vol. 2, p. 273-276. For the logic of such narratives in general, see P. GEARY, *Furta Sacra: Thefts of Relics in the Central Middle Ages*, Princeton NJ, 1990².

tercessor against the plague in 1126 was explicitly inspired by the legend of the origins of the Major Litany (25 April), according to which a severe plague was halted in Rome when Gregory organized a procession in the city:

> Since a major plague was approaching in the very month of April – the month when the Major Litany is performed, on the day of which Bl. Gregory saved the people of Rome from the plague with prayers – it was a heartfelt wish to turn to Bl. Gregory on the same day because of a similar plague, and to implore the Lord's mercy through him.[9]

In other words, even in a major center of Sebastian's cult like Soissons, if there was a plague saint in the twelfth century, it was not he but Gregory the Great. It seems that until the Black Death there was no interest in connecting the cult of Sebastian to the plague with the exception of Pavia where, according to Opicino de Canistris, writing in 1330, two kinds of ritual objects were blessed and distributed in the *ecclesia sancti Petri ad vincula* on his feast-day: little birds made of bread dough (*avicule panis*) were given to humans and beasts alike "in order to avoid pestilence" (*propter evitandam pestem*), and little arrows made of iron were given to men "in the memory of St Sebastian who was pierced by arrows, in order that he may protect them from injury caused by arrows" (*in memoriam sancti Sebastiani, qui fuit sagittis perfossus, ut eos a sagictarum lesione defendat*).[10] Whereas his protection from arrow shots is explained with reference to his legend, his protection from the plague needed no explanation in the local context.[11] Elsewhere in the same work Opicino describes the church of San Pietro in Vincoli as the one "in which there are relics of the martyr St Sebastian that helped to chase the plague away from the city of Pavia in the times of Guibert [i.e. Cunipert], King of the Lombards".[12]

---

[9] *Catalogus codicum hagiographicorum bibliothecae regiae Bruxellensis*, vol. 2, p. 246. For a reconstruction of the events of 589-590 in Rome, see A. T. HACK, *Gregor der Grosse und die Krankheit*, Stuttgart, 2012, p. 10-35. For the legend of the Major Litany, see A. VAUCHEZ, "Liturgy and Folk Culture in the Golden Legend", in *Id.*, *Laity in the Middle Ages: Religious Beliefs and Devotional Practices*, ed. and intr. by D. E. BORNSTEIN, trans. by M. J. SCHNEIDER, Notre Dame IN, 1993, p. 129-139.
[10] Anonymus Ticinensis (Opicino de Canistris), *Liber de laudibus civitatis Ticinensis*, ed. R. MAIOCCHI, F. QUINTAVALLE, RIS 11.1, Città di Castello, 1903, p. 32; F. GIANANI, *Opicino de Canistris, l'"Anonimo Ticinese" (Cod. Vaticano Palatino Latino 1993)*, Pavia, 1927, p. 104. For the author and his work, see *ibid.*, p. 7-12.
[11] To be sure, the meaning of bird symbolism is far from crystal clear to the modern reader (or to the present author, at least). As some sort of a parallel, there is a scene of bird hunting in the background of Botticelli's *St Sebastian* (Berlin, Staatliche Museen).
[12] Anonymus Ticinensis, *Liber de laudibus*, *op. cit.*, p. 8; F. GIANANI, *Opicino de Canistris*, *op. cit.*, p. 81.

That Sebastian's anti-pestilential capacities came to be trusted outside Pavia as well must have been due, in part, to the availability of the Pavian miracle as a historical precedent or proof during the Black Death. Otherwise it would be difficult to explain his connection to the disease; pointing to the arrows of his martyrdom seems to have been a retrospective attempt (medieval but later than the Black Death) to make sense of his relation to the plague.[13] Thus the bishop of Paris, Foulques de Chanac, in his letter of indulgence of 18 November, 1348 for the altar and relics of St Sebastian in the abbey church of Saint-Victor, referred to the story in the *Legenda aurea*, where James of Varazze retold it among the *post mortem* miracles attributed to the saint.[14] Or, Filippo di Neri dell'Antella, prior of the Florentine monastery of San Pier Scheraggio, who claimed to have recovered from the disease with the help of St Sebastian, was inspired to seek his assistance by the Pavian miracle which he found in "alcuna cronica romana", probably the *Historia Langobardorum* or a compilation based on it.[15]

---

[13] The arrow-plague association had, of course, existed since the arrows of Apollo in *Iliad* I, 9 ff. But as far as late medieval epidemics are concerned, the first text that, to my knowledge, uses the arrow image – the *Historia de Morbo* written by the Placentine notary, Gabriele de' Mussi, before 1356 – places it in a series of equally relevant metonymic references to sudden and massive death coming from a distance: darts, arrows, lightning, spears (*mortis jacula... sagita venenata... morbus incurabilis fulminabit... vibrata omnipotentis lancea, duris aculleis undique destinatis*). See A. W. HENSCHEL, "Document zur Geschichte des schwarzen Todes", *Archiv für die gesammte Medicin*, 2 (1841), p. 26-59, on p. 47-48. For the dating of this text, see A. G. TONONI, "La peste dell'anno 1348", *Giornale ligustico di archeologia, storia e letteratura*, 11 (1884), p. 139-152; for an English translation, see *The Black Death*, ed. trans. R. HORROX (Manchester, 1994), p. 14-26. If the means of martyrdom had been enough for Sebastian to become a plague saint, then St Thomas Apostle, who was killed by a spear and arguably a more important saint than Sebastian, should have preceded him in this capacity. See also the references in footnote 25 below.

[14] K. RESSOUNI-DEMIGNEUX, "La personnalité de saint Sébastien: Exploration du fonds euchologique médiéval et renaissant, du IVᵉ au XVIᵉ siècle", *Mélanges de l'École française de Rome. Moyen Âge*, 114 (2002), p. 557-579, on p. 569; James of Varazze, *Legenda aurea: Con le miniature del codice Ambrosiano C 240 inf*, ed. and comm. by G. P. MAGGIONI, 2 vols., Florence-Milan, 2007, chapter 23 (*De s. Sebastiano*), 1, p. 194-201 (plague miracle: p. 200). James also quoted it in one of his sermons for the feast of St Sebastian, but he kept it separate from his discussion of arrow-symbolism – the miracle account is meant to exemplify the power of Sebastian's relics; see James of Varazze, *Sermones de sanctis*, Strasbourg, 1484, *De sancto Sebastiano*, third sermon (without foliation). The arrow symbolism is discussed in the first sermon without reference to the plague. For other cases of visiting his relics in Soissons and in a monastery of St Peter in Hainaut in 1349, that is, after and, possibly, following the lead of the bishop of Paris, see Gilles Li Muisis, "Chronicon minus", in *Recueil des Chroniques de Flandre*, ed. J.-J. DE SMET, 4 vols., Brussels, 1837-1865, here vol. 2, p. 303-448, on p. 381-382.

[15] F. CARDINI, "Una nuova fonte sulla peste del 1348 ad Avignone, Firenze e Siena: il culto di S. Sebastiano e Filippo dell'Antella", *Bullettino senese di storia patria*, 82-83 (1975-1976), p. 372-384.

Nevertheless, even during the Black Death and its aftermath the association between St Sebastian and the plague failed to become fully fledged. Although in 1349 the Benedictine chronicler of Tournai, Gilles li Muisis, noted down a contemporary prayer to St Sebastian against the plague,[16] the *Missa pro evitanda mortalitate* instituted by Pope Clement VI against the epidemic in 1348, and subsequently included in a large number of missals, did not yet turn to Sebastian for help; it named as holy intercessor the Virgin Mary alone.[17] And even later, many sermons written for his feast paid little or no attention to his anti-pestilential capacities, and continued to praise him as a martyr in a traditional manner.[18]

One of the earliest post-Black Death representations of the saint, Giovanni del Biondo's *St Sebastian Triptych* painted around 1375 and now in the Museo dell'Opera del Duomo in Florence, shows the attempt to execute him by arrow shots on the central panel and four scenes from his life on the inner sides of the wings. Given that one of these scenes is the miracle of Pavia, the connection between the altarpiece and the plague is a strong one, especially if its dating is correct and it was indeed painted right after the 1374 epidemic.[19] Similarly, Josse Lieferinxe's *Retable of St Sebastian* from the once Notre-Dame-des-Accoules in Marseille (1497-1499) represented St Sebastian flanked by St Anthony and St Roche on the central panels (now lost), and the life of the saint on eight side panels with one of them (now in The Walters Art Museum in Baltimore) dedicated to his intercession for Pavia.[20] In *c.* 1448 a processional banner, a *gonfalone*, with the image of St Sebastian was painted in Foligno with a worshipper at his feet holding a scroll that reads: "Who entrusts oneself to God and St Sebastian won't ever die from the plague" (*Chi a Dio et sam Sobbastiano se racomanda mai de morbo non morirà*).[21] In Siena, in 1476, the *Palio* was cancelled because of fear of the plague, and the

---

[16] Gilles Li Muisis, "Chronicon minus", *art. cit.*, p. 382 and 385-386.
[17] J. VIARD, "La messe pour la peste", *Bibliothèque de l'École des Chartes*, 61 (1900), p. 334-338.
[18] O. GECSER, "Sermons on St Sebastian after the Black Death", in *Promoting the Saints: Cults and Their Contexts from Late Antiquity until the Early Modern Period. Essays in Honor of Gábor Klaniczay for his 60th Birthday*, ed. O. GECSER et al., Budapest-New York, 2011, p. 261-272.
[19] S. BARKER, "The Making of a Plague Saint: Saint Sebastian's Imagery and Cult before the Counter-Reformation", in *Piety and Plague: From Byzantium to the Baroque*, ed. F. MORMANDO, T. WORCESTER, Kirksville MO, 2007, p. 90-131, on p. 100-102.
[20] M. R. KATZ, "Preventative Medicine: Josse Lieferinxe's Retable Altar of St Sebastian as a Defense Against Plague in 15th Century Provence", *Interfaces*, 26 (2006-2007), p. 59-82.
[21] M. SENSI, "Santuari politici 'contra pestem': L'esempio di Fermo", in M. SENSI, *Santuari, pellegrini, eremiti nell'Italia centrale*, 3 vols., Spoleto, 2003, vol. I, p. 333-380, on p. 348.

money reserved for it was spent to make a silver statue of St Sebastian.[22] Some broadsheets printed in Germany in the second half of the fifteenth century represented him in the moment of being shot by the archers and had a prayer underneath the image naming him as a holy helper against the plague.[23]

Nevertheless, many – possibly most – representations of St Sebastian lack an explicit reference to the plague or it is difficult to connect them precisely enough to a local outbreak. His martyrdom with arrows piercing his body, the most frequently depicted episode of his legend, is too multivalent to be taken as a clear reference to the disease in itself. It is meant to be an example of *imitatio Christi* in the first place. In Giovanni del Biondo, for example, he is not merely tied to a pole or column but he is also elevated above the head of his executors by standing on a small wooden shelf attached to the pole, which makes him similar to Christ on the cross. Such an elevated position, not very practical for the archers, remained characteristic of his Italian representations throughout the fifteenth century, even if the wooden shelf came to be replaced by a marble pedestal.[24]

Moreover, the arrows themselves, as we have already seen in his Pavian commemoration, refer more directly to arrow shots than to the plague – even if they did become a major visual sign of pestilence in post-Black Death iconography.[25] Being the patron saint of archers seems to have been a more explicit – if not necessarily more typical – reason than his anti-pestilential capacities for dedicating religious or civic associations to St Sebastian. In Bruges, although the city was severely hit by the Black Death, it was the guild of archers that appeared under Sebastian's patronage from 1396 onwards. The connection with the archers must have also been supported by the fact that

---

[22] "Cronaca Senese di Tommaso Fecini (1431-1479)", in *Cronache Senesi*, ed. A. LISINI, F. IACOMETTI, Bologna, 1931-1937, vol. 2, p. 837-874, on p. 873; D. WEBB, *Patrons and Defenders: The Saints in the Italian City State*, London, 1996, p. 211.

[23] P. HEITZ, *Pestblätter des XV. Jahrhunderts*, Strasbourg, 1918², nos. 18-19; W. L. SCHREIBER, *Handbuch der Holz- und Metallschnitte des XV. Jahrhunderts*, vol. 3, Leipzig, 1927, nos. 1678-1679; *Origins of European Printmaking: Fifteenth-Century Woodcuts and Their Public*, ed. P. PARSHALL et al., Washington-New Haven, 2005, nos. 5, 36, 96, p. 73-75, 157-159, 302-307. See also H. DORMEIER, *"Ein geystliche ertzeney fur die grausam erschrecklich pestilentz*: Schutzpatrone und frommer Abwehrzauber gegen die Pest", in *Das große Sterben: Seuchen machen Geschichte*, ed. H. WILDEROTTER, M. DORRMANN, Dresden, 1995, p. 54-93, esp. p. 63.

[24] See the corpus of images with further literature in S. BARKER, "The Making of a Plague Saint"; L. MARSHALL, "Reading the Body of a Plague Saint: Narrative Altarpieces and Devotional Images of St Sebastian in Renaissance Art", in *Reading Texts and Images: Essays on Medieval Renaissance Art and Patronage*, ed. B. J. MUIR, Exeter, 2002, p. 237-271.

[25] E. HAGEMANN, *Der göttliche Pfeilschütze: Zur Genealogie eines Pestbildtypus*, St. Michael, 1982; P. DINZELBACHER, "Die tötende Gottheit: Pestbilder und Todesikonographie als Ausdruck der Mentalität des Spätmittelalters und der Renaissance", in *Zeit, Tod und Ewigkeit in der Renaissance Literatur*, ed. J. HOGG, vol. 2, Salzburg, 1986, p. 5-138.

according to his *passio* he was a soldier, just like St George, the patron of the local crossbowmen. Moreover, openly in response to increased military needs under Charles the Bold, a second St Sebastian archery guild was established in Bruges – right outside the city walls – in 1476.[26] Between the middle of the fifteenth century and the first decades of the sixteenth, 26 towns and cities in the medieval diocese of Würzburg chose St Sebastian as the patron and a further six as a co-patron of a confraternity, but seeking protection from the plague appears only once as the explicit *raison d'être* of these institutions, whereas archery is the most frequent one (among the sufficiently documented cases). It is also true, however, that the majority of their members were not archers – in contrast to the Bruges guilds, they were legally separate from the urban militia – and in many cases the immediate motivation behind their institution was, apparently, a preexisting altar or chapel of St Sebastian which the members wanted to take care of.[27] A confraternity of St Sebastian in Alsace was first mentioned in the extant sources in 1439 and it was followed by twenty-one similar institutions until 1562. In most of the cases the circumstances of their foundation are not known but in those few cases in which they are, they seem to be related to the companies of archers and not (or not directly) to the plague.[28] In Venice, there were at least five confraternities dedicated, partly or entirely, to St Sebastian by the beginning of the sixteenth century. Two of them were related to guilds, the arrow makers and the glassworkers, but in only one case does their *mariegola* (collection of official documents) connect the existence of the confraternity to the anti-pestilential function of the saint.[29]

Besides the fact that the association between St Sebastian and the plague largely remains unstated, these examples also suggest the late emergence of his role as a patron of confraternities. To be sure, the dedication of ecclesiastical institutions to specific saints is typically known from last wills, and

---

[26] A. BROWN, *Civic Ceremony and Religion in Medieval Bruges, c. 1300-1520*, Cambridge, 2011, p. 139, 146, 256.
[27] L. REMLING, *Bruderschaften in Franken: Kirchen- und sozialgeschichtliche Untersuchungen zum spätmittelalterlichen und frühneuzeitlichen Bruderschaftswesen*, Würzburg, 1986, p. 238-257.
[28] M.-M. ANTONY-SCHMITT, *Le culte de saint Sébastien en Alsace: médecine populaire et saints guérisseurs. Essai de sociologie religieuse*, Strasbourg, 1977, p. 43-58; unfortunately, the author provides little in terms of factual information, and tends to see the effects of the plague everywhere without the warrant of documentary evidence.
[29] G. VIO, *Le Scuole Piccole nella Venezia dei Dogi: Note d'archivio per la storia delle confraternite veneziane*, Costabissara (Vicenza), 2004, no. 108, 238 (*frezzaroli* – arrow makers), 296 (*verieri* – glassworkers), 737, 799 (protection from the plague), p. 157, 286, 345-348, 758-759, 816-819; in one further case (no. 726, p. 751), it is not clear if the confraternity really came into existence after the official approval by the Council of Ten in 1449.

older wills have a smaller chance to survive than newer ones – not to mention the further chronological bias that results from the diffusion of the very practice of drawing up (notarized) testaments. But belatedness in the case of St Sebastian does not seem to follow from the loss of earlier sources. Based on the data collected by Jacques Chiffoleau from testaments of residents in the Comtat region (without Avignon) between *c.* 1320 and *c.* 1480, the number of newly mentioned confraternities bearing the name of St Sebastian lagged well behind the overall number of such institutions appearing in the sources for the first time until the middle of the fifteenth century, even if we grant that all anonymous confraternities were in fact dedicated to St Sebastian; after 1450, however, it started to outgrow the general trend significantly (see Figure 1).[30]

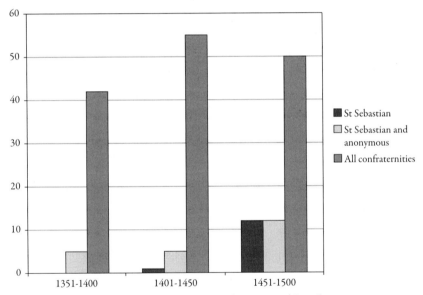

Figure 1: The growth of St Sebastian confraternities (their first appearance in the sources) in the Comtat region without Avignon (source: see footnote 30)

---

[30] J. CHIFFOLEAU, *La comptabilité de l'au-delà. Les hommes, la mort et la religion dans la région d'Avignon à la fin du Moyen Âge (vers 1320 – vers 1480)*, Rome, 1980, Annex 3, p. 448-453. Chiffoleau himself analyzes these data in slightly different timeframes; see *ibid.*, p. 270 and 382. Other sources also suggest a late growth of Sebastian-patrocinia in the region; see *ibid.*, p. 383-386.

St Roche: the quintessential plague saint

The reason for Sebastian's unsystematic or indefinite association with the plague lies, first of all, in the generally late diffusion of venerating saints for particular types of assistance they were supposedly prone to offer.[31] Moreover, the function itself of protecting from the plague was connected to more than one saint, in fact to quite a number of them, already before the appearance of St Roche on the scene. Among these other saints the Virgin Mary, especially in the form of the *Schutzmantelmadonna* or *Madonna della Misericordia* was probably the most important, but many other holy men and women, including – particularly in Italy – local saints, assumed this role occasionally.[32]

In contrast to these 'occasional helpers' much less attached to the disease than Sebastian, St Roche seems to have been venerated as a plague saint and mainly as a plague saint right from the beginning. That it only *seems* is because the unfolding of his veneration in its earliest phase is still quite unclear. Although the feast of a St Roche in the month of August is already mentioned in the civic statutes of Voghera in 1389, it is far from clear that it refers to the same St Roche or, if so, whether he was already associated with the plague at that time.[33] The earliest evidence of his having been venerated as a plague saint comes from murals painted in the 1450s and 1460s in the medieval diocese of Novara in Lombardy. In these early images – which preceded the appearance of the first known *vitae* by some twenty years – Roche is not yet represented with his usual companions, a dog or an angel, but he already

---

[31] See O. Gecser, "Holy Helpers and the Transformation of Saintly Patronage", *art. cit.*

[32] For a classification of saints whose protection from the plague was sought in the late Middle Ages, see H. Dormeier, "Laienfrömmigkeit in den Pestzeiten des 15./16. Jahrhunderts", in *Maladies et société (XIIe-XVIIIe siècles)*, ed. N. Bulst, R. Delort, Paris, 1989, p. 269-306, on p. 294-298; N. Bulst, "Heiligenverehrung in Pestzeiten: Soziale und religiöse Reaktionen auf die spätmittelalterlichen Pestepidemien", in *Mundus in Imagine: Bildersprache und Lebenswelten im Mittelalter. Festgabe für Klaus Schreiner*, ed. A. Löther *et al.*, Munich, 1996, p. 63-97; M. Sensi, "Santuari, culti, riti 'ad repellendam pestem' tra medioevo ed età moderna", in M. Sensi, *Santuari, pellegrini, eremiti, op. cit.*, vol. 1. p. 381-395, esp. p. 381-383. See also L. Marshall, "Manipulating the Sacred: Image and Plague in Renaissance Italy", *Renaissance Quarterly*, 47 (1994), p. 485-532 and *Ead.*, "Confraternity and Community: Mobilizing the Sacred in Times of Plague", in *Confraternities and the Visual Arts in the Italian Renaissance: Ritual, Spectacle, Image*, ed. B. Wisch, D. Cole Ahl, Cambridge, 2000, p. 20-45.

[33] G. Forzatti Golia, "Il culto di San Rocco a Voghera e nel territorio Pavese", in *San Rocco: Genesi e prima espansione di un culto; Incontro di studio – Padova 12-23 febbraio 2004*, ed. A. Rigon, A. Vauchez, Brussels, 2006, p. 117-159, on p. 120; H. Dormeier, "Un santo nuovo contro la peste: Cause del successo del culto di San Rocco e promotori della sua diffusione al Nord delle Alpi", *ibid.*, p. 225-243, on p. 226.

appears as a pilgrim (modelled, primarily, on the iconography of St James the Greater), with the plague wound or bubo on one of his upper thighs.[34]

In the last ten or fifteen years the received view on the date and filiation of Roche's early *vitae* has been significantly revised by Pierre Bolle. Bolle has originally argued that all known fifteenth-century biographies of the saint – including the so-called *Acta Breviora* previously regarded as the earliest – go back to Francesco Diedo's *Vita Sancti Rochi* (1479), and there is no need to suppose that the common source was a lost Italian text from around 1400.[35] More recently – trying to accommodate the implications of a newly discovered Latin *vita* copied by the Veronese burgher, Bartolomeo dal Bovo in his family book in 1487, and to find a better place in his filiation scheme for Domenico da Vicenza's *Istoria di San Rocho* (1478-1480) – he has reached a new conclusion according to which the latter two and Diedo's *Life* had a common, now lost, source, and many of the later texts, including the *Acta Breviora*, depend not on the *Vita Sancti Rochi* but on the *Istoria di San Rocho*.[36]

---

[34] D D. RIGAUX, "Le dossier iconographique de saint Roch: Nouvelles images, nouvelle chronologie", in *San Rocco, op. cit.*, p. 245-268. Antonio Vivarini's *St Anthony altarpiece* from Pesaro (1464, Pinacoteca Vaticana) and Bartolomeo Vivarini's *Sacra conversazione* (1465, Naples, Museo di Capodimonte), which M. T. SCHMITZ-EICHHOFF, *St. Rochus: Ikonographische und Medizinhistorische Studien*, Cologne, 1977, p. 58-59, thinks to exhibit the "früheste sichere Datierung" among images of St Roche, do not, in fact, represent him but Vitus in the first, and James the Greater in the second case. H. DORMEIER, "St. Rochus, die Pest und die Imhoffs in Nürnberg vor und während der Reformation: Ein spätgotischer Altar in seinem religiös-liturgischen, wirtschaftlich-rechtlichen und sozialen Umfeld", *Anzeiger des Germanischen Nationalmuseums* (1985), p. 7-72, on p. 13 and p. 60, n. 72 (with further literature).

[35] P. BOLLE, "Saint Roch de Montpellier: doublet hagiographique de Saint Raco d'Autun. Un apport décisif de l'examen approfondi des incunables imprimés anciens", in *'Scribere sanctorum gesta': Recueil d'études d'hagiographie médiévale offert à Guy Philippart*, ed. E. RENARD et al., Turnhout, 2005, p. 525-572. Diedo's *vita* (*BHL* 7273) was published, in a Latin and in an Italian version separately, in Milan, in 1479; the *Acta Breviora* (*BHL* 7275) appeared for the first time in the *Hystorie plurimorum sanctorum* in Cologne, in 1483. The Bollandists edited them – in *AASS*, Aug. III, p. 399-410 – from two handwritten copies based on early printed editions; the Bollandist editions are reprinted with some emendations and modern Italian translations in A. FANELLI, *Le due più antiche biografie del '400 su s. Rocco*, Conversano, 1996. P. BOLLE, "Saint Roch de Montpellier", *art. cit.*, p. 551-552, has shown that the Bollandist editions contain a number of errors. A collation of the Bollandist editions with the earliest incunabula by Pierre Bolle is available (together with the edition of other early texts of Roche's hagiographical *dossier*, including the Italian version of Diedo's *vita*, and the Lives mentioned in footnote 36 below) at www.sanroccodimontpellier.it under "Testi, Textes, Texts, Textos" (last accessed: 17 April, 2015). P. BOLLE, "Saint Roch de Montpellier", *art. cit.*, has suggested that the cult of St Roche goes back to that of bishop Raco/Rocco of Autun. For this suggestion, see R. GODDING, "San Rocco di Montpellier, un doppione agiografico? Culto e leggenda di San Rocco d'Autun", in *San Rocco, op. cit.*, p. 71-82 and the references in footnote 36 below.

[36] P. BOLLE, "Saint Roch, une question de méthodologie", in *San Rocco, op. cit.*, p. 9-56; P. BOLLE, "San Rocco di Montpellier: Una lunga ricerca tra archivi, leggende e nuove

The basic elements of the life of St Roche in this complex web of narratives are the following. Roche was a nobleman (from Montpellier or from England) who, after the death of his parents, distributed his wealth among the poor and set out on a pilgrimage to Italy.[37] Close to Rome, he stopped in Aquapendente and Cesena ravaged by a severe plague, and healed many of those who contracted the disease. He spent three years in the Eternal City as the guest of a cardinal and met the pope who recognized him as a man of God. After the death of the cardinal, Roche left Rome, and visited a number of places in central and northern Italy to care for the sick, especially those suffering from the plague. In Piacenza he himself became ill with pestilence, and retreated to a hut in the surrounding woods, where he was fed by a dog carrying bread in his mouth from the table of his master. The rich master of the dog, Gothard, became Roche's disciple and started to lead an eremitic life, begging food from others instead of relying on his fortune, while Roche looked after the plague patients in the urban hospital, curing many of them. After the plague ended in the city, a celestial voice announced that he, too, was healed. Now he decided to return to his homeland but on the way, passing through a city immersed in war, the local ruler – a relative of his who failed to recognize him – put him in prison supposing that he was a spy. He died in prison after five years, but before his death, according to Domenico da Vicenza and Francesco Diedo, an angel appeared to him inquiring about his last wish. Roche asked God to allow that everyone who would pray for his intercession against pestilence be protected from it; an inscribed tablet found next to his corpse revealed that his wish came true. In the text copied by Bartolomeo dal Bovo, the angel is left out, but the tablet does state that "if someone has devotion for the suffering of our Lord Jesus Christ and for me, Roche, he will remain unharmed by any plague or illness" (*si quis habebit in devotionem passionem domini nostri Yhesu Christi et me Rochum, liber sit ab omni peste infirmitateque*).[38] The earliest extant biographies, if they

---

scoperte", in *San Rocco di Montepellier: Studi e ricerche (Atti delle Giornate internazionali di San Rocco, Caorso e Cremona, 2-3 ottobre 2009)*, ed. P. Ascagni, N. Montesano, Tolve (Piacenza), 2015, p. 7-56 (also available online at www.ascagnipaolo.it/1/upload/san_rocco._convegno_di_studi.pdf, last accessed: 20 April, 2015). For the text copied by Bartolomeo dal Bovo, see F. Lomastro, "Di una *Vita* manoscritta e della prima diffusione del culto di San Rocco", in *San Rocco, op. cit.*, p. 98-116 (edition on p. 108-116). Domenico da Vicenza's *Istoria* was published in Milan, in 1478-1480; see also the webpage in footnote 35 above.

[37] On the hagiographical type of holy pilgrims that formed the basis of the legend of St Roche, see A. Vauchez, "Un modèle hagiographique et cultuel en Italie avant Saint Roch: le pèlerin mort en chemin", in *San Rocco, op. cit.*, p. 57-69; A. Vauchez, "San Rocco: L'ultimo santo laico del Medioevo", in A. Vauchez, *Esperienze religiose nel Medioevo*, Rome, 2003, p. 81-97, on p. 89-92.

[38] F. Lomastro, "Di una *Vita* manoscritta", *art. cit.*, p. 115.

mention it at all, give 1327 as the date of his death, that is, they place his life before the great epidemic of the mid-fourteenth century.

In 1469, the Council of Twelve Wise Men, the urban government of Voghera, decided to set up a committee for examining the relics of St Bovo, a Provençal pilgrim who had been venerated as the patron of the city for centuries. The decision was motivated by the news coming from Pavia, Voghera's main rival, that the body of the saint had recently been found there, in one of their own churches. Apart from finding the precious corpse intact under the main altar of the *ecclesia Sancti Bobonis*, the committee also claimed to have found, in the hospital church of Sant'Enrico, the earthly remains of another holy pilgrim, St Roche. By that time – as we have seen above – his cult had been identifiably connected to the plague, and some of his characteristic iconographic features were already present in his earliest visual representations in an area right to the north of Voghera. Thus even if the St Roche mentioned in the statutes of the city in 1389 may not have been him, or not yet related to pestilence, the St Roche of the newly discovered relics must have been regarded as the plague saint widely known ever since. The Venetians clearly had the same opinion when a few years later, in 1485, they translated the relics to Venice, to the Scuola Grande di San Rocco.[39]

Despite all attempts by hagiographers to make his cult look more official – from Roche's meeting with the pope in Rome in all early *vitae* through Diedo's bolder claim that the veneration of the saint was approved by the Council of Constance – St Roche has never been canonized.[40] Liturgical texts for his feast appear even later than his *vitae*: the earliest missal containing a mass in his honor was printed in Venice in 1483/1484.[41] His veneration was supported by laymen in the first place, motivated by their belief in his prophylactic capacities. It spread from Lombardy to the Veneto, facilitated by Lombard migrants, as in the case of Padua from 1468 onwards,[42] and, somewhat later, by the relic translation from Voghera to Venice. From the Veneto it was carried north of the Alps by students who studied in Padua, by pilgrims who travelled

---

[39] For the events in Voghera, see FORZATTI GOLIA, "Il culto di San Rocco", *op. cit.*, p. 131-136; for the cult in Venice, see H. DORMEIER, "Venedig als Zentrum des Rochuskultes", in *Nürnberg und Italien. Begegnungen, Einflüsse und Ideen*, ed. V. KAPP, F.-R. HAUSMANN, Tübingen, 1991, p. 105-127.

[40] H. DORMEIER, "*Ein geystliche ertzeney*", *op. cit.*, p. 70-72; A. VAUCHEZ, "San Rocco: L'ultimo santo laico", *op. cit.*, p. 83 and 92-93. The bishop of Padua, Pietro Barrozzi, during his pastoral visitations in 1489, criticized the dedication of ecclesiastical institutions to Roche because he was not canonized; see A. RIGON, "Origini e sviluppo del culto di San Rocco a Padova", in *San Rocco, op. cit.*, p. 177-209, on p. 188-189.

[41] H. DORMEIER, "St. Rochus, die Pest und die Imhoffs", *art. cit.*, p. 12-13.

[42] A. RIGON, "Origini e sviluppo", *art. cit.*, p. 181-184.

to and came back from the Holy Land through Venice, and by merchants who traded in oriental luxuries imported by the Venetians. The earliest German life of the saint, the *History von Sand Roccus / Das Leben des heiligen herrn sant Rochus* was published in Vienna in 1482 and in Nuremberg in 1484; it is a translation-adaptation of an Italian original ("Die history ist von welisch auf teutsch pracht, in der loblichen Stat zu Wienn in Osterreich"), probably Domenico da Vicenza's *Istoria di San Rocho*.[43] The St Roche altarpiece in the church of Sankt Lorenz in Nuremberg, the earliest pictorial legend of the saint north of the Alps (completed shortly before 1493), was commissioned by Peter Imhoff the Elder, a leading official of the Fondaco dei Tedeschi in Venice, whose half-brother was a member of the Scuola Grande di San Rocco.[44]

But why another saint against the plague if there were already many who could be called on – St Sebastian, first of all? Heinrich Dormeier has suggested that the biographical connection, Roche's having contracted the disease himself, recovered from it and healed others, as well as the divine revelation of his specialty, made him significantly more authentic in this role than Sebastian or other saints. According to Mario Sensi, previous plague saints were merely expected to protect from the plague, whereas Roche was seen able to cure it.[45]

In addition to these explanations, I would like to emphasize two further points. One is that many sources suggest – especially the massive appearance of confraternities dedicated to and images representing him – that the cult of St Sebastian underwent a revival in the second half of the fifteenth century, that is, at the very moment when St Roche appeared on the scene. To what extent this revival was related to the plague is an open question but it does not necessarily mean that the two saints were considered rivals. Partly they seem to have been held responsible for different kinds of supernatural assistance, as in the case of the protestant reformer, Johannes Agricola, who recalled that in his youth, when he was afraid, he turned to the saints and, among others, "Saint Roche had to serve against the plague, St Sebastian against [arrow] shots".[46] Partly they reinforced each other in promising an even more effective protection from the plague as in many pictorial representations where they appear side by side.[47]

---

[43] *Das Leben des heiligen sant Rochus (1482-1484)*, ed. P. BOLLE, www.sanroccodimontpellier.it under "Testi, Textes, Texts, Textos" (last accessed: 29 April, 2015), p. 11. For its source, see P. BOLLE, "San Rocco di Montpellier", *art. cit.*, p. 28-30.
[44] H. DORMEIER, "St. Rochus, die Pest und die Imhoffs", *art. cit.*, p. 35-38.
[45] H. DORMEIER, "Un santo nuovo contro la peste", *art. cit.*, p. 228-321; M. SENSI, "Santuari, culti, riti", *art. cit.*, p. 383.
[46] Quoted in G. KAWERAU, *Johann Agricola von Eisleben: Ein Beitrag zur Reformationsgeschichte*, Berlin, 1881, p. 9.
[47] Dominique Rigaux has argued that the coupling of St Roche in his early Italian representations with St Sebastian, a well-known (plague) saint, served to legitimize Roche, a new saint,

The other point I would like to emphasize concerning the rapid emergence of St Roche as a plague saint, is how obscure the earliest Lives are about the place of his death. With the exception of the *Acta Breviora* – which says explicitly that he died in *Angleria*, that is, Angera in Lombardy, but that may well be just a rationalization of *Anglia* found in its source, Domenico da Vicenza – they are amazingly unspecific, especially if we compare it to how well they document the other stations of his journey. They do not say more than an *oppidum in Gallia* (Diedo) or *partes suas* (the Life copied by del Bovo), and later fifteenth-century Lives continue to do the same.[48] The simplest explanation for leaving this important detail in the dark is that they, most probably, did not know about the invention of his relics in Voghera. But, whatever the explanation, the fact remains that Roche's fifteenth-century hagiographers did not advertise his grave as a pilgrimage site; they were silent about the possibility of visiting his relics. This attitude is in harmony with Roche's minimalist requirements in exchange for his intercession against the plague: it is enough to pray to or have devotion for him. Thus his cult – in its blueprint constructed by the hagiographers, at least – looks rather delocalized or decentralized, not connected to relics and sacred places and, hence, easy to transport anywhere with the help of (mechanically reproduced) texts and images.

St Sebastian in Hungary before and after the Black Death

The liturgical cult of St Sebastian is already attested in Hungary in the eleventh century. His *nativitas* (together with that of St Fabian, on 20 January) is included in the *Szelepcsényi* or *Nitra Evangelistary* (Nitra, Archív nitrianskej kapituly, no. 118) and the *Esztergom Benedictionale* (Zagreb, Metropolitanska knjižnica, MR 89).[49] This is, after all, not very surprising as the feast of Fabian and Sebastian belongs to the Gelasian-Gregorian calendar that formed the common basis of all local calendars. It is more difficult, on the other hand, to assess the local importance of the feast. In the calendar of a late-twelfth-century sacramentary, the so-called Pray Codex (Budapest, OSZK, MNy1), for example, it appears in red letters, just as in a breviary

---

in his capacity as intercessor in general, and intercessor against the plague in particular. See D. RIGAUX, "Le dossier iconographique", *art. cit.*, p. 260. At the same time, however, given the ambiguities or the multivalence of Sebastian's figure, his association with the plague could also be strengthened by the presence of St Roche.

[48] See the synoptic table in P. BOLLE, "Saint Roch de Montpellier", *art. cit.*, p. 551 or *Id.*, "San Rocco di Montpellier", *art. cit.*, p. 23.

[49] P. RADÓ, *Libri liturgici manuscripti bibliothecarum Hungariae et limitropharum regionum*, Budapest, 1973, p. 234; M. I. FÖLDVÁRY, *Az Esztergomi benedikcionále. Irodalom és liturgia az államalapítás-kori Magyarországon*, Budapest, 2014, p. 32.

made around 1370 in Esztergom (Budapest, OSZK, Cod. Lat. 408).[50] It looks similarly important in two of the earliest printed missals, that of Esztergom from 1484 and that of Pécs from 1486/1488.[51]

The importance suggested by these latter sources, however, is not corroborated by synodal documents even in the case of Esztergom. The feast is missing from the first surviving list of major holidays (*festivitates feriande*) sanctioned by the synod of Szabolcs (under the auspices of King Ladislas I) in 1092.[52] It is also missing from the oldest synodal list of major holidays of the diocese of Esztergom composed around 1390, as well as from the respective constitutions of the local synods of 1450, 1460, 1489 and 1493 held in the same diocese. Similarly, the synod of the bishopric of Nitra (Nyitra) in 1494 did not require anyone *servilibus operibus abstinere* on 20 January, and this day was not named among the *festivitates colende* in the bishopric of Veszprém in 1515 nor in the bishopric of Oradea in 1524.[53] The list of major holidays appended to the *statuta* of the diocesan synod of Esztergom in 1510, under Archbishop and Cardinal Tamás Bakócz, did include *Fabiani et Sebastiani*; this list, however, refers not to the local practice, as in the case of other diocesan synods from late medieval Hungary, but to the liturgy of the papal court.[54]

---

[50] K. Kniewald, "A Pray-kódex Sanctoraleja", *Magyar Könyvszemle*, 63 (1939), p. 1-53; J. Dankó, *Vetus hymnarium ecclesiasticum Hungariae*, Budapest, 1893, p. 438; P. Radó, *Libri liturgici*, no. 2 and 88, p. 40-76 and 328-331.

[51] Esztergom: *Missale Strigoniense 1484, id est Missale secundum chorum almae ecclesiae Strigoniensis, impressum Nurenbergae apud Anthonium Koburger, anno Domini MCCCCLXXXIIII)*, ed. B. Déri, Budapest, 2009, p. 7. Pécs: *Missale Quinqueecclesiense*, Basel, 1486/1488; G. Borsa, "Problematische Angaben in der Bibliographie von Weale-Bohatta zu den für Ungarn gedruckten Meßbüchern", *Gutenberg-Jahrbuch*, 66 (1991), p. 127-134.

[52] L. Závodszky, *A Szent István, Szent László és Kálmán korabeli törvények és zsinati határozatok forrásai*, Budapest, 1904, p. 79.

[53] Esztergom, *c.* 1390: L. Solymosi, "Az esztergomi egyházmegye legrégebbi ünneplajstroma (Szent Adalbert, Szórád-András és Benedek tisztelete az erdélyi szászoknál)", in *R. Várkonyi Ágnes emlékkönyv születésének 70. évfordulója ünnepére*, ed. P. Tusor, Z. Rihmer, G. Thoroczkay, Budapest, 1998, p. 88-95, on p. 93; Esztergom 1450, 1460, 1489: I. Batthyány, *Leges ecclesiasticae Regni Hungariae et provinciarum ei adiacentium*, 3 vols., Alba Iulia, 1785-1827, vol. 3, p. 490-491, 518, 565-566; Esztergom 1493, Veszprém 1515, Nitra/Nyitra 1494: K. Péterffy, *Sacra concilia Ecclesiae Romano-Catholicae in regno Hungariae celebrata ab anno Christi MXVI. usque ad annum MDCCXXXIV.*, 2 vols., Vienna-Bratislava, 1742, vol. 1, p. 219, 243, 281; Oradea/Nagyvárad 1524: S. Jaczkó, *Az 1524. évi váradi zsinat és határozatai*, PhD diss., Debrecen, 2011, p. 211 (reproduction of the original document – Hungarian National Archives, DL 29416 – in the appendix).

[54] I. Batthyány, *Leges ecclesiasticae, op. cit.*, vol. 3, p. 659-660. Here, instead of the customary heading *festivitates colende/feriande* (and a few introductory sentences frequently added to it), this last section of the constitutions is entitled *festum pallacii* (!), and the list ends with the sentence *Item festa principalia illius loci, ubi Papa cum sua curia residet*. Nevertheless, the fact that the names of the months are also given in contemporary Hungarian (*Bodogazzonho, Beythelwhó, Beythmáshó*, etc.) suggests that this calendar was intended for local use.

The picture changes again if we look at the use of the feast in dating legal documents. Apparently, the earliest charter dated with reference to Sebastian's feast-day in medieval Hungary was written at Zalakomár, in the western part of the country, in 1263.[55] Two further thirteenth-century cases, from 1295 and 1297, come from two very different parts of the kingdom, the Premonstratensian priory of Ság (modern-day Šahy, Slovakia) and the Transylvanian Chapter of Alba Iulia (Romania),[56] suggesting that by then this form of dating was not an isolated local phenomenon. From the fourteenth century, using *Fabiani et Sebastiani* for this purpose became fairly common. Searching through the digitized version of charters (or *regesta* of charters) from medieval Hungary edited between the 1830s and today, I found approximately 35 from the first half of the fourteenth century, roughly the same amount from the period between 1350 and 1400, and some 90 cases from the first half of the fifteenth century.[57] The numbers are certainly not exact, but even if they were, they would not be particularly relevant because in themselves they merely reflect the number of (a part of the) charters issued around 20 January; and, thus, their increase in itself means not more than the increase of notarial activity in this period of the year, which – with the overall

---

It may have been related in some or other way to Bakócz's aspirations to the papal throne in 1513, when, eventually, Pope Leo X was elected, Bakócz receiving merely eight votes in the conclave. P. ENGEL, *The Realm of St Stephen: A History of Medieval Hungary*, London, 2005, p. 362.

[55] *Sopron vármegye története: Oklevéltár*, ed. I. NAGY, Sopron, 1889-1891, vol. 1, no. 17, p. 26-27. The practice of providing the name of an ecclesiastical feast, or the temporal distance from such a feast (so and so many days before or after it) as an indication of a charter's date of issue (or the date of an event mentioned in it), appeared in Hungary around 1200 and became more common from the second half of the thirteenth century. See Zs. SIMON, "Adatok szent Szaniszló, Kriszpin, Otília, Praxedis és Rókus középkori magyarországi kultuszához az egyházi ünnepek szerinti keltezések alapján", in *Arcana tabularii: Tanulmányok Solymosi László tiszteletére*, ed. A. BÁRÁNY, G. DRESKA, K. SZOVÁK, Budapest-Debrecen 2014, vol. 1, p. 157-174, esp. p. 159-161; I. SZENTPÉTERY, *Chronologia: A közép- és újkori időszámítás vázlata*, ed. and suppl. G. ÉRSZEGI, T. RAJ, L. SZÖGI, Budapest, 1985, p. 43. For the diffusion of this dating practice elsewhere, with further literature, see P. RÜCK, "Zur Verbreitung der Festdatierung im 13. Jahrhundert in Urkunden aus dem Gebiet der Schweiz", *Archiv für Diplomatik, Schriftgeschichte, Siegel- und Wappenkunde*, 38 (1992), p. 145-192.

[56] G. FEJÉR, *Codex diplomaticus Hungariae ecclesiasticus ac civilis*, Buda, 1829-1844, t. 6, vol. 1, p. 371 (or again in t. 11, p. 420); Zs. JAKÓ, *Erdélyi okmánytár*, 3 vols., Budapest, 1997-2008, vol. 1, p. 316.

[57] *Digital Library of Medieval Hungary*, http://mol.arcanum.hu/medieval (with search functions available in English and Hungarian; last accessed: 29 March, 2015). The reliability of data gained from this source is affected by the multiple editions of the same charter (or its *regesta* or medieval copies), the occurrence of medieval (or later) forgeries, and the fact that the biggest projects of editing charters from medieval Hungary did not get much further than the middle of the fifteenth century. The numbers are merely approximate due to the occurrence of ambiguous cases.

growth of notarial activity in the fourteenth and fifteenth centuries – had to increase anyhow. It makes more sense to compare it to alternative forms of dating based on different feasts.

A suitable set of comparative material is provided by charters dated with reference to Epiphany as it was, of course, a major holiday right from the Christianization of Hungary onwards.[58] Using the database of charters and photographic reproductions of charters kept in the Hungarian National Archives, I counted all documents drawn up between 17 and 29 January that referred to either of the two feasts.[59] The interval is placed evenly between the octave of Epiphany (13 January) and Candlemas (2 February), the next major holiday, to mark off a period when it may have been the most convenient to use *Fabiani et Sebastiani* (including its octave). The results show a clear relative growth of dating with the latter feast in the fourteenth and fifteenth centuries (see Figure 2); the absolute growth, again, does not mean much, given the general rise of charter production in the period.

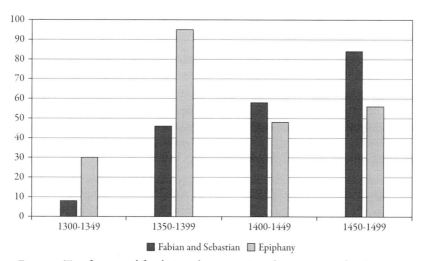

Figure 2: Two feasts used for dating charters written between 17 and 29 January in any year from 1300 until 1499 in the Kingdom of Hungary

---

[58] See footnotes 52-53 and 55 above.
[59] *Database of Archival Documents of Medieval Hungary*, http://mol.arcanum.hu/dldf (with search functions in German, English and Hungarian; last accessed: 29 March, 2015). This database has only sporadic cases for dating with the two feasts before 1300 (I found one for Fabian and Sebastian, and two for Epiphany) but it has the advantage over the *Digital Library of Medieval Hungary* that it allows searches for specific time periods.

In a cautious interpretation of these results, those involved in drawing up charters in late medieval Hungary increasingly tended to think that using *Fabiani et Sebastiani* would be easily intelligible to anyone qualified to read these documents. Note that the process is self-reinforcing: other things being equal, the more someone entitled to produce official documents saw the feast used for such a purpose, the more he must have been inclined to follow suit. In principle, given its self-reinforcing character, the increasing occurrence of *Fabiani et Sebastiani* in charters may have taken place independently of changes in other facets of the cult, such as liturgical celebrations, naming patterns, or church dedications. But even in this case it certainly needed an initial motivation to reach a critical mass. Was this initial motivation the plague or related to the plague?

It is difficult to give a conclusive answer. As we have seen, dating with *Fabiani et Sebastiani* started earlier than the Black Death, and we do not know when it reached the critical mass because our data is only good for assessing relative and not absolute growth. Remember that published charters yielded a higher number of occurrences for the period between 1300 and 1349 than the database of the National Archive used for making the bar chart. Since elsewhere the feast was more important, especially in Italy, the initial motivation could come from other sources as well. The earliest extant text written in medieval Hungary about St Sebastian, a sermon *de sancto Sebastiano*, appears in a Dominican sermon collection composed around 1300 in Buda.[60] In this short text he is celebrated as a martyr and his role of intercessor against the plague is – not surprisingly – not even mentioned; but it is not by chance that he appears for the first time in a Dominican *sermonarium* as the Blackfriars dedicated more sermons to him before the Black Death than any other religious order in medieval Europe.[61] In addition, Sebastian was among the more important saints with eight miniatures dedicated to his *vita* in the so-called Hungarian Angevin Legendary, a lavishly decorated hagiographical picture book based on the *Legenda Aurea*, which was made in the first half of the fourteenth century – either in Hungary or in Italy – for a member of the Hungarian royal dynasty, a branch of the Angevins of Naples.[62]

---

[60] *Sermones compilati in studio generali Quinqueecclesiensi in regno Ungarie*, ed. E. Petrovich, P. L. Timkovics, Budapest, 1993, no. 32, p. 80-81. The collection is falsely called in its *codex unicus* as "Pécs University Sermons". E. Madas, "A Dominican Sermon Collection", *Budapest Review of Books*, 6 (1996), p. 415-419.
[61] O. Gecser, "Sermons on St Sebastian", *art. cit.*, p. 265 and 267.
[62] For the debates about the exact dating, place of production and commissioner of the manuscript, see B. Zs. Szakács, *The Visual World of the Hungarian Angevin Legendary*, Budapest-New York, 2016, p. 7-11. For the legend of St Sebastian, see *ibid.*, p. 92.

The initial motivation may have been related to naming patterns as well. Although the available studies of personal names used in various sources of medieval Hungarian history have a largely linguistic focus – so they tend to be statistically non-representative of the surviving texts (not to mention the problem of the surviving sources themselves not being statistically representative of the real patterns) – the diffusion of "Sebastian" in various social environments is not entirely unclear.

After some earlier occurrences referring to clerics exclusively, we have already a servant (*servus*) and a bell-ringer (*pulsator*) called Sebastian in two villages belonging to the priory of Dömös in 1138, two serfs (*iobagiones*) who were the sons of a certain Sebastian on the lands of the priory of Tihany in 1211, or a count (*comes*) Sebastian from the diocese of Oradea in 1213 – just to name a few of the known examples.[63] Thus by the beginning of the thirteenth century, the name was used in all social milieus all over the kingdom, even if we cannot assess how frequently or compare its popularity with that of other names.

For the period between 1301 and 1341 – that is, right before the Black Death – all occurrences of personal names in the Kingdom of Hungary have been collected from the overwhelming majority of published and authentic charters by Mariann Slíz. This collection permits some statistical comparisons: 40 different persons were called Sebastian (again from all social environments) in the sources under scrutiny, which was a rather low figure if compared not only to those 1378 called John, but also to those 142 called Blaise (another saint widely associated with disease) or even those 45 called Fabian; on the other hand, it fared better than Francis (a relatively new name) borne by 22 persons.[64]

Unfortunately, the information available for the period after the Black Death is far more sporadic. The names of serfs in more than hundred settlements on a large estate in South-West Hungary, listed in three closely interrelated charters from 1389, show proportions similar to those found in pre-Black Death documents: Sebastian was the name of 8 persons, John of 220, Blaise of 55, Fabian of 21, and Francis of 15.[65] Based on an analysis of naming patterns in published and unpublished sources from northeast Hungary (the Upper Tisza Region) between 1401 and 1526, Sebastian

---

[63] K. Fehértói, *Árpád-kori személynévtár (1000-1301) – Onomasticon Hungaricum: Nomina propria personarum aetatis Arpadianae (1000-1301)*, Budapest, 2004, p. 701-702.
[64] M. Slíz, *Anjou-kori személynévtár 1301-1342*, Budapest, 2011, p. 61-65 (Blaise: *Blasius* with variants *Balaseus* and *Balas*), 131-132 (Fabian: *Fabianus* and *Fabyanus*), 135-136 (Francis: *Franciscus* with a range of variants), 189-231 (John: *Johannes* – without popular variants like *Ivan* or *Iwan*), and 440-441 (Sebastian: *Sebastianus* with variants *Sebascianus, Sebe*, and *Sebeuk*).
[65] K. Fehértói, "Egy XIV. századi nagybirtok jobbágyainak személynévanyaga", *Magyar Nyelv*, 64 (1968), p. 317-331.

continued to lag behind even Fabian until the last quarter of the fifteenth century (see Figure 3).⁶⁶

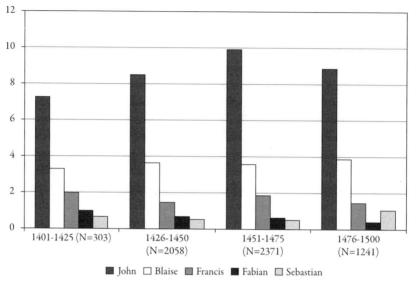

Figure 3: Relative frequency of personal names in the Upper Tisza region (1401-1526); percentages of the total number of cases in a given time interval; source: see footnote 66

In spite of their deficiencies, all these data suggest that the Black Death did not change significantly the popularity of the name "Sebastian". Interestingly enough, Fabian (the generally less known saint of 20 January) seems to have been slightly more popular than Sebastian in this respect until about 1475 – possibly because some people, for the sake of brevity, may have referred to 20 January as St Fabian's day, contributing to a greater familiarity of this name. If anything, only the increase of Sebastian's popularity as a name-giver to the disadvantage of Fabian in the same capacity after 1475 can be attributed to the effects of the plague – not the Black Death but subsequent, late medieval outbreaks.⁶⁷ Thus it would be difficult to conclude that the critical mass in dating charters with *Fabiani et Sebastiani* was reached in concomitance with an increase in naming persons after St Sebastian, but the general diffusion of

---

⁶⁶ J. N. FODOR, *Személynevek rendszere a kései ómagyar korban. A Felső-Tisza-vidék személyneveinek nyelvi elemzése (1401-1526)*, Budapest, 2010, p. 125-130.
⁶⁷ Nevertheless, one of the major deficiencies of the post-Black Death data discussed here is the lack of information about major cities – typically not located in the areas studied so far – where (according to my impression) several persons were called Sebastian in the fifteenth century.

the name in the kingdom as well as its stable if not very high frequency could contribute to make his feast seem more suitable for this purpose.

A further manifestation of the cult that could have initiated a shift in using 20 January as a point of reference in charters – or, in general, could have intertwined with its other manifestations and strengthen them – are the altars, churches, religious houses or confraternities bearing the name of the saint. The earliest known ecclesiastical institution dedicated to St Sebastian in the country, an *ecclesia beatorum Fabiani et Sebastiani martirum* at Fábiánsebestyén (letter K in Figure 4), was first mentioned in 1389. Until the beginning of the sixteenth century, it was followed by a moderate number of other similar *patrocinia* (see Figure 4).[68]

---

[68] *A*: Košice (Kassa/Kaschau) Franciscan church, altar of St Sebastian (hereinafter: S.); L. Kemény, *A reformáczió Kassán: Oklevéltárral*, Košice, 1891, p. 6; I could not verify the existence of a St S. confraternity in the same town indicated by L. Pásztor, *A magyarság vallásos élete a Jagellók korában*, Budapest, 1940 (repr. 2000), p. 33. *B*: Prešov (Eperjes/Preschau), Carmelite church, altar of Sts F. and S. (hereinafter: F. and S.); B. Iványi, *Eperjes szabad királyi város levéltára, 1245-1526*, 2 vols., Szeged, 1932, no. 587, vol. 2, p. 242. *C*: Trnava (Nagyszombat/Tyrnau), church of Sts F. and S.; A. Mező, *Patrocíniumok a középkori Magyarországon*, Budapest, 2003, p. 84. *D*: Bratislava (Pozsony/Pressburg); 1481: St Martin collegiate church, altar of Sts F. and S.; 1494: Franciscan church, chapel of St S. (belonging to the confraternity of St S.); E. Hoffmann, "Pozsony a középkorban: Elfelejtett művészek, elpusztult emlékek", *Magyarságtudomány*, 3 (1937), p. 65-121, on p. 79; T. Ortvay, *Pozsony város története*, 4 tomes, 7 vols., Pozsony, 1892-1912, t. 2, vol. 1, p. 267 to be read with the corrections of J. Majorossy, "Late Medieval Confraternities in Pressburg", in *Pfarreien in Mitteleuropa im Mittelalter: Deutschland, Polen, Tschechien und Ungarn im Vergleich*, ed. N. Kruppa, L. Zygner, Göttingen, 2008, p. 339-361, on p. 350. *E*: Sopron, chapel of Sts F. and S. (belonging to the confraternity of Sts F. and S.); J. Házi, *Sopron szabad királyi város története*, 2 tomes, 13 vols., Sopron, 1921-1943, t. 1, vol. 6, no. 41, p. 44-45. *F*: Győr, cathedral, altar of F. and S.; V. Bedy, *A győri székesegyház története*, Győr, 1936, p. 88. *G*: Esztergom, cathedral, an *altar sancti Sebastiani martyris* mentioned in 1379, an altar of Sts F. and S. is mentioned in 1502; F. Kollányi, ed., "Visitatio capituli E. M. Strigoniensis anno 1397", *Történelmi Tár*, 24 (1901), p. 71-106 and 239-272, on p. 256; A. Végh, *Buda város középkori helyrajza*, 2 vols., Budapest, 2006-2008, vol. 2, p. 137, no. 485. *H*: Buda (Budapest), Church of Mary Magdalen, altar of F. and S.; A. Szebeni, A. Végh, "A budavári volt helyőrségi templom", *Budapest Régiségei*, 35 (2002), p. 427-457, on p. 430. *I*: Pécs, Church of St Bartholomew, altar of Sts F. and S.; I. Nagy et al., *A zichi és vásonkeői gróf Zichy-család idősb ágának okmánytára*, 12 vols., Budapest, 1871-1931, vol. 11, p. 344-345, no. 190. *J*: Szentsebestyén (near Karcag), church of St S.; Mező, *Patrocíniumok, op. cit.*, p. 84. *K*: Fábiánsebestyén, church of Sts F. and S.; Mező, *Patrocíniumok*, p. 84; I. Gyárfás, *Jász-kúnok története*, 4 vols., Kecskemét, 1870-1885, vol. 3, p. 511. *L*: Sombor (near Hida/Hidalmás, Romania), donation for the church of the Virgin Mary, *ad honorem sanctorum Fabiani et Sebastiani martyrum unam columpnam lapideam cum ymaginibus eorundem sanctorum depingere faciant*, most probably a reliquary for the already existing altar; Zs. Jakó, *A kolozsmonostori konvent jegyzőkönyvei*, 2 vols., Budapest, 1990, no. 2342, vol. 1, p. 799-800; the donation may not be unrelated to the fact that the donator and his wife were setting out for Rome as pilgrims; for a column-shaped reliquary of St S. from Tongres, see R. Bartlett, *Why Can the Dead Do Such Great Things?, op. cit.*, p. 303. *M*: Şoimeni, chapel of Sts F. and S.; A. Mező, *Patrocíniumok, op. cit.*,

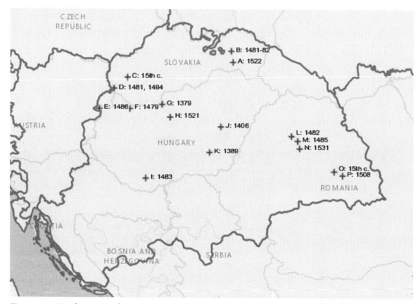

Figure 4: Ecclesiastical institutions dedicated to St Sebastian in Medieval Hungary with the date of their first appearance in the sources
(for the place names and sources, see footnote 68)

Although, except for Sopron, Şoimeni (Sólyomkő) and Keisd (Saschiz/Százkézd; Figure 4, letters E, M, and P), we do not know when these institutions were placed under the patronage of St Sebastian, it seems reasonable to suppose that not a long time had to elapse before they first appeared in the sources. It would certainly be very difficult to argue for a pre-Black Death origin of any of these institutions, but it would not be an easy job either to date them generally to the immediate aftermath of the great plague. Evidently, there were epidemics in Hungary between the Black Death and the 1470-1480s. The best available list contains 5 for the second half of the fourteenth and 21 for the fifteenth century, among which those of 1360, 1381, 1410,

---

p. 84 (writes, erroneously, 1458 as its first mention); Zs. JAKÓ, *A kolozsmonostori, op. cit.*, no. 2516, vol. 2, p. 17. *N*: Cluj-Napoca (Kolozsvár/Klausenburg), Dominican church, chapel of Sts. F. and S.; E. JAKAB, *Oklevéltár Kolozsvár története első kötetéhez*, Buda, 1870, p. 374. *O*: Sighişoara (Segesvár, Schäßburg), Dominican nunnery of St S.; A. MEZŐ, *Patrocíniumok, op. cit.*, p. 84. *P*: Keisd, altar of the Holy Cross and St S. (belonging to the confraternity of shoemaker apprentices); F. MÜLLER, *Deutsche Sprachdenkmäler aus Siebenbürgen: Aus schriftlichen Quellen des zwölften bis sechzehnten Jahrhunderts*, Sibiu, 1864, p. 161. I made a digital version of Figure 4 available at http://worldmap.harvard.edu/maps/patr_seb. The layer of the medieval boundaries around 1500 was adapted by Jerome Chia-Rung (Center for Geographic Analysis, Harvard University) from a map available at www.euratlas.com.

1456, 1480 and 1495 are said to have been exceptionally severe.[69] So there were plenty of occasions for founding such institutions or for mentioning them in relation to a donation, a last will or something similar. It is difficult not to suspect that they were not mentioned earlier because they were not there.

Dating most of these dedications to the second half of the fifteenth century is corroborated by a similarly late appearance of explicit textual connections between Sebastian and the plague. The short series of sources to this effect is opened by the Observant Franciscan, Pelbart of Timişoara (Temesvár, d. 1504), at the end of the fifteenth century, who notes in his sermon for the feast of the saint that it is "common knowledge that the intercession of St Sebastian is more effective against the plague than anything else," and relates the Pavian story from the *Legenda aurea* to substantiate this statement.[70] This latter story is the only *post mortem* miracle in the narrative part of an Old Hungarian sermon for the feast of Sts Fabian and Sebastian in the so-called Debrecen Codex (Debrecen, TREKK, R. 524) written in 1519,[71] while the Old Hungarian sermon by the so-called Anonymous Carthusian (Budapest, OSZK, Mny 9, shortly before 1526), leaves out the Pavian episode, in spite of its source having been Pelbart and the *Legenda aurea*, but it is with reference to Sebastian's "saintly merits" and "saintly intercession" that it pleads God to "keep us from all evil, pestilence and deadly enemies of other kinds".[72]

Of course, these late references to Sebastian and the plague can be attributed to a loss of earlier manuscripts as well. But taken together with the generally late indications of Sebastian-*patrocinia*, as well as the apparently tardy growth of his relative popularity as a name giver, this may fit in the Europe-wide revival of his cult in the second half of the fifteenth century – mentioned at the end of section one – that seems to be implied by the sudden proliferation of religious associations dedicated to him and images representing him. It makes sense to suppose that in an area where his public cult was previously rather limited, its growth was inspired by a parallel growth in neighboring areas, especially Italy and the German Lands.

The visual representations of the saint in Hungary are latecomers too;[73] and just as the charters mentioning the *patrocinia* say nothing about the

---

[69] I. Szabó, "Hanyatló jobbágyság a középkor végén", *Századok*, 72 (1938), p. 10-59, on p. 36-37.
[70] *Pomerium sermonum de sanctis*, Augsburg, 1502, sermon 47 (unnumbered pages).
[71] *Debreceni kódex, 1519: A nyelvemlék hasonmása és betűhű átirata*, ed. Cs. Abaffy, A. Reményi, intr. by E. Madas, A. Reményi, Budapest, 1997, p. 315-317.
[72] *Érdy codex*, ed. Gy. Volf, Budapest, 1876, p. 298.
[73] D. Radocsay, *A középkori Magyarország táblaképei*, Budapest, 1955, index, *s. v.* "Szt. Sebestyén", lists altogether twelve surviving panel paintings, all of which stem from the second half of the fifteenth or the beginning of the sixteenth century; the same chronology

motivations of the founders, the panel paintings and sculptures representing him do not exhibit any unambiguous reference to the disease – like many of their foreign counterparts. One of the twenty-four panels of the St Andrew (or All Saints) altar in the St Gilles parish church in Bardejov, for example, apparently the oldest extant representation of St Sebastian from medieval Hungary made around 1460, shows the suffering of a Christ-like figure; the inclusion in the same panel of the beheading of St Fabian points in a similar direction.

No altarpiece of St Sebastian has survived from medieval Hungary, although we know that one was in the making for his altar in the Carmelite church of Prešov in 1481-1482, right after one of the exceptionally severe plagues in 1480.[74] Thus the extant panels and sculptures belonged to altars of other saints and the date of their creation – if it can be established with sufficient precision at all – can hardly be explained with reference to specific outbreaks. But we can still ask the question whether the inclusion of his images in various polyptychs, like that of Bardejov, was motivated by expecting him to offer assistance in pestilential times, even if this may not have been the only motivation and, more significantly, the final product could elicit a range of associations different from the disease.

We have seen that the feast of Sts. Fabian and Sebastian was not particularly important in medieval Hungary. The number of *patrocinia* was rather limited and typically did not coincide with the provenance of the extant visual representations. Hence, it was far from evident to choose Sebastian as a pictorial or sculptural subject. In addition, archer societies which usually chose him as their patron saint did not exist in Hungarian cities, while there was a tendency to represent him together with several other saints who could be invoked against various ailments or difficulties. This was already the case with the St Andrew (or All Saints) altar at Bardejov, which also comprises among others an image of Sts Anthony the Abbot, Catherine of Alexandria,

---

holds for the eleven surviving and identified wooden statues of the saint according to *Id., A középkori Magyarország faszobrai*, Budapest, 1967, s. v. "Szt. Sebestyén"; the provenance of the twelve panels and the eleven statues is known to overlap in two cases, those of Bardejov and Levoča. Although the iconographic attributes of St Sebastian make him relatively easy to identify even in fragmentary representations, no mural depicting him seems to have survived in any condition save one in Sâncraiu de Mureș (Marosszentkirály/Weichseldorf, Romania) found, identified, and dated to the twelfth or thirteenth century in 1894. See D. RADOCSAY, *A középkori Magyarország falképei, op. cit.*, Budapest, 1954, p. 174.

[74] See footnote 68, item A, and footnote 69 above; B. F. ROMHÁNYI, "Késő középkori számadáskönyvek, a koldulórendi kolostorok gazdálkodásának tükrei", in *Arcana tabularii, op. cit.*, vol. 1, p. 837-853, on p. 841.

Barbara, Christopher, Cosmas and Damian, Dorothy, George, Lawrence, Margaret of Antioch and Wolfgang.[75] Given the circumstances described above, it is reasonable to suppose that here, as in similar retables, Sebastian was included as the plague specialist.

The arrival of St Roche in Hungary

In Hungary as elsewhere, the association of St Sebastian with the plague is more pronounced, when he is coupled with St Roche, the plague saint *par excellence*. The earliest example of this coupling in medieval Hungary is the Virgin Mary altarpiece from Arnutovce (Arnótfalva), where the two saints are on different panels, but both of them are on the inner sides of the wings of a triptych facing each other. Earlier research dated the altarpiece to the marriage of its supposed commissioners, Stephen Szapolyai, count of Spiš (the region where Arnutovce is located) and his wife Hedwig of Cieszyn (Teschen) in 1483. The name of the wife fits the presence of St Hedwig on one of the panels, while the fact that the husband is called Stephen and his brother Emerich would explain why only St Stephen and St Emerich from the triumvirate of the *sancti reges* of Hungary are depicted on the altar wings, leaving out St Ladislas, the most popular of the three. Nevertheless, as János Végh has recently argued, 1483 is too early in stylistic terms, and it is better to date the work to the 1490s, but before 1497, the completion date of the Madonna of Janovce (Jánosfalva) attributed to the same painter, Master Martin.[76] In addition to the stylistic problems, by dating the altarpiece to 1483 we would make the appearance of St Roche one of the earliest outside Italy, contemporary to his first visual representations in Germany in the early 1480s, all of which are printed and not painted.[77]

A similar problem of premature representation of St Roche in Hungary is posed by the Virgin Mary altarpiece in the fortified church of Biertan (Birthälm/Berethalom, Romania). The movable wings of the middle tier of the retable have four series of saints on their workday sides, three of them all-female, one all-male. On the all-male panel, from left to right, Roche is followed by St Michael, St Sebastian and St Joseph. This panel is consensually regarded as contemporary to the Presentation of Jesus panel on the

---

[75] D. RADOCSAY, *A középkori Magyarország táblaképei*, *op. cit.*, p. 264-265, 285-286 and 342-343.
[76] J. VÉGH, "Szent Rókus ábrázolása egy szepességi táblaképen", *Ars Hungarica*, 39 (2013), p. 236-241.
[77] H. DORMEIER, "St. Rochus, die Pest und die Imhoffs", *art. cit.*, p. 15.

feast-day side, which bears the date of 1483.[78] The altarpiece was refurbished in 1515 when new panels were added in the upper and the lower tiers, and the frames of the earlier panels were also replaced: on the new frames the name of each saint is inscribed above his or her head. What is striking in the figure of Roche (identified by an inscription on the frame) is that the plague wound on his right upper thigh is largely hidden behind the hanging folds of his cloak. The solution to this problem is that this Roche must have originally been James the Greater, modelled on an engraving by Martin Schongauer datable to *c.* 1470-1482.[79]

That this is not just a renaming but a repainting of the figure is made clear by the painter's attempt to place the wound or bubo on the right upper thigh in spite of the difficulties posed by the cloak and by painting Roman pilgrim's badges on Roche's hat (Veronicas cloth in the middle flanked by what seems to be two crossed keys of St Peter) instead of the scallop shell of Compostela that must have been there originally; the absence of both the dog and the angel was absolutely not unusual – rather the norm than the exception – not only in his early Italian but also in his early German iconography up till *c.* 1500.[80] Compared to the Biertan panel, the painter or the commissioner of the Arnutovce polyptych, where the saint wears a scallop shell on his hat, seems to have had a vaguer idea of what kind of pilgrim St Roche was.

Apart from the Arnutovce and Biertan panels, Roche is known to have been visible in Hungary until the beginning of the sixteenth century on the retable of Bruiu (Braller/Brulya, Romania),[81] on the *Pietà altarpiece* in Bardejov,[82] and in the form of two wooden statues in Levoča[83] and Šiba

---

[78] E. SARKADI NAGY, *Local Workshops – Foreign Connections: Late Medieval Altarpieces from Transylvania*, Ostfildern, 2012, p. 33-59 (esp. p. 33-35 for the dating in previous scholarship) and no. 7, p. 128-133.

[79] F. W. H. HOLLSTEIN, *German Engravings, Etchings and Woodcuts c. 1400-1700*, Amsterdam, 1954, no. 44; M. LEHRS, *Geschichte und kritischer Katalog des deutschen, niederländischen und französischen Kupferstichs im XV Jahrhundert*, Vienna, 1908, vol. 5, no. 214.44; A. BARTSCH, *Le Peintre graveur*, Vienna, 1801-1821, vol. 6, no. 136.36. This solution has been pointed out to me by Emese Sarkadi Nagy, the foremost expert of the Biertan altarpiece, who was kind enough to answer my questions about it.

[80] D. RIGAUX, "Le dossier iconographique", *art. cit.*, p. 258; H. DORMEIER, "St. Rochus, die Pest und die Imhoffs", *art. cit.*, p. 15-16.

[81] Now in the parish church of Cisnădi (Heltau/Nagydisznód, Romania). See E. SARKADI NAGY, *Local Workshops – Foreign Connections, op. cit.*, p. 153-155.

[82] D. RADOCSAY, *A középkori Magyarország táblaképei, op. cit.*, p. 275 (considers it undatable); J. VÉGH, "Szent Rókus ábrázolása", *art. cit.*, p. 240 (dates it to *c.* 1520); I. GERÁT, *Legendary Scenes: An Essay on Medieval Pictorial Hagiography*, Bratislava, 2014, p. 111-112 (leaves it undated).

[83] D. RADOCSAY, *A középkori Magyarország faszobrai, op. cit.*, p. 194 (dates it to 1500-1510); J. HOMOLKA, *Gotická plastika na Slovensku*, Bratislava, 1972, fig. 134, cat. no. 52, p. 400 (dates it to *c.* 1500).

(Szekcsőalja, Slovakia).[84] In contrast to these visual representations, there is no further sign of a contemporary cult of the saint. Roche does not appear in any extant missal or breviary demonstrably used in Hungary, and no ecclesiastical institution was dedicated to him before the seventeenth century.[85] Although his feast (16 August) was used to date three entries of the municipal account book of Bistriţa (Beszterce, Romania) in 1512 and 1514, this seems to have remained the exception.[86] Roche does not figure in any collection of *vitae* or sermons on saints produced in Hungary in the period in question.

In such a situation the cult must have had a lay or unofficial character, maybe even more than elsewhere. It was probably motivated and transmitted by personal experiences abroad, connections with foreigners through trade, pilgrimage, or study, as well as books and (mechanically reproduced) images introduced to the country from elsewhere. Francesco Diedo was the Venetian ambassador to the Hungarian court in 1469-1470, during the reign of Matthias Corvinus, but as his stay in the country antedated the composition of his *Vita Sancti Rochi* by ten years, he may not have been familiar with the saint yet.[87] Nevertheless, a few years later, John of Lazo, archdeacon of Telegd (Tileagd, Romania) was, quite probably, among the first northerners who witnessed the cult of St Roche in Venice. He was one of the (otherwise exclusively German) pilgrims led by Felix Fabri to the Holy Land in 1483-1484; and, since he was invited by Fabri personally and they remained inseparable all the way from Venice, John must have been in his company when, having learned that their Venetian innkeeper might have died in pestilence, they turned to the new saint for help – as Fabri tells in his travelogue:

> With those who had remained [i.e. did not run away to Padua to avoid the vicinity of the supposed plague victim] I took a boat to the church of St Roche in the city of Venice, and we prayed to the aforementioned saint,

---

[84] D. Radocsay, *A középkori Magyarország faszobrai*, op. cit., p. 211-212 (dated to 1500-1520); J. Végh, "Szent Rókus ábrázolása", art. cit., p. 240.
[85] S. Bálint, *Ünnepi kalendárium: A Mária-ünnepek és jelesebb napok hazai és közép-európai hagyományvilágából*, 2 vols., Budapest, 1977, vol. 2, p. 191-195.
[86] Zs. Simon, "Adatok szent Szaniszló", art. cit., p. 165-166. Roche also appears in an indulgence issued in Rome for a church in Cluj / Kolozsvár between 1513 and 1517 but the fragmentary state of the document (or, at least, its transcript) does not make it possible to understand the nature of the link between the saint and the church; see E. Jakab, *Oklevéltár*, op. cit., p. 329.
[87] For Diedo's life, see G. Tournoy, "Francesco Diedo, Venetian humanist and politician of the Quattrocento", *Humanistica Lovaniensia*, 19 (1970), p. 201-234; *Id.*, "Diedo, Francesco", in *Dizionario Biografico degli Italiani*, vol. 39, Rome, 1991, p. 769-774. For the *vita*, see footnote 35 above.

who is a special supporter of those fearing from pestilence, that we would not be infected.[88]

As to written sources of Roche's life available in late medieval Hungary, the Augustinian Friar and humanist, Giacomo Filippo Foresti of Bergamo, in the second edition of his renowned *Supplementum chronicarum* published in 1485 in Venice – that is, in the very year when the relics found in Voghera were obtained by the Venetians – included a short account of the saint's life still missing from the first edition of 1483. This short account appeared in subsequent editions of the work with minor modifications.[89] The Franciscan library of Gyöngyös has preserved four exemplars, and a fifth one also used in medieval Hungary has survived in the Brukenthal Museum in Sibiu.[90]

The *Supplementum chronicarum* was the direct source of a similar epitome of the life of St Roche in the *Liber chronicarum* of Hartmann Schedel, published in Latin and German in 1493, in Nuremberg.[91] Schedel also included an image of the saint in his book in which – as quite an interesting example of iconographic contamination – instead of a baculum he holds a spear or an oversized arrow, which Schedel may have thought more congruent with the theme of the plague. A copy of the German version of the work – *Das Buch der Chroniken* – was bought one year after its publication by Vincent of Izsép, a Hungarian student at the University of Cracow.[92] We, of

---

[88] *Fratris Felicis Fabri Evagatorium in Terrae Sanctae, Arabiae et Egypti peregrinationem*, ed. K. D. HASSLER, 3 vols., Stuttgart, 1843-1849, vol. 1, p. 101 (at the end of the sentence I emended *ne inficiantur* to *ne inficiamur*). As to John's having been inseparable from Fabri, see e.g. *ibid.*, vol. 2, p. 108: *non enim peregrinationem illam assumsisset, nisi sub mea confidentia, qui erat purus Hungarus, non unum verbum teutonicum sciens, sed in latina lingua et sclavonica et italica et hungarica peritus erat [...] mihi adhaesit semper*; or vol. 3, p. 173 (entry in Egypt): *a Venetiis usque huc individui fuimus*. For John's life and surviving poems, see S. V. KOVÁCS, "A humanista Lászai János", *Filológiai Közlöny*, 17 (1971), p. 344-366 (who, on p. 347, claims without any proof that John joined the others in Jaffa only). For a comprehensive discussion of medieval Hungarian pilgrims abroad, see E. CSUKOVITS, *Középkori magyar zarándokok*, Budapest, 2003.
[89] Jacopo Filippo FORESTI, *Supplementum chronicarum*, Venice, 1485, lib. 13, an. 1327, fol. 294r; see also *Id., Supplementum chronicarum orbis ab initio mundi*, Venice, 1490, lib. 13, an. 1327, fol. 214v; *Id., Novissime historiarum omnium repercussiones*, Venice, 1506, lib. 13, an. 1327, fol. 332v. Foresti dedicated another work of his, the *De plurimis claris selectisque mulieribus*, Ferrara, 1497, to Beatrix of Aragon, Queen consort of Hungary.
[90] Cs. CSAPODI, K. CSAPODINÉ GÁRDONYI, *Bibliotheca Hungarica: Kódexek és nyomtatott könyvek Magyarországon 1526 előtt*, 3 vols., Budapest, 1988-1994, no. 1450 (ed. of Venice, 1486), no. 1486, 1488, 1489, 2067 (ed. of Venice, 1492-1493).
[91] Hartmann Schedel, *Liber Chronicarum*, Nuremberg, 1493, fol. 227r; *Id., Das Buch der Chroniken*, Nuremberg, 1493, fol. 227r.
[92] Cs. CSAPODI, K. CSAPODINÉ GÁRDONYI, *Bibliotheca Hungarica*, op. cit., no. 1939. For the *possessor*, see K. SCHRAUF, *Registrum bursae Hungarorum Cracoviensis. A krakkói magyar tanulók-háza lakóinak jegyzéke (1493-1558)*, Budapest, 1893, p. 3 and 53.

course, do not know if he ever read the section on St Roche – or if anyone in the country read its counterpart in the *Supplementum chronicarum* – but the information was available, and given the success of both of these works and the massive destruction of Hungarian libraries in the sixteenth and seventeenth centuries, it is reasonable to suppose that there were many more exemplars of these and other accounts of Roche's life in Hungary.

In spite of having been credited with the same kind of assistance, St Sebastian and St Roche represent two different trajectories of becoming plague saints in the late Middle Ages. In the case of Sebastian, the main hagiographic text that defined his identity for centuries, the *Passio S. Sebastiani*, does not connect him to the disease. His cult became widespread but, before the Black Death, he was not invoked against the plague outside Pavia, and it was his Pavian plague miracle narrated by Paulus Diaconus and James of Varazze that served as a historical proof of the efficaciousness of praying for his intercession and visiting his relics in 1348-1349. The emergence of his identity as a widely known plague saint had apparently started in the core territories of his cult where his relics were available, and only later spread to the fringes like Hungary where there is no sign of any Sebastian *patrocinium* or, by implication, any Sebastian relic before the Black Death. Although the feast of Sts. Fabian and Sebastian was already used to date legal documents in Hungary before the mid fourteenth century – which may have been related to foreign influences, including that of the Dominicans and the Angevin dynasty – the late appearance of ecclesiastical institutions dedicated to the saint suggests that these were largely unrelated to the dynamic of dating charters. That most of the St Sebastian *patrocinia* surface in the source material as late as the second half or the end of the fifteenth century cannot be explained by the growing importance of the liturgical cult either, but it does coincide with the beginnings of his representation on altarpieces, the growth of his popularity as a name-giver in rural areas, and the first occurrences of attributing anti-pestilential capacities to him in hagiographic texts in Hungary, as well as with a revival of the cult in other regions of Europe. His images in Hungarian churches were as multivalent as elsewhere but since the earlier, pre-Black Death layers of his veneration must have been much weaker in Hungary than in the core territories of the cult, and since his patronage of archers, the other main specialty of Sebastian in the late Middle Ages was not characteristic of Hungarian towns and cities, protection from the plague seems to be the only reasonable explanation of why benefactors of churches and commissioners of polyptychs chose him and not some other martyr. As a consequence, his identity as a plague saint may have been less ambiguous in Hungary than elsewhere.

In contrast to St Sebastian, Roche was born, as it were, to be a plague saint. Although the beginnings of his cult are still very much in the dark, when he did appear in an identifiable form on murals in Lombardy in the 1450s and 1460s, he was already associated to pestilence – at least as someone who miraculously recovered from it. From the earliest vitae onward his relevance for the plague was multiply reinforced: he was shown not merely to have survived the disease himself, but to have cured many others as well and, what is more, to have been promised by God that anyone praying to him against the plague would enjoy divine grace. His cult had no identifiable center until the translation of his relics from Voghera to Venice, but even thereafter his cult spread more through texts and images (mainly from the printing press) than through pilgrimages and relics. His veneration in late medieval Hungary was largely limited to visual representations in churches in the Spiš region and in Transylvania. In the absence of other manifestations of the cult, public or private, it seems to have been promoted by individuals familiar with it as travelers (merchants, students, pilgrims) or as owners of foreign books or (mechanically reproduced) images, and who wanted to create visual reminders or claims of his prophylactic capacities. His coupling with St Sebastian could serve as a way of introducing him in his anti-pestilential function but, inversely, his presence could also reinforce Sebastians's identity as a plague saint.

Les saints libérateurs des Turcs en Hongrie à la fin du Moyen Âge

Enikő Csukovits
(*Budapest*)

La journée du 25 septembre 1396 fut une journée de deuil pour l'Europe chrétienne[1]. L'armée du sultan Bajazet Ier battit ce jour-là l'armée des croisés à Nikopol (Nicopolis), près du Bas-Danube. Conduite par le roi de Hongrie et composée de chevaliers français, bourguignons et allemands, cette armée de croisés qui franchit le Danube en août avait pour but de combattre les Turcs et de les expulser du continent européen. Elle atteignit Nikopol, verrou du Bas-Danube, le 12 septembre. L'armée principale du sultan, arrivée quinze jours après celle des Chrétiens pour délivrer la forteresse, infligea à ceux-ci une cuisante défaite. La plupart des combattants périrent sur le champ de bataille ou furent faits prisonniers. Même le roi de Hongrie Sigismond de Luxembourg eut le plus grand mal à avoir la vie sauve. Parmi les prisonniers de guerre du sultan, les plus illustres étaient Jean de Nevers, héritier du duc de Bourgogne, et le fameux maréchal Boucicaut, parangon des chevaliers. Le prix à payer pour obtenir leur libération s'éleva à deux cent mille florins d'or, une somme vertigineuse qui nécessita une collaboration paneuropéenne[2].

---

[1] Sur le sujet traité dans la présente contribution, voir E. Csukovits, « Miraculous escapes from Ottoman captivity », dans *Ransom Slavery along the Ottoman Borders (Early Fifteenth-Early Eighteenth Centuries)*, éd. G. Dávid et P. Fodor, Leyde-Boston, 2007, p. 1-18 ; *Ead.*, « Dalla cattività turca alla soglia degli apostoli », dans *Gli archivi della Santa Sede e il regno d'Ungheria (sec. 15-20). In memoriam di Lajos Pásztor*, éd. G. Platania, M. Sanfilippo, P. Tusor, Budapest-Rome, 2008 (Collectanea Vaticana Hungariae, 4), p. 3-10.

[2] J. Delaville le Roulx, *La France en Orient au XIVe siècle : expéditions du maréchal Boucicaut*, Paris, 1886 ; A. S. Atiya, *The Crusade of Nicopolis*, Londres, 1934 (reprint 1978) ; *Nicopolis, 1396-1996*, éd. J. Paviot, M. Chauney-Bouillot, Dijon, 1996 (Annales de Bourgogne, 68). Parmi les sources imprimées sur la bataille, voir en particulier *Le Livre des faicts du bon Messire Jean Le Maingre, dit mareschal Boucicaut*, éd. D. Lalande, Genève, 1985 ; *Chronique du Religieux de Saint-Denys contenant le règne de Charles VI de 1380 à 1422*, 2 vol., éd. M. L. Bellaguet, Paris, 1994 ; Jean Froissart, *Chroniques*, 4 vol., éd. P. F. Ainsworth et G. T. Diller, Paris, 2001.

Les saints et leur culte en Europe centrale au Moyen Âge (XIe-début du XVIe siècle), éd. par Marie-Madeleine de Cevins et Olivier Marin, Turnhout, 2017 (Hagiologia, 13), p. 109-121.

Selon la Chronique du religieux de Saint-Denis, « il n'y avait point de famille dans le royaume qui n'eût à déplorer quelque perte domestique[3] ». Or les pertes du contingent franco-bourguignon étaient très en-deçà de celles subies par les Hongrois, dont l'armée affrontait également pour la première fois les troupes ottomanes. Ce qui en Occident était un désagrément temporaire, assorti certes de pertes humaines et matérielles, devint en Hongrie un fardeau quotidien qui pesa pendant plusieurs siècles sur les habitants du pays. Car la saignée ne se limita pas à Nikopol, mais elle se répéta à un rythme tel que la population, armée ou non, éprouva dans sa chair de façon continue ce que signifiait le voisinage des Ottomans.

Les premières incursions turques remontent à 1390, l'année qui suivit la bataille de Kosovo Polje. Elles frappèrent les régions méridionales du pays, notamment la Syrmie (en hongrois Szerémség) et le Temesköz. L'année suivante, les Turcs envahissaient de nouveau la Syrmie, détruisant plusieurs villes ; puis en 1392, une attaque visa le Temesköz. Les bataillons hongrois dépêchés en hâte sur les lieux ne trouvèrent à leur arrivée que les ruines fumantes des destructions opérées par les Turcs, aussitôt repartis chargés de butin et de prisonniers. Si, dans les décennies suivantes, les pillards ottomans continuèrent à cibler ce secteur, ils jetèrent également leur dévolu sur de nouveaux comitats, élargissant continuellement leur rayon d'action[4].

Au début du XVe siècle, des groupes armés turcs firent irruption en Croatie et en Slavonie, réputées sûres jusqu'alors. Dans les années 1420, ce fut le tour de la Transylvanie, attaquée depuis la Valachie. Une des villes les plus importantes du pays, Brassó (actuelle Braşov, en Roumanie), fut alors mise à sac. Désormais, le royaume de Hongrie était contraint de se protéger sur toute la longueur de ses frontières méridionales, soit près de 800 kilomètres. C'est à partir des années 1520 que les Turcs commencèrent à conquérir des territoires hongrois. Mais ce n'était là que la phase terminale d'une longue

---

[3] *Chronique du Religieux*, op. cit., p. 522-523.
[4] F. SZAKÁLY, « Phases of Turco-Hungarian Warfare before the battle of Mohács (1365-1526) », *Acta Orientalia Scientiarum Hungaricae*, 33 (1979), p. 65-111 ; P. ENGEL, *The Realm of St Stephen. A History of Medieval Hungary, 895-1526*, Londres-New York, 2001, p. 202-203, 231-243, 283-297, 306-309, 367-370 ; P. ENGEL, Gy. KRISTÓ, A. KUBINYI, *Histoire de la Hongrie mediévale*, t. 2, *Des Angevins aux Habsbourgs*, Rennes, 2008, p. 120-123, 137-140, 146-150, 198-209, 257-267, 342-343, 372-375, 396-400. Dans la longue liste des travaux remarquables sur la lutte contre les Turcs, voir en particulier Gy. RÁZSÓ, « A Zsigmond-kori Magyarország és a török veszély (1393-1437) », *Hadtörténelmi Közlemények*, 20 (1973), p. 403-441 ; P. ENGEL, « A török-magyar háborúk első évei 1389-1392 », *Hadtörténelmi Közlemények*, 111 (1998), p. 561-577 (également publié dans P. ENGEL, *Honor, vár, ispánság. Válogatott tanulmányok*, Budapest, 2003, p. 555-577) ; Id., « Ungarn und die Türkengefahr zur Zeit Sigismunds (1387-1437) », dans *Das Zeitalter König Sigismunds in Ungarn und im Deutschen Reich*, éd. T. SCHMIDT et P. GUNST, Debrecen, 2000, p. 55-71.

suite d'intrusions et d'attaques qui avaient causé d'énormes pertes humaines et matérielles depuis au moins cent trente ans, c'est-à-dire pendant cinq à six générations. Dans le secteur méridional du royaume, près de 90 % des villages disparurent. Et l'impact des attaques turques toucha, directement ou indirectement, l'ensemble de la population du pays[5]. Vers la fin du XVe siècle, il ne se comptait pas une famille noble dont aucun membre n'eût pris part aux guerres contre les Turcs ; tandis que la masse des contribuables supportait un fardeau fiscal de plus en plus lourd pour la défense des frontières méridionales. L'objectif principal des attaquants turcs était le pillage. Et le butin le plus recherché n'était autre que les hommes, faciles à vendre sur le marché des esclaves.

On ne sait pratiquement rien du sort de la plupart des malheureux prisonniers qui tombèrent entre les mains des Turcs, pas même leur nombre global approximatif. Chaque incursion ottomane pouvait entraîner le rapt de plusieurs milliers d'hommes. Dans son traité sur les coutumes des Turcs, *Georgius de Hungaria*, ancien prisonnier capturé en 1438 en Transylvanie, écrit : « Comme je l'ai moi même entendu dire, ils [les Turcs] prennent parfois une telle multitude de prisonniers qu'un homme peut être échangé contre un chapeau »[6]. Il est encore plus difficile d'évaluer la proportion des évadés, de ceux qui réussirent à rentrer, plusieurs années ou décennies après leur capture. Dans l'ensemble, les prisonniers avaient peu de chances d'être libérés. Les notables, les nobles et leur famille ont généralement été relâchés, du moins lorsqu'ils étaient retrouvés par leurs proches, moyennant une rançon très élevée. Mais la plupart des captifs – hommes et femmes – de condition paysanne ne pouvaient guère compter sur leur rachat. Il ne leur restait que la fuite, périlleuse. Sur la foi de son expérience personnelle, *Georgius de Hungaria* considérait l'évasion comme une initiative vouée à l'échec. « Ils essaient de fuir de différentes façons, quoique sans succès, puisqu'il n'y en a que quelques-uns qui peuvent recouvrer leur liberté par la fuite. Et c'est encore plus difficile s'ils sont déjà outre-mer. Dans la pratique, les Turcs ont des moyens variés et très nombreux pour entraver les évasions et poursuivre, puis retrouver finalement les fugitifs. De plus, ceux qui sont retrouvés et ramenés en captivité doivent endurer des souffrances redoublées[7] ».

---

[5] P. ENGEL, « A török dúlások hatása a népességre : Valkó megye példája », *Századok*, 134 (2000), p. 267-321.
[6] Georgius DE HUNGARIA, *Incipit prohemium in tractatum de moribus, conditionibus et nequicia Turcorum*, Urach, 1481. Traductions hongroises : L. TARDY, *Rabok, követek, kalmárok az oszmán birodalomról*, Budapest, 1977, p. 49-153 (p. 67 pour la citation) ; E. FÜGEDI, *Kimondhatatlan nyomorúság. Két emlékirat a 15-16. századi oszmán fogságról*, Budapest, 1976.
[7] L. TARDY, *Rabok, követek, op. cit.*, p. 70-71.

Pour les Hongrois infortunés qui tombèrent entre les mains des Turcs, la captivité fut très certainement l'épreuve la plus terrible de leur existence. Dans leur affliction, ils ne pouvaient compter que sur leur propre habileté, ou sur quelque assistance spirituelle, cette dernière étant de toute façon nécessaire pour trouver la motivation indispensable à toute entreprise ou action individuelle. Aussi n'est-il pas surprenant de constater que, sur le territoire de la Hongrie médiévale, le gros des récits de libération se rencontre dans les recueils de miracles rédigés auprès des lieux de pèlerinage.

Les plus illustres foyers de pèlerinage de la Hongrie tardo-médiévale sont énumérés dans trois sources narratives, nées respectivement sous la plume de Petrus Ranzanus, d'Antonio Bonfini et de Nicolas Oláh[8]. Elles mentionnent, dans l'ordre, la relique du Saint Sang de l'abbaye de Báta ; la sépulture du fondateur de la monarchie hongroise, saint Étienne, et celle de son fils, le prince Émeric, à Székesfehérvár; celle du roi-chevalier saint Ladislas à Nagyvárad (Oradea, en Roumanie) ; enfin, la tombe du célèbre prédicateur franciscain observant Jean de Capistran, à Újlak (Ilok, en Croatie)[9]. À ces quatre lieux de pèlerinage de renommée nationale, Miklós Oláh ajoute la relique de saint Jean l'Aumônier à Buda et celle de saint Paul l'Ermite à Budaszentlőrinc[10].

Parmi les six lieux cités, deux seulement disposent d'un recueil de miracles qui a été préservé : Újlak et Budaszentlőrinc. Le recueil concernant Újlak rapporte des prodiges survenus entre 1458 et 1461 ; celui de Budaszentlőrinc, rédigé par Valentin Hadnagy, concerne la période 1422-1505. Jean de Capistran mourut en octobre 1456, quelques mois après la victoire de Belgrade, dans le couvent franciscain observant de la ville d'Újlak. Le jour même de son enterrement, de nombreux miracles se produisirent. Relatés de façon

---

[8] Petrus Ransanus, *Epithoma rerum Hungararum*, éd. P. KULCSÁR, Budapest, 1977 ; *Antonii Bonfinii Asculani Rerum Hungaricarum Decades*, éd. I. FÓGEL, B. IVÁNYI, L. JUHÁSZ, t. I-IV, Leipzig-Budapest, 1936-1941 ; Nicolaus Olahus, *Hungaria – Athila*, éd. C. EPERJESSY et L. JUHÁSZ, Budapest, 1938.

[9] Je me bornerai ici à citer les textes concernant les sanctuaires mentionnés dans l'ouvrage de Ransanus. Báta : *Batensis a Bata nominatus, qui vicus quidem est sed nobilis ob situm in eo monachorum ordinis sancti Benedicti monasterium, quod fama illustrissimum est propter evidens illud miraculum, quo in sacra hostia sanguis cum portiuncula quadam Christi carnis videtur, ut affirmant innumeri, qui viderunt* ; Fehérvár : *Est illic basilica olim a beato Stephano condita, ... eo nobilissima, quod in ea conditur eiusdem regis ac beati Emerici filii eius venerabile corpus* ; Oradea / Várad : *ubi est Varadinum oppidum illustre basilica, in qua beati Ladislai sacrum corpus sepultum est* ; Ilok / Újlak : *occurrit deinde Huliac, in quo oppido Ioannis Capistrani viri dei corpus conditur, quod divina virtute multis fertur clarere miraculis*. Petrus Ransanus, *Epithoma, op. cit.*, p. 61, 62, 68, 83.

[10] *Haec praeter situm atque architecturam tum regiam, tum corpore divi Ioannis Eleemosynarii insignis fuit*. Nicolaus Olahus, *Hungaria, op. cit.*, 8.5 ; *Supra mons divi Pauli cernitur sylvosus monasterio fratrum Eremitarum et corpore Pauli primi eremitae olim clarus, ibid.*, 9.12.

plus ou moins concordante selon les témoignages recueillis pour instruire son procès en canonisation (ouvert en 1460), ils sont plus de cinq cents au total[11]. En ce qui concerne la relique de saint Paul l'Ermite, ses gardiens enregistrèrent continuellement les miracles survenus depuis son obtention en 1381, auprès de la République de Venise. Cette liste servit probablement de base au travail du moine paulinien Valentin Hadnagy, auteur d'un livre imprimé en 1511 sous le titre de *Vita divi Pauli*[12].

Les deux listes de miracles contiennent principalement des descriptions de guérisons. Les autres thèmes sont moins nombreux, mais malgré tout homogènes, puisqu'ils rapportent tous des délivrances miraculeuses. Parmi les miracles recueillis pour Jean de Capistran, 4,6 % (c'est-à-dire 23 cas) racontent comment le saint obtint la libération de ceux qui l'avaient imploré. Dans le cas de saint Paul Ermite, le total s'élève à 18 cas, qui représentent 20 % de tous ses prodiges[13]. Certains des miraculés étaient tombés aux mains de l'ennemi, d'autres avaient été capturés par des brigands, d'autres encore avaient été emprisonnés pour leurs torts ou à la suite de fausses accusations. Près de la moitié des captifs mentionnés étaient prisonniers des Turcs – ce qui désigne clairement ceux-ci comme les adversaires de la Hongrie et de sa population.

Nombre des récits consignés dans ces recueils de miracles rapportent avec une minutie remarquable les circonstances de la capture, les souffrances endurées par les prisonniers pendant leur captivité, mais aussi les instruments de leur libération. Ils offrent une image assez fidèle des tribulations des communautés hongroises qui vivaient à proximité des Turcs et montrent le rôle de la foi chrétienne dans la survie de ces populations menacées au quotidien. Les textes, couchés par écrit en latin, portent la trace visible du caractère vivant des dépositions effectuées dans la langue maternelle des témoins.

Parmi les anciens captifs, on ne rencontre qu'un seul combattant. Il s'agit du noble Démétrius Kónya, habitant du village de Szaján (Sajan), dans le

---

[11] St. ANDRIĆ, *The Miracles of St John Capistran*, Budapest, 2000. Ce dossier a été étudié en premier lieu par E. FÜGEDI, « Kapisztránói János csodái. A jegyzőkönyvek társadalomtörténeti tanulsága », dans E. FÜGEDI, *Kolduló barátok, polgárok, nemesek. Tanulmányok a magyar középkorról*, Budapest, 1981, p. 7-56. Une partie du recueil de miracles a été publiée en hongrois. Texte du procès-verbal du 25 avril 1460, avec 188 miracles : A. HEGEDÜS, *Népélet és jogalkotás a középkori Újlakon*, Újvidék, 1983, p. 9-89 ; recueil de János Geszti, avec 111 miracles : E. MADAS, G. KLANICZAY, *Legendák és csodák (13-16. század). Szentek a magyar középkorból*, II, Budapest, 2001 (Milleniumi magyar történelem. Források), p. 403-478.
[12] Valentinus Hadnagy, *Vita divi Pauli*..., Venetiis, 1511 ; éd. bilingue latin-hongrois G. SARBAK, *Miracula sancti Pauli primi heremite. Hadnagy Bálint pálos rendi kézikönyve, 1511*, Debrecen, 2003. Voir encore E. MADAS, G. KLANICZAY, *Legendák, op. cit.*, p. 369-402. L'analyse de la source a été effectuée par É. KNAPP, « Remete Szent Pál csodái. A budaszentlőrinci ereklyékhez kapcsolódó mirákulumföljegyzések elemzése », *Századok*, 117 (1983), p. 511-557.
[13] St. ANDRIĆ, *The Miracles, op. cit.*, p. 304.

Temesköz. Il avait partagé le sort de l'oncle du roi Mathias Corvin, Michel de Szilágy, ancien régent et capitaine de Hongrie Supérieure tombé entre les mains des Turcs après une bataille d'importance secondaire en 1460. Démétrius raconte qu'il a été ferré avec des fers lourds, puis vendu à un homme originaire de Raguse pour six pièces d'or. Son maître lui promit de le libérer pour 40 ducats, après quoi il porta la somme à 110 ducats. C'est à ce moment-là que Démétrius fit le vœu de visiter la tombe de Capistran. Ce vœu étant reproduit mot pour mot dans le recueil de miracles, il vaut la peine d'en donner le texte intégral : « O Dieu éternel, créateur de tout, viens à mon secours dans ma vieillesse, prends-moi en ta miséricorde, et libère-moi d'entre les mains de mes ennemis par les mérites du bienheureux père [Jean de Capistran]. Je jure et je promets de visiter dévotement le tombeau de cet homme de Dieu, sitôt que je serai libéré et rentré à la maison[14] ». Le secours attendu ne tarda pas à arriver : un Hongrois donna à Démétrius la clé de ses fers, et comme il n'était plus entravé dans ses mouvements, celui-ci parvint à quitter le lieu de sa détention, la forteresse de Szendrő (Smederevo, en Serbie), puis gagna Belgrade (alors sous régime hongrois) après quatre lieues de marche. Il ne dit pas un mot du sort de ses compagnons, mais il est peu probable qu'ils aient été aussi chanceux que Démétrius Kónya. On sait par exemple que, peu après sa capture, Michel de Szilágy a été conduit à Constantinople par les Turcs pour y être exécuté[15].

Les autres prisonniers implorant l'aide de saint Paul ou de saint Jean de Capistran et faisant vœu de visiter leur sépulture avaient été capturés par surprise dans leurs maisons ou sur leurs terres par les bandes ottomanes. Grégoire, tailleur de Felfalu (Suşeni, dans le comitat de Baranya), piochait sa vigne. Un dénommé Étienne, du comitat de Temes, était aux champs, tandis qu'Étienne Horvát et ses compagnons moissonnaient quand ils ont été faits prisonniers par les Turcs[16].

Plus les captifs étaient éloignés de leur terre natale, plus leur délivrance s'avérait difficile. Les plus chanceux échappaient aux mains ottomanes au moment de l'attaque contre leur ville ou village. C'est ainsi qu'une femme noble

---

[14] *O Deus eterne, qui cunctorum es conditor, adiuva meam senectutem, fac meum hodie talem misericordiam, ut per merita beati patris merear de manibus iniquorum liberari. Voveo et promitto, ut cum libertati mee restitutus fuero domumque usque pervenero, sepulcrum cuiusdam hominis Dei devote volo visitare.* St. ANDRIĆ, *The Miracles*, p. 401, Appendix 8 ; E. MADAS, G. KLANICZAY, *Legendák, op. cit.*, p. 414.

[15] *Antonii Bonfinii*, IV, p. 12 (4.1.140) ; E. CSUKOVITS, *Dalla cattività turca, op. cit.*, p. 4-6.

[16] St. ANDRIĆ, *The Miracles, op. cit.*, p. 400, Appendix 7 ; G. SARBAK, *Miracula sancti Pauli, op. cit.*, p. 94, n° 40 (*quidam Stephanus tn campi medio per eosdem circumvallatus...*) ; St. ANDRIĆ, *The Miracles, op. cit.*, p. 403, Appendix 11 ; E. MADAS, G. KLANICZAY, *Legendák, op. cit.*, p. 460.

habitant près de Temesvár (Timisoara, en Roumanie) réussit à s'enfuir dans la forêt voisine, avec ses enfants[17]. Mais ceux qui ne trouvaient pas de refuge au moment de l'attaque étaient pris, ligotés, enchaînés et étroitement surveillés pendant leur longue marche vers les frontières méridionales du royaume, le long de la Save ou du Danube. Tous les récits de miracles mentionnent des fers et des cordes. Obstacles à la libération, ils étaient les premiers à s'ouvrir ou se détacher au moment de celle-ci. Le tailleur Grégoire, blessé pendant sa capture dans les vignes, avait la main ligotée au cou, avant de parvenir à couper la corde avec son couteau. Ayant retrouvé sa liberté de mouvement, il courut dans la forêt, où ses poursuivants ne purent le rattraper[18]. Accompagné de nombreux autres prisonniers, Paul, menuisier de Cseri (Sacoşu Turesc), dans le comitat de Temes, avait été traîné par les Turcs jusqu'au Danube, à cinq journées de marche de sa terre natale. La nuit, Paul réussit à desserrer les liens de ses mains avec ses dents, puis à défaire les cordes liant ses pieds. Il parvint ainsi à s'éloigner à reculons du groupe des gardes[19]. Benoît, fait prisonnier aux environs de Makó (Macău), fit vœu à saint Paul et put ensuite, grâce à ses prières, briser les fers qui encerclaient son cou, qui se détachèrent comme s'ils étaient faits de cire[20].

Étienne Horvát, qui avait été emmené au-delà de la Save, donc hors du royaume de Hongrie, avait été ligoté d'une manière particulièrement cruelle, parce qu'il avait tué un Turc pour se défendre. Plié en deux, la tête au niveau des genoux, il avait été attaché par les mains et les pieds à une poutre en attendant son exécution, prévue pour le jour suivant. Il échappa à la mort en déliant ses cordes, ouvrit la porte et s'enfuit, laissant sa femme entre les

---

[17] *Altera vero matrona cum circa festum Margarithe circa Temeswaar Turcis omnis beluina crudelitate depopulantibus sola cum suis parvulis cuiusdam silve densitatem intrasset.* G. SARBAK, *Miracula sancti Pauli, op. cit.*, p. 92 n° 34 et p. 94 n° 40.

[18] *...manibusque ligatis fune in colle misso captivus deducitur,... ruptis manuum suarum colligacionibus cultellum de vagina eduxit, funem de collo suo precidit et de manibus eorum exiliens acupedio cursu vastam silvam peciit et Turcis eum acriter insequentibus per Dei propiciacionem ac meritorum beati patris suffragacionem rursum ab eis capi non potuit sed saluber evasit.* St. ANDRIĆ, *The Miracles, op. cit.*, p. 400, Appendix 7.

[19] *...ipsum nephandissimi Treuci cum aliis multis captivum abduxissent venissentque secum iuxta flumen Danobii essetque in nocte fortiter legatus..., Cum igitur sic orasset rescipiens hinc inde cepit dentibus suis ligaturam manuum dissolvere, quam cum solvisset similiter et de suis pedibus dissolvit surgensque cum bona confidencia et paulatim exivit de medio eorum quasi vigilancium.* St. ANDRIĆ, *The Miracles, op. cit.*, p. 402, Appendix 10 ; E. MADAS, G. KLANICZAY, *Legendák, op. cit.*, p. 458.

[20] *...quendam Benedictum nomine cum aliis multis capiendis in captum cum omnibus suis aspectaverunt usque ad fluvium Mwrvva dictum, duobus miliaribus ad Mako. Cumque nimium afflictus votum ad sanctum Paulum emisisset, in quandam silva Turcis ab eo elongatis cathenam ferream collo circumligatam cum coltello quasi ceram liquidam scidit et simul cum sociis liber evasit...* G. SARBAK, *Miracula sancti Pauli, op. cit.*, p. 96 n° 47.

mains des Turcs[21]. Le récit ne précise pas quel fut le sort de son épouse, sans doute parce que son mari ne savait rien d'elle au moment de sa déposition. On connaît en revanche les tribulations de deux autres femmes, Hélène de Gara, qui implora l'aide de Jean de Capistran, et Anne, habitante de Szentmárton près de Gara, qui s'en remit à Paul l'Ermite. Tombée en captivité avec plusieurs autres personnes, Hélène fit preuve d'une ingéniosité, d'un courage et d'une fermeté hors du commun. Elle était déjà arrivée en Serbie quand, à la suite de son vœu, le verrou de ses fers s'ouvrit. Elle eut la présence d'esprit de remettre en place le verrou pour attendre le moment opportun. Quand elle put enfin s'évader, elle passa quatre jours et quatre nuits sans manger ni boire afin d'atteindre la Save... où elle fut reprise par les Serbes, qui la vendirent comme esclave. Selon sa déposition faite sous serment à Újlak, elle fut revendue cinq fois avant de pouvoir enfin rentrer chez elle[22]. Dix ans plus tard, en 1471, Anne fut également emmenée en captivité au-delà de la Save. Elle parvint à s'évader nuitamment, après son vœu, mais retomba en captivité une fois arrivée à la Save. « Par une manière de miracle », les Serbes qui l'avaient capturée, « enclins à la miséricorde », la relâchèrent et l'aidèrent même à traverser le fleuve[23]. Hélène de Gara n'était pas la seule à avoir changé de maître à plusieurs reprises. Valentin d'Erdőd, tombé lui aussi aux mains des Turcs, a été revendu plusieurs fois. Chaque fois qu'il s'évada, il fut repris, jusqu'à sa libération finale par un miracle[24].

---

[21] *...captivum et ligatum duxissent ultra flumen Zawe essetque fortiter astrictus diris vinculis et diversimode tormentatus ita ut caput suum infra ad pedes reflexissent manusque et pedes suos ad trabem sursum ligassent..., ligaminibus tam manuum, quam etiam omnium aliorum membrorum apertisque paulatim ianuis exivit de medio eorum, remanente uxore sua in manibus ipsorum...* St. ANDRIĆ, *The Miracles*, op. cit., p. 403, Appendix 11 ; E. MADAS, G. KLANICZAY, *Legendák*, op. cit., p. 460.

[22] *...quo facto lingua compedis de sera ita exilivit ac si dura malei percussione fuisset propulsata; verum cernens mulier propter Turcorum custodias ad fugiendum tempus non esset opportunum, ipsius sere linguam restituit in locum suum... Apto itaque tempore ad fugiendum considerato cordas quibus manus sue erant ligate dentibus dissolvit et... prosiluit... et quatuor diebus et noctibus absque omni alimento sed gaudens per processum vie usque ad Zawe fluvium pervenit, sed eam iterum Rasciani captivarunt et rursum vendiderunt. Quinque itaque vicibus successim vendita dum fuisset...* St. ANDRIĆ, *The Miracles*, op. cit., p. 399, Appendix 5.

[23] *...prima fuit relicta quondam Mathie Magni Anna dicta de Zenthmartnii prope Gara, cum per sevissimos Turcos circa festum beati Jacobi fuisset capta et deducta ad civitatem Parodiina, recordata meritorum beati Pauli votum vovit visitare reliquias eiusdemet sequenti nocte Turcis dormientibus per omnia castra eorum libera evasit at cum per Rascianos (circa Zawam veniens) iterum detenta fuisset. Idem quod prius vovens modo mirabili per eosdem Rascianos intuitu misericordie dimissa et per aquam transvecta...* G. SARBAK, *Miracula sancti Pauli*, op. cit., p. 92 n° 34.

[24] *...ipse cum per Turcos in captivitatem deductus et ibi pluribus vicibus venditus fuisset nonnullies per fuge presidium ab ipsis liberati attemptans semper recaptivatus extitit...* St. ANDRIĆ, *The Miracles*, op. cit., p. 398, Appendix 3.

Les cas réunis dans les recueils de miracles étudiés montrent que les captifs ne pouvaient compter sur aucune assistance extérieure pour obtenir leur libération. Dans la liste des exemples dont on dispose, un seul rapporte qu'une attaque surprise menée par les Hongrois facilita la délivrance. Le premier jour de l'an 1461, Barthélemy, habitant d'Erdővég (Erdevik) dans le comitat de Valkó, fut capturé par les Turcs. Ceux-ci firent halte avec leurs prisonniers dans une ville serbe proche de la Save. Le jour même, une troupe hongroise arrivée de Belgrade fit brusquement irruption dans la ville, qu'elle pilla et incendia en massacrant, capturant et mettant en fuite les Turcs qui s'y trouvaient. Barthélemy profita de la confusion pour s'échapper et rejoignit les soldats venus de Belgrade[25]. Mais en ce qui concerne les autres libérations miraculeuses, non seulement les troupes hongroises chargées de défendre les zones exposées ne jouent aucun rôle dans les libérations, mais elles ne semblent même pas constituer un espoir pour les captifs. Les témoins implorent l'assistance divine pour se libérer, sans attendre une armée de secours, sans même prier pour qu'elle arrive.

Rares étaient les captifs qui comptaient sur leur rachat par leurs proches ou par eux-mêmes, car les Turcs n'avaient pas pour habitude d'enlever des foules d'habitants de leurs villages pour en tirer ensuite des rançons. Seuls deux hommes ont eu (ou auraient eu) la possibilité de se racheter : Démétrius Kónya, le soldat capturé pendant une bataille, ainsi qu'un bourgeois nommé Mathieu, qui habitait dans la bourgade de Kő, près du Danube. Les Turcs devaient considérer ce dernier comme un homme riche, puisqu'ils réclamèrent initialement 200 pièces d'or pour sa délivrance, mais se contentèrent finalement de dix pièces, grâce au miracle[26].

Les captifs qui traversaient le Danube ou la Save se trouvaient en territoire ennemi. Vivant sous obédience turque, les Serbes manifestaient peu d'empathie pour les prisonniers hongrois, essayant au contraire d'en tirer profit. Le seul décisif sur le plan psychologique devait se situer à la hauteur de l'ancienne capitale serbe, Smederevo. Car là, les captifs avaient encore un petit espoir de parvenir à s'enfuir, tandis que chaque lieue parcourue en

---

[25] *Et ecce eodem die Ungari de castro Albanandor armatis manibus irruentes contra civitatem predictam spoliantes ac conburrentes eam funditus et quos potuerunt ex Treucis trucidarunt, quosdam autem captivos duxerunt, reliquos vero in fugam converterunt. Juvenis autem sepedictus fugam peciit ante Turcos ad silvam, qui eum prosequentes nec invenire valentes, ex alia parte circuiens iunxit se Ungaris liberatus de manibus pessimorum, cum quibus venit ad predictum castrum...* St. ANDRIĆ, *The Miracles, op. cit.*, p. 402, Appendix 9 ; E. MADAS, G. KLANICZAY, *Legendák, op. cit.*, p. 435-436.

[26] *...Turcus non eum libertati sue dare nisi ducentis florenis persolutis, verum omnipotens Deus per merita beati patris ei graciam contulit, quod pro decem tantum florenis eum emisit et usque ad metas Hungarie sociavit.* St. ANDRIĆ, *The Miracles, op. cit.*, p. 399, Appendix 6a.

direction du Sud amenuisait leurs chances d'être libérés. Le retour devenait extrêmement difficile pour ceux qui avaient été transférés à l'intérieur de l'Empire ottoman. Enlevé avec sa femme, Blaise Sárkány de Csanád passa dix années aux mains des Turcs. Ils eurent tous deux de la chance dans leur malheur, puisqu'ils ne furent pas séparés et eurent même deux filles, nées en captivité. La famille fut finalement vendue en Terre Sainte, mais n'y demeura pas longtemps : son maître ayant été exécuté par le sultan, elle put rentrer en Hongrie[27]. Mais Blaise de Szentgyörgy, du comitat de Somogy, dut passer vingt-deux années en Turquie avant d'obtenir son élargissement[28].

Quel qu'ait été leur rôle personnel dans leur libération, les captifs croyaient fermement que celle-ci était due à l'intervention du saint qu'ils avaient invoqué. Aussitôt après leur délivrance, ils accomplissaient leur vœu en visitant la sépulture de saint Paul l'Ermite ou de saint Jean de Capistran pour leur rendre grâce. Épuisé par sa fuite, Démétrius Kónya n'eut pas la force de tenir sa promesse pendant un certain temps. On lit dans le recueil de miracles : « Aussitôt sa santé recouvrée, il se rendit à la sépulture du saint conformément à son vœu, et il a dit et redit maintes fois qu'il était convaincu que, sans la bonté de Dieu et les mérites du bienheureux père, il n'aurait jamais réussi à sortir de sa captivité[29] ». Ces dépositions étaient souvent prononcées devant une foule nombreuse. Libéré par les soldats de Belgrade, Barthélemy d'Erdővég fut sollicité par un prédicateur d'Újlak pour monter en chaire avec lui et proclamer à haute voix les circonstances de sa libération, à titre d'illustration du sermon du jour, devant la multitude assemblée pour entendre le prêche[30].

Un autre usage voulait que les miraculés déposent les preuves de leur libération sur le tombeau du saint intercesseur, à la manière des béquilles devenues inutiles aux malades guéris qui s'accumulaient sur les lieux de pèlerinage. Pendant sa fuite, le menuisier Paul, enlevé à Cseri, avait gardé les cordes qui avaient ligoté ses mains et ses pieds et qu'il avait tranchées avec

---

[27] *Quidam Blasius Saarkan de Chanadino cum uxore per Turcos captus et ad Turciam deportatus, cum ibidem decem annis detentus, duas filias genuisset. Et tandem ultra mare ad sepulchrum Domini venditus fuisset, votum fecit ad sanctum Paulum... Voto emisso dominum suum zoltanus iugulans una cum uxore et liberis evasit.* G. SARBAK, *Miracula sancti Pauli, op. cit.*, p. 94 n° 43.

[28] St. ANDRIĆ, *The Miracles, op. cit.*, p. 405, Appendix 14.

[29] *...recuperataque sanitate veniens secundum promissionem suam ad sepulchrum viri Dei et merita eiusdem beati patris defuisset (!), nunquam potuisset de captivitate ipsorum liberari.* St. ANDRIĆ, *The Miracles, op. cit.*, p. 401, Appendix 8.

[30] *...de hinc ad Vylac iuxta quod promiserat, quem predicator traxit super ad ambonem iuxta se stare et fecit ipsum alta voce clamare coram omni multitudine ibidem tunc verbum Dei audiencium, quod eodem die Deus omnipotens quo ipsum oravit pro sua liberacione meritis eiusdem beati patris de manibus iniquorum eripuisset.* St. ANDRIĆ, *The Miracles, op. cit.*, p. 402, Appendix 9 ; E. MADAS, G. KLANICZAY, *Legendák, op. cit.*, p. 435.

les dents pour les emmener à Újlak. Ces cordes « pendaient au tombeau du bienheureux père », rapporte le registre[31]. Les plus importants lieux de pèlerinage de la Hongrie étaient pleins de cordes et de chaînes déposées de la même façon. On en trouvait aussi dans les grands centres de pèlerinage de rayonnement international. Les sources allemandes mentionnent les cordes suspendues dans la cathédrale d'Aix-la-Chapelle par les Hongrois libérés de la captivité turque[32]. Cordes et fers étaient utilisés comme ex-voto par les miraculés de toutes les couches sociales. Membre d'un des plus importants lignages du baronnage hongrois, Jean de Gara fut capturé au cours d'une bataille en 1415. L'histoire de son vœu est racontée dans une chronique et même dans une chanson de geste. Nous savons ainsi que Gara s'est voué à la relique la plus illustre du pays, le Saint Sang de l'abbaye de Báta, pour obtenir sa libération. « Quand il recouvra sa liberté après une longue captivité, il déposa ses chaînes d'un poids considérable dans l'abbaye de Báta, pour la mémoire de la postérité, pour accomplir son vœu et pour la gloire du précieux Sang de notre Seigneur et Rédempteur[33]. »

Les histoires consignées dans les recueils étudiés, réalistes, ne comportent aucune trace de mysticisme. Les cordes et les chaînes ne sont jamais déliées et coupées directement par Paul l'Ermite, Jean de Capistran, la Vierge ou quelque autre saint invoqué, mais toujours par le captif lui-même. Les saints n'indiquent pas non plus la route à prendre pour s'enfuir, ni ne procurent de gîte ou de nourriture pendant la fuite, laquelle peut durer plusieurs journées. Leur concours est d'un autre ordre. Ce sont eux qui donnent du courage, de la persévérance dans l'épreuve, eux aussi qui renforcent l'élément central de l'identité des captifs, celui de l'appartenance à la Chrétienté, même dans un environnement païen. Là réside leur principale contribution au processus de libération. Aux yeux des Hongrois captifs, les Turcs sont des infidèles (*infidelissimi*), infâmes (*nephandi*) et sauvages (*sevissimi*), au milieu desquels et le corps et l'âme des Chrétiens se trouvent en danger mortel[34]. Cette conception

---

[31] *...venit ad sepulchrum beati patris una cum aliis votivis iuxta promissum suum, portans secum ligaturas illas, que modo stant suspense ante tumulum ipsius beati patris in testimonium sue optate liberacionis...* » St. Andrić, *The Miracles, op. cit.*, p. 403, Appendix 10 ; E. Madas, G. Klaniczay, *Legendák, op. cit.*, p. 458.
[32] E. Thoemmes, *Die Wallfahrten der Ungarn an den Rhein*, Aachen, 1937, p. 30.
[33] *Johannes enim de Gara [...] post multos sue captivitatis dies libertate potius, pondus feramentorum ingens, quibus vinctus erat, in monasterio de Batha ad gloriam preciosissimi sanguinis domini redemptoris nostri pro illius, quod ibidem voverat, redemptione voti futuram ad memoriam reliquit*. Johannes de Thurocz, *Chronica Hungarorum*, I, éd. E. Galántai et J. Kristó, Budapest, 1985, p. 223-224.
[34] St. Andrić, *The Miracles, op. cit.*, p. 402-403, Appendix 9, 10, 11 ; G. Sarbak, *Miracula sancti Pauli, op. cit.*, p. 92 n° 34.

est exprimée dans les prières et invocations des captifs. Ligoté atrocement et redoutant une mort imminente, Étienne Horvát « invoquait la bonté de Dieu en disant : Seigneur Jésus Christ, j'implore ta clémence humblement et dévotement, ne laisse point ton serviteur indigne finir misérablement sa vie par les mains de ces païens infidèles, mais par les mérites du bienheureux père frère Jean de Capistran, daigne me délivrer de leurs mains »[35]. Au milieu du campement turc, le menuisier Paul feignait de dormir et priait ainsi : « Seigneur Dieu tout puissant, montre aujourd'hui ta vertu à travers ton serviteur, et par les mérites du bienheureux père frère Jean de Capistran, délivre-moi d'entre les mains de ces ennemis de toute la Chrétienté. Ne me laisse pas perdre la foi catholique que j'ai professée dans l'eau baptismale, ni tomber en désespérance par la multiplication de mes péchés et encourir la damnation éternelle. Car je préfère vivre, Seigneur, dans le royaume bienheureux, plutôt que de subir les cruelles tortures sans fin dans le feu éternel[36] ».

Le menuisier fait prisonnier à Cseri n'avait, à ce qu'il semble, aucune formation théologique particulière, ni aucune conscience identitaire dépassant celle du commun. Cet été de 1461, ligoté dans un camp près du Danube, il n'était point le premier à associer captivité turque et damnation éternelle, ni le premier à accoler le terme « ennemi de la Chrétienté » au nom des Turcs. Sa prière et les pensées exprimées à travers elle reflètent les mentalités hongroises du XVe siècle[37]. Cette attitude, complétée par l'expérience personnelle d'une longue captivité, est encore mieux exprimée par *Georgius de Hungaria*, fait prisonnier en 1438, dans son traité publié en 1480 : « dans cette servitude, l'affliction de l'âme et de l'esprit est tellement grande et tellement amère, qu'elle est à peine comparable avec celle de la mort même. Que peut faire

---

[35] *...oravit Domini bonitatem dicens: Domine Ihesu Christe humiliter et devote tuam exoro clemenciam út non dimittans me indignum famulum tuum per manus istorum infidelium paganorum mala morte meam finire vitam et per merita beati patris fratris Johannis de Capistrano eripere me digneris de manibus eorum.* St. ANDRIĆ, *The Miracles, op. cit.*, p. 403, Appendix 11 ; E. MADAS, G. KLANICZAY, *Legendák, op. cit.*, p. 460.

[36] *Domine Deus omnipotens, ostende in me hodie servo tuo virtutem tuam et per merita beati patris fratris Johannis de Capistrano, libera me de manibus inimicorum tocius christianitatis, ne amissa fide catholica quam professus sum in fonte baptismatis incidam ex multiplicacione peccatorum meorum in desperacionem et inde perveniam ad eternam dampnacionem, plus enim vellem domine regno beatorum perfrui quam eternis ignibus attrociter perpetue cruciari.* St. ANDRIĆ, *The Miracles, op. cit.*, p. 402-403, Appendix 10 ; E. MADAS, G. KLANICZAY, *Legendák, op. cit.*, p. 458 ; E. FÜGEDI, *Kapisztránói János csodái, op. cit.*, p. 49 ; St. ANDRIĆ, *The Miracles, op. cit.*, p. 243.

[37] E. CSUKOVITS, « 'Le serpent tortueux' et 'les satellites de Satan' : l'image de l'ennemi dans les narrations des chartes de donation des rois Anjou en Hongrie », dans *La diplomatie des États angevins aux XIIIe et XIVe siècles*, sous la direction de Z. KORDÉ et I. PETROVICS, Rome-Szeged, 2010, p. 345-347.

cette âme misérable, quand elle aperçoit que le bien lui est interdit, tandis que le mal rôde tout autour d'elle ? Elle voit régner sur elle l'ennemi de la Croix du Christ, elle sent peser sur elle le travail immense et les diverses occupations, elle sent qu'elle est séparée du bercail du Christ et livrée aux gueules et aux griffes des loups. [...] Il est certain que, si elle avait la possibilité de choisir, elle choisirait la mort au lieu d'une telle vie[38]. »

Conséquence de son voisinage forcé avec la puissance turque, le royaume de Hongrie alimenta pendant plusieurs siècles les marchés aux esclaves de l'Empire ottoman. À partir des années 1390, des dizaines de milliers de captifs hongrois eurent le sentiment d'être « livrés aux loups », pour reprendre l'expression de l'ancien prisonnier *Georgius* – entré ensuite chez les Dominicains. Dans cet état douloureux de détresse, c'est leur foi chrétienne qui était seule susceptible de fournir la pierre angulaire de leur être, en même temps que la garantie de la préservation de leur identité, même dans l'hypothèse où ils ne reverraient jamais plus leur terre natale. La vigueur de leur sentiment d'appartenance à la Chrétienté peut être démontrée également par des données chiffrées. Tandis que la population des territoires orthodoxes tombés sous domination ottomane s'est convertie massivement à l'islam, dans les pays de la Chrétienté latine, on trouve très peu d'exemples d'islamisation – ni collective, ni même individuelle. Les registres des forteresses turques des XVIe et XVIIe siècles prouvent que très peu de Hongrois se convertirent à la religion de Mahomet pendant les cent cinquante années d'occupation ottomane[39].

---

[38] L. TARDY, *Rabok, követek*, op. cit., p. 68-69.
[39] K. HEGYI, « Etnikum, vallás, iszlamizáció. A budai vilájet várkatonaságának eredete és utánpótlása », *Történelmi Szemle*, 40 (1998), p. 229-259 ; Id., *A török hódoltság várai és várkatonasága*, 3 vol., Budapest, 2007 (História Könyvtár, Kronológiák, adattárak, 9).

II
L'EMPRISE DES ORDRES MENDIANTS

Shaping the Sainthood of a Central European Clarissan Princess

The Development and Fate of the Earliest Hagiographic Texts on Agnes of Bohemia and St Clare's Epistolary Tradition

Christian-Frederik FELSKAU
(*Berlin and Cologne*)

For Ada-Brunkosch, Ziguzago and Ruhpell

When on 2 March 1282, the Přemyslid princess Agnes "recommended her soul into the hands of our Heavenly Father", as stated in the saint's legend *Candor lucis eterne*, "the sisters [of her community] filled up with complaints the monastery and wetted their virgin faces with plenty tears".[1] In fact, the death of the Central European royal proponent of what historians call "evangelical awakening" meant a huge turning point in the history of the first established Clarissan house north of the Alps, founded by the daughter of king Ottokar I (*c.* 1155-1230).[2] Despite the condolences of an "endless mass" seeking

---

[1] This source (henceforth: *CLE*) is cited hereafter from J. K. VYSKOČIL, *Legenda blahoslavené Anežky a čtyři listy sv. Kláry*, Prague, 1932, here p. 121. First edition of the legend by W. SETON, *Some New Sources for the Life of Blessed Agnes of Bohemia* (British Society of Franciscan Studies, 7), London-Aberdeen, 1915, repr. Cambridge, 2010.

[2] On the monastery: H. SOUKUPOVÁ, *Anežský klášter v Praze*, Prague, 2011; Chr.-Fr. FELSKAU, *Agnes von Böhmen und die Klosteranlage der Franziskaner und Klarissen in Prag*, 2 vols., Nordhausen, 2008. Monographs on the Order of the Poor Clares in the Middle Ages: B. ROEST, *Order and Disorder. The Poor Clares between Foundation and Reform*, Leiden-Boston, 2013; on its initiation: C. ANDENNA, "Dalla Religio pauperum dominarum de Valle Spoliti all' Ordo Sancti Damiani. Prima evoluzione istituzionale di un ordine religioso femminile nel contesto delle esperienze monastiche del secolo XIII", in *Die Bettelorden im Aufbau. Beiträge zu Institutionalisierungsprozessen im mittelalterlichen Religiosentum*, ed. G. MELVILLE, J. OBERSTE, Münster-Hamburg-London, 1999, p. 429-492. See also Chr.-Fr. FELSKAU, "Agnes und die anderen: Der Anteil der Frauen am evangelischen Aufbruch in Böhmen und Mähren während der ersten Hälfte des 13. Jahrhunderts", in *Církev, žena a společnost ve středověku. Sv. Anežka a její doba*, Ústí nad Orlicí, 2010, p. 21-42.

*Les saints et leur culte en Europe centrale au Moyen Âge (XI*ᵉ*-début du XVI*ᵉ* siècle)*, éd. par Marie-Madeleine de CEVINS et Olivier MARIN, Turnhout, 2017 (*Hagiologia*, 13), p. 125-171.

© BREPOLS PUBLISHERS DOI 10.1484/M.HAG-EB.5.113970

to touch or at least to see Agnes' corpse in the subsequent days, driven by the hope to obtain healing from it, only a few contemporaries could recall all the important steps which had shaped Agnes' life since her birth most probably in 1211.[3]

Agnes' Deeds and Her Death, a Brief Recollection of Facts

Born as the ninth and presumably last daughter of king Ottokar's second marriage with the Árpád princess Constance (*c.* 1180-1240),[4] Agnes spent some years of her childhood first in the Cistercian nunnery of Trebnitz/Trzebnica in Silesia under the guidance of her aunt and future St Hedwig of Andechs (1174-1243)[5] and afterwards in the Premonstratensian monastery of Doxan/Doxany, a monastic spot in Northern Bohemia for raising daughters of the ruling Přemyslids.[6] Due to ambitious plans of her father, she was then sent to the Viennese court of the Babenbergs, close allies of the Bohemian

---

[3] Citation: *CLE*, p. 122. On the phenomenon: R. BARTLETT, *Why Can the Dead Do Such Great Things? Saints and Worshippers from the Martyrs to the Reformation*, Princeton, 2013, here p. 239-250. For 1205 as Agnes' birth year argue: J. BERAN, *Blahoslavená Anežka Česká*, Rome, 1974, p. 17s.; J. POLC, *Agnes von Böhmen 1211-1282. Königstochter – Äbtissin – Heilige* (Lebensbilder zur Geschichte der böhmischen Länder, 6), Munich, 1989, p. 11; W. SETON, *Some New Sources*, p. 45. Cf. the catalogue of the exhibition dedicated to the princess' 800th anniversary in the monastery, nowadays called "Agnes cloister": *Svatá Anežka Česká. Princezna a řeholnice*, Prague, 2011, here p. 11. Most recent monography on her deeds and commemoration: H. SOUKUPOVÁ, *Svatá Anežka Česka*, Prague, 2015.

[4] Since František Palacký, some historians consider Guiglielma di Chiaravalle (*c.* 1212-1282), the foundress of a lay community near Milan and declared heretic (inquisitorial trial in 1300), as Agnes' younger sister: B. NEWMAN, "Agnes of Prague and Gulgielma of Bohemia", in *Medieval Holy Women in the Christian Tradition c. 1100 – c. 1500*, ed. A. MINNIS, R. VOADAN, Turnhout, 2010, p. 557-580.

[5] On the Central European adoption of new models of religious life and sanctity: G. KLANICZAY, *Holy Rulers and Blessed Princesses: Dynastic Cults in Medieval Central Europe*, Cambridge, 2000; Fr. MACHILEK, "Die Přemysliden, Piasten und Arpaden und der Klarissenorden im 13. und frühen 14. Jahrhundert", in *Westmitteleuropa, Ostmitteleuropa, Vergleiche und Beziehungen, Fs. für Ferdinand Seibt zum 65. Geburtstag*, ed. W. EBERHARD et al., Munich, 1992, p. 293-306.

[6] On Trebnitz: H. GRÜGER, "Der Konvent von Trebnitz (Trzebnica) bis zum Ende der habsburgischen Gegenreformation", *Archiv für Schlesische Kirchengeschichte*, 51-52 (1994), p. 159-175; K. CHARVÁTOVÁ, *Dějiny cisterckého řádu v Čechách 1142-1420*, vol. I, Prague, 1998, p. 291-336. Hedwig's legend: *Legenda o sw. Jadwize. Legende der hl. Hedwig*, ed. W. MROZOWICZ, Tr. EHLERT, Wrocław, 2000; about her canonisation: O. KRAFFT, *Papsturkunde und Heiligsprechung. Die päpstlichen Kanonisationen vom Mittelalter bis zur Reformation. Ein Handbuch*, Köln-Weimar-Wien, 2005, here p. 588s. On Doxan: J. PRAŽÁK, "Privilegium Přemysla I. pro Doksany a jého konfirmace z r. 1276. Poznámky k dějinám doksanského klášterectví ve XII a XIII století", *Sborník archivních prací*, 5 (1955), p. 159-203. The princess' commemoration in the necrologue of the monastery (1373): *Necrologium Doxanensis*, ed. B. DUDÍK, Wien, 1880, here p. 14.

king at that time. But thwarting Ottokar's plan, Leopold VI of Babenberg (1176-1230) arranged a marriage between his own daughter Margaret (1204-1286) and the Hohenstaufen prince Henry (VII, 1211-1242), for which Agnes had to return to Prague in 1225, where she became the subject of further dynastic ambitions, once again with the Hohenstaufen dynasty, but more concrete with the Plantagenets in England.[7] All these initiatives failed, let it be due to Agnes' growing religious zeal as the hagiographic tradition claims,[8] let it be for political reasons.

The death of her father and the ascension to the throne of her most intimate brother Wenceslas I (1230-1253) paved the way to Agnes' conversion probably in 1231.[9] In close reconciliation with the Apostolic See and after the arrival of some Damianite sisters from Trento in the Trentino region (founded in the 1220s),[10] Agnes, inspired by the models of her cousin, the future St Elizabeth of Hungary/Thuringia (1207-1231) and of Clare of Assisi (1194-1253), founded a hospital and an attached monastery of the newly established *ordo Sancti Damiani*[11] at the edge of the settlement which was constituted as the Old Town of Prague precisely in this period.[12] She entered the monastery of St Francis in a solemn ceremony at Pentecost 1234 or 1235 and was invested by the already settled Friars Minor of the local friary of

---

[7] J. ŽEMLIČKA, "Tradice babenbersko-přemyslovských manželských svazků", in *Česko-rakouské vztahy ve 13. století*, ed. M. BLÁHOVÁ, I. HLAVÁČEK, Prague, 1998, p. 69-75; for the latter cf. still *Royal and other historical letters illustrative of the reign of Henry III* (Royal Society, 27), 2 vols., ed. W. W. SHIRLEY, London, 1862, 1866, here vol. 2, p. 252, no. 213; *Codex diplomaticus et epistularis regni Bohemiae*, vol. III, ed. G. FRIEDRICH et al., Prague, 1942, 1962, 2000, here III/1, p. 257s., no. 266 (source collection cited henceforth as CDB).

[8] *CLE*, p. 104. On this topic: A. KUZNETSOVA, "Signs of Conversion in *Vitae sanctorum*", in *Christianizing peoples and converting individuals*, ed. G. ARMSTRONG, I. WOOD, Turnhout, 2000, p. 125-132.

[9] On his rulership: Vr. VANÍČEK *Velké dějiny zemí Koruny české II: 1197-1250*, Prague-Litomyšl, 2000, p. 318-361.

[10] See J. HÖRMANN-THURN UND TAXIS, "Frauenklöster im mittelalterlichen Tirol und Trentino – Ein Überblick", in *Frauenklöster im Alpenraum*, ed. Br. MAZOHL, E. FORSTER, Innsbruck, 2012, p. 15-44, here 32s.; S. TOVALIERI, "Damianite e Clarisse in Trentino e in Alto Adige nel XIII e XIV secolo", *Collectanea Franciscana*, 74 (2004), p. 557-580, here p. 568; J. HÁJÍČEK, "O původu řeholních sester sv. Anežky České, klarisek Benigny a Petrušky", *Heraldika a genealogie*, 3-4 (2003), p. 177-184.

[11] Chr.-Fr. FELSKAU, "*Imitatio* und institutionalisierte Armenfürsorge: Das 'Modell Elisabeth' und die *mulieres religiosae* in Ostmitteleuropa (c. 1200-1280)", in *Elisabeth und die neue Frömmigkeit in Europa*, ed. Chr. BERTELSMEIER-KIERST, Frankfurt a.M., 2008, p. 52-76.

[12] T. KALINA, "Příspěvek k založení Starého Města a k vývoji jeho areálu ve 13. století", *Historická geografie*, 8 (1972), p. 73-104; P. STÁTNÍKOVÁ et al., *Dějiny Prahy I. Od nejstarších dob do sloučení pražských měst (1784)*, Prague/Litomyšl, 1997, here p. 55-58; Chr.-Fr. FELSKAU, *Agnes von Böhmen, op. cit.*, p. 398-408.

St James (since 1232) as abbess.[13] Moved by the *vita apostolica* which Clare of Assisi sought to implement for her community at San Damiano, the Bohemian princess fought, as documented by a series of papal letters, for the right to live without possession and to obtain an individual rule, a rule which must have been very close to what Francis' spiritual companion received on her death bed in August 1253 for her own community (*Regula Clarae*).[14] As an outcome of Agnes' insistence on a life *sine proprio*,[15] her hospital was detached in the course of the years 1237-1239 and substituted by a male Franciscan friary, creating thus the Order's first double cloister.[16] While the hospitalitarian community was turned into an *ordo canonicus* and in the 1250s approbated as the unique religious order of Bohemian origin, the Crosiers with the Red

---

[13] *Sincerum animi carissima*. CDB III/1, p. 87, no. 80; *CLE*, p. 106. On the already existing local Franciscans: L. J. SKRDA, *Kostel svatého Jakuba v Praze*, Prague, 1902. The *Annalium Pragensium* I (or *Cosmas Chronicle*), in ed. R. KÖPKE, W. WATTENBACH, Hannover, 1851 (*Monumenta Germaniae Historica*, Scriptores, 9), p. 169-181, here p. 171, are recounting for the year 1232: *fratres minores receperunt domum Pragae*.

[14] Papal letters to Agnes addressing aspects of regulation: (a) Gregory IX: CDB III/1, p. 85-87, no. 79 (30.8.1234), p. 135s., no. 110 (18.5.1234, mentioning Agnes' first *supplicatio*, promise to keep hospital and monastery united), p. 144-147, no. 118 (25.7.1235, confirmation of possessions, liturgical rules), p. 189, no. 155 (4.4.1237, regulations on liturgy and mess), p. 189s., no. 156 (dispens on fasting, strong disclosure), p. 193-195, no. 159 (14.4.1237, confirmation of possessions, liturgical regulations), p. 195-198, no. 160 (14.4.1237, detachment of the hospital), p. 227s., no. 182 (15.4.1238, acceptance of Agnes' resignation of the hospital, concession of the right to refuse property), p. 233, no. 187 (5.5.1238, abatement of the rule's austerity due to climatic conditions), p. 235-237, no. 189 (9.5.1238, acceptance of Agnes' resignation on the abbacy), p. 237-239, no. 190 (11.5.1238, refutation of Agnes' proposal for a rule, obligation to follow the Ugolinian Rule), CDB III/2, p. 260s., no. 203 (18.12.1238, *Ex parte carissime*, regulations on fasting according to the Ugolinian Rule); (b) Innocent IV: CDB V/1, p. 107s., no. 29 (easements on food and garments due to climatic reasons), p. 108-110, no. 30 (13.11.1243, explanations on the implimentation of the Benedictine Rule after Agnes' request for an own rule), p. 110s., no. 31 (25.11.1243, reconfirmation of the right to live without possession). The approved rule of St Clare: *Escritos de Santa Clara y documentos complementarios* (Biblioteca de autores cristianos 314), ed. I. OMAECHEVARRIA, Madrid, 1982, p. 266-289. L. KNOX, *Creating Clare of Assisi. Female Franciscan Identities in Later Medieval Italy*, Leiden-Boston, 2008; J. MUELLER, *The privilege of Poverty: Clare of Assisi, Agnes of Prague and the struggle for a Franciscan rule for women*, Pennsylvania, 2006; Ch. CREMASCHI, *Donne emerse dell'ombra. L'erdità di Chiara d'Assisi: il Duecento*, Assisi, 2011; M. P. ALBERZONI, "Elisabeth von Thüringen, Klara von Assisi und Agnes von Böhmen. Das franziskanische Modell der Nachfolge Christi diesseits und jenseits der Alpen", in *Elisabeth von Thüringen – eine europäische Heilige*, ed. D. BLUME, M. WERNER, Petersberg, 2007, p. 47-56.

[15] E. SCHLOTHEUBER, "Klara von Assisi und Agnes von Prag. Die Besitzlosigkeit als besondere Herausforderung für Frauengemeinschaften", in *Svatá Anežka Česká a velké ženy její doby. Die heilige Agnes von Böhmen und die großen Frauengestalten ihrer Zeit*, ed. M. ŠMID, Fr. ZÁRUBA, Prague, 2013, p. 56-73.

[16] On double cloisters of the Franciscans: St. HAARLÄNDER, "Doppelklöster und ihre Forschungsgeschichte", in *Fromme Frauen – unbequeme Frauen: weibliches Religiosentum im Mittelalter*, ed. E. KLUETING, Hildesheim 2006, p. 27-44.

Star,[17] Agnes received on 15 April 1238, shortly after her retirement from the office of abbess and the renouncement of every power related to her hospital, the privilege to reject property (*Pia credulitate tenentes*).[18] With modifications though, she had to observe the Benedictine rule imposed by Hugolino of Ostia, the later Pope Gregory IX, on this *religio nova* as on numerous other similar orientated female institutions.[19]

That Agnes' decease, according to Bohemian contemporary chronicles, received only marginal attention outside the monastic and urban walls and, moreover, beyond the Přemyslid realm,[20] is evidently connected with the political and economic crisis the core lands of the Bohemian crown were facing at that time. After the death of her nephew and supporter, king Ottokar II (1253-1278), who had embellished the monastic site with the construction of the splendid Redeemer's chapel, but succumbed to the forces of Rudolph of Habsburg (1218-1291) on the battle of the Marchfeld in 1278, an era of civil war and famines had dawned in Bohemia, from which the country only gradually

---

[17] Chr.-Fr. FELSKAU, "Das Franziskushospital in Prag und das Matthiasstift in Breslau. Über den schwierigen Beginn einer Beziehungsbalance beim Aufbau eines ostmitteleuropäischen Hospitalordens, der Kreuzbrüder mit dem roten Stern", in *Wanderungen und Kulturaustausch im östlichen Mitteleuropa. Forschungen zum ausgehenden Mittelalter und zur jüngeren Neuzeit*, ed. H.-W. RAUTENBERG, Munich, 2006, p. 59-92; *Id.*, "Agnes' gestiftete *caritas*: Von der Spitalbruderschaft Sankt Franziskus in Prag zu den Kreuzbrüdern mit dem roten Stern in Böhmen, Mähren und Schlesien, mit Seitenblick auf europäische Hospitalordensgründungen", in *Svatá Anežka Česká a velké ženy její doby, op. cit.*, p. 100-124. Map of the Order's thirteenth-century possessions in A. WOJTYŁA, *Idea ordo militaris w sztuce barokowej krzyżowców czerwoną gwiazdą*, Wrocław, 2012, p. 37. A general history still provides W. LORENZ, *Die Kreuzherren mit dem roten Stern*, Königstein, 1964.

[18] CDB III/1, no. 182, p. 227s. Cf. the *privilegium paupertatis* to Clare of Assisi with the incipit *Sicut manifestum est* (17.9.1228) in *Escritos de Santa Clara*, p. 232: *Nella tua tenda per sempre (sl 61,5). Storia delle Clarisse. Un'avventura di ottocento anni*, ed. R. BARTOLINI, Assisi, 2005, table II, p. 137-139, counting four monasteries till 1253, and in total twelve till 1350 which received this privilege. B. ROEST, *Order and Disorder, op. cit.*, p. 33 and 53.

[19] *Gregorio IX e gli ordini mendicanti. Atti del XXXVIII convegno internazionale della Società Internazionale di Studi Francescani e del Centro Interuniversitario di Studi Francescani*, Spoleto, 2011; G. P. FREEMAN, *Clarissen in de dertiende eeuw, drie studies. Drei Studien zur Geschichte des Klarissenordens im 13. Jahrhundert*, Utrecht, 1997. Out of the vast literature discussing the institutionalizing period of the Poor Clares: L. KNOX, "Audacious Nuns: Institutionalizing the Franciscan Order of Saint Clare", *Church History*, 69 (2000), p. 41-62; M. P. ALBERZONI, *La nascita di un'istituzione. L'Ordine di S. Damiano nel XIII secolo*, Milano, 1996.

[20] *Vypravování o zlých letech po smrti krále Přemysla Otakara II.*, in FRB II, p. 335-367, here p. 340. N. KERSKEN, "Das přemyslidische Böhmen in der zeitgenössischen Historiographie des Reiches", in *Böhmen und seine Nachbarn in der Přemyslidenzeit*, ed. I. HLAVÁČEK, A. PATSCHOVSKY, Ostfildern, 2011, p. 385-436, here p. 428, lists Heinrich von Heimburg as the only non-Bohemian contemporary historiographer who mentions Agnes' death.

recovered in the second half of the 1280s.[21] Maybe due to this situation of political instability, the body of the Princess was laid fully two weeks in the choir of the St Francis Church before the Minister General of the Order, Bonagratia Tielci of St John in Persiceto (1279-1283/84), could commit her to burial.[22]

Medieval Canonisation Attempts and the Production of Hagiographic Texts

The first request for canonization is recounted by the Bohemian Cistercian monk Peter of Zittau/Petr Žitavský (1275-1339) in his *Chronicon Aulae regiae*, composed soon after 1316.[23] Peter is reporting about an assembly convoked by the last Přemyslid queen Elizabeth/Eliška Přemyslovna (1292-1330), the wife of John of Luxembourg, on Saint Martin's day (11 November) 1328, in the Bohemian residential place.[24] The chronicler, but also the petitioners do not miss to refer explicitly to the miserable conditions which prevented the proper recognition of the saintly life of princess Agnes in previous times.[25] Peter then informs us that at this meeting some letters, composed by high clergymen and citizens, were put together with a petition from the queen and sent to Pope John XXII asking for the canonization of Elizabeth's great-great aunt.[26] Among the promoting councillors were those of Prague's Old Town (Nicholas), of Kutná Hora/Kuttenberg (Hermann Vlkoš) and two *magistri*

---

[21] M. BLÁHOVÁ, "Hladomor v Čechách roku 1282 a jeho reflexe v české středověké historiografii", in *Ponížení a odstrčení: Města versus katastrofy: sborník příspěvků z 8. vědeckého zasedání Archivu hlavniho města Prahy* (Documenta Pragensia), ed. J. PEŠEK, Prague, 1998, p. 161-170.

[22] The bishop of Prague, Tobias of Bechyně (1278-1296), as well as several abbots of neighboring monasteries were indisposed to take over this duty.

[23] K. CHARVÁTOVA, "Cistercian monks and Bohemian kings in the times of Peter of Zittau", in *Chronicon Aulae regiae. Die Königsaaler Chronik. Eine Bestandsaufnahme*, ed. St. ALBRECHT, Frankfurt a. M., 2013, p. 63-74.

[24] The chronicle in: *Fontes rerum Bohemicarum*, Tomus I-V, ed. K. J. EMLER, J. ERBEN, Prague, 1874, 1882, 1884, 1893, here vol. IV, p. 3-337 (collection henceforth cited as FRB; the chronicle *ChAR*). Cf. P. KUBÍN, "Anežka a Eliška Přemyslovny. Pokus o svatořečení v královské rodině", in *Ve znamení zení Koruny české. Sborník k šedesátkým narozeninám profesorky Lenky Bobkové*, ed. L. HRABOVÁ, Prague, 2006, p. 186-197. On the author: J. SPĚVÁČEK, "Petr Žitavský a počátky lucemburské dynastie v českých zemích", *Mediaevalia historica Bohemica*, 3 (1993), p. 177-197.

[25] *ChAR*, p. 291: *Que in quidem lucerna pro dominorum varietate, qui in regno Bohemie post felicis memorie domini Wenceziai, Boemie et Polonie regis, obitum in ipso regno Boemie successerunt, sic occulta fuit sub modio, quod virginis ipsius vita et sanctitatis ad apostolice sedis et vestram non pervenit. Sed nunc in regno ipso stabilitate divina miseracione concessa illustris domine etc.*

[26] Ibid.: *...ibique devocionem et intentionem suam de canonizacione iam dicte virginis exposuit; litteras quoque intercessorias ad dominum Johannem papam pro eodem negocio tam prelatorum quam civium obtinuit, quas cum suis propriis epistolis domino apostolico destinavit.*

iudicorum, both from royal towns in the sphere of influence of the Cistercian monastery of Sedletz/Sedlec, namely Gotzlin from Kolin (35 km east of Prague) and Hanzlin from Tschaslau/Čáslav near Klattau.[27] The background of Elizabeth's initiative sheds further light on some side ambitions in play, since she had lived after the failed rebellion against her husband, the first "foreign" king John the Blind (1296-1348) from the Luxembourg dynasty, mostly in her possessed Leibgedingestadt Mělník evidently due to her backing of the insurgents, and returned to Prague only in 1325. One year before this gathering, she had sent several letters to the Apostolic See in which she sought papal support for awarding prebends and positions to relatives and high Prague citizens.[28] Even more interestingly, at the time of this convention the Bohemian bishop John of Dražice (1301-1343) stayed at the Papal court due to suspected heresy, an accusation partially promoted by the Friars Minor of Prague.[29]

The evidence for the second request for canonization is preserved, together with most parts of the legend *CLE*, in a *folio* bundle of the Franciscan friary of Šibenik on the Dalmatian coast.[30] This plea consists of three petitions (*supplicae*) written firstly by the Bohemian-Polish provincial minister Nicholas (1333-1338),[31] secondly by an anonymous abbess of the Poor Clares,[32] and thirdly by an unnamed lay person probably from Prague. It is noteworthy

---

[27] M. MUSÍLEK, "Zajetí českého panstva patriciátem v sedleckém klášteře a v Praze roku 1309. Příspěvek k vývoji pražského a kutnohorského patriciátu na přelomu 13. a 14. století", in *Sedlec. Historie, architektura a umělecká tvorba sedleckého kláštera*, ed. R. LOMIČKOVÁ, Prague, 2009, p. 139-164.

[28] RBM III, p. 538-541, no. 1372-1375; *Jean XXII (1316-1334). Lettres communes analysées d'après les registres inédits d'Avignon et du Vatican*, 16 vols., ed. G. MOLLAT et al., Paris, 1904-1947, here t. IV, no. 30053-30055, 30058, 30060, 30068; cf. Zd. HLEDÍKOVÁ, "Češi u římské kurie za prvních tří avignonských papežů", *Český časopis historický*, 102 (2004), p. 249-271, here esp. p. 267-269.

[29] Chr.-Fr. FELSKAU, *Agnes von Böhmen, op. cit.*, p. 611-619.

[30] Šibenik, Library of the Friars Minor in Šibenik, bundle 36; cited henceforth according to the current edition: P. KUBÍN, "Počátky anežské hagiografie. K otázce stáří a autorství Candor lucis eterne a tzv. šibenických žádostí o Anežčinu kanonizaci", in *Svatá Anežka Česká a velké ženy její doby, op. cit.*, p. 80-99. H. SOUKUPOVÁ, *Svatá Anežka, op. cit.*, p. 216s., recently suggested to identify the provincial minister with another provincial minister Nicholas, thus inverting the chronology of canonisation requests; arguing against: P. KUBÍN, "The Earliest Hagiography of St Agnes of Bohemia († 1282)", *Hagiographica*, 22 (2015), p. 265-290, here p. 280-289.

[31] W. DERSCH, "Die Provinzialminister der Böhmisch-polnischen Provinz", *Franziskanische Studien*, 1 (1914), p. 193-203, here p. 196. The precise period of his ministry is not determined beyond all doubt. P. KUBÍN, *Počátky anežské hagiografie*, p. 85s.; Nicholas' mentioning in RBM IV, p. 37-39, no. 109 (29.11.1334). The other Bohemian Provincial Nicholas is mentioned in two charters from 1275 and 1279. CDB V/2, p. 450, no. 777; CDB V/3, p. 396s, no. 1627.

[32] J. K. VYSKOČIL, *Legenda, op. cit.*, p. 300, identifies the author as the second subsequent abbess of the monastery, Agnes of Beřkovic, who was a beneficiary of Agnes' posthumous miracle (M23). She was probably a close relative of Martin of Beřkovic and Jaroš of Beřkovic. Zd. KALISTA, *Legenda o blahoslavené Anežce České*, Prague, 1941, p. 119.

that this initiative, triggered by the two Franciscan orders and a related party in 1338 or a bit earlier, took place at a time in which the theoretic fundament of the Order, the principle of absolute poverty, had faced strong persecution and in which Pope Benedict XII, after a a short period of mutual examination, was accused by adherents of the dismissed Minister General Michael of Cesena (*c.* 1270-1342) of continuing the harsh politics of his predecessor John XXII.[33]

The third and final of traceable initiative for Agnes' canonization before the Hussite Reformation which saw the expulsion of the sisters (refuge site: Jungfernteinitz/Panenský Týnec, founded around 1278)[34] was carried out by the John the Blind's son, the Roman and Bohemian king Charles IV (1316-1378), probably around 1353, the year of his visit to Agnes' double cloister, or sometime in 1355, the year of his imperial coronation in Rome.[35] His court historian, the Franciscan theologian, bishop and diplomat Giovanni Marignolli (John of Marignolla) (1290-*c.* 1357) gives the first hint to this attempt in his chronicle written in the late 1350s.[36] In the chapter *ingressus in cronicam Boemie*, he mentions in a closer context of Charles' visit to the Clarissan monastery in Prague where a miraculous handing over of Saint Nicholas' arm relic happened, Agnes' saintly life and her miracles of which one rescued the life of the future king and *consanguineus*; it finishes with the note that Charles made the *sacro collegio* aware of her merits.[37]

---

[33] Possible connections between the legend's tone and the parallel disputes on poverty discusses: Chr.-Fr. FELSKAU, "*Vita religiosa* und *paupertas* der heiligen Agnes von Prag. Zu Bezügen und Besonderheiten in Leben und Legende einer späten Heiligen", *Collectanea Franciscana*, 70 (2000), p. 413-484.
[34] On the Hussite and post-Hussite fate of the monastery: H. SOUKUPOVÁ, *Anežský klášter*, *op. cit.*, p. 254-365. On the Poor Clares of Panenský Týnec, founded by the regional noble family of the Žerotin/Zerotyn and established by sisters from Prague still: N. N., "Týnec Panenský – Panenský klášter klarisek", *Soupis památek* (1897), p. 85-89. The family was also beneficiary of a miracle of Agnes (MT1). The abbreviations for the miracles adopted here are based on the classification scheme of Chr.-Fr. FELSKAU, *Agnes von Böhmen, op. cit.*, p. 1209-1235, annex VII.2.
[35] See E. WIDDER, *Itinerar und Politik. Studien zur Reisegesellschaft Karls IV. südlich der Alpen*, Wien, 1993, esp. p. 25-52.
[36] In: FRB III, p. 487-606; mention of the miraculous reception of St Nicholas' arm relic (Charles' finger began to blee suddenly), *ibid.*, p. 521. On the chronicle: K. ENGSTOVÁ, "Marignolova kronika jako obraz představ o moci a postavení českého krále", *Mediaevalia historica Bohemica*, 6 (1999), p. 77-94. The king's religiosity discusses M. BAUCH, "Öffentliche Frömmigkeit und Demut des Herrschers als Form politischer Kommunikation. Karl IV. und seine Italienaufenthalte als Beispiel", *Quellen und Forschungen aus italienischen Archiven und Bibliotheken*, 87 (2007), p. 109-138. Agnes had received several precious relics by Pope Innocent IV; cf. *Regesta Pontificum Romanorum inde ab Anno post Christus Natum MCXCVIII ab Anno MCCCIV*, t. I-II, ed. A. POTTHAST *et al.*, Berlin, 1874, repr. Graz, 1957, here II, no. 1163/14087. See briefly Vl. J. KOUDELKA, "Tři dopisy bl. Anezce", *Nový Život*, 36 (1984), p. 88-90.
[37] FRB III, p. 521: *Excitans non solum Germaniam, Poloniam, Vngeriam et Boemiam, verum eciam Romanam ecclesiam ad dulcia cionnubia, agni amplexanda, inter quas precipua neptis*

According to later traditions, initially from the pen of the remarkably well informed Franciscan chronicler Bartholomew of Pisa († 1401) and afterwards taken over by other Bohemian sources, Emperor Charles passed this endeavor for canonization to his son, king Wenceslav IV (1361-1419) who, as one may assert, never found the conditions for pushing forward this prestigious step.[38]

With regard to the content and the direction of these three initiatives, we grasp deeper insight only of the first royal and the Orders' one. Astonishingly, we find relatively poor information on Agnes' merits within the queen's supplica (*PetEl*). Apart from mentioning the miracles during and after her lifetime, basically only the number of years she stayed in the Poor Clares' monastery of Prague are noted, omitting every foundation activity and skipping any reference to her religious goals.[39] Even remarks on her pre-conversional life are completely lacking. The letter closes with the plea to ascribe this virgin to the *cathalogo sanctorum*.[40] In contrast, the petitions on the Orders'

Agnes, illustris regis Ottakari filia, spreto imperiali seu regali connubio ac se ipsa, facta virginis perfectissima ymiatrix Virginis filio perfectissima caritate coniuncta post sancte Clare virginis religionem ymitatricis paranymphi seraphici viri Francisci Minorum et predicte religionis fundatoris per vite labilis gloriosum decursum ipsi coniuncta in celis, quem in terris tota devocione dilexit, pertis miraculis choruscare non cessat, suis profigiis et beneficiis excitans et inducens gloriosissimum consangwineum suum Karolum Quartum, Romanorum imperatorem illustrissimum semper Augustum, ut menor beneficiorum forte in suo corpore ostensorum clamare non cesset, donec excitet piis clamoribus apostolicum dormientem cum sacro collegio, ut dignetur in terris reddere clariorem et celebrem, quam Christus gloriosam fecisse in celis tot signis ostendit ecclesie militanti. On the concept of female royal sanctity, 'Geblütsheiligkeit' (*beata stirps*): G. KLANICZAY, "Pouvoir et idéologie dans l'hagiographie des saintes reines et princesses", in *Hagiographie, idéologie et politique au Moyen Âge en Occident*, Turnhout, 2012, p. 423-446.
[38] Bartholomew's report on Agnes' life entered the *Acta Sanctorum* under the title *Compendium Pisanum*; cf. *Acta Sanctorum*, Mart. I, Antwerp, 1668, p. 502-532, here 508s. (cited henceforth *ComPi*); it was part of his extensive work on the Franciscan Orders, their founding figures and saints: *De conformitate vitae S. Francisci*, ed. in *Analecta Franciscana*, 4 (1906), p. 1-632 and 5 (1912), p. 1-504; C. ERICKSON, "Bartholomew of Pisa, Francis exalted: 'De conformitate'", *Mediaeval Studies*, 34 (1972), p. 253-274. About the content of his description, see Chr.-Fr. FELSKAU, *Agnes von Böhmen, op. cit.*, p. 831-833.
[39] *ChAR*, p. 292: *Verum quia divine largitatis immensitas munificencie sue mensuram non ponit, nec collata semel libertas fastidium ei prestat, illis quos eidem regno patres contulit et patronos dedit adhuc et virginem innocencie agnam et nominis appellacione Agnetem, que felicis memorie domini Przemisl sive Othakari, Boemie quondam regis, filia ex utroque parente stirpe regali progenita, sic iuventutis sue florem virtutum decore vestitit, quod ab ineuntis etatis sue primordiis ad patriam visa fuit festinare celestem. In ordine tandem sancte Clare conversacione degendo sanctissima vite sue terminum sic explevit, quod hoc, quod feliciter inchoaverat, felicius consumavit. Cui pro perfeccione vite laudabilis tantam Dominus contulit graciam et virtutem, quod in vita et in morte et post mortem tanta miraculorum claritate refulsit, quod evidenter patuerunt et patent cottidie sue indicia sanctitatis* [expanded spacing Chr.-Fr. Felskau].
[40] *Ibid*. On the meaning of this term see: Th. WETZSTEIN, *Das Kanonisationsverfahren im europäischen Spätmittelalter*, Köln-Weimar-Vienna, 2004, here p. 359.

behalf a couple of years later already show an abundance of information albeit their distinct perceptive tone. The recipient of this series of letters is identified as the Apostolic See, but empty spaces where the office bearer should be inserted refer to an insecure situation, or eventually a prophylactic intention in the moment of their composition. The author of the first letter (*PetNic*) introduces himself as the minister of the "Bohemia Franciscan province" which only can be a strong allusion to a serious threat of a split between the Polish and the Bohemian part of the province's official unity.[41] What follows is a deep appraisal of Agnes' religious life, now stressing all three foundations of the princess (hospital, female plus male monastery), and by that applying the elaborated Franciscan concept of *plantula* which hagiographers have stressed at length to characterize the relationship between Saint Francis and Clare.[42] To underscore the eligibility of the request, *PetNic* moreover emphasizes that honorable testimonies for Agnes' miracles exist.[43] Even more informative and

---

[41] Photographic reproduction of the first letter and parts of the second one in: *Svatá Anežka Česká*, p. 59. On the struggles within the province: Zd. SMEJKAL, *K dějinám národnostích sporů u českých františkánů (1256-1517)*, Olomouc, 1939. An introduction on the history of the province offers J. KŁOCZOWSKI, *Klöster und Orden im mittelalterlichen Polen*, Osnabrück, 2012, p. 107-119, 254-265; H.-J. SCHMIDT, "Contested Frontiers: Mendicant Provinces Between Germany and Poland During the Late Middle Ages", in *Monasteries on the Borders of Medieval Europe*, ed. E. JAMROZIAK, K. STÖBER, Turnhout, 2013, p. 129-148, here p. 136-137.
[42] P. KUBIN, *Počátky anežské hagiografie, op. cit.*, p. 90s.: *Sanctissimo in Christo patri et domino ...* [name is blanked – Chr.-Fr. F.] *sacrosancte Romane ac universalis ecclesie digno pontifici frater Nicolaus ordinis fratrum minorum in provincia Bohemie humilis minister* [sic] *et servus cum fratribus eiusdem provincie universis orationes devotas et pedum oscula beatorum.* [...] *Inde mundi iam eciam occasu urgente Agnetem felicem uirginem sancte Clare in regno Bohemie, plantulam generosam utpote sancta* [sic] *et illustri Regni Bohemie et Vngarie stirpe progenita, tamquam solem in altissimis Dei orientem in ornamentum eiusdem sancte matris ecclesie lucmque credencium destinauit, que velut aromatum arcola delicata manu pigmentarii exculata celestis sanctique spiritus austro proflata productis ex se fructibus honoris et honestatis instar cynamonii et balsami aromatizans non solum in regno Bohemie memorato sed eciam in terris adiacentibus suauem difundit sue fragranciam sanctitatis. Nam manens in habitu seculari ora-tionibus, ieuniis ac elemosynis insistebat nec non monasteria pro fratribus minoribus et sororibus ordinis sancte Clare et pro infirmis hospitale solempne* [sic] *in civitate pragensi de suis sumptibus fieri procuravit, ut autem non solum sua sed eciam se ipsam offeret holocaustum Domino medulatum regalibus spretis honoribus et diviciis, omnibusque mundi oblectamentis ad ordinem sancte Clare convolavit, in quo quasi auri vas solidum ornata fuit omni perfestione virtutum.* The edition is hereafter cited as *PetNic*. On the concept: A. MARINI, *"Ancilla Christi, plantula sancti Francisci. Gli scritti di Santa Chiara e la Regola"*, in *Chiara di Assisi. Atti del XX Convegno Internazionale di Studi Francescani*, Assisi, 1993, p. 107-156.
[43] *PetNic*, p. 90s.: *Propter quod Deus, bonorum retributor cunctorum, eam non solum in vita, sed eciam in morte et post mortem virtute sue dextere multis miraculis decoravit, sicud in partibus nostris rerum evidenciam testis clamat* [expanded spacing Chr.-Fr. F.]. Here we encounter for the first time the threefold distinction of miracles (in life, at death, and posthumous). On their relevance for canonisation inquiries: Chr. KRÖTZL, *"Fama sanctitatis. Die*

revealing, however, is the content of the second, the abbess' letter (*PetSor*), when she states that a *descriptione vitae* was accomplished, not only for the sisters themselves but also for other religious and lay persons, amongst them the Holy See, illustrating the miraculous merits of Agnes, confirmed by a *proprio iuramento* of the witnesses.[44] Also the third and much shorter letter (*PetAn*) from the lay person emphasizes the imitations provoked by the *virgo gloriosa* and the miracles accomplished by her.[45]

The two initiatives for canonization illustrate a considerable increase of knowledge about Agnes and her deeds during probably less than a decade. The information on her life and afterlife at the end consists of all relevant foundation activities and even some news related to her pre-conversional period were added, ready to be sent to the unnamed Papal authority together with the Orders' petitions. The growth of knowledge about Agnes' *summa vitae* goes along with a change of perspective, from the secular-royal to the monastic-Franciscan view.[46] The only vague report of a similar initiative by the Luxembourg king Charles IV, though, does not make any reference to the production of written records. Considering the preceding endeavors, it seems plausible that the composition of relevant material for the canonization was already determined or even submitted at this stage.

Though profound studies on the inner- and contextual links between requests for canonisation and hagiographic material are lacking, such an approach turns out to be very revealing in the case of the Bohemian princess. In striking accordance to the two agencies of promotion, the royal and the Franciscan one, the earliest hagiographic production on Agnes comprises likewise two branches of texts, an outer-Franciscan and a Franciscan one. The first is

---

Akten der spätmittelalterlichen Kanonisationsprozesse als Quelle zu Kommunikation und Informationsvermittlung in der mittelalterlichen Gesellschaft", in *Procès de Canonisation au Moyen Âge. Aspects juridiques et religieux*, ed. G. KLANICZAY, Rome, 2004, p. 223-244.

[44] *PetNic*, p. 92s.: *Quantis quoque coruscaverit miraculorum prodigiis in vita, in morte et post mortem ex descriptione vite ipsius luculenter apparet, quam Sanctitate Vestre transmittimus per presentes* [expanded spacing Chr.-Fr. F.].

[45] *Ibid.*, p. 94: *Ut igitur precelse virgini memorate digna laudum munia sonoraque preconia a christifidelibus devotis mentibus impendantur, coram Vestram Bwatudine flexis poblitis humiliter et affectuose rogamus, quatenus eam sanctorum kathalogo annotare velitis* [...].

[46] Though one would expect that the Order was the first to promote the canonisation of one of its members, a sequence of hagiographic initiatives happened where the secular or royal initiative was preceding the monastic, Franciscan one. Such a pattern is not as unusual considering for instance the cases of the Franciscan patron king Louis IX of France or the Franciscan tertiary Margarete of Cortona, but moreover of the "terciary" princess Elizabeth of Hungary/Thuringia; the Franciscan hagiographies in these cases were rather "late comers".

represented by so called *Vita Prima*, the second is connected with the already introduced *Candor lucis eterne*.[47]

For centuries, the broader public knew only about the *Vita Prima*, published together with further hagiographic material from the Bollandist's collection *Acta Sanctorum* (1668, record for March): an embellished version of this life (*Vita Secunda*), the already mentioned description of Agnes' deeds by Bartholomew of Pisa (*Compendium a Pisano scriptum*), a Baroque short story written by Georg Barthold Pontanus of Breitenberg from Brüx/Most († 1616) from the late sixteenth century (*Compendium a Pontano scriptum*),[48] and finally Clare's four letters to Agnes (*EpCl.1-4*).[49] The entrance of this material was the result of the efforts of the two Bohemian Jesuits, John Tanner (1623-1694) and Georg Kruger (1608-1671).[50] While Kruger decribed the *Vita Secunda* correctly as a re-translation of a mingling of two later lost manuscripts, one in Czech (*Codex Velesvavinus*) and the other in Latin (*Codex Crumloviensis*), Tanner explained his submitted *Vita Prima* as being a transcript of an "old Latin manuscript" stored in Prague.[51] Although these manuscripts were lost, an early Czech version published in 1643 by the Jesuit Georg Ferus/

---

[47] The appropriate distinction between pre-canonizational and post-canonizational legends hitherto has not been substantiated by comparative studies. See recently the suggestion of Chr.-Fr. FELSKAU, *Agnes von Böhmen, op. cit.*, p. 711. For Clare of Assisi, it is just worth to point to the miracles recounted during the canonization process; cf. M. PATTENDEN, "The Canonisation of Clare of Assisi and Early Franciscan History", *Journal of Ecclesiastical History*, 59 (2008), p. 208-226, here p. 212-214. *Santa Chiara di Assisi. I primi documenti ufficiali: Lettera di annunzio della sua morte, processo e bolla di canonizzazione*, ed. G. BOCCALI, Assisi, 2002.

[48] This story is prevailingly based on the older chronicles of Wenzel Hajek of Lobotschan († 1533) and bishop John Dubravius (1542-1553). J. ROYT, "Bemerkungen zur Ikonographie und zum Kult der böhmischen Landespatrone im 17. und 18. Jahrhundert in Böhmen", in *Die Heiligen und ihr Kult im Mittelalter*, ed. E. DOLEŽALOVÁ et al., Prague, 2010, p. 243-274, here p. 246. The texts, partially submitted by the Bohemian Jesuits John Tanner (1623-1694) and George Kruger (1608-1671), are published in *Acta Sanctorum*, Mart. I, Antwerp, 1678, p. 502-532.

[49] The letters henceforth cited according to J. K. VYSKOČIL, *Legenda blahoslavené Anežky, op. cit*. On the general issue: K. CHEREWATUK, U. WIETHAUS, "Introduction: Women Writing Letters in the Middle Ages", in *Dear sister: medieval women and the epistolary genre*, ed. K. CHEREWATUK, U. WIETHAUS, Pennsylvania, 1993, p. 1-19.

[50] Introductionary: P. CEMUS, *Bohemia Jesuitica*, Prague, 2010; M. SVATOŠ, "Quellen und Formen des Patriotismus der Jesuiten der Böhmischen Provinz im XVII. und XVII. Jahrhundert", in *Lesestoffe und kulturelles Niveau des niederen Klerus: Jesuiten und die nationalen Kulturverhältnisse. Böhmen, Mähren und das Karpatenbecken im 17. und 18. Jahrhundert*, ed. I. MONOK, P. ÖTVÖS, Szeged, 2000, p. 92-100.

[51] *AS Martius I*, p. 504; Codicum horum MSS. quibus Crugerus usus est, alter appelatur Crumloviensis, alter Veleslavius. Cf. J. NECHUTOVÁ, *Die lateinische Literatur des Mittelalters in Böhmen*, Köln-Weimar-Vienna, 2007, p. 144-146. See Tanner's still unevaluated letter to Papenbroich (13.3.1670), preserved at the Bibliothèque des Bollandistes, Ms. Boll 66, fol. 47. Overall evaluation of the Bollandists' work: J. M. SAWILLA, *Antiquarianismus, Hagiographie und Historie im 17. Jahrhundert. Zum Werk der Bollandisten. Ein wissenschaftlicher Versuch*, Tübingen, 2009; on their philological work: M. FERRARI, "Mutare non lubuit: Die

Jiří Plachý (1585-1655) under the title *Žiwot Swaté Anežky* indicates that such a witness must have existed.[52] Later investigations brought to light that with regards first to the discovery of fragments of a rhymed legend written in the 1360s which derives from the Poor Clare's monastery of Eger/Cheb (founded around 1273),[53] second to the *Život blahoslavené panny Anežky* written by the chaplain Šimon in 1524 (a Czech translation of the *Compendium Pisanum*),[54] third the *Vita Beatae Agnetis* from the circle of the Crosiers with the Red Star, composed in the 1650s on the basis of the *Vita Prima*, but moreover with the first more widerly known Czech version of the *Candor lucis eterne*, namely Ferus' second publication *Život blahoslavené Anyžky panny, řadu svaté Kláry* from 1666,[55] the local hagiographic tradition must have been much broader at the end of the Middle Ages and the Early modern times than historians for long assumed.[56]

---

mediävistische Philologie der Jesuiten im frühen 17. Jahrhundert", *Filologia mediolatina*, 8 (2001), p. 225-250.

[52] Prague, Narodní knihovna v Praze (library henceforth cited as NKP), sign. 54 H 6489; J. K. VYSKOČIL, *Legenda blahoslavené Anežky*, passim, and V. BOK, "Einige Beobachtungen zur lateinischen Legende über Agnes von Prag und zu ihren mittelalterlichen deutschen und tschechischen Übertragungen", in *Selecta Bohemico-Germanica, Tschechisch-deutsche Beziehungen im Bereich der Sprache und Kultur*, ed. E. EICHLER, Münster-Hamburg-London, 2003, p. 163-178, did not come across this source.

[53] Cheb, Státní okresní archiv Cheb (henceforth cited: SOACh), svazek 469; V. BITNAR, "Neznámá hymna o blah. Anežce České", *Déšť růží*, 9/1 (1937) p. 17-22, 9/2 (1937) p. 47-52, 9/3 (1937) p. 82-85, 9/4 (1937), p. 112-118. Edition: M. MLADĚJOVSKÁ, *Legenda o blahoslavené Anežcé Chebské zlomky*, Prague, 1948; BAUMANN, "Die Egerer Fragmente der alttschechischen Agneslegende", *Bohemia*, 19 (1978), p. 321-330. This legend which must have consisted of 1500-2000 verses presents Agnes in its surviving parts as a mystic saint communing with the heavenly Father. The fragmentary manuscript was part of the rich liturgical library the Cheb monastery of the Poor Clares must have possessed. Several liturgical books, amongst them a very rare sequence on St Clare, *Ave preclara virgo Clara*, survived. L. LEHMANN, "Eine Sequenz aus Eger [3 Sequ]", in *Die heilige Klara in Kult und Liturgie*, ed. L. LEHMANN, J. SCHNEIDER, Norderstedt, 2012, p. 125-129. On the monastery, attributed to the Poor Clares in 1287: A. RÖTTGER, P. GROSS, *Klarissen. Geschichte und Gegenwart einer Ordensgemeinschaft*, Werl, 1994, p. 45; E. WAUER, *Entstehung und Ausbreitung des Klarissenordens, besonders in dendeutschen Minoritenprovinzen*, Leipzig, 1906, here p. 140s.; Id., *Die Anfänge des Klarissenordens in den slawischen Ländern*, Leipzig, 1903.

[54] The text is incorporated into a collection of Franciscan hagiographies, see: Prague, NKP, sign. XVII F 7. On this source: J. K. VYSKOČIL, *Legenda blahoslavené Anežky, op. cit.*, p. 46-52.

[55] Prague, NKP, Sign. 54 H 2043: *Žiwot blahoslavené Anyž ky Panny Ržadu Swaté Kláry, Dcery Krále Přemysla Ottakara, Sestry Wáclawa Krále Českého. Od starožitného Spysowatelé Česky sepsaný a nynj w těmž starodáwnjm Českém Gazyku pro wětssý Wjru wydaný.* Wytisstěný w Praze v Vrbana Goliáše Léta Páně, 1666.

[56] Vl. KYBAL, *Svatá Anežky Česká*, Prague, 2001, analysed extensively the relations between the Medieval and the Baroque sources; his book was published postum decades after the completion of Kybal's work in 1955; see the preface.

The second medieval hagiographic branch, the tradition of *Candor lucis eterne*, came to our knowledge with the publication of a Latin manuscript of the Bamberg library examined by the British Franciscan researcher Walter Warren Seton (1882-1927) in 1915.[57] Seton was also the first to discover parts of an hitherto unknown broader reception of Agnes in the era of the Order's reform, editing out of a set of similar manuscripts a fifteenth century Middle-High-German translation of the legend from the same library (*Ba2*) in his book.[58] He did not come across the discovery of another Latin version stored in a Milanese library of St Ambrose, nor could he foresee the Šibenik findings with the mentioned petitions. Nearly parallel to the notice on the bundle in the Dalmatian friary, the Moravian Franciscan Observant Jan Kapistran Vyskočil (1886-1956) delved deeper into the textual tradition of Agnes' early hagiography examining and editing a hitherto neglected Latin manuscript from a codex of mixed liturgical texts stored in the Metropolitan chapter library in Milan (*Ambrosiana*), the oldest preserved witness of *CLE*.[59] This had already been discovered at the turn of the century by Achille Ratti, the later Pope Pius XI.

The distinctions between the two main branches, the legend and the *Vita*, were analysed by the exiled Czechoslovak cardinal Josef Beran († 1969), but his book published in 1974 received, mostly due to political reasons, only scant attention.[60] Beran's examination, however, provides key insights into

---

[57] Bamberg, Staatsbibliothek (library henceforth: BSB), Msc. hist. 146 E VII 19: fol. 1v-138v: M.-H. Germ. version of *SCV*; fol. 139r-157v: M.-H. Germ. version of *EpCl.1-4*; fol. 157v-158v: M.-H. Germ. version of *BenCl-A*; fol. 158v-217r: Latin (!) version of *CLE*. Fr. LEITSCHUH, *Katalog der Handschriften der Königlichen Bibliothek zu Bamberg*, 1. Bd., 2. Abt., Bamberg, 1895, p. 241-243. W. SETON, *Some New Sources, op. cit.*, p. 17s.; J. KIST, *Das Klarissenkloster in Nürnberg bis zum Beginn des 16. Jahrhunderts*, Nürnberg, 1929, here p. 120; early dating from: H. WEILER, *St.-Clara Vita. Textkritische Edition und Wortschatz-Untersuchung*, unpubl. dissertation, Innsbruck, 1972, p. 30.

[58] Bamberg, BSB, Msc. hist. 147 E VII 54; fol. 3v-162v: M.-H. G. version of *LegMai* (Bonaventure's legend of Francis); fol. 162v-210v: M.-H. G version of *CLE*; Fr. LEITSCHUH, *Katalog der Handschriften*, p. 243-245. Attribution to Nuremberg: E. SCHRAUT, *Stifterinnen und Künstlerinnen im mittelalterlichen Nürnberg (Ausstellungskatalog)*, Nürnberg, 1987, p. 35; J. KIST, *Das Klarissenkloster in Nürnberg*, p. 120, 129, identifies the scribe as Margareta Wisentauer, abbess of the monastery in the years 1395-1397 and 1401-1403.

[59] Milan, Archivio e Biblioteca Capitolare della Basilica di S. Ambrogio (Bibl. Ambrosiana), M-10. For the Šiberck legend, see above. A. RATTI, "Storia e agiografia. Quarantadue lettere originali di Pio II relative alla guerra per la successione al reame di Napoli. Un codice pragense a Milano con testo inedito della vita di S. Agnese di Praga", *Rendiconti. Reale istituto lombardo di scienze e lettere*, serie II 29 (1896), p. 392-396, here p. 394. Short description: *Svatá Anežka Česká, op. cit.*, p. 178s. See also: J. KALIVODA, „Rari nantes in gurgite vasto. Anežská hagiografie v víru staletí", in *Církev, žena a společnost ve středověku*, p. 153-171; *Id.*, "Rukopisná tradice anežské legendy Candor lucis aeternae", *Listy filosofické*, 127 (2004), p. 19-36; C. ALZATI, *Ambrosiana Ecclesia. Studi su la chiesa Milanese e l'ecumene cristiana fra tarda antichità e medioevo*, Milano, 1993, here p. 298.

[60] Cf. above, n. 3.

our knowledge on the production of the early hagiographic material, while it challenges Vyskočil's hitherto undisputed verdict that the *Vita Prima* tradition came later than the legend.[61]

Reading the *Vita Prima* carefully, we encounter a hagiographer who does not write from the perspective of a friar; clearly he wasn't a member of the Franciscan Order.[62] The first of the three chapters of the text extensively deals with the royal ancestry of Agnes, starting with the appraisal of her parents and pinpointing the relationship to St Elizabeth. When the author recounts Agnes' saintly and royal kindred and decisive moments of her secular life, he includes a lengthy description of the dynastic plans and her role within the Přemyslids' and imperial politics.[63] More significantly, during the description of her monastic life in the second chapter opening with her conversion, the author uses a register apparently distant from the one of an Order's representative; this chapter emphasizes the solemn ceremony of her entrance into the cloister followed by a rather brief account of thirteen miracles *in vita*. When the hagiographer describes Agnes' foundation initiatives, he knows only of the hospital *ad imitationem S. Elisabethae*, here labelled as *nosocomium*, and the Poor Clare's monastery, while he ignores completely the erection of a Franciscan friary.[64] The third chaper entails a decription of Agnes' decease followed by the report of miracles occurring during the disposal of her corpse and after the funeral, in total twenty three. It ends nearly abruptly with a short intercession. Concerning the authorship of this outer-Mendicant but clerical hagiography, researchers' suggestion to identify him with Ulrich of Paběnic († 1334), the general vicar of the Prague bishop and master of the Crosiers with the Red Star, is with regards to content and chronology coherent, but not proven.[65]

---

[61] BERAN, *Blahoslavená Anežka, op. cit.*, p. 251, 301. Instead: J. POLC, *Agnes von Böhmen, op. cit.*, p. 170.

[62] According to Cr. ANDENNA, "Heiligenviten als stabilsierende Gedächtnisspeicher in Zeiten religiösen Wandels", in *Literarische und religiöse Kommunikation in Mittelalter und Früher Neuzeit. DFG-Symopsion 2006*, ed. P. STROHMEIER, Berlin-New York, 2009, p. 526-573, here p. 535, the external-institutional perspective defines the goal of the writer to preserve a cultural memory.

[63] *Vita Prima*, p. 509s and (more extensively) *Vita Secunda*, p. 513-517.

[64] *Vita Prima*, p. 510: *Iam deballata aliquot conflictionibus carne Agnetis, protinus sic mundo gravis incubuit. Accersitis quippe discalceatis hominibus, ad normam Divi Francisci viventibus, didicit ab iis fastigium melioris vitae, quam B. Clara soror eiusdem Sancti studiose lectabatur, in egestate volunarie suscepta, et corporis voluptatum contemptione, iudiciique sui alterius placitis subiectione constare. Quamobrem nihil morata preciosum illium muliebrem mundum inter pauperes distrahit; nosocomium ad imitationem S. Elisabethae cognatae sue, perpetibus redditibus fruens, sub nomine D. Francisci prope Pontem constituit;* [...] *virginibus quoque D. Clarae, se per despicientiam rerum omnium confirmare volentibus, peramplum aedeficium sub Servatoris nomine, omni templi ornatu exaggeratum, concinnavit.*

[65] J. ŠUSTA, *České dějiny II, část 1. Soumrak Přemyslovců a jejich dědictví*, Prague, 1935, p. 512; J. BERAN, *Blahoslavená Anežka, op. cit.*, p. 311-313; Chr.-Fr. FELSKAU, *Agnes von Böhmen,*

On the other hand, *CLE* comprises, apart from the recount of the failed wordly dynastic plans and the entrance ceremony, a much more profound description of the conversion of Agnes, listing all three foundations and noting the idea of model and imitation to which Franciscan hagiography frequently alludes. The author's register and vocabulary identify him as a Friar Minor, in particular when he uses phrases common and particular for the Franciscan perception of conversion and religious orientation.[66] The hagiographer connects Agnes' wish for a life in poverty with the evangelical advice and puts the description of her *conversio* into a dramatic climax.[67] How closely the Order's initiative for canonization is connected with the text of the Milan manuscript of *CLE* becomes evident by juxtaposing crucial passages of the concluding paragraph of the *vita*, that is the epilogue, and the conversion report with *PetNic*.[68] The description of the secular life of the princess as well as her *conversio*, the monastic life and the death illustrate that the knowledge of Agnes and her deeds had been augmented since the precedent canonization attempt, but was captured within the monastic walls.

Already at the beginning of *CLE*, in the prologue, the reader grasps an instructive glance of the author's interest and strategy.[69] Apart from the customary proclamation of modesty, the hagiographer explains basic parameters

---

op. cit., p. 666s.; D. Dvořáčková-Malá, "Panovnický dvůr ve středověku. Struktura, prostor a reprezentace", in *Dvory a rezidence ve středověku. II. Skladba a kultura dvorské společnosti*, Prague, 2008, p. 11-37, here p. 20s.

[66] C. Bohl, "Belehren und Bekehren. Das Sante Francisken leben des Lamprecht von Regensburg als Zeugnis franziskanischer Bildung, Seelsorge und Frömmigkeit Mitte des 13. Jahrhunderts in Deutschland", in *Europa und die Welt in der Geschichte. Festschrift zum 60. Geburtstag von Dieter Berg*, ed. R. Averkorn et al., Bochum 2004, p. 574-592.

[67] *CLE*, p. 106: *Edocta uero a fratribus quod regula memorata intrare uolentibus ordinem supradictum secundum tenorem sacri ewangelii suadet omnia sua uendere et ea pauperibus erogare, Cristoque pauperi in paupertate & humilitate famulari, celesti munditate perfusa 'hoc est' ait 'quod cupio, hoc est quod totis precordiis concupisco'.*

[68] E. g. *CLE, De miraculis virtute divina patratis* (as part of the epilogue), p. 124: [...] *Agnetem felicem virignem sancte Clare in regno Bohemie plantulam generosam; diffundit fragranciam sanctitatis*. *PetNic*, p. 90.

[69] *CLE*, p. 100: *Tandem reuerendi patris mei ministri super hoc obediencinali precepto constrictus negocium super uires meas assumpsi, mallens sub sarcina tanti laboris humiliter parendo* [...]. *Sed quia non sumus sufficientes cogitare aliquid a nobis sed sufficiencia nostra ex deo est, qui misericordia sua grata operatur in nobis et uelle et perficere pro bona uoluntate, ideo adiutorii mei totam fiduciam ponens in ipso de hac eximia uirgine alia scribere non intendo quam ea que habere potui ab hiis personis, que uirtutum eius magnalia conuersando cum ipsa suis oculis conspexerunt, quarum assercioni ob uite ipsarum meritum non facile quis potest refragari – et mira que per ipsius merita tam in uita quam post felicem eius transitum dominus dignanter effecit, aliqua quidem uisa, alia uero ab hiis quibus acciderant narrata et sub fideli asseueracione recepta ad meam noticiam peruenerunt. In processu uero huius hystorie non secundum semper ordinem temporis res gestas descripsi propter confusionem uitandem, sed quecumque alicui materie competebant siue eodem siue diuersis patrata forent temporibus, pro simplicitatis mee modulo sicut*

of his approach and aim: first, he was commissioned by his minister to write this legend; second he composed the elements by adopting at least two methods, namely by writing down his own observations as an eye witness and then by reporting the recounts of others witnesses; third he organized this material not in a chronological manner *(ordo temporis)* but in a textual sequence in order to maintain the interest of his audience.[70] We thus may classify this text between an eye witness report and a report with recollections of contemporaries.[71] At the end of the prologue, the hagiographer, certainly of Bohemian origin, provides a content, explaining that the text to come is divided into eleven chapters and will finish with final remarks on the miraculous power demonstrated by the divine Father through the princess, basically referring to the miracle report. What follows, however, is not completely compatible with these introductory remarks, since the legend is devided into twelve chapters adjoined by an epilogue, the miracle report, and a revealing, but also neglected *nota*. This concluding passage gives a brief summary of Agnes' most important deeds, partially in contrast with what the preceding parts are telling,[72] in general designed to add chronological data to the events occuring after Agnes' death. The subsequent historical remarks mention briefly king Ottokar's death, the storage of his corpse at the Franciscan church, here erroneously attributed to the one in Iglau/Jihlava (founded 1245/before 1257), and the ruling

---

compendiosus et conuerniencius potui, coaptaui, ut breuitate gaudentes materiam fastidiendi non habeant, et ut affectus fidelium ad imitacionem huius praeclare uirginis ardencius inflammetur.
[70] Philological classification of hagiographies: E. FEISTNER, *Historische Typologie der deutschen Heiligenlegende von der Mitte des 12. Jahrhunderts bis zur Reformation*, Wiesbaden, 1993.
[71] *CLE*, p. 100: *Sed consideracione sollerti ad hoc insufficientem me senciens et indignum calamum a scribendo continui, pauens imperito sermone fuscare quod claris et magnis laudum preconiis fuerat depromendum* [...] *In processu vero huius hystorie non secundum semper ordinem temporis res gestas descripti propter confusive eodem sive diversis patrata forent temporibus, pro simplicitatis mee modulo sicut compendiosius et conveniencius potui*. This differentiation applies: Fr. LOTTER, "Methodisches zur Gewinnung historischer Erkenntnisse aus hagiographischen Quellen", *Historische Zeitschrift*, 229 (1979), p. 298-356, here p. 320-322.
[72] Most interestingly, the *nota* parallelizes Agnes' foundations with the Francis' foundation of the three Orders. Cf. *CLE*, p. 135: *Anno domini millesimo ducentesimo tricesimo quarto fratres intraverunt Bohemiam. Anno domini millesimo ducentesimo tricesimo sexto in Christo devota virgo domina Agnes, soror Wencesslai qurti regis Bohemie, suscepit ordinem sancti Francisci. Ad cuius imitacionem, sicut pater sanctus Franciscus sub typo trium ordinum tres ecclesias erexit, ita ipsa tres sellempne ecclesias construxit in Praga. Primam videlicet in honore salvatoris omnium, in qua se cum sororibus suis recollegit. Secundam in honore sancte die genitricis Marie et beati Francisci pro fratribus minoribus iuxta se divina sibi et sororibus administrantibus. Terciam in hospitali suo eciam in honore sancti Francisci pro ordine cruciferorum tunc de novo per fratres minores de mandato ipsius domine Agnetis creato* [...]. This passage is a strong reference to the beginnings of the Friars Minor as a hospitalitarian community. Cf. M. P. ALBERZONI, *Elisabeth von Thüringen, op. cit.*, esp. p. 50.

of the Brandenburg duke Otto IV (*c.* 1238-1309) as well as the famines which occurred during this period.[73] The reader's irritation about the obvious discrepancies grows, when we recognize that historical data between the *nota* and the core part of the legend, that is the description of Agnes' life, do not correspond to each other nor does the *nota* list Agnes' foundation activities in the aforementioned chronological order or style. These inconsistencies must reflect a complex composition process of the *CLE* manuscript from Milan. In order to understand the "texture of the text" we can already assume that the author of this witness has woven together layers of the textual corps which was to some extent already formulated or written by distinct scribes and adjoined. At the final step of this *réécriture*, the amalgamation of the added elements *(prologus, epilogus, nota)* to the core part happened rather in haste, without a final proof of consistency.[74] Due to this observation, an earlier and shorter, but even monastic version of the legend must have been written, probably right after the protagonist's death, presumably composed by the Franciscan chaplain and later minister Theodoricus (rul. 1285-1297) as Vyskočil proposed; subsequently, this prototype was amended by the addition of concluding text elements like the *nota*.[75] The intertextual similarities between the Order's petition and the interpolated parts of *CLE* lead to the assertion that the redactor of the Milan manuscript accomplished his work in close chronological and spatial connection with the corresponding initiative sometime between 1334 and 1339.[76]

The Franciscan authorship of the legend is not only perceivable by the appraisal of the highest poverty *(paupertas altissima)*, and its esteem of cardinal John Gaetanus Orsini, the later Pope Nicolas III.[77] It becomes even more evident when highlighting the strategies of insertion of textual elements, the narratology, and the register. Altogether this brings about a *franciscanisation*

---

[73] *CLE*, p. 135: *sicut ipse Rudolfus fratribus minoribus vulnera monstravit in Yglavia*. On Ottokar's fight on the Moravian battlefield: J. ŽEMLIČKA, *Přemysl Otakar II. Král na rozhraní věků*, Prague, 2011, here esp. p. 475. Probably, the writer was confusing Ottokar's favour for the city (privilege from 1270) with the Franciscan church of Znaim/Znojmo, where the corpse was temporarily stored. Otto was the guardian of the infant Wenceslas III (rul. 1305-1306); cf. Vr. VANÍČEK, *Velké dějiny země Koruny české III*, Prague-Litomyšl, 2002, p. 359-403.
[74] M. VAN UYTFANGHE, "Le remploi dans l'hagiographie: une 'loi du genre' qui étouffe l'originalité?", in *Ideologie e pratiche del riempiego nell'alto medioevo*, Spoleto, 1999 (Settimane di studio del Centro italiano di studi sull' alto medioevo, 46), p. 359-412.
[75] J. K. VYSKOČIL, *Legenda blahoslavené Anežky, op. cit.*, p. 69.
[76] The scribe inserts at the end of the fourth letter of Clare the letters P (probably an abbreviation for "pater") and B (Bartholomew?), between both a drawing of a chalice, see: *CLE*, fol. 56v, p. 149.
[77] Analysis: Chr.-Fr. FELSKAU, *Agnes von Böhmen, op. cit.*, p. 320s., 754-762. On the political background see the study of U. HORST, *Evangelische Armut und päpstliches Lehramt. Minoritentheologen in Konflikt mit Papst Johannes XXII. (1316-1334)*, Stuttgart, 1996, here p. 18, 48.

of an already existing stock equivalent to that what recounts the *Vita* tradition. The author (or redactor) did not start from zero, but had a textual basis at hand which he expanded and deepened, with a critical bias towards the ruling last Přemyslid queen on the one hand,[78] with an emphasis on Agnes as an adherent and legitimate successor of St Francis, Claire and Elizabeth on the other, but in all with a hasty amalgamation of elements. Already Vyskočil discovered that some miracles are corresponding to what we find in Clare's legend *Legenda Sanctae Clarae Virginis* (henceforth: *SCV*), most probably composed by the Order's official hagiographer Thomas of Celano († 1260).[79] That the Bohemian author was consulting at length this legend of the foundress of the Poor Clares becomes evident already at the level of the chapters' headings.[80] Apart from Clare's legend, the hagiographer of the princess adopts textual components of other hagiographies, though the adoptions as in the case of the Bonaventurian legend of St Francis are much weaker. However, the takeover of the models set by the Italian saints of the Order and their biographers for the composition of texts for their Central European saints exemplifies on the level of literary productivity a broad transfer of cultural patterns.[81] In addition, Agnes' hagiographer may have consulted other, rather local hagiographies like at least the *legenda maior* of her aunt Hedwig, written before 1300 by an anonymous cleric. From the *Legenda maior Hedwigis* he borrows a few headlines but also some further formulations.[82]

---

[78] The reproach of having disregarded the canonization of Agnes is wrapped in one miracle recount, stating Agnes' initial reluctance to heal the queen's child, Charles IV, cf. *CLE*, p. 124s. (M3): '*Cur pro te orabo?' At regina nimium consternata corruit ante cratem dicens 'Avia ora pro me, quia de loco isto non recedam, sed pocius hic iacebo et in cordis anustia moriar, nisi pro me ad domimum intercedas!*' Only after the subsequent miracle which secured the health of Elizabeth herself, the latter promises to espouse Agnes' canonization.

[79] The legend published in: *Fontes Francescani* II (Medioevo Francescano, 2), ed. E. MENESTÒ, St. BRUFANI, Assisi, 1995, p. 2403-2453 (henceforth cited according to this publication); *Escritos de Santa Clara*, p. 127-197. Arguing for this attribution of authorship: M. GUIDA, *Una leggenda in cerca d'autore, la Vita di santa Chiara d'Assisi. Studio delle fonti e sinossi intertestuali*, Bruxelles, 2010.

[80] J.-Cl. POULIN, "Un élément négligé de critique hagiographique: les titres de chapitres", in *Scribere sanctorum gesta. Recueil d'études d'hagiographie médiévale offert à Guy Philippart*, ed. É. RENARD *et al.*, Turnhout, 2005, p. 309-342.

[81] P. MESSA, "L'agiografia francescana e la posterità di Chiara d'Assisi", in *Da santa Chiara a suor Francesca Farnese. Il francescanesimo femminile e il monastero di Fara in Sabina*, ed. S. BOESCH GAJANO, T. LEGGIO, Rome, 2013, p. 69-74, examines the dependencies of the legend of Saint Kinga/Kunigunde (1224-1292), the foundress of the Poor Clare's cloister in Stary Sandecz, on Bonaventure's second legend on Saint Francis, *LegMai*.

[82] *Legenda maior sanctae Hedwigis*, in: *Acta Sanctorum*, Oct. VIII, ed. J. BOLLANDUS *et al.*, Brüssel, 1853, p. 224-264; recent edition of the Hedwig's hagiography: *Legenda o św. Jadwidze. Legende der hl. Hedwig*, ed. W. MROZOWICZ, Tr. EHLERT, Wrocław, 2000; analysis: Chr.-Fr. FELSKAU, *Agnes von Böhmen, op. cit.*, p. 718-723.

The Miracle Recount as a Key to the Understanding of Textual Genesis

The implementation of miracle reports within hagiographic texts illustrates the author's intention to apply a given model to the *vita* of his protagonist. At the same time, it provides significant insights into this composition process of the texts themselves. This holds true especially with regards to the texts on princess Agnes.[83] Though a terminological clarification of the term 'miracle' still remains under discussion,[84] it is legitimate to adopt the basic distinction of Agnes' own hagiographer, differentiating them into *miracula in vita* (V), which comprise the revelation of the saint's birth to her mother queen Constance[85] or other divine foreseeings, miracles during the corpse's exhibition (MT), and finally the *miracula post mortem* (M), all subsumed under the term *signa*.[86] In both branches: the *Vita Prima* and *CLE*, the report on the miracle participants, whether those *in vita* or *post mortem*, is exceptionally elaborated because the beneficiaries, moreover when of secular origin, are mentioned prevailingly with full and identifiable names. This does not only allow us to establish a topographic network, a "hagio-geography", and a social frame of miraculous participation.[87] The rather exceptional level

---

[83] Latest on *CLE*: V. Bok, *Einige Beobachtungen zur lateinischen Legende*, p. 164s.

[84] Kl. Herbers, "Miracula – Definition, Entwicklungstendenzen und Forschungsfragen", in *Mirakelberichte des frühen und hohen Mittelalters*, ed. Kl. Herbers et al., Darmstadt, 2005, p. 14-17; M. Goodich, *Miracles and Wonders. The Development of the Concept of Miracle, 1150-1350*, Aldershot-Burlington, 2007.

[85] *CLE*, p. 101s. (Re1). On this type of prediction: A. Marini, *Agnese di Boemia*, Rome, 1991, here p. 133-141.

[86] On the narrative components of miracles: G. Klaniczay, "Ritual and Narrative in Late Medieval Miracle Accounts. The Construction of the Miracle", in *Religious Participation in Ancient and Medieval Societies*, ed. S. Katalaja-Peltomaa, V. Vuolanto, Rome, 2013, p. 207-224.

[87] Of all identifiable beneficiaries of Agnes' miracles, a clear concentration on Prague and the Northern Bohemian parts of the kingdom is observable. Apart from the Moravian locations Lešan and Tassow, both relatively close to the Bohemian frontier, nearly no beneficiary derives from the Moravian bishopric. Interestingly enough, it is only the high noble family of the Sternbergs, which due to its split into two branches of Bohemian and Moravian Sternberg occurring at the end of the thirteenth century, provides a more intensive recognition of Agnes' miraculous merits within the Eastern country of the Bohemian crown lands. Leaving the royal kindred aside, the Sternbergs, the strongest supporters of Agnes' hospitalitarian community, eventually founders of the Olomouc monastery of the Poor Clares in the 1250s, and loyal to the Přemyslids, rank within the very small group of triple beneficiaries. Such a prominent position maintains only the noble family *de Squorcz* with one lifetime miracle in the presence of sister Domka, the daughter of Domislas of Squorz (V13, M31, M52) and two posthumous miracles; the intensity of participation, but also the characteristics of the miracles – amongst them the rare miracle of rescue – indicate that the princess and her community maintained close connections

of accuracy together with the referral to historical events permit examination of these recounts as a tool for reconstructing the composition process at least of this part of the legend as Václav Bok, based on the analysis of Beran and Vyskočil, acknowledged.[88] *CLE* consists of 60 *signa* in total, of them 22 during Agnes' lifetime, three *miracula* occuring during the corpse's disposal, and 32 *miracula post mortem*, of which three are rather generic references to her miraculous deeds without indication of concrete events. This amount of miracles does not equal either in number or in elaborateness those reported in the *Vita Prima*, which strengthens the opinion that the development of knowledge on Agnes follows the described tendency from poor to rich also in terms of the miraculous reports.

Table 1: Text elements and miracles of *CLE* with missing text elements in *Vita Prima*

Prologue	Notes on Agnes' secular & monastic life	Miracles during corpse exhibit	Epilogue	Miracle report *post mortem*	Nota
	CLE: 22 *signa* / Vita Prima: 13 *singna*	CLE: 3 *miracula* / Vita Prima: 1 miraculum	1 general remark on Agnes' miracula	CLE: 31 *miracula* / Vita Prima: 23 *miracula*	
	Mentioned in the prologue of CLE			Mentioned in the prologue of CLE	

Detailed composition and timing:

Pro-logue	Notes on Agnes' secular + monastic life	Miracles during corpse exhibit	Epi-logue	Royal miracles	Basic miracle cluster	Miracles under Franciscan guidance	First miracle addition	Unstable reported miracle	Partially irregular dispersed miracles, unstable tradition	Miracles also in the legend branch, unstable tradition	Nota
	MT2 (Sternberg)			M1-4	M5-16	M17-21 M25	M22-23	M24 (Sternberg)	M26, M27-30	M(3)1-32	
	MX, M3-5, M11, 15, M16E, M21	MT1+3									

| 1334/ 1338-1339 | 1282–1328 | 1282–1328 | 1334 /1338-1339 | 1317-19 1322-28 | Before 1316? | After 1316 before 1334/ 1338-39 | Before 1316 | Around or shortly after 1329 | Around 1328/29? | Around 1328/29? | 1334 /1338-1339 |
| | 1328-1338 | 1328-1338 | | | | | | | | | |

Starting with the miracula in lifetime, the very first miracle reported in both hagiographic branches, that is the angel's revelation to the pregnant

---

to members of this family. Citation from H. RÖCKELEIN, "Über Hagio-Geo-Graphien. Mirakel in Translationsberichten des 8. und 9. Jahrhunderts", in *Mirakel im Mittelalter. Konzeptionen, Erscheinungsformen, Deutungen*, ed. M. HEINZELMANN *et al.*, Stuttgart, 2002, p. 166-179.
[88] V. BOK, *Einige Beobachtungen*, p. 166s. For the geographic distribution of Agnes' miracles, see the table in Chr.-Fr. FELSKAU, *Agnes von Böhmen, op. cit.*, p. 1225, annex VII.3.

mother of the coming saint, resembles the identical report in Clare's legend *SCV* though to a certain extend topical for hagiographic texts.[89] But subsequently, the *Vita Prima* is missing some miracles closely connected with internal affairs of the Poor Clare's monastery, namely the biblical miracles presented by the way also in *SCV*, namely the unexplainable discovery of fish and bread by the porter of the monastery,[90] as well as the observation of a strange light on Agnes' face by a sister, but also Agnes' revelation of her long life to the provincial minister of the Friars Minor.[91] Noteworthy are three other miracles omitted in the *Vita Prima*: the unexplainable finding of apples in the monastic garden and, indeed astonishingly, two miracles witnessed by Agnes' royal kindred – her relevation to the brotherly king Wenceslas concerning the outcomes of his Austrian politics as well as a devil's expulsion from the corpse of a *domina soror Elisabeth imperatorice* (V11), possibly referring to queen Elizabeth.[92] The shortage of internal or Franciscan miracles supposedly reflects the distinct authorship, but the lack of these two latter miracles refer to the assumption that at the composition stage of *Vita Prima* not all was known about Agnes' impact on the health and wealth of the contemporary ruling dynasty in Bohemia.

Focussing at a second step on Agnes' *miracula post mortem* as a separate report, their structure is comparably complex and underlines the assertion that the composition of *CLE* already in its oldest Milanese witness had run through various layers of re-writing. In accordance with the hagiographer's remarks, we are able to cluster the miracles after Agnes' lifetime in typological units and by that convincingly prove the writer's working method.[93]

---

[89] See here *Vita Prima*, p. 509. A similar information on the angel's revelation came up in the inquistorial records of Agnes' alleged biological sister Guiglielma. *Milano 1300. I processi inquisitoriali contro le devote e i devoti di santa Guglielma*, ed. M. BENEDETTI, Milano, 1999, p. 172.

[90] Cf. *SCV*, p. 2424s; *CLE*, p. 110, 114 (V1+2, V8a+b: finding of bread and fish, but also the unnatural detection of an apple used for a subsequent healing miracle). Models are here the two gift miracle of Jesus, the feeding of the five thousand or 'bread miracle' (Mk 6, 35-44; Lk 9, 10-17) and the miraculous fishing (Lk 5, 1-11). The fish miracle is, due to local conditions in Assisi, turned into an oil miracle. For hagiographies entailing this type of miracle: C. HESS, *Heilige machen im spätmittelalterlichen Ostseeraum. Die Kanonisationsprozesse von Brigitta von Schweden, Nikolaus von Linköping und Dorothea von Montau*, Berlin, 2008, p. 51-68.

[91] *CLE*, p. 114 (Re3): *Quam revelacionem ut audiverat provinciali ministro et aliquibus aliis personis sub specie magni secreti reservavit.*

[92] On the structural affinities of the miracle recounts between *CLE* and the legends of Clare (*SCV*) and Hedwig see Chr.-Fr. FELSKAU, *Agnes von Böhmen, op. cit.*, p. 779-796.

[93] Table taken from *Ibid.*, p. 651, table 10.

Table 2: *Post mortem* miracle sequences in *CLE* and their spatial-typological structure

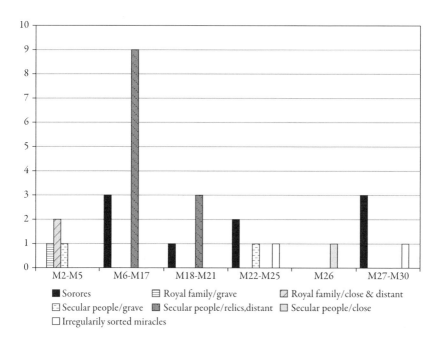

The first sequence (M2-M5), included also in the *Vita* tradition, is composed of a series of miracles with the involvement of the royal kindred: the daughter of queen Judith/Guta (1271-1297), the wife of king Wenceslas II (rul. 1278-1305), is healed during a visit to the cloister, then the first born son of queen Elizabeth, the first petitioner of Agnes' canonization, is healed after a cloister visit and Agnes' invocation; finally Elizabeth is healed after the birth of her second son. This sequence, however ends with the healing of a child of a prestigious Prague citizen after the Papal permission to its kindred to enter the monastery.[94] The next and longest sequence (M6-M17) starts with three miracles under the participation of inmates, followed by eight respectively nine miracles from which external or secular people benefit.[95] The ninth of this miracle sequence is missing already in the

---

[94] *CLE*, p. 124-126. The most frequent type of healing miracles introduces: R. A. SCOTT, *Miracle Cures. Saints, Pilgrimage, and the Healing Powers of Belief*, Berkeley-Los Angeles-London, 2011; H. LUTTERBACH, "Der Christus medicus und die *sancti medici*. Das wechselvolle Verhältnis zweier Grundmotive christlicher Frömmigkeit zwischen Spätantike und Früher Neuzeit", *Saeculum*, 47 (1996), p. 239-281.

[95] *CLE*, p. 127-129, with the following participants/beneficiaries: Domka of Squorz, Jutta of Lyznik, Wracka of Ujezd, Ludkaw of Turnov, Cunso of Hermanycz and his servant, *virgo*

vita tradition, thus it might be that this miracle indicates the start of a subsequent textual cluster though it is addressing still an external participant. The *nucleus*, the narratological content of the following miracle sequence M18-M21, which is totally omitted in the *Vita* tradition, remains nearly always identical: people, often women or children, get healed through the water taken from Agnes' grave after flooding or through the hair of Agnes, all of them accomplished with the intervention of the local Friars Minor as transmitters or mediators of the liquids or materials.[96] These Franciscan wonders are an indication that the "franciscanisation" of the content from the *Vita* branch to the legend observable already in the parts recounting the saint's life cover also the miracle part. This "Franciscan miracle section" is followed by an unstable reported and clustered sequence of four miracles (M22-25), of which one (M24) is even irregularly sorted at least in the *CLE* tradition, since it represents there – but not in the *Vita Prima* (!) – a *miraculum in vita*, carried out for the benefit of the noble woman and *amatrix Agnetis* Scholastica of Sternberg.[97] Before the scribe of *CLE* concludes with two rather unconcrete descriptions of Agnes' miraculous merits, he incorporates a final miracle sequence which is present again in both traditions. This sequence (M27-M30) consists of various miracles enacted within the monastic walls, one of them again irregularly placed because the scribe tells about the miraculous survival of Agnes' chair during a fire, evidently still during her earthly existence.[98]

Wanka of Prague, Christian (daughter of the Franciscan *procurator* Gottfried), Martin of Prague and his wife, *domina* Dobroslava from Slany, nobleman Tasso, Hynko of Duba, Wenceslav (notary of the *miles* of Proczywczonis), and Marzicus of Hoholycz. I. HLAVÁČEK, "Adel und Nicht-Adel an der Schwelle von der Přemysliden- zur Luxemburger-Zeit in Böhmen", in *Zwischen Nicht-Adel und Adel*, ed. K. ANDERMANN, P. JOHANEK, Stuttgart, 2001, p. 157-178.

[96] *CLE*, p. 130s. Beneficiaries of this miracle set: Margareta (daughter of the Prague *cives* James), *vir* Albert of Prague, "many sick people", Markward of Wlassim and 15 feverish people. Terminology according to HESS, *Heilige machen, op. cit.*, p. 52-54. On the distribution of male or female beneficiaries of healing miracles see the findings of S. KATAJALA-PELTOMAA, *Gender, Miracles, and Daily Life. The Evidence of Fourteenth-Century Canonization Processes*, Turnhout, 2009, here p. 29 (table) and 34.

[97] *CLE*, p. 130; *Vita Prima*, p. 512, § 15. Beneficiaries: Constance (later abbess), Agnes of Sberzkowicz, Scholastica (wife of Harbard of Zerotyn and grandmother of Scolastica of Sternberg), Hostyrhilda (wife of Jaroslaus of Sternberg). J. TANNER, *Geschichte derer Helden von Sternen oder deß Geschlechtes von Sternberg*, Prague, 1732, p. 132. Modern overview on the family's history Fr. PALACKÝ, Zd. STERNBERG, *Dějiny rodu Sternbergů. Geschichte der Familie Sternberg*, Moravský Beroun, 2000. The family's position within the Bohemian higher nobility: J. JUROK, *Česká šlechta a feudalita ve středověku a raném novověku*, Nový Jičín, 2000, esp. p. 14; D. DVOŘÁČKOVÁ, J. ZELENKA, *Panovnický dvůr za vlády Přemyslovců*, Prague, p. 122s.

[98] *CLE*, p. 133s. Beneficiaries: Domka (daughter of Domaslaus of Squorcz), *multi audientes*, Elizabeth (daughter of Albert of Lubsycz) and Sdynka Paulikonis, Jutka of Lesszan.

Such irregular sorted miracles (here M24, M30) we encounter also in other legends as for instance in the legend of St Clare.[99]

The prominent royal miracles do not only illustrate the endeavour to present Agnes as the saviour of the ruling dynasty, they provide at the same time access to the dating of these reports. While the healing of the future king can be reconstructed and attributed to the years 1317-1319, the healing of Guta of Habsburgs daughter Marketa who died in 1322 finishes with the words: *pluribus postmodum annis supervixit*, which means that the writing of this passage must have happened several years after that event. The *Vita* tradition instead describes that miracle only in one sentence without any notice on Guta's later decease, which on the contrary does not indicate a safe *terminus ante quem*.[100] The miracles related to queen Elizabeth permit some far-reaching conclusions, since they entail a passage in which the presumed saint is complaining about Elizabeth's insufficient support of and belief in her veneration. Again, we may deduce from such unscrupulous attitude that the scribe does not derive from a court circle, but rather from a monastic one. On the other hand, this obvious distance to the ruling family does not necessarily indicate the legend's composition before or after the queen's attempt for canonization in 1328. In addition, the miracle sequence reporting several healing acts through Agnes' relics distributed after the flooding of the cloister offer a contribution to the chronological stipulation. These events refer to the flood of the Moldave in 1316, which enforced the replacement of Agnes' sarcophagus from lower parts of the Saint Francis chapel to a more secure place.[101] Was this the moment when the secular royal information started to dissolve from the monastic one or vice versa? One crucial textual piece which may provide access to the genesis of both traditions are the prominent miracles connected with the Sternberg family, one occurring during the disposal of the saint's corpse.[102] After the royal family, the Sternbergs were the most powerful promoters of the Order of the Crosiers with the Red Star,[103] but also strong supporters of the Poor Clares, in particular their Moravian branch. Their impressive support for the Poor Clares at the episcopal Moravian seat Olomouc from

---

[99] Cf. the examples cited in M. GUIDA, *Una leggenda in cerca d'autore*, op. cit., p. 188.

[100] *Vita Prima*, p. 5112, § 16. Consult the observations of V. BOK, *Einige Beobachtungen*, op. cit., p. 167. More striking is the implementation of miracle M24, reported in the *Vita* tradition as a *post mortem* miracle, but as a miracle *in vita* in the *CLE* tradition (see *CLE*, p. 133, 174, no. 254).

[101] This transfer can be viewed as a second, forced *translatio* of the saint after the funeral; cf. H. RÖCKELEIN, *Über Hagio-Geo-Graphien*, op. cit., p. 166-179.

[102] MT2, M24, and M25: *CLE*, p. 122 and 132.

[103] The first minister general of the Prague settlement of this community was a member of the Sternberg dynasty; most probably, the Order's *signum*, approved in the 1250s, makes reference to them in sign and name; cf. A. WOJTYŁA, *Idea ordo militaris*, op. cit., p. 379, annex III, s. 2.

the foundation to the period of the legend's composition and in particular in the years between 1329 and 1332 may have been a good reason for the writer's intervention, increasing the prominence of the Sternbergs by this healing miracle when deferred into the lifetime of the presumed saint.[104]

The differences between the accuracy and the amount of reported information and miracles in the both branches of hagiographic texts on the princess strongly support the idea that the process of hagiographic production was oscillating between the involved agencies. In a first stage, the information on the life of Agnes was recollected within the Franciscan double monastery but never received external attention or exploitation; in a second stage, the clerical circle at the Bohemian royal court was grasping the core information of this probably already existing written account, rewriting it for the purpose of an intended canonization process; at a third step the given material returned to the local Franciscan-Clarissan circle, where it was embellished and rewritten again by a set of miracles, the addition of concluding passages, and slight, but inconsistent modifications of the existing Franciscan narrative material; this was conducted on behalf of the provincial Nicholas for the purpose of canonization. The adjustment of this material, the arrangement of narrative elements, and the inclusion of existing models within this procedure of rewriting were triggered by the strategy of producing a *cohérence supranationale*, a coherence of female Franciscan hagiography in a Central European Context.

(Re-)Constructed Affinity – The Rule of Saint Clare, Her Four Letters And Agnes' Reception in the fourteenth-fifteenth Century

Princess Agnes' compliance to the ideals of "female Franciscanism" is demonstrated at its best by the foundations with which she sought, as her legend proficiently points out in its conversion chapter, to combine a *vita apostolica* for which Clare was scrambling and a way of life following St Elizabeth's

---

[104] Introductionary: *Encyklopedie moravských a slezských klášterů*, ed. D. FOLTÝN *et al.*, Prague, 2005, p. 485-489; E. WAUER, *Entstehung und Ausbreitung des Klarissenordens*, *op. cit.*, p. 99, n. 1, corrects an earlier dating to 1329 connecting it to the donation charter of Diviš' of Sternberg (29.6.1329; RBM II, p. 619, no. 1575); see also RBM III, p. 846s., no. 2173 (1.11.1332): Margarethe of Sternberg, the widow of Zdislai of Sternberg bequeaths a huge donation (the village Sthernow) to the Olomouc Poor Clares; their daughters Agnes and Elizabeth (eventually the abbess?) were inmates of the local monastery; the donation charter considers also the local Franciscans with an annuity; further notifications of the Sternbergs: John of Sternberg, canon at the Prague church: RBM II, p. 542 no. 1384 (3.11.1327); Zdeslaus senior and his son Zdeslaus junior, chamberlain of the *czuda* (i.e. governor, *Landeshauptmann*): RBM II, p. 307, 318, no. 750, 752, 782 (all 1322). The support of the Sternbergs and their affined family of the Zierotin for the Crosiers and the Poor Clares investigates Chr.-Fr. FELSKAU, *Agnes von Böhmen, op. cit.*, p. 599, table 9.

extraordinary model of charity.[105] In addition, it is strengthened by Agnes' probably persistent approach to the Papal *curia* for obtaining an own rule.[106] On the hagiographic level, the affinity towards the Umbrian foundress of the Order is mirrored by the dependance of the *Candor lucis eterne* on the legend of St Clare. The close relationship between the Umbrian founding figure of the Order and her Central European follower is in addition strengthened by a few documents, that is the rule granted to Clare's community in Assisi and, most of all, Clare's four surviving letters to Agnes.[107]

The particular rule, promulgated shortly before Clare's decease by Pope Innocent IV to the community of San Damiano (*Solet annuere*, 11 August 1253) after a preceding approbation by cardinal protector Rainald of Jenne, the later Pope Alexander IV (*Quia vos*, 16 September 1252),[108] is considered by historians as the impressive fruit of Clare's fight for a religious life under the spiritual guidance (*cura monialium*) of the Friars Minor and the auspices of "highest poverty" (*altissima paupertas*), chastity and penance.[109] Unlike the *privilegium paupertatis* which was granted to several Clarissan houses on the Italian peninsula and

---

[105] *CLE*, p. 106. The assumption that the complex "At Saint Francis" was established as a counterweight to the asserted German dominated local community of St James can not be upheld considering the early influential Friars like Konrad of Worms or the reconstructed list of guardians. Cf. *Urkundenbuch der Kustodien Goldberg und Breslau*, Teil 1: *1240-1517* (Monumenta Germaniae Franciscana, 2. Abt., Band 1), ed. Chr. REISCH, Düsseldorf, 1917, p. 8s., no. 37s; W. DERSCH, "Die Provinzialminister", *art. cit., passim*. The combination of the 'hospitalitarian type of architecture' and the traditional monastic building plan recognizes W. SCHENKLUHN, *Architektur der Bettelorden. Die Baukunst der Dominikaner und Franziskaner in Europa*, Darmstadt, 2000, p. 89; see also C. JÄGGI, *Frauenklöster im Spätmittelalter. Die Kirchen der Klarissen und Dominikanerinnen im 13. und 14. Jahrhundert*, Petersberg, 2006, p. 40-45, 202-205.

[106] The research on Agnes' approach summarizes N. KUSTER, "Eine neu entdeckte Lichtgestalt. Forschungsbericht zu Klara von Assisi", in *Klara von Assisi. Zwischen Bettelarmut und Beziehungsreichtum. Beiträge zur neueren deutschsprachigen Klara-Forschung*, Münster, 2011, p. 213-236, here p. 223.

[107] An overview on English (published) studies dedicated to the letters: *The Writings of Clare of Assisi. Letters, Form of Life, Testament and Blessing*, ed. M. BLASTIC *et al.*, New York, 2011, p. 27-29.

[108] On the office: Cr. ANDENNA, "Le cardinal protecteur dans les ordres mendiants: une personne d'autorité?", in *Les personnes d'autorité en milieu régulier. Des origines de la vie régulière au XVIIIᵉ siècle. Actes du 7ᵉ colloque international du CERCOR*, ed. J.-Fr. COTTIER *et al.*, Saint-Étienne, 2012, p. 289-313, here p. 298, 304s.

[109] Out of the innumerable studies: A. BONI, "La legislazione clariana nel contesto giuridico delle sue origini e della sua evoluzione", *Antonianum*, 70 (1995), p. 47-98; Fr. COSTA, "Le Regole Clariane. Genesi e confronto", *Miscellanea Franciscana*, 98 (1998), p. 812-835. On the discovery of the bull: St. BRUFANI, A. BARTOLI LANGELI, "La lettera Solet annuere di Innocenzo IV per Chiara (9 agosto 1253)", *Franciscana*, 8 (2006), p. 63-108. On the manuscript tradition: *Il vangelo come forma di vita. In ascolto di Chiara nella sua Regola*, Padova, 2013, p. 39-70, followed by an extensive analysis of the sources of the *forma vitae*.

beyond, amongst them Agnes' monastery in Prague,[110] Clare's rule was explicitly designed to pertain only to her community of San Damiano,[111] while most of the Franciscan inspired female institutions had to follow a rule based rather on traditional Benedictine regulations (August 1247, *Cum olim vera religio*).[112] However, a clear exception with regards to the dominating attempt of unifying these female houses under one rule was made in the case of the institutions founded by the princess Isabelle of France (1224-1269) at Longchamp near Paris, founded in 1255, with its later erected regional affiliated houses in 1259.[113]

Though it is assumed that several communities of the growing Damianite (or Clarissan Order, as it was named from 1263 on) followed "ideally" Clare's rule during the lifetime of the foundress,[114] formal evidence for a strict extension of this regulation during the thirteenth century survived only in the case of Agnes'

---

[110] Initially, this privilege was commissioned to the houses of Monteluce (1229) and Monticelli (1230), but later on was issued for several houses, which were not always interested in a literal observation of a life *sine proprio* but applied it moreover for spiritual matters. P. HÖHLER, "Frauenklöster in einer italienischen Stadt. Zur Wirtschafts- und Sozialgeschichte der Klarissen von Monteluce und der Zisterzienserinnen von S. Giuliana in Perugia (13. – Mitte 15. Jahrhundert)", *Quellen und Forschungen aus italienischen Archiven und Bibliotheken*, 67 (1987), p. 1-107; M. CUSATO, "From the Perfectio Sancti Evangelii to the Sanctissima Vita et Paupertas: An Hypothesis on the Origin of the *Privilegium Paupertatis* to Clare and Her Sisters at San Damiano", *Franciscan Studies*, 64 (2006), p. 123-144. See also the map in *Nella tua tenda per sempre, op. cit.*, [799-805], table II, listing the following recipients till 1253: Burgos, Saragozza, Zamora, and Olite on the Iberian Peninsula; Reims in France, Firenze, Siena, Assisi in Italy; Trnava and Prague in Central Europe. Cf. *Sainte Claire d'Assise et sa postérité. Actes du colloque international organisé à l'occasion du VIIIe centenaire de la naissance de sainte Claire*, ed. G. BRUNEL-LOBRICHON et al., Paris, 1995, appendix I (till 1253).

[111] Th. MAIER, "*Forma vitae*. Eine Interpretation der Ordensregel der heiligen Klara von Assisi", in *Klara von Assisi, op. cit.*, p. 327-374.

[112] This rule of Innocent (*Escritos de Santa Clara*, p. 242-264) took over many elements of the Ugolinian *Forma vitae* issued in 1245. In brief: B. ROEST, *Order and Disorder, op. cit.*, p. 48-51. See also: G. CASAGRANDE, "La regola di Innocenzo IV", in Clara Claris Praeclara. *Ricerche dell'Istituto Telogico e dell'istituto di Scienze Religiose di Assisi*, Assisi, 2004, p. 71-82.

[113] The rule in: *Escritos de Santa Clara, op. cit.*, p. 289-324. On the life and impact of the princess: S. FIELD, *Isabelle of France. Capetian Sanctity and Franciscan Identity in the Thirteenth Century*, Notre Dame/Indiana, 2006; G. MŁYNARCZYK, *Ein Franziskanerinnenkloster im 15. Jahrhundert. Edition und Analyse von Besitzinventaren aus der Abtei Longchamp*, Bonn, 1987. On the proliferation of the rule, cf. Chr.-Fr. FELSKAU, "*Hoc est quod cupio*. Approaching the Religious Goals of Clare of Assisi, Agnes of Bohemia, and Isabelle of France", *Magistra*, 12/2 (2006), p. 1-28.

[114] Cf. the list of N. KUSTER, "San Damiano und der päpstliche Damiansorden. Die spannungsvolle Geschichte der Klarissen im Licht der neuesten Forschung", *Collectanea Franciscana*, 82 (2012), p. 253-340, here p. 335; see B. ROEST, *Order and Disorder, op. cit.*, p. 53; *Nella tua tenda per sempre, op. cit.* [799-805], table III, calls this rule *Regola Prima*, attributing it to the following monasteries till 1350: Benavente, Trnava/Tyrnau (close to Pressburg/Bratislava in presentday Slowakia, founded in 1238), Aix-en-Provence, Napoli, Trieste, Reims, but excluding Prague. Basis: *Sainte Claire d'Assise et sa postérité, op. cit.*, appendix II, which counts among the 430 monsteries in 1350 only seven following this first rule. The assumption of E. WAUER, *Entstehung und Ausbreitung des Klarissenordens*, p. 95s.; repeated by M. SENSI,

community in Prague and of the Přemyslid-Piast foundation in the Silesian capital Breslau/Wrocław, comissioned by the princess's younger sister Anne († 1265) and her kindred.[115] At Wrocław, Anne had founded after the decease of her husband Henry II († 1241), with the strong support of Alexander IV in 1256/57, and in striking parallel to the Prague model, the monastery of the Poor Clares in vicinity to an allegedly 1253 (re-)founded, but already existing hospital which soon became a second 'mother house' of the newly established Order of the Crosiers with the Red Star.[116] In June 1262, thus only a couple of months prior to the passing of a new, unifying rule for the Poor Clares' houses (*Religiosam vitam*, 18 October 1263) replacing his predecessor's regulation, Pope Urban IV granted to this royal foundation of the *ordo sancti Damiani* Clare's particular rule.[117]

According to the statement of the *Candor lucis eterne*, Agnes of Bohemia received still before, namely from Alexander IV, the right to follow Clare's rule which the latter had sent first to Prague as a legitimate of "heritage of succession". Interestingly, this claim for legitimacy is explained by the close discipleship between both women, emphasizing the consolation Clare as a spiritual authority gave through her letters. This description is embedded into the concept of *sequela* or, from the other perspective, of *plantula* widely exploited by Franciscan hagiographers.[118] The *Vita* tradition instead is providing slightly different, more

---

"Mulieres in ecclesia". *Storie di monache e bizzoche*, 2 vols., Spoleto, 2010, here t. I, p. 311, no. 90, that the Order's house in Bratislava received this rule, is lacking evidence.
[115] See G. P. FREEMAN, "Klaras Kloster als Modell für die ersten Damianitinnen", in *Klara von Assisi – Gestalt und Geschichte*, Mönchengladbach, 2013, p. 31-62, here p. 54. The granting of Clare's rule to the foundation of Queen Sancia of Mallorca or Naples (1285-1345) in 1327 by John XXII discusses: Chr. ANDENNA, "Secundum regulam datam sororibus ordinis sancti Damiani. Sancia e Aquilina: due esperimenti di ritorno alle origini alla corte di Napoli nel XIV secolo", in *Franciscan Organisation in the Mendicant Context. Formal and informal structures of the friars' lives and ministry in the Middle Ages*, ed. M. ROBSON, J. RÖHRKASTEN, Münster, 2010, p. 139-178. The document published in *Jean XXII (1316-1334). Lettres communes*, t. VI, p. 503, no. 28397.
[116] *Schlesisches Urkundenbuch. Dritter Band 1251-1266*, ed. W. IRGANG, Köln-Wien, 1984, p. 131-133, no. 193-195 (henceforth: SUB); Prz. WISZEWSKI, "Herzogliche Stifter und Frauenklöster in Schlesien (13. – Mitte 14. Jahrhundert)", in *Monarchische und adelige Sakralstiftungen im mittelalterlichen Polen*, ed. E. MÜHLE, Berlin, 2012, p. 455-482, here p. 457s.
[117] Wrocław, Archiwum Państwowe we Wrocławiu. Rep. 63, no. 20 (A); ed.: SUB III, p. 273s., no. 414. Briefly on the rule amongst numerous studies: G. BARONE, "La regola di Urbano IV", in *Clara Claris Praeclara, op. cit.*, p. 83-95.
[118] *CLE*, p. 108s.: *Cum autem sanctitas eius mirabilis ad aures sanctissime Clare virginis prevenisset, illa tam nobili prole divina gracia fecun gaudens, magnificavit altissimum eamque crebrius suis graciosis literis materne reverenter ac affectuosissime consolans, studiose in sancto proposito confortavit regulamque suam per bone memorie dominum Innocencium quartum confirmatam veluti pignus hereditarie successionis eidem transmisit. Quam agna Cristi devote suscipiens denuo per felicis recordacionis dominum Alexandrum quartum pro se et sororibus sui monasterii perpetuis temporis obtinuit confirmari.* German translation: Candor lucis eterne, *op. cit.*, p. 35. A. MARINI, "Ancilla Christi, plantula sancti Francisci. Gli scritti di Santa Chiara e la Regola", in *Chiara di Assisi*, p. 107-156; *Id.*, "Pauperem Christum, virgo pauper,

vague information within a similar context just mentioning Agnes' devout request (*petiit*) to follow this rule.[119] The presumed evidence for the granting of the rule is found in a nineteenth century collection of documents and other reports compiled by Johann Florian Hammerschmid (1652-1735) as an apograph from an chartulary of the Prague Crosiers with the Red Star composed in the previous century which comprises this confirmation to Agnes and her community supposedly granted by the mentioned Pope on 4 May 1260.[120] Though Alexander's high esteem for the Bohemian princess is perceivable by only two additional letters sent to her,[121] this document is not free of doubt: the usage of Order's title *ordo sanctae Clarae* by the Papal chancery at this stage causes irritations since this title was used only after Urban's regulation three years later, in 1263.[122] Probably due to generally insecure forms of tradition and this observation, many recent investigations on Agnes and her monastery remain cautious or silent about their statements on this document.[123] Regardless whether the Clarissan community was sticking to the rule of living without possession or not, its economic situation must have been awkward in the first half of the fourteenth century as we learn from a bishops appeal to collect alms for it in 1342.[124]

---

amplectere. Il punto su Chiara ed Agnese di Boemia", in *Chiara e la diffusione delle Clarisse nel secolo XIII, Atti del convegno di studi in occasione dell'VIII centenario della nascita di Santa Chiara, Manduria, 14-15 dic. 1994*, ed. G. ANDENNA, B. VETERE, Lecce, 1998, p. 121-132; Id., "La 'forma vitae' di san Francesco per San Damiano tra Chiara d'Assisi, Agnese di Boemia ed interventi papali", *Hagiographica*, 4 (1997), p. 179-195.

[119] Cf. *Vita Prima*, p. 509: *Clara audita fama illius gratulata, mittens ab Innocentio IV regulas confirmatas, quas & haec ab Alexandro IV confirmari denuo petiit*.

[120] CDB V/1, p. 345s., no. 223; RBM II, p. 761, no. 1769; cf. Fl. HAMMERSCHMID, *Monasterium S. Agnetis sacrarum virginium clarissarum ord. S. Francisci*, Old Prague, reprint 1845, p. 80-83 (Prague, NKP, sign. I D 40); cf. Chr.-Fr. FELSKAU, *Agnes von Böhmen, op. cit.*, p. 311.

[121] CDB V/3, p. 127-129, no. 1147s. (27.4.1259): *Insinuavit nobis carissima in Christo filia nostra Agnes soror monasterii sancti Francisci Pragensis ordinis sancti Damiani, quod dilecta in Christo filia nobilis mulier... ducissa Poloniae germana sua cupiens ad gloriam celestis*.

[122] G. P. FREEMAN, *Klaras Kloster, op. cit.*, p. 55, no. 64, mentions a few episcopal and Franciscan documents, using this title for the Order prior to its official announcement; cf. the examination by Chr.-Fr. FELSKAU, *Agnes von Böhmen*, p. 315s. The usage of this expression by the Papal chancery at this stage remains unique and questionable. Noteworthy, in the very same year (before April 1260), King Ottokar II granted to the Crosiers with the Red Star at Prague a village, making reference to his *amita nostra* (Agnes), *ordinis sancte Clare*; CDB V/1, p. 334s., no. 215.

[123] The interpretation of M. KREIDLER-KOS, "Klara von Assisi – Zwischen Bettelarmut und Beziehungsreichtum", in *Lebendiger Spiegel des Lichts, op.cit.*, p. 1-18, here p. 13, thus is not virtually correct. See for instance J. MUELLER, *The privilege of Poverty, op. cit.*, p. 125-129, who does not make any reference to this document.

[124] Bishop John IV of Dražice on April 1342; mentioned by V. TOMEK, *Dějepis mesta Prahy II, op. cit.*, Prague, 1899, here p. 200. See recently E. DOLEŽALOVÁ, "The Inquisition in Medieval Bohemia: National and International Contexts", in *Heresy and the Making of European Culture. Medieval and Modern Perspectives*, ed. J. SIMPSON, A. ROACH, Farnham, 2013, chapter 15.

The second pillar of the discerned particular affinity between the Bohemian princess and the Umbrian foundress of the Poor Clares consists of four letters addressed to Agnes (henceforth: *EpCl.1-4*). Leaving aside the insecure tradition of one or two *epistolae* to Ermentrude of Bruges, presented firstly in Wadding's *Annales Minorum* but recently excluded by most scholars from their reflections, they are considered the most significant part of Clare's epistolary heritage;[125] moreover, they are seen as evidence of the extraordinary spiritual and human relation between the Umbrian founding figure and the Central European princess. At least since the discovery of the letters in the Milan manuscript of *CLE* and their fragmentary tradition in the Šibenik bundle, they are considered by scholars unanimously as authentic.[126] The objection that the theological elaborateness leastways of the fourth letter does not fit with Clare's assumed modest education was replied by the argument that the authoress most likely received support from an educated brother, eventually brother Leo, in the times of her growing illness.[127] The correspondence subsequently was subject to numerous studies examining their stylistic arrangement, the theological ideas,[128] their references to the Bible, their appraisal of the Franciscan concept of poverty or their interdependence to other sources on or of Clare, like her (disputed) testament, her rule, and the epistolarian exchange between the Roman *curia* and Agnes. While a critical codicological, intertextual investigation on it reflecting also the Late Medieval Observant recourse on prior sources and pious intentions is still missing,[129] remarkable aspects of the *Überlieferungsgeschichte* of these texts like the disjointed tradition of *CLE* and *EpCl.1-4* within the (non-Franciscan)

---

[125] L. WADDING, *Annales Minorum*, vol. 4, Quarracchi, reprint 1931, here p. 30s (ad annum 1258). See the introduction of E. PAOLI in: *Fontes Francescani II*, ed. S. BRUFANI et al., Assisi, 1995, p. 2223-2260, esp. p. 2251-2254; *Clare of Assisi – The Lady*, p. 51, includes them into the corpus; *La letteratura francescana*, vol. I: *Francesco e Chiara d'Assisi*, ed. CL. LEONARDI, Firenze, 2004, like many others, does not. See the remarks of J. MUELLER, *A Companion to Clare: Life, Writing, and Spirituality*, Leiden, 2010, p. 15, no. 17; *Francis and Clare – the complete Works*, ed. R. ARMSTRONG, New Jersey, 1986, p. 207.
[126] M. BARTOLI, *Klara von Assisi. Die Geschichte ihres Lebens*, Werl, 1993, p. 22s.; P. L. BARABÁS, "Le lettere di Santa Chiara alla Beata Agnese di Praga", in *Santa Chiara d'Assisi. Studi e Cronaca del VII Centenario 1253-1953*, Assisi, 1954, p. 123-143.
[127] See K. ELM, "Klara von Assisi und Agnes von Prag – Na Františku und San Damiano", in *Franziskus von Assisi. Das Bild des Heiligen aus neuer Sicht*, ed. D. R. BAUER, H. FELD and U. KÖPF, Köln-Weimar-Vienna, 2005, p. 227-250; on *EpCl.4* see the observations of T. JOHNSON "Clare, Leo, and the Authorship of the Fourth Letter to Agnes of Prague", *Franciscan Studies*, 62 (2004), p. 91-100.
[128] For the most important contributions consult the bibliography at L. LEHMANN, *Die Briefe der hl. Klara*, p. 11s.
[129] Introductionary: B. ROEST, "The Poor Clares during the Era of Observant Reforms: Attempts at a Typology", *Franciscan Studies*, 69 (2011), p. 343-386.

Milanese codex[130] as well as the distinct letters' addressees remain nearly undisputed.[131] Even the observation that none of the petitions for canonization in the 1330s mentions this important correspondence did not cause further inspection although it must lead to the conclusion that in the composing phase of the legend these documents were not known. In sum, the general spatial and chronological linkage between letters and legend was lacking detailed knowledge.

Since the oldest witness of the letters is handed down together with Agnes' legend, it is worthwhile to contextualize the tradition of both texts, integrating their codicological as well as historical context. Systematically, this tradition can be distinguished into three types: first a contextual one of *EpCl.1-4* and *CLE* and their Middle-High German translations; second the witnesses of *EpCl.1-4* without connection to the Agnes legend; third *CLE* and their Middle-High German translations without the epistolarian appendage. Focussing first on the manuscripts with the Bohemian legend, research has determined in total three Latin witnesses and eight Middle-High German translations ranging from the late fourteenth century to the early sixteenth century:

Table 3: Witnesses of *Candor lucis eterne* (current repositories) and their origin, chronological order

Category	Abbr. (Storage place)	Description
\multicolumn{3}{c}{CLE, Latin}		
#1	*Mi* (Milano)	oldest witness, *c.* 1333/38, Prague; published by Vyskočil
#2	*Ši* (Šibenik)	probably second half 14th c., probably Prague?; unpublished

---

[130] J. K. Vyskočil, *Legenda blahoslavené Anežky*, p. 16-18. Between *CLE* and *EpCl.1-4* are incorporated two apocryphal letters of St Ignatius, which are first known from the end of the thirteenth century: H. J. Sieben, "Die Ignatianen als Briefe. Einige formkritische Bemerkungen", *Vigiliae Christianae*, 32 (1978), p. 1-18.

[131] Only the first and the third letter allow a clear identification of their addressee whereas the second and the fourth letter leave room for interpretation. *EpCl.1*, p. 139: *Venerabili et sanctissime virgini, Domine Angneti, filie excellentissimi ac illustrissimi regis Bohemie*; *EpCl.2*, p. 142: *Filie Regis regum, ancille Domini dominancium, sponse dignitissime Ihesu Christi et ideo regine prenobili domine Agneti*; *EpCl.3*, p. 144: *In Christo sibi reverendissime domine ac pre cunctis mortalibus diligende sorori Agneti, illustris regis Bohemie germane*; *EpCl.4*, p. 147: *Anime sue dimidie et precordialis amoris armarie singularis, illustri regine, agni regis eterne sponse, domine Agneti, matri sue et karissime ac filie inter omnes altas speciali*.

Category	Abbr. (Storage place)	Description
#3	Ba1 (Bamberg)	around 1360/1380/end of 14th c., Poor Clare's monastery of Nuremberg, scribe: Katharina Hoffmann (abbess 1380-1393); published by Seton
	CLE, Middle-High-German	
#1	Ba2 (Bamberg)	end of 14th / beg. of 15th c., Nuremberg[131]
#2	Mü1 (Munich)	third quarter of 15th c., North-Bavarian monastery, probl. Nuremberg (reformed 1452)[132]
#3	Wi (Vienna)	[1435], 1501, 1507; transcript, probabl. of Nicholas Glassberger; Nuremberg[133]
#4	Wo (Wolfenbüttel)	15th c., Silesian female monastery, possibly Wrocław, probabl. Clarissan[134]

---

[132] Published by W. SETON, *op. cit.* (see above, n. 57).

[133] Munich, Bayerische Staatsbibliothek (henceforth BSM), Cgm. 539; Legendary as part of the compendium 'Heiligen Leben, Januar – April, September – Dezember', fol. 232r-261v: M.-H.Germ. version of *CLE* with deviating epilogue, cf. W. SETON, *Some New Sources, op. cit.*, p. 19; dating and provenience: K. SCHNEIDER, *Die deutschen Handschriften der Bayerischen Staatsbibliothek München V/IV*, Wiesbaden, 1978, p. 104s; briefly: W. WILLIAMS-KRAPP, *Die deutschen und niederländischen Legendare des Mittelalters. Studien zu ihrer Überlieferungs-, Text- und Wirkungsgeschichte*, Tübingen, 1986, p. 317s.

[134] Vienna, Österreichische Nationalbibliothek, cod. 13.671, Legendary; fol. 1r-29v: "Hie vahet an daz leben und lesen der kúnigin agnes von behim, die sancte claren orden lebet sechs und vierzig Iar [sic]"; *EpCl.1-4*: fol. 31r-37r. *Verzeichnis der altdeutschen literarischen Handschriften der Österreichischen Nationalbibliothek*, vol. III, Berlin, 1961, p. 1329, describes it as a collected manuscript written in Gothic character by three scribes.

[135] Wolfenbüttel, Herzog August Bibtliothek, Cod. Guelf. 132 Helmst.; fol. 153r.-205r.: M.-H.Germ. version of *SVC* and *LbAA*; fol. 205r-213v: M.-H.Germ. version of *EpCl.1-4*; fol. 213v-214r: M.-H.Germ. version of *KlaBen.*; fol. 257v-287r: M.-H.Germ. version of *CLE* (W. SETON, *Some New Sources, op. cit.*, p. 19 f.); E. NEUNER, *Textkritische Edition der mittelhochdeutschen Klara-Predigten des Prager Codex XVI D 16 samt vollständigem Glossar*, Diss., Innsbruck, 1971, p. 38-42; M. BORKOWSKI, *Two medieval German translations of the letters of St Clare of Assisi to Blessed Agnes of Prague and the Benediction of St Clare*, Diss., Chapel Hill, 1974, p. xlviii-xlix. Due to the close spiritual and personal connections between the Clarissan house in Breslau and the one in Prague, one tends to attribute this witness to the Silesian community, cf. J. KĘBŁOWSKI, *Klasztor, kościół ss. Urzulanek i Mauzoleum Piastów Wrocławskich*, Wrocław, 1998. On the examination of the library's manuscripts: V. HOHNEMANN, "Fromme Frauen oder ungebärdige und verdorbene höhere Töchter? Eine Verbotsliste des Provinzials Ulrich vom Hagen aus dem Jahre 1365 für die Breslauer Klarissen (mit Abdruck und Übersetzung des Texts)", *Wissenschaft und Weisheit*, 75 (2012), p. 237-258, here p. 238.

Category	Abbr. (Storage place)	Description
# 5	Be1 (Berlin)	mid 15th c., female Dominicans, Saint Nikolas *in undis*, Strasbourg (reformed 1431)[135]
# 6	Pra (Prague)	after 1465, Poor Clares of Eger (reformed by Nuremberg 1465)[136]
# 7	Be2 (Berlin)	1492-98, Poor Clares of Söflingen/ Ulm (reformed by Pfullingen 1485)[137]
# 8	Stu (Stuttgart)	(1490-1511?) / beginning of 16th c., Poor Clares of Pfullingen (reformed 1484)[138]

The eight Middle-High German versions can be distinguished into two general branches, one closer to the Latin original (*Ba2, Mü1, Pra*, 'Sondergut': *Wo*), the other more distant and without deeper knowledge on local names and topographies (*Wi, Be2, Be1, Stu*).[140] As the table shows, the shift from the Latin to vernacular traditions and the proliferation of the

---

[136] Berlin, Staatsbibliothek zu Berlin – Preußischer Kulturbesitz (henceforth: SBB), Germ. quart. 189; according to H. HORNUNG, *Daniel Sudermann als Handschriftensammler*, Diss., Tübingen, 1956, p. 90s., of "lower Alsatian" origin. On the monastery's library: A. RÜTHER, H.-J. SCHWIEGER, "Die Predigthandschriften des Straßburger Dominikaerinnenklosters St. Nikolaus in undis", in *Die deutsche Predigt im Mittelalter*, ed. V. MERTENS, Tübingen, 1992, p. 160-193; H.-J. SCHIEWER, *Die Handschriften aus dem Straßburger Dominikanerinnenkloster St. Nikolaus in undis und benachbarte Provenienzen*, Tübingen, 2000; W. WILLIAMS-KRAPP, *Die deutschen und niederländischen Legendare*, p. 39; Zd. UHLÍŘ, *Literární prameny svatováclavského kultu a úcty ve vrcholném a pozdním středověku*, Prague, 1996, here p. 49-57.

[137] Prague, NKP, XVI D 16, fol. 133-140: *CLE*. Of interest here also the incorporated letter of bishop Thybaldus on the socalled Portiuncula decree; partially ed.: E. NEUNER, *Textkritische Edition, op. cit., passim*. Cf. M. BORKOWSKI, *Two medieval German translations, op. cit.*, p. xli-xliii.

[138] Berlin, SBB, Sign. Germ. oct. 484; therein fol. 177r-214v: M.-H.Germ. version of *CLE*; fol. 215r-222v: M.-H.Germ. version of *EpCl.1-4*; fol. 222v-223r: M.-H.Germ. version of *BenCl-A*.; W. SETON, *Some New Sources, op. cit.*, p. 20s., notices the Upper-German, Swabian idiom; cf. M. BORKOWSKI, *Two medieval German translations*, p. xxvi-xxix. On the monastery, founded in 1239 and supporting the Nuremberg community in the phase of its incorporation into the Order of the Poor Clares: K. S. FRANK, *Das Klarissenkloster Söflingen: ein Beitrag zur franziskanischen Ordensgeschichte Süddeutschlands und zur Ulmer Kirchengeschichte*, Stuttgart, 1980.

[139] Stuttgart, Württembergische Landesbibliothek, cod. HB I 26, here fol. 37r-72v; M.-H. Germ. version of *CLE*, mixed manuscript, on the monastery (founded 1250): R. WAIBEL, *750 Jahre Klarissenkloster der heiligen Cäcilie in Pfullingen: 1252-2002*, Pfullingen, 2002; in short: A. RÖTTGER, P. GROSS, *Klarissen, op. cit.*, p. 34. About its scriptorium: F. HEINZER, "Bücher aus der Klausur – Das abgewandte Leben der Pfullinger Klarissen im Spiegel ihrer Bibliothek und Schreibtätigkeit", in *Franziskus, Klara und das Pfullinger Kloster. Vorträge anlässlich des 750-jährigen Jubiläums der Ersterwähnung des Klarissenklosters Pfullingen*, Pfullingen, 2003, p. 40-61.

[140] V. BOK, *Einige Beobachtungen, op. cit.*, p. 171-174; *Id.*, "Zwei deutsche Übertragungen der lateinischen Kanonisationslegende über Agnes von Böhmen", in *Editionsberichte zur*

Middle-High German versions of the Agnes legend finds its starting point at the Nuremberg monastery of the Poor Clares in the second half of the fourteenth century. In this monastery, the last Latin transcript was composed, as we learn from a colophone, by Katharina Hoffmann, detectable as abbess in the period 1380-1393, and, most probably parallel to it, the first of at least three known translations of *CLE* was conducted. The geographic distribution of the vernacular legends underlines how the liturgical remembrance of the Přeymslid princess moved from its homeland to adjacent territories after the Hussite Reformation – though the knowledge of her never ceased completely. The local chronicles of that era report only in scarce words on the princess, but with a content which exceeded the information held by the *Vita Prima*.[141]

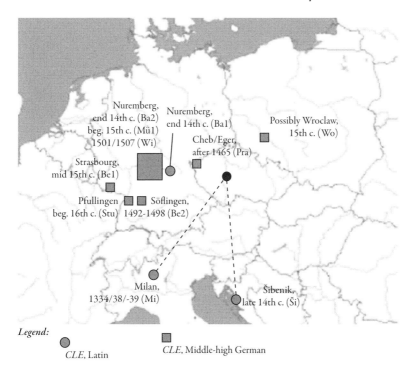

Figure 1: Geographic distribution of the textual witnesses of *Candor lucis eterne*

---

mittelalterlichen deutschen Literatur. Beiträge der Bamberger Tagung 'Methoden und Probleme der Edition mittelalterlicher deutscher Texte', ed. A. SCHWOB, Göppingen, 1994, p. 181-184.
[141] *Chronica Bohemorum ab initio gentis ad annum 1438*, in *Monumenta Historica Boemiae usquam antehac edita*, colligit P. G. DOBNER a S. Catharina e clericis regularibus scholarum, t. III, Prague, 1774, p. 32-56, here p. 49; and *Series ducum et regum Bohemiae* (c. 1459), in *Scriptores rerum Bohemicarum*, t. II, Prague, 1784, p. 427-434.

The initial activities of the Nuremberg monastery of the Poor Clares testify an early, but strong endeavor of strengthening the Order's tradition and primary ideas, long before the Observance movement put its feed into this community (1452) and the intensive literal and logistic undertakings of Nicholas Glassberger († 1508) with his particular interest in the affairs in his Bohemian homeland were unfolded.[142] These first attempts to reinforce the Order's origins and principles – in a way a 'pre-Observant-reform' – were accompanied by a considerable artitistic and literal production.[143] The transcription and later on the translation of the Latin version of *CLE* was embedded into a textual corpus of hagiographic texts which in its basic composition included the Clare legend then called *Admirabilis femina*,[144] her canonization bull, a brief collection of Clare's biographical data, and a rhymed prayer 'Sand Claren bvch' for which the initial researcher on it, Kurt Ruh, labelled it *Klarenbuch*.[145] In one of its embellished branches this collection of hagiographic recounts comprised the following texts: the legend of Clare's sister

---

[142] W. SETON, *Nicholas Glassberger and His Works*, Manchester, 1923; see Glassbergers *Maior Chronica Bohemorum moderna* (Brno, Statni Oblastni Archiv, G 12 (= Ceroni) II 292), in this book, p. 1-109. See also: *Schreib die Reformation von München gancz daher. Teiledition und historische Einordnung der Nürnberger Klarissenchronik*, ed. L. VOSDING, Nürnberg, 2012, with a partial edition of the convent's chronicle. F. MACHILEK, "Klosterhumanismus in Nürnberg um 1500", *Mitteilungen des Vereins für Geschichte des Stadt Nürnberg*, 64 (1977), p. 10-45.

[143] Cf. the splendid altarpiece of Clare, manufactured around/after 1360; reproduced in: *Krone und Schleier. Kunst aus mittelalterlichen Frauenklöstern, Ausstellungskatalog*, Munich, 2005, p. 509-515; Fr. M. KAMMEL, *Verborgene Schönheit. Spätgotische Schätze aus der Klarakirche in Nürnberg. Katalog zur Ausstellung im Germanischen Nationalmuseum*, Nürnberg 2007, p. 107s. For the textual production see the famous book of St Mary: B. JUNG, *Das Nürnberger Marienbuch. Untersuchungen und Edition*, Tübingen, 2004, here esp. p. 34*-39* (the library of the monastery), p. 69*-71* (the manuscripts entering the monastery after 1410).

[144] See also: J. SCHNEIDER, "Klara nördlich der Alpen: Das Nürnberger *Sand claren bvch*", in *Lebendiger Spiegel*, p. 143-160, here p. 148. Many manuscripts contain only Clare's legend without the discussed adjoined texts; selected witnesses with closer geographical or contextual affinity: Munich, BSM, Cgm 5235 (Poor Clares of Cologne, last quarter of 14th c.); Nuremberg, Germanisches Nationalmuseum Nürnberg (henceforth: GNM), Hs. 7206 (Dominican monastery of Nuremberg, rhymed legend on Clare, 15th c.; J. SCHNEIDER, " 'Freu dich Klara'. Eine mittelhochdeutsche Reimlegende [FrKl]", in *"Vena vivida – Lebendige Quelle". Texte zu Klara von Assisi und ihrer Bewegung I: Deutsche und niederländische Zeugnisse zur hl. Klara*, Münster, 2008, p. 65-84, here 65). In addition also Augsburg, Universitätsbibliothek Augsburg, Cod. II.1.2°222/2. At Wrocław, further manuscripts consisting of the legend and other Clarian texts are stored, deriving certainly from the local Poor Clares. G. BOCCALI, "Tradizione manuscritta delle legende di Santa Chiara", in *Clara Claris praeclara, op. cit.*, p. 419-500, here p. 438, 440.

[145] K. RUH, *s. v.* "St. Klara-Buch", in *Die deutsche Literatur des Mittelalters*, vol. 4, ed. W. STÜMMLER *et al.*, Berlin-New York, 1983, col. 1183s.; *Id.*, "Das 'St. Klara-Buch' ", *Wissenschaft & Weisheit*, 46 (1983), p. 192-206; introductionly: K. HOFFMANN, "Aus dem 'St.-Klara-Buch' [KlB]. Eingeleitet und übersetzt von Johannes Schneider OFM", in *'Vena vivida', op. cit.*, p. 29-64, here p. 32-35, with a list of the distinctive material ('Sondergut') of this *compendium*. The basic branch edited by: H. FLESSA, *Thomas von Celano: 'Legenda*

Agnes of Assisi (1197/98-1253; *Legenda beatae Agnetis Assisiensis*; henceforth: *LbAA*), Clare's four letters, her blessing for Agnes, commonly attributed to the Bohemian foundress (*BenCl-A*),[146] and finally the legend of the Přemyslid princess; it came into existence eventually in the 1360s-70s, due to the work of a certain lecturer Johannes, and became an important source for many female communities of the Franciscan Observant reform movement in the German speaking territories and beyond.[147] Could the interlinkage of the letters and *Candor lucis eterne* have been the result of a confused attribution and *EpCl.2* or *EpCl.4* addressed to another Agnes, Clare's biological sister or the contemporary Clarissan Agnes de Peranda (or of Barcelona, † 1281) who probably had stayed in Assisi and founded a Damianite community in the Catalan town in 1237?[148] Although the addressee of *EpCl.1* and *EpCl.3* does not allow diverse attributions and notwithstanding our current knowledge that the content of *EpCl.2* (admonishment to follow the advice of the dismissed minister Elias) and *EpCl.4* suggest convincingly an attribution to the Bohemian princess, it is worth considering contemporary implication and ignorance in play. Such a perspective might explain particularities related to their discovery and to the process of their connection with her legend.

Whereas the information on Agnes of Barcelona is pretty vague and does not provide any provable indication of an Iberian-Umbrian net of communication during Clare's lifetime, the postum and hagiographic perception of Agnes of Assisi is deeply intertwined with the one of her elderly sister which coaxed scholars repeatedly to warn of mistakes.[149] Agnes of Assisi entered the

---

Sanctae Clarae Virginis'. Die mittelhochdeutsche Übersetzung des Codex 14711 aus dem Germanischen Nationalmuseum Nürnberg, Würzburg, 1964.

[146] Oldest witness in *Ba1*. Edition: W. SETON, "Some New Sources for the Life of Blessed Agnes of Bohemia including some chronological notes and a new text of the Benediction of Saint Clare", *Archivum Franciscanum Historicum*, 7 (1914), p. 185-190, here p. 189s.; *Klara-Quellen*, *op. cit.*, p. 88. Medieval Dutch translations of the blessing collects D. DE KOK, "S. Clarae benedictionis textus Neerlandici", *Archivum Franciscanum Praedicatorum*, 27 (1934), p. 387-397. According to J. MUELLER, *A Companion to Clare*, *op. cit.*, p. 17, this text is likewise of questionable authenticity.

[147] The unique known Umbrian adoption of the *Klarenbuch* can be found in the first vernacular legend on Saint Clare written by Battista Alfani around 1490. K. HOFMANN, "Aus dem 'St.-Klara-Buch'", *op. cit.*, p. 36; Edition: *Vita et leggenda della seraphica vergine Sancta Chiara distinta in capitoli composta in volgare da sr. Battista Alfani*, ed. G. BOCCALI, Assisi, 2010, here esp. p. 253s., 276, with references to the closer relationship between Clare and her sister Agnes.

[148] *EpCl.4*, p. 148, mentions the regards of Clare's biological sister, which excludes that the latter was the addressee. On the foundress: N. JORNET I BENITO, "Agnès de Peranda i Clara de Janua: dues figures carismàtiques o la fundació del monastir de sant Antoni de Barcelona", *Duoda*, 22 (2002), p. 41-54.

[149] G. JAKSCHE, *Die selige Agnes von Prag*, Munich, 1989, p. 33. False attributions of art historians and other researchers when it comes to representations of Agnes are not such rare.

community of San Damiano following the conversion of Clare, became later on the abbess of the monastery of Monticelli (near Florence) and is supposed to have founded further female Franciscan houses in Mantua, Venice and Padua; shortly before the death of her sister she returned to San Damiano and died also only a few months after Clare's decease. Her legend *Admirabilis femina* which functioned as the crucial text within the development of the *Klarenbuch* recounts the close relationship between the two sisters, an intimate relation which is moreover strengthened by declarations of Clarissans during the canonization process of Clare.[150] The legend of Agnes, *LbAA*, is integrated into the *Chronica XXIV Generalium* which is supposed to be written by the Franciscan Arnald of Sarrant, lecturer at the *Sacro convento* in 1356 and, if they are identical, provincial minister in the long period from 1361-1383.[151] Although we lack a witness of this chronicle prior to Glassberger's revision more than a hundred years later and we can not assess the interventions and modifications made by him, the prominent position of this text – the first female legend in the collection of reports and legends, even prior to Clare's *vita*! – and the integration of one undated letter addressed to her sister (*EpAgn*) catches more attention.[152] It is noteworthy that we finally become aware of a correspondence between Clare and a pen friend named Agnes who wasn't of Bohemian origin. At the same time, but certainly before the year 1400, the Nuremberg Dominicans who stood in good relation with the neighbouring Clarissans, composed the German legendary called *Der heiligen Leben*, which entails a short description of the life of Agnes of Assisi, though of distinct provenance.[153] On the other hand, the Clarissans of this

---

Cf. M. PROKOPP, "Die hl. Agnezka an dem Altarfresko von Simone Martini in der Hl. Elisabethkapelle in der Unterkirche von San Francesco in Assisi", in *Svatá Anežka Česká a velké jeny její doby*, p. 197-208, here p. 208, interpreting Agnes of Rome as Agnes of Bohemia in a famous depiction of Simone Martini (1284-1344).

[150] *Santa Chiara di Assisi. I primi documenti ufficiali, op. cit.*, here 1, 55 and 6, 49.

[151] Latest: J. SCHNEIDER, *Arnald von Sarrant (?). Das Leben der heiligen Agnes von Assisi und ihr Brief an ihre Schwester, die heilige Agnes*, in *Klara von Assisi, op. cit.*, p. 507-528. Source: "Chronica XXIV Generalium Ordinis Minorum", *Analecta Franciscana*, 3 (1897), p. 1-616 (henceforth: *ChXXIVGen*); M. T. DOLSO, *La Chronica XXIV generalium. Il difficile percorso dell'unità nella storia francescana*, Padova, 2003.

[152] *ChXXIVGen* p. 174-181 (*EpAgn* + *LbAA*). German translation: J. SCHNEIDER, *Arnald von Sarrant (?)*, p. 520-522, here esp. no. 57. *EpAgn* is inserted into WADDING, *Annales Minorum, ad annum 1221*, no. 20, right before *EpCl.1*. See also *Escritos de Santa Clara, op. cit.*, p. 361-365, dating this letter to the year 1232.

[153] V. STADLER, "Von sant Klarn, Das Klara-Leben im frühneuhochdeutschen Legendar 'Der Heiligen Leben' " in *"Vena vivida", op. cit.*, p. 109-126. The veneration of Clarissan women within the female Dominican Order still lacks substantial examination. See A. WILLING, *Die Bibliothek des Klosters St. Katharina zu Nürnberg: Synoptische Darstellung der Bücherverzeichnisse*, vol. 1, Berlin, 2012, p. lxxxvii, n. 211. See also E. L. LINDGREN, *Sensual*

town close to the Bohemian border maintained close relations to the Order's houses in Prague and Cheb/Eger (the latter pertained, like the Nuremberg community, to the Franciscan province *Saxonia*)[154] saw from the 1350s-60s onwards a "re-franciscanisation" of their community, apparently launched without any reinforcement from outside, which led to an increase of artistic production as verified among others by a famous alterpiece.[155]

As demonstrated, the reawakening of spiritual origins was shaped by an accompanying production of hagiographic material and the development of the *Klarenbuch*. The Middle-High German manuscripts even preceding the latest Latin version of the Agnes legend already comprise an early stage of this re-collection. Their first witness includes only a fragment of the first letter to Agnes, the following ones already show the complete set. This means that the letters were not an integral part of the *CLE*-tradition, but an element of a textual corpus concentrating on Clare and her sister. The Latin witness of *CLE* from Nuremberg, indicating the transition to the Middle-High German versions of the Bohemian legend, provides further evidence for the assertion that earlier hagiographic information on the Umbrian Agnes and her close ties to Clare must have existed.[156] In this crucial manuscript, we find, after the translation of *Admirabilis femina* an abbreviated Middle-High German version of this *LbAA* with *EpAgn*; the Middle-High German versions *EpCl.1-4* are placed right between this letter and the Latin version of *CLE* which attests that both texts already had a disjointed history. These observations carry a more systematic differentiation of the introduced three types of traditions of hagiographic sources on the Bohemian Agnes, distinguishing those incorporated into the elaboration of the *Klarenbuch* and those without connection to it.

Encounters. Monastic Women and Spirituality in Medieval Germay, New York, 2009, focussing on the 'Schwesternbücher' of the Dominicans.

[154] K. SIEGL, "Das Salbuch der Egerer Klarissen v. J. 1476 im Egerer Stadtarchiv", *Mitteilungen des Vereins für Geschichte der Deutschen in Böhmen*, 42 (1904), p. 207-252, 293-317, 450-479; 43 (1905), p. 77-105; H. GRADL, *Monumenta Egrana: Denkmäler des Egerlandes als Quellen für dessen Geschichte*, 2 vols., Eger, 1888-1889, here vol. I, p. 135, no. 367 (14.1.1273). See also the miracle M12 / M5 in *CLE*, p. 128s. On the inter-regional relations: R. ZAORAL, "Wirtschaftsbeziehungen zwischen Bayern und Böhmen. Die Handelskontakte Prags mit Eger, Regensburg, Nürnberg und Venedig im 13. Jahrhundert", in *Bayern und Böhmen. Kontakt, Konflikt, Kultur*, ed. R. LUFT, L. EIBER, Munich, 2nd ed., 2007, p. 13-34.

[155] Taken from: FR. M. KAMMEL, *Verborgene Schönheit, op. cit.*, p. 19, Ill. 20; and *Krone und Schleier, op. cit.*, p. 509-515. See further illustrations in P. SCHNEIDER, *Tafelmalerei in Nürnberg 1350-1550*, Königstein i. T., 1993, p. 20-23.

[156] The oldest Italian vernacular version reaches back till the end of the fourteenth century: 'Clara in claustro latebat in mundo clarebat', cioè *Legende antiche in volgare di santa Chiara di Assisi (sec. XIV-XV)*, ed. G. BOCCALI, Assisi, 2010, esp. p. 261-277.

Table 4: Contextual typology of the tradition of *CLE* and *EpCl.1-4*
in chronological order

Category, first level	Category, second level	Abbreviation (Language; dating)
A: *EpCl.1-4* in contextual tradition of *CLE*	A.1.: without 'Klarenbuch', after *CLE*	*Mi* (L; c. 1330)
		Ši (L; *EpCl.2*-frag., *EpCl.3+4*; 2nd half 14th c.)[156]
		Be2 (G; 1490s)
		Wi (G; probl. 1501)
		Žiwot blah. Anyžky (T; 1666)[157]
	A.2.: with 'Klarenbuch', *LbAA*, after *CLE*	*Ba1* (L; c. 1380)
		Wo (G; 15th c.)
		Pra (G; after 1465)
B: *EpCl.1-4* without contextual tradition of *CLE*	B.1.: with *SCV*, 'Klarenbuch-early stage' and *LbAA*	*Dre1* (G; *EpCl.1* – fragment, 1350?)[158]
		Dre2 (G; 1356/74.)[159]
		Ba3 (G; late 14th c.)[160]

---

[157] On the library and the church of the local Franciscans: M. OREB, "Samostan sv. Frane u Šibeniku", in *Kulturna baština samostana sv. Frane u Šibeniku*, ed. Grg. NOVAK, Vj. MAŠTROVIĆ, Zagreb, 1968, p. 7-38, here p. 10-12; Ž. TOLI, "Redovništvo u šibenskoj biskupili u srednjem vijeku", in *Sedam stoljeća Šibenske biskupije. Zbornik radova sa znanstvenog skupa Šibenska biskupija od 1298. do 1998*, Šibenik, 2000, p. 549-582, here p. 558-566.

[158] According to V. BOK, *Einige Beobachtungen, op. cit.*, p. 167, this source is a clear indication that a Czech translation was accomplished already in the fourteenth century. This lost manuscript could have been a direct model of the *Vita Secunda*.

[159] Dresden, Sächsische Landesbibliothek – Staats- und Unversitätsbibliothek Dresden (SLUB), m. 282, Bl. 1-4: *Daz ist der vor brive...*; Bl. 4-100': Klarenbuch incl. *SCV* with the ending: *Hie hat seind Claren puch ein ende*; bl. 110'-114: *Disse Priffe sand...* (= *EpCl.1*). Provenance: Nuremberg, monastery of the Poor Clares. *Katalog der Handschriften der Sächsischen Landesbibliothek zu Dresden*, Dresden, 1981, p. 520s.

[160] Dresden, SLUB, m. 281 (b); fol. 1r-150v: Middle-High German versions of *SVC* and *LbAA*; fol. 150v-175r: M.-H.G. version of *EpCl.1-4*; fol. 175r-176v: M.-H.G. version of *BenCl-A*. W. SETON, *Some New Sources*, p. 20. Provenance: Nuremberg, monastery of the Poor Clares. *Katalog der Handschriften der Sächsischen Landesbibliothek zu Dresden, op. cit.*, p. 519s.

[161] See above; W. SETON, *Some New Sources*, p. 18s. Provenance: Nuremberg, monastery of the Poor Clares, scribe Margarethe Wiesenthau, the successor of Katharina Hoffmann, probably till 1403. Analysis: M. UMIKER, "Un'antica raccolta di fonti su Chiara d'Assisi: Il 'Sand Claren Bvch' di Norimberga", *Collectanea Franciscana*, 85 (2015), p. 207-235.

Category, first level	Category, second level	Abbreviation (Language; dating)
	B.2.: with 'Klarenbuch', *LbAA*	*Nü* (G; before 1380)[161]
		Mü3 (G; 2nd half 14th c.)[162]
	B.3.: with 'Klarenbuch', without *LbAA*	*Ka* (G; 1490s)[163]
	B.4.: with *Chronica XXIV Generalium* (embellished by Glassberger)	*Ha* (L; *EpCl.1*-fragment; c. 1491)[164]
	B.5.: without 'Klarenbuch'	*Mü2* (G; 1487/90)[165]

---

[162] Nürnberg, GNM, cod. 147III, containing also the rhymed legend on Clare. On fol. 127r-141v: *EpCl.1-4* (cf. *Kataloge des Germanischen Nationalmuseums Nürnberg. Die Handschriften des Germanischen Nationalmuseums Nürnbergs in 5 Bänden*, ed. L. KURRAS, Wiesbaden, 1974-1994, here vol. I, p. 64s.); see B. JUNG, *Das Nürnberger Marienbuch*, p. 34*. On this legend still instructive: L. OLIGER, "Documenta Gaudia sancte virginis Clare seu Vita eius versificata", *Archivum Franciscanum Historicum*, 12 (1919), p. 110-131, here p. 122-131 (with edition).

[163] Munich, Bayerisches Nationalmuseum, Mss. 3603, with the following sequence: Papal letter to Clare, *SCV*, canonization bull and life data of Clare, again *SCV*, *LbAA*, *EpCl.1-4*, *BenCl-A.*, *LegMai* (Bonaventure), recounts out of the Order. Cf. M. BORKOWSKI, *Two medieval German translations*, p. xxxvi-xxxviii. On its provenance: J. HAMBURGER, "Am Anfang war das Bild: Kunst und Frauenspiritualität im Spätmittelalter", in *Studien und Texte zur literarischen und materiellen Kultur der Frauenklöster*, p. 1-44, here p. 41, ill. 16, states Regensburg as possible provenance (Poor Clares?). Dating: B. JUNG, *Das Nürnberger Marienbuch*, p. 34*.

[164] Karlsruhe, Badische Landesbibliothek, sign. Cod. Thennenbach 4. Main scribe: Magdalena Steimerin; secondary scribe and illustrator: Sybilla of Bondorf, around 1493; presumably accomplished for the Poor Clares of Straßburg ('St. Klara auf dem Wörd'); edition of the investigated part: M. BORKOWSKI, *Two medieval German translations, op. cit.*, p. 1-73. The additions within *SCV* summarizes: CL. BRUINS, *Chiara d'Assisi come altera Maria: le miniature della vita di Santa Chiara nel manoscritto Thennenbach-4 di Karlsruhe* (Iconographia francescana, 12), Rome, 1999, p. 40-44. Description: U. BODEMANN, "Von Schwestern für Schwestern. Miniaturzyklen der Klarissin Sibylla von Bondorf und ihre Funktion", in *Frauen – Kloster – Kunst, op. cit.*, p. 197-212. Instead, *Mü2* with a Bavarian idiom classification including the narrative elements of the *ars dictaminis*. See also: A. WINSTON-ALLEN, " 'Nonnenmalerei': Iconography in Convent Women's Art of the Upper Rhine Region", in *Kulturtopographie des deutschsprachigen Südwestens im späteren Mittelalter. Studien und Texte*, ed. B. FLEITH, R. WETZEL, Berlin-New York, 2009, p. 141-156.

[165] Hall, Franziskanerkloster, cod. P 37 F; cf. L. LEHMANN, "Die Briefe der hl. Klara", in *Klara-Quellen, op. cit.*, p. 13-19, here p. 15; description of the codex and transcript of *EpCl.1* in *ChXXIVGen*, p. xvi, 183-186, note 7.

[166] Munich, BSM, Cod. Germ. 5730; scribe: Johannes Franck of Würzburg; description and dating: E. WUNDERLE, *Die mittelalterlichen deutschen Handschriften der Bayerischen Staatsbibliothek München, Vorläufige Beschreibungen*, on: http://daten.digitale-sammlungen.

Category, first level	Category, second level	Abbreviation (Language; dating)
C: *CLE*-tradition without appendage of *EpCl.1-4*	C.1.: without *EpCl.1-4* and 'Klarenbuch'	*Ba2* (G; end 14th c.)
		Mü1 (G; beg. 15th c.)
		Stu (G; beg. 16th c.)
	C.2.: without *EpCl.1-4* and 'Klarenbuch', but with *SCV*	*Be1* (G; mid 15th c.)

The outstanding literal production of the Nuremberg Clarissans was followed by a document which probably derives from the Poor Clares of Regensburg, a community founded in the late 1220s first as a member of the Order of Saint Mary and incorporated into the Clarissan Order around 1269.[167] Only four of all known witnesses which include a description of the life of the Přemyslid princess remain without these important texts (i.e. the *Klarenbuch*); they derive first of all again from Nuremberg (*Ba2*, then *Mü1*) – the first a remarkable Clarissan manuscript consisting of Middle-High German versions of *LegMai* and *CLE*, the second a Franciscan *Heiligen Leben* –, then a legendary from the female Dominican monastery of Strasbourg (*Stu*), and finally as part of a mixed manuscript of the Poor Clares of Pfullingen (*Be1*), entailing even secular travel reports like the one of Felix Fabri (1439-1502).[168]

How, when and under which conditions did the amalgation of Agnes' legend and the letters happen? The first linkage of Clare's correspondence with Agnes and *CLE* most probably did not occur in Bohemia nor within the Franciscan Order. The unpublished and still only superficially examined chronicle of the Italian Franciscan Elemosina, composed in the 1330s, knows

---

de/~db/0003/bsb00034946/images/; Fl. Sepp, B. Wagner, St. Kellner, "Handschriften und Inkunabeln aus süddeutschen Frauenklöstern in der Bayerischen Staatsbibliothek München", in *Nonnen, Kanonissen du Mystikerinnen. Religiöse Frauengemeinschaften in Süddeutschland*, ed. E. Schlotheuber *et al.*, Göttingen, 2008, p. 317-372, here p. 357; with *LegMai* (Bonaventure's legend of Saint Francis). Provenance: monastery of the Poor Clares in Munich (S. James at the Anger), first mention of the community in 1257. Inventory provides recently M. Hömberg on: http://www.phil-fak.uni-duesseldorf.de/forschung/schriftlichkeit-in-sueddeutschen-frauenkloestern/muenchen-klarissenkloster/.

[167] N. N., "Geschichte des Klarissenklosters in Regensburg", *Franziskanische Studien*, 35 (1953), p. 346-373; D. Engel, "Die Klarissen in Regensburg", *Bavaria Franciscana Antiqua*, 2 (1954) p. 44-77; more recent: M. Bresky, *Wirtschaftsgeschichte des Klarissenklosters in Regensburg vom 13. Jahrhundert bis zum Beginn des 16. Jahrhunderts*, Regensburg, 1987.

[168] See the comments of W. Williams-Krapp, *Geistliche Literatur des späten Mittelalters. Kleine Schriften*, ed. Kr. Freienhagen-Baumgart, K. Stegherr, Tübingen, 2012, p. 35-48. On the scriptorium: F. Heinzer, *Klosterreform und mittelalterliche Buchkultur im Deutschen Südwesten*, Leiden/Boston, 2008, here esp. p. 508-510.

of at least of two letters when citing the correspondence between Prague and Assisi.[169] But even this reduced knowledge was lost till the end of the fourteenth century as traceable in the chronicle of Bartholomew of Pisa who, while being well informed about the affinity of the two leading women of the early Franciscan movement, neglects this aspect completely.[170] The scenario therefore is very plausible that the legend arrived in Italy at the very beginning of the reign of Charles IV in Bohemia or eventually with the Bohemian Franciscan request for canonization some years before. The discovery of the letters happened only a few years later and became first known and documented by the canons of Saint Ambrose in Milan, where Charles received the crown of the Lombardy on 6 January 1355.[171] It is not far-fetched to assume that the scribe of the Milanese manuscript either was not sure if all of Clare's four *epistolae* justifiably were to be connected with the Bohemian princess or received the letters sometime after the legend was written down in the chapter's scriptorium. This would explain his hesitation or impracticality to annex the letters to *CLE*, but to put another text in-between. Charles IV, who was not much of a friend of the Franciscan Order but promoted the cult of Ambrose in his reign and even founded a monastery consecrated to this saint in the recently established New Town of Prague, staffed with clergy from the Milanese chapter, could have given the deciseve push in this process.[172] He

---

[169] *Chronicon seu Liber ystorie* (*c.* 1336), Paris, Bibliothèque nationale de France, Lat. n. 5006, here fol. 146r. On the text and its author: Fr. Fossier, "Les chroniques de fra Paolo da Gualdo et de Fra Elemosina", *Mélanges de l'École française de Rome*, 89 (1977), p. 411-483; I. Heullant-Donat, "Livres et écrits de mémoire du premier XIVe siècle: le cas des autographes de fra Elemosina", in *Libro, scrittura, documento della civiltà monastica e conventuale nel basso Medioevo (secoli XIII-XV)*, ed. G. Avarucci et al., Spoleto, 1999, p. 239-260.

[170] *ComPi*, p. 509: *Huius beatae Agnetis famam beata Clara cum audisset, per nuntios, quos ipsa sanctae Clarae direxerat, Dominum Deum laudavit, et dictae sanctae Agneti aliqua misit, videlicet Pater noster, velum, scutellam, in qua sancta Clara comedebat, et cyphum et nonnulla alia, quae cum summa devotione ab ipsa sancta Agnete sunt suscepta; per quae Deus multa signa fecit meritis beatae Clarae; quae imnia auro et gemmis ornata, in dicto monasterio reservantur.*

[171] RI VIII n. 1963a, in *Regesta Imperii Online*, http://www.regesta-imperii.de/id/1355-01-06_1_0_8_0_0_2227_1963a (Accessed on 17 April 2015). The hint provide P. Crosseley, Z. Opačić, "Prag. Die Krone des böhmischen Königtums", in *Karl IV. Kaiser von Gottes Gnaden. Kunst und Repräsentation des hauses Luxemburg 1310-1437*, ed. J. Fajt, Munich-Berlin, 2006, p. 197-217, here p. 204. On Charles cultural-political connections with the Lombardy region: D. Zaru, "De Prague à la Lombardie. Reliques et culte des saints durant la deuxième moitié du XIVe siècle", *Convivium*, s.n., 1 (2014), p. 102-114.

[172] M. Bauch, "Der Kaiser und die Stadtpatrone: Karl IV und die Schutzheiligen der Städte im Reich", in *Städtische Kulte im Mittelalter*, ed. S. Ehrich, J. Oberste, Regensburg, 2010, p. 168-188, here p. 182, speaks virtually of an aversion of the Luxembourg for the Franciscans, understandable with regards to their preceding support of his opponent Louis the Bavarian; L. Bobková, "Das Ende einer Herrschaft – Karl IV. als Gegenkönig und Nachfolger Ludwigs des Bayern", in *Ludwig der Bayer. Wir sind Keiser! (Ausstellungskatalog)*, Munich,

thus may well have been the deliverer of the legend, but even more the mentor of all the steps following the Order's petitions and of the transmission of the material, the "return" of this knowledge to Bohemia.

The chronicle of the historian at Prague, Přibík Pulkava of Radenín († 1380), very much supports this interpretation: the first Latin version of his *Chronicon* written in the 1370s omits this aspect of relationship between Clare and Agnes whereas the vernacular translation, started probably at the end of his life or latest in the 1390s, mentions "many letters" which were exchanged between them:

> Léto božie tisíc dvě stě a osm Constancia žena Přěmyslavova urodila Václava, jěsto potom byl markrabí moravským. Agnežku, ještо za Fridrika za ciesaře nechtěla jíti, jeho ciesařstvím vzhrděla, ale nebeskímu choti svú vieru a svú čest a čistotu zachovala. Nebo ta jistá dievka klášter s. Clary u věčšiem městě pražském, jěsto u s. Františka slove, založivši, v něm jeptišku ostala. V ňemžto sčěstně odpočívá mnohými divy i za živa stkvějíci sě přěslavně. Tato jistá panna dóstojná byla jest také zákonnicí, jenžto mnohé l i s t y ona k niej a ona k niej sobě sta psale. Toho léta také bylo na slunci pokaženie.[173] [Expanded spacing Chr.-Fr. Felskau]

To conclude, the gateway for the transfer and increase of knowledge coming from the East (Agnes' legend) and the South (Clare's letter) was evidently the Clarissan monastery at Nuremberg, the "beloved city" of Charles IV.[174] With its productivity in the decades from 1350 onwards, this institution functioned as a mediator and creator of a new set of vernacular hagiographic texts; moreover, it provided an important literal fountain for the spiritual

---

2014, p. 89-94; J. HEMMERLE, "Karl IV. und die Orden", in *Kaiser Karl IV. Staatsmann und Mäzen*, ed. F. SEIBT, Munich, 1978, p. 301-305; H.-J. SCHMIDT, "The Imperial Dynasty of Luxemburg, the Emperors, and the Mendicant Orders in the Fourteenth Century", in *Religious and Laity in Western Europe 1000-1400. Interaction, Negotiation, and Power*, ed. JAMROZIAK, J. BURTON, Turnhout, 2006, p. 147-166, here p. 165s. On the foundation cf. V. LORENC, *Nové město pražské*, Prague, 1973, p. 121; *Encyklopedie českých klášterů*, ed. P. VLČEK et al., Prague, 1997, p. 490-499.

[173] Pulkavae, *Chronicon*, in: FRB V, p. 3-207; the Old-Czech version edited: *ibid.*, p. 208-326, citation on p. 290; modern Czech translation: *Kroniky doby Karla IV.: František Pražský – Kronika, Beneš Krabice z Weitmile – Kronika pražského kostela, Přibík z Radenína, řečený Pulkava – Kronika česka, Jan Marignola – Kronika Česká, Neplach – Stručné sepsání Kroniky římské a české*, ed. M. BLAHOVÁ, Prague, 1987, p. 269-444; short description: NECHUTOVÁ, *Latinská literatura, op. cit.*, p. 140.

[174] See briefly: L. BOBKOVÁ, "Norimberk, město Karla IV", *Documenta Pragensia*, 29 (2010), p. 15-24; the codification of the Golden Bull at the turn of the years 1355/56 could have been a rightful occasion, but only one possibility out of his frequent sojourns in the town, placed at the road of the *Via Regia*.

orientation of the subsequent Observant movement in that region.[175] The linkage of legend and letters continuously was accompanied by a precarious appraisal of the latter's attribution, especially since it became so much intertwined with the hagiographic information on Agnes of Assisi.[176] To a large extent, this combination of texts shaped the perception of Agnes of Bohemia as the Central European heir, intimate combatant and royal representative of the foundress' concept of an evangelical life.

In Nuremberg, but soon after in the Bohemian communities of the Poor Clares and in the houses of the Crosiers with the Red Star, powerful support bases of the Luxembourg dynasty in this period, the veneration of the Princess culminated – the "network was formed" and reached with the textual witness of Šibenik even the Dalmation coast,[177] locally biased by the aim to confirm the glory of the realm and the ruling dynasty for which her healing miracles paved the way. In this time, the Crosiers of the Red Star commissioned the most precious medieval donation image of Agnes during the term of Grand Master Leo (1352-1363);[178] the Poor Clares of Eger wrote the rhymed legend on her, based on *CLE*,[179] while the sisters from Nuremberg started to match their literal aknowledgment of the Umbrian foundress – always combined with the admonishment of the original rule, the *regula sancta* or *sacra*

---

[175] S. MENGIS, *Schreibende Frauen um 1500: Scriptorium und Bibliothek des Dominikanerinnenklosters St. Katharina St. Gallen*, Berlin-Boston, 2013, here p. 163, with further evidence of the Clarissan scriptorium of Nuremberg.

[176] For instance, in the manuscript Dresden, ms. 281, the depiction of Clare admonishing two sisters is placed right before *EpCl.1-4*. One may ask: did the illuminator have both Agneses in mind, the spiritual and the biological one?

[177] Quote based on T. SNIJDERS, *Manuscript Communication. Visual and Textual Mechanics of Communication in Hagiographical Texts from the Southern Low Countries, 900-1200*, Turnhout, 2015, p. 273. The mediation or transportation of the legend including the petitions might have been the result of the travel of bishop Albert of Sarajevo to the consecration of the Franciscan church in Český Krumlov/Böhmisch Krummau in autumn 1358; Albert († 1388) was theologian at the Prague university, anointed by Charles IV. See Chr.-Fr. FELSKAU, *Agnes von Böhmen, op. cit.*, p. 685s.

[178] V. BĚLOHLÁVEK, *Dějiny českých křižovníků s červenou hvězdou*, Prague, 1930, here p. 25-56; P. BRODSKÝ, "Neznámá miniatura mistra křižovnického breviíře", *Časopis narodního muzea, řada historická*, 154 (1985), p. 121-124; *Galerie křižovníků. Schatzkammer der Kreuzherren mit dem roten Stern. Katalog der ständigen Ausstellung im Konventsgebäude in Prag 1*, Mělnik, 1994; W. LORENZ, *Die Kreuzherren, op. cit., passim*; Chr.-Fr. FELSKAU, "Autonomie und Zusammengehörigkeit im ordo cruciferorum cum stella rubea: Die Hospitäler St. Franziskus in Prag und St. Matthias in Breslau als 'Mutterhäuser' des Ordens (1310-1490)", in *Slezsko země koruny české. Historie a kultura 1300-1740*, ed. H. DANOVÁ, J. KLÁPA, L. STOLÁROVÁ, Prague, 2008, p. 31-50.

[179] J.-Y. TILLIETTE, "Hymnes et séquences hagiographiques: formes et fonctions de la réécriture lyrique des vies de saints", *Hagiographica*, 10 (2003), p. 161-181. At Eger, the early veneration of Agnes can be seen also in an antependium form 1285 (Muzeum Cheb, i. č. E 3092); cf. SOUKUPOVÁ, *Svatá Anežka, op. cit.*, p. 184, 192s.

regula[180] – with the new material on the Bohemian princess they received.[181] The legend from the *Franziskaner-Stadt* Eger demonstrates how willingly local monastic agencies were able to transform the sainthood of the princess at this stage into a mystic character for the sake of their own interpretation and in the style of contemporary rhymed legends, a *translatio sanctitatis* which the Crosiers of Prague applied in their own manner when they highlighted the merits of the *fundatrix* of their house.[182]

The "renaissance" of Agnes' remembrance certainly was pushed by the discovery of Clare's letters, but went beyond and reached a yet unseen intensity. As much as this refreshment of the past might be interpreted as a subtle reflex on the proliferation of the Plague in Central Europe, in Nuremberg and in Prague.[183] This development was apparently in the interest and under the promotion of Charles IV. The veneration of his relative backed his intention to strengthen the spiritual legitimacy of his rulership. On a symbolic, subtextual level, it served as a means to attest the rightful and god-given

---

[180] *CLE*, p. 106: *Huius sacre regule professione se uinciens districtione obediencie que prepollet uistimis, quasi vite hostie pacificorum mactabat assidue propriam uoluntatem. Toto nempe mentis conamine regulari obseruancie intendebat non iota statutorum uel apicem pretermittens, ut sine offendiculo uiam mandatorum dei percurreret superiorumque iussionibus quoad uixit cum humilitate et reuerencia magna parebat.* See also the statutes of Nuremberg Tertiaries from 1456 with a miniature eventualy refering ot Agnes of Bohemia: *Franziskus – Licht aus Assisi. Katalog zur Ausstellung im Erzbischöflichen Diözesanmuseum und im Franziskanerkloster Paderborn,* ed. Chr. STIEGEMANN et al., Paderborn, 2011, p. 251, no. 28.

[181] Cheb, Státní okresní archiv Cheb, sign. 469, image taken from H. SOUKUPOVÁ, *Anežský klášter, op. cit.*, p. 252; another sixteenth-century transcript (1580-1582) of the fourteenth century described in: *Svatá Anežka Česká, op. cit.*, p. 180, n. 132.

[182] P. DINZELBACHER, "Movimento religioso femminile e santità mistica nello specchio della *Legenda sanctae Clarae*", in *Chiara di Assisi*, p. 3-32, describes Clare as the first "proto-mystical saint". Citation taken from: V. V. FILIP, "Die Bettelorden in Eger", in *Bausteine zur deutschen und italienischen Geschichte. Festschrift zum 70. Geburtstag von Horst Enzensberger,* ed. M. STUIBER, M. SPACCHINI, Regensburg, 2014, p. 155-174. From the Eger Clarissans also an antiphon of Saint Clare is known (Nuremberg, GNM, Hs. 81767). On the manuscripts from the local male monastery: J. LIŠKOVÁ, *Liturgické knihy chebského františkánského konventu,* unpublished dissertation, Prague, 1991. I deeply thank the author for providing me with the manuscript. Further manuscripts from Eger stored at Prague, NKP: sign. XVI E 15 (*speculum perfectionis* and further Franciscan legends, 15th-16th c.); sign. Brst. 39 (mystical tractates); probably also Sign. Brst. 8 (Passional entailing the legend of the 11,000 virgins and extract of an Elizabeth legend, 13th-14th c.). V. BOK, "Zur literarischen Situation im Böhmen des 14. Jahrhunderts", in *Literatur im Umkreis des Prager Hofes der Luxemburger,* ed. J. HEINZLE, Berlin, 1994, p. 10-27.

[183] Prague had to cope with at least three epidemic waves in the 1350s, 1360s and early 1370s. Cf. D. MENGEL, "A Plague on Bohemia? Mapping the Black Death", *Past & Present,* 211 (2011), p. 3-34.

transition from the Přemyslid to the Luxembourg kingship in the lands of the Bohemian crown.[184]

With a retardation of several decades, but still before the Observant movement could formulate a renewed perspective on the Order's male and female pioneers, the promotion of Agnes' memory was shaped by the pattern of a saintly Central European princess – not so innovative, not so spectacular, and not so stirring as the first protagonists of the evangelical awakening offered a century before, but absorbed by a net of contemporary implications and now appreciated by a generation which perceived the Poor Clares as part of the "establishment". Apart from individual factors, this unseasonable delay would be the decisive reason for the final failure of promoting her cult in the later Middle Ages. Due to the infavorable spiritual, social and political development in Agnes' homeland after the end of the Luxembourgs, the profound knowledge of her merits, refreshed during the Observant movement, remained unstable and required further centuries to become an undisputed part of her commemoration – in Bohemia as well as within the Order of the Poor Clares in both regions, North and South of the Alps.[185]

---

[184] In terms of patriotic protection, the rescuing of the *civitas* Assisi by Clare (see *SCV*, p. 2428s.) can be interpreted as a counterpart to Agnes' saving of the ruling dynasty. M. PATTENDEN, "The Canonisation of Clare", p. 215. On the general topic: G. SIGNORI, *Patriotische Heilige? Begriffe, Probleme und Traditionen*, in *Patriotische Heilige. Beiträge zur Konstruktion religiöser und politischer Identitäten in der Vormoderne*, ed. H. BAUER, G. SIGNORI, Stuttgart, 2007, p. 11-32.

[185] Cf. the first chronicle exclusively dedicated to the history of the Order of the Poor Clares, written by Marianus of Florence (1477-1523), "Libro delle degnità Fra Mariano da Firenze O.F.M., Libro delle degnità et excellentie del Ordine della seraphica madre delle povere donne sancta Chiara da Assisi", ed. G. BOCCALI, *Studi Francescani* 83 (1986), p. 31-360, here p. 165: "Divulgandosi per tutta la Magna la fama della beata Agnesa incomincioronsi ad hedificare et multiplicare li monasterij sotto la regola di santa Chiara". Ch. MERCURI, "Raccolte agiografiche e osservanza francescana", in *Europa sacra. Le raccolte di vite di santi e la costruzione delle identit. politi-che in Europa fra medioevo e età moderna*, ed. S. BOESCH GAJANO, R. MICHETTI, Rome, 2001, p. 281-294. A full investigation on Agnes' importance during the establishment of the Clarissan observant movement in Central Europe and adjacent regions is still missing.

The Oldest Legend of Francis of Assisi and his Stigmatization in Old Hungarian Codex Literature (*c.* 1440-1530)*

Eszter KONRÁD
(*Budapest*)

Since the time of their settlement in the territory of the Kingdom of Hungary in 1229, the Order of the Friars Minor made great contributions to the formation of the late medieval saintly ideal, making efforts to popularize especially the saints of their own orders both on institutional and less formal levels. By the early sixteenth century almost all of the most famous Franciscan saints were present in some form in sermon collections, legendaries, liturgical and prayer books produced in Hungary and some of them were also represented in visual arts. However, none of the saints of the mendicant orders, considering also the saints and blessed of the Order of Preachers, turn up in the Hungarian codex literature as many times as St Francis of Assisi between the late fourteenth and the mid-sixteenth century: several Old Hungarian codices contain writings on him of different length and of different genres, ranging from sermons to prayers.

Since it is not possible to treat all the codices and to exhaust all aspects of the vernacular hagiographic and sermon literature written about him, the first part of this paper proposes to examine in detail the earliest surviving prose text written in the Hungarian vernacular, the legend of Francis of Assisi and his companions in the *Jókai Codex* (*c.* 1440). The second part explores the most distinctive theme of his sanctity, the stigmatization: following a

---

* I am grateful to Edit Madas and Gábor Klaniczay for their comments to the earlier drafts of this paper. All the translations, unless otherwise indicated, are mine. Since the linguistic aspect of the Old Hungarian texts here is not of primary importance, I have changed the special linguistic characters to their closest 'normal' correspondences, and when it was needed, I also introduced punctuation in the texts.

Les saints et leur culte en Europe centrale au Moyen Âge (XI-début du XVI* siècle)*, éd. par Marie-Madeleine de CEVINS et Olivier MARIN, Turnhout, 2017 (*Hagiologia*, 13), p. 173-194.
© BREPOLS PUBLISHERS   DOI 10.1484/M.HAG-EB.5.113971

brief overview of the transformation of the early Latin accounts, I examine how this event was reflected in the Hungarian devotional literature.

Hagiographic and sermon literature on mendicant saints in Hungary

Latin collections of sermons and legends of Franciscan or Dominican provenance that contained writings on the saints of the mendicant orders were composed or used in Hungary from the late thirteenth century onwards, such as the so-called *Sermones compilati in studio generali Quinqueecclesiensi in regno Ungarie*, the sermons of the *Divisions of the Codex of Alba Iulia* as well as codices of the *Legenda Aurea* completed with the legends of those saints who had special veneration in Hungary. A considerable amount of sermons on the saints of the Order of the Brothers Minor were included in the *De sanctis* parts of the collections of Hungarian Observant Franciscan preachers, the *Pomerium sermonum* of Pelbartus de Themeswar (c. 1440-1504) and the *Biga salutis* of Osualdus de Lasko (c. 1450-1511) that appeared in print in the last years of the fifteenth century.[1] Some parts of the sermons of Pelbartus composed for the feast of Francis also found their way to vernacular literature, as we shall see in the second part of this paper.[2] About the same time, also vernacular hagiographic and sermon literature started to flourish in Hungary: legends, *exempla* and sermons were compiled, translated and adapted to the Hungarian vernacular. These are preserved in the so-called Old Hungarian codices, composed between c. 1370 and 1539 and named for their place of origin, content, discoverer, owner, or some outstanding figure of Hungarian culture.[3] However, the oldest surviving hagiographic prose text written in the Hungarian vernacular, an early version of the legend of St Francis and his companions in the *Jókai Codex* seems to have existed already in the late fourteenth century but it did not survive. This date is quite

---

[1] For an overview of the hagiographic and sermon literature in Hungary until the first quarter of the sixteenth century, see G. KLANICZAY, E. MADAS "La Hongrie", in *Hagiographies: International History of the Latin and Vernacular Hagiographical Literature in the West from its Origins to 1550*, vol. 2, ed. G. PHILIPPART, Turnhout, 1996 (Corpus Christianorum, Hagiographies, 2), p. 103-160. For an informative summary of the two Observant Franciscan preachers' lives and works, see B. KERTÉSZ, "Two Observant Friars Minor (Franciscan Observants) in the Late Middle Ages: Pelbart of Temesvár and Oswald of Lasko", in *Infima aetas Pannonica. Studies in Late Medieval Hungarian History*, ed. P. E. KOVÁCS, K. SZOVÁK, Budapest, 2009, p. 60-78.

[2] Pelbartus composed altogether six sermons for the feast of Francis and one for his stigmatization, Osualdus three sermons for his feats and one for his translation.

[3] 1370 is the supposed date after which the early translation of the *Jókai Codex* was made, and 1539 is the year when the latest of them, the *Kulcsár Codex* was composed.

late compared to emergence of the French and German (ninth century) or Italian (twelfth century) vernacular hagiography, but it is roughly the same time when the earliest hagiographic pieces in the Czech and the Polish vernacular were composed.[4]

Old Hungarian Codex Literature

The emergence of the vernacular religious literature was strongly related to the Observant reforms in the fifteenth century as well as to the change in the devotional life of women. The majority of the surviving 46 Old Hungarian codices (or fragments of codices) were related to the Order of Minor Brothers and the Order of Preachers[5] as they were responsible for the *cura monialium* of the female counterparts of their orders. Both orders had their important female monasteries in the surroundings of Buda, the political seat of power: the Dominican monastery on the Rabbits' Island (*Insula Leporum*) and a Clarissan monastery in Óbuda.[6] The royal foundations of dynastic monasteries served as residences for princesses and the daughters of the high nobility.[7] They played an important role in manuscript production: there existed a high-quality *scriptorium* in the Dominican monastery on the Rabbits'

---

[4] Cf. H. BIRNBAUM, "The Vernacular Languages of East Central Europe in the Medieval Period", in *'The Man of Many Devices, Who Wandered Full Many Ways...'. Festschrift in Honor of János M. Bak*, ed. B. NAGY, M. SEBŐK, Budapest, 1999, p. 384-396; T. DUNIN-WASOWICZ, "Hagiographie polonaise entre XIe et XVIe siècle", in *Hagiographies, op. cit.*, vol. 3, ed. G. PHILIPPART, Tunhout, 2001 (Corpus Christianorum, Hagiographies, 3), p. 193-194.
[5] In addition to the Franciscans and Dominicans, also the Pauline, the Premonstratensian and the Carthusian Orders produced codices. In some cases, however, the provenance of a codex is debated or unknown. For an introduction to the Old Hungarian codex literature, see A. DÖMÖTÖR, *Régi magyar nyelvemlékek: a kezdetektől a XVI. század végéig* [Old Hungarian texts from the beginnings to the end of sixteenth century], Budapest, 2006, p. 52-95.
[6] For the history of the Dominican monastery on the Rabbits' Island, see A. HARSÁNYI, *A domonkos rend Magyarországon a reformáció előtt* [The Dominican Order in Hungary before the Reformation], Debrecen, 1938, reprinted in Budapest, 1999, p. 104-112. For the Clarissans at Óbuda, see J. KARÁCSONYI, *Szent Ferencz rendjének története Magyarországon 1711-ig* [History of the Order of St Francis in Hungary up to 1711], vol. 2, Budapest, 1924, p. 450-457, 482-509.
[7] For the Dominican monastery on the Rabbits' Island, see G. KLANICZAY, "Családi kolostor: a szent hercegnők uralkodói rezidenciája" [Dynastic monasteries: the royal residence of the holy princesses], in *A tudomány szolgálatában. Emlékkönyv Benda Kálmán 80. születésnapjára*, ed. F. GLATZ, Budapest, 1993, p. 13-26, at p. 18-21; Id., *Holy Rulers and Blessed Princesses: Dynastic Cults in Medieval Central Europe*, Cambridge, 2002, p. 262-264. The same can be said about the Clarissan monastery of Óbuda: it was an educational centre of the Angevin royal house and Hungarian high nobility, especially during the lifetime of Elizabeth Piast, under whose supervision young girls were educated.

Island where some nuns were active scribes.[8] Of the codices that I treat in this paper, the *Virginia Codex* is the only one that is related to this place: despite its Franciscan content, the codex was copied by the Dominican nuns on the island, which suggests literary connection with the Clarissan monastery of Óbuda.[9] The flourishing of the production of the vernacular codices came to an end due to the ongoing Ottoman threat of Buda: the fleeing Dominican and Clarissan nuns took some of their codices with themselves to the northern part of the country; this is how many of the Old Hungarian codices survived.

The texts of the vernacular codices in almost all cases go back to Latin sources but in many instances reveal the medieval authors', compilers' or translators' interventions to the sources in terms of the selection, organization and appropriation while writing for an audience for whom the Hungarian vernacular seemed to be a more suitable language to convey their message. The only indication that comes directly from the author himself concerning his intended audience is in the *Érdy Codex* (1526-27). The Carthusian monk wrote in the Latin *Prologue* to his work that he was urged to write in the vernacular by the just claim of lay brothers and nuns from various religious orders, among them his sister, too. The Carthusian Anonymous maintained that the Lutheran 'heresy' can be stopped by means of writing, preaching and teaching.[10]

The *Jókai Codex*

Among the Old Hungarian codices in which Francis of Assisi figures, the *Jókai Codex* is of central importance. It is a Franciscan compilation from the deeds of Francis and the early brethren and the oldest codex written entirely

---

[8] On the nun scribes, see L. HAADER "Arcképtöredékek ómagyar scriptorokról" [Portrait fragments of the scribes of Old Hungarian codices], in *'Latiatuc feleym...'. Magyar nyelvemlékek a kezdetektől a 16. század elejéig* (The exhibition of the National Széchényi Library, 29 October 2009 – 28 February 2010), ed. E. MADAS, Budapest, 2009, p. 53-78. On the influence of the observant reform reflected in the readings of the Dominican nuns, see S. LÁZS, "A Nyulak szigeti domonkos apácák olvasmányainak korszerűsége" [The up-to-dateness of the readings of the Dominican nuns of the Rabbits' island], p. 123-139 in the same volume.
[9] The literacy of the Dominican and Clarissan nuns in Hungary was discussed comprehensively by Á. KORONDI, *A misztika a késő középkori magyar nyelvű kolostori kódexirodalomban* [Mysticism in the late medieval Hungarian codex literature of nuns' convents], Kolczsván, 2016, p. 55-85.
[10] Shelfmark: Országos Széchényi Könyvtár, MNy 9. Edition: *Érdy Codex*, ed. Gy. VOLF, 2 vols., Budapest, 1876 (Nyelvemléktár, 4-5), p. xxii-xxiv.

in vernacular.[11] The *Jókai Codex* is emblematic in the sense that it originated from a religious order whose apostolic mission made the use of vernacular of central importance.[12] Since it is not likely that definite answers will be given concerning the place of origin, the translator/compiler, and the audience of the codex, I limit myself to the (re)-examination of its sources and the themes covered, as these two seem to be the firm grounds on which further hypotheses are based.

Although based on the watermarks the *Jókai Codex* was made around 1440, it was supposedly copied from an earlier Hungarian translation traditionally dated to after 1370.[13] The codex was copied by a single hand, it consists of 81 paper leaves, and almost its quarter is missing.[14] Not always perfectly coinciding but still close Latin textual parallels were identified to the whole codex:[15] 28 chapters correspond to the *Actus beati Francisci et sociorum eius*,[16] 29 chapters to the *Speculum perfectionis*,[17] 3 chapters have textual paral-

---

[11] Shelfmark: Országos Széchényi Könyvtár, Budapest MNy 67. The codex was first published by Gy. VOLF, *Jókai-Codex (Ehrenfeld-Codex)*, Budapest, 1878 (Nyelvemléktár, 7). Its full facsimile edition is *Jókai-kódex*, ed. D. SZABÓ, J. LOTZ, Budapest, 1942 (Codices Hungarici, 1). The codex was edited again by J. P. BALÁZS, *Jókai-kódex, XIV-XV. század. A nyelvemlék betűhű olvasata és latin megfelelője* [Jókai Codex, 14th-15th century. The diplomatic transcription and the Latin correspondence of the Hungarian linguistic record] Budapest, 1981 (Codices Hungarici, 8). I will refer to this edition in my study.

[12] There are at least nine Old Hungarian codices that contain writings on St Francis of Assisi but in this paper I do not treat the *Simor Codex* (1508), the *Lobkowitz Codex* (1514), the *Domonkos Codex* (1517), the *Debreceni Codex* (1519), and the *Teleki Codex* (1525-1531).

[13] For the traditional dating of the earlier translation of the *Jókai Codex*, see *Jókai-kódex*, op. cit., p. 10. A slightly later dating of the Jókai Codex is to c. 1448; see DÖMÖTÖR, *Régi magyar nyelvemlékek*, op. cit., p. 57.

[14] For the missing pages see *Jókai-kódex*, op. cit., p. 10.

[15] L. KATONA, "Az Ehrenfeld- és Domonkos-codex forrásai" [The sources of the Ehrenfeld and Domonkos Codices], *Irodalomtörténeti Közlemények*, 13 (1903), p. 59-78; *Jókai-kódex*, op. cit., p. 11-13, 18.

[16] *Actus beati Francisci et sociorum eius*, ed. P. SABATIER, Paris, 1902 (Collection de documents pour l'histoire religieuse et littéraire du Moyen Âge, 4); a new edition of the text together with the *Fioretti* was made by J. CAMBELL, M. BIGARONI, G. BOCCALI, Assisi, 1988, p. 107-593; in case the numeration of the chapters in Cambell's addition is different from Sabatier's, I indicate it. The new addition is also reported in *Fontes Franciscani*, ed. E. MENESTÒ, S. BRUFANI, G. CREMASCOLI, E. PAOLI, L. PELLEGRINI, S. DA CAMPAGNOLA; apparatuses by G. M. BOCCALI, Assisi, 1995, p. 2085-2219.

[17] The first edition of the work is *Speculum perfectionis seu S. Francisci Assisiensis Legenda antiquissima, auctore fratre Leone*, ed. P. SABATIER, Paris, 1898 (Collection de documents pour l'histoire religieuse et littéraire du Moyen Âge, 1); the second is *Le Speculum perfectionis ou Mémoires de frère Léon sur la seconde partie de la vie de Saint François d'Assise*, ed. P. SABATIER, A. G. LITTLE, 2 vols., Manchester, 1928-1931, I, p. 1-350; also reported in *Fontes Franciscani*, op. cit., p. 1849-2053.

lels with the *Codex Latinus 77* of the National Széchényi Library,[18] the prayer to the Crucified can be found the *De Conformitate Vitae Beati Francisci ad Vitam Domini Iesu* of Bartholomew of Pisa,[19] and the final list of eight miracles is translated from the treatise of miracles from Bonaventure's *Legenda maior*.[20]

The date of composition of the latest source of the *Jókai Codex* is vital for the dating of the supposed earlier translation. In case the *De Conformitate* composed between 1385 and 1390 and approved by the General Chapter of the Franciscan Order in 1399[21] was indeed among the sources of the early translation of the *Jókai Codex*, then it is more likely that it was made after 1390, around 1400. It is also possible that the source of the prayer to the Crucified was not the *De Conformitate* but some earlier source instead, or that this section was added later to an already existing vernacular translation of the legend.[22]

The overwhelming majority (*c.* 85%) of the sources of the surving part of the *Jókai Codex*, – the *Speculum perfectionis*, the *Actus beati Francisci* as well as three additional chapters that I will discuss below – originated from a Spiritual Franciscan environment. Motivated partly by the call of the General Chapter of Padua in 1276 to collect the deeds and the sayings of Francis and his early companions that were in danger of oblivion after that the General Chapter of Paris in 1266 had ordered the distruction of all previously composed legends, the *zelanti* were quite active in the compilation of such works.

---

[18] The codex was described by L. KATONA, "Az Ehrenfeld- és Domonkos-codex forrásai", *op. cit.*, at p. 65-66.

[19] Editio princeps: BARTHOLOMEUS DE PISIS, *Liber conformitatum: Vitae beati Francisci ad vitam Domini Iesu*, Milan, 1510. The modern edition of the text is *De Conformitate vitae beati Francisci ad vitam Domini Iesu auctore Fr. Bartholomaeo de Pisa*, in *Analecta Franciscana*, 4-5 (1906-1912). For the dating of its composition and its approval by the Order, see the *Praefatio*, at p. xi-xii. The prayer to the Crucifix is at p. 521-522. According to the author of the *De Conformitate*, the friar to whom the Crucifix spoke was the English Franciscan John Pecham (*c.* 1230-1290).

[20] Bonaventurae de Balneoregio, *Legenda maior s. Francisci* in *Legendae s. Francisci Assisiensis saeculis XIII e XIV conscriptae* in *Analecta Franciscana*, 10 (1926-1941), p. 555-652. The *Tractatus de miraculis* is at p. 627-652. The treatise is also reported with the same title in the bilingual edition of the works of Bonaventure: *Sancti Bonaventurae Opuscula Franciscana (Sancti Bonaventurae Opera*, XIV/1) and in *Fontes Franciscani, op. cit.*, p. 912-961.

[21] *Jókai-kódex, op. cit.*, p. 10.

[22] The same prayer but with an ending different from the one reported in the *De Conformitate* is reported in G. M. DREVES, *Analecta hymnica medii aevi*, XXXI, Leipzig, 1898, p. 53-54. The two manuscripts signaled by Dreves that have a slightly different ending are: Cod. Palat. Matriten 2 N 4 dated to the thirteenth-fourteenth century and the Cod. Londinen Reg.7 A VI, dated to the fourteenth-fifteenthth century, so it is theoretically possible that the source of the prayer to the Crucifix was not the *De Conformitate*.

The early thirteenth-century compilations like the *Speculum* and the *Actus* and they – despite their unofficial character –, diffused quite quickly in the Franciscan Order, if not on their own, then as parts of other works, as they were regarded as complementary material to Bonaventure's *Legenda maior*. The late fourteenth-early fifteenth-century *Codex Latinus 77* of the National Széchényi Library, which shows close textual parallels to the *Jókai Codex*, begins with the incipit *Fac secundum exemplar* and thus belongs to the group of manuscripts referred to as the *Avignon Compilation*.[23] The earliest manuscript of this group was compiled in the first half of fourteenth century by a Franciscan who was a student in Avignon. Although the eleven manuscripts of this group – dated almost all to the second part of fourteenth and fifteenth century – have a rather varied structure, they usually contain the short version of the *Speculum perfectionis*, a part of the *Actus*, the *Vita secunda* of Thomas of Celano, an excerpt from the *Legenda maior*, collections of edifying anecdotes, historical documents and several other writings as well as a set of seven chapters of which three are present in the *Jókai Codex*.[24]: "Hogÿ kelnekuala neky az baratok kyk regulat tartanakuala" (*Legenda vetus*, Ch. 3: *Exemplum de praedicta voluntate*); "Az tudomanrol kÿt zent ferencz eleue meg mondott" (*Legenda vetus*, Ch. 4: *De scientia quam praedixit*); "Angÿalnak yzanÿv yelenetyrewl" (*Legenda vetus*, Ch. 5: *Ad idem de apparitione stupenda angeli*).[25] The issues concerned in these chapters were sensitive ones for the Spiritual branch of the Franciscans and they frequently turn up also in other texts: the prediction of the future tribulations of the Order, poverty, the role of learning, the seeking of the initial observance and the place of Our Lady of the Portiuncula. This set of seven chapters either fully or partially, can be found in a number of writings originating from the Spirituals, among others

---

[23] For the most recent and exhaustive study on the *Avignon Compilation*, see E. MENESTÒ, "La '*Compilatio Avenionensis*': una raccolta di testi francescani della prima metà del XIV secolo", *Studi medievali*, 44 (2003), p. 1423-1541.

[24] Paul Sabatier regarded these seven chapters to be the part of a hypothetical legend that he called "*Legenda vetus*" and he edited them as "S. Francisci Legendae veteris fragmenta quaedam", in *Opuscules de critique historique*, vol. 3, Paris, 1902, p. 87-109. The seven chapters are the following: (1) *De statu malo futuro fratrum*; (2) *De intentione S. Francisci*; (3) *Exemplum de praedicta voluntate*; (4) *De scientia quam praedixit*; (5) *De apparitione stupenda angeli*; (6) *De euntibus inter infideles*; (7) *De loco S. Mariae de Angelis*. Another version of the *De apparitione* can be found in the *Actus* (Ch. 25: *De statua simili statue Nabuchodonosor*), in *Fontes Franciscani, op. cit.*, p. 2138-2142. In the text I refer to the chapter number of the *Legenda vetus*.

[25] *Jókai-kódex*, p. 266-273. It was Arnold Magyar who identified the three chapters with Sabatier's *Legenda vetus*. See A. MAGYAR, "Eine Vergessene Franziskus-Handschrift: Der Jókai Codex von Budapest", *Archivum Franciscanum Historicum*, 62 (1969), p. 662-677, at p. 675.

in Angelo Clareno's *Expositio super regulam fratrum Minorum* (1321-1323) and his *Historia septem tribulationum Ordinis Minorum*.[26] It can be assumed that they were circulating together in the 1310s and possibly derived from Conrad of Offida or from his entourage.[27] Consequently, it was not only the *Avignon Compilation* through which these three chapters could fare to the *Jókai Codex*. Moreover, the manuscripts of the *Avignon Compilation* do not contain two chapters of the *Actus* that are organic part of the *Jókai Codex*.[28] Whereas the prayer to the Crucified and the list of miracles at the end of the *Jókai Codex* can be additions to its 'core', the translations of Ch. 39 and 45 of the *Actus* fit perfectly in the sequence of the chapters of the Hungarian codex.[29] Nevertheless, the striking resemblance between the *Avignon Compilation* and the *Jókai Codex* in their content makes possible to hypothesize that the 'core' of the latter was not put together by the Hungarian compiler/translator but was translated from an already existing Latin compilation, made up of excerpts from the *Actus*, the *Speculum perfectionis* and the set of the seven chapters, that were relatively widespread in the period.[30]

Various hypotheses have been offered concerning the audience: the Clarissan nuns of Óbuda, the tertiary communities of Buda who were under the direction of the Observant Franciscans from 1445 onwards,[31] or a male com-

---

[26] According to Menestò, the sixth chapter of this set can be found already in the *Regula Non Bullata* (1221), and the seventh one in the *Compilatio Assisiensis* (1244-1260). See E. MENESTÒ, *La 'Compilatio Avenionensis'*, *op. cit.*, p. 1512-1513. For the full list of works in which these chapters were reported, see *Francis of Assisi: Early Documents*, 3 vols., ed. R. J. ARMSTRONG, J. A. W. HELLMANN, W. J. SHORT, New York, 1999, in vol. 3, p. 110-113 (hereafter referred to as *FA: ED*).

[27] See the introduction of Sylvain Piron to the French translations of excerpts from Angelo Clareno's *Historia septem tribulationum Ordinis Minorum*, in *François d'Assise. Écrits,Vies, témoignages*, ed. J. DALARUN et al., Paris, 2010 (Sources Franciscaines), vol. 2, p. 2563-2575, p. 2571-2572.

[28] See the table of comparison in A. MAGYAR, "Eine Vergessene Franziskus-Handschrift: Der Jókai Codex von Budapest", *art. cit.*, at p. 670-676.

[29] *Jókai-kódex*, *op. cit.*, p. 146-148, "Frater leorol mykoron latta uala zent ferenczet fewlttewl fel emeletlennÿ" (*Actus*, Ch. 39: *De fratre Leone quando vidit sanctum Franciscum elevatum a terra et vidit et palpavit eius stigmata*); p. 174-176, "Mykeppen frater Egyed vonot kÿ nemÿ mestert ew ketsegebelewl" (*Actus*, Ch. 45 = 67² in: *Qualiter, dicente fr. Egidio: Virgo ante partum, Virgo in partu, Virgo post partum, orta sunt tria lilia*); reported in *Fontes Franciscani*, p. 2166-2167, 2218-2219.

[30] On the problems concerning the early translation of the *Jókai Codex*, see D. FALVAY, E. KONRÁD, "Osservanza francescana e letteratura in volgare dall'Italia all'Ungheria: ricerche e prospettive", in *Osservanza francescana e cultura tra Quattrocento e primo Cinquecento: Italia e Ungheria a Confronto*, ed. F. BARTOLACCI and R. LAMBERTIN, Rome, 2014, p. 161-186, at p. 175-178.

[31] J. HORVÁTH, *A magyar irodalmi műveltség kezdetei: Szent Istvántól Mohácsig* [The origins of Hungarian literature: from St Stephen to Mohács], first published in Budapest, 1931; reprint: Budapest, 1988, p. 101-109, at p. 104-105. Yet, the fact that the *Jókai Codex*

munity for whom going around begging was a usual activity and who, as the scribal additions reveal, should be warned against intemperance in eating[32] and to the scorn of money.[33] The only argument in favour of the Clarissan nuns as the destined readers of the *Jókai Codex* can be that almost all the later surviving vernacular codices were translated for and copied by nuns. I have not found any hint in the text that would particularly suggest a female audience.

The first thematic unit of the *Jókai Codex* (*Actus*, Ch. 1-9; 31-33; 38-40 [= 65²] 41-43, 45 [= 67²]) presents the early days of the community through the relationship among Francis and his companions. The saint's *Christiconformitas* is elaborated in this section and culminates with his stigmatization in the very middle of this part. The second part of the same unit continues with the narration of the mystical experience and the miracle stories related to the companions, including also Clare of Assisi. The second thematic unit (*Speculum perfectionis* 12-14; 18; 20-2; *Actus* 67; *Speculum perfectionis* 25-26; 28-29) deals with the issues related to absolute poverty: begging for alms, renunciation of worldly goods, the prohibition to get in physical contact with money and further episodes concerning the *usus pauper*, as well as the care for the poor and the sick. The third unit (*Speculum perfectionis* 49; 51-53; 56-58) is concerned with obedience, discipline, and peace within the Order. With his humility manifested in different situations Francis wants to show example to his companions. Although at first it seems that the episodes of the fourth major unit (*Speculum perfectionis* 79; 66; 68-73; 81; 85-86; the so-called *Legenda vetus*, 3-5) are of miscellaneous content, they are all related to the zeal of the Poverello to instruct the brethren by showing them the contrast between real and worldly knowledge, that conversion is a result of praying and compassion, that the observation of the *Rule* is necessary. Francis foretells the tribulations of the Order, which is the result of the friars' estrangement from his original intentions, especially in the field of studies, *usus pauper*, and humility. The fifth unit (*Actus* 10; 13-14; 16; 18-19; 24-23) is heavily damaged, but on the basis of the surviving pages it is apparent that it consists of miscellaneous episodes: the approaching death of the saint is mentioned, but then

---

was written in northern dialect does not seem to support this assumption; cf. *Jókai-kódex, op. cit.*, p. 10.

[32] *Jókai-kódex, op. cit.*, p. 180: "Azert penzt ne zeressetek mert czalard" [Thus do not love money because it is deceitful].

[33] *Jókai-kódex, op. cit.*, p. 192: "azert legÿen egÿarant eteltek nem hogy egÿ zaja keduen egyek smasnak ne legÿen mytt az ellenne ennÿ" [Thus you should have equal portion of food, and do not allow that one eat as much as (s)he wishes, and nothing is left to the other]. The examples are highlighted in J. KASTNER, *A Jókai – kódex és az obszerváns kódexirodalom* [The Jókai Codex and the Observant codex literature], Budapest, 1933, p. 1-19, at p. 10-11.

comes an episode relating his revelations and conversations with God, and also two stories about his special relationship with animals is narrated, one of them is the taming of the wolf of Gubbio. The next unit is a short poem, in which an unnamed friar – who in the Jókai Codex can be interpreted as St Francis – (*De Conformitate*, p. 521-522) turns to the Crucified for consolation, who, in turn, narrates Francis his Passion. The fragmentary poem separates the stories of St Francis and his companions from the last section of the codex, the raising of eight dead thanks to the intercession of the saint.

Since the *Jókai Codex* is quite a faithful translations of Latin texts, its original features are limited to the organization of the material. On the one hand, the sequences of the episodes show a conscious effort for a thematic arrangement; for instance, the episodes from the life of the Poverello and his companions are separated from his *post mortem* miracles by a poem that evokes the Passion of Christ. On the other hand, the explanatory additions that show the intervention of the translator or the scribe who wrote the legend down in order to make the text more comprehensible to its readers or to add his own conclusion or advice on some of the issues treated.

What are the reasons of relating the *Jókai Codex* to the Observant Franciscans? As it has been shown, the overwhelming majority of the codex goes back to Latin works originated from the Spirituals. Although the Observant movement cannot be regarded as the direct continuation that of the Spirituals, it is undeniable that some of the recurring themes in the *Jókai Codex*, such as evangelic poverty, obedience, scorn for secular knowledge were crucial issues also for the Observant Franciscans.[34] It should be noted, too, that the date of the *Jókai Codex* coincides with the period of the expansion of the Observants in Hungary who within a few years (1448) would obtain a permission to, separating from the Observant province of Bosnia, establish an autonomous Hungarian vicariate.[35] All this, however, cannot be considered as decisive evidence in favour of the Observant provenance of the codex.

---

[34] It should be added, however, that the objection to learning was characteristic of the early Observants, motivated more by the fear that the engagement in science would be an obstacle for the aspired humility and simplicity. On the Observants' initial distrust in learning and their subsequent re-orientation to the pursuit of studies, see B. ROEST, *A History of Franciscan Education (c. 1210-1517)*, Leiden, 2000, p. 153-171.

[35] For a recent and detailed history of the Observant presence in fourteenth-century Bosnia and the creation of the independent Observant province in Hungary, see M.-M. de CEVINS, *Les Franciscains observants hongrois de l'expansion à la débâcle (vers 1450 – vers 1540)*, Rome, 2008, at p. 31-42.

The evolution of the stigmatization narratives

The *Jókai Codex* attests how rich an inventory of the life and deeds of St Francis and his companions was translated to the Hungarian by the mid-fifteenth century. Many of these episodes, although sometimes in different forms or translated from other works, can be found in other Old Hungarian codices. Among the most diffused stories and *exempla* from the hagiography of Francis, one finds episodes about his early companions, Masseus and Rufino, some stories about the saint's special relation to animals, the quite popular '*exemplum* of the three spears'. Nevertheless, the most emblematic episode of the legend of Francis is his stigmatization. The five wounds of the saint have been in the centre of attention since the time it became known that this divine gift was given to him. In the course of time, as usual, the earliest accounts have been enriched with new details, rewritten and reinterpreted.[36] I give a short summary of the evolution of the stigmatization in the early biographies of the saint in order to show the new elements incorporated in the Latin accounts of the stigmatization that served as a basis for the Hungarian translations.

The desire of the faithful for the bodily imitation of the suffering Christ goes back chiefly to three passages of St Paul's letter to the Galatians, especially on Gal 6,17: *Ego enim stigmata domini Iesu in corpore meo porto*. After some late antique and early medieval antecedents, this concern became central in the wake of the religious renewal of the twelfth century,[37] and got its archetypal expression, when after the death of Francis in 1226 Minister General Elias of Cortona informed the friars about the five wounds that

---

[36] See the works by A. VAUCHEZ, "Les stigmates de saint François et leurs détracteurs dans les derniers siècles du Moyen Âge", *Mélanges d'archéologie et d'histoire*, 80 (1968), p. 596-625; O. SCHMUCKI, "The Illness of St Francis of Assisi before His Stigmatization", *Greyfriars Review*, 4 (1990), p. 31-61; Id., "The Illnesses of Francis during the Last Years of His Life", *Greyfriars Review*, 13 (1999), p. 21-59; C. FRUGONI, *Francesco e l'invenzione delle stimmate: Una storia per parole e immagini fino a Bonaventura e Giotto*, Turin, 1993; G. CONSTABLE, *Three Studies in Medieval Religious and Social Thought*, Cambridge, 1998, p. 143-247; R. C. TREXLER "The Stigmatized Body of Francis of Assisi: Conceived, Processed, Disappeared", in *Frömmigkeit im Mittelalter: Politisch-soziale Kontexte, visuelle Praxis, körperliche Ausdrucksformen*, ed. K. SCHREINER and M. MÜNTZ, Munich, 2002, p. 463-497; S. M. BENFATTI, *The Five Wounds of Saint Francis: A Historical and Spiritual Investigation*, Charlotte, 2011.
[37] On the comments on St Paul's verses on the stigmata in the Late Antiquity and the early Middle Ages, see C. MUESSIG, "L'evoluzione della spiritualità delle stimmate prima di San Francesco d'Assisi", in *Discorsi sulle stimmate dal Medioevo all'età contemporanea / Discours sur les stigmates du Moyen Âge à l'époque contemporaine*, ed. G. KLANICZAY, Rome, 2013 (Archivio italiano per la storia della pietà, 26), p. 21-42; cf. G. CONSTABLE, *Three Studies in Medieval Religious and Social Thought*, op. cit., p. 194-195.

appeared on Francis shortly before his death.[38] Two years later, the first biographer of Francis, Thomas of Celano, presented the event in a more detailed manner: he introduced a crucified Seraph as the agent of the stigmatization, dated it to two years earlier than the death of the saint, locating it to the hermitage of the Mount la Verna. Subsequently also the testimony of Brother Leo became crucial because he was with Francis at that time, and received an autograph from him, upon which he wrote a gloss that claims that the *laudes* were written by Francis after the vision and the message of the Seraph and the impression of Christ's stigmata on his body.[39] In Bonaventure's *Legenda maior*, about the feast of the Exaltation of the Cross, in a vision, the crucified Christ appears from among the six wings of a Seraph. Francis understands from this vision what is going to happen to him, and as it is disappearing, the marks of nails begins to appear in his hands and feet.[40]

The papacy's position concerning the stigmatization has changed considerably in the decades after Francis's death in 1226. While in the canonization bull *Mira circa nos* issued on 19 July 1228 by Pope Gergory IX there is but a rather slight hint to his wounds,[41] starting with his bull *Non minus dolentes* issued on 31 March 1237 the Holy See stood by the authenticity of the stigmata and issued eight more bulls condemning those who would deny it. A further set of new details were added to the account in 1282 when Minister General Bonagrazia Tielci ordered an inquiry into the circumstances of the stigmatization. In line with the new pieces of information, the date of the stigmatization was fixed to 17 September, the feast of the Exaltation of the Holy Cross. The institution of the Feast of the Stigmata was mentioned as early as the Chapter of Cahors in 1337 but the first legislative text comes only from the Chapter of Assisi in 1340.[42]

According to the protocol that recorded the results of the inquiry of Bonagrazia Tielci, known as *Instrumentum de stigmatibus b. Francisci*, a

---

[38] *Epistola encyclica de transitu S. Francisci a fr. Helia tunc ordinis vicario generali ad omnes provincias ordinis missa*, in Legendae S. Francisci Assisiensis saeculis XIII et XIV conscriptae, *Analecta Franciscana*, 10 (1926-1941), p. 523-528.

[39] S. M. BENFATTI, *The Five Wounds of Saint Francis, op. cit.*, p. 44-51. For the reconstruction of the sources on the stigmata of Francis, see J. DALARUN, "À cette époque le bienheureux François avait des cicatrices aux mains et aux pieds et au côté", in *Discorsi sulle stimmate dal Medioevo all'età contemporanea, op. cit.*, p. 43-92.

[40] For Bonaventure's account on the stigmatization, see the *Legenda maior*, Ch. 13, in *Fontes Franciscani*, p. 889-898, at p. 889-892.

[41] J. DALARUN, "The Great Secret of Francis", in *The Stigmata of Francis of Assisi: New Studies, New Perspectives*, ed. M. CUSATO, J. DALARUN and C. SALVATI, New York, 2006, p. 9-26, at p. 10-11.

[42] *Francis of Assisi: Early Documents, op. cit.*, in vol. 3, p. 661. Hereafter referred to as *FA: ED* III.

lay brother, in front of six witnesses, made a deposition of a revelation how St Francis himself appeared and shared with him the 'truth' concerning the stigmatization.[43] This record provides some previously unheard details and clarifications of the event: an angel tells Francis to be prepared for what God wants to do to him; it takes place at dawn of the day of the Exaltation of the Cross; it was not an angel but Christ who appeared to him in the appearance of a Seraph. Two of the novelties of the *Instrumentum* are of particular relevance for us. First, it reports a conversation between Christ and Francis who commands three times the saint to give him whatever alm he has in his robe, and each time he finds a precious gem in it, signifying the three Orders that would spring out from the community. Second, the protocol also speaks about a direct physical contact between Christ and Francis, and that the impression of the wounds was quite painful: "After that, the Lord himself placed his hands on my body, and impressed those stigmata first to my hands, second to my feet and third to my side with the feeling of extremely strong pain and crying out each time.[44]" It is Brother Conrad who eventually finds the unconscious Francis.

The last narrative directly related to the Hungarian vernacular literature on the stigmatization of Francis is in the *Actus* (Ch. 9). This account is surprisingly short compared to the length of the whole chapter.[45] Although the author of the *Actus* had access to the *Instrumentum*,[46] for the stigmata narrative he used rather Bonaventure's *Legenda maior* and the antiphons written for the Feast of the Stigmata.[47] The description of the stigmatization in the *Actus* is only one brief paragraph that tells that around the feast of the Exaltation of the Holy Cross, Christ appeared under the form of a winged Seraph as though crucified and impressed both the nails and the stigmata on the hands and feet and side of Francis. The vision appeared at night with such splendour that it illuminated the mountains and valleys, and were witnessed by shepherds. The reason why these stigmata had been impressed on

---

[43] The text was edited in *Analecta Franciscana*, 3 (1897), p. 641-645. On the manuscript tradition of the text and its importance among the other stigmata-accounts, see I. HEULLANT-DONAT, "Pourquoi enquêter sur la stigmatisation de François d'Assise? Remarques sur l'*Instrumentum de stigmatibus beati Francisci* (1282)", in *Discorsi sulle stimmate dal Medioevo all'età contemporanea*, op. cit., p. 93-124.
[44] *Instrumentum de stigmatibus beati Francisci* in *Analecta Franciscana*, 3 (1897), p. 644: *Post ipse Dominus manus suas corpori meo applicuit et primo manibus, secundo pedibus, tertio lateri mihi stigmata ista impressit cum vehementissimo doloris sensu et cum magno qualibet vice clamore.*
[45] *Fontes Franciscani*, op. cit., p. 2106-2109.
[46] Cf. HEULLANT-DONAT, "Pourquoi enquêter?", art. cit., p. 111-113.
[47] *FA: ED* II, p. 458, note 'a'.

him is not perfectly clear, but as Francis himself said to his companions, this mystery being put off for the future. The authenticity of the story is underscored:

> Brother James de Massa received this account from the mouth of Brother Leo, and Brother Ugolino of Monte Santa Maria had it from the mouth of this Brother James, and I, the writer, had it from the mouth of Brother Ugolino. All these were men worthy of trust in all things.[48]

Thanks chiefly to the *Instrumentum*, more dramatic and detailed versions of the miracle, such as the *Considerazioni sulle stimmate* appended to the *Fioretti*, the free adaptation of the *Actus* in the Tuscan vernacular,[49] as well as further Latin accounts of the stigmatization were composed: one of them, as well as the one reported in the *Actus* became part of the Hungarian devotional literature.

The stigmatization in the Old Hungarian codex literature

After this general survey of those Latin accounts of the stigmatization that can be in one way or another associated with the narratives translated to the Hungarian vernacular, let us turn now to the Jókai, the Virginia and the Lázár Zelma codices that narrate what happened on the Mount La Verna.[50] The chapter "Aluerna hegye megleleserewl" [On finding the Mount Alverna] of the *Jókai Codex* gives a rather faithful translation *Actus* that narrates how his stigmatization took place with the exception that apart from two shepherds, no further witnesses are mentioned,[51] although its Latin parallel, the *Actus* makes a strong claim on authenticity.[52] The stigmata are mentioned again in the chapter about the *levitatio* of Francis, (*Actus* 39) witnessed by Brother Leo, who is described as the only person who could touch the wounds and regularly change the bandages on them.[53] In the next chapter

---

[48] *Fontes Franciscani, op. cit.*, p. 2109: *Hanc ystoriam habuit fr. Iacobus de Massa ab ore fr. Leonis; et fr. Hugolinus de Monte S. Marie ab ore dicti fr. Iacobi, et ego qui scribo ab ore fr. Hugolini, viri fide digni et boni.* The English translation is from *FA: ED* II, p. 458.

[49] The text of the *Actus* and that of the *Fioretti*, although not completely identical, is published in the *Actus beati Francisci et sociorum eius* in CAMBELL's edition. See footnote 17.

[50] The mystical aspect of hagiographic texts written in Hungarian (Sts Francis, Catherine of Siena, Margaret of Hungary) was treated by Á. KORONDI, *A misztika, op. cit.*, p. 179-196.

[51] *Jókai-kódex, op. cit.*, p. 119.

[52] *Fontes Franciscani, op. cit.*, p. 2109: *Quare vero apparuerunt stigmata s. Francisci, nondum per omnia notuit; sed, sicut ipse sociis revelavit, hoc prefertur magnum misterium in futurum. Hanc ystoriam habuit fr. Iacobus de Massa ab ore fr. Leonis; et fr. Hugolinus de Monte S. Mariae ab ore dicti fr. Iacobi; et ego qui scribe ab ore fr. Hugolini, viri fide digni et boni.*

[53] See footnote 30.

of the *Jókai Codex*, entitled "Zent sebekrewl ualo czuda" [Miracle about the holy wounds] (*Actus* 40 = 65²), a Dominican friar denies the authenticity of Francis' stigmata and tries – unsuccessfully – to destroy the fresco in the refectory that represents the saint with the wounds.[54]

Whereas in the *Jókai Codex* the episode of the stigmatization is clearly the translation of the laconic account of the *Actus* without any additional details on the part of the translator, a few decades later a much longer Latin text about the same event was translated to the Hungarian vernacular: it survived in two independent translations in the *Virginia*[55] and *Lázár Zelma* codices. The two translations go back to the same Latin text which appeared in print both as the part of the *Speculum vitae beati Francisci et sociorum eius* (1504) as well as in Sermo 75 of the *Pomerium de Sanctis: pars aestivalis* of Pelbartus de Themeswar (1499).[56] We can read both in the *Speculum vitae* and the sermon of Pelbartus that the stigmata narrative comes from a certain *Vita sociorum sancti Francisci* which unfortunately cannot be identified today. The work gives a much more elaborated version of the stigmatization since much of the information coming from the *Instrumentum* – although probably through intermediary works – was incorporated in the account that can be summed up as follows: while Francis is spending the Lent of St Michael on the Mount La Verna, as he goes out one day to pray early in the morning he sees a Seraph descending with burning fire and the crucified Christ appears between the wings. Francis marvels greatly and rejoices but Christ warns him of secrecy and tells him to be prepared as he will perform a wonderful miracle to him. As Francis claims to be ready, Christ holds out his right hand and puts it above that of Francis, who immediately cries out his name and collapses. Christ urges him to get up again, and he performs the same act with Francis's right hand, then his feet. The climax of the stigmata account is the impression of the side wound when Francis asks who would be able to endure such pain, Christ responds to him:

> 'What would you have done then if you had suffered all the beatings, the crowning of thorns, the slaps, the spitting and other harsh torments that

---

[54] *Jókai-kódex, op. cit.*, p. 152-160.
[55] Shelfmark: K 40 in the manuscript collection of the Library of the Magyar Tudományos Akadémia (Hungarian National Academy of Sciences, Budapest). Edition: *Virginia-kódex, XVI. század eleje: a nyelvemlék másolata és betűhű átirata* [Virginia codex, the beginning of the sixteenth century: the facsimile and the diplomatic transcription of the Old Hungarian codex], ed. Zs. Kovács, Budapest, 1990 (Régi Magyar Kódexek, 11). The stigmatization is at p. 105-111.
[56] Editio princeps: *Speculum vitae beati Francisci et sociorum eius*, Venice, 1504; Pelbartus de Themeswar, *Sermones de sanctis II. [Pars aestivalis]*, Hagenau, 1499.

I suffered for the people?' Rising up Francis said: 'I am ready for what you want.' And Jesus embraced him and placed his side to the side of Francis and immediately impressed the wound on his side. So Francis cried out 'O pious Jesus' and fell on the ground like a half-dead. And meanwhile Christ vanished.[57]

The account ends with the apparition of Brother Leo – not Conrad as in the *Instrumentum* – who finds the unconscious Francis about whom he thinks to have died due to his exaggerated abstinent lifestyle.

Like in the *Instrumentum*, there is no doubt in the *Vita sociorum sancti Francisci* that it was the crucified Christ who appeared to Francis under the form of a seraph, but neither the appearance of the stigmata is described, nor the nails are mentioned here. The pain of Francis caused by the stigmata is expressed in a different way: he cries out and collapses after each impression of a wound. The accentuation of the physical torment the saint had to suffer during the stigmatization and Christ's recalling of his own Passion in the *Vita sociorum sancti Francisci* fits quite well to the fourteenth-fifteenth-century tradition of affective piety.[58]

Despite their common Latin source, the significance of stigmata narratives is different in the two codices. The Virginia Codex was made sometime before 1529 and contains a mirror of confession, a collection of episodes from the life of St Francis, fragments of a sermon and translation of the abbreviated version of the *Regula monacharum* but was copied by a Dominican nun. It belongs to the family of *Conformitas* since the greatest part of the codex treats the conformity of Francis to Christ. The stigmatization is only one of the several characteristics that made him similar to the Saviour, but in the codex equal importance is given to other aspects of the life of the saint: how God made Francis similar to the other saints, *exempla* that tell about not only his but also his companions' eminence in humility and obedience.

In the *Lázár Zelma Codex*, a collection of prayers and devotional writings made in Transylvania for private use for a Clarissan nun around 1525, the same stigmatization episode functions as a "very beautiful and devout" prayer.[59] The

---

[57] *Speculum vitae*, op. cit., fol. 232a: *Quid fecisses tunc, si verbera et spinee corone punctiones, alapas, sputa et alias penas quos ego per hominibus suscepi, sustinuisses?' Surgens ergo Franciscus dixit: 'Quod iubes paratus sum'. At Iesus amplexus illum iunxit latus lateri beati Francisci, et statim impressit plagam lateralem. Tunc Franciscus exclamans: 'O pie Iesu!' Cecidit in terram quasi semi mortuus. Et Christus interim disparuit.*
[58] On the Passion in the Hungarian devotional literature, see Á. KORONDI, *A misztika*, op. cit., p. 170-200.
[59] Shelfmark: K 41 in the manuscript collection in the Library of the Hungarian Academy of Sciences [Magyar Tudományos Akadémia]. Edition: *Lázár [Zelma]-kódex: XVI. század első fele. A nyelvemlék hasonmása és betűhű átirata* [*Lázár Zelma Codex*: the first half of

direct source of the stigmata account of the *Lázár Zelma Codex* was Pelbartus de Themeswar whose exhortation to pray to the saint's intercession for eternal bliss for life after death at the end of his sermon was also translated.[60]

The descriptions of the Seraph in the Hungarian translations are also slightly different from the Latin: in the *Lázár Zelma Codex* between the wings of the Seraph there was an army of angels surrounding the crucified Christ, and the *Virginia Codex* gives a detailed account of the Seraph of six wings based on the traditional biblical description of Isaiah 6:2.[61] Other remarkable scribal additions can be found in the *Virginia Codex*. Whereas in the Latin text the crucified Christ asks Francis to prepare himself (*Para te, Francisce!*) for receiving the wounds, in the *Virginia Codex* Christ urges him to 'Prepare yourself for peace!' (*zerezd magadat bekesegre*), then to 'Prepare yourself for suffering!' (*zerezd magad zenuedesre*)and then 'Prepare yourself to get closer to hil!' (*zerezd hazza magad enelfelieben*), the first referring the mission of Francis, the second to his imitation of Christ, and the third to his strive to elevate his soul to God.[62] Apart from some further minor additions and changes to the Latin source, the two translations do not show any major intervention.

In addition to the three vernacular narratives, the stigmata of Francis (but not his stigmatization) turn up also in the *Érdy Codex* (1526/27) which is the most comprehensive surviving collection of sermons and legends intended for public reading by a Carthusian monk in Lövöld (Veszprém county, today Városlőd, Hungary). In the *De sanctis* part of the *Érdy Codex* the Carthusian Anonymous included a high number of "modern" saints, of whom many belonged to or was associated with the two great mendicant orders, of whom the Franciscans were represented by Francis of Assisi, Clare of Assisi, Anthony of Padua, and Elizabeth of Hungary, the latter associated with the Third Order.[63] The sermon written for the feast of Francis is based on sermo 45 (De tribus excellentiis beati Francisci) of *De laudibus sanctorum* by the Franciscan Roberto Caracciolo, although the Carthusian monk chose a different *thema* for his sermon: *Ego enim stigmata domini Iesu in corpore meo*

---

sixteenth century. The facsimile and the diplomatic transcription of the Old Hungarian codex], ed. Cs. N. ABAFFY, Budapest, 1992 (Régi Magyar Kódexek, 14). The stigmatization is at p. 319-337.
[60] *Lázár Zelma-kódex, op. cit.*, p. 337.
[61] *Lázár Zelma-kódex, op. cit.*, p. 321; *Virginia-kódex, op. cit.*, p. 105.
[62] *Virginia-kódex, op. cit.*, p. 107.
[63] The sermon on St Clare of Assisi is at p. 195-202, the legend on Anthony of Padua is at p. 464-474, that of Elizabeth of Hungary is at p. 476-487, and that of Francis of Assisi at p. 366-375 in the *Érdy-codex*.

porto (Gal 6:17).⁶⁴ This passage has been generally associated with St Francis and his wounds and was recited in the readings of the liturgy and in the office on the feast of St Francis.⁶⁵ A noteworthy characteristic of the vernacular sermon is that the author directs his audience's attention Francis's stigmata and in this way he underlines the saint's conformity to Christ, whereas in the much longer sermon of Caracciolo he used as a model the stigmata is only mentioned twice.⁶⁶ The fact the Italian Franciscan dedicated a whole sermon to the stigmata of Francis in the *De laudibus sanctorum* may be an explanation why the Carthusian Anonymous, who composed only a single sermon on the saint, intensified this aspect of his holiness.

In the introduction to the sermon the Carthusian Anonymous compares St Francis to St Paul: while the latter bore in his soul the cross and the holy wounds of Jesus Christ, the former bore them on his body. In the introduction after the epistle the stigmatized Francis is presented as "the image, the mark, the example and the follower of the son of God, and the renovator of the corruption of all Christianity".⁶⁷ The Carthusian monk built his sermon around the same three *capituli* as Caracciolo. These *capituli* are illustrated by a copious number of exemplum-like episodes from his hagiography, taken mostly from Bonaventure's *Legenda maior*: (1) the reasons why Francis was granted the wounds of Christ and sent here by God to preach penitence just

---

⁶⁴ Robertus Caracciolus, *Sermones de laudibus*, Venice, 1490: "Sermo quadragesimusquinto De tribus excellentiis beati Francisci", fol. 141a-144c. It should be noted that the theme of Caracciolo's "Sermo quadragesimusquarto de sacris admirandisque stigmatibus seraphici Francisci", fol. 138a-141a of the collection is built on the same theme. For the analysis of this sermon, see C. MUESSIG, "Roberto Caracciolo's Sermon on the Miracle of the Stigmatization of Francis of Assisi", *Anuario de Estudios Medievales*, 42/1 (2012), p. 77-93.

⁶⁵ P. BERHIDAI, "Szent Ferenc képe a XV. századi magyarországi irodalomban" [The image of St Francis in the fifteenth century Hungarian literature], in *Európa védelmében: Kapisztrán Szent János és a nándorfehérvári diadal emlékezete*, ed. K. PEREGRIN, L. VESZPRÉMY, Budapest, 2013, p. 111-118, at p. 117. On Caracciolo as the source of the Carthusian Anonymous sermon on St Francis, see D. RAPAVI, "A Karthauzi Névtelen Szent Ferenc-napi beszéde a rendi elfogultság tükrében" [The Carthusian Anonymous's sermon on the feast of St Francis in the light of monastic bias], unpubl. MA thesis, Budapest, Eötvös Loránd Tudományegyetem, 2007, p. 4-25. Recently, C. RADÓ TÓTHNÉ has discussed the use of some of Caracciolo's sermons (Sts. Francis of Assisi, Anthony of Padua and Catherine of Siena) in the Érdy Codex in her doctoral dissertation *Robertus Caracciolus OFM prédikációs segédkönyveinek magyarországi felhasználása* [The use of the model sermons of Robertus Caracciolus in Hungary], unpubl. PhD thesis, Piliscsaba, Pázmány Péter Katolikus Egyetem, 2014, p. 86-187.

⁶⁶ Robertus Caracciolus, *Sermones de laudibus*, "Sermo quadragesimusquinto De tribus excellentiis beati Francisci", *op. cit.*, fol. 141c, 142a.

⁶⁷ *Érdy-codex, op. cit.*, p. 367: "isten ffya abrazattyanak kepeenek, yegyeenek, peldayanak es kowetoyeenek es mynd egheez kereztttyenseegben valo romlasnak meg wyoytoyanak".

before the end of the world, (2) his virtues: piety, poverty, austerity, humility and patience, (3) the different kinds of divine gifts God granted to glorify him. The Carthusian Anonymous alludes to the stigmata of Francis in the first and third sections, but he does not assign them central role in the sermon. In the first section, the author considers the wounds of Francis as a proof of his faithfulness:

> It was due to his great mercy that the Lord God sent our father St Francis with his wounds in order to induce and inflame the hearts that are arid, dry, and cold and lack divine love. And we should not marvel that people consider him more faithful because of the visible sign that was inflicted on him, the seal of the son of God, that is his holy wounds, for the salvation of this world; at which we, my beloved fellows, should not marvel. But rather be deeply grateful to the Lord God.[68]

In the third section, elaborating the various ways the Lord magnified him, the Carthusian monk, praising Francis's perfect detachment from the world, urges his listeners to the *sequela Christi* and advises them to look at the crucifix of the blessed Jesus Christ in order to find the path and weapon of Christ they should follow, and to look at the face of Francis and the wounds he took up in order to understand the way how Christ should be followed.[69] By the end of the sermon, the Carthusian monk talks about "noble and pious virgins from the order of our father St Dominic could have this gift of the great divine grace also in our times, at which Christian people cannot but marvel.[70]" This "gift" refers again to the stigmata, which were also given not only to St Francis but to other holy people, including women, most notably the Dominican tertiary Catherine of Siena whose sermon the Carthusian Anonymous included in his collection, but it remains unclear to which other Dominican stigmatized saints he alluded.[71] Nevertheless, in the sermon on

---

[68] *Érdy-codex, op. cit.*, p. 368: "Azert az ew nagy kegyelmessegeebol tewee wr isten hogy zent ferencz atyankkat az ew zent sebeywel el kyldenee hogy az meg azot, zaradot es hydegodt isteny zeretetneel kyl valo zyweket ffeel gheeryeztenee es gywlaztanaa. Es hogy ynkab meg hynnenek ewneky ollyan nylwan valo yegy alat mert twlaydon ez vylagnak Idvessegeert bochatatott volna isten ffyanak peechetywel az az a zent sebeywel kyn zerelmes atyamffyay ne keel chwdalnwnk. De ynkab nagy halakat raytta adnwnk az kegyelmes wr istennek (...)".
[69] *Érdy-codex, op. cit.*, p. 373.
[70] *Ibid.*: "Meely nagy Isteni malaztnak ayandekaat tebbeknek ees olwaswnk enghettethween lenny. Zent Damonkos atyank zerzetybol: nemes ayoytatus zent zyzeket: wgyan my ydettewnk ees, kyn kerezttyen emberek lehetetlenkeppen nem keel chodalkony".
[71] The sermon on St Catherine of Siena is in *Érdy-codex, op. cit.*, p. 396-413. On the other stigmatic women of the Italian Dominicans after Catherine, like Columba of Rieti, Lucia Brocadelli, Osanna Andreasi and Stefana Quinzani, see the works of T. Herzig, especially her *Savonarola's Women: Visions and Reform in Renaissance Italy*, Chicago, 2008; Ead., *Christ*

St Catherine of Siena the Carthusian Anonymous' says explicitly that "Jesus allowed only St Paul, St Francis and St Catherine virgin, his spouse, to have the sign of salvation, the holy and worthy wounds.[72]"

Although in the general opinion of the various religious orders Catherine of Siena was a saintly woman who had the stigmata, the idea scandalized the Franciscans. The Franciscan Order claimed that Francis was the only person who really bore the wounds of Christ in his body, and no one else could have it, or at least, not visibly.[73] The Dominicans were eager to prove that Catherine was indeed the bearer of the holy wounds and opposed to Francis's corporeal stigmata, they developed the theology of invisible ones.[74] Catherine of Siena was canonized in 1461 by Pope Pius II and although in the canonization bull her stigmatization was not mentioned, in the Processo Castellano, an early fifteenth-century attempt by Tommaso Caffarini to have her canonized and her *Legenda* written by Raimondo da Capua her stigmatization was discussed exhaustively.[75] The stigmata of Catherine caused a long and fierce debate between the two mendicant orders: in 1475 Pope Sixtus IV prohibited her representation with "Christ's Stigmata", and several Franciscan preachers, among them Roberto Caracciolo who, despite having a high opinion of Catherine, challenged her veneration as a stigmatic saint.[76] In the Latin sermon the Carthusian Anonymous used as model for his sermon on Catherine of Siena, Caracciolo argued that she was a saint because of being a virgin, prophetess, and visionary, but not a stigmatic.[77] The Carthusian monk

---

Transformed into a Virgin Woman: Lucia Brocadelli, Heinrich Institoris and the Defense of the Faith, Rome, 2013 (Scritture nel Chiostro – Temi e Testi 114).

[72] *Érdy-codex, op. cit.*, p. 411: "… iesus ez vylaghnak meg valto yegyt az zent melto sebeket enghette vona, hanemczak uzent palnak, zent ferencznek es ez zyz zent katherina yegeseenek".

[73] For an overview of the debate concerning the visual representation of the stigmata of Catherine of Siena, see D. GIUNTA, "The Iconography of Catherine of Siena's Stigmata", in *A Companion to Catherine of Siena*, ed. C. MUESSIG, G. FERZOCO, B. M. KIENZLE, Leiden, 2012, p. 259-294; in the same volume, C. MUESSIG, "Catherine of Siena in Late Medieval Sermons", p. 203-226.

[74] For Catherine of Siena and the debate on the stigmata, see C. MUESSIG, "The Stigmata Debate in Theology and Art in the Late Middle Ages", in *Authority of the Word. Reflecting on Image and Text in Northern Europe, 1400-1700*, ed. W. MELION, C. BRUSATI, K. ENENKEL, Leiden, 2012, p. 481-504.

[75] For the canonization of Catherine of Siena, see G. FERZOCO, "The *Processo Castellano* and the Canonization of Catherine of Siena", in *A Companion to Catherine of Siena, op. cit.*, p. 185-202; O. KRAFFT, "Many Strategies and One Goal", in *Catherine of Siena: The Creation of a Cult*, ed. J. E. HAMBURGER and G. SIGNORI, Turnhout, 2013, p. 25-46.

[76] C. MUESSIG, "The Stigmata Debate in Theology and Art in the Late Middle Ages", *art. cit.*, p. 498.

[77] Robertus Caracciolus, *Sermones de laudibus sanctorum* (Reutlinger, 1495), fol. 220b-225b; quoted in C. MUESSIG, "Catherine of Siena in Late Medieval Sermons", *art. cit.*, p. 220.

thus did not include Caracciolo's long justification why the Sienese *mantellata* was not a stigmatic; for him she was, insomuch that he called his audience attention to the Dominican holy virgins in the sermon composed for the feast of St Francis.[78]

We have seen that from the beginning of the fifteenth century the latest there was a demand for a *Franziskusbuch*, a standard work in the Franciscan (nuns') convents, in the Hungarian vernacular. The *Jókai Codex* was made to satisfy this need, although the circumstances of its origin and target audience are not clear, and nor the milieu from where its Latin sources come, neither internal evidence provide any secure reference to this. The only certainty is that it was destined to a community that was not educated in Latin but was supposed to be interested in everything about Francis. An obligatory component of such work was his stigmatization, and the *Jókai Codex* indeed reports the brief account of the *Actus*, as well as other episodes related to the saint's stigmata. There is no doubt in the codex about the authenticity of the wounds of Francis, and it is the stigmatization itself and its physical effect on the rest of his life rather than the circumstances of this event that stand in the foreground. The two early sixteenth-century Hungarian accounts on the stigmatization in the *Virginia* and *Lázár Zelma* codices, however, were translated from a not identified but a presumably contemporary *Vita sociorum sancti Francisci*, that provides an expanded and rather affective presentation of the event. The two different translations may imply that it was considered to be a suitable piece of reading for a female audience. The stigmatization of Francis has gained considerable spiritual charge in the course of time, yet it preserved its basis, the saint's *Christiconformitas*. The structure and the style made the stigmatization narrative befitting to stand on its own among other prayers, as in the case of the *Lázár Zelma Codex*. The examined Old Hungarian codices show that the stigmatization or the stigmata of Francis were reported in codices of different provenance (Franciscan/Clarissan, Dominican and Carthusian), written for private and community use alike. The Carthusian Anonymous in his collection of sermons destined to use for

---

[78] The Carthusian Order had a significant role in the propagation of the cult of Catherine of Siena in the late fourteenth and early fifteenth century: Stefano Maconi, who was the disciple and one of the principal secretarians of the saint, and who entered on her advice the Carthusian Order in 1381 and when he became the abbot of the order in 1398 he moved to Seitz, Styria, where he dedicated himself the diffusion of Catherine's *Legenda maior* by having copies made and sending one to each Carthusian monasteries. For Maconi, the disciple of Catherine, see D. MOVRIN, "The Beloved Disciple: Stephen Maconi and St Catherine of Siena", *Annual of Medieval Studies at CEU*, 10 (2004), p. 43-52; on his activity for the preservation of her memory, see S. NOCENTINI, "Lo 'scriptorium' di Tommaso Caffarini a Venezia", *Hagiographica*, 12 (2005), p. 79-144, at p. 87-93.

community reading composed a sermon on St Francis in which the stigmata, as a distinctive feature of his sanctity, are emphasized; yet, the author also added, possibly for the sake of his female audience, that Francis was not the only one with this divine privilege but it was given also to saintly women of the Dominican Order.[79]

---

[79] Since the original version of this paper was submitted in 2015, I could not take into consideration the new results of the recently published work of S. Lász, *Apácaműveltség Magyarországon a XV-XVI. század fordulóján: az anyanyelvű irodalom kezdetei* [The culture of nuns in Hungary at the turn of the fourteenth and fufteenth centuries: the beginnings of vernacular literature], Budapest, 2016.

Medieval Hagiography of St Hyacinth

Anna ZAJCHOWSKA
(*Warsaw*)

The corpus of medieval hagiography of St Hyacinth, the first Polish Dominican, is exceptionally modest. It consists of a fourteenth-century life by the Dominican *lector* Stanislaus, based mostly on a lost thirteenth-century *liber miraculorum*; dozens of miracle accounts from the end of the fifteenth century; and – provided that we understand the Middle Ages broadly enough, which is well-grounded in the case of Poland – the sixteenth-century "Song about St Hyacinth" written by Nicholas Hussoviensis, a Polish Renaissance poet. The short list is supplemented with hagiographical works devoted to other saints which shed (a dim) light on the figure of St Hyacinth: the life of an eleventh-century bishop of Krakow, Stanislaus, and the sermon on St Dominic by Peregrinus of Opole. Some hagiographical motifs related to Hyacinth are found also in a sermon delivered at the chapter of the Polish Dominican province at the beginning of the sixteenth century. Besides that, scholars dealing with the cult of St Hyacinth have at their disposal also a relatively small number of diplomatic and historiographic sources related to the efforts at the canonization of the Polish Dominican.

The canonization efforts, crowned with success in 1594 only, represent the *leitmotif* of the first, exceptionally long stage of the cult of the saint who died in 1257. Almost all listed sources concerning St Hyacinth are into a smaller or higher extent connected to the canonization efforts. However, the chronological limit of the paper is not the year 1594, but 1527. This date represents a breakthrough in the development of the cult of St Hyacinth. Until then, the founder of the Polish Dominican province, as Pope Leo X writes in his *breve* of 1527, had been surrounded by the devotion from the part of the faithful, who considered him as a saint and believed in the efficacy of his intercession, but they did not have the certainty whether they were allowed to do so.[1] Only by the act of 2 February 1527 the pope dispelled these doubts and officially approved the cult of St Hyacinth, restricting it, however, to the Dominican churches within the Polish province. From this date until his canonization, the scope of the official cult was being gradually broadened. Therefore, until the moment when the mentioned *breve* was issued, we can talk about an unofficial pre-canonization cult, while after this date, although Hyacinth was not inscribed in the catalogue of the saints yet, we have to do with a cult formally approved by the Church authorities.[2] Before we turn to the description of the hagiography concerning St Hyacinth and its relation

---

[1] Cf. the *breve* published by Severinus LUBOMELIUS in: *De vita, miraculis et actis canonisationis Sancti Hyacinthi confessoris Ordinis Fratrum Praedicatorum libri quattuor*, Rome, 1594, p. 233-235.

[2] Although the pre-canonization cult of St Hyacinth has already been the subject of many studies, there is still no exhaustive monograph of the topic. The scholars were interested in his cult as a side issue of their research concerning the life of St Hyacinth. For example: J. WORONIECKI, *Św. Jacek Odrowąż i wprowadzenie zakonu Kaznodziejskiego do Polski*, Katowice, 1947; J. KŁOCZOWSKI, "Św. Jacek", in *Hagiografia polska. Słownik bio-bibliograficzny*, ed. R. GUSTAW, vol. I, Poznań, 1971. The studies directly connected with the cult of St Hyacinth were conducted by Zdzisław Obertyński, who reconstructed the course of efforts at canonization of Hyacinth, and Aleksandra Witkowska, who devoted a special article to the cult of Hyacinth, which analyses the medieval miracle collections and studies medieval pilgrimage cults in Krakow. Jan Andrzej Spież reached important results at the occasion of his study of the cult of Blessed Czesław. The work of Zdisław Obertyński – Z. OBERTYŃSKI, "Dzieje kanonizacji św. Jacka", *Prawo Kanoniczne*, 4 (1961), no. 1-4 –, although extremely valuable, is based on a selective source query. The author relies mainly on the work of Seweryn Lubomelczyk from the period after the canonization, and does not include original documents related to the canonization process. A. WITKOWSKA, "Kult Jacka Odrowąża w średniowiecznym Krakowie", in *Christianitas in cultura Europae. Księga jubileuszowa Profesora Jerzego Kłoczowskiego*, ed. H. GAPSKI, part 1, Lublin, 1998 (hereafter: WITKOWSKA, "Kult Jacka Odrowąża"); Ead., "Miracula małopolskie z XIII i XIV wieku (Studium źródłoznawcze)", *Roczniki Humanistyczne*, 19/2 (1971); Ead., *Kulty pątnicze piętnastowiecznego Krakowa*, Lublin, 1984; J. A. SPIEŻ, "Średniowieczne świadectwa życia i kultu błogosławionego Czesława", in *Dominikanie w środkowej Europie w XIII-XV wieku. Aktywność duszpasterska i kultura intelektualna*, ed. J. KŁOCZOWSKI, J. A. SPIEŻ, Poznań, 2002, p. 87-108. Another important group of works is related to edition and analysis of sources concerning the cult of St Hyacinth. We have to mention, first of all, the extensive study of Raymond J. Loenertz on the Life of St Hyacinth by lector Stanislaus (J.-R. LOENERTZ, "La vie de S. Hyacinthe du lecteur Stanislas envisagée comme source historique", *Archivum Fratrum Praedicatorum*, 22 (1952), p. 294-316), and the edition of letters requesting the canonization ascribed to Zbigniew Oleśnicki, prepared by Maria Kowalczyk. The volume published on the occasion of 750th anniversary of the death of Hyacinth contains Polish translation of almost all sources concerning the cult of St Hyacinth, including a fifteenth-century collection of miracles unpublished until then. Its Latin version, prepared among others by the author of this article, appeared a year later in *Studia Źródłoznawcze*. M. ZDANEK, A. ZAJCHOWSKA, "Mirakula świętego Jacka z lat 1488-1500. Edycja krytyczna", *Studia Źródłoznawcze*, 46 (2009), p. 95-105. We are still waiting for a new critical edition of the Life. M. KOWALCZYK, "Starania kardynała Zbigniewa Oleśnickiego o kanonizację św. Jacka Odrowąża", in *Dominikanie w środkowej Europie, op. cit.*, p. 65-72.

to the development of his cult, let us provide some basic information about the saint himself.

Biography of St Hyacinth

St Hyacinth belonged to the first generation of the Polish Dominicans and the Dominicans in general. He was a canon of the chapter of Krakow, active by the side of his relative, bishop of Krakow, Iwo Odrowąż. The bishop encouraged him and two other Poles to accept the habit from the hands of St Dominic in Rome. After their noviciate,[3] Hyacinth, together with Herman Germanus and Czeslaus set on a journey to Krakow, on their way founding a convent in Austrian Friesach, where Herman stayed. In 1222 the convent of the Holy Trinity in Krakow was established with the help of Bishop Iwo. Other centres started to form shortly after the Krakow convent. The foundation of the convents in Prague and Wroclaw, and also in Gdańsk and Kiev, is also related to the saint's activity. Although he laid the foundation for the development of the Polish province of the Order, St Hyacinth did not stand at its head, but devoted himself to missionary and pastoral activities. In 1225 he set together with several friars to the north in order to establish a convent in Gdańsk, which could serve as a foothold for the Dominican missions among the Prussians. St Hyacinth dedicated the following years of his life to the missionary activity, working in Prussia and above all in Rus. After around ten years of missionary activity, Hyacinth returned to Krakow and most probably fully occupied himself with preaching. He died on 15 August 1257.

Already from this short biographical sketch – which contains, *nota bene*, most of the information which can be mined from the preserved sources – Hyacinth emerges as a typical Mendicant saint of the thirteenth century. However, it is not his life but his broad-based miracle-working activity which has become the essential content of his cult. It is not by chance that one of the earliest preserved records devoted to him, which comes from the acts of the general chapter, talks about him as somebody who has the power to raise people from the dead, and does not mention a word either about his merits for the order or about his christianization mission.

---

[3] Historians have been debating the chronology of the events related to St Hyacinth's stay in Rome. The length of his noviciate is the subject of the particularly fervent discussion.

Corpus Hagiographicum sancti Hiacynthi

The thirteenth century: *Liber miraculorum, Vita s. Stanislai, Acta Capitulorum Generalium, sermo Peregrini Opoliensi*

The earliest evidence of the cult of St Hyacinth comes from the second half of the thirteenth century already. Almost immediately after his death, the Dominicans started to write down the accounts of the miracles accomplished through his intercession.[4] This constituted the beginning of the nowadays lost *Liber miraculorum*, which would become the basic source for the Life of St Hyacinth written by *lector* Stanislaus a hundred years later. The book of miracles started to be recorded possibly already in 1268, that is, 11 years after the saint's death. A "miracle office", established specifically for that purpose, most probably functioned at the Krakow Dominican convent; its activities have been thoroughly studied by Raymond J. Loenertz. The analysis of the group of persons involved in the miracles written originally in the *Liber miraculorum* and subsequently incorporated in the Life by *lector* Stanislaus has shown that a majority of them belonged to the nobility of Little Poland, especially to those with family ties to the saint. Thus, it was mostly a local cult, which only occasionally exceeded the boundaries of the diocese.[5]

This earliest phase of the cult is confirmed by the thirteenth-century Life of St Stanislaus written by, *nota bene*, a Dominican, Vincent of Kielcza.[6] His mention of the tomb of St Hyacinth as a point of reference proves that this place was well-known and recognized already at that time.[7] The third trace of the earliest manifestations of the cult of the deceased founder of the Polish

---

[4] The work on the register of miracles was undertaken at the time when the General Chapter of the Dominican Order issued in 1256 the recommendation to collect testimonies about saintly members of the order. Cf. for example Z. OBERTYŃSKI, "Dzieje kanonizacji", *art. cit.*, p. 80.

[5] J. WORONIECKI, *Św. Jacek, op. cit.*, p. 259, A. WITKOWSKA, "Miracula", *art. cit.*, p. 121.

[6] J. KŁOCZOWSKI, "Św. Jacek", *art. cit.*, p. 446-447.

[7] Vincent of Kielcza, *Vita sancti Stanislai episcopi Cracoviensis. Vita maior*, ed. W. KĘTRZYŃSKI, Lwów, 1884 (Monumenta Poloniae Historica, 4), p. 433. In the same place Vincent mentions that besides St Stanislaus there are six more saints in Poland, who in God's eyes enjoy the same merits as the martyr-bishop. The editor of the text, W. Kętrzyński, saw also St Hyacinth among those anonymous saints. See Vincent of Kielcza, *op. cit.*, p. 433, n. 1. A. Witkowska questions this opinion and maintains that the note could concern "solely St Adalbert and Five Brethren". A. WITKOWSKA, *Kulty, op. cit.*, p. 80. Kętrzyński's opinion is confirmed by the text of Thomas of Sycow, "De inventione et bina translatione assium Beati Iacinthi", in *De vita et miraculis sancti Iacchonis (Hyacinthi) Ordinis Fratrum Praedicatorum auctore Stanislao lectore Cracoviensi eiusdem ordinis*, ed. L. ĆWIKLIŃSKI, Lwów, 1884, p. 894-899 (Monumenta Poloniae Historica, 4), which interprets the passage of the Life of St Stanislaus in the same spirit.

Dominicans, which is listed equally by all scholars, is the abovementioned record in the acts of the General Chapter of the Order of Friars Preachers, convoked in Bordeaux in 1277. They describe the state of the Polish province as following: "in the Krakow convent [two friars] lie – Friar Hyacinth, who has the power to raise from the dead, and Vitus, a bishop, who has the power to work miracles".[8]

For sure, the Dominicans promoted the cult of "their own" saint not only by collecting the miracles accomplished through his intercession, but also by preaching sermons. The evidence of this is found in the miracle accounts which *lector* Stanislaus inserted in his Life of the saint. The account no. 42 from 1284 reads that Mileszka, who turned to St Hyacinth for help in her need, knew about the efficacy of his intercession thanks to the sermons she had heard;[9] then, chapter 52 of the year 1352 informs us that one of the miracles which took place at the saint's tomb was recounted during a sermon.[10] Unfortunately, none of these sermons have been preserved until our times. The only extant preaching text touching on the saint is the sermon for the feast of St Dominic by the Dominican Peregrinus of Opole, who lived at the turn of the thirteenth and fourteenth centuries (born around 1260, died after 1333). Peregrinus acknowledges the founder of the Order of Preachers with many titles, among others he describes him as the father of martyrs and saints. He names among his sons, besides Peter of Verona, Jordanus, and Czeslaus, also Hyacinth.[11] Taking into consideration the broad diffusion of Peregrinus' sermons throughout whole Europe, this short *passus* should be given a big significance in the propagation of Hyacinth's cult.[12] However, we have to take this mention with caution because of its unclear date of origin. Although a critical edition of the sermons of Peregrinus of Opole is available,

---

[8] *Anno Domini MCCLXXVII in Capitulo Generali Burdegalis celebrato erant conventus Fratrum et sororum tot.* [...] *In provincia Poloniae conventus Fratrum XXXVI, monasteria Sororum duo. In cracoviensi jacet frater Jacons potens in mortuis suscitandis et Vitus episcopus potens in miraculis patrandis.* See *Scriptores Ordinis Praedicatorum*, ed. J. QUETIF, J. ECHARD, vol. I, Paris, 1719, p. 1; translation after: A. WITKOWSKA, "Kult Jacka Odrowąża", art. cit., p. 170. See also J. WORONIECKI, *Św. Jacek, op. cit.*, p. 260; J. KŁOCZOWSKI, "Św. Jacek", *art. cit.*, p. 447; Z. OBERTYŃSKI, "Dzieje kanonizacji", *art. cit.*, p. 80. The quoted passage comes from Bernard Gui.

[9] *De vita et miraculis sancti Iacchonis (Hyacinthi) Ordinis Fratrum Praedicatorum auctore Stanislao lectore Cracoviensi eiusdem ordinis*, ed. L. ĆWIKLIŃSKI, Lwów, 1884, p. 884.

[10] *De vita et miraculis sancti Iacchonis, op. cit.*, p. 893-894.

[11] *Peregrini de Opole sermones de tempore et de sanctis*, ed. R. TATARZYŃSKI, Warsaw, 1997, p. 602.

[12] There are approximately around 300 extant manuscripts with the sermons by Peregrinus; by the early sixteenth century there were also nine printed editions. See R. TATARZYŃSKI, "Einteitung des Herausgebers", in *Peregrini de Opole, op. cit.*, p. lvi.

it is based only on a rather small part of the enormous number of manuscripts containing this collection. Already an examination of the base manuscripts of the edition shows that the sermon on the feast of St Dominic with the mention of St Hyacinth is found only in two fifteenth-century manuscripts, nowadays kept in Gniezno. An extensive manuscript research would be needed in order to determine the time and the place in which the passage mentioning St Hyacinth among the spiritual sons of St Dominic found its way into the sermon collection. However, it is worth noting that the omission of Thomas Aquinas among the enumerated Dominican saints could be an argument in favour of an early dating of the sermon. As we know, he was canonized in 1323, whereas the sermon collection of Peregrinus has been dated approximately to the years 1297-1304.[13] If we accept that the mention of St Hyacinth originates from Peregrinus himself, the sermon closes the short list of the earliest pieces of evidence of pre-canonization cult of St Hyacinth.

The findings of Loenertz confirm the hypothesis which was earlier proposed by Jacek Woroniecki. According to him, the first efforts at the official canonization fall into the earliest stage of Hyacinth's cult, namely to the year 1289.[14] Still, even if these assumptions are correct, these efforts most probably did not exceed the boundaries of Poland at that time. They fit into the religious landscape of Krakow in the second half of the thirteenth century. All mentioned sources concerning the first Polish Dominican – *Liber miraculorum*, the mention in the *Life of St Stanislaus*, and the record in the acts of the general chapter – inform us, above all, about the tomb of St Hyacinth as the place of the miraculous events ascribed to the intercession of the deceased Dominican. In this way, the Dominican Church of the Holy Trinity became one of the *loci sacri* of medieval Krakow. It had a prestigious meaning not only for the Friars Preachers, but also for the city and the local Church.[15] It is important, as in the second half of the thirteenth century we can observe an increasing need to introduce and support the cults of local saints in Krakow Church. Until the canonization of St Stanislaus (in 1253) Krakow could not boast a saint of its own. Only the second half of the thirteenth century, with the canonization of the martyr-bishop and with the emerging unofficial cults of Hyacinth and Princess Salomea connected to the Franciscans,

---

[13] *Ibid.*, p. xlviii-xlix.
[14] The evidence of this was to be the exceptionally high number of miracles noted under this date, and also the mention of the canonization in the chapter 49 of the Life by lector Stanislaus. J. WORONIECKI, *Św. Jacek, op. cit.*, p. 260-263; *De vita et miraculis sancti Iacchonis, op. cit.*, p. 890-891.
[15] A. WITKOWSKA, *Kulty, op. cit.*, p. 78.

brought about a change in this respect.[16] The leading role in the propagation of all new cults can be ascribed to the Mendicants – Franciscans and Dominicans.[17] It is evident in the case of two Mendicant saints – Hyacinth and Salomea, but Krakow Dominicans were also involved in the actions related towards the canonization of the Krakow bishop (Stanislaus). Suffice it to say that the author of his canonization life and of the office dedicated to him was a Dominican – Vincent of Kielcza. The Dominicans were members of the delegation of the Krakow bishop sent to the Apostolic See concerning the canonization.[18] One of the scholars – Maria Starnawska – even argues that the steps undertaken with the relics of St Dominic which preceded his canonization served for the bishop of Krakow as the model of the procedure preceding the canonization of St Stanislaus. The idea to elevate the remains of the candidate for sainthood already before his official canonization was allegedly suggested to the Krakow official by the Friars Preachers.[19] Starnawska assumes that St Hyacinth himself took part in the pre-canonization elevation and even delivered a sermon at the occasion.

The fourteenth century: *De vita et miraculis sancti Jaczkonis*

The fourteenth century seems to have been a period of certain stagnation in the development of the cult of Friar Hyacinth. Paradoxically, one of the main sources which allow us to recreate at least an outline of the saint's biography and the beginnings of his cult originated at this time. It is *De vita et miraculis sancti Jaczkonis* of *lector* Stanislaus, who was the first to describe the "biography" of St Hyacinth. He collected and described all miracle accounts known to him, that is, besides the abovementioned *liber miraculorum* from the end of the thirteenth century also the records of miracles from the years 1329-1331, the times contemporary to Stanislaus.[20] It was the key work for the further development of the hagiography concerning St Hyacinth, as all later authors of Hyacinth's lives would draw on it until the sixteenth century at least.[21]

---

[16] A. WITKOWSKA, *Kulty, op. cit.*, p. 77; *Ead.*, "Miracula", *art. cit.*, p. 61-66 and 114-138.
[17] A. WITKOWSKA, "Kult Jacka Odrowąża", *art. cit.*, p. 78-79.
[18] A detailed treatment of this topic in M. STARNAWSKA, in "Dominikanie, św. Jacek i elewacja szczątków św. Stanisława przez biskupa Pradotę", *Mendykanci w średniowiecznym Krakowie*, ed. T. GAŁUSZKA, K. OŻÓG, A. ZAJCHOWSKA, Kraków, 2008, p. 407-424.
[19] *Ibid.*, p. 413.
[20] Z. OBERTYŃSKI, "Dzieje kanonizacji", *art. cit.*, p. 84.
[21] M. ZDANEK, "Figury biblijne w literackim wizerunku świętego Jacka w świetle jego najstarszej hagiografii", *Przegląd Tomistyczny*, 14 (2008), p. 57.

The life contains a number of elements characteristic for a hagiographic legend (etymology of his name, description of childhood, description of virtues and death) and at the same time it is a rather typical example of Mendicant hagiography. On the level of facts, it relies to a great extent on the life of St Dominic. Scholars dealing with this *vita* are increasingly inclined to see the analogies not as the result of the schematic approach of its author, but rather as the Order's *mimesis* – the conscious desire of Hyacinth himself to imitate the holy founder.[22] *Lector* Stanislaus thus emphasises the features typical for Mendicants – the pastoral engagement of Hyacinth, which was closely related to the ascetic practices (nightly prayer, fasting, the gift of tears) – also present in the life of Dominic. The similarity of Hyacinth to St Dominic has also been noted by Dominic de Castelnedulo, the author of the office, based on the *Vita* of *lector* Stanislaus, written only after the official approval of the cult.[23] In the life of Hyacinth we can also find a whole repertory of biblical motifs typical for the Dominican hagiography – first of all, references to Christ, and then to St Paul and Elias.[24] An overwhelming part of the life is, however, filled with miracle accounts – those accomplished both during his life and – mostly – after his death.

The reasons why *lector* Stanislaus undertook to write a life of St Hyacinth are not clear. Some scholars believe that he was prompted by the renewal of the canonization efforts;[25] it could have been the result of the general recommendations of the Order to collect the evidence concerning its members of saintly reputation, not directly connected to the canonization efforts.[26] The construction of the life itself allows us to presume that it was written with the preaching and liturgical uses in mind.

It should also be mentioned that in the middle of the fourteenth century the Kingdom of Poland continued to be divided into a number of principalities which competed among each other. The rivalry translated itself also to the renewal of local cults. The Piast princes tried to increase the political prestige

---

[22] J. Woroniecki, *Św. Jacek, op. cit.*, p. 279.
[23] M. Zdanek, "Figury biblijne", *art. cit.*, p. 47.
[24] *Ibid.*, p. 58-59.
[25] *Ibid.*, p. 86.
[26] *Acta Capitulorum Generalium Ordinis Praedicatorum*, ed. B. M. Reichert, vol. 2, Rome, 1889, p. 230, 241. Jacek Woroniecki holds the same view and supplements the list of reasons of interest in Hyacinth with general revival in the order after the canonization of St Thomas Aquinas, and also with the hypothesis concerning the personal engagement of bishop of Krakow, Nanker, who came from the same place as St Hyacinth. Z. Woroniecki, *Św. Jacek, op. cit.*, p. 266-267. The Dominican historian also accepts that, even if there had been some efforts at canonization then, they must have been obstructed by the epidemics of plague which devastated Western Europe at that time: *ibid.*, p. 267.

of their principalities through the promotion of local patrons, aspiring at the same time to spread their cults to the remaining lands. In this context we can talk about a peculiar "hagiographic rivalry".[27] It is difficult to estimate the degree into which this competition concerned the cult of St Hyacinth, because there are no sources which would confirm that anyone else beyond the group of the Krakow Dominicans was engaged in the development and support of the cult.

Anyhow, even if some actions had been undertaken towards the canonization, they did not bring any result, and the cult died out for at least 100 years, and revived in the mid-fifteenth century. Importantly, not only the Dominicans – like earlier – but also the bishop of Krakow and the royal court were engaged in this renewal.

The fifteenth century: *Miracula sancti Jackonis* and Leander Alberti, *De Viris illustribus*

The fifteenth century in Krakow has been described as a *saeculum aureum* thanks to the boom of the local saints' cults. Aleksandra Witkowska – the most distinguished scholar of Polish medieval hagiography – talks about a new fashion of pilgrim cults which can be observed at the turn of the fourteenth and fifteenth centuries. Importantly, they all had their centres in the capital of the kingdom – Krakow. Besides the canonized saints – Stanislaus and Florian – the cults of numerous others flourished at that time: Queen Hedwig/Jadwiga, Princess Salomea, Jan Kanty (John Cantius), Bishop Prandota, Szymon of Lipnica, and, from the second half of the fifteenth century onwards, also Hyacinth. Various Krakow sanctuaries in a way competed to attract the highest number of pilgrims, which got reflected in their material benefits. In this competition the Dominicans had undoubtedly the advantage of the preaching and confessing service that they practiced, and especially the special papal privileges which allowed them to grant absolution for the sins which were canonically reserved for the bishop.[28] Surely – in a similar way like it functioned in other convent churches – the pilgrimage cult was accompanied with paraliturgical worship, which attracted the pilgrims.[29] The analysis of available sources shows that the cult of Hyacinth, similarly to those of other Krakow saints, was closely connected to his relics and his

---

[27] A. WITKOWSKA, "Miracula", *art. cit.*, p. 61.
[28] A. WITKOWSKA, *Kulty, op. cit.*, p. 107.
[29] *Ibid.*, p. 108.

tomb. The saint was supposed to be, first of all, a miracle-worker, and not an example to imitate.[30]

The *spiritus movens* of the fifteenth-century revival of the cults of local saints was Cardinal Zbigniew Oleśnicki. It was from his initiative that the miracles accomplished through the intercession of Queen Hedwiga started to be collected, the elevation of the relics of Bishop Prandota was carried out, and the memory of the Dominican martyrs of Sandomierz was recalled.[31] The bishop played his part also in the propagation of the cult of Hyacinth.

Maria Kowalczyk has recently shown that two letters with a petition to initiate the canonization of St Hyacinth, which present the reasons supporting these efforts, one addressed to the pope and another to the cardinal college, are to be ascribed to the Krakow cardinal, who acted with the support of Queen Sophia.[32] Maria Kowalczyk presents a cautious hypothesis that the delegation with the letters to the pope set on a journey to Rome between 1449 (when Oleśnicki was awarded the title of cardinal) and 1455 (the cardinal's death).[33] At that time the Life of St Hyacinth by Stanislaus had been certainly known in the cathedral milieu, as Jan Długosz used a copy of the Life which was kept in the cathedral treasury when he was editing a part of his *Annales* concerning St Hyacinth and the beginnings of the Dominicans in Poland.[34]

Besides the revival of the cult supported by the local Church and the royal court, in the second half of the fifteenth century the conditions within

---

[30] Cf. A. WITKOWSKA, *Kulty, op. cit.*, p. 109. The content related to the cult of Krakow saints still awaits a detailed study, which will surely shed new light also on the religious content of the cult of St Hyacinth in the fifteenth century.

[31] M. KOWALCZYK, "Starania kardynała", *art. cit.*, p. 65. Cf. also *Hagiografia polska*, vol. I, ed. R. GUSTAW, Poznań, 1971, p. 432-455.

[32] The manuscript of Biblioteka Jagiellońska/Jagiellonian Library, shelfmark 1961, contains besides the speeches of the envoys delivered on the occasion of handing over to the pope the cardinal's letters a letter of Queen Sophia addressed to the bishop of Rome in support of the efforts of Oleśnicki (see M. KOWALCZYK, *op. cit.*, p. 66-67). Both Zdzisław Obertyński and Jacek Woroniecki refuted the proposition of ascribing those letters to Oleśnicki, and pointed to Cardinal Frederick as their author (Z. OBERTYŃSKI, "Dzieje kanonizacji", *art. cit.*, p. 89 and J. WORONIECKI, *Św. Jacek, op. cit.*, p. 269). They did so on the basis of the mention that 240 years had passed since the death of St Hyacinth. Maria Kowalczyk disputes the view of these two scholars and argues in a convincing way that the letters were actually written by Oleśnicki, on the basis of the manuscripts of the Jagiellonian Library 42 and 1961. The latter contains two speeches delivered in front of the pope on behalf of Cardinal Oleśnicki before and after handing over the letters in support of the canonization of St Hyacinth and the letter of Queen Sophia supporting these efforts. M. KOWALCZYK, "Starania kardynała", *art. cit.*, p. 65-67.

[33] M. KOWALCZYK, "Starania kardynała", *art. cit.*, p. 67.

[34] *Ioannis Dlugossii Annales seu Cronicae Incliti Regni Poloniae. Liber septimus et octavus*, ed. D. TURKOWSKA, Warsaw, 1975, p. 116-117.

the Order of Preachers itself were favourable for the efforts at the canonization of St Hyacinth. Pope Pius II announced as saints the Dominican Vincent Ferrer in 1455 and the Dominican tertiary, Catherine of Siena, in 1461. This must have encouraged the Polish Friars Preachers to take up actions to have St Hyacinth elevated to the altars.

At least from the beginning of the 1480s the cult of St Hyacinth started to revive. Two pieces of information concerning miraculous events which took place at the tomb of St Hyacinth are related to this period. In 1480 Mikołaj Pilecki got miraculously healed: he lost his voice as a result of uttering a blasphemy and regained it only after his mother Sophia invoked St Hyacinth for intercession.[35] The second record comes from a later provincial, Andrew of Parczow, who recalled that during his youth – which falls into the first half of the 1480s – he had ordered to guide the possessed to the tomb of St Hyacinth.[36]

Another hagiographical work, the continuation of Hyacinth's *liber miraculorum* from 1488-1500, captures the cult renewal. It is not much known and practically not analyzed until now. On the one hand, it could have been inspired by the dynamic development of the cults of Krakow saints, in which the cult promoted by the Dominicans from the convent of the Holy Trinity must have played its part. On the other hand, it could have responded to the needs of the renewed efforts at the official canonization undertaken by both the Dominicans and the local Church.

The evidence of the renewed enthusiasm is also the fact that the life written by *lector* Stanislaus, supplemented with the miracles which took place after 1352, was delivered to the General Chapter in Ferrara in 1494. A passage about Hyacinth appears in the chronicle of Hieronym Borselli in 1498; and the work *De Viris illustribus* written by Leander Alberti in 1517 contains a biography of St Hyacinth, written on the basis of the work of *lector* Stanislaus.[37]

---

[35] S. Lubomelius, *De vita, op. cit.*, p. 195. The account of the miracle was submitted during the information process in Krakow in the years 1523-1524 and it has all features of reliability. Only the date might seem too early. Mikołaj Pilecki of Leliwa reached the age of maturity, i.e. 14 years of age, before 1496, and thus was born before 1482. His mother Sophia was daughter of Jan Odrowąż of Szczekocin and Wojciechow and she is recorded as the first wife of Jan Pilecki in the sources in 1481. See F. Sikora, "Pilecki Mikołaj", *Polski Słownik Biograficzny*, vol. 26, Wrocław, 1981, p. 264-266.

[36] Thomas of Sycow, *De inventione, op. cit.*, p. 898.

[37] Z. Obertyński, "Dzieje kanonizacji", *art. cit.*, p. 87, 91. We have to add that, besides the work of Leander Alberti on the Life of St Hyacinth by *lector* Stanislaus, he relies on the part devoted to the Polish province of the Dominicans in the chronicle of the generals of the Order of the Preachers by Hieronim Borselli. See Z. Obertyński, "Dzieje kanonizacji", *art. cit.*, p. 87 and A. M. Walz, *Compendium Historiae Ordinis Praedicatorum*, Rome, 1930, p. 151.

Another proof of the efforts undertaken at the end of the fifteenth century is the record in the acts of the bishop's court of Krakow dated on 3 August 1497. The decision ordered Mikołaj Kamieniecki of Pilawa, the mayor of Krakow and Sandomierz, to return the money which he borrowed in emergency, although he had earlier donated it to the convent of the Holy Trinity for the uses related to the canonization of St Hyacinth, who was famous for various miracles.[38]

The passage with a description of Krakow in the World Chronicle of Hartmann Schedel, dated to 1493, also informs us about the popularity of the cult of Hyacinth, at least within Krakow milieu, which he gained as a result of the events described above. The author mentions that the tomb of a saintly man Hyacinth, a companion of St Dominic, who is not counted among the number of saints, but is famous for various miracles, including resurrection of three dead, is found in the church of the Holy Trinity.[39]

Another element supplementing the picture of the efforts to propagate of Hyacinth cult and his canonization is the only known pre-canonization image of St Hyacinth dated to around 1500.[40] It depicts the vision of

---

[38] Archiwum Kurii Metropolitalnej w Krakowie/Archives of the Metropolitan Curia in Krakow, *Acta Officialia Cracoviensia*, vol. 17, p. 393. I thank for this record to Dr Maciej Zdanek, who found it and made it available to me.

[39] *Ad edem namque gloriosissime Trinitatis sic vocatum est celebris Ordo Praedicatorum. In ea vero sacra ede multe sanctitatis vir Jacinthus nondum in numerum sanctorum rilatus, magnis mirabilis redolet, divi Dominici comes, qui adhuc vivens tres mortuis in vitam reduxit.* Hartmann Schedel, *De Cracovia urbe regia Sarmacie*, Kraków, 1849, p. 5. Aleksandra Witkowska called attention to this mention in her work on the pilgrimage cults of the fifteenth-century Krakow. See A. WITKOWSKA, *Kulty, op. cit.*, p. 113.

[40] *Katalog Zabytków Sztuki*, vol. 4, part 3/2, ed. A. BOCHNAK, J. SAMEK, Warsaw, 1978, fig. 305 and literature which refers to it includes a stained glass window from around 1430 which allegedly represents St Hyacinth, which is allegedly confirmed by an inscription underneath. However, the inscription dates back to the twentieth century only, and the stained glass depicts St Thomas Aquinas. Cf. *Malarstwo tablicowe w Małopolsce*, vol. II, part 3, ed. A. S. LABUDA, K. SECOMSKA, Warsaw, 2004, p. 131-134 and *ibid.*, L. KALINOWSKI, "Malarstwo witrażowe", p. 200. In this place we should also list another mention concerning a pre-canonization image of St Hyacinth. Seweryn of Lubomel, when describing the miracle of St Hyacinth crossing Dneper with the Holy Sacrament and a figure of Mary in his hands with dry feet, while he was fighting a demon in the middle of the river, mentions that an image depicting this scene has been present on the wall of the Dominican church in Krakow, close to the main altar, for 280 years. See S. LUBOMELIUS, *De vita, op. cit.*, p. 38 and 124. When we consider that Lubomelczyk published his work in 1594, we would have to accept that the image he mentioned dated back to the early fourteenth century. However, it is the only extant mention on this topic. Its existence, and at least its early dating, is questioned by the fact that the description of the cited miracle is not found in the Life by lector Stanislaus, who wrote his work in the mid-fourteenth century in the convent in Krakow, and thus would have had to know the painting and also the story which it was supposed to illustrate. It is difficult to find a reason why he would have omitted such a spectacular miracle in his

St Hyacinth, described in the fourteenth-century Life, in which Mary with Child appeared to him in order to confirm that his prayers carried through her intercession were pleasing to God and they would all be heard.[41]

The renewal of the cult of St Hyacinth in the Krakow convent itself – especially when compared with other Krakow centres – came exceptionally late. One of the authors of the continuation of the saint's *liber miraculorum* observes with bitterness that the memory of a certain miracle had vanished *propter incurabilitatem fratrum*. Later, Mikołaj/Nicholas Hussoviensis would also complain about the negligence on the side of the friars with respect to sustaining the cult. The *incurabilitas* led even to forgetting the exact place of burial of Hyacinth. When in 1543 it was necessary to inspect the relics for the needs of the canonization process, the friars were not able to indicate the place where to look for them.[42] It shows that the continuity of the cult was broken at some point.

The sixteenth century: *Mikołaj Hussoviensis, sermo Iacobi Ioanides Strelleris*

It was necessary to wait till the sixteenth century until not only the miracle-working activity of Hyacinth but also his religious life started to arouse the interest of hagiographers. The first traces of such hagiographic writing are found in a sermon delivered in 1514 by Jakub Joanides Streller, a Dominican of Wrocław, at the provincial chapter in Łowicz. He names St Hyacinth, with a description *divus*, together with Blessed Czesław as examples of the friars who cared about the common good and the glory of God. The preacher presents both of them as models of religious life. It is interesting that in so doing he refers not so much to the biographical details from the lives of the

---

Life of St Hyacinth. It is worth mentioning that the miracle of crossing the river Dneper with dry feet, so frequently found in the iconography of St Hyacinth after the canonization, was most probably described for the first time at the time of the first diocesan canonization process in 1523 (see S. LUBOMELIUS, *De vita, op. cit.*, p. 124-125). It is to be noted in this place that there is unfortunately no monograph on the iconography of St Hyacinth, which would surely supplement our knowledge on the topic of the saint's cult. A synthesis of the known representations of St Hyacinth by M. Jacniacka is found in *Encyklopedia katolicka,* vol. VII, Lublin, 1997, col. 641-642. *Malarstwo gotyckie, op. cit.*, p. 233-234 and *ibid.*, J. GADOMSKI, "Malarstwo tablicowe w Małopolsce", p. 286. There is also a bibliography on the described monument.
[41] S. LUBOMELIUS, *De vita, op. cit.*, chapter V.
[42] These events are described in the work of Thomas of Sycow, *De inventione, op. cit.*, p. 894-899.

Dominicans, but to the elements of the programme of the reformers of the Polish province of the Dominican Order.[43]

The attempts to initiate the canonization process which started at the end of the fifteenth century ended with a success – in 1523, after solving all the procedure problems, the diocesan enquiry was open.[44] While not going into the details of the turbulent history of the process, we have to mention that the documents gathered during its course were sent to Rome, where they fell victim to the turmoil of history – they got lost in 1527, during the *sacco di Roma*.[45]

The process is extremely important from the viewpoint of scholarship concerning medieval hagiography of St Hyacinth. Its atmosphere gave rise to a precious monument of Latin Polish literature – the song about St Hyacinth by Mikołaj/Nicholas Hussowczyk/Hussovianus, dated to 1525.[46] The author stays faithful to the narrative of *lector* Stanislaus on the layer of history, with an exception of a highly interesting passage devoted to St Hyacinth's stay in Kiev. The poet mentions the great honour that the father of the Polish Dominicans enjoyed in entire Rus. According to Hussowczyk the local population preserved the memory of Hyacinth's sainthood, built churches dedicated to him and was willingly giving his name to their children. In this regard the author refers to some unspecified books which dealt with the devotion towards Hyacinth in those areas.[47] Unfortunately, none of these sources are extant today and it is impossible to confirm whether the story of the sixteenth-century poet is only a product of his imagination or whether it contains a grain of truth. However, most probably, his work expressed an oral tradition which demonstrated the viability of Hyacinth's cult, which is confirmed also in the testimonies of the witnesses in the canonization process. Two miracle collections of 1518-1519 and 1523-1524 contain a number of testimonies concerning the Russian mission of Hyacinth, which were not present in contemporary hagiography. It means that their memory was cultivated and transmitted orally.[48]

---

[43] J. A. SPIEŻ, *Średniowieczne świadectwa życia i kultu, op. cit.*, p. 105-106; *Acta capitulorum provinciae Poloniae Ordinis Praedicatorum*, vol. I, ed. R. F. MADURA, Rome, 1972, p. 197.
[44] Z. OBERTYŃSKI, "Dzieje kanonizacji", *art. cit.*, p. 100-101.
[45] They were found only on 15 July 1580 in the archives of Paul V from the times of his cardinalate, when upon an intervention of the provincial of Polish Dominicans Pope Gregory XIII threatened with excommunication *ipso facto* all who would unlawfully own them. *Ibid.*, p. 122.
[46] *Ibid.*, p. 101-102.
[47] N. HUSSVIANUS, "De vita et gestis Divi Hyacinthi", in *Nicolai Hussoviani Carmina*, ed. I. PELACZAR, Krakow, 1894, ver. 239-248, p. 75.
[48] M. ZDANEK, "Figury biblijne", *art. cit.*, p. 25-26.

Although the efforts at the beginning of the sixteenth century did not directly result in canonization, they brought about a breakthrough in the cult of St Hyacinth: the abovementioned approval (of 11 February 1527) by the papal tribunal of the public cult related to the image of St Hyacinth and the observance of his feast on 16 August in all chapels and churches of male and female Dominican convents of the Polish province with a special mass and breviary office.[49] It was the first official act concerning the cult of St Hyacinth, equivalent to the later introduced act of beatification.[50] From that moment on we can talk about an official cult of the saint, whose development goes beyond the chronological frame of this paper. The efforts which lasted almost three and a half centuries culminated in the canonization which took place in Rome on 17 April 1594. Local canonization festivities took place in Krakow in July of the same year.

As we know, André Vauchez distinguished two models when studying medieval saints' cults. He maintains that the Mediterranean, especially Italy, was dominated by the cults which originated in the admiration of the way of life of a person considered as a saint and in the emotional relationship towards him/her. In turn, outside of the Mediterranean, during entire Middle Ages, the saint was recognized above all as a dead person who worked miracles, and whose life and circumstances of death were only of secondary importance.[51]

The research into the pre-canonization hagiography and cult of St Hyacinth confirms the thesis of the French scholar. Both during his life and after his death, St Hyacinth was regarded first of all as a powerful miracle-worker, through whose intercession the faithful could obtain the grace they needed. Of course, it does not mean that the exemplary character of his life was completely overlooked. *Lector* Stanislaus in his fourteenth-century devoted entire first part of his Life of St Hyacinth to strictly biographical information about the saint, pointing to his education, piety, and his faithfulness to the religious vocation. Only the sixteenth century brought about, in a broader extent, interest not only in miracles but also in the life of the saint, especially his contribution to the spread and strengthening of the Catholic faith in Poland and Eastern Europe, which was described with some exaggeration.

---

[49] Z. OBERTYŃSKI, "Dzieje kanonizacji", *art. cit.*, p. 105-106.
[50] *Ibid.*, p. 106.
[51] A. VAUCHEZ, *Sainthood in the later Middle Ages*, Cambridge, 1997, p. 216-217.

Les martyrs dominicains de Hongrie
et leur insertion réussie dans la mémoire hagiographique
de l'Ordre des frères Prêcheurs

Anne Reltgen-Tallon
(Paris)

Le matériel hagiographique fourni au XIIIe siècle par la province dominicaine de Hongrie constitue sans aucun doute un très bon exemple d'exportation d'un culte local, ou plus exactement d'une mémoire hagiographique locale, à l'échelle de la Chrétienté – dans le cadre particulièrement favorable, il est vrai, d'un ordre religieux fortement centralisé et propre à faciliter la diffusion rapide, du moins en son sein, de nouvelles dévotions ou de nouveaux modèles de sainteté. Cela dit, même eu égard à ce contexte particulier, la contribution hongroise au renouvellement du sanctoral dominicain à partir du milieu du XIIIe siècle se signale véritablement comme non négligeable, surtout si on la compare à celle des autres provinces de l'ordre pouvant être qualifiées de périphériques.

Il s'agit en l'espèce d'une sainteté non canonisée, comme pour l'immense majorité des Prêcheurs faisant à cette époque l'objet d'une quelconque vénération au sein de leur famille religieuse, puisque les deux seuls saints canonisés de l'ordre sont pour le XIIIe siècle saint Dominique, le fondateur, et saint Pierre martyr, l'inquisiteur assassiné en 1252 dans le Milanais et porté sur les autels dès l'année suivante[1]. Cela n'exclut cependant pas la floraison d'un matériel hagiographique secondaire consacrant de nombreuses figures dotées d'une réputation de sainteté à l'intérieur de la famille dominicaine. Car à partir du milieu du XIIIe siècle, on assiste à une véritable politique de développement d'une hagiographie collective de

---

[1] Sur les circonstances de cette canonisation, voir G. Merlo, « Pietro di Verona. S. Pietro martire. Difficoltà e proposte per lo studio di un inquisitore beatificato », dans *Culto dei santi, istituzioni e classi sociali in età preindustriale*, éd. S. Boesch Gajano et L. Sebastiani, L'Aquila-Rome, 1984, p. 483.

Les saints et leur culte en Europe centrale au Moyen Âge (XIe-début du XVIe siècle), éd. par Marie-Madeleine de Cevins et Olivier Marin, Turnhout, 2017 (*Hagiologia*, 13), p. 211-225.

l'ordre, parallèlement à la littérature dédiée à ses saints canonisés[2]. De ce point de vue, il existe d'ailleurs une similitude assez nette avec l'histoire de l'ordre franciscain qui, selon des modalités et malgré une tradition hagiographique très différentes, peu de temps seulement avant les Prêcheurs, s'efforce aussi de promouvoir l'idée de son excellence collective à travers sa capacité à générer, souvent et partout, de nouvelles figures de saints[3]. Une telle concomitance n'est évidemment pas fortuite. Elle s'explique en grande partie par le contexte polémique qui commence alors à se développer à l'encontre de l'ensemble des ordres mendiants, entraînant en retour chez ces derniers le développement d'une littérature marquée du sceau de l'apologétique[4].

Chez les Prêcheurs, l'un des premiers textes représentatifs de cette tendance, et sans conteste l'un des plus célèbres, n'est autre que la collection de récits exemplaires rassemblés par le provincial de Provence Gérard de Frachet dans les années 1250 sous le titre de *Vitas fratrum*[5], évidemment inspiré de celui des *Vitas Patrum*, en référence à la grande tradition érémitique des Pères du Désert[6]. L'histoire de ce texte est probablement beaucoup plus complexe qu'on ne l'a cru longtemps[7] : sans doute, en effet, résulte-t-il de la fusion de différents projets et y a-t-il eu plusieurs interventions dans sa composition, en-dehors de celle de Gérard de Frachet – en particulier, selon toute vraisemblance, celle du maître général Humbert de Romans lui-même. Il existe, certes, ce que l'on peut considérer comme une version canonique du texte, celle qui fut approuvée par le chapitre général de 1260 en vue d'une diffusion

---

[2] Voir notamment à ce sujet L. CANETTI, « Da san Domenico alle *Vitae fratrum*. Pubblicistica agiografica ed ecclesiologia nell'*Ordo Praedicatorum* alla metà del XIII secolo », *Mélanges de l'École française de Rome. Moyen Âge*, 108 (1996), p. 165-219 (repris dans *Id.*, *L'invenzione della memoria. Il culto e l'immagine di Domenico nella storia dei primi frati Predicatori*, Spolète, 1996, p. 451-478) ; A. RELTGEN-TALLON, *La mémoire d'un ordre : les « hommes illustres » dans la tradition dominicaine (XIIIe-XVe siècle)*, thèse de doctorat d'histoire de l'Université de Paris X – Nanterre, 1999, t. 1, p. 101 et suiv.

[3] R. PACIOCCO, *Da Francesco ai « Catalogi sanctorum ». Livelli istituzionali e immagini agiografiche nell'ordine francescano (secoli XIII-XIV)*, Assise, 1990.

[4] Voir à nouveau L. CANETTI, « Da san Domenico », *art. cit.*, et A. RELTGEN-TALLON, *La mémoire d'un ordre*, *op. cit.*

[5] Gérard de Frachet, *Vitae fratrum Ordinis Praedicatorum*, éd. B. M. REICHERT, Rome-Stuttgart, 1897 (Monumenta Ordinis fratrum Praedicatorum historica, 1), p. 1-320.

[6] A. BOUREAU, « *Vitae fratrum, Vitae patrum*. L'Ordre dominicain et le modèle des Pères du désert au XIIIe siècle », *Mélanges de l'École française de Rome. Moyen Âge – Temps modernes*, 99 (1987), p. 79-100.

[7] C'est ce qu'a montré : S. TUGWELL, « L'évolution des *Vitae fratrum*. Résumé des conclusions provisoires », dans *L'ordre des Prêcheurs et son histoire en France méridionale*, Toulouse, 2001 (Cahiers de Fanjeaux, 36), p. 415-418.

exclusivement interne à l'ordre[8]. Mais la tradition manuscrite montre qu'un certain nombre d'additions continuèrent d'être effectuées par la suite.

Et c'est justement à l'une de ces additions postérieures, conservée dans neuf des manuscrits connus contenant les *Vitas fratrum*[9], que remonte la première introduction, dans la mémoire hagiographique de l'ordre, d'un groupe d'individus originaires de la province de Hongrie. À vrai dire, il s'agit même d'une véritable petite chronique de l'histoire de cette province, insistant particulièrement sur le caractère missionnaire de celle-ci et ses succès en la matière[10]. L'auteur en est connu, puisqu'il se nomme lui-même : il s'agit d'un certain *Svipertus*, ou Svipert, du couvent de *Porrochia*[11], ou Porroch, dont il a été prieur[12]. Selon ses propres dires, il a écrit son texte en 1259 ou peu après[13], ce qui donne à penser que la rédaction de celui-ci s'inscrit bien dans le cadre des grandes commandes de matériel hagiographique lancées dans les années 1250 par les chapitres généraux pour alimenter, précisément, le corpus des *Vitas fratrum*. S'il ne fut pas intégré à la version canonique de celles-ci, c'est sans doute parce qu'il ne parvint pas à temps pour l'approbation de 1260. L'éventuel lien avec l'entreprise de récolte de nouveaux récits pour les *Vitas fratrum* expliquerait en tout cas la place du matériel hagiographique dans cet écrit, qui se présente comme une histoire de la province de Hongrie, mais cherche surtout manifestement à faire connaître à l'ensemble de l'ordre les hauts faits des frères de cette province et, par ailleurs, les miracles des reliques de saint Pierre Martyr qui y étaient conservées[14].

La présence de celles-ci en ces lieux et à cette époque – six ans seulement après la canonisation de l'inquisiteur, dans une province assez éloignée du théâtre de sa vie et de son martyre – est tout à fait intéressante. Elle résulte très probablement d'une demande des frères de ce couvent de Porroch. Certes, que le second saint canonisé de l'ordre dominicain ait été connu assez rapidement à l'intérieur de celui-ci n'a rien de surprenant. Mais cet intérêt pour lui plutôt que pour le fondateur, dans une province située aux marges

---

[8] Comme l'indique la lettre qu'Humbert de Romans leur adjoignit alors en guise de prologue. Gérard de Frachet, *op. cit.*, p. 4-5.
[9] S. Tugwell, « Notes on the life of saint Dominic, VI : Dominic would-be missionary. Appendix I : the *Relatio de missionibus provinciae Hungariae* », *Archivum Fratrum Praedicatorum*, 68 (1998), p. 86.
[10] D'où le titre que lui donne son éditeur le plus récent : *Relatio Sviperti de missionibus provinciae Hungariae*, éd. S. Tugwell, « Notes », *art. cit.*, p. 86-92.
[11] Toponyme mystérieux, que l'éditeur des *Vitas fratrum* et de leurs annexes – dont la *Relatio* – identifie avec l'actuelle ville de Patak [Sárospatak]. Gérard de Frachet, *op. cit.*, p. 305, note a.
[12] *Cum populus venisset ad ecclesiam fratrum nostrorum de Porrochia [...] etiam ego Svipertus tunc prior eiusdem conventus. Relatio Sviperti, op. cit.*, p. 92.
[13] *Sed etiam noviter anno domini M°CC°LIX°. Ibid.*
[14] *Ibid.*

de la Chrétienté, s'explique sans doute par le sentiment que son culte avait de meilleures chances de s'implanter dans des régions récemment et tragiquement sensibilisées à la question du martyre, notamment lors de l'invasion tatare de 1241. Les Prêcheurs hongrois ayant payé un lourd tribut à cette occasion, la promotion du culte de saint Pierre Martyr pouvait leur apparaître d'autant plus opportune qu'elle permettait également de l'associer à celui, purement local, de leurs confrères morts dans ces circonstances. Si ces derniers ne pouvaient, quant à eux, prétendre à l'honneur des autels[15], ils n'en partageaient pas moins la palme du martyre, aux yeux des survivants, avec le saint milanais.

Ainsi l'évocation des miracles accomplis au couvent de Porroch, à la fin du récit de Svipert, n'est-elle pas fortuite. Elle résonne au contraire comme un rappel de la tonalité de l'ensemble de son récit, lequel met en avant, parmi les frères s'étant illustrés d'une manière ou d'une autre dans cette histoire de la province de Hongrie, l'importance de la sainteté martyre.

Parmi ces Prêcheurs morts pour la foi figurent, bien entendu, les victimes des Tartares [ou Tatars], mais aussi celles, plus anciennes, des Coumans – beaucoup moins nombreuses, puisqu'il n'y en a que deux[16]. Cela ne les empêche pas de figurer en bonne place aux côtés des premières dans le récit de Svipert, qui insiste par ailleurs longuement, sans doute pour faire bonne mesure, sur la dureté de leur apostolat en terre païenne (comme on le verra plus loin). Ce traitement très circonstancié contraste assez nettement avec la sobriété du récit concernant la façon dont les Tartares, quant à eux, massacrèrent plus de quatre-vingt-dix frères dans les tourments les plus variés :

> Survint alors, selon le jugement caché de Dieu, la persécution des Tartares, qui non seulement empêcha cette prédication de nos frères, mais obligea même beaucoup d'entre eux à rejoindre plus vite le royaume des cieux ; au point que ce sont environ quatre-vingt-dix frères de notre ordre, les uns tués par l'épée, les flèches ou les lances, les autres brûlés par le feu, qui se sont envolés pour le Royaume des cieux[17].

---

[15] Sur les réticences croissantes de la papauté, à partir du dernier tiers du XIIIe siècle, face au modèle de la sainteté martyre, voir A. VAUCHEZ, *La sainteté en Occident aux derniers siècles du Moyen Âge*, 2e éd. Rome, 1988, p. 487-488.
[16] *Relatio Sviperti*, *op. cit.*, p. 88.
[17] *Supervenit autem occulto Dei iudicio Tartarorum persecutio, que non solum dictam predicacionem fratrum nostrorum impedivit, sed eciam multos ad regnum celorum festinantius ire compulit, adeo ut circiter nonaginta fratres nostri ordinis alii gladiis, alii sagittis, alii lanceis interfecti, alii ignibus concremati, ad regnum celorum convolaverunt. Ibid.*, p. 90.

Il est vrai que les faits parlent ici d'eux-mêmes, et que la concision pouvait être un procédé rhétorique tout aussi efficace qu'une longue digression pour frapper les esprits. Le caractère spectaculaire de cet épisode tartare explique d'ailleurs sans aucun doute la fortune de ce groupe de martyrs dans l'hagiographie dominicaine ultérieure : d'abord par son adjonction assez rapide aux *Vitas fratrum*, dont témoigne le groupe de manuscrits ayant conservé le texte de Svipert à la suite de celles-ci ; puis par son utilisation dans les sources dominicaines ultérieures qui présentent la même tendance que l'œuvre de Gérard de Frachet à une hagiographie de groupe.

Le premier de ces textes est l'édition donnée par Bernard Gui, au début du XIVe siècle, du traité des gloires de l'ordre, le *De quatuor in quibus Deus Praedicatorum Ordinem insignivit*, écrit par son confrère limousin Étienne de Salagnac en 1277[18]. Ce dernier avait inventé, en troisième partie de son œuvre, un genre nouveau dans la littérature dominicaine et appelé à une certaine fortune au sein de celle-ci : le catalogue des hommes illustres[19], véritable déclinaison typologique des grandes figures de la famille des Prêcheurs, dans une perspective qui n'était plus exclusivement hagiographique mais faisait toute leur place, en particulier, aux écrivains et aux prélats[20]. Néanmoins, les « frères ayant souffert pour la foi » y apparaissaient encore au premier rang[21]. C'est à l'intérieur de cette rubrique que Bernard Gui inséra les martyrs de Hongrie, dans un décalque assez fidèle du texte de Svipert, explicitement cité d'ailleurs, mais comme une partie des *Vitas fratrum*[22].

La probable absence de ces martyrs dans l'état initial du texte n'est guère surprenante : d'abord, parce que c'est un traité clairement inachevé qu'a laissé Étienne de Salagnac, selon le propre témoignage de Bernard Gui[23] ; ensuite,

---

[18] Ce traité n'est parvenu jusqu'à nous que dans différentes versions corrigées et augmentées par Bernard Gui à partir de 1304. Sur l'histoire compliquée de ce texte, voir l'introduction de l'éditeur, ÉTIENNE DE SALAGNAC – BERNARD GUI, *De quatuor in quibus Deus Praedicatorum ordinem insignivit*, éd. T. KAEPPELI, Rome, 1949 (Monumenta Ordinis fratrum Praedicatorum historica, 22), p. V-XXIV.

[19] Cette partie s'intitule précisément « De illustri prole ». *Ibid.*, p. 19.

[20] *Ibid.*, p. 31-123.

[21] *Fratres passi pro fide. Ibid.*, p. 20-30.

[22] *Addita sunt hec duo capitula sequencia de* Vitis fratrum *extracta* (*Ibid.*, p. 25), peut-on en effet lire en marge du texte dans un certain nombre de manuscrits, et en particulier dans le seul qui soit entièrement de la main de Bernard Gui (Toulouse, Bibl. municipale, codex 490, fol. 4r-50r). C'est la raison pour laquelle il est choisi comme texte de référence par l'éditeur, bien qu'il ne soit pas le plus ancien.

[23] Voici en effet ce qu'il écrit dans la lettre par laquelle il adresse au maître général Aymeric de Plaisance, en 1304, sa compilation historique relative à l'ordre des Prêcheurs et qui s'ouvre, précisément, sur son édition du *De quatuor* : *Primo tractatus quidam brevis religiosi viri vite venerabilis fratris Stephani de Salanhaco, mee Lemovicensis dyocesis, de quatuor in quibus Deus Predicatorum ordinem insignivit, quem de manu sua conscriptum, nondum tamen ad plenum*

parce qu'il est tout à fait possible que le premier n'ait jamais eu entre les mains qu'un seul exemplaire des *Vitas fratrum*, lequel ne contenait peut-être pas les additions postérieures à 1260[24]. Bernard Gui, à l'inverse, a beaucoup voyagé et eu accès à une documentation abondante. Cela lui a très probablement donné aussi une vision plus globale de la réalité de son ordre, et rend d'autant plus significatif son choix d'inclure les martyrs de Hongrie dans la liste des héros dominicains morts pour la foi.

Mais cela montre également la part considérable de hasard qui préside à la circulation de ce type de matériel hagiographique : faute d'un accès de Bernard Gui à ceux des manuscrits des *Vitas fratrum* contenant la *Relatio* de Svipert de Porroch, celle-ci serait très probablement tombée dans l'oubli, et les glorieux martyrs des Coumans et des Tartares avec elle. À preuve, le contre-exemple donné par un récit pourtant voisin contenu dans une collection d'*exempla* dominicains très comparable aux *Vitas fratrum*, et d'ailleurs rigoureusement contemporaine, mais qui, contrairement à celles-ci, ne fit l'objet d'aucune approbation particulière par les chapitres généraux et, par conséquent, ne connut pas la même diffusion au sein de l'ordre, si bien qu'elle resta longtemps en-dehors du répertoire habituel de sources des hagiographes dominicains : il s'agit du *Livre des Abeilles* de Thomas de Cantimpré[25], rédigé lui aussi dans les années 1250 dans une visée consolatoire à l'intention de confrères exposés aux rigueurs de la lutte avec le clergé séculier[26], auxquels il propose toutes sortes de récits édifiants visant à les conforter dans leur propos religieux, présentant leur ordre comme une société parfaite, à l'instar de celle des abeilles[27]. On trouve dans cet ensemble un *exemplum* mettant en scène un duc hongrois devenu Prêcheur après avoir abandonné le pouvoir à ses fils. Lettré et grand prédicateur, il apparaît surtout comme véritablement

---

usque digestum neglectumque ab omnibus curavi sollicite recolligere ne periret, cum videretur penitus derelictus, ipsumque compingens quasi noviter reformavi. Ibid., p. 3-4.

[24] On ne sait guère, sur la biographie de Salagnac, que ce que nous en dit Bernard Gui dans l'*explicit* qu'il ajoute au traité, où il affirme avoir fait profession entre ses mains (*Ibid.*, p. 184), ainsi que dans les notices qu'il lui consacre dans ses listes des prieurs des couvents de Limoges et Toulouse. BERNARD GUI, *De fundatione et prioribus conventuum provinciarum Tholosanae et Provinciae Ordinis Praedicatorum*, éd. P. A. AMARGIER, Rome, 1961 (Monumenta Ordinis fratrum Praedicatorum historica, 24), p. 51 et 60-62. Mais tout cela met en lumière une carrière très locale, qui ne permit probablement guère au frère limousin de voyager en-dehors des limites de sa province.

[25] Sur l'auteur comme sur son œuvre, voir l'introduction à la traduction partielle de H. PLATELLE, *Les exemples du « Livre des Abeilles ». Présentation, traduction et commentaire*, Turnhout, 1997, p. 11-18 en particulier.

[26] A. RELTGEN-TALLON, *La mémoire d'un ordre, op. cit.*

[27] Étudiée par l'auteur quelques années auparavant à l'occasion de la rédaction de son *De natura rerum*. H. PLATELLE, *op. cit.*, p. 17.

héroïque lorsque, alors que tous fuient devant l'avance tartare, il demeure sur place pour assister les plus faibles qui, eux, ne peuvent fuir. À leur retour, ses confrères le retrouvent mort au pied de l'autel, étendu les bras en croix et martyrisé avec des raffinements de cruauté[28]. L'épisode est donc particulièrement édifiant. Mais en dépit de cela, et malgré l'intérêt porté par les hagiographes dominicains de la fin du XIIIe siècle aux faits liés à l'invasion tartare, dont atteste le relatif succès de la *Relatio* de Svipert de Porroch, il ne fut pas repris avant le milieu du XVe siècle, lorsque l'Allemand Johannes Meyer, l'un des premiers écrivains dominicains à renouer avec le genre littéraire du catalogue d'hommes illustres inauguré par le traité d'Étienne de Salagnac[29], l'inclut dans son *De Viris illustribus Ordinis Praedicatorum*[30], en 1466[31], suivi à la fin du siècle par le Bolonais Jérôme Borselli dans sa Chronique des maîtres généraux[32] – la plus encyclopédique sans doute de toutes celles qui avaient jusqu'alors été consacrées à l'histoire de l'ordre, et qui, partant, incorpora de nombreux matériaux hagiographiques jusqu'alors laissés de côté dans ce type d'écrits plus historiographiques[33].

---

[28] Thomas de Cantimpré, *Bonum universale de Apibus*, Douai, 1627, p. 421-422 : *Dux quidem in Hungaria potentissimus relictis in principatu filiis ordinem Praedicatorum intravit. Erat autem sufficienter litteris instructus, et factus est egregius ac devotissimus praedicator. Irruentibus ergo Tartaris et priore domus cum fratribus fugiente petivit idem frater quondam dux ut in solacium dimitteretur debilium populorum, dicens se confectum senio, et etiamsi non occideretur a Tartaris in proximo tamen moriturum. Permissus ergo remansit in domo fratrum et admonitione dulcissima pauperibus et debilibus qui fugam inire non poterant ad patientiam confortatis ipse usque ad irruptionem barbarorum pronus in oratione et lacrymis in ecclesia in modum crucis extensus ante altare iacebat, et sic ab impiis est occisus. Recedentibus ergo Tartaris ad domum fratres reversi sunt, et fratrem quondam ducem lanceis terebratis pedibus et manibus atque confossis omnibus membris et cerebro excusso de capite coram altari ut dictum invenerunt.*
[29] Le seul à l'avoir précédé en ce sens est le Bourguignon Laurent Pignon, le premier Prêcheur après Salagnac-Gui à dresser un catalogue d'hommes illustres de son ordre qui ne soit pas uniquement une liste d'écrivains, et ce dès les premières années du XVe siècle. Voir à son sujet l'introduction de l'éditeur : LAURENT PIGNON, *Catalogus fratrum spectabilium Ordinis fratrum Praedicatorum*, éd. G. MEERSSEMAN, Rome, 1936 (Monumenta Ordinis fratrum Praedicatorum historica, 18), p. VII-XXII.
[30] J. MEYER, *De Viris illustribus Ordinis Praedicatorum*, éd. P. VON LOË (Quellen und Forschungen zur Geschichte des Dominikanerordens in Deutschland, 12), Leipzig, 1918, p. 40. Pour une présentation de l'auteur et de ses écrits, voir A. BARTHELMÉ, *La réforme dominicaine au XVe siècle en Alsace et dans l'ensemble de la province de Teutonie*, Strasbourg, 1930, p. 155 et suiv., à compléter par W. FECHTER, « Meyer, Johannes », dans *Die deutsche Literatur des Mittelalters. Verfasserlexikon*, 6, Berlin-New York, 1987, col. 474-490.
[31] Comme on peut le lire à la fin du prologue. J. MEYER, *De Viris, op. cit.*, p. 17.
[32] J. BORSELLI, *Cronica Magistrorum Generalium Ordinis Praedicatorum*, Bologne, Bibl. Univ., cod. lat. 1999, fol. 41r.
[33] G. PASQUALI, « Gerolamo Albertucci de' Borselli OP (1432-1497). Ricerche bio-bibliografiche », *Rivista di Storia della Chiesa in Italia*, 25 (1971), p. 59-82.

Cela dit, l'insertion, même tardive, d'un tel récit dans la littérature auto-célébrative des Prêcheurs montre que l'intérêt se maintient dans les rangs de ces derniers, deux siècles plus tard, pour la glorieuse geste des frères de Hongrie lors de l'invasion tartare. Les martyrs évoqués par le texte de Svipert de Porroch connaissent d'ailleurs un sort comparable : absents, après l'œuvre de Salagnac-Gui, de la littérature dominicaine du XIVe siècle, désormais plus tournée vers l'exaltation des figures de la sainteté savante que vers les catégories hagiographiques plus traditionnelles[34], on les retrouve cependant eux aussi chez Johannes Meyer, dans son *De Viris* comme dans sa chronique de l'ordre[35].

Cet intérêt renouvelé pour la sainteté martyre de Hongrie se traduit enfin, au début du XVIe siècle, par l'introduction d'une nouvelle source dans la tradition relative aux Prêcheurs martyrs des Tartares – une source qui n'est pas parvenue jusqu'à nous, mais dont on peut montrer l'existence et la circulation à partir d'autres textes[36], qui, en l'incorporant, ont consacré pour longtemps sa place dans la mémoire dominicaine[37]. Pourtant, un tel texte était plus que suspect : bien que probablement d'origine hongroise, compte tenu de l'importance de la matière relative à cette province dans ce qui se présentait comme un catalogue de martyrs, il n'en comportait pas moins un certain nombre de distorsions de la réalité historique des faits, en particulier lorsqu'il associait aux quelque quatre-vingt-dix victimes des Tartares déjà connues depuis la fin du XIIIe siècle comme un groupe anonyme, la figure de l'un des principaux acteurs de la fondation de la province dominicaine de

---

[34] A. RELTGEN-TALLON, *La mémoire d'un ordre*, op. cit., t. 2, p. 262-321.

[35] J. MEYER, *De Viris*, op. cit., p. 41 et *Id.*, *Chronica brevis ordinis Praedicatorum*, éd. H. SCHEEBEN, Leipzig, 1933 (Quellen und Forschungen zur Geschichte des Dominikanerordens in Deutschland, 29), p. 31-32.

[36] Comme l'a bien montré R. LOENERTZ, « Un catalogue d'écrivains et deux catalogues de martyrs dominicains », *Archivum Fratrum Praedicatorum*, 12 (1942), p. 279-303.

[37] Le premier à l'utiliser est le Milanais Ambrogio Taegio, qui comme Borselli écrit à la charnière des XVe et XVIe siècles. Ce sont cependant deux recensions différentes qu'il a utilisées d'une part dans le tome III de ses *Monumenta Ordinis fratrum Praedicatorum historica* (Rome, *Archivum Generale Ordinis Praedicatorum*, ms. XIV-53, fol. 142rv) – où, en-dehors de sa part personnelle limitée à une *Chronica brevior Ordinis Praedicatorum* (*Ibid.*, fol. 1-91v), sont surtout rassemblées des copies de documents pour le reste de sa compilation historique – et dans son *De insigniis Ordinis Praedicatorum* (*Archivum Generale Ordinis Praedicatorum*, ms. XIV-54, fol. 126v-127v) dont se rapprochent davantage les sources ultérieures, en particulier : Leandro ALBERTI, *De Viris illustribus ordinis Praedicatorum*, Bologne, 1517, fol. 59rv, et Francesko DIACCETO, *Vita dell'inclito et santissimo Domenico*, Florence, 1572, p. 205-206, qui ont probablement utilisé la même source, mais dans des recensions légèrement différentes, comme le montrent les quelques discordances qui existent entre ces différents textes (*cf. infra*).

Hongrie, frère Sadoch[38]. Si celui-ci était déjà évoqué par Svipert de Porroch pour sa vision, dès la première nuit de l'arrivée en Pannonie des cinq frères envoyés par le chapitre général de 1221 pour y fonder une province[39], d'une multitude de démons se lamentant de l'extension prochaine de l'ordre dans ces régions, en aucun cas la *Relatio* n'évoquait les circonstances de sa mort ; tout au plus signalait-elle, à propos de la suite de sa carrière, qu'il devint plus tard prieur du couvent de Zagreb[40]. Quant à frère Paul, le véritable fondateur de la province de Hongrie, puisqu'il était à la tête du petit groupe de frères envoyés en 1221[41] et fut donc probablement par la suite le premier provincial[42], il devient également dans ce texte le martyr qu'il n'était nullement sous la plume de Svipert de Porroch[43], non plus, quant à lui, par association avec les quatre-vingt-dix victimes des Tartares, mais par assimilation avec les frères qui, envoyés de Hongrie comme inquisiteurs en Bosnie et Dalmatie, y tombèrent sous les coups, cette fois, des hérétiques[44].

Au-delà de ces affabulations manifestes, l'intérêt d'un tel texte est de montrer l'identification désormais pleine et entière, en ce début du XVIᵉ siècle, de la sainteté dominicaine de Hongrie avec un modèle avant tout martyrial. On voit en effet ici que le souvenir des pères fondateurs devait toujours être présent dans la province à cette époque mais que, sous peine de faire pâle figure à côté des héros tombés pour la foi à la faveur de l'histoire tourmentée de ces régions, les premiers se devaient d'être associés aux seconds dans un même culte ; et cela aussi bien en Hongrie même, dont est probablement

---

[38] Ambrogio Taegio, *Monumenta, op. cit.*, t. III, éd. part. R. Loenertz, *art. cit.*, p. 284, n° 5 ; *Id., De insigniis*, éd. part. R. Loenertz, *art. cit.*, p. 297, n° 6 ; Leandro Alberti, *op. cit.*, fol. 59r. En revanche, rien de tel chez Diacceto (ce que commente R. Loenertz, *art. cit.*, p. 288).

[39] *Acta capitulorum generalium Ordinis fratrum Praedicatorum*, I (1220-1303), éd. B. Reichert, Rome, 1898 (Monumenta Ordinis fratrum Praedicatorum historica, 3), p. 2.

[40] *Relatio Sviperti, op. cit.*, p. 88.

[41] *Ibid.*, p. 86.

[42] Certes, nous sommes un peu livré aux conjectures quant au titre qui était le sien, tant est encore floue l'histoire institutionnelle des débuts de l'ordre, notamment en ce qui concerne les structures de gouvernement. Voir à ce sujet les remarques de S. Tugwell, « The evolution of Dominican structures of government, II : the first Dominican provinces », *Archivum Fratrum Praedicatorum*, 70 (2000), p. 5-109, en particulier p. 50.

[43] « A metamorphosis as mythical as any that we read about in Ovid », comme l'a bien montré S. Tugwell, « Was *Paulus Hungarus* really Dalmatian ? », *Archivum Fratrum Praedicatorum*, 79 (2009), p. 21.

[44] Ambrogio Taegio, *Monumenta, op. cit.*, t. III, éd. part. R. Loenertz, *art. cit.*, p. 284, n° 6 ; *Id., De insigniis*, éd. part. R. Loenertz, *op. cit.*, p. 298, n° 11 ; Francesco Diacceto, *op. cit.*, éd. part. R. Loenertz, *art. cit.*, p. 284, n°6. Cette fois, c'est Alberti qui est muet sur le sujet. Voir les remarques de R. Loenertz, *art. cit.*, p. 290. Mais si Paul de Hongrie ne figurait pas parmi eux, ces martyrs de Bosnie et de Dalmatie étaient bien présents dans le texte de Svipert de Porroch. *Relatio Sviperti, op. cit.*, p. 90-91.

originaire le catalogue dont il vient d'être question, qu'en-dehors de celle-ci, puisque la version des faits qui y était donnée fut reprise sans sourciller par les hagiographes dominicains contemporains, en particulier en Italie, lieu probable de la première circulation du texte.

Voilà qui pourrait au premier abord surprendre de la part de membres d'un ordre mendiant censé incarner un modèle de sainteté différent, avant tout centré sur la conformité au modèle de la *vita apostolica* plus qu'à celui du martyre, dont la thèse d'André Vauchez a bien montré qu'il pouvait être qualifié d'archaïque face à la modernité précisément incarnée, en particulier, par les Mendiants à partir de la fin du XIIIe siècle. Mais le même auteur a également mis en évidence une géographie différentielle de la sainteté dans les derniers siècles du Moyen Âge, opposant ce modèle, moderne et très méditerranéen, des ordres mendiants, à celui, plus traditionnel, des pays de l'Europe du Nord et de l'Est[45]. Or, les martyrs dominicains de Hongrie se situent d'une certaine façon à l'intersection de ces deux ensembles ; du coup, leur intégration réussie dans le « panthéon » dominicain pourrait signifier le succès d'une stratégie assez efficace de la part de l'ordre en termes d'intégration de ses espaces les plus périphériques. Le fait que les martyrs des Tartares jouissent assez rapidement d'une réputation de sainteté auprès de leurs confrères hongrois peut en effet être la marque d'une culture religieuse propre à ces derniers ; mais leur prise en compte dans des textes qui souvent résultent d'une commande officielle des instances dirigeantes des Prêcheurs, et font l'objet d'un étroit contrôle de leur part, témoigne d'une véritable politique d'auto-représentation s'efforçant d'articuler mémoire locale et mémoire de l'ordre – ce dont témoigne l'ensemble des *Vitas fratrum*[46], par exemple. Cela suppose, évidemment, une certaine forme de respect pour les différentes expressions de cette mémoire locale : en l'espèce, la reconnaissance d'une identité particulière de la province dominicaine de Hongrie, qui en fait une sorte de marche avancée de la Chrétienté face aux nouveaux périls barbares[47], où la place privilégiée du martyre parmi les différents modèles de sainteté proposés aux frères s'explique par le caractère crucial du témoignage que bon nombre d'entre eux sont amenés à porter, parfois de la façon la plus héroïque, dans l'un des derniers lieux de la confrontation de l'Église avec les païens.

---

[45] A. Vauchez, *La sainteté, op. cit.*, p. 487-488.
[46] A. Reltgen-Tallon, *La mémoire d'un ordre, op. cit.*, t. I, p. 146.
[47] Comme j'ai essayé de le montrer dans A. Reltgen-Tallon, « Vers un autre Sud ? Les marges orientales de la chrétienté comme nouvelle terre de mission dans l'imaginaire dominicain du Moyen Âge », dans *Tous azimuts... Mélanges de recherches en l'honneur du Professeur Georges Jehel*, Amiens, 2002, p. 421.

Mais pour qu'une telle intégration de la mémoire locale à la mémoire collective de l'ordre soit réussie, il ne suffit sans doute pas de ce seul effort de compréhension du centre pour la périphérie : encore faut-il que les spécificités de celle-ci, en termes hagiographiques, soient compatibles avec les exigences particulières de l'ecclésiologie dominicaine envisagée cette fois depuis le centre. Pour expliquer l'adoption assez rapide, par les hagiographes dominicains du Midi français d'abord, puis ceux des autres provinces, des martyrs de Hongrie, il faut donc se demander comment celle-ci pouvait servir une politique hagiographique plus générale de l'ordre, en dehors du seul souci, par ailleurs manifeste, de renforcement d'une cohésion identitaire que l'expansion géographique rapide de la famille dominicaine pouvait paraître menacer.

Pour répondre à cette question, il peut être utile de revenir sur la proximité clairement suggérée par la *Relatio* de Svipert de Porroch entre les Prêcheurs hongrois morts pour la foi et le second saint canonisé de l'ordre, saint Pierre Martyr. La promotion du culte de ce dernier servait en effet un but politique évident de la papauté[48], mais également l'apologétique dominicaine, en cette période où l'ordre se voyait incriminé de toutes parts, comme l'ensemble des ordres mendiants, certes, mais plus particulièrement sans doute pour son association étroite à la répression inquisitoriale[49]. Pouvoir opposer aux martyrs des hérétiques ceux de la foi catholique était, à l'évidence, une réponse possible contre l'accusation qui était faite aux frères d'avoir du sang sur les mains[50]. Cependant, la politique hagiographique en faveur des inquisiteurs assassinés n'était pas sans risques, car elle présentait l'inconvénient de renforcer, d'une certaine façon, l'assimilation entre Prêcheurs et inquisiteurs. Par conséquent, la possibilité offerte par l'épisode tartare de mettre en avant d'autres figures de martyrs dominicains que ceux de l'Inquisition était particulièrement bienvenue, en associant quant à elle l'activité des frères non plus à la répression antihérétique, mais à une vocation missionnaire beaucoup plus proche, sans doute, du modèle apostolique, si central dans la spiritualité mendiante.

Symptomatiquement d'ailleurs, cette dimension est également très fortement revalorisée dans l'hagiographie contemporaine relative à saint Dominique, à commencer par les *Vitas fratrum* auxquelles fut précisément adjointe la *Relatio* de Svipert de Porroch : on trouve en effet en seconde partie de

---

[48] G. Merlo, « Pietro di Verona », *art. cit.*
[49] Comme l'a bien montré A. Vauchez, « Les réactions face aux ordres mendiants dans les chroniques rédigées en France au XIIIe siècle », dans *Finances, pouvoirs et mémoire. Hommages à Jean Favier*, éd. J. Kerhervé et A. Rigaudière, Paris, 1999, p. 539-548.
[50] G. Merlo, « Pietro di Verona », *art. cit.*

celles-ci un supplément à la Vie de saint Dominique dont l'apport principal, par rapport aux différentes légendes jusqu'alors rédigées au sein de l'ordre pour les besoins de la liturgie dominicaine, consiste précisément dans une accentuation du caractère héroïque de la sainteté du fondateur et l'évocation plus appuyée qu'auparavant de son aspiration au martyre[51]. Plus loin, en outre, c'est dans des termes comparables qu'est décrit l'apostolat des premiers frères dans le Languedoc cathare, évoquant les souffrances du missionnaire : « Depuis près de quarante ans les frères de ces régions combattaient dans le froid, la nudité et toutes sortes de tribulations[52] ». Passage qu'il est tentant de rapprocher de celui de Svipert de Porroch sur l'œuvre d'évangélisation menée par les Prêcheurs de Hongrie auprès des Coumans : « Ils parvinrent jusqu'à eux, près d'un grand fleuve appelé Dniepr, où bien souvent ils eurent à souffrir de la faim et de la soif, du manque de vêtements et de toutes sortes de persécutions[53] » ; les deux textes étant indépendants l'un de l'autre, une telle proximité ne peut s'expliquer que par une sensibilité hagiographique commune à l'ensemble de l'ordre à cette époque, et caractérisée par le souci de revaloriser le modèle de la sainteté martyre en tant que liée à une activité missionnaire.

La même impression ressort d'ailleurs de la lecture de la première véritable Vie de saint Pierre Martyr qui fut rédigée dans les rangs des Prêcheurs, celle que l'on trouve, encore et toujours, dans les *Vitas fratrum*, au début de la cinquième partie relative aux morts édifiantes survenues dans l'ordre et qui s'ouvre, sans surprise, sur l'évocation de ses martyrs. Il est en effet manifeste que l'auteur a ici voulu insister, autant que sur la mort brutale du saint, sur une vie entièrement consacrée à la défense de la doctrine : dès l'enfance, lorsque le jeune Pierre argumentait contre les croyances de son milieu familial hérétique[54] ; puis au sein de l'ordre des Prêcheurs, où il s'illustra en particulier par de nombreuses disputes[55] ainsi que par un certain type de miracles ordonnés à la défense et illustration du dogme catholique

---

[51] En particulier avec l'introduction de l'épisode dans lequel saint Dominique, après avoir été délibérément égaré par un hérétique dans un lieu plein de ronces et d'épines qui lacèrent ses jambes et ses pieds nus, loin de se plaindre, se félicite de pouvoir ainsi se purger de ses péchés en répandant son sang. Gérard de Frachet, *op. cit.*, p. 68.
[52] *Cum [...] fere XL annis fratres de partibus illis in fame et siti, in frigore et nuditate et in tribulacionibus multis certaverint. Ibid.*, p. 231.
[53] *[...] Pervenerunt ad eos iuxta magnum fluvium qui dicitur Deneper. Ubi frequenter fame et siti et nuditate ac varia persecutione afflicti [...]. Relatio Sviperti, op. cit.*, p. 88.
[54] Gérard de Frachet, *op. cit.*, p. 236-237.
[55] *Ibid.*, p. 237-240.

contre le dualisme cathare, *in vita*[56] comme *post mortem*[57] ; enfin, à l'instar du saint fondateur de son ordre, par son aspiration à ne pas mourir pour une autre cause que la défense de la vraie foi[58]. Et par la suite, les différentes Vies de saint Pierre Martyr rédigées dans les rangs des Prêcheurs ne cessèrent de développer à son propos ce thème d'une sainteté doctrinale autant que martyre[59].

On comprend mieux, dès lors, le succès d'un texte comme celui de Svipert, en parfaite résonance avec l'hagiographie dominicaine contemporaine. Le texte insiste sur la dureté, mais également les succès de l'apostolat auprès des Coumans, beaucoup plus que sur l'héroïsme des frères qui y trouvèrent la mort. Il souligne même, à propos de l'épisode tartare, que la véritable catastrophe survenue alors, plus encore que la mort de quatre-vingt-dix frères de l'ordre, était l'interruption de leur prédication et, partant, la mise en péril du début de conversion des Coumans. À n'en pas douter, cette insistance sur une facette résolument moderne de la sainteté martyre, mettant l'accent sur l'impossibilité de dissocier celle-ci du zèle apostolique au cœur de la vocation mendiante, est l'une des clés du succès de la *Relatio* de Svipert de Porroch auprès de ses confrères de l'ensemble de la Chrétienté.

L'un des meilleurs témoignages que l'on puisse en trouver est sans doute la façon tout à fait originale dont celle-ci fut intégrée à la dernière grande compilation hagiographique dominicaine du XIIIᵉ siècle : il s'agit paradoxalement, en apparence du moins[60], de la nouvelle Vie de saint Dominique rédigée

---

[56] Ainsi, par exemple, lorsqu'à la suite d'un défi que lui lance un hérétique, il réalise un miracle pour mettre à l'abri du soleil la foule venue l'écouter en prononçant les paroles suivantes : « Afin que le vrai Dieu se manifeste comme le créateur de l'univers visible et invisible, pour conforter les fidèles et confondre les hérétiques, je lui demande qu'un nuage descende et vienne s'interposer entre le soleil et le peuple » (*Ad hoc, ut verus Deus appareat creator visiblium et invisibilium et ad consolacionem fidelium et ad confusionem hereticorum, rogo eum, ut descendat nubecula aliqua et interponat se inter solem et populum*). *Ibid.*, p. 238.

[57] Notamment dans les deux miracles par lesquels le saint accorde la survie de leur progéniture à venir à deux femmes ayant déjà donné naissance à plusieurs enfants morts-nés et le suppliant de leur venir en aide à ce sujet. *Ibid.*, p. 241 et 246-247. Comment ne pas voir ici, contre la doctrine cathare, une approbation à peine implicite de la procréation ?

[58] *Aliter quam pro fide Christi. Ibid.*, p. 237.

[59] A. RELTGEN-TALLON, *La mémoire d'un ordre*, op. cit., t. 2, p. 249-261.

[60] Car ce texte ne se veut pas seulement une nouvelle Vie de saint Dominique, plus complète que les précédentes, mais une hagiographie collective de l'ordre et de ses premiers frères, comme l'explique clairement l'auteur dans le prologue : *Est autem ex hoc libellus iste prolixior, quod gesta magistri Reynaldi, et obitum ejus, et quorum aliorum Patrum, et quae ad commendationem Ordinis spectant, plenius inserta continet et adscripta [...] ut cum quanta gloria et religione Praedicatorum institutus sit Ordo, et sanctorum Patrum eumdem fundantium eximia devotio et praeclara discretio posteris innotescat. Nec volo, quod Legendae vocabulo censeatur, sed libellus de Vita et obitu et miraculis sancti Dominici, et de Ordine, quem instituit,*

sur près d'une dizaine d'années[61] par le frère thuringien Thierry d'Apolda[62]. Elle présente un aspect compilatoire et se caractérise par l'adjonction aux légendes antérieures, refondues à cet effet, du matériel bolonais jusqu'alors laissé de côté par celles-ci et rapporté par le provincial Conrad de Trebensee[63] à son retour du chapitre général de Lucques[64]. Parmi ces ajouts figure une version assez largement récrite de la *Relatio* de Svipert, et surtout une version tronquée, puisqu'elle s'arrête juste avant l'épisode tartare[65] : comment mieux dire que celui-ci, malgré son cortège de martyrs, ne présentait aux yeux de l'auteur aucun intérêt ? Ce qui, à l'inverse, souligne l'attention qu'il portait aux paragraphes précédents relatifs aux Coumans. Celle-ci était peut-être due à l'héroïsme de la prédication des frères impliqués, voire à leurs deux martyrs, mais plus encore à l'issue de leur mission qui se solda, *in fine*, par la conversion de tout un peuple[66].

Ainsi peut-on considérer que le sort réservé par la littérature dominicaine du XIIIe siècle aux martyrs de Hongrie est un bon exemple de la façon dont

---

nominetur. Thierry d'Apolda, *Libellus de vita et obitu et miraculis sancti Dominici et de ordine quem instituit*, *AASS*², Aug. I, Paris-Rome, 1867, p. 559.

[61] Comme le montrent les commandes de deux maîtres généraux, Munio de Zamora en 1289 (*Ibid*. p. 372) et Nicolas Boccasini, le futur Benoît XI, en 1296, à qui l'ouvrage fut envoyé l'année suivante (*Ibid*., p. 372-373).

[62] Sur sa vie et son activité d'hagiographe, voir M. WERNER, « Die Elisabeth-Vita des Dietrich von Apolda als Beispiel Spätmittelalterlicher Hagiographie », dans *Geschichtsschreibung und Geschichtsbewusstsein*, éd. H. PATZE, Sigmaringen, 1987, p. 523-541.

[63] Sur l'identification du « Gerardus » nommé par Thierry dans sa préface (Thierry d'Apolda, *op. cit.*, p. 559 : *cf. infra*), voir B. ALTANER, *Der heilige Dominikus. Untersuchungen und Texte*, Breslau, 1922, p. 191.

[64] *Tandem dilectus Pater noster, Frater Gerardus, Priori provincialis Theutoniae, rediens de generali Capitulo, in Luca celebrato, detulit quaedam praeclara gesta sancti Dominici de Bononia* [...] *Praeterea dicta illustrium virorum, videlicet novem Fratrum, quorum testimonia credibilia nimis, auctoritate domini Gregorii noni approbata, etiam aliis praeferenda, Patris nostri eximiam praedicant sanctitatem. Accedunt ad haec revelationes Sanctorum, quae spernendae non sunt, relationesque veterum fidelissimae, et omni credulitate dignissimae*. Thierry d'Apolda, *op. cit.*, p. 559.

[65] *Ibid.*, p. 612-613.

[66] Dignement célébrée, quant à elle, aussi bien par Thierry d'Apolda (*Ibid.*) que déjà par Svipert de Porroch. On lit dans la *Relatio Sviperti* (p. 88-89) : *Tandem placuit altissimo respicere laborem et constantiam fratrum et dedit eis gratiam ut audirentur a dictis paganis, et sic primo omnium ducem unum nomine Burchi cum aliquibus de familia sua baptizaverunt.* [...] *Posthunc Benborch ducem nobiliorem cum mille circiter de familia sua ad fidem Ihesu Christi convertuerunt*. On trouve également un écho du retentissement qu'eut ce beau succès de la mission dominicaine dans les deux brèves chroniques adjointes aux *Vitas fratrum*, comme la *Relatio* de Svipert, dans certains manuscrits et éditées pour cette raison à la suite de celles-ci, en regard l'une de l'autre. *Cronica Ordinis prior*, éd. B. REICHERT, Rome, 1896 (Monumenta Ordinis fratrum Praedicatorum historica, 1), p. 338 ; *Cronica Ordinis posterior*, éd. B. REICHERT, Rome, 1896 (Monumenta Ordinis fratrum Praedicatorum historica, 1), p. 337.

ses auteurs s'efforcèrent de résoudre les difficultés liées à une double exigence parfois contradictoire : d'une part, la nécessaire insertion de la mémoire des provinces périphériques, fût-elle caractérisée par une sensibilité religieuse très particulière, à celle de l'ensemble de l'ordre, et d'autre part la fidélité à une politique hagiographique qui fût le reflet fidèle de l'ecclésiologie des Prêcheurs. Pour pouvoir adopter pleinement et promouvoir ce modèle de sainteté en apparence archaïque qu'était le martyre, ils firent en effet le choix de le moderniser par le rapprochement avec celui de l'apôtre, permettant ainsi sa récupération au profit de la promotion de l'idéal mendiant par excellence, le *zelus animarum*. Ainsi les martyrs de Hongrie purent-ils être promus au rang de frères « illustres » de l'ordre, contribuant par leurs mérites au rayonnement de la famille dominicaine tout en incarnant de façon presque paradigmatique l'une des facettes les plus essentielles de son identité.

Sainteté et observance franciscaine en Europe centrale : Bernardin de Sienne et Jean de Capistran

Ludovic VIALLET
(*Clermont-Ferrand*)

Il faut se méfier des apparences : « l'Observance » chez les Frères mineurs ne peut être définie par la seule obsession du littéralisme de la Règle, malgré le caractère extrême qu'a pris, au sein de l'Ordre, la question de l'*observatio* de celle-ci. Bien d'autres textes ont servi de références aux hommes qui portaient la réforme : des constitutions et des statuts, certes, mais aussi des écrits hagiographiques, car la force des modèles y a joué un rôle majeur et structurant[1]. Pour l'histoire du mouvement observant *sub vicariis*, qui a fini par triompher au début du XVIe siècle (mais à quel prix!), celui de Bernardin de Sienne a été déterminant. On voudrait ici reprendre le dossier de deux saintetés qui furent comme « emboîtées », l'une d'elle se construisant par la promotion de l'autre, dans une forme de dialectique qui les renforça chacune mais n'évita ni les ambiguïtés, ni les ferments de division.

La sainteté de Bernardin : une sainteté identitaire, au service du combat

La construction de la sainteté de Bernardin et, corrélativement, du modèle projeté dans et hors de l'Ordre franciscain ne peut se comprendre que si l'on considère la situation au sein de ce dernier au cours des décennies 1440-1450. Il faut en effet souligner l'importance de ces quelques années qui furent le cadre

---

[1] Ceci est à replacer dans une évolution plus large, à l'échelle du monde des réguliers. Maria Pia Alberzoni a récemment souligné combien, à partir du début du XIIIe siècle, la règle perdit « en bonne partie sa valeur de point de référence pour la réalisation d'un idéal de vie religieuse » et acquit une dimension plus juridique, laissant à d'autres types de textes, et avant tout à l'hagiographie, « la fonction d'indiquer les idées-guides de la spiritualité » pour les différents mouvements. M. P. ALBERZONI, « Le idee guida della spiritualità », dans *Mittelalterliche Orden und Klöster im Vergleich. Methodische Ansätze und Perspektiven*, éd. G. MELVILLE, A. MÜLLER, Münster, 2007, p. 63 (traduit par mes soins).

Les saints et leur culte en Europe centrale au Moyen Âge (XIe-début du XVIe siècle), éd. par Marie-Madeleine de CEVINS et Olivier MARIN, Turnhout, 2017 (*Hagiologia*, 13), p. 227-243.

de la canonisation du réformateur siennois, de l'institutionnalisation décisive de l'Observance autonome, du départ de Jean de Capistran hors d'Italie et d'un véritable changement de *climat* qui s'est opéré alors, la recherche de solutions encore consensuelles – dont témoignent les Constitutions de 1430 – laissant place à des comportements plus radicaux, notamment dans le contexte de la longue tournée de Capistran et ses disciples en Europe centrale. À l'attitude des réformateurs observants *sub vicariis* font écho les griefs des « Conventuels » favorables à une réforme (les « Martiniens » ou plutôt *Reformaten* emmenés par le provincial de Saxe Matthias Döring), pour qui le choix de l'autonomie, donc le primat accordé à la pauvreté (et à des positionnements jugés trop extrêmes) par les Observants italiens aux dépens de l'unité de l'Ordre était considéré comme une trahison de l'injonction d'obéissance aux ministres laissée par François[2]. Est-il besoin de souligner, en outre, que ce face-à-face s'inscrivait dans le contexte, lourd de tensions et de ressentiments, du règlement d'un schisme au cours duquel Capistran et Döring – pour ne citer qu'eux – s'étaient retrouvés dans des camps opposés, celui du pape et celui du Concile ?

Vers 1450, l'autorité de Bernardin pouvait encore être invoquée par les partisans d'une voie moyenne fondée sur la *moderatio* dans la mise en pratique du *propositum* franciscain. On pensera, en particulier, à la lettre qu'il avait envoyée le 31 juillet 1440 aux Observants italiens, dont il était alors le vicaire général, afin de leur transmettre les déclarations de son confrère Nicolas d'Osimo, lettre qui reflétait le souci d'œuvrer en faveur de l'*usus moderatus* tout en prenant en compte « la qualité des personnes, la variété des périodes, les conditions de lieux et les autres circonstances »[3]. On sait aujourd'hui que le positionnement de Bernardin, dans le processus de distinction entre « Observants » et « Conventuels » à l'œuvre au cours des décennies 1430-1440,

---

[2] Ce face-à-face a été au cœur de mon enquête *Les sens de l'observance. Enquête sur les réformes franciscaines entre l'Elbe et l'Oder, de Capistran à Luther (vers 1450 – vers 1520)*, Münster, 2014, à laquelle je me permets de renvoyer pour de plus amples développements.
[3] *Chronica Fratris Nicolai Glassberger Ordinis Minorum Observantium* (*Analecta Franciscana*, 2, 1887, p. 303-304) : *Item, quod superfluitas vel curiositas non debet discerni respectu necessitatis arctae seu usus arcti quoad statum Fratrum Minorum, sed moderati, cum usus moderatus non potest dici superfluus vel curiosus et per consequens vitiosus, immo secundum regulam et omnimodam veritatem omnino licitus, ut patet ex praeallegato dicto Nicolai. Et quia moderatio dicti usus debet attendi secundum qualitatem personarum et varietatem temporum et locorum conditiones et alias occurrentes circumstantias, superfluitas et curiositas non potest faciliter discerni: propterea per subditos non debet iudicari nec potest, sed per Ministros et Custodes, vel eos, quibus ab ipsis committitur, qui de talibus super eorum conscientiam debent discrete iudicare, ut patet ex declaratione domini Nicolai, ibi*: insuper, *et* § Quamquam. Nicolas d'Osimo était alors commissaire du ministre général pour la province de Saint-Ange. Ses déclarations, écrivit Bernardin, avaient fait l'objet d'un examen attentif et de discussions, notamment par Jean de Capistran (*ibid.*, p. 303).

n'a pas été aussi tranché que ce que les constructions postérieures de l'historiographie franciscaine ont pu faire croire[4] ; la proclamation de sa sainteté, et plus encore l'usage que fit Capistran de cette sainteté, l'amenèrent davantage du côté de l'Observance *sub vicariis*. Structurant avant tout l'ensemble dit « cismontain », polarisé *ab origine* sur la péninsule italienne, Capistran (vicaire général cismontain jusqu'au printemps 1452, puis nommé commissaire général outre-Alpes par son successeur Marc de Bologne) a développé en Europe centrale une pastorale qui s'adressait à la masse des fidèles par le *medium* d'une prédication fondée largement sur le visuel et le miraculeux, faisant de la sainteté de Bernardin la pierre angulaire de son charisme de thaumaturge. Tandis que le conflit avec les Conventuels éclatait dans toute sa violence lors du chapitre général tenu à L'Aquila en 1452, la mission fut pour lui l'occasion d'arrimer définitivement la figure de son maître et ami à l'Observance des vicaires. La sainteté de Bernardin, lorsqu'elle fut proclamée en 1450 (en grande partie grâce à Capistran), revêtit presque immédiatement une dimension civique, d'ailleurs multipolaire – à L'Aquila, où reposait le corps, Sienne, Pérouse, Ferrare notamment[5]. Le parcours de prédicateur de Capistran, dans les mois puis les années qui suivirent, fut l'instrument essentiel de la propagation de la dévotion bernardinienne hors d'Italie, mais aussi un moyen de ramener cette dévotion dans le giron de l'ordre franciscain et de mieux affirmer le caractère « pan-observant » de la sainteté de Bernardin[6]. Capistran a donc fait de celle-ci un instrument de combat au service de l'Observance *sub vicariis* ; par là-même, elle a été tirée hors du consensus.

---

[4] L. Pellegrini, « Bernardino da Siena, il minoritismo e l'Osservanza: ambiguità e ambivalenze. A partire da Monteripido », dans *Giacomo della Marca tra Monteprandone e Perugia. Lo 'studium' del Convento del Monte e la cultura dell'Osservanza francescana. Atti del Convegno Internazionale di Studi (Monteripido, 5 novembre 2011)*, éd. F. Serpico, L. Giacometti, Pérouse, 2013, p. 21-35, en particulier p. 32-34. Voir également D. Solvi, « Il culto dei santi nella proposta socio-religiosa dell'Osservanza », dans *I Frati osservanti e la società in Italia nel secolo XV. Atti del XL Convegno internazionale della Società internazionale di studi francescani (Assisi-Perugia, 11-13 ottobre 2012)*, Spolète, 2013, p. 144.
[5] Voir la belle étude de : D. Arasse, « *Fervebat pietate populus*. Art, dévotion et société autour de la glorification de saint Bernardin de Sienne », *Mélanges de l'École française de Rome. Moyen Âge – Temps modernes*, 89 (1977), p. 189-263. Sur la canonisation et l'hagiographie de Bernardin, voir *Il processo di canonizzazione di Bernardino da Siena (1445-1450)*, éd. et intro. L. Pellegrini, Grottaferrata, 2009 (Analecta Franciscana, 16, n. s. 4), ainsi que *L'agiografia su Bernardino Santo (1450-1460)*, éd. D. Solvi, Florence, 2014.
[6] Ce qui n'empêcha pas le colétan Boniface de Ceva, ministre provincial de France au début du XVIe siècle, de déclarer, avec un sens certain de la polémique, que Bernardin étant mort dans l'obéissance aux ministres *inter ipsos fratres vicarianos nullus unquam sanctus extitit canonizatus*. Voir M. Bihl, « Fra Bonifacio da Ceva († 1517) e i suoi giudizi su Bernardino da Siena », *Studi Francescani*, 42 (1945), p. 171.

Dans le sud de la province franciscaine de Saxe, le succès de Capistran comme prédicateur fut bien plus important que son succès comme réformateur, alors qu'en Pologne nombre de couvents furent réformés ou créés sous son impulsion. Partout, cependant, l'importance qu'il fit jouer à la sainteté de Bernardin marqua d'une forte empreinte la façon dont furent perçues l'Observance *sub vicariis* ou même les communautés de tertiaires dans sa mouvance : en Silésie et en Pologne, où les deux grands couvents de Breslau (Wrocław) et Cracovie, fondés par Capistran, étaient dédiés à Bernardin, les Franciscains réformés reçurent le nom de « Bernardins », qui exprime bien l'impact de la pastorale énergique menée par le réformateur et ses disciples en faveur du culte du prédicateur siennois, mais aussi la nouveauté que prit le mouvement aux yeux de fidèles pour qui il s'agissait quasiment du développement d'un nouvel ordre religieux. À Kamenz (lieu de l'unique fondation observante de Haute Lusace), par exemple, le 20 avril 1498, une délibération du Conseil de ville autorisant les tertiaires à acheter un jardin évoque celles-ci comme les jeunes femmes vivant sous « la troisième règle de saint Bernardin »[7].

Toutefois, compte tenu des tensions entre mouvements réformateurs, au début du XVIe siècle, en Silésie et Haute Lusace, l'hostilité des *Reformaten* envers les « Bernardins » se traduisit par un certain dénigrement de la canonisation de Bernardin de Sienne. La chronique d'un observant anonyme en témoigne, dans le contexte des tentatives menées pour réaliser l'union en vertu des statuts promulgués par Jules II le 1er juillet 1508. À Neisse (Nysa), en janvier 1510, le custode Benoît de Löwenberg aurait tâché d'obtenir le soutien des fidèles afin d'expulser les Observants du couvent de Sainte-Croix *rebelles et inobedientes* au Siège apostolique. Parmi les arguments utilisés, tels qu'ils ont été rapportés par le chroniqueur, on trouve le reproche d'avoir honte du nom de saint François, reproche assorti d'une remise en cause de la sainteté de Bernardin de Sienne, dont la canonisation, erreur de l'Église, n'aurait été due qu'à la séparation entre Conventuels et Observants[8].

---

[7] *Codex Diplomaticus Saxoniae regiae*, II, 7 (*Urkundenbuch der Städte Kamenz und Löbau*), éd. H. KNOTHE, Leipzig, 1883, p. 135-136, n° 181 : *Freitagis noch ostern hot der erbar roth denn juncffrawen der dritten regil wff ir ansuchen, sancti Bernardini, irlewbet, den garten Symon Remisch zu sich zu kewffen.*

[8] F. DOELLE, *Die Observanzbewegung in der sächsischen Franziskanerprovinz bis zum Generalkapitel von Parma 1529*, Münster, 1918, p. 226 (Beilagen, 7) : *Allegantes contra nos, quod non haberemus studia neque horas caneremus, ipsi essent de vera et regulari observancia, nostram observanciam non mediocriter infamantes, asserentes nos verecundari paterni nominis sancti Francisci, et faceremus nos nuncupari Bernrnardinenses et ipse sanctus Bernhardinus, si non esset canonisatus propter separacionem a conventualibus, nunquam canonisaretur, quasi ecclesia errasset in sua canonisacione. Ecce perfidia pessimorum obstinatorum deformatorum!*

La sainteté de Capistran, ou l'usage ambigu des reliques

L'image de Bernardin a été au cœur de toute une stratégie du miraculeux, dénoncée comme une véritable supercherie par les adversaires de Capistran, tel Matthias Döring dans un passage violemment critique de la *Continuation de la Chronique de Dietrich Engelhusen* :

> Cette même année [1453], le frère Jean de Capistran, envoyé dans le royaume de Bohême, certes d'abord brûlant du désir du martyre, refusa ensuite d'y entrer s'il n'avait pas de sauf-conduit. L'hérésiarque Jean Rokycana soutint, dans ses écrits et ses prêches, qu'il était le précurseur de l'Antéchrist. En effet, contournant la Bohême, tantôt en Autriche, tantôt en Bavière, tantôt en Saxe, Thuringe, Silésie, tantôt en Pologne, tantôt en Moravie, il prêcha par l'intermédiaire d'un traducteur, mécontent si quelque part il n'était pas reçu avec grand tumulte de procession, et quelque importantes que semblaient être, dans ses préceptes, leurs prétentions au mépris du monde, à lui et à ses religieux, ils avaient cependant l'habitude de réclamer des mets raffinés et les meilleurs vins, d'obtenir les applaudissements des hommes et leur affluence, d'envoyer des messagers pour les annoncer, d'exalter le toucher du bord du vêtement du frère Jean compte tenu des nombreux et grands miracles qu'il avait faits[9]. Il fut ainsi mis en valeur, de telle sorte qu'il ne pouvait supporter patiemment une parole qui lui fût contraire. Afin que la foule le vît, il avait coutume de célébrer des messes en des lieux profanes préparés avec grand faste pour cela sur le marché des villes, dans lesquelles il y avait pourtant nombre d'églises consacrées et de monastères, et il ne prêchait en aucun lieu qui n'ait été beaucoup rehaussé et orné. [...] et si quelque individu avec un membre atrophié ou quelque boiteux, par une confiance née de la rumeur propagée par les messagers, pensait se tenir mieux, ses[10] compagnons le pressaient de s'avancer, criant et appelant le peuple à crier 'Jésus' avec grand tumulte ; ils emportaient leurs bâtons et béquilles et les suspendaient dans l'église devant l'image de saint Bernhard [*sic*]. Le bruit courait toutefois que beaucoup de ces [infirmes] ainsi guéris retombaient et réclamaient leurs bâtons. Il reçut de nombreux nouveaux membres dans sa famille, de toute provenance, et afin de les rassembler, demanda des lieux aux seigneurs et aux communautés pour construire des monastères appelés de l'observance, et réussit à causer un grand trouble dans et autour de la province de Saxe[11].

---

[9] Je traduis ici « *et de factis multis et magnis miraculis per fratrem Johannem prefatum fimbriam magnificare* », sans certitude.

[10] Ndt : de Capistran.

[11] « Mathias Dörings Fortsetzung der Chronik von Dieterich Engelhusen », dans *Riedel's Codex diplomaticus Brandenburgensis. Sammlung der Urkunden, Chroniken und sonstigen Geschichtsquellen für die Geschichte der Mark Brandenburg und ihrer Regenten*, IV/1, Berlin, 1862, p. 225 : *ipso eodem anno* [1453] *dictus frater Johannes de Capestrano missus ad regnum Bohemie, primo quidem fervens ad martirium, post recusavit intrare, nisi haberet salvum*

Jean de Capistran montra une image de saint Bernardin à Breslau le dimanche *Judica me* (18 mars 1453) avec, selon le clerc Sigismond Rosicz, *speculum terribile alias ein Hirnschedel* (*Hirn-Schädel*, « crâne-cerveau »)[12]. La prédication de Leipzig, à l'automne 1452, confirme – sans grande surprise – qu'il sortait parfois de son vêtement une véritable tête de mort pour la brandir devant son auditoire, en particulier au cours de ses sermons sur la mort et le Jugement[13]. À Breslau, cela fut le cas lors d'une homélie construite à partir de Jean 8, 52 (*Abraham mortuus est et prophetae mortui sunt*) évoquant la mort[14] et au cours de laquelle il précisa que le crâne était un miroir plaçant chaque fidèle face à lui-même[15]. D'autres sources montrent qu'il présentait à la foule

---

conductum. Johannes autem Rockenczan heresiarcha scribendo asseruit et predicando, quod esset precursor antichristi. Ipse namque circueundo Bohemiam, nunc in Austria, nunc Bavaria, nunc Saxonia, Thuringia, Slesia, nunc Polonia, nunc Moravia predicavit per interpretem, male contentus, sicubi cum multo tumultu processionis non recipebatur, et quantumcunque videbatur contemptum mundi cum suis tamquam religiosis observacionibus pretendere, exquisitos tamen cibos et meliora vina expetere, applausus hominum, et eorum concursus procurare, cursores preconisantes premittere, et de factis multis et magnis miraculis per fratrem Johannem prefatum fimbriam magnificare soliti erant. Sicque pretensus apparuit, ut verbum sibi contrarium pacienter ferre non posset. Et ut videretur coram hominibus in locis prophanis ad hoc in foro civitatum cum multo apparatu preparatis, ubi tamen ecclesiarum solempnium et monasteriorum erat numerus, missas celebrare consweverat, nec in aliquo loco nisi multum exaltato et ornato predicabat. [...] et si quis contractus vel claudus ex confidencia orta ex rumore premissorum se putavit melius stare, illum procedere socii sui compulerunt, clamantes et magno cum tumultu populum ad clamandum ihesus provocantes; tulerunt eorum baculos et sustentacula, suspendentes ea in ecclesia coram ymagine sancti Bernhardi [sic]. Fama tamen erat, quod sic curati recidivantes baculos ut plurimum repecierunt. Hic recepit multos undecunque venientes ad suam familiam, et loca pro construendis monasteriis de observancia nuncupandis, pro illis recolligendis, peciit a Dominis et communitatibus, et optinuit in provincia Saxonie et aliarum magnam turbacionem.

[12] S. Rosicz, *Gesta diversa transactis temporibus facta in Silesia et alibi*, éd. dans *Scriptores rerum silesiacarum*, t. 12, Breslau, 1883 (*Geschichtschreiber Schlesiens des XV. Jahrhunderts*), p. 63 : *Predicavit die cinerum in ecclesia sancte Elisabeth deinde in foro salis quasi singulis diebus latine* [14 février], *dominica judica ostendit speculum terribile alias ein Hirnschedel et imaginem sancti Bernhardi* [18 mars] *factaque fuit solemnis processio de foro salis per dominum episcopum ambarum ecclesiarum parochialium et patris et fratrum ad novam hereditationem in nova civitate pro fratribus noviter erectam.*

[13] Voir J. Hofer, « Zur Predigttätigkeit des hl. Johannes Kapistran in deutschen Städten », *Franziskanische Studien*, 13 (1926), p. 149-150 ; J. Neubner, « Die Sachsenfahrt des hl. Johannes Capistrano », dans *St.-Benno-Kalender 1931*, Dresde, 1931, p. 55. La mort et le Jugement furent des thèmes abordés par Capistran à Leipzig : voir L. Łuszczki, *De Sermonibus S. Ioannis a Capistrano. Studium historico-criticum*, Rome, 1961, p. 277-278 (et l'index chronologico-thématique, p. 308), qui souligne le degré d'intensité extrême – rarement atteint selon lui chez Capistran – de cette prédication sur la mort, sans toutefois mentionner l'usage d'un crâne.

[14] L. Łuszczki, *De Sermonibus, op. cit.*, p. 164, n° 652 et p. 170, n° 709.

[15] E. Jacob, *Johannes von Capistrano*, Breslau, 1905-1911, II, Dritte Folge, p. 135, cité par G. Buchwald, « Johannes Capistranos Predigten in Leipzig 1452 », dans *Beiträge zur Sächsischen Kirchengeschichte*, 26 (1912), Leipzig, 1913, p. 149.

la barrette d'ecclésiastique (*biretum* ou *pileolum*) de Bernardin. Il le fit dès le 14 février 1451 à Brescia, dans un extraordinaire engouement populaire décrit par Cristoforo da Soldo dans sa *Cronaca*[16]. Capistran effectuait des guérisons miraculeuses au nom de Bernardin, tenant à la main la barrette de celui-ci lorsqu'il effectuait sur les malades le signe de la croix au nom du Père, du Fils, du Saint-Esprit et… de saint Bernardin[17].

L'épisode de la réforme du couvent des Clarisses de Nuremberg, le 24 juillet 1452, est également significatif. Capistran, qui n'était pas officiellement chargé de la réforme, se livra à un véritable rituel purificateur. Il fit un sermon aux sœurs, réunies dans le réfectoire, les exhorta à respecter l'observance régulière et à imiter leur mère sainte Claire; puis il imposa les reliques de saint Bernardin sur chacune d'elles et certaines recouvrèrent la santé[18]. Avant de quitter le monastère, il en visita et purifia tous les « lieux » (*Lustratis deinde omnibus monasterii locis*), puis il revint à ses activités habituelles dans le couvent des frères et partit pour Bamberg. En fait, le réformateur italien mit en œuvre, face à ses sœurs clarisses, un procédé devenu quasiment routinier depuis le début de sa mission, puisque lors de son séjour viennois ses après-midis et ses débuts de soirée étaient consacrés à la rencontre des malades qui l'avaient attendu au couvent des Mineurs, comme le montre le véritable emploi du temps donné par Glassberger :

> Le sermon fini, retourner au monastère de son ordre, et sexte et none accomplies, aller voir les malades, rester longtemps auprès d'eux, imposer les mains sur tous, approcher la barrette et le sang de saint Bernardin, qui avait dit-on coulé de ses narines à sa mort, sur chacun d'eux (ils étaient de façon avérée rarement moins de cinq cents), prier pour tous en s'agenouillant; après cela dîner, accorder une audience à ceux qui se présentent, ensuite dire les vêpres. Ceci terminé, retourner vers les malades et s'occuper d'eux jusqu'à la nuit; et alors seulement, après complies et les autres prières choisies avec

---

[16] Voir J. HOFER, *Johannes Kapistran. Ein Leben im Kampf um die Reform der Kirche*, t. 1, Rome-Heidelberg, 1964, p. 313-320 (« Die Heiligsprechung Bernhardins »), p. 353-357 (« Große Volksmission in Brescia ») et p. 360 (commentaire de l'illustration : retable réalisé par Jean Figuera pour le couvent de Cagliari, en Sardaigne). Dans la *Cronaca (1437-1468)*, le passage sur le séjour à Brescia, du 9 au 16 février 1451, se situe aux p. 865-869 de l'édition de Milan, 1732 (*Rerum Italicarum Scriptores*, 21-3), aux p. 100-103 de celle de Bologne, 1938.

[17] Autre témoignage, celui de la chronique des évêques de Spire, qui mentionne l'ostension d'un *Hubel* ou *Häubel*, c'est-à-dire d'un bonnet ou d'une coiffe d'ecclésiastique. Voir F. J. MONE, *Quellensammlung der badischen Landesgeschichte*, t. 1, 1848, cité par F. FALK, « St. Johann von Capistrano in Deutschland », *Der Katholik*, 71 (1891), p. 151.

[18] *Chronica Fratris Nicolai Glassberger* […], p. 341 : *Finita collatione, imposuit beatus Pater singulis sororibus reliquias sancti Bernardini, ex quibus aliquae sorores consecutae sunt sanitatem ob merita Sancti, propter ipsarum devotionem.* Glassberger rapporte ici sans doute un élément de la mémoire collective du couvent de Nuremberg, où plusieurs proches de Capistran séjournèrent ou moururent et où lui-même passa la fin de sa vie en étant confesseur des Clarisses.

soin, donner le corps au repos, s'abandonner le moins possible au sommeil, trouver trop peu de temps pour revoir les livres de la Sainte Écriture[19].

En plus de la barrette de Bernardin, Capistran avait emporté du sang de ce dernier – il en laissa au long de son parcours – ainsi que, vraisemblablement, un de ses habits[20]. La principale relique qu'il utilisa, toutefois, fut la fameuse barrette, qu'il nous faut bien distinguer du crâne présenté manifestement à la foule à plusieurs reprises. La distinction est nécessaire, car en passant de l'un à l'autre on passe d'un procédé didactique, ou de communication, à un pouvoir thaumaturgique ; elle l'est d'autant plus qu'au fil des jours et des mois, il n'est pas certain que la confusion ne se soit pas insinuée dans les esprits de fidèles qui, rappelons-le, ne pouvaient comprendre les paroles du prédicateur qu'à condition de saisir celles du traducteur posté plus ou moins loin d'eux. Il semble qu'au début du XVIIe siècle, en effet, si l'on se base sur le récit de Johann Jacob Vogel, annaliste de la ville de Leipzig, dont l'erreur peut fort bien témoigner de toute une tradition, le crâne-miroir de la mort ait été considéré comme la tête de Bernardin[21].

Johannes Hofer et à sa suite Ottokar Bonmann ont pu affirmer que les manifestations suscitées dans la foule par la personne même de Capistran étaient désormais moins dues à ses talents de prédicateur, ou même à sa réputation de sainteté, qu'à la renommée des guérisons qu'il effectuait. Il était dépositaire d'un charisme de thaumaturge mis au service de l'Ordre, puisque ses interventions étaient suivies de la prise d'habit de dizaines de jeunes novices et suscitaient l'afflux de candidats. Il est étonnant de constater de quelle façon le réformateur a utilisé le charisme de l'évêque siennois en faisant, pour ainsi dire, du neuf avec du vieux. Lorsqu'il élevait la relique du saint pour la

---

[19] *Ibid.*, p. 336 : *Finito sermone, ad coenobium sui Ordinis reverti, ac Sexta et Nona completis, infirmos visere, diu apud eos morari, manus omnibus imponere, birretum sancti Bernardini et cruorem, quem illi mortuo e naribus fluxisse ferunt, singulis aegrotantibus admovere, quos raro infra quingentos fuisse constat, precari supplex pro omnibus; exinde coenare, demum his, qui se accedunt, audientiam praebere, mox Vesperas dicere. Hisque completis, ad aegrotos reverti atque cum his usque ac noctem se exercere; tumque demum, Completorio et aliis dilectis precibus expletis, corpus quieti dare, minimum esse quod somno indulgeret, nihil ad revisendos sacrae Scripturae codices pauxillum furari temporis.*

[20] Je ne peux attester pour ma part que l'usage de sa barrette, mais il est vrai que dans les affaires de Capistran inventoriées après sa mort, le 3 décembre 1456, se trouvait au moins un morceau de tissu de laine imprégné du sang de Bernardin. Voir M. BARTOLI, « La biblioteca e lo *scriptorium* di Giovanni da Capestrano », *Franciscana*, 8 (2006), p. 241.

[21] J. J. VOGEL, *Leipzigisches Geschichtsbuch oder Annales*, Leipzig, 1714, p. 56 : « Und als er einsmahls nach gehaltener Predigt auff dem Marckte einen Kopff eines verstorbenen Heiligen von der Cantzel gezeiget, sind dadurch in die 60 Universitäts-Verwandten bewogen worden, dass sie das weltliche Leben verlassen und zu Franciscaner-Mönchen sich einkleiden lassen ».

présenter à la foule et que celle-ci s'exclamait « Miséricorde ! Miséricorde ! » (comme l'après-midi du dimanche 14 février 1451 à Brescia ou en août 1452 à Arnstadt)[22], Capistran renouait avec les pratiques de *disciplinamento* mises en œuvre deux siècles auparavant dans les cités italiennes, en une pastorale et un rapport au Sacré au sujet desquels on peut parler d'« archaïsme innovateur » – un « archaïsme » qui fut aussi « rénovateur » et constitua le pendant de la « restauration innovatrice »[23] incarnée par le projet des Observants sur le plan social. Ainsi, pour répondre à la (fausse) question posée par Olivier Marin dans ce volume, avec la geste de Capistran nous n'avons pas affaire à une adaptation à une « mentalité archaïque » propre à l'Europe centrale, mais aux caractères d'une pastorale importée d'Italie et adaptée à un territoire considéré comme territoire de mission, avec un « modèle martyrial » propre à la géopolitique des lieux. Quant au processus enclenché par l'usage des reliques d'un saint, il est sans doute caractéristique d'une tendance naturelle de la canonisation « populaire », à travers les âges : *mutatis mutandis*, Capistran est un peu comme le Théo du cimetière municipal de Toulouse qui, à la fin du XXe siècle, se consacrait tout entier à sainte Héléna, prétendant effectuer des miracles au nom de cette femme morte un siècle auparavant et dont il détenait une relique (un minuscule bout de robe) ; le « médiateur de la médiatrice » finit par être considéré, par les habitués du cimetière, comme un saint[24]. Avec en plus, toutefois, pour le réformateur italien, la force de frappe de l'institution et des serviteurs du projet observant.

On ne reviendra pas ici sur les miracles réalisés par Capistran avec les reliques de Bernardin : après Stanko Andrić, Anna Zajchowska et Marcin Starzyński les ont étudiés récemment à partir de la section « polonaise » du *Liber miraculorum sancti Bernardini* (Paris, BnF), due au frère Conrad de Freystadt[25]. Les miracles réalisés par le réformateur italien au cours de sa mission en

---

[22] Avec une variante : « Jésus et Miséricorde ». Voir J. BÜHRING, « Johanns von Capistrano, des andächtigen Vaters Aufenthalt in Arnstadt 1452 », *Alt-Arnstadt. Beiträge zur Heimatkunde von Arnstadt und Umgebung*, 3 (1906), p. 88.
[23] Selon le mot de Grado G. Merlo, « Observance », dans *Dictionnaire encyclopédique du Moyen Âge*, éd. A. VAUCHEZ, t. 2, Paris, 1997, p. 1095.
[24] Voir l'étude d'E. BLANC, « Héléna : la sainte du cimetière », *Terrain*, 24 (1995), p. 33-42. « Le médiateur de la médiatrice » est le titre de la troisième partie de cet article.
[25] A. ZAJCHOWSKA, M. STARZYŃSKI, « Le culte de saint Bernardin de Sienne en Pologne médiévale dans l'optique du *Liber miraculorum sancti Bernardini* de Conrad de Freystadt », *Études franciscaines*, n. s., 7 (2014), p. 69-111, à partir de Paris, Bibliothèque nationale de France, ms. nouv. acq. lat. 1763, fol. 186r-190v. Conrad fut probablement accueilli dans l'Observance par Capistran à Nuremberg en juillet 1452 et présent à Cracovie lors du séjour du réformateur italien en 1453-1454. Sur les miracles attribués à Bernardin après sa mort, effectués par Capistran et consignés dans le *Liber miraculorum* de Paris, voir Ph. JANSEN, « Un exemple de sainteté thaumaturgique à la fin du Moyen Âge : les miracles de saint Bernardin

Europe centrale le furent très majoritairement par l'entremise des reliques de Bernardin ; la vague des actes prodigieux attribués à l'entremise de ce dernier faiblit après la mort de Capistran. Par-delà toute tentative de typologie, il est intéressant de saisir comment ces miracles furent perçus, c'est-à-dire à qui ils furent attribués, et comment il fallut, dans l'entourage de Capistran, « rectifier le tir ». Le témoignage du dominicain Jacques de Brescia (souffrant d'une infection du pouce) dans le *Liber miraculorum* est significatif : *audito transitu s(ancti) B(ernardini)...* (« Ayant entendu le passage de saint Bernardin [...] »)[26].

De la sainteté de Bernardin – donc du pouvoir de ses reliques, même portées par un autre – à celle de Capistran, tel fut le *passage* auquel durent œuvrer les artisans de l'hagiographie capistranienne, qui furent, il faut le souligner, des compagnons de route du prédicateur italien. Plus tard, d'ailleurs, une partie des actes miraculeux attribués à Bernardin et compris dans son *Liber miraculorum* furent assignés à Jean de Capistran après sa mort et transférés aux catalogues dressés dans le cadre de son propre processus de canonisation. Si, dans l'ensemble du *Liber miraculorum*, comme l'avait souligné Philippe Jansen, dominent largement (à hauteur des deux tiers) les miracles intervenus suite aux bénédictions de malades effectuées par Capistran avec des reliques de son maître, le chapitre « polonais » du recueil montre une surreprésentation imposante des miracles que l'on peut attribuer directement à saint Bernardin (82 des 94 miracles décrits)[27]. En revanche, toute l'hagiographie capistranienne « immédiate » (celle des années qui suivirent sa mort) travailla à tisser des liens très étroits entre la sainteté de Bernardin et celle à laquelle on aspirait pour Capistran. La comparaison entre les deux réformateurs italiens apparaît de plus en plus clairement dans la *vita* de Christophe de Varèse, puisqu'au fil du récit et à partir du franchissement des Alpes, les références à François s'effacent au profit de l'affirmation du

---

de Sienne », *Mélanges de l'École française de Rome. Moyen Âge – Temps modernes*, 96 (1984), p. 129-151.

[26] A. Zajchowska, M. Starzyński, « Le culte de saint Bernardin de Sienne », *art. cit.*, n° 94 (1432), p. 109 : *Ad laudem Domini nostri Iesu Christi et beatissimi Bernardini confessoris sui. Ego frater Jacobus de Brixa ordinis predicatorum exiguus, dum a puero ferme per XXV annos ex quedam incisione policis sinistre manus cartilago turpissimo modo infecto unguem digito minime cohereret permitteret, sed usque ad coronam digiti, unde unguis apparere incipit, semper divisa foret. Nec quovis medicorum presidio ad debitam coherentiam posset convalescere, sed ex contactu diversarum rerum sentire modo plures inmundicie non mediocriter horrorem excitantes detrimentis. Quod michi satis onerosum erat, quod minus equo sacris misteriis illum applicarem. Unde audito transitu s(ancti) B(ernardini), invocato nomine eius, remota meritis eiusdem illa scabiosa cartilagine unguis sensim digito herens ad perfectum usque succrevit, servata tamen cicatrice in ungue, in miraculi, ut reor, testimonium. Deo gracias ago coram Deo, veritatem expressi.*

[27] Ph. Jansen, « Un exemple de sainteté », *art. cit.*, p. 132 et A. Zajchowska, M. Starzyński, « Le culte de saint Bernardin de Sienne », *art. cit.*, p. 77.

lien de quasi-identification rattachant Capistran à Bernardin, jusqu'à la mise en parallèle des maux qui menèrent à leurs morts respectives[28].

À un tel degré, le processus n'a pas que des avantages pour l'hagiographe, qui doit surmonter un certain embarras. En évoquant les usages que fait Capistran de la barrette de Bernardin (chap. 172-173), il s'applique alors à corriger les dires de son maître, puisque celui-ci attribue ses miracles aux mérites de Bernardin – manifestation d'humilité, mais pas seulement, que Christophe de Varèse se doit de souligner, mais ne peut évidemment pas accepter :

> Néanmoins le serviteur fidèle, indifférent à la chaleur, ne craignant ni le froid, ni la pression populaire, ni les moqueries de ses adversaires, enflammé par un amour extrême, visitait les malades, les touchait avec les mains et les reliques de saint Bernardin qu'il emportait avec lui, les signait très dévotement. Ce n'est pas à lui que le père très humble attribuait les miracles et les prodiges qui étaient réalisés, mais aux mérites de saint Bernardin, dont il portait avec lui la barrette et avec laquelle il signait les malades quels qu'ils soient[29].

Puis un peu plus loin, au chapitre suivant :

> ainsi assurément, bien que ce saint homme attribuât les miracles aux mérites de saint Bernardin et s'efforçât de se cacher avec la barrette de celui-ci, se produisaient des merveilles en raison de sa très grande foi, de son très ardent amour [...] Car les malades, signés avec la barrette de saint Bernardin, n'obtenaient aucun bénéfice pour leur santé ; mais lorsqu'ils revenaient ensuite, touchés par les mains du Père, ils étaient guéris[30].

Au terme de cette séquence, tandis que le récit s'apprête à emmener le lecteur, non plus en Pologne et Silésie mais en Hongrie, le court chapitre suivant (chap. 174) a pour objectif de bien souligner que les miracles doivent être attribués aux mérites de Capistran. Un épisode abordé plusieurs chapitres auparavant fournit une clef de lecture, sinon des pratiques du saint, du moins

---

[28] *Vita S. Joannis a Capistrano, Scripta a Fr. Christophoro a Varisio, ex ms. Aracœlitano*, dans *Acta Sanctorum*, Oct. X, Bruxelles, 1861, p. 533, c. 192 : *Delatus ergo ad locum, in Vuilak positum, per plures dies valida fluxus aegritudine (qua et Sanctus Bernardinus obiit) laboravit : ita, ut nihil penitus retinere posset.*

[29] *Ibid.*, p. 528, c. 172 : *[...] nihilominus servus fidelis, non considerans aestus, non timens frigora, non pressuram populi, non irrisiones aemulorum, nimia charitate accensus, visitabat infirmos, tangebat manibus et cum Reliquiis Sancti Bernardini, quas secum deferebat, devotissime signabat. Non sibi attribuebat miracula humillimus Pater, et prodigia quae fiebant, sed meritis Sancti Bernardini, cujus biretum secum portabat, et cum eo aegrotos quoscumque signabat.*

[30] *Ibid.*, p. 528-529, c. 173 : *[...] sic profecto vir iste beatus, licet miracula meritis Sancti Bernardini attribueret, et cum bireto ipsius se abscondere niteretur, fiebant tamen mirabilia propter ipsius maximam fidem, ardentissimam charitatem [...] Nam saepe infirmi, cum bireto Sancti Bernardini signati, nullum sanitatis consequebantur beneficium ; sed postea revertentes et manibus Patris contrectati, sanabantur.*

de la façon dont Christophe de Varèse entend surmonter l'aporie à laquelle mène la glorification d'un homme fondée en partie sur la gloire d'un autre. La barrette de Bernardin est en effet à l'origine d'un bref processus de reconstruction hagiographique, lorsque au détour d'une description de miracle est affirmé le pouvoir thaumaturgique de Capistran, très tôt dans son parcours, par le biais de sa propre calotte. Ainsi, ce qu'avait fait le saint en Europe centrale grâce au *medium* de la relique de son maître, il l'avait déjà fait plus jeune, en une sorte de « relique vivante » :

> Alors que l'homme de Dieu avait à peine achevé sa troisième année dans l'Ordre, un jour qu'il marchait dans le cloître, il rencontra un homme en proie au délire, à l'esprit totalement dérangé ; pris d'une immense compassion pour lui et pleinement confiant dans les bienfaits de Dieu, il alla vers lui et imposa sa barrette sur sa tête. Alors, l'homme retrouva ses esprits et recouvra la raison[31].

Si l'hagiographe en vient à ce type de procédé, c'est aussi que du vivant même du réformateur italien des voix s'étaient probablement élevées pour relativiser, voire même nier les mérites du « proto-saint ». Le fait est signalé par l'autre grand biographe de Capistran, Nicolas de Fara, qui avait également franchi les Alpes avec lui :

> Nous passons sous silence les miracles réalisés en ce lieu, autant parce que les détracteurs de Jean les attribuent à Bernardin (puisque beaucoup, mais pas tous, sont intervenus au toucher de ses reliques) que pour ne pas dégoûter et épuiser le lecteur par un long discours[32].

Et Nicolas d'insister sur le fait que son héros avait déjà effectué des miracles du vivant de Bernardin, en plusieurs endroits d'Italie, ce qui ne pouvait être nié, comme le montre le bref récit de la guérison de l'insensé par le jeune frère Capistran grâce à sa propre barrette, que l'on trouve donc également chez Nicolas de Fara[33].

---

[31] *Ibid.*, p. 504, c. 52 : *Dum vir Dei vix adhuc tertium annum complevisset in Ordine, quadam vice per claustrum ambulans, obvium habuit quemdam mente captum, totaliter in capite destructum ; cui nimia compassione compatiens, et in beneficiis Dei plene confidens, accessit ad eum, et biretum suum capiti ejus imponens, ad mentem rediit, et sanitati est restitutus.*
[32] *Vita S. Joannis a Capistrano, Scripta a Fr. Nicolao de Fara, ex ms. Aracœlitano*, dans *Acta Sanctorum*, Oct. X, Paris, Bruxelles, 1861, p. 457, c. 53 : *Quae quidem miracula ideo silentio hoc in loco praetereamus, tum quia Joannis detractores ea sancto adscribant Bernardino, quandoquidem ad tactum suarum reliquiarum multa, etsi non omnia, facta fuisse contendant, tum quia, ne longiori oratione lectorem fastidiosum molestumque reddamus.*
[33] *Ibid.*, p. 458, c. 58 : *Ac ne putemus ea meritis Beati Bernardini tantum facta extitisse et non suis : similia ante dormitionem Bernardini per illum Dominum operatum fuisse, in plerisque Italiae partibus, non est qui inficiari possit. Nam hic, vivente adhuc in hoc saeculo Beato Bernardino, multa signa et prodigia fecit.* L'épisode de la barrette suit immédiatement (c. 59).

Dans le récit de Christophe de Varèse, le séjour de Capistran à Cracovie (de la fin de l'été 1453 au printemps 1454) est incontestablement marqué par une augmentation des miracles attribués à un vœu formulé explicitement à saint Bernardin par le bénéficiaire. Le miracle peut également être lié au fait d'être présent dans un lieu de culte qui lui a été dédié, ou à un vœu de se rendre ensuite dans une église Saint-Bernardin pour lui rendre grâce – et l'on a alors affaire à ce que Stanko Andrić appelle un miracle « recyclé », puisque l'enchaînement d'un vœu de visite à une église Saint-Bernardin puis d'un miracle se trouve au départ dans le *Liber miraculorum sancti Bernardini*[34]. Le discours hagiographique se fait l'écho et participe d'une pastorale de l'implantation qui, à l'instar des indulgences, vise à encourager la *visitatio* de nouveaux lieux de culte, puisqu'à Vienne, Breslau et Cracovie chaque fondation de couvent est suivie d'un miracle. Plus encore, sous le récit hagiographique, à visée didactique, on distingue la réalité d'une stratégie de communication qui met le miraculeux au service de la sacralisation d'un *lieu*, opération généralement effectuée pour les lancements de pèlerinages. L'épisode de la fondation du couvent de Breslau, à Pâques 1453, est significatif : le miracle y fait partie intégrante d'une séquence ritualisée, avec célébration, procession et prise de possession des lieux[35].

Dans le *Liber miraculorum*, plus de la moitié (47) des miracles décrits par Conrad de Freystadt sont intervenus en relation avec une visite à l'église des Observants de Cracovie récemment fondée dans le faubourg de Stradom. Anna Zajchowska et Marcin Starzyński ont souligné que ni les sources médiévales connues, ni la plus ancienne description des églises cracoviennes et de leurs reliques, *Bijoux de la ville capitale de Cracovie* (*Klejnoty stołecznego miasta Krakowa*, 1745) de Piotr Pruszcz ne font mention d'une quelconque relique de Bernardin qui aurait été conservée dans cette église[36]. Elle ne devint un centre de pèlerinage qu'après la mort de Simon de Lipnica (1482). On a là, peut-être, un indice de plus de la propension qu'eurent les fidèles de la fin du Moyen Âge à vénérer les représentations des saints davantage que leurs reliques, comme

---

[34] S. Andrić, *The Miracles of St. John Capistran*, Budapest, 2000, p. 195-196.
[35] *Vita S. Joannis a Capistrano, Scripta a Fr. Christophoro a Varisio*, op. cit., p. 527, c. 163 : *In eadem etiam civitate* [= Breslau] *vel suburbio ejus recepit locum, qui MCCCCLIII, in die parasceves, conclusa praedicatione Passionis Domini in civitate per Patrem, et Jesu posito in sepulcro, deferendo ipsum sepulcrum per Fratres cum maxima comitiva populi civitatis et cleri processionaliter ordinati, solemniter traditus est, et susceptus ad laudem et gloriam Dei et sancti Bernardini, in cujus titulo est consecratus. In quo positi sunt novitii, in Lipsk et alibi per eum vestiti ducenti usque hodie, et proficientes in vita et Observantia regulari. Quo in loco Domini cuidam vulnerato ad mortem, de cujus vita spes nulla erat promissus per alium amicum suum, scilicet quod si visitaret Ecclesiam sancti Bernardini sanitati pristinae restitutus esset.*
[36] A. Zajchowska, M. Starzyński, « Le culte de saint Bernardin de Sienne », art. cit., p. 80.

André Vauchez l'avait noté dans sa grande thèse[37] ; peut-être a-t-on là aussi, ou davantage, un indice supplémentaire que les Franciscains n'ont jamais fait jouer à la relique le rôle de « pile au cœur du sanctuaire »[38] polarisant la dévotion sur une localisation géographique précise que bien d'autres familles religieuses lui ont fait jouer. Les Mineurs, et particulièrement leurs tendances réformatrices, ont davantage trouvé leur compte dans la promotion de l'hostie, qui favorisait une religiosité particulièrement christo-centrée, certes, mais aussi une « mobilité sacrée » contre laquelle se multiplièrent les critiques au XVe siècle.

De la monstration de la barrette de Bernardin jusqu'aux massacres de Juifs, l'action de Capistran et de son entourage eut une totale cohérence dont la dimension économique, souvent invoquée à propos des Observants italiens, ne doit pas prendre le pas, dans les analyses, sur la dimension dévotionnelle et pastorale, poussée à l'extrême dans le contexte particulier de la tournée en Europe centrale. Il s'est agi de l'agencement de plusieurs éléments relevant du lien étroit, noué jusqu'à un extrême degré, entre le *faire voir* et le *faire croire*, au service du culte eucharistique comme du Nom de Dieu. L'action pastorale de Capistran et de ses compagnons, ayant pour pivot la sainteté de Bernardin de Sienne, insista probablement sur le Nom de Jésus comme elle insistait sur le Corps sanglant du Christ. Au printemps 1453, la persécution des Juifs de Silésie, accusés de profanation de l'hostie et de blasphème sur le Nom de Dieu, constitua ainsi non seulement le prolongement ou la conséquence de la pastorale du franciscain italien, mais l'un de ses éléments constitutifs, en une violence *exemplaire*, c'est-à-dire intégrée dans une séquence à valeur d'*exemplum* : une histoire simple à la fin édifiante[39].

De la sainteté-étendard à la figure « totémique »

Les traces du culte de saint Bernardin qui ont été repérées par les chercheurs, y compris en Pologne, sont en définitive assez peu nombreuses[40] ; elles s'inscrivent, en outre, dans une chronologie très resserrée, celle des années qui suivirent le passage de Capistran et la fondation des couvents de Breslau et Cracovie. Le fait que, sur le retable réalisé pour les Observants de Kamenz,

---

[37] A. VAUCHEZ, *La sainteté en Occident aux derniers siècles du Moyen Âge d'après les procès de canonisation et les documents hagiographiques*, Rome, 1981, p. 519-529.
[38] Pour reprendre une expression de Jacques Chiffoleau lors du colloque *Transferts de reliques et circulation des dévotions (milieu XIVe – milieu XVIIe s.)* organisé à Chambéry les 16-17 mars 2007 dans le cadre du programme *Identités franciscaines à l'âge des réformes*.
[39] Voir L. VIALLET, *Les sens de l'observance, op. cit.*, p. 141-152.
[40] A. ZAJCHOWSKA, M. STARZYŃSKI, « Le culte de saint Bernardin de Sienne », *art. cit.*, p. 83, à la suite de Jerzy Kłoczowski, qui a signalé la quasi-absence du prénom Bernardin chez les laïcs.

daté de 1513, Bernardin soit représenté aux côtés de saint François, entourant le Christ et au-dessus des religieux martyrisés au Maroc en 1220, témoigne moins d'un regain de ce culte qu'il ne dit quelque chose du « profil identitaire » de la sainteté bernardinienne – et peut-être, plus largement, du « profil identitaire » observant en Silésie et Haute Lusace : les retables qui y furent réalisés pour des églises de Franciscains observants au tout début du XVIᵉ siècle ont pour thème important, traité sous des formes archaïsantes, le combat contre l'infidèle[41]. Le choix des motifs iconographiques – qui exaltaient l'Église militante face à la menace de l'hérétique et accordaient une place majeure à l'Eucharistie – n'avait évidemment rien de fortuit, au moment où se faisait plus que jamais sentir le besoin de réaffirmer l'attachement, mis en doute par leurs adversaires au sein de l'Ordre, des « Bernardins » à la famille franciscaine.

En 1510, à Goldberg (Złotoryja), dans le contexte des tentatives de réunion évoquées au début de cette étude, la prédication d'un religieux représentant les *Reformaten* tendrait à confirmer que le nom même de « Bernardins » était au cœur des débats, tant il était aisé, pour les adversaires des Observants, d'en faire la preuve éclatante de leur sécession et de leur refus de l'union alors même, disait le frère, que « nous formons un tout et qu'il n'y a pas de 'Bernardins' ou de 'frères de saint Bernardin', mais que nous sommes tous franciscains »[42]. Ainsi, dans le contexte de fragmentation et de dissolution identitaire que connaissait l'Ordre des Mineurs au début du XVIᵉ siècle, émergeait un terme, celui de « franciscain », et les frères faisaient appel, en désespoir de cause, à l'Autorité par excellence, celle de leur père. La sainteté réformatrice et missionnaire de Bernardin de Sienne, propagée par Capistran, fut balayée d'un revers de main par certains religieux excédés. Les plaintes du gardien de Crossen (Krosno Odrzańskie) adressées au capitaine de Glogau (Głogów) contre « la nouvelle secte des Bernardins », le 8 septembre 1501, sont à ce titre significatives des crispations suscitées par la présence de religieux revendiquant leur différence : avant de s'en prendre à un mode de vie marqué davantage par l'insistance sur la clôture

---

[41] Voir J. Kostowski, « Die Ausstattung der Franziskanerobservanten-Kirchen in Schlesien und in der Oberlausitz im ausgehenden Mittelalter », dans *Böhmen – Oberlausitz – Tschechien. Aspekte einer Nachbarschaft*, éd. L.-A. Dannenberg, M. Hermann, A. Klaffenböck, Görlitz-Zittau, 2006 (Neues Lausitzisches Magazin, Beiheft 3), p. 79-88. Pour une mise en contexte de la réalisation du retable de Kamenz, voir J. W. Einhorn, « Unter den Fuß gebracht. Todesleiden und Triumph der franziskanischen Märtyrer von Marokko 1220 », dans *Europa und die Welt in der Geschichte. Festschrift zum 60. Geburtstag von Dieter Berg*, éd. R. Averkorn, W. Eberhard, R. Haas, B. Schmies, Bochum, 2004, p. 447-483.
[42] F. Doelle, *Die Observanzbewegung, op. cit.*, p. 85, n. 1 : *jam totum sumus unum, jam nulli sunt Bernhardinenses vel fratres s. Bern[ar]dini, sed omnes sumus Franciscini.*

et la réaffirmation de la césure entre clercs et laïcs (« ils ont honte de visiter les pauvres, de maison en maison, comme nous devons le faire selon notre règle... »[43]), il avait dirigé sa critique contre le fait de tromper les fidèles en se réclamant, par le nom même, de la sainteté – importée depuis des terres étrangères – d'un homme qui n'avait jamais créé d'ordre ni laissé de règle[44].

Lors de la période d'élaboration de la théologie réformatrice « luthérienne », puis au moment des choix décisifs, les Franciscains observants furent en première ligne, à Jüterbog pendant le Carême et le temps pascal 1519 face aux prêches de Franz Günthers et Thomas Müntzer, à Wittenberg lors de la *disputatio* d'octobre 1519. Les échanges, qui cherchèrent le discrédit de l'adversaire plus que l'approfondissement théologique, dévoilent le poids des héritages (en particulier celui des affrontements avec les réformes de Bohême) et renvoyèrent les frères à un questionnement sur leur propre histoire et leur identité, à travers le statut de François et de ses stigmates, mais aussi les places respectives du travail et de la mendicité ainsi que leur passé (et leur présent) d'incessantes querelles internes. L'appellation de « Franciscains » fut dénoncée, puisque le seul nom qui vaille, fondé sur le seul Christ, à l'intérieur d'une Église qui devait être unité, était celui de « Chrétien ». La critique, fondée en particulier sur Paul (1 Cor. 1, 10-13), concernait la division : se revendiquer d'un personnage, c'était rompre l'unité de l'Église en créant des *sectae*, après avoir rejeté le nom de Dieu. L'accusation fut utilisée par Luther dans son *De votis monasticis* de 1521[45]. À l'encontre des Franciscains, la critique réformée dépassait la seule question de l'unité de l'Église chrétienne ; ou plutôt, elle la poussait à son plus haut point, en faisant reposer

---

[43] Chr. REISCH, *Urkundenbuch der Kustodien Goldberg und Breslau, I : 1240-1517*, Düsseldorf, 1917, n° 751, p. 324 : « Dy alleyn dem vorgenanten orden gross vordriß und schaden thwen und eyn gar vil closter awßleschen ader off mynste geringern gotesdynst, geystliches leben und bruderliche lybe, wenne sy alleyne bütthen wellen eyn sthetin beyn edeln und reychen lewten, sich schemen von hawße czw hawße noch unserm regel dy armen pawr czw besuchen alß wyr armen mwssen thwen ». Passage en espacement développé par mes soins.

[44] *Ibid.* : « [...] dy newe secte der Bernhardiner, dy do sich krönen und rühmen eyner fremden heligket, durch welche sy betrigen dy werleth, zo doch S. Bernhardinus, als y mir got helffe und alle zeyne heligen, keynen orden und regel ny hot gemacht, sondern under der czvchth und regel S. Francisci, dem sy vorkysen eym namen und vorlogken, ist heligk gestorben ».

[45] *D. Martin Luthers Werke. Kritische Gesammtausgabe*, 8, Weimar, 1889, p. 618, l. 5-13 : *At institutio voti, dum docet opera, fidem evacuat (ut diximus) et inde abiecto nomine Dei suum erigunt. Neque enim Christiani amplius nec filii Dei, sed Benedictini, Dominicani, Franciscani, Augustiniani dicuntur: hos et suos patres prae Christo iactant. Neque enim hoc nomine salui et iusti fieri praesumunt, quod baptisati, quod Christiani sunt, sed hoc solo, quod sui ordinis nomen habent. Ideo in suum nomen confidunt, in hoc gloriantur, quasi baptismus et fides iam olim velut naufragio perierint. Non ergo assumunt et invocant nomen Domini nisi in vanum, sed nomen suum, quod per opera erexerunt.*

la menace sur le statut même de François – « autre Christ » – aux yeux de ceux qui s'en réclamaient. Pour Johann Eberlin von Günzburg (v. 1470-1533) comme pour d'autres, le *De Conformitate* de Barthélemy de Pise – approuvé au chapitre d'Assise de 1399, mais imprimé au début du XVIe siècle – ainsi que bien des sermons et des images témoignaient des tentatives pour élever François à la hauteur du Christ, en une véritable idolâtrie[46]. Comme l'a démontré Servus Gieben, l'emblème franciscain des « Conformités » était apparu à la fin du XVe siècle en terre flamande[47] : l'iconographie contemporaine de la canonisation de Bonaventure (1482) et un texte publié en flamand en 1518, *La vigne de saint François*, en attribuaient l'origine à un choix du Docteur séraphique ; il s'agissait encore de deux mains réunies par un même clou, soulignant l'éternelle union de chaque frère mineur, et de l'Ordre tout entier, au Christ crucifié. Le glissement se fit en quelques années, au tournant des XVe-XVIe siècles, puisque la forme « classique » de l'emblème (deux bras croisés montrant clairement, l'un, la plaie du Christ, l'autre, les stigmates de François) se trouve représentée dans la seconde édition du traité de Barthélemy de Pise, en 1513. À ce parallèle exaltant l'exceptionnelle conformité du Fondateur au Christ, par les stigmates, allait s'attaquer quelques décennies plus tard avec un extrême degré d'intensité le traité réformé d'Érasme Alber intitulé *Der Barfuser Muenche Eulenspiegel und Alcoran* (1542).

La critique violente du culte de leurs saints patrons par les Mendiants n'était pas nouvelle, puisqu'elle était déjà présente au XIIIe siècle[48]. Forçons le trait : identitaire, la sainteté de Bernardin l'a été ; et elle l'a tellement été, qu'elle n'a peut-être été que cela[49]. Celle de Capistran, même officieuse, l'est

---

[46] Le traité *De Conformitate vitae Beati Francisci ad vitam Domini Jesu redemptoris nostri* de Bartolomeo degli Albizzi a été d'abord imprimé à Venise, s. d., puis à Milan en 1510 et 1513. Sur les retombées de cette œuvre à l'époque moderne, voir notamment E. LABROUSSE, « Bayle et saint François », dans *Mouvements franciscains et société française, XIIe-XXe siècles (Études présentées à la Table ronde du CNRS, 23 octobre 1982)*, éd. A. VAUCHEZ, Paris, 1984, p. 149-155.

[47] S. GIEBEN, *Lo stemma francescano. Origine e sviluppo*, Rome, 2009, p. 12-17 et p. 34-35.

[48] Voir, pour le processus d'« exaltation hyperbolique » de la figure de saint François, l'étude classique d'A. VAUCHEZ, « Les stigmates de saint François et leurs détracteurs dans les derniers siècles du Moyen Âge », *Mélanges d'archéologie et d'histoire*, 80 (1968), p. 595-625, en particulier p. 606-608 et p. 618-623.

[49] Quelle qu'ait été par ailleurs l'ampleur du projet des réformateurs pour une *renovatio* de la société, s'accompagnant de l'assimilation du saint observant au prophète de l'Écriture (principalement Moïse) ou à l'apôtre néo-testamentaire (Paul), comme l'a souligné D. SOLVI, « Il culto dei santi », *art. cit.*, p. 152 – mais il convient de bien faire la part entre modèle identitaire et réalité sociale. Sur la dimension de modèle originel, dont il fallait être l'imitateur, que Bernardin de Sienne eut pour Jacques de la Marche et d'autres de ses compagnons, voir L. TURCHI, « Bernardino da Siena e la santità di Giacomo della Marca : dal 'prendere forma' del discepolo alla 'costruzione dell'immagine' del Maestro », dans

aussi devenue, à voir comment les édiles de la ville de Görlitz utilisèrent en février 1507, dans la *Recognitio* concédée au frère Martin Tinctoris, la référence au passage du prédicateur cinquante-quatre ans auparavant, ce qui leur permit de raccrocher leur action à un projet *observant*[50]. Dans le contexte de division et de rivalité entre branches de l'Ordre, qui impliquait la nécessité, inédite jusqu'alors, de se distinguer et d'être identifié, les saints des Observants ont eu tendance à être érigés en figures quasi *totémiques*. On touche ici, plus largement, à la question du modèle (François) et des modèles « intercalés » (entre le Fondateur et les frères) : des personnages qui ont défini, infléchi voire redéfini le *propositum* ; des figures auxquelles étaient rattachées un ensemble de valeurs, dans la fidélité à une image construite, plus ou moins proche de ce que chaque personnage avait été de son vivant ; des cautions spirituelles devenues, en quelque sorte, cautions identitaires et signes de reconnaissance, à l'instar – mais le cas est sans doute extrême – d'une stricte contemporaine de Bernardin de Sienne, Colette de Corbie, pour les frères « colétans »[51].

Gemma Lucens. Giacomo della Marca tra devozione e santità. Atti dei convegni (Napoli, 20 novembre 2009; Monteprandone, 27 novembre 2010), éd. F. SERPICO, Florence, 2013, p. 13-48.

[50] Sur ce document, édité par F. DOELLE, *Die Martinianische Reformbewegung in der Sächsischen Franziskanerprovinz*, Münster, 1916, Annexe 5, p. 151-153, voir L. VIALLET, *Les sens de l'observance, op. cit.*, p. 215-218. Cet acte est un véritable brevet de bonne vie franciscaine délivré à un religieux désireux de passer à l'Observance. Après un demi-siècle de prises de position et d'engagements réformateurs des autorités urbaines en faveur de la voie moyenne (mais dans une version plus stricte, sous l'égide du *visitator regiminis*) et dans le refus de l'Observance des vicaires, la référence à Capistran permettait de se placer dans le même héritage que la réforme longtemps rivale.

[51] Comment définir le rapport entre les Franciscains « colétans » (très proches, dans leur *propositum*, des *Reformaten* germaniques, car ils étaient, les uns et les autres, des « Martiniens ») et Colette de Corbie ? Remarques et pistes de réflexion dans L. VIALLET, « Colette of Corbie and the *de observantia* Franciscan Reforms in the First Half of the Fifteenth Century », dans *A Companion to Colette of Corbie*, éd. J. MUELLER, N. BRADLEY WARREN, Leyde, 2016, p. 76-100.

III
SAINTS D'IMPLANTATION ET SAINTS DE SOUCHE

Saint national ou saint européen ?
Les tribulations d'Adalbert de Prague et de ses reliques dans le temps et dans l'espace (X^e-XIIe siècles)

Geneviève BÜHRER-THIERRY
(Paris)

En 1979, dans sa communication intitulée « Saints d'implantation, saints de souche dans les pays évangélisés de l'Europe du Centre-Est », Aleksander Gieysztor étudiait à la fois les vocables des églises de la nouvelle Chrétienté, la diffusion des reliques et des noms des saints notamment en Pologne et en Bohême, et parvenait chaque fois à la conclusion qu'Adalbert de Prague avait été le premier – et longtemps le seul – « saint de souche » associé aux grandes figures que sont la Trinité, la Vierge, saint Pierre ou saint Jean Baptiste et aux saints militaires comme saint Georges ou saint Maurice[1]. Adalbert apparaît ainsi comme le prototype du saint autochtone de la nouvelle Chrétienté. Mais le fait qu'il soit reconnu comme saint patron de la Pologne, de la Bohême, voire de la Hongrie[2], amène à s'interroger sur ce que peut être son caractère de saint « national ».

Cet Adalbert, Vojtěch de son nom tchèque, est un personnage fascinant et particulièrement bien documenté, puisqu'il a bénéficié rapidement de la rédaction de *Vitae* par ses propres contemporains[3]. La première, dite *Vita Prior*, a été produite en Italie vers l'an 1000, à la demande de l'empereur Otton III, probablement par un moine de Saint-Boniface-et-Alexis de Rome, Jean Canaparius, ou bien, si l'on se rallie à l'hypothèse de Johannes

---

[1] A. GIEYSZTOR, « Saints d'implantation, saints de souche dans les pays évangélisés de l'Europe du Centre-Est » dans *Hagiographie, culture et sociétés (IVe-XIIe s.), Actes du colloque organisé à Nanterre et Paris (2-5 mai 1979)*, Paris, 1981, p. 573-584.
[2] Sur les relations d'Adalbert avec la Hongrie, dont je ne traiterai pas ici, on peut encore utiliser la synthèse de Th. VON BOGYAY, « Adalbert von Prag und die Ungarn – ein Problem der Quellen-interpretation », *Ungarn Jahrbuch*, 7 (1976), p. 9-36.
[3] Sur l'ensemble de cette production, I. N. WOOD, *The Missionary Life. Saints and the Evangelisation of Europe (400-1050)*, Londres, 2001, p. 207-239.

Les saints et leur culte en Europe centrale au Moyen Âge (XIe-début du XVIe siècle), éd. par Marie-Madeleine de CEVINS et Olivier MARIN, Turnhout, 2017 (*Hagiologia*, 13), p. 247-260.

Fried, dans l'entourage de l'évêque de Liège Notker[4]. La seconde, beaucoup plus longue, est l'œuvre de Brunon de Querfurt[5], qui l'a rédigée entre 1004 et 1008, en reprenant partiellement des éléments de la première *Vita*, alors même qu'il attendait en Pologne une opportunité pour partir évangéliser la Prusse[6].

Le carrefour du nouveau monde

Si l'on veut situer la naissance de Vojtěch – qui n'est pas encore Adalbert – vers 956 dans son contexte, on doit d'abord souligner qu'il voit le jour au sein d'une des familles les plus prestigieuses de Bohême, les Slavnikides, que l'historiographie traditionnelle représentait comme des concurrents directs de la puissance princière établie en Bohême par les Přemyslides depuis la fin du IXe siècle. On a plutôt tendance à considérer aujourd'hui Slavnik, le père de Vojtěch, comme un des représentants de la puissance přemyslide en Bohême orientale : vers 950, il s'installe à Libice, où Vojtěch est probablement né, et administre depuis ce siège l'ensemble de la région pour le compte du duc přemyslide. Il n'en reste pas moins que Slavnik et sa famille ne peuvent être décrits comme des « fonctionnaires », mais doivent être considérés comme des aristocrates qui déploient, en s'appuyant sur la faveur princière, une puissance qui peut finir par inquiéter le duc lui-même. Mais il faut aussi insister sur la situation « géopolitique » très particulière de la Bohême où Vojtěch est né, une région qui apparaît comme un véritable carrefour du nouveau monde qui s'ouvre vers l'Est.

---

[4] *Vies de saint Adalbert de Prague*, éd. J. KARWASINSKA, Varsovie, 1962-1969 (*Monumenta Poloniae Historica*, series nova, 4/2). Il existe trois rédactions de cette *Vita* dont la tradition est assez complexe. Voir la discussion ainsi qu'une nouvelle édition-traduction (en anglais) par C. GAȘPAR, « The Life of saint Adalbert, Bishop of Prag and Martyr » dans *Saints of the Christianisation Age of Central Europe (10th-11th c.)*, éd. G. KLANICZAY, Budapest, 2012, p. 79-181 – citée désormais, à partir de cette dernière édition, *Vita Prior*. L'attribution de ce texte au milieu liégeois, défendue par J. FRIED, « Gnesen-Aachen-Rom. Otto III. und der Kult des hl. Adalbert. Beobachtungen zum älteren Adalbertsleben », dans *Polen und Deutschland vor 1000 Jahren. Die Berliner Tagung über den Akt von Gnesen*, éd. M. BORGOLTE, Berlin, 2002, p. 235-279, a été étayée par J. HOFFMANN, *Vita Adalberti. Früheste Textüberlieferungen der Lebensgeschichte Adalberts von Prag*, Essen, 2005.
[5] *Vies de saint Adalbert de Prague*, éd. J. KARWASINSKA, Varsovie, 1962-1969 (*Monumenta Poloniae Historica*, series nova, 4/2) – désormais citée : Brunon. Sur l'ensemble de ces *Vitae*, voir en dernier lieu I. N. WOOD, « Hagiographie und Mission (700-1050) », dans *Credo : Christianisierung Europas im Mittelalter*, éd. Ch. STIEGEMANN, Paderborn, 2013, p. 121-129.
[6] Sur Brunon, R. WENSKUS, *Studien zur historisch-politischen Gedankenwelt Bruns von Querfurt*, Münster-Cologne, 1956 et plus récemment *Der heilige Brun von Querfurt : eine Reise ins Mittelalter*, éd. J. RUDOLPH et M. KÜHNEL, Querfurt, 2009.

Le duché de Bohême est un « État » tributaire de l'empire germanique depuis la fin du IXe siècle et il entretient des relations privilégiés avec les Saxons et les Bavarois[7], ces derniers ayant été particulièrement actifs dans le processus d'évangélisation de la région qui a débuté à l'époque carolingienne et ayant retardé aussi longtemps que possible la fondation d'un diocèse autonome, de manière à conserver l'autorité de l'évêque de Ratisbonne sur toute la zone. C'est pourquoi le diocèse de Prague n'a été créé qu'en 973, alors que toute la population était officiellement chrétienne depuis longtemps. Pour se dégager de la tutelle bavaroise, les grands de Bohême ont tissé de nombreux liens avec l'aristocratie saxonne tout au long du Xe siècle : le premier évêque attesté en 973 est d'ailleurs un Saxon issu du monastère de Corvey, et le nouveau diocèse fut rattaché non pas à la province ecclésiastique de Salzbourg – malgré les véhémentes protestations de l'archevêque – ni à celle de Magdebourg, qui commandait à l'ensemble des évêchés de mission (ce que Prague n'était pas), mais à celle de Mayence, qui représentait le cœur de la puissance ecclésiastique du royaume, créant ainsi un des rares cas de province ecclésiastique dont le territoire ne soit pas contigu[8].

Vojtěch est donc né en un lieu qui est déjà un carrefour d'influences, mais il est né aussi à un moment spécifique : vers 956, c'est-à-dire aux alentours de la bataille du Lechfeld (955), il représente cette génération qui voit s'ouvrir les frontières au centre de l'Europe, qui voit changer les équilibres et se construire de nouveaux pouvoirs. Il est né en quelque sorte sur une frontière, la frontière de la Chrétienté, au moment où la mission orientale prend un nouvel essor et gagne des territoires et des populations avec une rapidité surprenante. En effet, à peine cinquante ans après la bataille du Lechfeld, autour de l'an mil, deux grands ensembles chrétiens se sont constitués : d'une part autour de la dynastie des Arpads de Hongrie, dont Étienne, le premier roi, sera rapidement reconnu comme saint, d'autre part autour de celle des Piasts de Pologne, deux dynasties qui construisent leur pouvoir en transformant la société païenne en société chrétienne et notamment en fondant des centres de pouvoir religieux, comme les Přesmyslides l'avaient fait en Bohême un siècle plus tôt[9].

---

[7] Vue d'ensemble dans : M.-M. DE CEVINS, *L'Europe centrale au Moyen Âge*, Rennes, 2013, p. 53-60 ; point précis : F. GRAUS, « Böhmen zwischen Bayern und Sachsen. Zur böhmischen Kirchengeschichte des 10. Jahrhunderts », *Historica*, 17 (1969), p. 5-42.
[8] Pour une vue d'ensemble, J. KŁOCZOWSKI, « La nouvelle Chrétienté du monde occidental », dans *Histoire du christianisme, IV : Évêques, moines et empereurs (610-1054)*, éd. J.-M. MAYEUR *et al.*, Paris, 1993, p. 875-886.
[9] G. BÜHRER-THIERRY, *Aux marges du monde germanique : l'évêque, le prince, les païens (VIIIe-XIe s.)*, Turnhout, 2014, p. 251-264.

Vojtěch est élevé à Libice dans la maison de son père, puis il est envoyé parfaire son éducation à l'école cathédrale de Magdebourg, en 972. Les maîtres de cette école sont très réputés, mais le choix vient certainement de relations privilégiés entre la famille de Slavnik et la métropole saxonne, comme le montre aussi la transformation du nom de son fils qui prend le nom d'Adalbert, par référence à l'évêque saxon qui l'a confirmé : en abandonnant son nom slave de Vojtěch au profit de celui de l'archevêque Adalbert de Magdebourg, qui a été un des premiers ecclésiastiques en charge de la mission – quoique sans succès – vers le monde russe, Adalbert de Prague devient une figure emblématique à la fois de la mission vers l'Est et de l'allégeance à l'Église impériale, et par là-même, à l'empereur saxon.

En 983, Adalbert devient le second évêque de Prague, et le premier Tchèque à recevoir l'onction épiscopale. Il est investi de son évêché par l'empereur Otton II lui-même, au plaid de Vérone, quelques mois avant sa mort. Adalbert devient évêque lorsque s'ouvre le règne d'Otton III qui transforme radicalement la conception de l'empire germanique en l'imaginant – on peut même dire en le rêvant – comme un empire universel, c'est-à-dire sans limite et dont la puissance d'intégration doit passer d'abord par l'extension de la Chrétienté[10]. Adalbert participe à cette politique aux côtés d'Otton III, avec lequel il tisse des liens privilégiés sans être pour autant un pur instrument de la politique ottonienne, comme on va le voir.

La situation d'Adalbert en Bohême est rendue difficile par la concurrence accrue entre sa propre famille, les Slavnikides, et la famille ducale : si les Slavnikides ont développé des liens privilégiés avec l'aristocratie et les églises saxonnes, les Přemyslides sont restés plus proches de la Bavière et notamment du duc Henri (c'est-à-dire le futur empereur Henri II). Mais surtout, les Slavnikides utilisent leurs bonnes relations avec la dynastie impériale saxonne pour étendre leur domination au cœur de la Bohême, dans la région de Prague qui est le centre du pouvoir des Přemyslides. Il ne fait guère de doute que le choix d'Adalbert comme évêque en 983 est le fruit de cette alliance et déplaît probablement au duc de Bohême.

Les Přemyslides sont également fragilisés sur leur frontière orientale par la montée en puissance de la dynastie polonaise des Piasts, l'enjeu principal étant le contrôle de la Silésie, qui, pour l'heure, est aux mains des Tchèques ; or, les Slavnikides ont établi leur centre de pouvoir entre Prague et Cracovie, leurs forteresses dominent la grande route commerciale qui va de Ratisbonne à Kiev en passant par Prague et Cracovie, et dont les bénéfices font

---

[10] Voir par exemple G. Althoff, *Otto III.*, Darmstad, 1996 ou encore E. Eickhoff, *Kaiser Otto III. : die erste Jahrtausendwende und die Entfaltung Europas*, Stuttgart, 2000.

la fortune des lignages de l'aristocratie tchèque, au premier rang desquels la famille ducale[11]. La condamnation par Adalbert du trafic des esclaves chrétiens qui alimentait les caisses ducales n'est sans doute pas non plus du goût des Přemyslides.

Les Slavnikides qui fondent des églises, battent leur propre monnaie et ont mis la main sur le diocèse de Prague, se lient aussi par un pacte d'amitié avec le duc piast Boleslas le Vaillant (Chrobry) à la fin des années 980. Tous ces éléments exacerbent la compétition entre Slavnikides et Přemyslides, qui s'emploient à rendre la tâche d'Adalbert à Prague particulièrement ardue : le pouvoir épiscopal n'est pas suffisamment établi pour être capable de s'exercer hors de tout appui du pouvoir politique dont il reste dépendant[12]. Ce sont ces difficultés qui conduisent Adalbert à abandonner son siège une première fois en 988 et c'est ici que commencent les tribulations du saint évêque.

Les tribulations d'Adalbert de Prague

Chassé de son siège par l'hostilité des Přesmyslides à la fin des années 980, Adalbert aurait envisagé de se rendre en pèlerinage à Jérusalem et aurait même obtenu pour cela des subsides de l'impératrice Théophano. Accompagné de son demi-frère Radim, qui porte le nom latin de Gaudentius, et du prévôt de la cathédrale de Prague Williko, il se rend en Italie dans l'intention de résigner sa charge. Accueilli quelque temps au Mont-Cassin, il envisage de devenir définitivement moine au monastère Saint-Boniface-et-Saint-Alexis de Rome, sur l'Aventin.

Sa situation canonique est peu claire : il se considère lui-même destitué de sa charge de sa propre volonté, mais les moines du Mont-Cassin souhaitent le retenir pour utiliser ses prérogatives épiscopales, notamment pour consacrer leurs nouvelles églises. Quant au synode romain, il le considère toujours comme un évêque titulaire, mais qui a manqué aux devoirs de sa charge. C'est pourquoi l'archevêque de Mayence, Willigis, obtient facilement du pape qu'il le renvoie sur son siège épiscopal, où Adalbert retourne en 992.

Entre-temps, en Bohême, la situation s'est encore détériorée. Adalbert ne peut agir selon son gré, il est également démuni devant la désobéissance du troupeau qu'on lui a confié, ces ouailles ne l'écoutent pas et ne comprennent

---

[11] P. CHARVÁT, « Bohemia, Moravia and Long-Distance Trade in the 10th and 11th centuries », *Quaestiones medii aevi novae*, 5 (2000), p. 255-266.
[12] A. GIEYSZTOR, « *Sanctus et gloriosissimus martyr Christi Adalbertus* : un État et une Église missionnaire aux alentours de l'an Mille » dans *La conversione al cristianesimo nell'Europa dell'alto medioevo* (Settimane di studio del Centro italiano di studi sull'alto medioevo, 14), Spolète, 1967, p. 611-648.

pas ses sermons[13] : en gros ils ne voient pas en quoi ce qu'ils font est répréhensible, dès lors qu'ils sont baptisés et donc, en principe, chrétiens[14]. Ce qu'Adalbert leur reproche touche d'ailleurs différents domaines de l'organisation de la société et au premier chef l'inobservance des règles de l'union chrétienne à plusieurs niveaux : ils s'adonnent à la luxure, ils épousent leurs proches parents et ils pratiquent la polygamie. En outre, même les clercs sont mariés et commettent éventuellement des adultères avec les épouses des autres : l'épisode de la matrone adultère égorgée sur l'autel même de la cathédrale aurait conduit Adalbert à renoncer définitivement à occuper son siège épiscopal[15]. Mais il est clair que c'est aussi l'hostilité grandissante entre les Přemyslides et la famille d'Adalbert qui le pousse à quitter son siège une nouvelle fois, vers 994-995, peu de temps avant que la famille ducale n'organise le massacre de tous les Slavnikides dans leur résidence de Libice.

Seuls en réchappent Adalbert et son demi-frère Gaudentius qui sont à Rome, et un autre de ses frères, nommé Soběslav, qui se trouvait dans l'armée impériale et cherche refuge auprès de Boleslas le Vaillant en vertu du pacte d'amitié qui lie les deux familles – et qui doit sembler de plus en plus suspect au pouvoir ducal, dans un contexte où les Piasts sont en train de mettre la main sur la région de Wrocław et Cracovie.

Adalbert retourne à Rome donc, et s'emploie à convaincre le pape Grégoire V, mais aussi l'empereur Otton III avec qui il s'est lié d'amitié lors de son premier séjour, qu'il lui est devenu impossible de demeurer à Prague pour des raisons politiques, malgré les protestations de son archevêque. Comme le pape refuse toutefois de retirer à Adalbert sa charge épiscopale, ce dernier obtient de pouvoir l'exercer comme évêque missionnaire, auprès des païens. En guise de préparation à cette mission, Adalbert entreprend à l'automne 996 un pèlerinage en Francie, à l'occasion duquel il se recueille sur les tombeaux des plus grands saints du monde occidental : saint Martin à Tours, l'apôtre de la Gaule, saint Benoît à Fleury et son disciple saint Maur à Glanfeuil, mais aussi saint Denis aux portes de Paris. On observe que tous ces monastères sont directement liés au pouvoir royal. Il passe ensuite par Mayence, où il

---

[13] *Vita Prior*, cap. 13, p. 126 : [Adalbert vient se plaindre et demander conseil au pape en 989] *Commendatus inquid, mihi grex audire me non vult, nec capit sermo meus in illis in quorum pectoribus daemonicae servitutis imperia regnant; et ea regio est, ubi pro iusto virtus corporis, pro lege voluptas dominatur.*

[14] Sur cette question du processus d'acculturation, G. BÜHRER-THIERRY, *Aux marges du monde germanique, op. cit.*, p. 268-275.

[15] Brunon, cap. 11, p. 12 : *Populus autem erat durae cervicis; servus libidinum factus, miscebantur cum cognatis et sine lege cum uxoribus multis. […] Ipsi clerici palam uxores ducunt, contradicentem episcopum iniquo odio oderunt et sub quorum tutela qui fuerunt, contra ipsum maiores terrae concitaverunt.*

rencontre à nouveau Otton III, et par Magdebourg, avant de se rendre en Pologne, à Gniezno, auprès du duc Boleslas le Vaillant dont il attend des moyens matériels pour mettre en œuvre la mission en Europe orientale. Accompagné de son demi-frère Gaudentius, Adalbert se décide à aller prêcher l'Évangile chez les Pruthènes – ou Prusses –, des populations baltes établies au-delà de la Vistule, sur lesquelles Boleslas envisage sans doute d'étendre son influence, sinon sa domination, dans un processus exactement comparable à celui mis en œuvre par les Carolingiens au IXe siècle et les Ottoniens au Xe.

Adalbert et ses compagnons se rendent au printemps 997 au *castrum* de Gdańsk, où ils prêchent et baptisent, avant de s'embarquer sur un bateau fourni par Boleslas, avec une escorte de trente guerriers qui s'en retournent dès le débarquement sur un des îlots du delta marécageux. La mission, protégée par un noble local, entre dans un *mercatus* qu'on peut identifier comme un *emporium* (peut-être celui de Truso). On retrouve ici toutes les caractéristiques de ces missions du monde nordique où les *emporia* sont souvent les lieux de la première implantation chrétienne[16].

Toutefois, pour la mission d'Adalbert, la tentative de conversion n'est absolument pas couronnée de succès : les missionnaires sont immédiatement traduits devant un « tribunal » qui leur reproche d'avoir passé illicitement la « frontière » dans le dessein de changer le droit coutumier et l'ordre local[17]. Le soir même, on les rembarque sur l'autre rive, c'est-à-dire en Poméranie polonaise ; après cinq jours de discussion, les missionnaires se résignent à rentrer à Gdańsk, lorsqu'ils sont attaqués par un petit groupe mené par un prêtre païen : Adalbert est décapité et sa tête fichée sur un pieu en signe d'avertissement[18]. Les autres missionnaires s'empressent de retourner chez Boleslas, qui négocie à prix d'or avec les Pruthènes le rapatriement de l'ensemble du corps d'Adalbert pour l'ensevelir à Gniezno, dans l'église que son père avait faite construire, à proximité immédiate de sa résidence.

La vie d'Adalbert a donc été marquée par une pérégrination dont on voit bien, si on fixe les lieux sur une carte, qu'elle dessine celle de l'Europe chrétienne : son exil est calqué sur les dimensions de l'empire ottonien et s'ouvre

---

[16] Comme c'est le cas notamment à Birka et à Haithabu. Voir par exemple St. LEBECQ, « *Religiosa femina nomine Frideburg*. La communauté chrétienne de Birka au milieu du IXe siècle d'après le chapitre 20 de la *Vita Anskarii* » dans *Id.*, *Hommes, mers et terres du Nord au début du Moyen Âge*, vol. 1 : *Peuples, cultures, territoires*, Villeneuve d'Ascq, 2011, p. 141-149 et G. BÜHRER-THIERRY, *Aux marges du monde germanique*, *op. cit.*, p. 223-236.
[17] *Vita prior*, cap. 28, p. 172 : *Nobis et toto huic regno, cuius nos fauces sumus, communis lex imperat et unus ordo vivendi ; vos vero, qui estis alterius et ignotae legis, nisi hac nocte discedatis, in crastinum decapitabimini.*
[18] Sur le récit du martyre, G. BÜHRER-THIERRY, « Autour du martyre de saint Adalbert », dans E. BOZOKY, *Les saints face aux barbares au haut Moyen Âge*, Rennes, 2017, p. 147-160.

vers la nouvelle Chrétienté. Tous les lieux mentionnés dans les *Vitae* d'Adalbert sont peu ou prou en relation directe avec le pouvoir impérial, royal ou ducal: Adalbert vit dans un monde structuré par des centres de pouvoir qui sont à la fois politiques et religieux, reflétant ainsi le système idéologique d'avant la Réforme grégorienne. Les déplacements d'Adalbert s'inscrivent dans l'espace de l'empire universel imaginé par Otton III, depuis le centre de la chrétienté – Rome –, jusqu'aux confins: Gdańsk et les rives de la Vistule, et on doit à ce titre attirer l'attention sur les passages qui montrent, du point de vue des sources chrétiennes, la mission comme une force de pénétration du sacré chrétien dans le monde païen[19]: en tant qu'évêque et donc, par excellence, consécrateur, Adalbert transporte le sacré avec lui. On est là dans une conception de la sacralité qui se réfère bien aux personnes consacrées et non aux lieux, sacré chrétien dont le dieu est partout transcendant, par opposition au sacré païen, incarné dans des lieux précis[20].

C'est cette antinomie et l'idée d'une parcelle de sacré chrétien véhiculée par la présence d'Adalbert que reflètent les hagiographes lorsqu'ils imaginent les païens hostiles, exigeant avant toute chose que l'évêque et ses compagnons rebroussent chemin et quittent les lieux, parce que leur seule présence pervertit l'ordre naturel des éléments[21]. Du point de vue des hagiographes, c'est bien la transgression de ces limites spatiales qui conduit Adalbert au martyre, transgression qui marque l'accomplissement de sa pérégrination terrestre, des grands centres de pouvoirs de l'empire, comme Magdebourg où il a été élevé et Mayence dont il dépend, jusqu'au centre romain de la Chrétienté, en passant par les tombeaux des saints tutélaires que sont Martin, l'apôtre par excellence, Benoît, le fondateur du monachisme occidental, vénéré à Fleury et au Mont-Cassin, et Denis, l'évêque de Paris qu'on pensait être le disciple de saint Paul. C'est en quelque sorte la concaténation de tous ces éléments qui prend corps dans le martyre d'Adalbert, comme le rappelle la profession de foi que la *Vita Prior* lui attribue:

> *Tunc sanctus Adalbertus, quis et unde esset, vel ob quam causam illuc veniret, interrogatus, talia econtra miti voce respondit: Sum nativitate Sclavus, nomine Adalbertus, professione monachus, ordine quondam episcopus, officio nunc vester apostolus*[22].

Comme tout martyr, Adalbert commence alors une nouvelle vie.

---

[19] Brunon, cap. 25, p. 32: *Exeuntes exite de finibus nostris; si cicius non retro pedem ponitis, crudelibus penis afflicti mala morte peribitis.*
[20] Sur cet aspect, voir G. Bührer-Thierry, *Aux marges du monde germanique*, op. cit., p. 346-350.
[21] Brunon, cap. 25: *Propter tales, inquiunt homines, terra nostra non dabit fructum, arbores non parturiunt, nova non nascuntur animalia, vetera moriuntur.*
[22] *Vita Prior*, cap. 28, p. 172.

Les reliques d'Adalbert

Adalbert est rapidement devenu l'un des symboles de la nouvelle Chrétienté. Boleslas le Vaillant s'est empressé de racheter sa dépouille qu'il a fait ensevelir au centre de son pouvoir, à Gniezno. La présence matérielle du saint corps a immédiatement des conséquences importantes sur l'organisation des pouvoirs dans toute la région.

Otton III a sans doute été profondément ému par le martyre de son ami, ce qui l'a probablement conduit à prendre le parti des Piasts, protecteurs des Slavnikides, contre les Přemyslides. Ce rapprochement entre Otton III et Boleslas le Vaillant conduit d'abord à l'érection de Gniezno non seulement comme église épiscopale, mais surtout comme chef-lieu de province ecclésiastique, la première province autonome de la nouvelle Chrétienté. Or, comme Johannes Fried l'a démontré dans une longue publication[23], si le demi-frère d'Adalbert, Gaudentius, qui avait participé à la mission et assisté au martyre de son frère, a été le premier archevêque de Gniezno, il a d'abord porté un titre très particulier, qu'on trouve notamment dans un diplôme d'Otton III daté du 2 décembre 999 et donné à Rome[24] : *archiepiscopus sancti Adalberti martyris*, alors qu'on attendrait, si ce n'est « archevêque de Gniezno », du moins archevêque des Polonais, voire des Slaves. Johannes Fried a essayé de montrer que ce titre n'était pas attaché à un siège, mais était valable pour l'ensemble des pays slaves, ce qui expliquerait pourquoi les annales d'Hildesheim par exemple, énoncent que la nouvelle province s'étendait sur sept évêchés suffragants, alors que Gniezno n'en a jamais compté que quatre[25].

Même si tout le monde n'est pas convaincu par la démonstration, le titre porté, peut-être quelques mois seulement, par Gaudentius révèle l'importance de ce qu'on peut appeler « le gisement de sacralité » fondé à Gniezno par la dépouille d'Adalbert : après la pérégrination d'Adalbert jusqu'aux confins du monde chrétien, on assiste à une « relocalisation » de sa puissance sacrée au cœur du pouvoir polonais des Piasts, ce qui explique d'une part que ces derniers n'entendent pas le céder, d'autre part que beaucoup d'autres souhaitent s'en emparer.

Le premier est sans aucun doute l'empereur Otton III en personne, qui se rend à Gniezno « en pèlerinage » sur la tombe d'Adalbert en l'an mil. Ce voyage a bien sûr aussi un but politique et demeure partout célébré comme

---

[23] J. Fried, *Otto III und Boleslaw Chrobry : das Widmungsbild des Aachener Evangeliars, der Akt von Gnesen und das frühe polnische und ungarische Königtum*, Stuttgart, 1989.
[24] Éd. Th. Sickel, Hanovre, 1893 (*Monumenta Germaniae Historica*, Diplomata, II/2), n° 339, p. 768.
[25] J. Fried, *Otto III. und Boleslaw Chrobry, op. cit.*, p. 81-100.

la reconnaissance de la Pologne, à travers une cérémonie d'origine byzantine où Otton manifeste l'association de Boleslas à l'empire comme *frater et cooperator imperii, populi Romani amicus et socius*, si l'on en croit la chronique tardive de Gallus Anonymus[26]. C'est également à cette occasion qu'Otton III a confié à Boleslas une réplique de la Sainte-Lance, comme signe du rang élevé du prince polonais dans l'empire. Mais il ne fait pas de doute non plus qu'un des objets du pèlerinage était de récupérer la dépouille d'Adalbert, dont Otton souhaitait faire un des grands saints de l'empire, et il est probable que la réplique de la Sainte-Lance fît partie du « troc » imaginé par Otton.

Boleslas n'envisage pas cependant de laisser l'empereur repartir avec la dépouille du saint et un texte plus tardif attribue même aux *cives* de Gniezno le refus de laisser transférer l'ensemble du corps d'Adalbert à Rome, au motif qu'il est « leur » apôtre[27]. L'empereur doit finalement se contenter d'un seul bras, à partir duquel Otton distribue des fragments et pourvoit essentiellement les lieux centraux de l'empire, Aix-la-Chapelle, Rome et Ravenne, entre 999 et 1001. En Italie, Otton fonde également une chapelle sur des reliques d'Adalbert, à mi-chemin de Subiaco et du Mont-Cassin. On trouve encore des reliques à Terracine, dans le Latium, et à Sant'Alberto, près de Pereum, donc à proximité de Ravenne, mais aussi de l'ermitage de Romuald où s'était retiré Brunon de Querfurt. L'église paroissiale conserve encore aujourd'hui un doigt de saint Adalbert. Mais l'essentiel des reliques est déposé sur l'Isola Tiberina de Rome, dans l'actuelle église *San Bartolomeo apostolo*, qui était à l'origine dédiée aussi à saint Adalbert. Otton III avait obtenu ces reliques de saint Barthélemy à Bénévent au printemps 999 et la dédicace de l'église aux deux saints – aux deux apôtres donc – a été conjointe[28]. En Germanie, c'est Notre-Dame d'Aix la Chapelle qui recueille une partie des reliques du saint, mais Otton en cède aussi des fragments à l'évêque Notger de Liège et à la grande abbaye de Reichenau, où il séjourne probablement avec son précieux bagage lors de son dernier voyage vers Rome[29].

---

[26] Gallus Anonymus, *Gesta principum Polonorum* 1, 6, éd. P. W. KNOLL et F. SCHAER, Budapest-New York, 2003, p. 36. Sur le souvenir de cette rencontre dans la culture politique polonaise, H. HEIN-KIRCHER, « Akt von Gnesen. Ein Gipfeltreffen im Jahr 1000 », dans *Deutsch-Polnische Erinnerungsorte, 2: Geteilt/Gemeinsam*, éd. H.-H. HAHN et R. TRABA, Paderborn, 2014, p. 81-92.

[27] *De translatione sancti Adalberti*, éd. G. WAITZ, Hannover, 1888 (*Monumenta Germaniae Historica*, Scriptores, XV/2), p. 708.

[28] U. DERCKS, « Die Adlerkapitelle in der Krypta von San Bartolomeo all'Isola in Rom », dans *Europas Mitte um 1000. Beiträge zur Geschichte, Kunst und Archäologie*, éd. A. WIECZOREK et H. M. HINZ, vol. 2, Stuttgart, 2000, p. 809-812. L'église est fondée sur un ancien temple d'Esculape lui-même bâti sur une source.

[29] A. GIEYSZTOR, *L'Europe nouvelle autour de l'an mil. La papauté, l'empire et les « nouveaux venus »*, Rome, 1997, p. 18-21.

Malgré une historiographie militante qui explique volontiers qu'on se trouve là en présence d'un « réseau spirituel monté en Occident autour d'un évêque né en Bohême, greffé sur un espace bien déterminé : la *Respublica Christiana* qui transcende toutes les origines, vecteur d'une identité culturelle savante et ecclésiastique, dénominateur commun de l'Occident médiéval »[30], la tentative d'implanter le culte de saint Adalbert dans l'empire se révèle rapidement être un échec. D'une part, parce que le rêve d'empire universel d'Otton III disparaît avec lui dès 1002, d'autre part parce qu'il ne s'agit là nullement d'un « réseau » mais au contraire de pôles exclusivement liés soit à l'empereur lui-même, soit à l'entourage monastique d'Adalbert, mais assez peu liés entre eux. Ce qu'on peut dire en revanche, c'est que le culte d'Adalbert est polarisé autour de trois grands centres, Aix-la-Chapelle, Rome et Gniezno, et que le centre le plus important demeure la capitale des ducs polonais : dès les premières années du règne d'Henri II, Adalbert apparaît nettement comme le protecteur de la puissance polonaise, contre l'empereur lui-même et même contre les Tchèques.

Henri II, comme on le sait, n'a pas du tout la même conception de l'empire et des affaires slaves que son prédécesseur Otton III[31] : il est en particulier inquiet devant la puissance montante de Boleslas le Vaillant, qui refuse de lui faire hommage, et entend l'y contraindre par des moyens militaires. Il est logique dans ces conditions que l'empire apporte à nouveau son soutien aux Přemyslides de Bohême.

En juillet 1005, Henri prépare sa campagne contre Boleslas. Au plaid de Dortmund il crée une association de prières avec des familles saxonnes qui étaient connues pour être des amies de Boleslas et des Slavnikides, mais il complète aussi la fondation d'Otton III en faveur d'Adalbert à Aix-la-Chapelle : il lui donne en particulier la dîme de tous les revenus du fisc à Walcheren, Goslar et Dortmund, ainsi que la chapelle d'Ingelheim et le monastère du Luisberg à Aix, accomplissant ainsi la fondation d'Otton III[32]. Adalbert sera honoré aussi à Merseburg et Magdebourg, deux centres de pouvoir traditionnellement hostiles à Boleslas. Henri neutralise ainsi la force symbolique pro-polonaise de saint Adalbert. Il cherche à limiter la colère du saint et à en faire son obligé – avec succès, semble-t-il, car l'armée impériale n'a jamais

---

[30] T. DUNIN-WASOWICZ, « Le culte de saint Adalbert vers l'an mil et la fondation de l'église saint Adalbert à Liège », dans *La collégiale Saint Jean de Liège, 1000 ans d'art et d'histoire*, éd. J. DECKERS, Liège, 1981, p. 35-38.
[31] B. SCHNEIDMÜLLER, *Otto III. – Heinrich II. Eine Wende?*, Stuttgart, 2000 et S. WEINFURTER, *Heinrich II. (1002-1024). Herrscher am Ende der Zeiten*, Ratisbonne, 1999.
[32] *Die Urkunden Heinrichs II. und Arduins*, éd. H. BRESSLAU, Berlin, 1900 (*Monumenta Germaniae Historica*, Diplomata, 3), n° 99, p. 123-124 (donné le 7 juillet 1005 à Dortmund).

pénétré si loin dans les terres polonaises[33]. On est ici dans une situation d'affrontement, où il s'agit de neutraliser une puissance sacrée qui est explicitement liée à un lieu, Gniezno, à un peuple, les Polonais, et à une dynastie, les Piasts[34].

Enfin, il faut noter que si les Tchèques prennent une part active dans cet affrontement militaire, ils n'ont aucune part au pouvoir sacré de saint Adalbert, qu'ils ont rejeté de son vivant. Il semble pourtant, si on en croit Brunon de Querfurt, que les Tchèques ont réclamé eux aussi la dépouille de saint Adalbert des les premières années du XIe siècle, au motif qu'il était « leur » évêque. Comme leur demande n'a pas été entendue, ils ont cru bon, profitant de l'affaiblissement des Piasts à la fin des années 1030, d'aller eux-mêmes le chercher.

Adalbert, saint national des Tchèques ou des Polonais?

On retrouve ici l'ancienne rivalité opposant les Tchèques et les Polonais dont on a déjà parlé et qui recoupe des rivalités internes à l'empire, notamment entre Saxons et Bavarois. Henri II a durablement affaibli la puissance des Piasts en menant une lutte sans merci contre Boleslas le Vaillant jusqu'en 1025. Dans les années 1030, les Přemyslides reprennent l'avantage et tentent de reconquérir la Silésie. En 1039, une expédition menée par le duc Břetislav Ier (1034-1055) et l'évêque Séverin de Prague (1031-1067) parvient non seulement à prendre Cracovie, mais à pousser jusqu'à Gniezno, où ils entreprennent de piller la cathédrale, s'emparent des reliques d'Adalbert et les ramènent triomphalement à Prague – d'où il avait été chassé 45 ans auparavant[35]. Du coup, le culte d'Adalbert semble tomber en désuétude dans la capitale polonaise, laquelle souffre également de la désaffection du prince Casimir (1038-1058), qui lui préfère le siège de Cracovie. Jusqu'à ce que le chapitre de la cathédrale « retrouve » dans les années 1090 les reliques qui auraient été dissimulées à la convoitise des Tchèques: le culte d'Adalbert connaît alors un nouvel essor, qui passe par une nouvelle consécration de la cathédrale de Gniezno, en 1097, avec translation solennelle des reliques d'Adalbert, par l'invention de son chef en 1127 et, bien entendu, par la commande des fameuses portes de

---

[33] J. FRIED, *Otto III. und Boleslaw Chrobry, op. cit.*, p. 110.
[34] Sur cette politique d'Henri II à la frontière, G. BÜHRER-THIERRY, *Aux marges du monde germanique, op. cit.*, p. 321-346.
[35] Le récit se trouve essentiellement dans la chronique de Cosmas de Prague, rédigée au début du XIIe siècle: Cosmas Pragensis, *Chronica Boemorum*, éd. B. BRETHOLZ, Berlin, 1923 (*Monumenta Germaniae Historica*, Scriptores, NS 2), II/3-6, p. 84-91. Sur les implications de cette expédition de vol de reliques, G. BÜHRER-THIERRY, *Aux marges du monde germanique, op. cit.*, p. 280-283.

bronze. Au début du XIIe siècle, le prince Boleslas Bouchetorse soutient le culte d'Adalbert en offrant à la cathédrale un nouveau reliquaire et en faisant frapper une monnaie, où on le voit aux pieds du saint[36]. Or Boleslas mène aussi une politique très agressive à l'égard des populations païennes au-delà de la Vistule : selon le chroniqueur contemporain Gallus Anonymus, qui écrit dans les années 1113-1116, saint Adalbert lui-même se serait montré lors d'une campagne militaire, l'épée à la main et monté sur un cheval blanc, apparition qui aurait mis les païens en fuite[37]. C'est aussi sur l'autel de saint Adalbert dans la cathédrale de Gniezno que le duc de Poméranie devra déposer son offrande symbolisant sa dépendance politique et spirituelle envers le prince Boleslas.

Doit-on conclure qu'Adalbert est un saint « national » polonais ? Il est vénéré, sans nul doute, aujourd'hui encore comme un des patrons de la Pologne – mais aussi de la Bohême, de la Hongrie et de la Prusse. Force est de constater que si sa sainteté rejaillit sur l'ensemble de la terre de Bohême d'où il est issu, son culte ne présente là que très peu d'éléments autochtones[38], et qui sont, de plus, des éléments tardifs[39] : si on le compare à l'autre grand saint « national » de la Bohême, saint Venceslas, on peut observer que les *Vitae Adalberti* sont dues à des auteurs extérieurs à la Bohême, tandis que Venceslas bénéficie d'au moins trois textes du Xe siècle rédigés à coup sûr en Bohême[40]. Les origines du culte d'Adalbert ne sont pas non plus autochtones, on n'en a aucune trace avant 1039 et la perte des reliques par le chapitre cathédral de Gniezno n'empêchera pas les Polonais de continuer à célébrer le culte d'Adalbert, qui joua un rôle non négligeable dans le processus d'unification de la Pologne[41]. Les magnifiques portes de bronze racontant la passion de saint Adalbert, qui ornent la cathédrale de Gniezno depuis le début du XIIe siècle, montrent que l'ancrage de son culte n'a pas été remis en cause par le vol de ces reliques. Ici encore, on se trouve dans une logique de compétition qui empêche finalement Adalbert de devenir un authentique saint « national » ; mais

---

[36] P. Skubiszewski, « La porta della cathedrale di Gniezno », dans *Le porte di bronze dell'Antichità al secolo XIII*, Rome, 1990, p. 247-270, ici p. 266.
[37] Gallus Anonymus, *Gesta Principum Polonorum* II, 6, *op. cit.*, p. 130.
[38] F. Graus, « St. Adalbert und St. Wenzel. Zur Funktion der mittelalterlichen Heiligenverehrung in Böhmen », dans *Europa slavica – Europa orientalis. Festschrift für Herbert Ludat zum 70. Geburtstag*, Berlin, 1980, p. 205-231.
[39] F. Machilek, « Die Adalbertsverehrung in Böhmen im Mittelalter », dans *Adalbert von Prag. Brückenbauer zwischen dem Osten und Westen Europas*, éd. H.-H. Henrix, Baden-Baden, 1997 (Schriften der Adalbert-Stiftung-Krefeld, 4), p. 163-184.
[40] Sur les trois textes de la Légende *Crescente Fide*, la Légende en Vieux-Slave et la Légende de Christian, voir I. N. Wood, *The Missionary Life*, *op. cit.*, p. 187-192.
[41] A. Gieysztor, « Gens Polonica : aux origines d'une conscience nationale », dans *Études de civilisation médiévale. Mélanges Edmond-René Labande*, Poitiers, 1974, p. 351-362.

c'est ce qui lui vaut aujourd'hui d'être célébré comme un des premiers saints « européens ». Ainsi le millénaire de son martyr en 1997 a-t-il été marqué par plusieurs publications qui insistent toutes sur ce caractère « européen » d'Adalbert, « Brückenbauer zwischen Ost und West », qui incarnerait un « véritable universalisme européen et occidental dans sa spiritualité, sa religiosité, sa conception de l'Église et sa culture »[42]. Si Otton III a échoué à construire un culte impérial – c'est-à-dire européen – de saint Adalbert[43], les conditions dans lesquelles se développe son culte ont fait de lui un saint qui transcende très largement les appartenances nationales et sert en fait à chacun des pouvoirs princiers d'Europe centrale dans son processus de construction identitaire et nationale[44]. Adalbert n'est ni un saint européen, ni un saint de souche, c'est un saint « transnational ».

---

[42] E. NITTER, « Adalbert, der zweite Bischof von Prag – Brückenbauer zwischen Ost und West », dans *Den Reich komme. 89. Katholikentag vom 10. bis 14. September 1986 in Aachen*, éd. Zentralkomitee der deutschen Katholiken, Dokumentation, II, Paderborn, 1987, p. 1419-1430, ici p. 1427.
[43] P. KUBÍN, « Die Bemühungen Ottos III. um die Einsetzung eines Heiligenkultes für Bischof Adalbert von Prag » dans *Böhmen und seine Nachbarn in Přemyslidenzeit*, éd. I. HLAVÁCEK et A. PATCHOWSKY, Ostfildern, 2011, p. 317-340, arrive à la même conclusion.
[44] Pour une évaluation de l'usage politique du culte de saint Adalbert dans la longue durée, S. SCHOLZ et E. JANUS, « Heiliger Bonifatius und Heiliger Adalbert. Vom Märtyrertod zum Symbol der europäischen Einigung », dans *Deutsch-Polnische Erinnerungsorte*, 3 : *Parallelen*, éd. H.-H. HAHN et R. TRABA, Paderborn, 2012, p. 128-146.

The Old and the New:
St Stanislaus and Other Cults in Krakow

Stanislava KUZMOVÁ
(*Oxford*)

My paper presents the cult of St Stanislaus, as the first Pole to be canonized, with focus on the challenges posed by the rise of Stanislaus cult to the earlier cults in Krakow (especially that of St Florian), as well as the challenges that he faced from the new late medieval cults.

In the first part, I will show how St Stanislaus was canonized in the mid-thirteenth century, although the new saint faced problems which were related to his being essentially an old figure in terms of relative chronology – especially in Rome. In Krakow, however, his novel character celebrated success, also at the expense of an old saint, imported ancient martyr Florian, who had been invoked as the local patron before him. The image and cult of St Stanislaus, however, besides his traditional type of sanctity of a bishop and martyr, had some "modern" features. Nevertheless, in the late Middle Ages, from the thirteenth to fifteenth century, Krakow and Polish lands saw an increasing number of other and "more modern" saintly candidates as well, although not officially recognized by canonization. This evidence suggests that the region was not *a priori* cold towards new sainthood and perhaps nor to the modernized religious feelings.

At the turn of the twelfth and thirteenth centuries, traces of devotion towards Stanislaus, former bishop of Krakow, increasingly appear in a variety of sources. A chronicler describes his death as a martyrdom suffered for his flock, the faithful invoke his intercession in health problems and other difficulties, he appears to several persons, his remains are elevated to a more honourable place and the dignitaries petition for his canonization in Rome, which succeeds in 1253. Thus, the local bishop, who represented a rather traditional type of sainthood, achieved this honour more than 150 years after his death, and ultimately became the patron-saint not only of Krakow, but of Poland.

Les saints et leur culte en Europe centrale au Moyen Âge (xie-début du xvie siècle), éd. par Marie-Madeleine de CEVINS et Olivier MARIN, Turnhout, 2017 (*Hagiologia*, 13), p. 261-280.
© BREPOLS PUBLISHERS   DOI 10.1484/M.HAG-EB.5.113976

Sources from the earlier period are mostly silent or vague concerning the bishop's holiness, although – according to the later tradition – some devotion towards him probably existed ever since his death in the conflict with King Boleslaus II of Poland in 1079, especially in the milieu of the cathedral chapter.[1] Later sources inform about the miraculous events immediately after his death as tokens of his sanctity and about the translation of his body from the place of his martyrdom to the new burial place in the cathedral ten years after his death. To be sure, early thirteenth century certainly was a period of cult revival – if not its birth. It seems that already then the hagiographers and promoters had to come to terms with the long time which passed since the holy man's lifetime. First hagiographic account concerning Bishop Stanislaus appeared in the Chronicle of the Poles of Master Vincent, as part of the description of the rule of King Boleslaus II, his glory and fall. The bishop, as a good shepherd of his flock, chastised the king for his cruel behaviour towards his subjects, for which he was killed by the furious king; his body was cut into pieces and scattered, but his limbs were allegedly found miraculously reintegrated on the following day.[2] This was the type of sanctity which fitted contemporary ideals of bishop, as the good shepherd and defender of the faithful, although the characterization of the bishop is only general.

Thirteenth-century lives of the bishop provide some information about the situation in the earlier period and devotion from the part of a rather limited circle around the cathedral – most of this, however, at least the more

---

[1] The *Cronicae et Gesta principum Polonorum* (1110-1114) written by an anonymous author, who is widely known as Gallus Anonymus, contains in the chapters 27-28 of the First Book a vague account about the nameless bishop whose death was the cause of the king's exile. Gallus Anonymus, *Cronicae et Gesta Ducum sive Principum Polonorum*, ed. K. MALECZYŃSKI, Warsaw, 1952 (*Monumenta Poloniae Historica*, series nova [hereafter: *MPH SN*], 2), p. 52-53, and an English translation in *Gesta Principum Polonorum: The Deeds of the Princes of the Poles*, transl. P. W. KNOLL and F. SCHAER, Budapest-New York, 2003, p. 96-99. For more details, see my description in *Preaching Saint Stanislaus: Medieval Sermons on Saint Stanislaus of Cracow, His Image and Cult*, Warsaw, 2013, p. 21-26. For the debate about the actual history of St Stanislaus (*factum sancti Stanislai*) and his pre-canonization cult, see among numerous works: G. LABUDA, *Święty Stanisław. Biskup krakowski, patron polski. Śladami zabójstwa – męczeństwa – kanonizacji*, Poznań, 2000, p. 50-76; *Id.*, "Wznowienie dyskusji w sprawie męczeństwa i świętości biskupa krakowskiego Stanisława", *Nasza Przeszłość*, 108 (2007), p. 5-57; J. RAJMAN, "Przedkanonizacyjny kult św. Stanisława biskupa", *Nasza Przeszłość*, 80 (1993), p. 5-49; T. GRUDZIŃSKI, *Boleslaus the Bold, called also the Bountiful, and Bishop Stanislaus: The Story of a Conflict*, Warsaw, 1985; M. PLEZIA, *Dookoła sprawy świętego Stanisława. Studium źródłoznawcze*, Bydgoszcz, 1999 – first published in *Analecta Cracoviensia*, 11 (1979), p. 251-413.

[2] Magister Vincentius, *Chronica Polonorum*, ed. M. PLEZIA, Krakow, 1994 (*MPH SN*, 11), p. 55-60. The passage is often analysed together with the respective passage in the anonymous *Gesta*, see works cited in the previous note.

specific information, concerns the period in the early thirteenth century, at the earliest – that is, the time preceding and the events leading to the elevation and canonization; and at the same time, the recurrent theme is certain negligence, oblivion (as intended by Boleslaus II when he ordered to cut the bishop's body into pieces and scatter them). The devotion towards the long-dead bishop, whose remains were buried in the cathedral in Krakow, was spreading beyond the narrow circles and intensified, accompanied with new forms of worship, attracting pilgrims and visitors asking for intercession, and thus overcoming negligence and oblivion of the previous decades and generations. Several miraculous apparitions, noted in the life and the miracle collection, allegedly encouraged the bishop to undertake the action. A German noblewoman was told in a dream vision, repeated twice, to go to the bishop and convince him to elevate the saintly man's relics, otherwise she would not be healed.[3] Similarly, a knight had a vision in which he met the former bishop, Wislaus (1229-1242), who was not allowed to enter the Krakow cathedral and celebrate a holy mass there. When the knight asked him for the reasons, he explained that he had neglected the veneration of the saintly bishop buried in the cathedral. Wislaus regretted this and urged the knight to go to his successor in the office, Bishop Prandota, in order to amend this. One of his arguments was that even more miracles could be accomplished through his bones after they are elevated than up to that time by virtue of Stanislaus's episcopal ring. He also reminded him of the nature and cause of his death, due to which the saintly man (*sanctus vir*) merits veneration.[4]

The changing situation prompted elevation of the desired relics, which took place most probably in 1244. It was the first step in initiating the official canonization. According to the later *vita* of Stanislaus, Bishop Prandota (1242-1266) together with the cathedral chapter elevated the relics from the ground, washed them in wine and water and placed them in a container

---

[3] The vision of a German noblewoman appears in *Miracula sancti Stanislai* (hereafter: *Miracula*), ed. W. Kętrzyński, Lviv, 1884 (*MPH*, 4), Art. 27, p. 305-306; and *Vita sancti Stanislai episcopi Cracoviensis (Vita maior)* (hereafter: *Vita maior*), ed. W. Kętrzyński (*MPH*, 4), III/5, p. 397-398.

[4] The vision of Count Falus in *Miracula*, Art. 35, p. 311; and *Vita maior*, III/4, p. 395-396: *Non permittor ibi venire, quia tot annis fui in ipsa ecclesia et sustinui corpus sancti Stanislai tantum iacere in terra et procurare neglexi, ut corpus eius a terra levaretur et idcirco hiis indumentis exspolior, sed tu vade et dicas episcopo Prandote, quod ipse non negligat predictum sanctum virum elevare de terra. Et ipse testis respondit: Non credet mihi. Et ipse vir venerandus dixit: Tunc dicas ei: trunce, trunce, quare non advertis, quali morte mortuus est et pro qua causa? Quare non attendis, quanta et qualia miracula fiunt per anulum suum? Si per ipsius anulum fiunt tanta, quanta fierent per ossa eius, si levarentur de terra.*

above the ground.⁵ The *elevatio* undertaken by the bishop, without the papal consent, i.e. before the candidate had been canonized, was possibly the initiative of the Dominicans, with whom the bishop closely cooperated. There was the precedent of the elevation of St Dominic which the friars used as a way to bolster his cult and force the beginning of the canonization procedure; however, at this period the rules for elevation and canonization were only being defined, and continued to be broken even later.⁶

The Church dignitaries petitioned for canonization in Rome in 1250.⁷ The board of investigators with papal mandate started the local enquiry *in partibus* and collected the depositions of the beneficiaries and witnesses of the attested miracles. The report (which is not extant) perhaps included a description of the candidate's life and death, and listed miracles which took place especially within the decade since the elevation. It was presented in Rome a year later but did not achieve immediate success.⁸ A new commission led by a papal legate, the Franciscan James of Velletri, was instructed to comprehensively investigate the case.⁹ They had to re-examine the miracles

---

⁵ *Vita maior*, III/7, p. 399-400. The elevation is also described in the *Vita Kyngae*, ed. W. Kętrzyński (*MPH*, 4), p. 711, with emphasis on Princess Kinga's part in it. In describing the canonization process of St Stanislaus and the development of his cult, I rely on my more detailed analysis in *Preaching Saint Stanislaus, op. cit.*, p. 27-32, etc.

⁶ The argument about the Dominicans' initiative was formulated by Polish historian: M. Starnawska, "Dominikanie, św. Jacek i elewacja szczątków św. Stanisława przez biskupa Prandotę", in *Mendykanci w średniowiecznym Krakowie*, ed. T. Gałuszka, K. Ożóg, A. Zajchowska, Kraków, 2008, p. 407-424; Ead., *Świętych życie po życiu. Relikwie w kulturze religijnej na ziemiach polskich w średniowieczu*, Warsaw, 2008, especially p. 204-207, 285-293, 297. For the initiative of the Dominicans, see also G. Labuda, *Św. Stanisław, op. cit.*, p. 157. For the practice of episcopal elevation, see A. Vauchez, *Sainthood in the Later Middle Ages*, Cambridge, 1997, p. 32, 91-94.

⁷ For the canonization process of Stanislaus, see *Vita maior*, III/7, p. 399-400; and the studies by A. Witkowska, "The thirteenth-century *miracula* of St Stanislaus, Bishop of Krakow", in *Procès de canonisation au Moyen Âge: Aspects juridiques et religieux*, ed. G. Klaniczay, Rome, 2004, p. 149-163; Ead., "Miracula małopolskie z XIII i XIV wieku", *Studium źródłoznawcze, Roczniki Humanistyczne*, 19/2 (1971), especially p. 43-52; G. Labuda, *Św. Stanisław, op. cit.*, p. 156-162; *Papsturkunde und Heiligsprechung. Die päpstlichen Kanonisationen vom Mittelalter bis zur Reformation. Ein Handbuch*, ed. O. Krafft, Köln-Weimar-Wien, 2005, p. 500-518.

⁸ "Magister Jacobus doctor decretorum et magister Gerardus canonici Cracouienses cum Predicatoribus et Minoribus pro canonizacione beati Stanyzlai certi nuncii et procuratores eiusdem negocii ad Romanam curiam destinantur". A contemporary note in the *Rocznik kapitulny krakowski* (The Annals of the Krakow Chapter), which noted several steps in the procedure; see *Najdawniejsze roczniki krakowskie i kalendarz* (The oldest Krakow annals and calendar), ed. Z. Kozłwska-Budkowa, Warsaw, 1978 (*MPH SN*, 5), p. 83.

⁹ The delegation bull *Licet olim venerabili*, 26 May 1252 is edited in *Kodeks dyplomatyczny katedry krakowskiej. Monumenta Medii Aevi Historica Res Gestas Poloniae Illustrantia* 1, ed. F. Piekosiński, Krakow, 1874 (hereafter *KDKK* 1), no. 33, p. 41-42. Another edition and a

collected by the first committee. The result of the second investigation is the juridical protocol of the *Miracula sancti Stanislai* (1252), containing 42 miracle testimonies with detailed information about circumstances, witnesses and chronology.[10] Another task was to find out more about the life of the bishop who had passed away so long ago, as well as his martyrdom and its causes – by examining the two hundred-year-old witnesses "mentioned in the acts" who had known the candidate's contemporaries and thus had second-hand information about his life, and also by inquiring about popular devotion and common opinion (*devotionem populi et famam communem*) concerning the candidate's death and sanctity.[11] The protocol of testimonies listed only miracles that happened long after the bishop's death and documented the fame of the candidate's sanctity. Given the gap between the candidate's life and the canonization process, instead of direct evidence, i.e. testimonies of his contemporaries about the virtuous life, the examiners relied on written sources and authentic archival documents: namely, a *liber cronicorum* which belonged to the chapter (i.e. presumably Master Vincent's *Chronica*), a *liber annalium* (i.e. the Old Annals of the Krakow Chapter, now lost), and an epitaph on the bishop's tomb.[12] There is no mention of a saint's *vita*. It is unclear what documents exactly the petitioners presented in Rome to support their

---

Polish translation by R. M. Zawadzki, "Innocentego PP. IV Bulla Kanonizacyjna Swietego Stanislawa oraz Bulla Delegacyjna dla Jakuba z Velletri", *Analecta Cracoviensia*, 9 (1979), the edition p. 42-45 and a description of the document, p. 28-29. Regestum in *Bullarium Poloniae* I, ed. I. Sulkowska-Kuraś and S. Kuraś, Rome-Lublin, 1982, no. 516; *Regesta pontificum romanorum*, ed. A. Potthast, vol. 2, Berlin, 1874, repr. Graz, 1957, no. 14604. See also R. Paciocco, *Canonizzazioni e culto dei santi nella* christianitas *(1198-1302)*, Assisi, 2006, p. 94-95.

[10] A contemporary copy in the form of a scroll (*rotulus*) is kept in the Archives of the Cathedral Chapter in Krakow. Edition: *Miracula*, p. 285-318. Edited bilingually with a Polish translation and attempted reconstruction of the missing articles, as "Cuda świętego Stanisława", ed. Z. Perzanowski and transl. J. Pleziowa, *Analecta Cracoviensia*, 11 (1979), p. 68-140. A detailed description of the MS. 228 in I. Polkowski, *Katalog, op. cit.*, p. 166-168; A. Witkowska, "Miracula małopolskie", *art. cit.*, p. 37; Z. Perzanowski, "Cuda", *art. cit.*, p. 47-50. Unfortunately, the beginning and the end of the protocol have not been preserved, so we do not have from this source the introductory information on the circumstances of the proceedings and the persons involved. For the *Miracula*, see A. Witkowska, "The thirteenth-century *miracula*", *art. cit.*, p. 149-163. See also a comprehensive analysis of the miracles and testimonies in the miracle collections in *Ead.*, "Miracula małopolskie", *art. cit.*, p. 43-52, 67-71, 82-84, 88-96 et *passim*.

[11] *KDKK* I, no. 33, p. 41.

[12] *Ibid.*, p. 41-42. For a plausible identification of the written sources see G. Labuda, *Św. Stanisław, op. cit.*, p. 157-158. For the epitaph, see M. Plezia, *Dookoła, op. cit.*, p. 101-105. For the practice of use of written documents instead of contemporaries' testimonies in the case of the candidates who were long dead, see A. Vauchez, *Sainthood*, p. 46-47 with a mention of St Stanislaus in note 57.

supplication. Traditionally, it was believed that the *Vita minor* was written before the canonization for these uses, but it is also possible that a certain text based on the passage of Master Vincent's *Chronica Polonorum* with the description of the martyrdom, its causes and subsequent miracles (although it had little about the candidate's life before the clash with the king) accompanied a list of miracles.[13] Besides this, the legate was even instructed to inquire about the possible uses of the proposed canonization (and subsequent cult) – and about the proximity of missionary regions.[14]

The repeated examination shows that there were some doubts concerning the canonization of Stanislaus in Rome. At the time when the papal curia in Rome was gradually taking control of the canonization, and establishing a more precise juridical form, some requests after an initial check did not proceed to trial, and some trials did not end successfully.[15] André Vauchez mentions a certain bias towards the candidates coming like Stanislaus from the margins of Christendom, including Poland, when the papacy was "*a priori* doubtful" and "had to be firmly persuaded that the cult was deep rooted and extended to the whole of a country".[16] However, the length of time that had elapsed since the bishop's death and the lack of contemporary evidence of his virtuous life and martyr's death seem to have caused some hesitation too, and the examination of the accounts in the chronicle and annals and their authenticity was not unproblematic.[17] Another piece of evidence of the difficulties is a letter of Cardinal John of Gaeta, the auditor of the case, to the Krakow Chapter, which praises the Polish postulators who had to go through unspeakable torments and close to a thousand "sharp obstacles and toothed objections", although so much evidence was diligently presented. He said, *quasi parabolice*, that the saint would probably have to perform a final miracle – to make the quarrelling cardinals agree; which happened in the end.[18] Later sources did indeed supply the decisive miracle, not metaphorically only: the *vita* explained that Cardinal Reginald (Rinaldo) of Ostia, the

---

[13] The dating and function of the *Vita minor* have been questioned and reconsidered in the last decades. There could have been "a pre-canonization life", now lost, which was reworked into the later thirteenth-century lives. Witkowska, unlike Labuda, maintains that the *Vita minor* was the oldest life written shortly before 1250 for the uses of the canonization supplication: "The thirteenth-century *miracula*", *art. cit.*, p. 150.

[14] KDKK I, no. 33, p. 41: *Inquiras insuper utrum Cracouiensis diocesis Paganis et Ruthenis scismaticis sit confinis, ut per hoc ex ipsorum confinio lucrum prouenire ualeat animarum.*

[15] For the evolution of the canonization procedure, see A. VAUCHEZ, *Sainthood, op. cit.*, p. 22-84; R. PACIOCCO, *Canonizzazioni, op. cit.*, p. 3-134.

[16] A. VAUCHEZ, *Sainthood, op. cit.*, p. 69-70.

[17] See also G. LABUDA, *Św. Stanisław, op. cit.*, p. 160.

[18] KDKK I, no. 37, p. 46-48. The last passage: *preposito procuratori diximus quasi parabolice, neccessarium habet Sanctus vester unum finaliter operari miraculum, quod discordantes in*

future Pope Alexander V (Pope 1254-1261) who succeeded Innocent IV, had opposed the canonization. The reason was, once again, that the events had occurred a long time ago (*antiquitatem temporis allegando*). When he fell seriously ill, but was healed through the miraculous apparition of Stanislaus, his hesitation disappeared.[19]

Finally Bishop Stanislaus was canonized by Pope Innocent IV in Assisi on 8 September, 1253.[20] He was the first canonized native saint and soon established as the patron of Krakow. What was the situation before that, however? Why did Krakow need to look for a patron in the thirteenth century? There was St Adalbert, the first patron of Poland, who, however, was not directly connected with Krakow, and his cult centre was in Gniezno; moreover, his relics were taken to Prague by Bohemians in 1038/9. The cathedral in Krakow was dedicated to St Wenceslas, the Bohemian martyr king (probably rather early, already in the tenth century; later joined by Stanislaus in the thirteenth century). Several decades before the interest in Stanislaus appeared with strength, however, another "foreigner" with ambitions to become the patron of the town and take roots there, arrived: St Florian, a Roman martyr. St Florian represents a different type of search for patron saint, and a different time period. He was an adopted saint, whose body was brought to Krakow from Italy in 1184, as the Annals of Krakow Chapter, and after them other Polish annals, noted: *Sanctus Florianus martir per Egydium episcopum Mutinensem apportatur et per Gedkonem episcopum Cracoviensem devotissime suscipitur*.[21] The *translatio* was most probably the common initiative of Gedko/Gedeon, Bishop of Krakow, and Casimir the Just, Prince of Krakow. The bishop needed the martyr's relics for the prestige of his diocese and Prince Casimir also needed to counterbalance the power of Gniezno with St Adalbert, among the competing principalities. His relics were deposited in the cathedral and in the church dedicated to him outside the city walls. The

---

miraculis mirabiliter faciat concordare. The letter is *sine dato et loco* according to the *KDKK*, but dated to 1253 by A. WITKOWSKA, "The thirteenth-century *miracula*", *art. cit.*, p. 153.

[19] See "De modo canonizacionis beati Stanislai et sanacione Domini Reynaldi Hostiensis episcopi, videlicet domini pape Alexandri", in the *Vita maior*, III/55, p. 434-436. The miracle is mentioned also by R. PACIOCCO, *Canonizzazioni*, p. 102 and note 11.

[20] For a description of the canonization, see the *Vita maior*, III/56, p. 436-438. The bull of canonization, *Olim a gentilium*, of 17 September 1253 is published in the *KDKK* 1, no. 38, p. 48-51; another edition and translation is by R. M. ZAWADZKI, "Bulla", *art. cit.*, p. 23-45, together with a description of its manuscripts; *Regesta pontificum romanorum*, ed. A. POTTHAST, vol. 2, no. 15137; *Bullarium Poloniae* 1, nos. 549-552 (to various addressees); see also *Papsturkunde und Heiligsprechung*, *op. cit.*, p. 500-518.

[21] *Rocznik kapitulny krakowski* (The Annals of the Krakow Chapter), in *Najdawniejsze roczniki krakowskie i kalendarz*, ed. Z. KOZŁOWSKA-BUDKOWA, Warsaw, 1978 (*MPH SN*, 5), p. 65.

collegiate church outside the walls of Krakow, most probably a common foundation of the prince and the bishop, was consecrated in 1216. The community around the church did not belong to the town of Krakow, but later got their own charter with town privileges as *civitas ad sanctum Florianum* (1366), first called Florentia, and then Kleparz/Clepardia.[22]

However, the popularity of St Florian as the main patron of Krakow did not last for long, and mostly did not get far beyond the circles of bishop and duke, and the churches with his relics. He was a saint without a biographical relation to Krakow, and for long remained such – until the legend of his translation was written, most probably sometime in the fourteenth century, usually accompanied with the martyrdom legend of the Roman tribute of Noricum; it was significant that he was a martyr and his relics were available in Krakow. Already when the church of St Florian was consecrated in 1216, a stronger cult of a native saint, Stanislaus, was nascent. The imported figure was overshadowed by the native saint who was well-suited to the local needs. The new cult has taken over the roles of Florian's cult. The changing preferences are well illustrated by several references in the miracle accounts collected for the purposes of the canonization process of Stanislaus. Two beneficiaries of miracles accomplished through St Stanislaus went to Krakow for the festivity of St Florian (interestingly, after Stanislaus was canonized, their feasts were very close: the feast of St Florian on 4 May, and that of martyrdom of Stanislaus on 8 May). A certain Richard with his pregnant wife came at the time of Florian's feast (*venisset b. Floriani festivitate invitante*), on the third night his wife gave birth to twins, a girl and a boy. When one of their newly-born babies died on the following day without baptism, Richard prayed to God for help through the merits of Stanislaus, the new native holy man, about whom they learned there. The boy came back to life for a day so that he could receive the sacrament.[23] Another woman came for the feast-day of St Florian in order to ask him for help with the mouth paralysis – *veniens Cracoviam ad festivitatem beati Floriani audivit de miraculis martyris Stanislai* (Vita). She went to Krakow to invoke the intercession of St Florian at the time of his feast in May, and there heard about the miracles of Stanislaus. She

---

[22] For more on the translation and the cult of St Florian in Krakow, see the comprehensive study of K. Dobrowolski, *Dzieje kultu św. Floriana w Polsce do połowy XVI w. Polsce*, Warsaw, 1923 (Rozprawy historyczne Towarzystwa naukowego Warszawskiego), vol. 2, no. 2, p. 92-116; J. Wyrozumski, "Skąd pochodził krakowski św. Florian?", *Rocznik Krakowski*, 14 (1998), p. 53-58; and M. Starnawska, *Świętych życie po życiu, op. cit.*, especially p. 281-285. The sources for the cult before the thirteenth century, for the period of its certain flourishment after the translation, are rather scarce.

[23] *De filio Richardi a morte suscitato, Vita maior*, III/8, p. 400. The account is not included in the extant part of the *Miracula*, it possibly got lost.

prayed for two days at his tomb but was not healed. On the third day, when a sermon was being delivered in the church where he was buried (cathedral), she prayed with tears in her eyes and her mouth suddenly got back to its place and she was healed from the disease of her head. It was testified by the woman (Kwietusza) herself, her husband and another woman (widow of count James) and the examiners confirmed that they had seen her alright.[24] Even the parish priest of St Florian Church in Krakow, Vitus, prayed to St Stanislaus around 1250 – he fell ill with a headache and pain in a half of his head, could not eat and talk for a week, then ordered to bring the ring of St Stanislaus with which he touched the painful places and he drank water into which he put the ring and got healed – he gave testimony in front of the canonization investigation committee himself, confirmed by two other witnesses.[25] These miracles are not only found as literary accounts in the Life of Stanislaus (*Vita maior*), but also as depositions (the latter two) in the judicial protocol for the canonization trial. These miracle accounts at the time of the campaign for a new saint have important functions: by relating the candidate with an established saint, the hagiographer of Stanislaus and "impressarios" of his cult in Krakow ("the miracle office" in the cathedral and local clerics, most importantly) spread the news about a new option of intercessor, legitimize his worship, and also show the continuity with the previous patterns of devotion towards Florian. The accounts also suggest certain competition between these two, and present the new option as a more efficacious one.

Later, there was an attempt to revive the cult of St Florian by strengthening his connection with Krakow. A legend of his translation to Krakow was written, describing it in a much more detailed way, and with some amount of fantasy, which was typical for this genre, it has to be said. The legend originated most probably in the fourteenth century in the circles of the collegiate church of St Florian in Krakow, although it is preserved in the manuscripts dating to the fifteenth century, in three various redactions.[26] Allegedly, the

---

[24] *De revoluto ore paralitico sanato*, Vita maior, III/23, p. 409, and *Miracula*, Art. XXVI, p. 305.
[25] *Miracula*, Art. XXXIX, p. 313, *Vita maior*, III/37, p. 418.
[26] *Translatio sancti Floriani*, ed. W. KĘTRZYŃSKI (*MPH*, 4), p. 757-762. See also *Acta Sanctorum*, Maii I, col. 466-467. For the translation legend, see also K. DOBROWOLSKI, *Dzieje kultu św. Florjana w Polsce, op. cit.*, especially p. 101-111; recently M. STARNAWSKA, *Świętych życie po życiu*, p. 281-285, and J. WYROZUMSKI, "Skąd pochodzil krakowski św. Florian?", p. 54-55. Dobrowolski, and after him Wyrozumski, date the legend rather to the second half of the fifteenth century only (although Dobrowolski's *terminus a quo* is mid-fourteenth century), Kętrzyński maintains that the fifteenth-century redactions had a fourteenth-century model, and Starnawska represents the group of historians who date the legend to the fourteenth century. Dobrowolski saw the revival of the cult, including the origin of the translation legend,

body was translated from Italy by Bishop Egidius of Modena thanks to Gedko/Gedeon, Bishop of Krakow, and Prince Casimir the Just. The legend starts with a story of a Polish young man (Bishop Gedko) who had an Italian good friend during his studies, allegedly in Padua – these two friends gave each other a promise to help if any of them got to a high position/benefice. When the Italian became the pope (Lucius III), he sent envoys to his friend Gedko, who had become bishop of Krakow by then, to ask him what he could do for him – the bishop replied that he had enough riches, gold and silver, but his Church lacked a holy patron and a guardian for the whole kingdom – and asked the pope to give him the relics of some of the holy martyrs. The legend recounts how the pope with the Polish envoys secretly went to the Church of St Lawrence behind the walls in Rome (Campo Verano), and opened the tombs of the martyrs. When the pope touched the body of St Lawrence with his crozier, the saint turned his face away from him; the same happened with St Stephen, neither of them willing to go to Poland. The pope explained that another martyr, St Florian, was lying under those two, but they could not move him because the pope was afraid of the anger of the Romans, since Florian was operating more miracles than the other two there. Then, however, St Florian reached out with his hand from under the two other martyrs, holding a card with an inscription: "I want to go to Poland" (*Ego volo/vadam Poloniam*). The envoys took the martyr's body with them and secretly transported him to Poland. When they approached the gates of Krakow, they could not move any further despite their efforts, and the saint said: "I will guard the city from this side against the Prussians, but after me, another patron of this glorious kingdom will come, who will reside in his cathedral, guarding the town from another side, from pagans and others". The prince and the bishop built a church dedicated to St Florian behind the city walls at the place, and placed the saint's arm and established prelates and canons with benefices there, while the rest of the relics was deposited in the cathedral church at the castle.

The Legend of translation brings up several problematic issues. Polish historians have demonstrated that the place of origin of the relics of St Florian was probably not Rome, but Bologna (Church of St Stephen). Besides that, several martyrs of that name, traditions related to them and their feast days got probably conflated, although in Polish legendaries St Florian is mostly presented as a Roman *princeps officii* in Noricum in the times of Emperor

---

only in the fifteenth century, starting with the statutes of 1436 (see below), following a period of decline which started from the time of the canonization of St Stanislaus in 1253.

Diocletian (284-305), with the feast on 4 May.[27] Interestingly, there is another hint at the confusion of Florians in the fourteenth century. A representative of the Canons Regular from Sankt Florian, in the Passau diocese near Linz in Austria, most probably requested the relics of St Florian in Krakow in 1323-1324. The convent, which was built according to the legend on the place where the Roman tribune and soldier martyr of that name was buried, did not have the relics of their patron and sought to acquire them in Krakow, which since 1184 possessed the relics of a saint named Florian, although not identical with the Roman tribune Florian, but only his namesake. However, they acquired the relics of Stanislaus, most probably instead of their desired ones, and with some liturgical works pertaining to him – which we can perhaps consider as another piece of evidence documenting the efforts of the local clergy to propagate the new saint at the expense of the old one. Then an altar of St Stanislaus was built in the convent church in Sankt Florian, and he was venerated in the convent during the following 200 years, but the cult did not spread from there, and declined from the sixteenth century.[28]

The main contrast between the cults of St Stanislaus and St Florian from the point of view of local faithful was the nature of their ties with Krakow, to which an anonymous sermon for the translation feast of St Stanislaus hints when it emphasises:

> our patron being of Polish nation did not want to have his body transferred to another country (*ad aliam patriam*), as many saints did, but to stay in this homeland (*in eadem patria*) and to have his body placed in the Castle of Krakow.[29]

The sermon possibly alludes to an older "imported" patron, St Florian – who "wanted to go to Poland", and in a way "betrayed" his home community.[30] Unlike numerous other patron-saints of various places (or even unlike

---

[27] For the discussion of various saints named Florian, the place of origin of the relics translated to Poland and the identification of the person, see especially J. WYROZUMSKI, "Skąd pochodził krakowski św. Florian?", *art. cit.*, p. 54-58. For the legend of the martyrdom of St Florian in Polish legend collections, see below.

[28] For more on the cult of St Stanislaus in Sankt Florian and a hypothesis about the request of the relics of St Florian and acquiring the relics of St Stanislaus, see K. DOBROWOLSKI, "Kult św. Stanisława w St. Florian w średnich wiekach", *Rocznik krakowski*, 19 (1923), p. 116-133.

[29] Sermon XLI (*De translacione sancti Stanislai*), manuscript Sandomierz, Biblioteka Seminarium Duchownego (Seminary Library) 428, fol. 81v: *Sic et beatus Stanislaus episcopus et patronus noster nacione Polonus existens, non ad aliam patriam corpus suum transferri voluit, sed in eadem patria in castro Cracoviensi honorifice collocari, cuius translacionem hodie solempniter peragit sancta mater Ecclesia.*

[30] Cf. above, *Translatio sancti Floriani*, ed. W. KĘTRZYŃSKI (*MPH*, 4), p. 757-762, quotation on p. 758.

"fashionable" imported relics), St Stanislaus was a native saint, his body was not translated from some far-away place, but only from the place of his martyrdom, nearby Skałka, to the cathedral church, and thus remained in his *patria*.

Moreover, the cult of St Stanislaus acquired a political dimension, which contributed to its success, among a number of other characteristics. According to the thirteenth-century *Vita*, the body of the martyr was said to have been cut into pieces after his death and scattered. However, the limbs were found miraculously reintegrated on the following day. The fate of the martyr's body was compared to the destiny of the Polish Kingdom: as a punishment for the crime of King Boleslaus II, Poland lost the crown and disintegrated into several principalities, but they were promised to reunite again one time. The author formulated a political programme for the restoration of the kingdom, with the centre in Krakow, and the saint as the guardian of the crown.[31]

The level and kind of proximity of these two saints with respect to the faithful in Krakow was different: in both cases, the relics, that is, "the dead saint", was accessible; but Stanislaus got the upper hand when the tie with "the living" aspect of the saint is concerned – he lived and was active in Krakow, while in the case of the ancient martyr, the narrative connection with the place was created only later, after his relics have reached the town (his translation was explained and accounts of apparitions were added up to strenghten the bond with the local community). The translation legend added the points which were important to fashion the saint as the patron of the community – which the cult of St Florian had ambitions to serve as: the connection with the place and community, the relics which facilitate the miracles and the protection against enemies.

Although as compared to the type of sainthood represented by the ancient martyr St Florian, Bishop Stanislaus, canonized after an official process in Rome, was a new, modern saint, he was certainly not a typical representative of new, "living", modern sainthood. It was visible already in the difficulties during the canonization process (and the hesitation in the curia because of the long time passed since the candidate's death and the lack of information

---

[31] For more on this, see among others especially a recent comprehensive monograph by W. DRELICHARZ, *Idea zjednoczenia królestwa w średniowiecznym dziejopisarstwie polskim*, Krakow, 2012, with regard to the cult of St Stanislaus especially p. 112-198. For a summary and references, see also St. KUZMOVÁ, *Preaching Saint Stanislaus, op. cit.*, p. 41-42; *Ead.*, "Division and Reintegration of St Stanislaus: A Political Analogy in Sermons?", in *Promoting the Saints' Cults and Their Contexts from Late Antiquity until the Early Modern Period: Essays in Honor of Gábor Klaniczay for His 60th Birthday*, ed. O. GECSER et al., Budapest, 2010, p. 141-153.

concerning his life). Still, the new mendicant orders, Dominicans and Franciscans, laboured for his canonization, supported and helped to propagate his cult, before his canonization and afterwards. They possibly urged the bishop to initiate the canonization proceedings, as they needed saints as examples that they could use in their preaching.[32] Mendicant friars took an active part in the canonization proceedings, their representatives were among the envoys who petitioned for the canonization – which can be seen as another example of the alliance between the friars and the bishop. With regard to the Franciscans, the place of Stanislaus' canonization ceremony – Assisi – should be noted.[33] Importantly, it was a Dominican, Vincent of Kielcza, who composed the hagiographical works about St Stanislaus (*Vita maior*) after the canonization, between 1257 and 1261,[34] at the request of Bishop Prandota and the cathedral chapter (*rogatu venerabilis patris domini Prandote Cracoviensis episcopi et capituli sui*).[35] The development of the canonization process shows that both miracles and virtues of the candidate were important and necessary for the official recognition of sainthood, they were interconnected and constituted "one package", and both these aspects could encourage devotion, and its renewal, of the faithful. At the outset both cults of Florian and Stanislaus were to a great extent bound to their shrines and relics as places of their presence and intercession, but usually a combination of more factors was needed for the devotion to persist – the narrative of their saintly lives, the repetitive ritual framework of commemoration in the context of liturgy, ideally with the occasion of preaching on them (normally when the feast was a *festum fori*). In terms of the type of life model, Bishop Stanislaus in the short account of Master Vincent's Chronicle was into some extent similar to Florian, as presented in the legend spread in the Middle Ages, imported as well (which was, besides the translation legend, a part of some legend collections in Poland

---

[32] G. LABUDA, *Święty Stanisław, op. cit.*, p. 156.
[33] On the other hand, the *Miracula* protocol contained only a few explicit mentions of the Mendicant orders that indicate their active part in the cult as far as the miracles are concerned. They appear as witnesses; sometimes the miracle beneficiaries came to them for confession after the miracle: *Miracula*, Art. 15, p. 297; Art. 22, p. 301; Art. 43, p. 316-317 (the same account, slightly modified in the *Vita maior*, III/21, p. 407-408). A boy called Stanislaus had been miraculously healed, then he entered the Franciscan order. *Ibid.*, III/27, p. 410-411.
[34] *Vita maior*, p. 319-438. It is listed in *BHL* under nos. 7833-7835. A Polish translation, "Żywot większy św. Stanisława", appears in *Średniowieczne żywoty i cuda patronów Polski*, transl. J. PLEZIOWA, ed. and introduction by M. PLEZIA, Warsaw, 1981, p. 247-344. An English summary and analysis are found in A. ROŻNOWSKA-SADRAEI, *Pater Patriae: The Cult of Saint Stanislaus and the Patronage of Polish Kings 1200-1455*, Krakow, 2008, p. 65-71.
[35] *Vita maior*, p. 363. The shorter of the two thirteenth-century lives, *Vita minor*, i.e. the legend which usually appears in the late medieval collections, is related to the *Vita maior*, although their relative chronology and the exact dating of the *Vita minor* are still debated, see above.

in the fourteenth and fifteenth centuries) – a courageous person opposing a powerful tyrant, showing fortitude and perseverance till the end.[36] The thirteenth-century proper hagiographic lives enriched the figure of St Stanislaus in terms of model of virtuous life and supplied much more detailed characteristic not limited to the conflict with the king and the bishop's death, starting from his childhood: he was a model cleric and bishop, according to the ideals of the thirteenth century, rather than the eleventh century.[37]

Already at the time when Stanislaus was canonized and his cult was spreading from its centre, there were other persons in Krakow who died in the odour of sanctity, connected with the mendicant orders. Although they neither achieved canonization, nor even an official process was initiated, the Dominicans and Franciscans were involved in propagation of their holiness; the shrines of these persons became the places of spontaneous devotion of the faithful, the friars initiated collecting miracle depositions, possibly with the intention of canonization supplication in mind, and their lives were written. The miracles of Princess Salomea of Galicia were collected by the Franciscans/Poor Clares shortly after her death (her body was translated from Skala to Krakow), in the period 1268-1273, then her life was also written around 1290.[38] Similarly, another princess from Hungary, Kinga, the wife of Boleslaus V the Chaste of Krakow, died in the odour of sanctity in the nunnery of Poor Clares in Stary Sącz; her life was written by a Franciscan friar in the fourteenth century and her miracles were collected around 1307-1312 and then were edited in 1329 (their second redaction).[39] In the Dominican

---

[36] For the legend of St Florian, see *Passiones vitaeque sanctorum aevi Merovingici et antiquorum aliquot*, ed. B. KRUSCH, Hannover, 1896 (*Monumenta Germaniae Historica*, Scriptores rerum Merovingicarum, 3), p. 65-71. The legend spread in Polish context, see Jakub de Voragine, *Złota legenda: Wybór*, ed. M. PLEZIA and J. PLEZIOWA, Warsaw, 1955, p. 251-258, the Polish translation of the legend on p. 253-256, then continued with Polish translation of the legend of the translation of St Florian, p. 256-258; the legend was later printed in legend collection of local patron saints: *Vita beatissimi Stanislai episcopi nec non legendae sanctorum Poloniae, Hungariae, Bohemiae, Prussiae et Slesiae patronum in Lombardica historia non contentae*, Cracoviae, Haller, 1511, fol. 98. See also *Acta Sanctorum*, Maii I, col. 462-463; K. DOBROWOLSKI, *Dzieje kultu św. Florjana w Polsce, op. cit.*, p. 95-101.

[37] For the characteristic of St Stanislaus as the model of virtues and ideal bishop in the lives, see my *Preaching Saint Stanislaus*, especially p. 36-39; and my article, "St Stanislaus of Cracow as a Model of Virtues in Sermons and Hagiography", in *Models of Virtues. The Role of Virtues in Sermons and Hagiography for New Saints' Cults (13th-15th centuries)*, ed. E. LOMBARDO, Padova, 2016, p. 121-136.

[38] *Vita sanctae Salomeae reginae Haliciensis*, ed. W. KĘTRZYŃSKI (*MPH*, 4), p. 770-796. A. WITKOWSKA, "Miracula małopolskie", *art. cit.*, p. 38-39, 52-55, etc.

[39] *Vita et miracula sanctae Kyngae ducissae Cracoviensis*, ed. W. KĘTRZYŃSKI (*MPH*, 4), p. 682-744. A. WITKOWSKA, "Miracula małopolskie", *art. cit.*, p. 39-41, 55-57, etc. For her

convent in Krakow, St Hyacinth/Jacek was venerated shortly after his death. His life written in the mid-fourteenth century by Stanislaus, the lector of the Dominicans in Krakow, informs us that depositions about his miracles (the *Liber miraculorum* which he used for writing the Life) were collected at his shrine by the lectors of the convent until 1289, and then again from 1329.[40] However, they did not enjoy an officially recognized cult until much later. As for Hyacinth, one miracle account talks about a woman who predicted his canonization, saying that he would do more damage to the hell than Bishop Stanislaus who was newly canonized then.[41] From this we can infer that the Dominicans intended to initiate canonization process at that time. These local cults connected to recently deceased persons in the Franciscan and Dominican convents, had prerequisites to become successful, they had features which would make the devotion towards them deeply rooted in the local space and vivid, perhaps an advantage which St Florian did not have. Still, these "modern" candidates for sainthood were not recognized officially as St Stanislaus was at the time. The authors of their lives and miracle collections made also effort to relate them to an established saint, Stanislaus in this case: Kinga was according to her *vita* one of the initiators of his canonization and his devotee; St Hyacinth went to preach on the occasion of his elevation/translation and on his way returned sight to two boys born blind,[42] at the day of his funeral Bishop Prandota had a vision in which two men appeared to him in the cathedral – St Stanislaus in pontifical attire accompanied by a man in Dominican habit with two golden crowns, whom Stanislaus introduced as friar Hyacinth, doctor and virgin, in eternal glory.[43] The prospects

---

hagiography, see A. WITKOWSKA, "Bł. Kinga w średniowiecznych przekazach hagiograficznych", in *Sancti, Miracula, Peregrinationes*, Lublin, 2009, p. 43-53. The model for these saintly princesses was probably St Hedwig of Silesia, another Piast princess, canonized in 1267. For the ideals of sainthood of dynastic princesses and these figures, see G. KLANICZAY, *Holy Rulers and Blessed Princesses: Dynastic Cults in Medieval Central Europe*, Cambridge, 2002, p. 195-294, especially p. 220-224.

[40] *De vita et miraculis sancti Iacchonis (Hyacinthi) Ordinis Fratrum Praedicatorum*, ed. L. ĆWIKLIŃSKI (*MPH*, 4), p. 818-894; A. WITKOWSKA, "Miracula małopolskie", *art. cit.*, p. 41-43, 57-60, etc.

[41] *De vita et miraculis sancti Iacchonis*, cap. XLIX, p. 890-891 (*Quomodo demones predixerunt canonizacionem beati Iaczonis*, dated to 1279). For more about the pre-canonization cult of St Hyacinth and further literature, see the study of Anna Zajchowska in this volume.

[42] *De vita et miraculis sancti Iacchonis*, cap. XXII, p. 861. See also St. KUZMOVÁ, *Preaching Saint Stanislaus*, *op. cit.*, p. 86-87.

[43] *De vita et miraculis sancti Iacchonis*, cap. XXV, p. 865. After his death Hyacinth is sometimes invoked in miracle accounts together with St Vitus, the Dominican friar and missionary bishop, as two Dominican holy men buried in the Church of Holy Trinity in Krakow, e.g. *ibid.*, no. XXX, p. 875; no. XXXVI, p. 879; no. XXXVIII, p. 881; no. XLVII, p. 888-889 – mentions a woman who set on a pilgrimage to the *limina sancti Stanislay et beatorum*

of more native saints, as envisaged by the cooperating bishop of Krakow and the Mendicant orders, are found in the *Vita maior* of St Stanislaus already: a man in one of the miracle accounts had a vision in which he was told that there have been until that time six saintly men in Poland, equal to Stanislaus in front of God due to their death and miracles. It is probable that the author had the deceased Dominican friars in mind as well.[44]

Let us look briefly at a later period. Both St Stanislaus and St Florian are visible in the religious landscape of Krakow. In the fifteenth century, the cult of St Stanislaus was well-established and safely functioned in both official and popular context, and spread throughout the Polish lands. His feast of martyrdom was a *festum fori* throughout the Polish dioceses, but the main centre of his cult remained in Krakow, concentrated in two places – his shrine in the cathedral at Wawel and the place of his martyrdom at Skałka/Rupella near the city. Sermons for his feasts preserved in manuscripts document the success of his cult too, and develop the content of his hagiography and cult in order to give a lesson to the faithful.[45] Skalka, with its miraculous pool, crystallized as the place of a more popular cult among various levels of population, publicized by Długosz (1415-1480), who wrote a new life and attached newly collected miracle accounts from the period around 1460.[46] The new initiatives came in connection with Bishop Zbigniew Oleśnicki, who supported the traditional patron cults of the city and the diocese: Stanislaus, Florian, and then, besides them also Adalbert and Wenceslas. In late Middle Ages all of them had their firm place in the pantheon of the local patrons, their festivities were regularly celebrated, often not only locally but reaching beyond the centre, still retaining an important connection to Krakow. Preachers had occasions to deliver sermons on these saints on their feast-days in front of clerical and lay audiences (most of the time these feasts were

---

uirorum Iaczchonis et Uiti episcopi Lumbuzani de ordine fratrum predicatorum and invoked the latter two for help with the pain of her feet.

[44] *Vita maior* III/54, p. 433: *adhuc in Polonia sunt sex sancti et electi Dei, quorum mors preciosa est in conspectu Domini, qui sunt equales coram Deo meritis beati Stanislai, quos Deus omnipotens signis et miraculis mirificabit et ostendet temporibus suis*. Wojciech Kętrzyński thought that these were Dominicans and bishops of Krakow, but Witkowska maintains that these are St Adalbert and Five brethren martyrs; A. WITKOWSKA, *Kulty, op. cit.*, p. 80-81.

[45] I have collected 80 various texts for the feasts of St Stanislaus in 100 codices and dealt with various aspects of his cult (especially the sermons on him) in my *Preaching Saint Stanislaus*, including the imitable and admirable dimensions of his image and cult (for this, see Chapter 4 and 5).

[46] Joannes Dlugossius, *Vita sanctissimi Stanislai episcopi Cracoviensis*. Opera omnia 1, ed. I. POLKOWSKI and Ż. PAULI, Krakow, 1887, p. 1-181. Another edition is included in the *Acta Sanctorum*: Joannes Dlugossius, *Vita sancti Stanislai episcopi Cracoviensis*, Acta Sanctorum, Maii II, p. 202-276. The *Vita* is listed in under nos. BHL 7839-7841.

prescribed as *festa fori*), the feasts of Sts. Stanislaus and Florian were celebrated with processions.[47] These patrons are listed in the synodal statutes of Bishop Zbigniew Oleśnicki from 1436: the statute raises the rank of the feast of St Florian to be venerated (in the liturgy of hours and of mass) in the diocese of Krakow on the same, high level as the other patrons of the kingdom – Adalbert, Stanislaus and Wenceslas; establishing special offices and devotional prayers to each of them on particular days of the week.[48] This was not only an effort to revive the cult of the old Florian, but also a framework for regular presence of these saints in the religious life of the community. They are also often depicted together as protectors of the community. Interestingly enough, exactly the four saints who are mentioned in the synodal statutes appear in the vision account of a certain woman Veronica recorded in the well-known book of Annals by Długosz, dated to 1438 – a couple of years after the statutes were issued. In her vision Veronica found herself in the Church of St Florian behind the walls, where she saw a multitude of people in procession, among them some in episcopal attire, others in knightly dress, both in white and red. Veronica followed the procession towards the city, when two of them, a man in pontifical attire and another one dressed as a knight approached her and talked to her. They turned out to be St Adalbert and

---

[47] For the liturgy related to these patrons of Krakow, see a more detailed summary by P. Kołpak, "Rola patronów Królestwa Polskiego w geografii póznośredniowiecznego Krakowa", in *Średniowiecze Polskie i Powszechne*, 10 (2014), p. 158-190. For the summary of Krakow celebrations related to St Stanislaus, see St. Kuzmová, *Preaching Saint Stanislaus*, op. cit., p. 113-117.

[48] *Statuty synodalne krakowskie Zbigniewa Oleśnickiego (1436, 1446)* (Krakow synodal statutes of Zbigniew Oleśnicki), ed. S. Zachorowski (Studya i materyały do historyi ustawodawstwa synodalnego w Polsce), vol. 1, Krakow, 1915, p. 43-47 (Art. 4, p. 44: Statutum de officiis et horis dicendis). On p. 47: *Etsi, ut sanctorum patrum edocemur scripturis, dominum in sanctis suis laudare iubemur, illos tamen specialis devocionis titulo attollere et dignis magnificare preconiis merito tenemur, quos divina dispensacione speciales ante faciem sedentis in throno intercessores sentimus et gaudemus nos habere patronos. Sane cum ecclesia nostra inter aliorum celestium civium venerandas reliquias gloriossimi martyris beati Floriani venerando corpore dotata sit, eius quoque interventu et meritis apud Deum totum hoc regnum Polonie credat se crebrius communiri, de fratrum nostrorum Capituli Cracoviensis previa deliberacione et assensu statuimus et presentibus ordinamus prenominatum gloriosum martyrem et patronum nostrum per totam nostram diocesim inter ceteros regni huius patronos insignes, videlicet Adalbertum, Stanislaum, Wenceslaum martyres pari devocione in horis canonicis et officiis divinis attollendum, colendum et venerandum, quodque de ipso huiusmodi officium feria quarta, de sancto Wenceslao tercia, de sancto Adalberto secunda et de beato Stanislao quinta feriis de cetero per totam nostram diocesim fiat et observetur temporibus perpetue duratis.* For Zbigniew Oleśnicki and his promotion of four main patrons of the diocese, Sts. Stanislaus, Florian, Wenceslas and Adalbert, with a special emphasis on the first two as particular Krakow patrons, see K. Dobrowolski, *Dzieje kultu św. Floriana w Polsce*, p. 92-116; M. Koczerska, *Zbigniew Oleśnicki i kościół krakowski w czasach jego pontyfikatu (1423-1455)*, Warsaw, 2004, p. 268-273.

St Florian, going to visit their "compatriots", Sts. Stanislaus and Wenceslas, to the cathedral at the castle hill of Wawel. Adalbert told her that the four of them had been assigned by God to their land as helpers and patrons, who speak on behalf of them in sight of God.[49]

Despite the efforts to revive the cult, its liturgical persistence in the city (*festum fori* on 4 May) and the presence of Florian among other patron saints, the transferred (and perhaps out-fashioned) cult proved rather weak in broader terms: there was no collection of his miracles (or is not preserved), and sermons on him have rather low profile in manuscripts (sometimes substituted with a legend), as compared to St Stanislaus, by any means. The collection of the cathedral preacher Paul of Zator (*c.* 1395-1463) is rather an exceptional case; it contains besides two sermons on St Stanislaus also four sermons on St Adalbert and other four on St Florian.[50] Still, one of Zator's sermons reminds that St Florian is not venerated in Poland as much as he

---

[49] Joannes Dlugossius, *Annales seu Cronicae incliti Regni Poloniae*, Liber 11-12 (1431-1444), ed. C. BACZKOWSKI *et al.*, Warsaw, 2001, Liber 12 (1438), p. 191-197 (*Mirabilis visio cuiusdam Cracoviensis virginis Veronicae*): *Ne timeas, inquit, scimus unde venis et quid videris, quod quia non intelligis, aperiemus tibi, et tu attende, quid te oporteat in re hac agere. Sic orsus subintulit: ecce ego et hic amantissimus socius meus, quem vides, sanctus et gloriosus martyr Florianus, visitavimus gloriosos patres concives nostros, sanctum Stanislaum et Wenceslaum, et ecclesiam ipsorum in castro sitam, quam inclitus confessor noster sanctus Stanislaus glorioso sanguinis sui martyrio, locum hunc omnipotenti Deo grato admodum sacrificio dedicavit et charum effecit. Nos enim quatuor, hi videlicet tres prenominati martires sancti et ego Adalbertus, dati sumus huic patriae in singulos coadiutores et patronos, qui incessanter assistimus ante conspectum Altissimi pro salute gentis huius.* The vision is the topic of the study of U. BORKOWSKA, "Przykład pobożności mieszczańskiej w XV wieku. Weronika z Krakowa", in *Sztuka i ideologia XV wieku. Materiały sympozjum Komitetu Nauk o Sztuce Polskiej Akademii Nauk, Warszawa, 1-4 grudnia 1976 r.*, ed. P. SKUBISZEWSKI, Warsaw, 1978, p. 111-121.

[50] St. KUZMOVÁ, *Preaching Saint Stanislaus*, p. 151-154. The devotion to St Florian in the fifteenth century was related also to the university clerics who held benefices at the Church of St Florian, since 1401 (like Bishop Zbigniew Oleśnicki). Sermons (and sermon materials) on St Florian are also included in the collections of John of Słupca, Paul of Zator (several manuscripts), John of Dąbrówka; *De sancto Floriano sermo* in the collection in Krakow, Biblioteca Jagellonica (hereafter BJ) 2340, fol. 150r-154r; *De sancto Floriano* in Krakow, Biblioteka Czartoryskich (Czartoryski Library, BCzart) 3413 III, fol. 74v-78v; related to *Sermo sancti Floriani* in BJ 1613, fol. 319r; BCzart 3793 II, p. 999-1001. For basic information about these authors and collections, see my *Preaching Saint Stanislaus*; also in the appendix for some references to St Florian in sermons on St Stanislaus and Adalbert, inspired by Peregrinus of Opole, from the collection of John of Dąbrówka, see *ibid.*, p. 450, 453. In several cases, the emphasis is on miracles and the power of his intercession in various phenomena, in other cases his martyrdom. Dobrowolski lists some sermons on St Florian in his *Dzieje kultu św. Florjana w Polsce*, 117-118 – he mentions manuscripts BCzart 3414, and Krakow PAN/PAU Library 1709.

would deserve, although he is their patron and defender, while in Austria they did not have his relics but showed him bigger devotion.[51]

In the fifteenth century, besides the continuity and revival of devotion towards older, established patron saints, a number of new cults started to emerge around several religious centres, both spontaneously and with institutional support of the bishop and the Mendicant orders. It is especially documented by collecting miracle depositions at the shrines of these persons. This period is called as a *felix seculum Cracovie* with a "confraternity" of holy men in the literature as early as in the sixteenth and seventeenth centuries.[52] In the fifteenth century, initiatives continued to boost several local cults and there were attempts to start canonization process in a couple of cases: Dominican Hyacinth (canonized in 1594) and Queen Hedwig of Anjou, which, however, were not successful at the time.[53] The body of former bishop Prandota, the supporter of the canonization of St Stanislaus, was elevated in the cathedral and Bishop Zbigniew Oleśnicki ordered to collect depositions concerning his miracles.[54] Other cults were connected with various local convents – again, these were the "living" saints, who died recently in odour of sanctity: Simon of Lipnica (died 1482) of the Observant Franciscans, Stanislaus Kazimierczyk

---

[51] *Sermo secundus de sancto Floriano*, manuscript Krakow, BJ 491, fol. 188r: *Dies hec gloriosi martiris ac militis Cristi martiris et amici Dei sancti Floriani, huius regni patroni, adiutoris et defensoris in tribulacionibus et periculis, quem tamen forsan debilius, et non ita ut meretur a nobis, honoramus. Licet enim suis sanctis reliquiis, sui corporis hanc patriam honoraverit, non tamen hunc honorem digna devocione ei rependimus. Quoniam ut fertur in partibus Austrie, ubi de ipsius reliquiis nihil habetur, homines ipsum maiori affectu et devocione honorant tanquam singularem ab igne protectorem, et in angustiis ad Deum intercessorem.* This is possibly also a hint at the supplication for the relics of St Florian by the representatives of the convent of Regular Canons from Sankt Florian.

[52] R. M. ZAWADZKI, "Mistrz Jan z Kęt i 'szczęśliwy wiek Krakowa'", in *Felix saeculum Cracoviae – krakowscy święci XV wieku. Materiały sesji naukowej Kraków, 24. kwietnia 1997 roku*, ed. K. PANUŚ and K. R. PROKOP, Krakow, 1998, p. 53-70. For a comprehensive overview and analysis of the miracle collections and cults in the fifteenth century, see A. WITKOWSKA, *Kulty pątnicze piętnastowiecznego Krakowa*, Lublin, 1984.

[53] For St Hyacinth, see the study of Anna Zajchowska in this volume, and M. KOWALCZYK, "Starania kardynała Zbigniewa Oleśnickiego o kanonizację św. Jacka Odrowąża", in *Dominikanie w środkowej Europie, op. cit.*, p. 65-72. For the memory of Hedwig in the milieu of the University of Krakow, see J. WOLNY and R. M. ZAWADZKI, "Królowa Jadwiga w tradycji kaznodziejskiej XV wieku", *Analecta Cracoviensia*, 7 (1975), p. 15-90. The commission to collect miracles at the shrine of St Hedwig was initiated by Bishop Wojciech Jastrzębiec in 1426 and there were some efforts during the times of Zbigniew Oleśnicki around 1450; a fragment in *Miracula beatae Hedwigis reginae Poloniae*, ed. W. KĘTRZYŃSKI (*MPH*, 4), p. 763-769. For her cult see A. WITKOWSKA, *Kulty, op. cit.*, p. 88-92.

[54] Miracle depositions were collected between 1454 and 1465. *Miracula venerabilis patris Prandothae episcopi Cracoviensis*, ed. W. KĘTRZYŃSKI (*MPH*, 4), p. 439-500; A. WITKOWSKA, *Kulty, op. cit.*, p. 40-44, 92-94. Prandota was praised for his merits for the canonization of St Stanislaus in *Miracula venerabilis patris Prandothae, op. cit.*, p. 442, 479.

(*c.* 1430-1489) of the Regular Canons at Kazimierz, Isaias Boner (died 1471) of the Augustinians,[55] theologian and university professor John of Kęty/Cantius (1390-1473) at the parish church of St Anne,[56] and so on. Their shrines attracted devotion of the faithful and pilgrims, local and from the surrounding region, their miracles were collected; Aleksandra Witkowska counted that 776 notes of miracles had been collected in Krakow about various saintly persons, both earlier and more recent, between 1430 and 1520.[57] But despite the efforts and the popular devotion, in the fifteenth century they did not achieve the official recognition like St Stanislaus, and thus also lacked the related liturgical framework; some of them succeeded later. The holy bishop was not just a subject of official liturgical cult – the interest on the popular part continued as well – St Stanislaus was the only saintly man in Krakow, whose miracles continued to be collected in the fifteenth century as well (as Aleksandra Witkowska noted[58]) and who proved successful among these new cults too and stood their pressure. Despite that he represented a traditional, old, type of sainthood, he was much more: not only a miracle-worker, an officially recognized patron of the community and kingdom, but, as sermons document, he was also an example of virtuous life especially for the bishops and priests, thus representing the moral reform of the clergy, so topical in the fifteenth century, an imitator of Christ in his life and his passion (in keeping with the contemporary devotional trends related to the passion and suffering of Christ) and as a good shepherd also an example of virtues to his flock and its protector.

---

[55] For the development of these new cults, see A. WITKOWSKA, *Kulty, op. cit.*, p. 94-106; for collections of miracles of Simon of Lipnica and Stanislaus Kazimierczyk, p. 47-55.
[56] A. WITKOWSKA, *Kulty, op. cit.*, p. 44-47; R. M. ZAWADZKI, "Mistrz Jan z Kęt", *art. cit.*, p. 53-70; *Id.*, *Spuścizna rękopiśmienna świętego Jana Kantego: studium kodykologiczne*, Krakow, 1995.
[57] A. WITKOWSKA, *Kulty, op. cit.*, p. 39.
[58] *Ibid.*, p. 82.

À la recherche des sources liturgiques et hagiographiques du culte des « saints rois » hongrois en Europe centrale[*]

Edit MADAS
(*Budapest*)

Si, au Moyen Âge, le culte liturgique officiel des saints hongrois s'est limité au territoire de la Hongrie, les textes liturgiques ou hagiographiques les concernant ont souvent traversé de diverses façons les frontières du pays. Dans la présente étude, nous nous intéresserons au culte en Europe centrale des trois saints de la dynastie arpadienne mentionnés ensemble comme *sancti reges Hungariae* : le roi Étienne († 1038), fondateur du royaume de Hongrie ; son fils, le prince Émeric († 1031) ; et le roi Ladislas († 1095), qui consolida le pays et l'Église. Le roi Étienne et le prince Émeric furent canonisés en 1083 à l'initiative du roi Ladislas, lequel fut lui-même canonisé cent ans plus tard, en 1192, par Béla III. Nous examinerons les raisons, les formes et les bornes géographiques du développement et de l'extension de leur culte, en nous appuyant principalement sur les sources liturgiques et hagiographiques du Moyen Âge extérieures à la Hongrie[1].

Le culte liturgique des saints est peut-être le plus facile à appréhender. En général, les calendriers des livres liturgiques donnent précisément le rang de la fête de chaque saint, et lors de la fête elle-même, on peut lire – en rapport avec celle-ci – des textes liturgiques propres ou généraux[2]. Bien qu'il n'y ait

---

[*] Cette contribution a été préparée dans le cadre des activités du groupe de recherches « Res libraria Hungariae » (Académie des Sciences de Hongrie, Bibliothèque Nationale de Hongrie).
[1] Pour une analyse des légendes dans un contexte européen, voir G. KLANICZAY, « Il culto dei santi ungheresi nel Medioevo in Europa », dans *La civiltà ungherese e il cristianesimo*, éd. J. JANKOVICS *et al.*, Budapest, 1998, vol. 1, p. 53-64 ; G. KLANICZAY, *Holy Rulers and Blessed Princesses : Dynastic Cults in Medieval Central Europe*, Cambridge, 2002 ; L. VESZPRÉMY, « Royal Saints in Hungarian Chronicles, Legends and Liturgy », dans *The Making of Christian Myths in the Periphery of Latin Christendom (c. 1000-1300)*, éd. L. B. MORTENSEN, Copenhague, Museum Tusculanum Press, 2006, p. 217-245. La présente contribution est le prolongement d'une étude antérieure : E. MADAS, « A magyar 'szent királyok' közép-európai kultusza liturgikus és hagiográfiai források tükrében », *Ars Hungarica*, 39 (2013), p. 145-152.
[2] On signale que le calendrier et le corpus du missel ou du bréviaire peuvent également différer, pour diverses raisons.

Les saints et leur culte en Europe centrale au Moyen Âge (XIᵉ-début du XVIᵉ siècle), éd. par Marie-Madeleine de CEVINS et Olivier MARIN, Turnhout, 2017 (*Hagiologia*, 13), p. 281-292.
© BREPOLS ☙ PUBLISHERS   DOI 10.1484/M.HAG-EB.5.113977

pas encore eu d'examen systématique des livres liturgiques des pays voisins de la Hongrie en relation avec les saints hongrois[3], nous aimerions attirer l'attention sur quelques exemples caractéristiques. Dans le missel de Gniezno-Cracovie publié à Strasbourg en 1490[4] figurent, accompagnées de leurs prières, les fêtes du 27 juin de saint Ladislas[5] et du 20 août de saint Étienne[6] – et ce bien qu'elles ne soient pas mentionnées dans le calendrier. Saint Émeric manque à l'appel. De même, dans le calendrier du missel de Prague publié en 1479[7], les saints hongrois n'apparaissent pas, alors que le corpus lui-même fait place à la fête de saint Étienne[8].

Les traces concrètes de leur culte liturgique sont le fruit d'une relation de voisinage, d'un contact direct avec les pays limitrophes. De la même manière, les saints tchèques et polonais sont présents dans les rites utilisés en Hongrie. Le bréviaire d'Esztergom imprimé en 1484 fait place au 28 septembre à saint Venceslas, avec six lectures s'appuyant sur sa légende[9]. Dans le bréviaire paulinien, on peut lire au 8 mai la légende de l'évêque saint Stanislas[10], et au 28 septembre celle de Venceslas, dans une version plus juste que celle du bréviaire d'Esztergom[11]. En analysant les fragments de *codices* liturgiques des archives de Sopron, Judit Lauf est récemment parvenue à isoler, à l'intérieur du rite de Passau, le rite de Vienne, dans lequel les saints hongrois trouvaient souvent également place. Il faut préciser que Sopron se situe à proximité de la frontière autrichienne et que ce sont les seules archives de la Hongrie d'aujourd'hui qui soient restées intactes depuis le Moyen Âge. Une partie des actes de Sopron a

---

[3] À titre d'exemple on se reportera à la monographie de Petr Kubín sur les saints tchèques : *Sedm přemyslovských kultů*, Prague, 2011.

[4] Budapest, Bibliothèque Universitaire, Inc. 882 : Missale Gnesnense-Cracoviense, Strasbourg, Johann Prüss, c. 1490.

[5] *Oratio*: Deus, qui beatum Ladislaum regem confessoremque tuum diversis miraculis decorasti...; *Secreta*: Mystica nobis prosit oblacio, Domine, que nos a reatibus...; *Complenda*: Refecti, Domine, benediccione solemni, quesumus, ut intercessione... La formule « regem nostrum et confessorem tuum » en vigueur dans les prières des missels hongrois est remplacée dans les missels étrangers par la formule « regem confessoremque tuum ».

[6] *Oratio*: Deus qui beatum Stephanum regem confessoremque tuum terreni imperii gloria et honore coronasti...; *Secreta*: Laudis tue, Domine, hostias immolamus in tuorum commemoratione sanctorum...; *Complenda*: Refecti cibo potuque celesti, Deus noster, te supplices exoramus, ut in cuius...

[7] *Missale Pragense of 1479*, éd. Z. V. Tobolka, Prague, 1931 (Monumenta Bohemiae Typographica, 9).

[8] *Oratio*: Deus, qui beato Stephano confessori tuo non solum regni coronam...; *Secreta*: Placeant tibi munera, omnipotens Deus, que tue clemencie deferimus...; *Complenda*: Sumpta sacrificia nos, quesumus Domine, a laqueis inimicorum nostrorum...

[9] Breviarium Strigoniense, Nuremberg, 1484 : *Beatus Venceslaus ex christianissimo patre, [duce] Bohemorum genitus...*

[10] Breviarium Ordinis Paulinorum, Venise, 1540 : *Beatus Stanislaus Cracoviensis episcopus...*

[11] *Beatus Venceslaus ex christianissimo patre, duce Bohemorum natus...*

été utilisée comme élément de reliure dans des fragments de *codices* apportés par les relieurs de Vienne à la fin du XVIIe siècle[12].

Regardons à présent plus à l'ouest. Le culte à Bamberg des saints rois de Hongrie a une explication non pas géographique, mais historique. Le diocèse de Bamberg et la cathédrale elle-même ont été fondés en 1007 par Henri II, beau-frère de saint Étienne et frère de la reine Gisèle. La fête de saint Étienne apparut pour la première fois dans un calendrier liturgique bambergeois en 1146, année de la canonisation de Henri II[13]. Son office comportait neuf lectures[14] ; autant dire qu'elle était d'une grande importance. Au début du XIVe siècle le prévôt de la cathédrale fit une fondation pour pouvoir célébrer dignement ladite fête, et en 1377 on éleva un autel en l'honneur des « trois saints rois de Hongrie » dans l'église Saint-Michel de Bamberg[15].

Le dernier élément que l'on peut mentionner à propos du culte liturgique nous vient d'encore plus loin, de Finlande. Le premier livre imprimé des Finnois, le *Missale Aboense*, missel de Turku qui vit le jour en 1488 à Lübeck, contient en annexe les fêtes des saints hongrois[16]. Ce phénomène surprenant vient de ce que le spécimen du missel de Turku était un missel dominicain imprimé à Venise en 1484[17], dans lequel les saints de la province dominicaine de Hongrie avaient pris place[18]. L'une des leçons que l'on peut tirer de l'exemple finnois est que la présence des saints hongrois dans un livre liturgique tient parfois au seul hasard.

L'importance du rôle des pèlerinages dans la diffusion du culte des saints est reconnue. Les Hongrois se rendaient massivement en pèlerinage à Aix-la-Chapelle, où le roi Louis le Grand avait fait élever en 1367 une chapelle abritant

---

[12] J. LAUF, « Verbindungen der mittelalterlichen liturgischen Praxis in Wien und Ödenburg », *Codices Manuscripti*, 73-74 (2010), p. 15-30 ; J. LAUF, « Beiträge zur liturgischen Praxis in der Diözese Wien und im Wiener Schottenstift auf Grund Ödenburger Handschriftenfragmente », dans *Quelle und Deutung*, I, éd. B. SÁRA, Budapest, 2014 (EC-Beiträge zur Erforschung deutschsprachiger Handschriften des Mittelalters und der Frühen Neuzeit), p. 89-104.
[13] R. KROOS, « Liturgische Quellen zur Bamberger Dom », *Zeitschrift für Kunstgeschichte*, 39 (1976), p. 144-145.
[14] G. SCHREIBER, *Stephan I. der Heilige. König von Ungarn, 997-1038. Eine hagiographische Studie*, Paderborn, 1938, p. 44.
[15] G. SCHREIBER, *Stephan I. in der deutschen Sakralkultur*, Budapest, 1938 (Études sur l'Europe centre-orientale, 15), p. 24-27.
[16] *Missale Aboense*, Lübeck, Bartholomeus Gothan, 1488. Cf. E. SÁMSON, « Adalék a magyar liturgiatörténethez. Magyar szentek tisztelete Finnország középkori liturgiájában », *Pannonhalmi Szemle*, 15 (1940), p. 238-240.
[17] *Missale secundum Ordinem Fratrum Predicatorum*, Venise, Nicolaus de Franckfordia, 1484.
[18] *Vanhimman suomalaisen kirjallisuuden käsikirja*, éd. T. LAINE, Helsinki, 1997, p. 104.

les reliques des trois saints hongrois, ainsi qu'à Cologne, le lieu de culte le plus important des trois rois mages. Peu de temps après, la chapelle Sainte-Catherine de l'église Saint-Maccabée des sœurs bénédictines de Cologne reçut une partie des reliques des saints hongrois d'Aix-la-Chapelle[19]. Autre souvenir de la vénération commune des saints rois par les pèlerins de cette région : un livre de prières de 1432 dans lequel on trouve, après des prières aux rois mages, une enluminure de pleine page (fol. 142v) représentant saint Émeric, saint Étienne et saint Ladislas, suivie d'un *suffragium* à saint Étienne[20].

Les canaux de diffusion des légendes des saints hongrois constituent une autre voie d'exploration possible. Il faut prendre en compte les légendes qui ont été composées, copiées, traduites et utilisées en dehors de la Hongrie. L'édition critique des légendes de saint Étienne, saint Émeric et saint Ladislas parut en 1938 dans le deuxième volume des *Scriptores rerum Hungaricarum*[21]. L'éditeur scientifique des textes, Emma Bartoniek, a pris naturellement en compte tous les manuscrits connus à l'époque et établi les *stemmata* illustrant la généalogie des textes, sans toutefois se préoccuper du contexte des légendes ni de la genèse des *codices*[22].

La tradition des textes sur saint Étienne étant la plus riche, elle nous servira ici d'exemple. À l'époque d'Emma Bartoniek, on connaissait onze légendiers de saint Étienne copiés ou utilisés à l'étranger[23]. Depuis, Florio Bánfi a découvert en 1948 un légendier conservé à Padoue qui contient, outre la légende des trois saints rois de Hongrie, celle de saint Gérard[24]. En 1968,

---

[19] G. Schreiber, *Stephan I. in der deutschen Sakralkultur, op. cit.*, p. 14.
[20] Munich, Bayerische Staatsbibliothek, Clm 21590. Selon Kinga Körmendy, le livre a pu être réalisé dans un territoire situé entre Passau, Ratisbonne et Nuremberg. K. Körmendy, « Egy 1432-ből származó imádságoskönyv magyar vonatkozásai », dans *Tanulmányok a középkori magyarországi könyvkultúráról*, éd. L. Szelestei N., Budapest, 1989, p. 259-272 ; Gy. Török, « Egy 15. századi imádságoskönyv a hónapképek és a magyar szent királyok ábrázolásával », dans *Tanulmányok a középkori magyarországi könyvkultúráról, op. cit.*, p. 273-296. Voir encore G. Klaniczay, *Holy rulers, op. cit.*, p. 393, fig. 91 (l'image est ici accidentellement reproduite à l'envers et la référence à Presbourg / Bratislava dans la légende renvoie à un autre codex).
[21] *Scriptores rerum Hungaricarum tempore ducum regumque stirpis Arpadianae gestarum*, vol. I-II, éd. E. Szentpétery, Budapest, 1937-1938. Reprint : éd. K. Szovák, L. Veszprémy, Budapest, 1999.
[22] Dans la postface de la réédition de 1999, la liste d'Emma Bartoniek est complétée par de nombreux éléments : vol. II, p. 363-460, 507-527.
[23] Budapest, Bibliothèque Nationale Hongroise (Országos Széchényi Könyvtár, ci-après OSzK), Cod. Lat. 17, Cod. Lat. 431 ; Heiligenkreuz, Stiftsbibliothek, Cod. 13 ; Lilienfeld, Stiftsbibliothek, Cod. 60 ; Melk, Stiftsbibliothek, Cod. 676 ; Vienne, Österreichische Nationalbibliothek, Cod. Lat. 832, Cod. Lat. 3662 ; Rein (Reun), Stiftsbibliothek, Cod. 69 ; Munich, Bayerische Staatsbibliothek, Clm 18624 ; Bruxelles, Bibliothèque Royale, Cod. (I) 982 ; Paris, Bibliothèque Mazarine, Cod. Lat. 1733.
[24] F. Banfi : « Vita di S. Gerardo da Venezia nel codice 1622 della biblioteca Universitaria di Padova », *Benedictina*, 2 (1948), p. 262-330. La légende de saint Étienne dans le codex 1622 se trouve aux fol. 128r-132v.

András Vizkelety établit et publia la première traduction de la légende de saint Étienne en allemand, à partir d'un recueil de légendes allemand conservé aujourd'hui à la Bibliothèque Széchényi[25]. En 1984, László Nagy découvrit dans un recueil conservé à Graz les légendes de saint Étienne, saint Émeric, saint Ladislas et saint Adalbert[26]. Nous-même, au cours de nos recherches sur la réception hongroise de la *Legenda aurea*, avons trouvé neuf manuscrits étrangers contenant la légende de saint Étienne. Ces 23 sources paraissent désormais suffisantes pour en tirer des conclusions générales sur leur provenance.

Trois légendes ont été composées en l'honneur de saint Étienne : la *Legenda maior* avant sa canonisation, la *Legenda minor* au début du règne du roi Coloman (après 1095), et la compilation des deux légendes par l'évêque Hartvik vers 1100. En 1201, le pape Innocent III approuva officiellement la version de Hartvik, laquelle devint la lecture exclusive de l'office de nuit de la Saint-Étienne. L'usage reléga de fait les deux autres légendes au second plan[27].

Le texte des légendes majeure et mineure est connu aujourd'hui grâce à quatre *codices*, où les deux légendes sont transmises ensemble. La variante la plus ancienne, celle du *Codex Ernst*, a été copiée en Hongrie probablement dans le *scriptorium* du monastère Saint-Martin à Pannonhalma dans la seconde moitié du XIIe siècle[28]. Le manuscrit contient les vies du saint patron (Martinellus) et du fondateur, Étienne (en 996). À l'origine indépendant, le livre se retrouve à la cour d'Ottokar II, plus exactement en la possession de Záviš Rosenberg. La famille Rosenberg (Rožmberk) avait fondé le monastère cistercien de Vyšší Brod (Hohenfurth) en Bohême méridionale, où notre codex fut corrigé dans le courant du XIIIe siècle avec beaucoup de soin (et une moindre compétence), puis utilisé en continu.

Les trois autres *codices* sont plus étroitement liés les uns aux autres. Il s'agit de trois légendiers monumentaux de Basse-Autriche (de quatre et six volumes), dont deux sont du XIIIe siècle (Heiligenkreuz, Lilienfeld) et le dernier du XVe (Melk). Ils font partie du célèbre *Magnum Legendarium Austriacum*, dont six exemplaires sont aujourd'hui connus, et qui réunit 21 volumes ;

---

[25] A. Vizkelety, « Eine deutsche Fassung der Stephanslegenda aus dem Jahre 1471 », *Magyar Könyvszemle*, 85 (1969), p. 129-145 ; Budapest, OSzK, Cod. Germ. 48.

[26] L. Szelestei N., « A Szent László-legenda szöveghagyományozódásáról (Ismeretlen legendaváltozat) », *Magyar Könyvszemle*, 100 (1984), p. 176-203 ; Graz, Universitätsbibliothek, Cod. Lat. 1232.

[27] G. Klaniczay, E. Madas, « La Hongrie », dans *Hagiographies : Histoire internationale de la littérature hagiographique latine et vernaculaire en Occident des origines à 1550*, éd. G. Philippart, vol. 2, Turnhout, 1996, p. 105-121.

[28] Voir E. Varjú, *Legendae S. Stephani regis. Szent István király legendái a legrégibb kézirat alapján, az Ernst-kódex hasonmásával*, Budapest, 1928 ; Budapest, OSzK, Cod. Lat. 431 ; *Ernst-Kódex (OszK, Cod. Lat. 431)*, I : Facsimile, vol. II : *Tanulmánykötet*, Budapest, Pannonhalma, 2016.

toutefois la fête de saint Étienne au mois d'août n'apparaît que dans les trois exemplaires ci-dessus mentionnés. Récemment a paru une étude importante de Diarmuid Ó Riain présentant les premiers résultats solides des nouvelles recherches sur le *Legendarium*. Selon lui, l'exemplaire primitif du légendier a été réalisé à la fin du XIIe siècle sur le territoire de l'actuelle Autriche, selon la plus grande probabilité à Admont. Désireuse de renforcer son pouvoir à travers le réseau des couvents, la dynastie de Babenberg a pu jouer un rôle dans la composition et la diffusion du légendier[29].

Pour le rédacteur, il était en tout cas important qu'Henri II, qui avait été récemment canonisé, eût sa place dans le légendier aux côtés du saint national des Tchèques, Venceslas, et du roi hongrois saint Étienne. Dans le cas de saint Étienne, il utilisa comme source une version semblable au *Codex Ernst*, version qui était reconnue tant à la cour royale que dans les cercles ecclésiastiques. Le travail de copie était mécanique, ce qui dans le cas des légendes d'Étienne aboutit du point de vue de la tradition des textes à une branche autrichienne indépendante[30].

Sur les 23 *codices* mentionnés de la légende de saint Étienne, utilisés ou réalisés à l'étranger, 19 présentent la version de Hartvik. Nous ne montrerons ici que quelques cas représentatifs. Au début – à l'instar des Légendes majeure et mineure – la version de Hartvik se diffusa de façon autonome. De fait, l'exemplaire le plus ancien que nous ayons conservé a été réalisé en Hongrie au tournant des XIIe et XIIIe siècles, puis par le biais des relations ecclésiastiques, il se retrouva bientôt à Augsbourg, où il fut relié à la fin d'un légendier augsbourgeois de même époque[31]. Plus tard, il arriva souvent qu'un exemplaire hongrois, à la suite de relations entre monastères d'un même ordre, se retrouve à l'étranger où il était sans nul doute utilisé.

Le fait que la légende soit intégrée dans un légendier étranger est le signe d'une progression de la réception, et d'un culte local véritablement vivant. L'exemple le plus manifeste à cet égard est la légende de saint Étienne en allemand mentionnée plus haut, que l'on peut lire dans un recueil de légendes à l'endroit correspondant du calendrier. La traduction a été faite à Bamberg à l'intention de frères laïques ou de sœurs ignorant le latin, pour lesquels le

---

[29] D. Ó. Riain, « The Magnum Legendarium Austriacum : a new investigation of one of medieval Europe's richest hagiographical collections », *Analecta Bollandiana*, 133 (2015), p. 87-165.
[30] E. Madas, « Die heiligen ungarische Könige in zisterziensischen Legendarien am Ende des 12. bis Anfang des 13. Jahrhunderts », dans *Zisterziensisches Schreiben im Mittelalter – Das Skriptorium der Reiner Mönche*, éd. A. Schwob, K. Kranich-Hofbauer, Bern, 2005 (Jahrbuch für Internationale Germanistik, Reihe A 71), p. 219-229.
[31] Budapest, OSzK, Cod. Lat. 17.

traducteur a retiré du texte original les détails de politique intérieure et ecclésiastique hongroise du XIe siècle, qui intéressaient peu l'auditoire allemand du XVe siècle[32].

Au XIVe siècle d'abord, puis d'une façon de plus en plus générale au XVe siècle, saint Étienne n'apparaît plus seul dans les légendiers étrangers, mais accompagné de saint Ladislas et de saint Émeric. Le plus ancien est le recueil de légendes de Graz mentionné plus haut. Les légendes des saints hongrois passèrent vraisemblablement des chartreux de Lövöld (aujourd'hui Városlöd, dans la région du lac Balaton) au monastère de Seitz, où l'on voulait obtenir du chapitre de l'ordre l'autorisation de célébrer les saints hongrois dans l'ordre même. Quoi qu'il en soit, les légendes étaient encore utilisées par la suite par les moines de Seitz[33]. À côté de cet exemple dû au hasard, le volume décoré de la *Legenda aurea* réalisé pour Frédéric III et dans lequel la légende des trois saints rois de Hongrie occupe une place de choix, traduit une représentation consciente du milieu de la cour viennoise[34].

Le recueil de légendes composé à la fin du XIIIe siècle par Jacques de Voragine est véritablement devenu populaire dans toute l'Europe aux XIVe-XVe siècles. Ici aussi le fonds a au début été complété en annexe par les saints locaux. Plus tard, les annexes ont été insérées dans le corps du texte qui suivait le calendrier. Saint Étienne figure dans neuf exemplaires de la *Legenda aurea* copiés et utilisés à l'étranger, seul parmi tous les saints hongrois dans quatre exemplaires, et avec saint Ladislas et saint Émeric dans les cinq autres. Mais, dans presque tous les cas, il se trouve en compagnie des saints polonais et tchèques Stanislas, Adalbert et Venceslas[35]. Si l'on projette sur une carte les *codices* contenant les légendes des saints hongrois, il apparaît que c'est l'usage autrichien et polonais qui domine, suivi par les *codices* d'Allemagne du sud et de Bohême, enfin par quelques exemples lointains des Pays-Bas et d'Italie[36].

Des trois saints hongrois, celui qui apparaît le plus souvent, comme nous l'avons signalé, est saint Étienne. Dans les anciens *codices*, cela n'a rien de

---

[32] A. Vizkelety, « Eine deutsche Fassung », *art. cit.*, p. 25.
[33] L. Szelestei N., « A Szent László-legenda », *art. cit.*, p. 26.
[34] E. Madas, « La Légende dorée – Historia Lombardica – en Hongrie », dans *Spiritualità e lettere nella cultura italiana e ungherese del basso Medioevo*, éd. S. Graciotti, C. Vasoli, Firenze, 1995 (Civiltà Veneziana Studi, 46), p. 53-61, ici p. 57-58.
[35] Barbara Fleith a pris en compte les volumes conservés de la *Légende dorée* et a répertorié dans tous les exemplaires les saints complétant le corpus original. Nous publions quant à nous les exemplaires extérieurs à la Hongrie dans lesquels se trouvent les légendes de saints hongrois. B. Fleith, *Studien zur Überlieferungsgeschichte der lateinischen Legenda aurea*, Bruxelles, 1991 (Subsidia Hagiographica, 72).
[36] Le nombre de légendes conservées ne reflète pas fidèlement le culte italien des saints rois hongrois. De leur côté, les sources liturgiques demeurent inexplorées.

surprenant puisque d'un point de vue européen, Émeric était moins important, et que le culte de saint Ladislas n'a commencé qu'au XIIIe siècle. Dès l'époque des Anjou, sur le modèle des rois mages, on représentait volontiers ensemble les « trois saints rois de Hongrie » – le vieux et sage saint Étienne, le roi d'âge moyen et de belle prestance saint Ladislas et le jeune saint Émeric[37]. Leur présence collective dans les légendiers est aussi la marque de ce culte collectif. Mais, tandis qu'à l'échelle nationale, le culte de saint Ladislas est plus varié, plus riche même que celui de saint Étienne (songeons à son iconographie autonome sur les peintures murales ou à la tradition populaire qui entoure sa figure), à l'étranger il n'apparaît jamais de façon isolée. Dans les légendiers publiés ou utilisés au-delà des frontières hongroises, la Hongrie est avant tout représentée par le fondateur du royaume, qui a converti son peuple à la foi chrétienne[38].

---

[37] Voir la note 20 et, en annexe, l'image qui y est mentionnée.
[38] Pour plus d'informations sur le roi saint Étienne : M.-M. de CEVINS, *Saint Étienne de Hongrie*, Paris, 2004.

ANNEXE

Légendes des « saints rois » de Hongrie
présentes dans les manuscrits médiévaux écrits ou utilisés hors de Hongrie

Bibliothèque	Type de manuscrit	Époque	Origine	Utilisé à	Légende de saint Étienne	saint Ladislas	saint Émeric
Budapest, Bibl. Nat. Cod. Lat. 431 (Codex Ernst)	trois légendes	XIIe s. (2e moitié)	Hongrie	Vyšší Brod OCist. Bohême	Légendes majeure et mineure	–	–
Heiligenkreuz OCist. Cod. 13	legendarium	XIIIe s. (1ère moitié)	Heiligenkreuz OCist. Autriche	Heiligenkreuz OCist. Autriche	Légendes majeure et mineure	–	–
Lilienfeld OCist. Cod. 60	legendarium	XIIIe s. (1ère moitié)	Lilienfeld OCist. Autriche	Lilienfeld OCist. Autriche	Légendes majeure et mineure	–	–
Melk OSB Cod. 676	legendarium	XVe s.	Melk OSB Autriche	Melk OSB Autriche	Légendes majeure et mineure	–	–
Budapest, Bibl. Nat. Cod. Lat. 17	legendarium	XIIe-XIIIe s.	Hongrie	Augsbourg	Légende de l'évêque Hartvik	–	–
Rein (Reun) OCist. Cod. 69	contenu mixte	XIIe-XIIIe s.	Rein OCist. Hongrie, Sopron	Rein OCist. Autriche	Légende de l'évêque Hartvik	–	+

289

Bibliothèque	Type de manuscrit	Époque	Origine	Utilisé à	Légende de saint Étienne	saint Ladislas	saint Émeric
Graz, UB Cod. Lat. 977	Legenda aurea (247)[39]	1346	Bohême OPraed.	St Lambrecht OSB Autriche	Légende de l'évêque Hartvik	+	–
Londres, B. L. Arundel 33	Legenda aurea (379)	XIVe s.	Mainz OCart.	Mainz OCart.	Légende de l'évêque Hartvik	–	–
Wilhering OCist. Cod. 27	Legenda aurea (998)	XIVe s.	Wilhering OCist. Autriche	Wilhering OCist. Autriche	Légende de l'évêque Hartvik	–	–
Graz, UB Cod. Lat. 1239	colligatum	XIVe s. (2e moitié)	Lövöld OCart. Hongrie	Seitz OCart. Autriche	Légende de l'évêque Hartvik	+	+
Vienne, ÖNB Cod. Lat. 832	colligatum	XIVe-XVe s.	Hongrie	Vienne OPraed.	Légende de l'évêque Hartvik	–	–
Budapest, Bibl. Nat. Cod. Germ. 48.	legendarium	XVe s.	Bamberg	Bamberg	Légende de l'évêque Hartvik en allemand	–	–
Munich, BSB Cod. Lat. 18624	contenu mixte	XVe s. (2e moitié)		Tegernsee OSB Bavière	Légende de l'évêque Hartvik	+	+
Vienne, ÖNB Cod. Lat. 3662	legendarium, colligatum	XVe s.	Hongrie	Mondsee OSB Autriche	Légende de l'évêque Hartvik	+	+
Bruxelles, B. R. Cod. (I) 982	legendarium	XVe s.	Rouge-Cloître Pays-Bas	Rouge-Cloître Pays-Bas	Légende de l'évêque Hartvik	–	–

[39] B. FLEITH, *Studien zur Überlieferungsgeschichte, op. cit.*, Appendix.

Bibliothèque	Type de manuscrit	Époque	Origine	Utilisé à	Légende de saint Étienne	saint Ladislas	saint Émeric
Paris, Bibl. Mazarine Cod. Lat. 1733	contenu mixte	XVe s.		Korsendonck OPraem. Pays-Bas	Légende de l'évêque Hartvik	+	+
Padoue, Bibl. Univ. Cod. Lat. 1622	legendarium	XVe s.		Chiesa di S. Sebastiano Rome	Légende de l'évêque Hartvik	+	+
Cracovie, Archiv. OPraed. Cod. R XV 35	Legenda aurea (324)	XVe s.	Pologne	Pologne	Légende de l'évêque Hartvik	+	–
Melk OSB Cod. 1824	Legenda aurea (416)	XVe s.	Autriche	Melk OSB Autriche	Légende de l'évêque Hartvik	+	–
Prague, N. K. Cod. XII. G. 1	Legenda aurea (724)	XVe s.	Bohême	Bohême	Légende de l'évêque Hartvik	–	–
Varsovie, B. N. Ms 3316	Legenda aurea (961)	1435	Pologne	Sieciechov OCist. dioec. Lublin, Pologne	Légende de l'évêque Hartvik	–	+
Vienne, ÖNB Cod. Lat. 326	Legenda aurea	1446-1447	Vienne	Vienne, Frédéric III	Légende de l'évêque Hartvik	+	+
Varsovie, B. N. Ms 8041	Legenda aurea (963)	XVe s.	Pologne? Hongrie?	Krasnik Pologne	Légende de l'évêque Hartvik	+	+
Weimar, T. L. Ms. Fol. 18	Legenda aurea (967)	XVe s.	Allemagne	Allemagne	Légende de l'évêque Hartvik	–	–

Some Structural Comparisons of Pictorial Legends from Medieval Hungary

Ivan GERÁT
(Bratislava)

Pictorial legends are a significant source of information for the question of how and why international and indigenous saints were worshipped. By representing events with a complex set of meanings, the cycles of images did much more than just propagating the person of a particular saint. To focus the attention of their target audience viewers on precisely selected structures of thinking, norms of behaviour and values, the pictorial narratives were mostly constructed from the well-known *topoi*.[1] Instead of trying to surprise their viewer, the traditional compositions were delivering more or less fixed and known messages. The identical or at least structurally analogous scenes were associated with more than one saint. The degree of similarity between the scenes was not always the same – the traditional compositions were sometimes modified when associated with a different saint. Seen from this perspective, the hagiographic landscape of medieval Hungarian kingdom does not appear as homogenous and simultaneously as differentiated as it might seem when one focussed only on the names of the saintly patrons represented in the pictorial legends. The functions of the pictorial narratives were influenced not only by a simple fact which saint was chosen as their main hero but also by a choice of the individual sequences from which the legend was built. These decisions might have reflected the degree of similarity or some specific differences in identities of social groups for which the images were produced.

A very impressive example of a hagiographic synthesis is offered by the legend of Saint Ladislas in the so-called Hungarian Angevin Legendary (Codex Vat. lat. 8541, fol. 80r-85v), created presumably in the second quarter of

---

[1] More detailed theoretical argumentation in I. GERÁT, *Legendary scenes: an essay on medieval pictorial hagiography*, Bratislava, 2013, p. 10-25.

Les saints et leur culte en Europe centrale au Moyen Âge (XIe-début du XVIe siècle), éd. par Marie-Madeleine de CEVINS et Olivier MARIN, Turnhout, 2017 (*Hagiologia*, 13), p. 293-310.

the fourteenth century.² The pictorial narrative consists of 24 images, accompanied by very short inscriptions (*tituli*). The known textual legends of the saint offer a commentary only to some scenes from this cycle. The reasons for an inclusion of topics not mentioned in the textual legends should be studied on the basis of the images. The narrative can be divided into shorter sequences of images according to dominating function. Some of these sequences and their functions were modelled on the basis of the well-known *vitae* of older saints, whose pictorial cults were spread across medieval Europe. Constructed in this way, the legend of Ladislas in the Angevin legendary associated many important motives of the European hagiography with the Hungarian national saint. What was the influence of this construction in the following centuries?

To answer this question, the pictorial narrative from the legendary can be compared with the images on altar retables, which were the most important medium of broader public communication in the late medieval period in the territory of Hungarian kingdom, with the peak of development in the decades around the year 1500. From this period of time, dozens of altar retables are preserved, many of them with pictorial legends of saints. Interestingly, there is no pictorial narrative with St Ladislas on the surviving retables. Nevertheless, the fact that there are no pictorial narratives about the holy king of Hungary does not mean the absence of meanings, carried by his legend in the legendary. Very similar sequences of images were associated with exactly the older saints imported from abroad who had inspired the legend of Ladislas in the legendary. This paper is offering a brief description of this phenomenon and attempts to explain it in the context of social history. The patrons of the altarpieces in multi-national towns, frequently merchants with a broad network of business partners at home and abroad were rarely interested in promoting the hagiographic constructions from the centre of the kingdom. Their interests in building smoothly functioning international communication networks were better served by focusing the attention on more universal saints, e.g. St Georges, St James of Compostella, St Anthony the Hermit, etc.³.

---

² *Magyar Anjou Legendárium*, ed. F. LEVÁRDY, Budapest, 1973; *Heiligenleben 'Ungarisches Legendarium': Codex Vat. lat. 8541*, Zürich, 1990; B. Zs. SZAKÁCS, *The Visual World of the Hungarian Angevin Legendary*, Budapest, 2016, p. 214-216; *Id*., "Between Chronicle and the Legend: Image Cycles of St Ladislas in fourteenth-century Hungarian Manuscripts", in *The Medieval Chronicle IV*, ed. E. KOOPER, Amsterdam-New York, 2006, p. 149-175. On Ladislas in general, see Z. MAGYAR, *Keresztény lovagoknak oszlopa. Szent László a magyar kultúrtörténetben*, Budapest, 1996.

³ About their cults in medieval Hungary see Z. MAGYAR, *Szent György a magyar kultúrtörténetben. A Kárpát-medence Szent György-hagyományainak néprajzi és művelődéstörténeti*

Construction of the legend in the Vatican Legendary

The first page of the legend of St Ladislas in the Vatican Legendary focusses on the image of the good king, his coronation by bishops (which is completely a-historical) and cooperation with the church, expressed by a procession, which might be a part of coronation ceremony.[4] A similarity between Ladislas and Jesus is stressed in two images. First, the arrival of the holy king into Székesfehérvár resembles Christ's entry into Jerusalem. Secondly, Ladislas – as a reaction to the hunger of his soldiers – performs a miracle like a Christ in the desert; the text of the legend refers to the manna, falling to the hungry Israelites.[5] The miraculous feeding, showing the animals bringing food after a prayer of the saint, was represented on other places of the legendary, e.g. in the life of St Blasius.[6]

The subsequent three pages of the legend concentrate on the fight of the king against demons.[7] Differently from the usual scenes in the legends of holy hermits, this sequence carries direct political meanings. It associates the anti-demonic struggle with the crusader-like fight of the Christian king against unbelievers, who are represented by the two nomadic nations. Firstly, Ladislas is represented ordering to burn down a seat of the Pechenegs.[8] Later, he personally takes part in the fight against the Cumanians, who are identified as *tartari* by the image *titulus*.[9] Between these images of military actions, there are four scenes focusing on a solitary fight of the saint against the devil during a nightly vigil in the church.

---

rétege, Budapest, 2006; L. KAKUCS, "Der mittelalterliche Jakobuskult in Ungarn", in *Der Jakobuskult in Ostmitteleuropa: Austausch, Einflüsse, Wirkungen*, ed. D. R. BAUER and K. HERBERS, Tübingen, 2003, p. 285-352; T. GRYNAEUS, "Die Antoniter in Ungarn", *Antoniter-Forum*, 13 (2005), p. 80-111.

[4] Hungarian Angevin Legendary, Vatican Library, Codex Vat. lat. 8541 (hereafter: HALVat), fol. 80r.

[5] Ex 16, 14-17; *Legenda sancti Ladislai regis*, ed. E. BARTONIEK and E. SZENTPÉTERY, Budapest, 1938, p. 520: *Quos ipse cum exercitu suo persequens venit in solitudinem magnam, nec habebant, quod manducarent. Et dum fame periclitaretur exercitus, evulsus est ipse seorsum ab eis, et in oratione prostratus implorabat misericordiam dei, ut qui quondam filios Israhel manna pluens nutrierat, christianum populum famis inedia non sineret interire. Cumque surgens ab oratione reverteretur, ecce grex cervorum et bubalorum obviat ei, et cum ipso simul in medium exercitum deposita feritate convenit. Legendy stredovekého Slovenska*, ed. R. MARSINA, Budmerice, 1997, p. 132.

[6] HALVat, fol. 52v: *de s. Blasio, Quomodo omnes fere portabant sibi uictualia*.

[7] *Ibid.*, fol. 81v-82r.

[8] *Ibid.*, fol. 81v: *Quomodo cremabatur domus bissenorum per exercitum*.

[9] *Ibid.*, fol. 82r: *Quomodo pugnabat cum tartaris*.

The solitary prayer of Ladislas in the church resembles the agony of Christ on the Mount of Olives by the motif of his sleeping companions.[10] In the next scenes, the devil in form of a death person (*dyabolus in forma mortui*) is attacking him by throwing firstly a drapery into his face (*proiecit sibi pallium ad faciem*) and later even the deathbed (*proiciebat cum feretro*). Working with the motif of the resuscitated corpse, the iconography achieves a remarkable degree of morbidity without using the repudiating effect to show the power of miracle in overcoming death like in many versions of Lazarus resurrected by Christ. This is a difference from the comparable scene occurring among the posthumous miracles of St James in the legendary.[11] In a more general sense, the fight of St Ladislas against demons resembles many other stories of the legendary, such as exorcisms performed by the apostles on possessed people or demoniac statues as well as solitary fight of hermits against the demons.[12] Usual theological interpretations of such scenes were stressing analogies with the temptations of Jesus by the demons.

The final victory of St Ladislas over the demon carries some Christological meanings, too. The saint raises against the devil a cross, taken from the altar.[13] In the subsequent military confrontation with the Cumanian, the red cross of a very similar shape is placed on the saint's white shield. This bridging

---

[10] *Ibid.*, fol. 81v: *Quomodo orabat in ecclesia*. About the christological image from the same manuscript, Hungarian legendary, New York, Pierpont Morgan Library, M 360, fol. VI: *Quomodo oravit in monte*.

[11] HALVat, fol. 34v-35r.

[12] *Ibid.*, fol. 24r: *Quando Symon Magus cecidit in terra* (popular scene from the life of Peter and Paul); fol. 14v: *Deliberatio multorum* (by St Paul); leaf from the Hungarian Angevin Legendary, St Petersburg, the Hermitage, 16934 16933; HALVat, fol. 17r: *Quomodo eiecit demones qui interficiebant homines* (St Andrew, three more scenes on fol. 18v); fol. 22v: *Quomodo per oraciones suas fracte sund ydole et templum* (St John the apostle); fol. 25r, 26v, 27r (St James and Hermogenes); fol. 31v: *Quomodo interfecerunt draconem per signum †* (St James); fol. 39r (St Mathew); Hungarian legendary, New York, Pierpont Morgan Library, M 360, fol. XX (St Bartholomew); HALVat, fol. 54v: *de sancto Georgio Quomodo interfecit draconem*; Hungarian legendary, New York, Pierpont Morgan Library, M 360, fol. XXIII (St Christoph); HALVat, fol. 56r: *Quomodo effugabant demones ante regem* (St Cosmas and Damian); fol. 62r: *Quomodo donatus eiecit demoniacum*; fol. 62v: *Quomodo eicerat draconem de lacu* (St Donat); fol. 73v: *Quomodo extraxerat unum draconem de lacu* (St Silvester); fol. 86r: *Quomodo demones corizabant ante ipsum in uno uiridario in forma puellarum* (St Benedict); fol. 87v: *quomodo unus dyabolus magne longitudinis erat decelo usque ad terram et angeli portabant animas. demones autem infra cadebant* (St Anthony the Hermit); fol. 91r: *Quomodo demones cruciabant ipsum* (St Francis); leaf from the Hungarian Angevin Legendary, St Petersburg, the Hermitage, 16934, 16934 (St Francis beaten by the demons); HALVat, fol. 94r: *Quomodo liberavit demoniacum* (St Egidius); Hungarian legendary Berkeley, Bancroft Library, f2MSA2M21300-37, f2MSA2M21300-37 (St Louis of Toulouse). See B. Z. SZAKÁCS, *A Magyar Anjou Legendárium, op. cit.*, fig. 30.

[13] HALVat, fol. 82r: *Quomodo portabat crucem contra demonem*.

with the help of the powerful symbol was used in order to integrate into the legend the fight of the holy king against the Cumanian abducting a Hungarian girl. This had been one of the most popular topics of early fourteenth century murals, which could not be ignored in the legendary, even if not present in the textual legends of the time. In the frescoes, there were some associations of the fight with the struggle against demons, but they were rather indirect. One of the earliest versions of the story was painted around 1317 on the wall of a sacristy in the Church of St Catherine in a village of Veľká Lomnica (in Hungarian Kakaslomnic).[14] In this fresco, the demonizing of the Cumanian was achieved through the form of his ugly, almost caricatural face with a smoke coming out of his mouth. The countenance which clearly resembled the usual image of devil was contrasted with the Christ-like face of the holy king, stylized according to the image of the crowning of Roger II by Christ, represented in the twelfth century mosaic in Martorana (Santa Maria dell'Ammiraglio), Palermo.[15] As far as there was no devil painted in the fresco, the reading of this layer of its meanings required some visual literacy. One more theological problem was hidden in the execution of the adversary. According to the oldest historical narrative of the chronicles, the final decapitation of the defended enemy was performed by the prince (not yet king) Ladislas. In the context of pictorial hagiography, the dirty work was delegated to the liberated girl, whose image after this shift of roles might resemble (at least to a viewer with some theological education) the heroic Judith killing the enemy of her nation. The punishment and murder of the beaten enemy by the girl was given even larger space of two scenes in the legendary. In the first one, the girl is cutting the legs of the wounded Cumanian.[16] In the second one, he is decapitated.[17] In both images, the saint is helping the girl by holding the hair of his adversary, which is a position known from the frescoes. Nevertheless, the authors of the legendary integrated the story in a very rich network of religious associations, starting with the already mentioned solitary fight of the holy king against the demons and ending with the miracles represented immediately behind the military action. The first of them was a healing of the wounded saint by the Virgin Mary.[18] This profoundly religious scene created a clear visual parallel with the rest of the saint in a lap of the

---

[14] I. GERÁT, *Svätí bojovníci v stredoveku: úvahy o obrazových legendách sv. Juraja a sv. Ladislava na Slovensku*, Bratislava, 2011.
[15] V. DVOŘÁKOVÁ, "La légende de saint Ladislas découverte dans l'église de Veľká Lomnica", *Buletinul Monumentelor Istorice*, 41 (1972), p. 25-42, here p. 36.
[16] HALVat, fol. 82r: *Quomodo tenebat per crines et puella incidebat pedes eius*.
[17] Ibid., fol. 83v: *Quomodo Comanum depilabat per crines et puella decollabat collum suum*.
[18] Ibid., fol. 83v: *Quomodo beata uirgo medicat ipsum*.

saved virgin, known from the frescoes.[19] Thus, an alternative interpretation was offered to the scene with undeniable erotic, appealing to medieval knights, who supported the creation of murals with this topic. The difference of meanings can be seen in the composition itself. While in the murals (e.g. in Kraskovo, Karaszkó) the king is taking a relaxed rest with his armour hanged on the nearby tree, in the legendary he retains all the attributes of his royal status (the crown) and sanctity (the halo). An alternative reading of the spiritual meaning of the image as a statement on the liberation of the soul could also have existed among the more educated clergy. Karel Stejskal already compared the image of the liberation of the girl with an example depicted in the contemporary Prague manuscript, the *Passionale Cunegundis*.[20] In a Neo-Platonic spirit, the ability to liberate the human soul, imprisoned in the material world is attributed to the heroic knight, who resembles Christ.

One more image was integrated into the legend to underline the religious meanings of the fight – the levitation of the saint, immersed in prayer.[21] Certain features of this image – e.g. the profile image of a hovering kneeling body with clasped hands might resemble a scene from the life of St Anthony, elevated by the angels.[22] Nevertheless, there are some differences between the two miracle images. Two angels help to lift up the body of St Anthony and two demons show their ugly faces in front of him. Contrastingly, Ladislas levitates without any visible help from outside and there are no demons which would disturb the peaceful atmosphere, achieved by the victorious fight of the saint. Ladislas seems to have been able to overcome the devil, whereas Anthony, beaten by demons, could only be saved by Christ.[23]

In the legendary, the military activity of the saintly king was fully integrated into the safe framework of Christian ideology. Ladislas was promoted as a ruler, able to achieve peace by fight as well as by means of diplomacy. The next page of the pictorial cycle starts with a picture of him exchanging a kiss of peace with the Bohemian king.[24] The peaceful character of the Hungarian

---

[19] *Ibid.*, fol. 83v: *Quomodo iacebat in gremio puelle.*
[20] K. STEJSKAL and E. URBÁNKOVÁ, *Pasionál Přemyslovny Kunhuty*, Praha, 1975, p. 29-36. A detailed study: G. TOUSSAINT, *Das Passional der Kunigunde von Böhmen: Bildrhetorik und Spiritualität*, Paderborn, 2003, p. 71-104.
[21] HALVat, fol. 83v: *Quomodo eleuatus est in aerem.*
[22] *The Visual World, op. cit.*, fol. 87r: *Quomodo fuit eleuatus per angelos in a(e)rem.* Similarity of image was addressed as a problem by B. Zs. SZAKÁCS, "Images from the Production Line. Constructing Saints' Lives in the Hungarian Angevin Legendary", *Ars*, 44 (2011), p. 182-193.
[23] This is happening in the first two scenes of his legend on the Leaf from the Hungarian Angevin Legendary, St Petersburg, the Hermitage, 16934, 16934; see B. Zs. SZAKÁCS, *The Visual World, op. cit.*, fig. 34.
[24] HALVat, fol. 84r: *Quomodo fuit osculatus cum rege bohemie.*

saintly king and his abilities to create alliances with other Christian rulers were stressed as the last event from his earthly life. Immediately after this scene, the final sequence starts, focusing on the passing away of the saint, his burial and the cult of his grave.

This sequence included two miracles – the first one of a carriage miraculously finding its way to the burial site and the second, manifesting the protective power of the saint and his ability to restore the order and justice by punishing an aristocrat who wanted to steal a silver plate from the grave. The specific aim of these narratives was to support the cult of Ladislas' grave in the Transylvanian town of Nagyvárad (*Waradinum*, today Oradea in Romania).

The miracle of the carriage founding its way to the burial place was quite frequently used *topos* in the Legendary itself.[25] It occurs not only on its well-known place in the legend of St James of Compostella, but also in the legend of the Hungarian bishop-martyr Gerhard.[26] Nevertheless, the procession, welcoming the saintly king, seems to be an original addition alluding to similar image in the opening sequence of the legend, in which Ladislas himself took part. Now, a bishop follows the carriage and another bishop walks behind two persons carrying crossed in the procession – the clerical control of the cult seems to be sufficiently promoted. This is valid for the subsequent image of the burial, too. The composition with bishops bowing behind the death body which is being put into a sarcophagus in the foreground resembles the *vita* of St Emeric of Hungary.[27] A similar formula was used many burial scenes in the legendary, with some minor variations in the number of depicted characters and their role, but the presence of the bishops remained constant. In case of Ladislas, there are two more moments making his cult complete. The popular devotion around the grave was expressed by an image of the pilgrims gathering around his sarcophagus.[28] This is a *topos*, too, present in the legendary e.g. in the vita of St James of Compostella.[29] The authority of Ladislas grave as a very special place was even more promoted by the two last scenes, devoted to the posthumous miracles, through which the saint helped to preserve justice. A nobleman, who tried to steal a silver plate, was punished by death and its

---

[25] Ibid., fol. 84r: *Quomodo currus ibat cum corpore waradinum*. The same miracle was represented in the *Chronicon Pictum*, p. 101.
[26] Ibid., fol. 31v: *Hic ducitur corpus sancti Jacobi in curru*; fol. 69v: *Quomodo currus ibat per se cum corpore ad chanadinum*.
[27] Ibid., fol. 78r. and fol. 85v: *Quomodo fuit sepultus*.
[28] Ibid., fol. 85v: *Quomodo populus adorabat circa sepulcrum*.
[29] Ibid., fol. 32r: *Quomodo venerunt populi orare ad sepulcrum*.

legitimate proprietor was allowed – in spite of his lower social status – to take the precious thing.[30]

Elements of the legend on altar retables

As far as we know, the pictorial legend of St Ladislas was never represented by a panel painting forming a part of an altar retable, a medium which began to flourish in the fifteenth century, with a culmination in the decades around 1500. Even without the legend of St Ladislas, many of the *topoi* used in this integrative hagiographic construction of his legend were used in the stories of more universal saints, again. The sequences identified in the cycle of the legendary can be looked for on the altar retables in the many towns of the country.

The first of them – the introductory images focusing on sacralising of the dynasty – was no longer of interest for the inhabitants of the cities. As a symptom of the decline of the popularity of monarchic values in municipal environment, the royal meanings, carried by this part of the legend disappeared from the narratives on retables without a replacement. The single retable devoted to the Hungarian royal saints – the one in Matejovce – focusses on the standing figures of St Stephen and St Emeric, omitting Ladislas.[31] The absence of Ladislas does not seem to be just a chance – there are no allusions to crusading activities of nobility on this retable.

Among the four narrative scenes on the retable wings, the nightly prayer of the young prince during which he promised virginity was a direct transposition of what was depicted in the life of Emeric, son of the Saint and King of Hungary Stephen I, in the Legendary.[32] The composition from the altar at Matejovce strongly resembles the solitary nightly prayer of Ladislas.[33] St Emeric kneels absorbed in prayer with folded hands in front of an altar above which an angel emerges, bearing a banderole in which virginity is praised: *Preclara est virginitas, virginitatem mentis et corporis a te exigo...* The idea of virginity penetrated Emeric's legend, although it was known that he was married. According to the legend, Emeric received God's call to

---

[30] *Ibid.*, fol. 85v: *Quomodo unus nobilis non potuit accipere scutellam arenteam* and *Quomodo pauper accepit scutellam.*
[31] G. Török, "A Mateóci Mester művészetének problémái", *Művészettörténeti Értesítő*, 29 (1980), p. 49-80; M. Novotná, "Oltár sv. Štefana a Imricha v Matejovciach", *Pamiatky a múzeá*, 56 (2007), p. 2-8.
[32] HALVat, fol. 78r: *Quomodo orabat in ecclesia et illuminata fuit ecclesia.*
[33] *Ibid.*, fol. 81v: *Quomodo orabat in ecclesia.*

virginity during a night of silent prayer in the old church at Veszprém.[34] In the background the kneeling figure represents Emeric's servant, the witness of the miracle. In spite of this difference from a solitary prayer of Ladislas, the compositions are very similar. The mystic character of the scene could make it relevant for the private devotion, popular in the later Middle Ages.[35]

Food miracles

The motive of the food being miraculously produced or brought after a prayer of the saint survived in the images of St Nicholas distributed grain from a ship in the harbour to each according to his or her need during famine in his diocese. Owing to a miracle, there was sufficient grain to satisfy the hungry for two years and even enough for sowing.[36] This miracle was depicted on the Hronský Beňadik Garamszentbenedek Altar of the Crucifixion from 1427 and in the the Prešov cycle.[37] From a conceptual point of view, this miracle represents a parallel to the miraculous feeding of the five thousands by Christ. In relation to the cult of the saint, it is a specific reference to his ability, not only to feed the hungry, but also to give general support and protection to life and fertility to the fields. The existence of such ideas in the Middle Ages is documented in various liturgical sources. In this context, it is also possible to speak of the "natural miracle" of new life, which retains a high level of emotional effectiveness in spite of various interpretations.[38] These ideas penetrated liturgical sources during the Middle Ages. A hymn

---

[34] *Legenda S. Emerici ducis*, ed. E. BARTONIEK and E. SZENTPÉTERY, Budapest, 1938, p. 453-454; G. TÖRÖK, "A Mateóci Mester", *op. cit.*, p. 64, 79; *Legendy stredovekého Slovenska*, *op. cit.*, p. 81; M. NOVOTNÁ, "Oltár sv. Štefana", *op. cit.*, p. 4.

[35] B. WILLIAMSON, "Altarpieces, liturgy, and devotion", *Speculum-a Journal of Medieval Studies*, 79 (2004), p. 341-406; I. BOCKEN, "Performative Vision: Jan van Eyck, Nicholas of Cusa and the devotio moderna", in *Ritual, Images, and Daily Life. The Medieval Perspective*, ed. G. JARITZ, Zürich-Berlin, 2012, p. 95-106.

[36] I. da Varazze, *Legenda aurea*, ed. G. P. MAGGIONI, Firenze, 2007, p. 46: *Frumentum autem secundum uniuscuiusque indigentiam uir dei distribuit ita ut miraculose duobus annis non tantum ad uictum sufficeret, sed etiam ad usum seminis abundaret*. Another depiction is found on the Altar of St Nicholas from Veľký Slavkov, 1503, now in Budapest, Magyar Nemzeti Galéria. See *A Magyar Nemzeti Galéria régi gyűjteményei*, ed. M. MOJZER, Budapest, 1984, text to ill. 84 (J. VÉGH). In some versions of the legend, this happened only after his death. K. MEISEN, *Nikolauskult und Nikolausbrauch im Abendlande. Eine kultgeographisch-volkskundliche Untersuchung*, Düsseldorf, 1931, p. 250.

[37] D. GRÚŇ, "Cyklus sv. Mikuláša z hlavného oltára farského kostola v Prešove. Interpretácia naratívneho celku", *Galéria – Ročenka SNG*, 2004-2005 (2006), p. 289-302, here p. 298-300.

[38] A. DE GROOT, *Saint Nicholas: a Psychoanalytic Study of his History and Myth*, Hague, 1965, p. 94.

from the influential Benedictine Abbey of Monte Cassino, based on the story of this miracle, presents Nicholas as the saint of grain (*frumenta sanctus*).[39]

The motive of miraculously produced food was represented with even more apparent visual similarity role on the High Altar of Sts. Anthony and Paul the Hermits at Sásová and on the Altar of St Anthony at Spišská Sobota.[40] Athanasius' Life of St Anthony describes events during journeys by the saint and his confrères through the desert.[41] The monks had no drinking water and would soon be in danger of death. After a prayer from Anthony, the Lord provided a new spring of water. At the same time, he helped the monks find the laden camel, which they had previously abandoned in despair and weariness.

Fighting the demons

The fight of the saintly king against the demons and against the Cumanian, which we have seen as a sophisticated visual argumentation to support unusual military activity of the saint was divided again into its two constitutive elements – spiritual and military fight.

The spiritual form survived and was developed above all on the above mentioned retables of St Anthony the Hermit. His confrontation with the demons included horrible moments of him being beaten, but, ultimately, he was granted victory and promised the glory and fame in the whole world by Christ. The danger of pagans attacking the land was modified according to what was felt to be the most important problem of contemporary Church. After the rise of the Hussite movement in the Kingdom of Bohemia, the image of the struggle with demons could refer to this historical reality.[42] In medieval Hungary, the image of the Arians destroying the altars on the retable at the Sásová Altar of Sts. Anthony and Paul the Hermits represents the most apparent hint to anti-heretic fight among the preserved panel paintings. In the altar shrine, the hermits piously venerate the Crucified Christ, while on the wings the dark forces prevail. On one side, demons beat a kneeling

---

[39] K. MEISEN, *Nikolauskult und Nikolausbrauch, op. cit.*, p. 250.

[40] L. CIDLINSKÁ, *Gotické krídlové oltáre na Slovensku*, Bratislava, 1989, p. 81 describes the scene as "St Anthony instructing the monks".

[41] Athanasius, *Vita Beati Antonii abbatis*, cap. 54 (ed. J. P. MIGNE, *Patrologia latina*, 73, col. 164-165).

[42] Specifically this concerns the story of St James and the sorcerer Hermogenes from around 1440, found on panels now in Prague (National Gallery), Vienna (Kunsthistorisches Museum), Nuremberg (Germanisches Nationalmuseum) and Brno (Moravská galerie). H. RÖCKELEIN, "Kult und Ikonographie Jacobus d. Ä. und die Entstehungsgeschichte des Altaraufsatzes", in *Das Hochaltarretabel der St. Jacobi-Kirche in Göttingen*, ed. B. CARQUÉ and H. RÖCKELEIN, Göttingen, 2005, p. 177-205, 182-193.

saint with clubs, while on the other, irate Arians smash an altar table with a hammer and iron bar. This association is based on reports of the looting of churches which already appears in the earliest life of St Anthony.[43] However, in these changed circumstances the subject acquired new relevance. The furious action and the features of the faces of the heretics, which verge on caricature, served to defame them in the eyes of the public. The parallel between the demons' attack on the saint and the attack of the heretics on the altar expresses the topicality of the theme of the struggle against demons in the effort of the Roman Church to oppose heresy just a few years prior to the arrival of the main wave of the Reformation. The peaceful city dwellers remembered well the lootings performed by the Hussites some decades ago and they certainly did not wish to see their lives and property endangered by imported religious controversies.

The military confrontation of the saint with the devil receded into the more traditional form of a fight of St George against the dragon, which could fulfil the important propagandist role of giving the military activities of the medieval nobility a religious aim, too. The saint retained all the attributes of a medieval knight, but his enemy was transformed into a fantastic animal carrying symbolic values. The episode of St George's legendary victory over the mythical monster enjoyed huge popularity in pictorial cycles and was the theme of numerous artworks.[44] A panel painting from the Altar of the Most Holy Trinity in Mošovce (Mosóc) (1471?) shows St George on a horse. On the left-hand side a princess watches the saint spear the dragon.[45] The masterpiece showing the same topic is the central relief of the retable of the Altar of St George at Spišská Sobota from 1516 (Figure 1, outside the text). Its affinity with the St George and dragon group in Levoča is well known.[46] The armoured knight on his horse brandishes his sword above the dragon,

---

[43] Athanasius, *Vita Beati Antonii*, cap. 82 (*op. cit.*, col. 155).

[44] See I. GERÁT, *Svätí bojovníci v stredoveku, op. cit.*

[45] Now in Martin, Slovenské národné múzeum, inv. n. KH 2286. A. GLATZ, *Gotické umenie zo zbierok Slovenského národného múzea v Martine*, Martin, 1985, p. 24-27.

[46] K. DIVALD, *Szepesvármegye művészeti emlékei*, Budapest, 1905-1907, vol. 2 (1906), p. 85-87; O. SCHÜRER and E. WIESE, *Deutsche Kunst in der Zips*, Brünn, Wien, Leipzig, 1938, p. 98-99, 228, 230; V. WAGNER, *Neskorogotická tabuľová maľba slovenská*, Turčiansky Svätý Martin, 1941, p. 33, 34, 37, 38; D. RADOCSAY, *A középkori Magyarország táblaképei*, Budapest, 1955, p. 171, 172, 448, 449; J. HOMOLKA, *Gotická plastika na Slovensku*, Bratislava, 1972, p. 274-275; A. GLATZ, *Kostol sv. Juraja v Spišskej Sobote*, Košice, 2001; Z. MAGYAR, *Szent György, op. cit.*, p. 82; J. VÉGH, "Ungarisch – mitteleuropäisch. Ist nationale Zugehörigkeit spätmittelalterlicher Künstler noch ein Problem?", *Acta Historiae Artium Hungariae*, 49 (2008), p. 220-234.

whose mouth has already been pierced by a lance.[47] The princess watches the struggle from a hillock in the background. She kneels and clasps her hands to pray that the struggle will turn out well. The same theme (but without the princess) was carved in 1519 on the high relief of the stone retable of the High Altar of the Church of St George in Svätý Jur (Szentgyörgy).

Levitation

We have seen above that the levitation of St Ladislas did have a visual parallel in the life of St Anthony. The topic of St Anthony raised by the angels but endangered by the demons survived on his retable in Spišská Sobota, in a painting inspired by Schongauer's engraving B47 (L. 54), but different in the use of the iconographic motif of four angels lifting the saint. With his supernatural protection St Anthony in Spišská Sobota appears to remain calm, absorbed in prayer. The combination of air-bound demons with elevation by angels is relatively rare. An iconographically related picture appears on a panel from the choir of Lübeck Cathedral, coterminous in date with the Spiš work to 1503.

The peaceful image of saintly king in levitation carries some associations with depictions from the life of St Mary Magdalene. According to the *Golden Legend*, she was raised by angels into the air on every canonical hour during the late phase of the life, when she lived as a hermit. During the elevation she was able to hear the superb singing of the heavenly choirs and was satisfied with extraordinarily tasty food.[48] The transported saint was usually depicted frontally, standing and clothed, as in the central relief of the altar from Rokycany from the 1480s.[49] A painting from about 1500 of Mary Magdalene carried by four angels appears on an altar from the Church of St James the Elder from the village of Jakub near Banská Bystrica

---

[47] This rare iconographic type appeared in the tympanum of the Romanesque portal of Ferrara Cathedral. Z. MAGYAR, *Szent György, op. cit.*, p. 82.

[48] I. da Varazze, *Legenda aurea, op. cit.*, p. 712: *Qualibet autem die septem horis canonicis ab angelis in ethera eleuabatur et celestium agminum gloriosos concentus corporalibus etiam auribus audiebat; unde diebus singulis hiis suauissimus dapibus satiata et inde per eosdem angelos ad locum proprium reuocata corporalibus alimentis nullatenus ignorabat.*

[49] Now in the Magyar Nemzeti Galéria, in Budapest. G. TÖRÖK, *Gótikus szárnyasoltárok a középkori Magyarországon. Állandó kiállítás a Magyar Nemzeti Galériában*, Budapest, 2005, p. 119. The carrying of the naked saint covered only by hair appears in a painting from about 1480 from the Church of St Magdalena in Mareit in Tyrol – according to the photograph on the server http://tethys.imareal.oeaw.ac.at/realonline (last accessed: 11 June 2012). In the older period, for example, on the Altar of the Resurrection at Klosterneuburg from 1456, the angels lift the saint against a golden background. See *Van Eyck to Dürer. Early Netherlandish Painting and Central Europe 1430-1530*, ed. T.-H. BORCHERT, Stuttgart, 2010, p. 447.

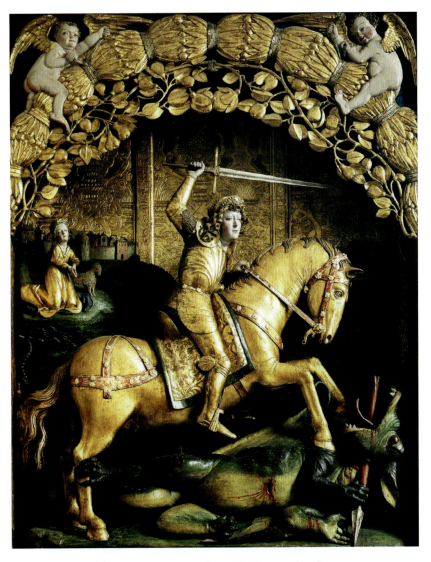

Fig. 1 : St George Fighting the Dragon (1516).
Spišská Sobota, High-Altar of St George.

(photo : Ivan Gerát)

Fig. 2 : Mary Magdalene Lifted by Angels.
Sv. Jakub near Banská Bystrica, Altar of St Mary Magdalene,
today in Banská Bystrica, Church of the Virgin Mary.

(photo : Jozef Medvecký)

Fig. 3 : The Remains of St James before Queen Lupa.
Panel from Sv. Jakub near Banská Bystrica,
today in Esztergom, Keresztény Múzeum [Christian Museum], inv. no. 55.42.7.

(photo : Keresztény Múzeum, Attila Mudrák)

Fig. 4 : The Pilgrims at the Grave of St. Anthony the Hermit (after 1500). Sásová, High-Altar of the Hermits Sts Anthony and Paul.

(photo : Ivan Gerát)

(Besztercebánya) (Figure 2, outside the text).[50] The saint depicted in semi-profile, kneels on the hands of one of the angels and raises her hands in the orant gesture. Another angel holds her bare feet. The two upper angels are positioned symbolically: one holds the saint's elbow, while the second supports her from behind.[51] Mary Magdalene is covered only by her long hair, leaving only her face, neck, hands and feet exposed. Her potentially problematic nakedness is further concealed by a narrow white cloth, draped from the saint's right hand so that it lies obliquely across her pudenda and left leg. As far as the position and form of the saint's body are concerned, the closest analogy is a fifteenth-century relief, now placed in the upper part of the Altar of the St Johns (1520) at Levoča. Such use of the work could be connected with the spiritual care of the sinner doing penance, which was the responsibility of the patron of the work – the highly educated Levoča (Lőcse) parish priest Johannes Henckel.[52] The picture of the body being carried could also recall the hermit saint's former sinful life. The undeniably erotic aspects of the pictures of Mary Magdalene in this period also became the subject of humanist criticism, based on a more rationalist and moralist understanding of piety.[53]

Cult of the grave

The miracles associated with the cult of the grave, especially survived in the well-known story of the carriage of St James of Compostella finding the place of its burial and the subsequent images of the pilgrims, visiting the grave. Since we have no panel painting of the miraculous journey of St Ladislas' remains to Oradea, we have to deal mainly with the legend of St James. The story of St James' remains is depicted on a panel from Sv. Jakub near Banská Bystrica (Figure 3, outside the text). On the actual picture showing the miracle, the two oxen are pulling a cart covered with a white sheet on which James lies with his hands crossed at the wrists. His legs extend beyond the left

---

[50] Now in the Chapel of Corpus Christi in the Roman Catholic Parish Church of the Assumption of the Virgin Mary in Banská Bystrica. A similar scene from 1518 appears on a panel from the Altar of the Apostles Sts. Philip and James the Younger from Mošovce, Martin Slovenské národné múzeum, catalogue no. KH 4979. See A. GLATZ, *Gotické umenie zo zbierok Slovenského národného múzea v Martine*, Martin, 1985, p. 56-58. To the cult of St James in medieval Hungary, see L. KAKUCS, "Der mittelalterliche Jakobuskult", *op. cit.*, p. 285-352
[51] The carrying occurs against a green natural background. A brown abyss opens below on the meadow. This motif may derive from the book of the Lives of the Saints. *Der Heiligen Leben. Sommer- und Winterteil*, Nürnberg, 1488, p. 151 (no. 72).
[52] J. VÉGH, "Der Johannesaltar des Stadtpfarrers von Leutschau Johannes Henckel", *Wiener Jahrbuch für Kunstgeschichte*, 46-47 (1993/94), p. 763-774, here p. 769.
[53] See T. COLETTI, *Mary Magdalene and the Drama of Saints. Theater, Gender and Religion in Late Medieval England*, Philadelphia, 2004, p. 214-216.

edge of the picture thereby emphasizing movement and inviting the viewer to imagine how the remainder of the scene unfolded beyond the edge. This representation technique has been used in the Legendary, too. The story in the panel painting includes some more elements: the centrally placed enthroned queen and the animals. The ill-disposed Queen Lupa gave the disciples of St James the Elder wild bulls, instead of oxen, to transport the apostle's body to her palace. However, thanks to a miracle, the bulls were tamed, allowing themselves be yoked like oxen in order to convey the saint's body to the palace. Following the queen's penitential conversion she changed her palace into a monastery, which, in turn, became a centre for the future pilgrimages.

From the point of view of the narrative of the St James cycle, the scene is the prelude to the picture of pious pilgrims. Two pilgrims, who respectfully take off their hats, approach from the left behind the throne. There would appear to be a mixed message for viewers since it is unclear whether the pilgrims are reacting adequately to the miracle or showing respect towards queen's majestic status. The cult of the grave has been furthermore supported by an image of pilgrims praying at the grave of the saint. The dead body of St James is surrounded by five pilgrims in the interior of a Gothic chapel.[54] The pious gestures and expressions of those present reflect the medieval pilgrim's fascination with the bodies of saints. A man approaching from the left is taking off his hat as a sign of respect, and points to the exact place where the shell is customarily placed on James' hat. However, in this case, the figure of the saint, served not only as a reference to the privileged aim of one of the most important places of pilgrimage in medieval Europe, but also as a model of behaviour.

The right-hand scene on the Sásová altar leads the viewer's eye into the interior of a chapel (Figure 4, outside the text). In the centre stands a large coffin covered by a black pall decorated with a rhythmically divided gold stripe. Five devout people can be seen around the coffin. It is likely that the three figures behind the coffin are pilgrims since the man has a pilgrim's stick and brown pilgrim's hat and the woman at the left has a similar hat tied on her back. The two figures in the foreground are absorbed in prayer: the woman has a rosary.[55] Between them a large candle-stick bears a candle, which is burning, or rather, on the point of flickering out. This motif symbolizes the

---

[54] The work is now in the Christian Museum at Esztergom, inv. n° 55.42.8. See P. Cséfalvay, *Christliches Museum Esztergom*, Szeged, 1993, p. 175.
[55] The man and woman were seen as the patrons of the altar – Königsberger and his wife by G. Endrődi, "Große Kunst 'aus Hass und Neid': Überlegungen zu Bauarbeiten und zur Ausstattung der Neusohler Pfarrkirche um 1500", *Acta Historiae Artium Hungariae*, 47 (2006), p. 37-78, here p. 15.

extinguishing of life and may point to observance of a vigil. Anthropologists state that watching over the coffin of the deceased, or, even hiring mourners, was part of the traditional customs of folk culture.[56] The Sásová picture leaves unresolved the question of what motivated people to visit coffins or tombs, but the practice does to some extent reflect the manifold significance of saint's bodily remains for medieval pilgrims. The medieval viewer of the picture may have had various reasons for making pilgrimages to important graves. In general the motivation was more than a mere expression of respect and prayer for the saint's soul, because it was associated with a belief in the extraordinary power of the person venerated. That is why miracles were expected to occur in such exceptional places. Indigent pilgrims might also be motivated by the almsgiving at more important graves on certain days, in return for which it was enough to pray.[57]

Some healing miracles occurred at the final resting places of saints. The importance of these places was emphasized in numerous stories about the posthumous miracles of saints (*capitola miraculorum*). Reports about posthumous miracles confirmed that the saint's grave retained exceptional power and that the saint was still alive and had not ceased to work miracles.[58] Reports of miracles attracted numerous pilgrims. A saint became the personal patron of healed people and those close to them. In times of need the pilgrims would pray to the saint in question. Naïve childlike trust in a saint, combined with an entrenched faith in a positive outcome, could initiate healing and in some cases this strong emotional basis may have allowed a real healing process to take place.[59]

Apart from satisfying spiritual needs, there was a more practical aspect to the cult of the final resting place of saints. Pilgrims coming to the graves of saints also had to satisfy needs pertaining to everyday life. When close to a famous saint, they sometimes became more generous. Thus, possession of relics also became an economic factor. More than one influential ecclesiastical or secular dignitary, who wished to establish a famous pilgrimage centre,

---

[56] S. KOVAČEVIČOVÁ, *Človek a jeho svet na obrazoch od stredoveku až na prah súčasnosti*, Budmerice, 2006, p. 55.
[57] More in R. KROOS, "Grabbräuche – Grabbilder", in *Memoria. Der geschichtliche Zeugniswert des liturgischen Gedenkens im Mittelalter*, ed. K. SCHMID and J. WOLLASCH, München, 1984, p. 285-353, on almsgiving p. 328-329.
[58] H.-W. GOETZ, "Wunderberichte im 9. Jahrhundert. Ein Beitrag zum literarischen Genus der frühmittelalterlichen Mirakelsammlungen", in *Mirakel im Mittelalter. Konzeptionen – Erscheinungsformen – Deutungen*, ed. M. HEINZELMANN, K. HERBERS and D. BAUER, Stuttgart, 2002, p. 180-226, here p. 212-217, 219.
[59] M. WITTMER-BUTSCH and C. RENDTEL, *Miracula. Wunderheilungen im Mittelalter. Eine historisch-psychologische Annäherung*, Köln-Weimar-Wien, 2003, p. 213.

considered the solution of practical problems as well as the conceptual aspect. On occasion the desire to acquire relics for religious or secular reasons was so strong that it led to theft, which was understood as a legitimate means of acquiring precious remains.[60] Moral doubts were assuaged by the argument that the powerful dead would not allow such manipulation if they did not agree. Therefore, the solemn ritual of transferring relics could also involve the despoliation of their graves. Fraud was also an influential factor in the struggle over possession of relics. The cult of relics was misused for commercial purposes, and false remains were sometimes offered.[61]

In the Middle Ages ownership of physical remains and the administration of the cult at a saint's grave represented more than a purely abstract spiritual treasure. The hope of a miraculous event in proximity to the saints' bodies often motivated people to undertake demanding pilgrimages to their resting place. Stories about transfers of the relics of saints sometimes include reports of miraculous healing of cripples, the deaf and the blind, and often also the possessed.[62]

The tomb of St Nicholas in Bari was famous for its many miracles. According to the *Golden Legend*, having been buried in a marble sarcophagus, a fountain of oil flowed from the saint's head, while a fountain of water flowed from his feet.[63] In about the 1470s, the master of an altar from Kremnica produced a work representing the theme.[64] In a Gothic church interior the large figure of the saint lies in an obliquely positioned sarcophagus around which hopeful afflicted people stand. In the foreground a woman with clasped hands kneels while her diminutive infant with hands on its chest lies

---

[60] P. GEARY, *Furta Sacra. Thefts of Relics in the Central Middle Ages*, Princeton, 1990.
[61] Evidence of this includes the fact that alleged skulls of St Elizabeth of Thuringia are found in Vienna, Brussels, Besançon, Bogota and Viterbo. F. DICKMANN, "Das Schicksal der Elisabethreliquien", in *St. Elisabeth – Kult, Kirche, Konfessionen. Katalog 700 Jahre Elisabethkirche in Marburg 1283-1983*, Marburg, 1983, p. 35-38 On the form of media presentation of relics see the studies in B. REUDENBACH and G. TOUSSAINT, *Reliquiare im Mittelalter*, Berlin, 2011.
[62] H. RÖCKELEIN, "Über Hagio-Geo-Graphien. Mirakel in Translationsberichten des 8. und 9. Jahrhunderts", in *Mirakel im Mittelalter. Konzeptionen – Erscheinungsformen – Deutungen*, ed. M. HEINZELMANN, K. HERBERS, D. BAUER, Stuttgart, 2002, p. 166-179, 167, 174.
[63] I. da Varazze, *Legenda aurea, op. cit.*, p. 50: *cum sepultus fuisset in tumba marmorea, a capite eius fons olei et a pedibus eius fons aque fluxit et usque hodie es eius membris sacrum resudat oleum ualens in salutem multorum.* » A similar story was told about the grave of St Elizabeth at Marburg. V. BELGHAUS, *Der erzählte Körper: die Inszenierung der Reliquien Karls des Grossen und Elisabeths von Thüringen*, Berlin, 2005, p. 137.
[64] Lúčky, altar of St Nicholas, originally from Kremnica, today in Budapest, Hungarian National Gallery, inv. n° 53.903. See G. TÖRÖK, *The Altarpiece of St Nicholas from Jánosrét in the Hungarian National Gallery*, Budapest, 1990.

alongside the saint on the mother's spread out cloak. The saint is expected to resurrect or heal the child. To the right of the kneeling woman, a leper with missing feet approaches and extends a diseased hand to the saint's grave. A group of disabled people can also be seen approaching the sarcophagus from the left. One is supporting himself on sticks; another has a blue hat pulled down to the eyes indicating blindness. The saint's grave is pivotal in the hopes of the suffering people.

Anti-Germanic meanings, a reason for the absence of Ladislas?

There appears an important question: why the retables omitted the image of the saintly king, even if they were using so many scenes similar to his legend? The reason for this decision might be hidden in the interests of the patrons of the retables, among which the local merchants – frequently of German origin – played an important role. They had their most important business partners or even distant relatives on the territory of the Empire, where the cult of Saint Ladislas was far less popular. There was a substantial portion of anti-German elements in the narrative on Ladislas in the so-called Illuminated chronicle. Ladislas with his brother and predecessor on the Hungarian throne *Geysa* managed to remove the legitimate king Salamo. The illuminations of the chronicle underline a collaboration of Salamo with the Emperor. In an illumination, which precedes his fight against Ladislas, he comes to Hungary together with the Emperor Henry IV.[65] The Hungarian crown is carried by the Emperor, which suggests Salamo's dependence on the influential neighbour. The symbol of the Hungarian monarchy even more humiliated in the picture of homage paid by Salamo to the Emperor – the crown has been put on the ground in an upside-down position.[66] Salamo took the Hungarian crown away from Hungary and it never came back. In one illumination of the codex, Ladislas has a vision seeing an angel putting the crown on the head of his brother Géza, who was the first to take power from Salamo.[67] Géza made a new crown, which was to be used in all following coronations of Hungarian kings.[68]

The anti-Germanic sentiments, expressed in these illuminations are associated with the fight of Ladislas against Salamo. An angel with a flaming

---

[65] Chronicon Pictum: Budapest, Országos Széchényi Könyvtár, Cod. 404, fol. 35r (*titulus* "De adventu imperatoris cum Rege Salomone genero suo"). See *Képes krónika. Faksimile*, ed. D. DERCSÉNYI, K. CSAPODINÉ GÁRDONYI, L. MEZEY, L. GERÉB, Budapest, 1964.
[66] Chronicon Pictum, fol. 45r.
[67] *Ibid.*, fol. 42r.
[68] P. VÁCZY, "The Angelic Crown", *Hungarian Studies*, 1 (1985), p. 15-16.

sword appeared above the saint and forced Salamo to run away from the fight in a battle near Bratislava castle.[69] The Hungarian crown appears in the hands of angels during the coronation of Ladislas.[70] In the legendary, the church ritual had been depicted without any angels. In the chronicle, the bishops are helped by the angels. The reader of the chronicle knew that the earthly Ladislas was never crowned, because the *de iure* legitimate king Salamo was still living. The image of heavenly coronation compensated for the insufficient power of human law, known to the reader of the Chronicle.[71] The stories of anti-German fight of the saintly king were appealing to Hungarian nobility, which was supporting the independence of the country from the Empire. The worshiping of the warrior king might be less attractive for the merchants, who had their most important business partners in German lands. Anyway, they were interested more in economic than military aspects of life, but they still appreciated the integrative social energy of Christian ideology.

---

[69] Chronicon Pictum, fol. 46r.
[70] *Ibid*.
[71] E. MAROSI, *Kép és hasonmás. Művészet és valóság a 14-15. századi Magyarországon*, Budapest, 1995, p. 78-79.

Les confréries, les métiers et le culte des saints dans la Bohême médiévale*

Hana Pátková
(Prague)

La documentation sur le culte des saints dans le milieu des confréries et des métiers est déjà bien connue[1], puisque même la littérature de vulgarisation destinée au large public des historiens amateurs y fait référence. Les informations les plus importantes sur l'activité de ces associations ont trait aux offices célébrés en l'honneur de tel ou tel patron, aux autels qui leur étaient consacrés, aux bannières processionnelles sur lesquelles figurait leur image. Les musées tchèques regorgent de témoignages matériels de ce genre : y abondent non seulement des étendards, mais aussi des tableaux, des sculptures, des parties d'autels, des armoiries funéraires exposées lors des obsèques des membres, etc. En cela, les confréries et les métiers de Bohême ne se distinguaient nullement des associations similaires répandues dans toutes les régions de l'Europe médiévale et moderne[2].

---

* Cet article a été conçu dans le cadre du programme PRVOUK P12 FF UK, à Prague, et de son sous-axe *Fontes*.

[1] H. Pátková, « Svatý Eligius, svatý Lukáš a cechovní patroni ve středověkých Čechách », dans *Světci a jejich kult ve středověku*, éd. P. Kubín, H. Pátková, T. Petráček Prague, 2006, (Sborník KTF UK. dějiny umění-historie, 4), p. 221-227 ; *Ead.*, « Der heilige Eligius, der heilige Lukas und die Zunftpatrone im mittelalterlichen Böhmen », *Colloquia mediaevalia Pragensia*, 11 (2010), p. 235-242.

[2] H. Pátková, *Bratrstvie ke cti Božie*, Prague, 2000, p. 20 et 109 ; plus récemment : *Ead.*, « Bruderschaften und Zünfte – Formen (und Grenzen) der Repräsentation », dans *Ecclesia als Kommunikationsraum in Mitteleuropa (13.-16. Jahrhundert)*, éd. E. Doležalová et R. Šimůnek, Munich, 2011, p. 185-192. Sur les confréries en Europe centrale et au-delà, voir : R. Ebner, *Das Bruderschaftswesen im alten Bistum Würzburg*, Würzburg, 1978 ; J. Krettner et T. Finkenstaedt, *Erster Katalog von Bruderschaften in Bayern*, Munich-Würzburg, 1980 ; T. Helmert, « Kalendae, Kalenden, Kalande », *Archiv für Diplomatik*, 26 (1980), p. 1-55 ; H. Hochenegg, *Bruderschaften und ähnliche religiöse Vereinigungen in Deutschtirol bis zum Beginn des zwanzigsten Jahrhunderts*, Innsbruck, 1984 ; B. Schwineköper (éd.), *Gilden und Zünfte*. Sigmaringen, 1986 ; L. Remling, *Bruderschaften in Franken*, Würzburg, 1986 ; P. Johanek (éd.), *Einungen und Bruderschaften in*

Si on l'examine plus attentivement, cette documentation en apparence solide et au-dessus de tout soupçon se révèle néanmoins problématique.

La première difficulté vient du fait que les documents et témoignages cités datent dans leur très grande majorité de l'époque moderne, et même souvent seulement des XVIIIe et XIXe siècles. Les sources antérieures sont, en revanche, peu nombreuses et même rarissimes en ce qui concerne le Moyen Âge. Si l'on se rappelle que les métiers étaient très répandus dans la Bohême médiévale, y compris dans les toutes petites villes, ce contraste entre les sources conservées et ce qui devait exister à l'époque est saisissant. Dans le cas des confréries, la documentation est encore moins abondante que pour les métiers, alors même qu'elles étaient omniprésentes en Bohême à la fin du Moyen Âge.

Parmi les sources textuelles, il faut d'abord faire état des statuts, étant donné que toute association devait s'en doter. Les plus anciens règlements d'une confrérie connus à ce jour datent seulement de 1327[3], et de 1318 dans le

---

der spätmittelalterlichen Stadt, Cologne-Weimar-Vienne, 1993 ; L. PITZL, *Spätmittelalterliche Priesterbruderschaften im Bereich der heutigen Diözese St. Pölten*, thèse soutenue à la faculté de théologie catholique de l'université de Vienne, 1981 ; *Quellen zur Geschichte der Kölner Laienbruderschaften vom 12. Jahrhundert bis 1562/63*, éd. K. MILITZER, t. 1-3, Düsseldorf, 1997, et t. 3, Nachträge, Düsseldorf, 1999 ; B. MEISTER, *Sie sollen bruderschaft halden : religiöses Engagement in den genossenschaftlichen Vereinigungen : Bruderschaften, Zünfte, Gesellenvereinigungen) der Stadt Altenburg im Spätmittelalter*, Beucha, 2001 ; R. von MALLINCKRODT, *Struktur und kollektiver Eigensinn : Kölner Laienbruderschaften im Zeitalter der Konfessionalisierung*, Göttingen, 2005 ; K. ROSENPLENTNER, *Saeculum Pium : die kirchlichen Bruderschaften in der Gesellschaftsordnung der Mark Brandenburg im Spätmittelalter*, Francfort-sur-le-Main, 2003 ; *Mittelalterliche Bruderschaften in europäischen Städten*, éd. M. ESCHER-APSNER, Francfort-sur-le-Main, 2009 ; B. KUMOR, « Kościelne stowarzyszenia świeckich na ziemiach polskich w okresie przedrozbiorowym », *Prawo kanoniczne*, 10 (1969), p. 289-356 ; E. WIŚNIOWSKI, « Bractwa religijne na ziemiach polskich w średiowieczu », *Roczniki humanistyczne*, 17 (1969), p. 51-81 ; H. ZAREMSKA, *Bractwa w średniowiecznym Krakowie*, Wroclaw-Varsovie-Cracovie-Gdańsk, 1977 ; *Ead.*, « Żywi wobec zmartych. Brackie i cechowe pogrzeby w Krakowie w XIV – 1. polowie XVI. w. », *Kwartalnik historyczny*, 81 (1974), p. 733-749 ; I. CZARCIŃSKI, *Bractwa w wielkich miastach państwa Krzyzackiego w średniowieczu*, Toruń, 1993 ; D. C. AHL et B. WISCH, *Confraternities and the visual arts in Renaissance Italy : Ritual, spectacle, image*, Cambridge, 2000 ; P. SCHMIDT, *Wandelbare Traditionen – tradierter Wandel : zünftische Erinnerungskulturen in der Frühen Neuzeit*, Cologne, 2009 ; A. DEHMER, *Italienische Bruderschaftsbanner des Mittelalters und der Renaissance*, Munich, 2004 ; M. RUBIN, « Stadtgeschichte und Laienfrömmigkeit. Das englische Beispiel », dans *Stadtgeschichtsforschung. Aspekte, Tendenzen, Perspektiven*, éd. F. MAYRHOFER, Linz, 1993, p. 37-53 ; *Ead.*, « Corpus Christi fraternities and late medieval piety », dans *Voluntary Religion*, éd. W. J. SHEILS et D. WOOD, Worcester, 1986 (Studies in church history, 23), p. 97-109.

[3] Il s'agit de la confrérie funéraire des chanoines de la cathédrale Saint-Guy, au château de Prague. H. PÁTKOVÁ, « Středověká bratrstva v katedrále sv. Víta v Praze », *Sborník archivních prací*, 47 (1997), p. 5-6.

cas des métiers[4]. Il faut aussitôt prendre garde au fait que ces premiers statuts émanent d'une confrérie de clercs, en la personne des chanoines de la cathédrale pragoise. Le milieu ecclésiastique entretenait un rapport à l'écrit bien plus étroit que les laïcs, et les chances de conservation de la documentation y étaient également bien supérieures. Quant aux statuts de métier cités, ils proviennent de la Vieille Ville de Prague : il s'agit des statuts des tailleurs, qui furent publiés par le conseil de ville. Leur contenu en fut directement affecté. L'administration citadine ne s'intéressait guère, en effet, aux activités religieuses et répugnait le plus souvent à y intervenir[5]. Aussi ce type de statuts se rapporte-il surtout aux conditions d'exercice des activités professionnelles. Des activités cultuelles, il ne retient que ce qui avait trait aux funérailles, comme par exemple l'obligation de participer au service funèbre d'un confrère décédé, les conditions qui y étaient mises et les sanctions prévues contre les absents. On ne trouve que rarement des dispositions supplémentaires relatives au culte, de manière pour ainsi dire adventice et involontaire – ainsi du fait que de la cire doit être offerte à une église, en guise d'amende pour une infraction qui n'a rien à voir avec le culte proprement dit. Les statuts des tailleurs pragois ne livrent par exemple aucun témoignage d'une hypothétique activité religieuse. Seuls font exception les statuts des peintres pragois, en 1348, dans lesquels les dispositions cultuelles se taillent la part du lion, les statuts des métiers du métal de Plzeň, datant des années 1480[6], ou encore les statuts des orfèvres pragois, en 1324, où les articles sur les conditions de travail coexistent avec des normes liturgiques. Bien sûr, il en va tout autrement des statuts des confréries, qui règlementent en détail les activités religieuses, mais dont on ne conserve que des épaves.

Un autre type important de sources est constitué des livres administratifs (*úřední knihy*) tenus par différentes corps constitués[7]. Y étaient enregistrées les affaires les plus diverses. Ordinairement, on y trouvait des statuts, des copies d'actes importants, des listes des membres, des procès-verbaux des conflits internes et de leur règlement, des informations comptables comme les cotisations des membres, le paiement des amendes, etc. Sans doute chaque association tenait-elle au bas Moyen Âge un tel livre, parfois même plusieurs. Mais il ne s'en est conservé qu'un petit nombre, et ils sont loin de toujours évoquer la part religieuse des activités.

---

[4] *Regesta diplomatica nec non epistolaria Bohemiae et Moraviae*, t. 3, éd. J. Emler, Prague, 1890, n° 423, p. 171-172.
[5] H. Pátková, *Bratrstvie ke cti Božie, op. cit.*, p. 74-79.
[6] J. Strnad, *Listář královského města Plzně a druhdy poddaných osad* 2, Plzeň, 1905, n° 122.
[7] H. Pátková, « *Volumus eciam, quod liber in pergameno fiat*. Úřední knihy středověkých bratrstev a cechů v Čechách », *Archivní časopis*, 56 (2006), p. 184-192.

Étant donné que la majorité absolue des associations corporatives connues était implantée en ville, la documentation urbaine, c'est-à-dire pour l'essentiel des annotations dans les registres urbains, constitue la principale source qui nous est parvenue du Bas Moyen Âge tchèque. Les informations les plus riches proviennent évidemment des testaments, car de nombreux testateurs, dans leur souci de s'assurer le salut, n'oubliaient pas de faire quelque legs à une confrérie. Les actes laissés par l'administration ecclésiastique sont nettement moins loquaces. Ils ne prêtent que peu d'attention aux confréries, sauf quand celles-ci regroupaient des clercs et requéraient l'autorisation épiscopale[8]. Pour le reste, les confréries et les métiers n'y apparaissent que fortuitement – par exemple, si l'une de ces associations détenait un droit de patronat sur tel bénéfice, les livres de confirmation de l'officialité (ou consistoire) pragoise, où étaient inscrites les nominations des clercs aux bénéfices, pouvaient en faire état. Mais ce n'est qu'à la toute fin du XVe siècle que l'autorité ecclésiastique s'est mise à confirmer les statuts des confréries, et même alors, cet usage releva plus de l'exception que de la règle.

L'utilisation de ces sources textuelles soulève des problèmes spécifiques d'interprétation. Le plus grave tient au fait que le mode de désignation des corporations n'est pas suffisamment discriminant pour permettre d'en reconnaître la nature. Alors que la terminologie tchèque actuelle distingue les métiers, entendus comme des associations professionnelles d'artisans ou, éventuellement, de marchands, et les confréries, des groupements à vocation religieuse et socialisatrice, tel n'est pas le cas dans la langue des sources médiévales. Les expressions de *confraternitas, fraternitas, Bruderschaft, bratrstvo, bratřina* étaient appliquées tant à des confréries de dévotion qu'à des métiers d'artisans. Les mots de *Zeche, cech* n'étaient pas moins équivoques[9]. Pour peu que les informations complémentaires fassent défaut, la nature concrète de la corporation en question demeure incertaine.

Quant aux sources matérielles et iconographiques, autant elles fourmillent à l'époque moderne, autant elles sont rares pour le Moyen Âge. Leur interprétation n'est pas non plus toujours simple. Prenons l'exemple des symboles d'une corporation donnée, présents dans l'espace sacré. Dans les villes de Prague, on conserve des témoignages de ce type dès l'époque pré-hussite. Ailleurs, comme à Most, ville de Bohême du Nord, ils remontent à la fin du Moyen Âge seulement. À Prague, il s'agit d'emblèmes héraldiques : mentionnons celui des peintres, dans le couvent Sainte-Agnès, ainsi que ceux des fourreurs, des tondeurs ou encore des brasseurs, qui proviennent

---

[8] H. Pátková, *Bratrstvie ke cti Božie*, Prague, 2000, p. 74-79.

[9] H. Pátková, *Bratrstvie ke cti Božie, op. cit.*, p. 70-73.

respectivement de l'église Saint-Gall[10], de l'église Saint-Pierre *na Poříčí* et de l'église Saint-Haštal (Castullus)[11]. Mais le problème est que l'on ne saurait dire avec certitude si ces emblèmes représentaient la corporation comme telle, ou seulement certains de ses membres. La situation est heureusement plus claire à Most, où l'église de la Vierge Marie, rénovée après un incendie en 1518, abritait des chapelles latérales ornées des emblèmes des artisans, mais aussi des emblèmes des métiers de la ville[12], ainsi qu'à České Budějovice, où des armoiries datant de la fin du XVe siècle (aujourd'hui disparues) étaient suspendues au-dessus de l'autel du métier[13].

Dans le paysage documentaire de la Bohême médiévale, l'ensemble d'objets issus du métier des orfèvres pragois est une exception de taille. Il s'agit d'abord de quatre manuscrits transmettant la légende et l'office de saint Éloi, dont deux ont été exécutés à grands frais (l'un est même orné d'enluminures), alors que les deux autres se présentent comme des recueils sans apprêt et de petit format. Le reste est composé d'une mitre reliquaire et d'un panneau reliquaire, d'une bourse, d'un éclat de la vraie Croix, ainsi que d'autres reliques comprenant un fragment du sceau de saint Éloi et son manipule[14].

Autant dire que les lacunes documentaires ne permettent de suivre et d'interpréter de manière détaillée le culte des saints que dans un petit nombre de cas. L'évolution religieuse de la Bohême nous autorise à diviser la fin du Moyen Âge entre la période antérieure aux guerres hussites – soit, approximativement, jusqu'en 1419 – et la période ultérieure, quand la majorité des habitants se mit à pencher pour le hussitisme. À la toute fin de la période considérée, commença parallèlement à se diffuser la réforme luthérienne. Rappelons aussi que le développement des villes et des formes de sociabilité qui y étaient liées fut en Bohême assez tardif, puisqu'il ne se fit pleinement sentir qu'au XIIIe siècle. Il fallut attendre la même époque pour voir l'administration ecclésiastique étendre son réseau territorial jusqu'au niveau des simples paroisses.

Les plus anciennes associations de métier sont probablement apparues dans les villes de Bohême à la fin du XIIIe siècle, mais les preuves de leur existence ne sont pas antérieures à la deuxième décennie du XIVe siècle (tels

---

[10] V. Denkstein, Z. Drobná et J. Kybalová, *Lapidárium Národního muzea*, Prague, 1958, p. 58.
[11] J. Jásek, « Cechovní symbolika před rokem 1400 », *Heraldická ročenka* (1997), p. 14.
[12] M. Myšička, « Řemeslná symbolika na pečetích, znacích a korouhvích na příkladu cechů města Mostu », *Sborník archivních prací*, 58 (2008), p. 352-354 ; H. Mannlová-Raková, *Kulturní památka Most. Děkanský kostel a jeho stavitelé*, Most, 1989, p. 29, 31, 89-90.
[13] České Budějovice, Archives publiques de la région de Třeboň – district de České Budějovice, corps de métier des bouchers I/1. H. Pátková, *Bratrstvie ke cti Božie, op. cit.*, p. 122.
[14] Voir ci-dessous, note 18.

les tailleurs de la Vieille Ville de Prague, que nous avons déjà mentionnés). Durant la troisième décennie sont également attestés des confréries de prêtres attachés à la cathédrale Saint-Guy[15]. C'est donc à partir de cette époque que l'on commence à trouver dans le milieu des métiers des témoignages d'un culte rendu à un saint en particulier : ainsi, dans le métier des peintres pragois en 1348, ou encore dans celui des orfèvres qui existait dès 1324, mais dont les activités cultuelles ne sont pas connues avant les années 1360. Il s'agit dans le premier cas de saint Luc[16]. Sa vénération trouve sa justification dans le fait qu'il fut, est-il dit explicitement, le premier à avoir peint la Mère de Dieu. En ce qui concerne les orfèvres, les sources se contentent de faire état d'un culte rendu à saint Éloi. Il en existe toutefois des preuves matérielles sans équivoque : la mitre reliquaire de saint Éloi et le groupe de quatre manuscrits transmettant son office et sa *Vita*, qui dérivent d'un unique modèle français. Leur genèse est traditionnellement mise en relation avec la visite de l'empereur Charles IV en France, en 1378 – ce qui n'est pas à exclure. Alors que saint Luc est un saint universellement connu et que sa vénération ne se limite pas au seul milieu des peintres, saint Éloi, même s'il était certainement déjà connu en Bohême avant 1378, n'y fit jamais l'objet d'un culte à grande échelle[17]. On peut donc dire que la nouveauté réside dans la connexion établie entre saint Luc et le métier des peintres, d'une part, ainsi que dans l'identification quasi exclusive de saint Éloi avec les orfèvres et les divers métiers du métal, d'autre part. Ce dernier ne se rencontre ailleurs que très exceptionnellement, par exemple dans quelques calendriers cisterciens et prémontrés, où une influence française est de nouveau probable.

Les autres documents du XIVe et du début du XVe siècle concernent des saints plus connus et plus largement honorés. Citons les merciers pragois (*institores*), qui faisaient célébrer des offices à l'église Saint-Nicolas, sans qu'on sache à quel autel[18], et à l'église Saint-Martin, ou encore les négociants pragois (*mercatores*), dont le chapelain était établi à l'église Sainte-Marie-devant-le-Tyn. Les *iuniores institores* faisaient célébrer la messe à l'église Saint-Gall, à l'autel des douze apôtres ; leur métier n'eut cependant qu'une existence éphémère, des années 1350 aux années 1380.

---

[15] H. PÁTKOVÁ, « Středověká bratrstva v katedrále sv. Víta v Praze », *Sborník archivních prací*, 47 (1997), p. 3-73.
[16] Prague, Archives de la Galerie nationale, AA 1207, p. 5. L'édition la plus récente se trouve dans H. PÁTKOVA, *Cechovní kniha pražských malířů 1348-1527*, Prague, 1996.
[17] D. STEHLÍKOVÁ, « Pražští zlatníci v letech 1400-1471 », *Staletá Praha*, 14 (1984), p. 171 (il ne s'agit cependant pas de saint Gilles) ; *De Noyon à Prague*, éd. H. PÁTKOVÁ, Prague, 2006.
[18] V. V. TOMEK, *Základy starého místopisu pražského*, 1, Prague, 1865, p. 60.

Par ailleurs, en 1397, le conseil de la Nouvelle Ville de Prague exigea que la confrérie commune aux menuisiers, aux tailleurs et aux pêcheurs fît représenter sur ses cierges la Passion du Christ et saint Venceslas. Il s'agissait d'une mesure toute circonstancielle : les tailleurs avaient voulu apposer sur les cierges l'emblème qui leur était propre, celui des ciseaux, ce qui fut perçu par les autres confrères comme une usurpation[19].

En ce qui concerne les confréries, on dispose également pour cette période de renseignements sur la confrérie des desservants (*ministri ecclesie*) de la cathédrale Saint-Guy[20]. Cette confrérie fondée en 1328 avait un autel consacré à l'Assomption de la Vierge Marie ; ses usages liturgiques se calquaient sur le calendrier diocésain. À la fin du XIVe siècle, il existait également une confrérie en l'honneur de la Vierge Marie à Kolín, en Bohême centrale, mais c'était probablement une corporation rassemblant tous les habitants de la ville.

En outre, à partir des années 1380, émergent à Prague des confréries du Corps du Christ ou, le cas échéant, du Corps et du Sang du Christ[21]. Leur organisation et leur composition étaient à l'évidence très disparates. La confrérie établie auprès de l'église Saint-Léonard, dans la Vieille Ville de Prague, se recrutait parmi les couches citadines, même si le roi Venceslas IV en personne y était inscrit[22]. En revanche, la confrérie de la Nouvelle Ville, établie auprès de la chapelle du Corps du Christ nouvellement construite, comptait parmi ses membres de nombreux personnages de la cour, en plus de quelques patriciens pragois. Elle semble avoir possédé ses propres insignes armoriés, puisqu'elle s'intitulait également la confrérie du cercle et du marteau (*circuli cum malleo pendente*)[23].

Les témoignages émanant des autres villes de Bohême – lesquelles ne pouvaient rivaliser ni en taille ni en importance avec Prague, centre incontesté du pays – sont beaucoup plus dispersés. Le tableau suivant en donne un aperçu[24] :

---

[19] V. J. SEDLÁK, *O počátcích erbů pražských cechů*, Prague, 1945, p. 15-16.

[20] H. PÁTKOVÁ, « Středověká bratrstva v katedrále sv. Víta v Praze », *Sborník archivních prací*, 47 (1997), p. 3-73.

[21] H. PÁTKOVÁ, « Die vorhussitischen Fronleichnamsbruderschaften in Böhmen », dans *Die 'Neue Frömmigkeit' in Europa im Spätmittelalter*, éd. M. DERWICH et M. STAUB, Göttingen, 2004. p. 77-83.

[22] E. ŠITTLER, « Kostel sv. Linharta a dům u Černého orla na Starém Městě pražském 2 », *Zprávy komise pro soupis stavebních, uměleckých a historických památek král. Hlav. Města Prahy*, 4 (1912), p. 109-113.

[23] M. POLÍVKA, « K šíření husitství v Praze. Bratrstvo a kaple Božího těla na Novém Městě pražském v předhusitské době », *Folia historica Bohemica*, 5 (1983), p. 95-118.

[24] La plupart des indications qui suivent sont empruntées à H. PÁTKOVÁ, *Bratrstvie ke cti Božie, op. cit.*, p. 111-140.

	Bohême du Nord-Ouest		
Most	1397	Bouchers	Autel Saint-Nicolas
Most	1411	Confrérie *Corpus Christi*[26]	
	Bohême du Nord-Est		
Hradec Králové	1399	Cordonniers	Autel Saint-Léonard
Turnov	1396	Drapiers	Messe en l'honneur de la Vierge Marie
	Bohême du Sud-Ouest		
Klatovy	1398	Drapiers	Autel Sainte-Marie-Madeleine
	Bohême centrale		
Kutná Hora	Années 1380	Confrérie du Corps du Christ et de sainte Barbe	Chapelle du même nom[27]
Sedlec (près de Kutná Hora)	1389	Confrérie du Corps du Christ et du Saint-Sépulcre	(confrérie attachée au monastère cistercien du lieu)[28]

---

[25] Prague, Archives du château de Prague, Archives du chapitre métropolitain, II-10, p. 136-139 ; K. KONRÁD, « O posvátném zpěvu staročeském I. Doba před Karlem IV. », *Cecilie*, 4 (1877), p. 41-43 ; J. N. CORI, *Geschichte der königlichen Stadt Brüx bis zum Jahre 1788*, Brüx, 1899, p. 65, 149 ; L. SCHLESINGER, *Stadtbuch von Brüx bis zum Jahre 1526*, Prague, 1876, p. 179 ; *Soupis česky psaných listin a listů* I, 2/1, n° 2784 ; T. V. BÍLEK, *Statky a jmění kollejí jesuitských, klášterů, kostelů, bratrstev a jiných ústavů v království českém, od císaře Josefa II. zrušených*, Prague, 1893, p. 422 ; Most, Archives publiques de la région de Litoměřice – district de Most, Archives municipales de Most, n° inv. 129, 130, 154, VII A/3.

[26] Prague, Archives du château de Prague, Archives du chapitre métropolitain, III-9, fol. 45v-46 ; *Regesta Bohemiae et Moraviae aetatis Venceslai IV* 1/6, éd. V. JENŠOVSKÁ, Prague, 1982, p. 1589, n° 6322 (la désignation du métier, sous le terme de 'czech', y est interprétée de façon incorrecte comme un toponyme tchèque) ; *Monumenta Vaticana res gestas Bohemicas illustrantia* 5/2, éd. K. KROFTA, Prague, 1905, p. 998 ; 7/1, éd. J. ERŠIL, 1998, p. 178 ; *Codex iuris municipalis regni Bohemiae* 2, éd. J. ČELAKOVSKÝ, Prague, 1895, p. 951 ; *Libri erectionum archidioecesis Pragensis saeculo XIV. et XV.*, 4, éd. C. BOROVÝ, Prague, 1883, p. 445-446, n° 615 ; *Libri confirmationum ad beneficia ecclesiastica Pragensem per archidioecesim* 8-10, éd. J. EMLER, Prague, 1889, p. 72 ; J. KURKA, *Archidiakonáty kouřimský, boleslavský, hradecký a diecese litomyšlská. Místopis církevní do roku 1421*, Prague, 1914, p. 132-135. On conserve le sceau de la confrérie, daté de l'année 1388 (Prague, Archives du château de Prague, Archives du chapitre métropolitain), qui porte une représentation de sainte Barbe.

[27] Archives nationales de Prague, pièces de provenances diverses, acte de Jean de Jenštejn du 30 mars 1389. *Monumenta Vaticana res gestas bohemiae illustrantia* 5, éd. K. KROFTA, Prague, 1889, p. 427, 492.

Il ressort de ce rapide tour d'horizon que les saints en question étaient dans leur immense majorité des figures universellement connues et honorées, non seulement en Bohême, mais à travers toute la Chrétienté. Il n'y a guère que deux exceptions à cette règle. Saint Éloi d'une part, qui était certes connu en Bohême, notamment dans les milieux cisterciens et prémontrés, mais dont le culte ne se répandit que sous l'influence française et demeura le monopole des orfèvres et, le cas échéant, des autres métiers du métal. Saint Venceslas, d'autre part, qui était au contraire un saint tchèque de souche et qui était perçu comme un saint patron généraliste, sans lien avec un type particulier de confrérie ou de métier. Voilà pourquoi, sur les cierges, son effigie pouvait servir de trait d'union entre des métiers aussi différents que les menuisiers, les tailleurs et les pêcheurs. Mis à part saint Éloi et saint Luc, les saints étaient polyvalents et n'avaient généralement pas de monopole sur tel ou tel métier en particulier. Même dans le cas de saint Luc, la vénération dont il faisait l'objet en Bohême n'avait que peu à voir avec les peintres. Leur statuts innovent toutefois en avançant que ce fut lui qui peignit la Vierge Marie. Il est possible que cet argument ait été importé d'ailleurs, peut-être d'Italie ou de France, où le culte de saint Luc était depuis longtemps bien établi dans le milieu des peintres. Quant au culte du Corps du Christ, on sait qu'il était partout très en faveur à l'époque[28]. Il ne faudrait d'ailleurs pas croire que les mentions du Sang du Christ figurant dans le nom des confréries de Prague et de Most annoncent l'utraquisme; elles font plutôt écho aux miracles des hosties sanglantes (Wilsnack), qui s'ébruitèrent rapidement en Bohême[29].

Le mouvement hussite changea radicalement la donne en Bohême. Le pays se partagea entre des régions majoritairement utraquistes et d'autres qui

---

[28] Voir par exemple P. BROWE, « Die Ausbreitung des Fronleichnamsfestes », dans *Jahrbuch für Liturgiewissenschaft*, 8 (1928), p. 107-143 ; *Id.*, « Entstehung der Sakramentprozession », dans *Bonner Zeitschrift für Theologie und Seelsorge*, 86 (1931), p. 97-117 ; X. HAIMERL, *Das Prozessionswesen des Bistums Bamberg im Mittelalter*, Munich, 1937 ; A. MITTERWIESER, *Geschichte der Fronleichnamsprozession in Bayern*, Munich, 1930 ; A. HÄUSSLING, « Literaturbericht zum Fronleichnamsfest », dans *Jahrbuch für Volkskunde*, 9 (1986), p. 228-238, 11 (1988), p. 343-250 ; A. LÖTHER, *Prozessionen in spätmittelalterlichen Städten*, Cologne-Weimar-Vienne, 1999 ; M. RUBIN, *Corpus Christi. The eucharist in late Medieval culture*, Cambridge, 1991 ; *Ead.*, « Fronleichnamsprozessionen », dans *Laienfrömmigkeit in späten Mittelalter*, éd. K. SCHREINER, Munich, 1992, p. 309-318 ; H. ZAREMSKA, « Procesje Bożego Ciała w Krakowie w XIV-XVI wieku », dans *Kultura elitarna i kultura masowa w Polsce późnego średniowiecza*, éd. B. GEREMEK, Cracovie, 1978, p. 25-40.

[29] *Wunder, Wallfahrt, Widersacher. Die Wilsnackfahrt*, éd. H. KÜHNE et K. ZIESACK, Ratisbonne, 2005 ; *Die Wilsnackfahrt. Ein Wallfahrts – und Kommunikationszentrum Nord- und Mitteleuropas im Spätmittelalter*, éd. F. ESCHER et H. KÜHNE, Francfort-sur-le-Main, 2006 ; C. Walker BYNUM, « Bleeding hosts and their German relics in late medieval northern Germany », *The medieval history journal*, 7 (2004), p. 227-241.

restèrent sous l'influence des catholiques, dits *sub una*. Alors que, chez les catholiques, les formes de la piété en général, et du culte des saints en particulier, ne cessèrent pas d'évoluer, souvent sous l'influence du reste de l'Europe catholique, il n'en alla pas de même chez les utraquistes[30]. Les plus radicaux d'entre eux prirent position contre le culte des saints ; leur critique n'épargna pas non plus l'ornementation des églises et des autels, les peintures et les sculptures, ce qui a eu pour effet de raréfier les sources conservées. Vis-à-vis des confréries, les réformateurs tchèques adoptèrent une attitude très réservée[31]. La majorité des utraquistes était certes modérée, mais il existait selon les lieux et les personnes une grande diversité de points de vue, qui se réfractaient aussi dans des rapports différenciés aux saints.

Toujours est-il que des associations professionnelles existaient du côté catholique comme utraquiste[32]. Si l'on considère séparément les deux milieux, la situation se présente de la manière suivante[33] :

a. Catholiques *sub una*

	Bohême du Sud		
České Budějovice	1478	Boulangers et meuniers	Vierge Marie
-	1482	Le grand métier (les métiers du métal ?)	Saint Éloi
-	1489	Bouchers	Vierge Marie
-	1495	Boulangers	Sainte Anne
-	v. 1500	Peintres et orfèvres	Saint Luc et saint Éloi
-	1515	Mégissiers	Saint Wolfgang
-	1518	Métiers du métal	Sainte Barbe
-	1521	Pêcheurs	Saint Pierre
Český Krumlov	1492	Drapiers	Vierge Marie
-	1492	Cordonniers	Sainte Catherine
-	1505	Métiers du métal	Sainte Barbe et saint Éloi
-	1505	Charpentiers	Saint Léonard

---

[30] Voir à ce sujet la monographie d'O. HALAMA, *Otázka svatých v české reformaci*, Brno, 2002.
[31] H. PÁTKOVÁ, *Bratrstvie ke cti Božie, op. cit.*, p. 96-99.
[32] H. PÁTKOVÁ, « Bractwa w czeskich miastach katolickich i utrakwistycznych », dans *Ecclesia et civitas. Kościół i życie religijne w mieście średniowiecznym*, éd. H. MANIKOWSKA et H. ZAREMSKA, Varsovie, 2002, p. 213-222.
[33] D'après les données fournies dans : H. PÁTKOVÁ, « Bratrstvie ke cti Božie », *op. cit.*, p. 111-140.

-	1512	Pelletiers	Saint Michel
-	1515	Brasseurs	Saint Laurent
-	1518	Potiers	Saint Wolfgang
-	1518	Tailleurs	Saint Venceslas
Kaplice	1481	Drapiers	Vierge Marie
Rožmberk-sur-Vltava	1506	Tisserands	Saint Venceslas
Benešov-sur-Černa	1519	Tisserands	Sainte Catherine
Lomnice-sur-Lužnice	1519	Tisserands	Sainte Barbe
Třeboň	1519	Tisserands	Saint Venceslas
Veselí-sur-Lužnice	1519	Tisserands	Sainte Apolline
Soběslav	1513	Boulangers	autel Saint-Pierre
Trhové Sviny	1520	Bouchers	Saint Venceslas, saint Nicolas
Prachatice	1461	Boulangers et meuniers	autel de la Vierge Marie
Bohême du Nord-Ouest			
Kadaň	1460	Tailleurs	Autel des saints apôtres
-	1460	Cordonniers	Autel *Corpus Christi*
-	1460	Boulangers	Autel de saint Louis et de saint Antonin
-	1460	Bouchers	Autel de la Vierge Marie
-	1520	Charrons	Saint François
Most	1518	Brasseurs	Chapelle Sainte-Barbe
-	1505	Compagnons boulangers	Autel Saint-Bernard
Jirkov	1509	Bouchers	Autel Saint-Nicolas et Saint-Martin
Bohême du Sud-Ouest			
Plzeň	1472	Drapiers	Autel Saint-Pierre
-	1486	Métiers du métal	Sainte Barbe
-	1512	Cordonniers	Autel Saint-Blaise

b. Utraquistes

Ville(s) de Prague				
Nouvelle Ville	1446	Forgerons	Saint André
Nouvelle Ville	1456	Brasseurs	Saint Venceslas
Nouvelle Ville	1457	Fabricants de planches et scieurs	Saint Joseph
Bohême centrale et occidentale			
Kutná Hora	1463	Monnayeurs	Chapelle des Rois mages dans l'église Sainte-Barbe ; En 1490, ils détenaient le droit de patronage sur l'église Saint-Venceslas, tout en possédant l'autel de la Vierge Marie et de Tous les saints dans l'église Saint-Jacques et l'autel Saint-André
-	1495	Mineurs[35]	Chapelle Sainte-Barbe
-	1463	Marchands d'argent et métaux	Église Saint-Georges
Jičín	1464	Tailleurs et tondeurs	Autel de la Vierge Marie
Rakovník	v. 1510-1520	Brasseurs	Saint Venceslas
Rokycany	1521	Brasseurs	Autel Saint-Venceslas

Tel est l'aperçu que l'on peut donner des dédicaces attestées parmi les métiers et les autres associations comparables.

Si l'on en vient maintenant aux confréries de dévotion, la situation est encore plus disparate entre les zones catholiques et utraquistes. Les régions catholiques du pays connaissaient au début du XVIe siècle : des confréries dédiées à sainte Anne, que ce soit au Sud ou au Sud-Ouest (Český Krumlov, Blatná, Horšovský Týn[35]) ; apparues dans les années 1480, des confréries du

---

[34] Le terme de *hašplíři* désigne spécifiquement ceux des mineurs qui assuraient le transport du minerai à l'aide de treuils.
[35] Český Krumlov, 1512 : Archives publiques de la région de Třeboň – district de Český Krumlov, Archives municipales de Český Krumlov, n° inv. 321, livre des testaments 1515-1581, p. 137-139 et suiv. Cf. H. Gross, « Mikuláše Slepičky z Nažic závět a její vykonání (1512) »,

Rosaire, liées à cette forme spécifique de dévotion mariale[36], non seulement au Nord-Ouest et à l'Ouest (Ústí nad Labem, Kadaň[37], Teplá[38], Tachov), mais aussi au Sud (České Budějovice); des confréries de saint Jacques, dispersées dans tout le pays (Kadaň, Broumov)[39], dont au moins une, à Plzeň, réunissait des pèlerins de Compostelle[40]; une unique confrérie dédiée au début du XVIe siècle à saint François, dans une ville où était établi un couvent de

Archiv český, 21 (1903), p. 489, 494. Horšovský Týn, 1511: cf. V. Ryneš, « Imagines miraculosae doby pobělohorské », *Český lid*, 54 (1967), p. 188; « Die St. Anna Wallfahrtsirche in Bischofteinitz », *Jahrbuch der Egerländer*, 6 (1959), p. 113; J. Hüttl, *Festschrift zum 600jährigen Stadtjubiläum der Kreisstadt Bischofteinitz* 1, s. l. 1951, p. 38; *Unser Heimatkreis Bischofteinitz mit den deutschen Siedlungen im Bezirk Taus*, Furth im Wald, 1967, p. 469; M. Kolář, « Rozrod Dobrohostův a osudy jejich. Příspěvek ku kolonisací Plzeňska », *Památky archaeologické a místopisné*, 8 (1868-1869), p. 489; J. Eckhardt, *Beiträge zur Geschichte der Stadt und der Herrschaft Bischof-Teinitz*, 1842, ms. Les archives publiques de la région de Plzeň – district de Domažlice, bibliothèque, p. 79-80, datent la fondation de la confrérie de 1516. Blatná, 1518: F. Dvorský, « Dopisy pana Zdeňka Lva z Rožmitála z let 1508-1535 », dans *Archiv český*, 8 (1888), n° 289, p. 224-225; M. Vrána, *Město Blatná. Obraz prehistorický, historický, kulturní, sociální a národohospodářský*, Blatná, 1926, p. 22.
[36] Ústí nad Labem, 1483: W. Hieke, A. Horčička, *Urkundenbuch der Stadt Aussig bis zum Jahre 1526*, Prague, 1896, p. 134; Kadaň, 1483: Archives publiques de la région de Plzeň – district de Chomutov, Archives municipales de Kadaň, livre urbain 1465-1522, fol. V 16v. Teplá, 1483: cf. notre note 39. České Budějovice, 1497: Archives publiques de la région de Třeboň – district de České Budějovice, Archives municipales de České Budějovice, testaments, Praxi untder chirchen 1497. Voir H. Pátková, « Wallfahrt und Bruderschaft in spätmittelalterlichen Böhmen », dans *Wallfahrt und Reformation. Pouť a reformacie. Zu Veränderung religiöser Praxis in Deutschland und Böhmen in der Umbrüchen der Frühen Neuzeit*, éd. J. Hrdina, Francfort-sur-le-Main, 2007 (Europäische Wallfahrtsstudien, 3), p. 139-144.
[37] H. Pátková, « Tzv. kniha růžencového bratrstva v Kadani jako pramen pro dějiny zbožnosti v pozdním středověku », *Porta Bohemica*, 5 (2009), p. 169-175.
[38] Prague, Archives nationales, NB XII/36. Sur la confrérie de Teplá, cf. les archives du château de Prague, Archives du chapitre métropolitain, VI.8, fol. 10r et suiv.; *Fest-Schrift zum siebenhundertjährigen Jubiläum der Gründung des Premonstratenser-Stiftes Tepl*, s. l. s. d. (1893), p. 10; B. Grassl, *Geschichte und Beschreibung des Stiftes Tepl*, Plzeň, 1929 (2), p. 20; H. Pátková, « Honoratiores ex statu ecclesiastico vel saeculari. Růžencové bratrstvo v Teplé na sklonku středověku », dans *Ve znamení zemí Koruny české. Sborník k 60. narozeninám prof. PhDr. Lenky Bobkové. CSc.*, éd. L. Březina, J. Konvičná, J. Zdichynec, Prague, 2006, p. 256-264.
[39] Kadaň, 1512: P. Hlaváček, « Kadaňská městská kniha jako pramen k dějinám pozdně gotického umění », dans *Gotické sochařství a malířství v severozápadních Čechách (Sborník z kolokvia konaného u příležitosti 70. výročí výstavy Josefa Opitze)*, Ústí nad Labem, 1999, p. 159; Archives du château de Prague, Archives du chapitre métropolitain, 1284 XLII 2; Broumov, Archives nationales, ŘB-B, actes, n° inv. 252.
[40] Plzeň, 1498: Archives municipales de Plzeň, livre des testaments 1468-1565, fol. 48r-v, 54v-55r, 60r, Dominicains de Plzeň, actes I/238, 239, 244, 417; J. Strnad, *Listář královského města Plzně a druhdy poddaných osad* 2, Plzeň, 1905, p. 384-387, 387-388, 588-589; J. Kocáb, M. Hruška, *Kniha pamětní král. Krajského města Plzně od roku 775 až 1870*, Plzeň, 1883, p. 61-62; V. Ryneš, « El culto de Santiago de Compostela en Bohemia », *Ibero-Americana Pragensia*, 8 (1974), p. 141.

Frères mineurs[41]; des confréries de *litterati* pratiquant le chant d'église[42], à Loket (Vierge Marie), Teplá[43], Ústí nad Labem (Vierge Marie et saint Venceslas, où il s'agissait d'une confrérie mixte, réunissant *litterati* et archers[44]) – on ne sait si la confrérie mariale attestée à partir de 1456 à Krupka, dans le Nord de la Bohême, en était également[45]; des confréries du Corps du Christ continuaient manifestement de fonctionner, comme à Most, ville demeurée catholique, tandis qu'une nouvelle apparut à České Budějovice. A Přeštice, dans le Sud-Ouest du pays, il existait aussi une confrérie dédiée à sainte Barbe au début du XVIe siècle. A Kájov, non loin de Český Krumlov, est attestée au même moment une confrérie Saint-Venceslas[46]. A České Budějovice, enfin, était active une confrérie dédiée à saint Wolfgang[47].

En milieu utraquiste, le début du XVIe siècle vit la fondation d'une nouvelle confrérie du Corps du Christ à Notre-Dame-devant-le-Týn, à Prague[48]. Elle avait le caractère d'une confrérie de *litterati*. Les confréries de ce genre se rencontraient en effet plus fréquemment dans les zones utraquistes qu'en terre catholique. Elles ne se consacraient pas au culte d'un saint en particulier, même si toutes honoraient la Vierge Marie.

Quant au culte rendu au *Corpus Christi*, il était à cette époque universel et alimentait la piété eucharistique aussi bien des catholiques que des utraquistes. Dans les villes, il s'exprimait de manière privilégiée lors de la procession de la Fête-Dieu, que les confréries et les métiers honoraient avec force bannières et luminaire[49].

---

[41] Český Krumlov, 1505: Archives publiques de Třeboň – district de Český Krumlov, Archives municipales de Český Krumlov, livre des testaments 1515-1582, p. 137-139 et suiv.; H. GROSS, « Mikuláše Slepičky z Nažic závět a její vykonání (1512) », dans *Archiv český*, 21 (1903), p. 489, 494; *Soupis česky psaných listin a listů* I 3/1, Prague, 1980, n° 4896; M. VOLF, *Popis městských archivů v Čechách*, Prague, 1947, p. 140.
[42] H. PÁTKOVÁ, « Die sogenannten Literatenbruderschaften in spätmittelalterlichen Böhmen », *Almanach Historyczny*, 3 (2001), p. 11-18.
[43] Prague, Bibliothèque nationale, Teplá A 47/1, *Annales monasterii* 1, fol. 118v.
[44] Ústí nad Labem 1490: W. HIEKE, A. HORČIČKA, *Urkundenbuch der Stadt Aussig bis zum Jahre 1526*, Prague, 1896, p. 151-153; *Dějiny města Ústí nad Labem*, Ústí nad Labem, 1995, p. 33.
[45] A. MÜLLER, *Quellen- und Urkundenbuch des Bezirkes Töplitz-Schönau bis zum Jahre 1500*, Prague, 1929, p. 231.
[46] Kájov, 1512, consécration en 1531: Archives publiques de la région de Třeboň – district de Český Krumlov, Archives municipales of Český Krumlov, livre des testaments 1515-1582, p. 137-139, 199.
[47] České Budějovice, 1496: Archives publiques de la région de Třeboň – district de České Budějovice, Archives municipales de České Budějovice, testaments, Ursula Damelin, 1498; *Soupis česky psaných listů a listin* I 3/1, Prague, 1980, n° 4778.
[48] H. PÁTKOVÁ, *Bratrstvie ke cti Božie, op. cit.*, en particulier p. 19-20, 118.
[49] Sur la participation des corps urbains aux processions et aux cortèges, voir H. PÁTKOVÁ, « Bruderschaften und Zünfte – Formen (und Grenzen) der Repräsentation », dans *Ecclesia*

Comme durant la période précédente, on constate qu'à cette époque aussi, la plupart des saints des métiers et des confréries étaient des saints universels, dont la vénération n'était pas limitée à ces seuls milieux. Un vocable préférentiel ne se remarque que dans le cas de saint Éloi, le patron des métiers du métal. D'autres cultes sont régionalement conditionnés, tel saint Wolfgang au Sud-Ouest et au Sud, où il est arrivé en provenance de Ratisbonne[50], quand ils ne bénéficient pas d'une popularité générale à la fin du Moyen Âge, comme saint Jacques, sainte Anne, sainte Barbe, sainte Apolline, sainte Catherine. La situation locale a pu aussi déterminer le choix du saint patron à Most, où le culte de saint Bernardin a manifestement été introduit par les Franciscains observants du cru[51], et à Kadaň, où coexistaient un couvent de Frères mineurs et un couvent plus récent de Franciscains observants. Exceptionnelle est la raison avancée pour justifier le culte rendu par les menuisiers pragois à saint Joseph, leur collègue.

Le rôle des saints de souche est, dans l'ensemble, très limité. Il n'apparaît vraiment au premier plan qu'avec saint Venceslas. Son culte bénéficie d'une faveur particulière chez les brasseurs, et ce, y compris en milieu utraquiste. Enfin, les milieux catholiques suivent la même évolution que le reste de l'Europe et en adoptent les nouvelles formes de piété, comme les confréries du Rosaire ou les saints et les saintes à la mode, tels que saint Jacques, sainte Barbe, sainte Anne ou sainte Catherine. En revanche, les utraquistes sont plus conservateurs : si tant est qu'ils ne répudient pas entièrement le culte des saints, ils s'en tiennent pour l'essentiel aux bonnes vieilles traditions.

Traduit du tchèque par Olivier Marin

---

als Kommunikationsraum in Mitteleuropa (13.-16. Jahrhundert), éd. E. DOLEŽALOVÁ et R. ŠIMŮNEK, Munich, 2011, p. 185-192.
[50] H. PÁTKOVÁ, « Bratrstva svatého Wolfganga v pozdně středověkých Čechách », dans *Za zdmi kláštera*, České Budějovice, 2010, p. 167-171.
[51] Les Franciscains observants de Bohême font l'objet des recherches de Petr Hlaváček.

Conclusions

Marie-Madeleine de Cevins
(Rennes)

Si, pour reprendre la célèbre formule de Lucien Febvre, l'historien part toujours avec en tête « une hypothèse de travail à vérifier », « la question qui a déclenché le mouvement ne reste pas identique à elle-même [...] : [au contact des données surgies de la documentation] l'hypothèse est reprise, corrigée, complétée et ainsi peu à peu naît et grandit la connaissance historique »[1]. Les éditeurs de ce volume s'étaient posés la question de l'existence d'un modèle de sainteté centre-européen au Moyen Âge, un modèle sinon véritablement original, du moins teinté d'une couleur régionale[2]. Cela revenait à éprouver la notion d'Europe centrale, appliquée à l'époque médiévale[3], selon le critère de l'hagiologie. Le clivage mis en relief voici plus de trente ans dans sa thèse par André Vauchez, qui opposait une zone « froide », réfractaire au changement, à une zone « chaude », dynamique et innovante, offrait à cet égard un point de départ à la fois commode et stimulant. L'auteur de *La sainteté en Occident* range l'Europe centrale dans la première[4]. Les contributions réunies dans ce livre incitent pourtant à ne pas placer trop hâtivement l'espace polono-bohémo-hongrois dans la moitié frileuse de la *christianitas*.

Jusqu'au XIVe siècle, l'attachement aux saints « anciens » – évêques, confesseurs, évangélisateurs ou martyrs des premiers siècles du christianisme,

---

[1] H.-I. Marrou, *De la connaissance historique*, Paris, 1954 (rééd. 1975), p. 118-119. La citation de Lucien Febvre est tirée de : L. Febvre, « Examen de conscience d'une histoire et d'un historien », dans *Id.*, *Combats pour l'histoire*, Paris, 1953, p. 8.

[2] On entend par « modèle de sainteté » le processus de reconnaissance d'un individu réputé saint, de sa « fabrication » à la diffusion de son culte et à l'épanouissement de celui-ci, voire à son extinction.

[3] Sur ce sujet largement débattu, voir les références fournies en introduction par Olivier Marin.

[4] André Vauchez a cependant apporté au tableau initial qu'il avait brossé dans *La sainteté en Occident aux derniers siècles du Moyen Âge d'après les procès de canonisation et les documents hagiographiques*, Rome, 1981, plusieurs correctifs dans son recueil d'articles *Saints, prophètes et visionnaires : le pouvoir surnaturel au Moyen Âge*, Paris, 1999.

Les saints et leur culte en Europe centrale au Moyen Âge (XIe-début du XVIe siècle), éd. par Marie-Madeleine de Cevins et Olivier Marin, Turnhout, 2017 (*Hagiologia*, 13), p. 327-350.

plutôt que frères mendiants, mystiques ou visionnaires –, ainsi qu'aux formes traditionnelles d'expression du culte des saints – inscription dans la liturgie et pèlerinages – prédomine sans nul doute dans toute l'Europe centrale. Le croisement des indices liturgiques, hagiographiques, homilétiques, iconographiques et des vocables d'églises met en évidence le poids écrasant des saints de l'Antiquité. Les figures évangéliques (les apôtres Pierre, Jacques et Jean, de même que Jean le Baptiste, Marie Madeleine, sans parler de la Vierge Marie), les archanges (en particulier Michel), ainsi que les évangélisateurs (Martin puis Lambert), les martyrs paléochrétiens (Laurent, Sébastien) et les guerriers de la foi (Georges, Maurice) fournissent le gros des dédicaces centre-européennes. Prenons le cas de la Hongrie, bien balisé par la recherche. La Vierge et les apôtres, ainsi que les martyrs et confesseurs arrivent en première place en Transylvanie, d'après les comptages effectués (C. FLOREA)[5]. Martin donne plus de deux cents vocables d'églises médiévales en Hongrie et une centaine de localités antérieures au XVIe siècle portent son nom[6]. Hors du champ dévotionnel, les saints des premiers temps du christianisme se retrouvent dans l'anthroponymie et servent de repères temporels, à en juger par leur utilisation récurrente dans la datation des chartes (O. GECSER). Enfin, ces saints-là étaient perçus comme aussi « efficaces » que les saints récents : les registres consignant les miracles attribués respectivement à Paul l'Ermite et à Jean de Capistran leur prêtent à tous les deux la même capacité à accomplir des prodiges (E. CSUKOVITS).

Soit. Mais les dédicaces des églises paroissiales de France du Nord – pour se limiter à une région familière aux lecteurs francophones – affichaient les mêmes préférences[7]. De plus, les signes de « réchauffement » de la sainteté se multiplient singulièrement en Europe centrale au XVe siècle. Le sanctoral s'y élargit, pour commencer. Les missels hongrois indiquent une inflation spectaculaire du nombre de saints fêtés dans le royaume de saint Étienne entre les XIIe et XVe siècles[8]. Le recensement exclusif des dédicaces des autels et des chapelles secondaires, érigés pour la plupart après 1300 mais non encore

---

[5] Les emprunts aux contributions rassemblées dans les pages qui précèdent sont signalés par le nom de leur auteur, donné en petites capitales et entre parenthèses.
[6] A. MEZŐ, *A templomcím a magyar helységnevekben (11-15. század)*, Budapest, 1996, p. 152-158.
[7] Voir les publications et références bibliographiques du projet « Inventaire des sanctuaires et lieux de pèlerinage chrétiens en France », coordonné par Catherine Vincent, sur l'URL http://sanctuaires.coldev.org/.
[8] Alors que le concile de Szabolcs (1092) prescrivait de fêter solennellement 23 saints, les missels tardifs (ceux de Bratislava pour les XIVe-XVe siècles, et celui de Pécs en 1499) honorent de messes spécifiques plus de deux cents saints différents. E. HERMANN, *A katolikus egyház története Magyarországon 1914-ig*, Munich, 1973, p. 178.

inventoriés, irait certainement dans le même sens. On entrevoit en parallèle un changement dans la perception de la sainteté. La réflexion entamée par les réformateurs tchèques à partir du milieu du XIVe siècle sur la nécessité de prendre exemple sur des individus contemporains (*sancti conviventes*) accompagné l'entrée en scène de nouvelles figures saintes en Bohême (P. KUBÍN, D. MENGEL). La Pologne et la Bohême ont vu éclore au XVe siècle le culte spontané de plusieurs *beati* assez proches dans le temps, ou bien réinventés (St. KUZMOVÁ).

On se gardera toutefois de généraliser tant le rythme et l'ampleur de ce renouvellement varient d'un pays à l'autre. À une Hongrie « froide », dans laquelle les nouveaux saints étaient imposés d'en haut – par les évêques, les hauts responsables réguliers et le roi –, tels Louis de Toulouse, Marguerite de Hongrie[9], voire Jean de Capistran[10], on sera tenté d'opposer une Pologne « chaude », caractérisée à la fois par l'actualisation de saints passablement anciens d'un strict point de vue chronologique – comme l'évêque et martyr Stanislas (St. KUZMOVÁ) – et la fortune exceptionnelle de saints récents, mendiants (de Hyacinthe à Bernardin de Sienne et Simon de Lipnica) et séculiers (l'évêque Prandota, Jean de Kęty...). La Bohême se rapproche de sa voisine slave si l'on inclut dans le champ d'observation les saints hussites – un parti-pris que justifie l'entremêlement des pratiques et des croyances des chrétiens de Bohême *sub una* d'une part et utraquistes d'autre part. Ils suscitèrent une vénération spontanée, populaire et féconde en textes hagiographiques, sans détrôner pour autant les intercesseurs traditionnels, d'après la liste des protecteurs choisis par les membres des métiers dans les villes de Bohême (H. PÁTKOVÁ).

Quels facteurs pourraient rendre compte de la relative lenteur de l'*aggiornamento* du sanctoral centre-européen ? Son urbanisation moindre, frein à la « modernisation » spirituelle, et donc à la propagation de nouveaux cultes (comme le suggérait André Vauchez), ne constitue pas une explication suffisante : les campagnes médiévales n'échappaient pas à la démultiplication des cultes (vocables, reliques et sanctuaires), ainsi que l'ont prouvé de récents travaux portant sur la France[11]. Aux marges orientales de la Hongrie et de la Pologne, les dévotions byzantines, nettement plus figées que celles

---

[9] Outre la synthèse de référence que l'on doit à Gábor Klaniczay (*Holy Rulers and Blessed Princesses. Dynastic Cults in Medieval Central Europe*, Cambridge, 2000 pour la traduction anglaise), voir en français : V. H. DEÁK, *La légende d'Avignon. Sainte Marguerite de Hongrie et l'hagiographie dominicaine au quatorzième siècle*, Paris, 2011 (trad. fr.).
[10] St. ANDRIĆ, *The Miracles of St John Capistran*, Budapest, 2000.
[11] Voir l'enquête sur les sanctuaires français mentionnée en note *supra*.

de la Chrétienté romaine, auraient-elles entretenu, par contagion, un certain conservatisme ?

En réalité, la place écrasante des églises paroissiales dans le tissu ecclésial biaise l'analyse[12]. Elles remontent pour l'essentiel aux XIIe et XIIIe siècles, autrement dit à une période où évêques et fondateurs puisaient encore largement dans le fonds des saints évangéliques ou paléochrétiens, en dépit de la difficulté à se procurer leurs reliques, disséminées depuis des siècles dans les sanctuaires d'Orient et d'Occident (D. MENGEL).

Qu'ils fussent « anciens » ou « modernes », les saints introduits d'autorité par les souverains, les évêques ou les supérieurs réguliers ont connu une fortune aléatoire. Louis de Toulouse, mis en avant pendant tout le XIVe siècle par les rois angevins de Hongrie, n'a guère déplacé les foules dans le bassin carpatique. Sigismond, exogène lui aussi, s'acquit au revanche une belle notoriété en Bohême. Il faut dire que Charles IV de Luxembourg n'avait pas lésiné sur les moyens : il se livra à une chasse aux reliques et aux indulgences effrénée, et programma judicieusement la *translatio* de Sigismond (1365) la veille de la très populaire Saint-Venceslas (D. MENGEL). Mais les instruments de promotion utilisés n'expliquent pas tout.

La palette d'exemples qui peuple ce volume le montre clairement : l'ingrédient principal de la réussite d'un candidat à la sainteté était sa capacité à se parer des traits, actes ou vertus dont les clercs, les souverains ou les fidèles avaient alors besoin. Par suite, le retour en force d'un saint déclassé pendant des siècles supposait de sa part une grande malléabilité. L'histoire du culte de Stanislas en Pologne est particulièrement instructive à cet égard. De cet évêque de Cracovie exécuté sur ordre de Boleslas II en 1079, on ne sait pratiquement rien. Ses promoteurs ont ainsi pu lui attribuer les qualités, le discours et les miracles qui servaient leurs idées et leurs ambitions. Alors que Cracovie s'était déjà appropriée un saint « ancien », Florian – dont la *translatio* polonaise date de 1184 –, c'est Stanislas (canonisé par Innocent IV en 1253) qui acquit la stature de saint national. Pourquoi ? Parce qu'il répondait simultanément au programme « théocratique » de la papauté (qui en fit une sorte de Thomas Becket polonais), aux attentes pastorales et identitaires des Franciscains et des Dominicains, ainsi qu'aux projets d'affirmation hiérarchique de l'évêque de Cracovie face à l'archevêque de Gniezno, puis enfin au programme de réforme pastorale relancé à partir du XIVe siècle par les évêques et les Mendiants polonais (St. KUZMOVÁ). De la même manière, en Bohême, le culte du moine Procope, ermite tchèque du XIe siècle, a été « réactivé »

---

[12] Paweł Kras avait attiré l'attention sur ce fait à propos de la Pologne, dans une communication malheureusement absente de ce volume.

– pour ne pas dire forgé de toute pièce – à partir du milieu du XIIe siècle. Le but poursuivi par les rédacteurs de sa *vita* était de protéger les Bénédictins de l'appétit des Prémontrés. Procope accéda peu après au rang de père fondateur du monachisme bohémien (P. Kubín).

On assiste en parallèle à la « modernisation » de plusieurs saints très anciens. Les deux martyres Catherine d'Alexandrie et Barbe doivent leur regain de popularité en Hongrie tardo-médiévale à des procédés de cléricalisation, à l'heure de la (re)valorisation du sacerdoce, ainsi qu'à leur association à la dévotion eucharistique, dans les textes et par l'image : cheveux courts pour Catherine, calice et hostie pour Barbe (C. Florea). En sens inverse, achevant de brouiller les repères chronologiques, les saints « anciens » étaient convoqués pour étayer de leur prestige et de leur antiquité les cultes montants : ainsi l'Arpadien Ladislas, que l'iconographie tardo-médiévale hongroise assimile plus ou moins explicitement au Christ, à saint Georges ou encore à saint Antoine (I. Gerát). L'homonymie fut mise à contribution. En témoigne la superposition iconographique et littéraire des deux Marguerite, celle d'Antioche et celle de Hongrie. Elle échoua à obtenir la canonisation en Curie de la dominicaine hongroise – malgré les démarches réitérées des derniers rois arpadiens puis de leurs successeurs angevins, jusqu'à Mathias Corvin au XVe siècle – mais elle élargit sa stature en Occident[13].

Ces procédés de substitution ne trahiraient-ils pas en définitive la frilosité hagiologique de l'Europe centrale ? Non, car la péninsule italienne en offre maints exemples, consignés notamment par André Vauchez[14]. À ce stade de la réflexion, on gagnerait plutôt à abandonner le schéma binaire opposant saints « anciens » et saints « modernes » : non seulement parce qu'il est impossible de s'entendre sur l'intervalle de temps qui séparerait objectivement ces deux groupes, mais aussi parce que les saints tombés dans l'oubli pendant des siècles puis revenus en force, après avoir été parés d'attributs exprimant les aspirations du moment, entrent dans les deux catégories à la fois.

André Vauchez l'avait déjà souligné dans sa thèse, les membres des ordres mendiants comptent parmi les principaux moteurs du renouvellement des modèles de sainteté à partir du XIIIe siècle. Curieusement, l'Europe centrale semble peu touchée par cette dynamique jusqu'au XVe siècle, en dépit de

---

[13] I. Orbán, « Adatok Antiochiai Szent Margit kultuszához », *Acta Iuvenum* 1986, p. 117-124 ; *Id.*, « Adatok Árpád-házi Szent Margit tiszteletéhez », *Aetas* 1986, p. 7-30 ; *Id.*, « Ecce, iam vici mundum ! » *Antiochiai Szent Margit tisztelete Magyarországon*, Budapest, 2001 ; S. Bálint, *Ünnepi Kalendárium. A Mária-ünnepek és jelesebb napok hazai és közép-európai hagyományvilágából*, Budapest, 1977, t. I, p. 156-160.
[14] *La sainteté en Occident, op. cit., passim.*

l'implantation précoce des Mendiants, de leur importance dans le maillage ecclésial (et régulier), de leur influence à la cour royale et de leur contribution majeure à la production de sermons *de sanctis*. Pour comprendre ce paradoxe, il convient d'apprécier plus finement la place des saints et *beati* mendiants en Europe centrale, d'identifier les acteurs de leur promotion et d'analyser les facteurs ayant permis celle-ci.

Vocables, calendriers liturgiques, images et textes hagiographiques ou homilétiques font peu de place aux Mendiants dans l'espace étudié. Certes, les chiffres ne disent pas tout : le rayonnement d'un seul saint mendiant pouvait fort bien écraser, par son envergure, des légions de frères anonymes ou dont le culte n'a jamais franchi les murs de leur couvent. Tel est le cas des fondateurs d'ordre ou de branches d'ordre. Les miracles les plus spectaculaires attribués à saint Dominique seraient survenus en Hongrie, probablement à Erd-Šomljo (en hongrois Érdsomlyó, aujourd'hui en Serbie), au milieu du XIIIe siècle[15]. Une église paroissiale des faubourgs de Buda a été placée sous le patronage céleste de Pierre de Vérone dès la fin des années 1250, laissant son nom au quartier environnant. François d'Assise occupe une place privilégiée dans la littérature religieuse hongroise de la fin du Moyen Âge, dans les sermons, les légendes mais aussi dans les prières composées en langue vernaculaire entre les années 1440 et 1520 (E. KONRÁD)[16]. En Bohême, peu avant que les Hussites ne rayent Dominique de leur calendrier, les hagiographes tchèques avaient parfaitement assimilé les motifs de l'hagiographie du *poverello* puisqu'ils en truffèrent la *vita* d'Agnès de Prague (Chr.-Fr. FELSKAU)[17]. Du côté des réformateurs, Bernardin de Sienne et Jean de Capistran se taillent la part du lion. Greffon introduit par Capistran, la figure de Bernardin éclipsa toutes les autres à partir des années 1450 chez les Observants polonais *sub vicariis*, qui s'identifièrent à lui au point de prendre son nom (*Bernardini*) – un phénomène resté absolument sans équivalent, en Italie comme au nord des Alpes (L. VIALLET). En Hongrie, où Jean de Capistran n'avait pas la dimension de fondateur de l'Observance franciscaine qui lui était reconnue en Pologne, il a suscité une vénération spontanée aussitôt après sa mort à Ilok en 1456. Elle

---

[15] Mise au point récente sur la relation de ces miracles : A. GYÖRKÖS, « Magyar vonatkozású domonkos rendi történetek a XIII. században », dans *A Domonkos rend Magyarországon*, Piliscsaba-Budapest-Vasvár, 2007, p. 49-60.

[16] Thèse en cours à la Central European University (Budapest), sous la direction de Gábor Klaniczay.

[17] Indice concordant même s'il est évidemment plus convenu, le préambule des lettres de confraternité adressées par les supérieurs mendiants aux clercs et laïcs hongrois mentionne la *devotio* de ces derniers envers l'Ordre mais aussi envers son fondateur (François, Dominique ou Augustin). M.-M. de CEVINS, *Koldulórendi konfraternitások a középkori Magyarországon (1270 k. – 1530 k.)*, Pécs, 2015, p. 147.

surprit par son expression parfois spectaculaire le chroniqueur Jean de Tagliacozzo, pourtant accoutumé aux formes de « dévotion panique » (A. Vauchez) qui entouraient les *beati* péninsulaires[18].

L'Europe centrale n'a pas été pour autant la matrice de saints mendiants à laquelle on aurait pu s'attendre. On y repère une quinzaine de *beati* mendiants, à laquelle vient s'ajouter une centaine de martyrs pour la plupart anonymes (A. TALLON). Si l'on écarte Élisabeth de Hongrie – qui a passé le plus clair de son existence en Thuringe et n'a jamais été affiliée à un ordre mendiant –, aucun n'a obtenu de reconnaissance officielle en Curie. Les autres connurent généralement un rayonnement provincial (à Cracovie, pour Hyacinthe et les *beati* « bernardins » de la fin du XVe siècle, les deux frères du couvent franciscain d'Esztergom mentionnés dans une liste commémorative de la fin du XVe siècle[19]), éventuellement lignager (dans le cas de Marguerite de Hongrie et d'Agnès de Bohême), ou rigoureusement cantonné à leur ordre (Agnès, chez les Clarisses).

En outre, ils ne présentent pas toujours un profil hagiographique exclusivement mendiant. Les figures féminines incarnent le type bien connu de la sainte aristocratique compensant son extraction sociale par la pratique de la charité et de l'humilité radicales[20]. C'est à leur fonction de pasteur ou de gardien de l'orthodoxie que l'évêque Jacques de Strepa et son compatriote, l'inquisiteur Jean de Schwenkenfeld, doivent respectivement leur célébrité en Pologne. Les frères tombés sous les coups des païens ou des Infidèles illustrent certes la vocation missionnaire qu'accaparèrent en quelques décennies Prêcheurs et Mineurs aux confins de la Chrétienté. Mais c'est seulement au XVe siècle que les hagiographes dominicains posèrent les victimes hongroises des Tatars en apôtres plutôt qu'en martyrs, reliant ainsi leur activité à la vocation première de leur ordre (A. TALLON).

On observera que les réguliers d'autres ordres ne faisaient pas toujours mieux. Si Brigitte de Suède connut un large succès en Pologne et en Bohême (dont témoigne entre autres la traduction précoce de ses œuvres en langue vernaculaire), on ne rencontre point de candidat à la sainteté chez les Ermites de saint Paul, pourtant solidement implantés en Hongrie depuis le début du XIVe siècle. Les *beati* mendiants subissaient par ailleurs la concurrence croissante des séculiers en Pologne et en Bohême, où la figure du saint évêque puis

---

[18] Jean de Tagliacozzo parle de *nimia et inordinata Hungarorum devotio*. St. ANDRIĆ, *The Miracles, op. cit.*, p. 67-70, 74.
[19] J. KARÁCSONYI, *Szent Ferencz rendjének története Magyarországon 1711-ig*, t. I, Budapest, 1922, p. 163-165.
[20] G. KLANICZAY, *Holy Rulers, op. cit.*

celle du saint prêtre bénéficièrent d'un regain de faveur à la fin du Moyen Âge[21]. Enfin, sous bénéfice d'inventaire, l'Europe centrale n'est pas en reste par le nombre de saints mendiants qu'elle a donnés en comparaison de la France du Nord, de l'Angleterre ou des pays allemands. La péninsule italienne – exceptionnellement prolifique, mais peuplée de figures n'ayant connu, sauf exception, qu'une notoriété locale –, ne saurait servir d'étalon absolu à l'ensemble de l'Occident latin.

Jusqu'à l'extrême fin du Moyen Âge, la promotion des saints mendiants centre-européens fut souvent le fait de puissants personnages (souverains, princes, évêques, seigneurs-patrons). Après Étienne V et Ladislas IV au XIIIe siècle, Charles-Robert Ier d'Anjou et son épouse piastienne Élisabeth ont multiplié les requêtes auprès des instances suprêmes de l'ordre des Prêcheurs et de la papauté pour faire reconnaître publiquement la sainteté de Marguerite de Hongrie (selon les hypothèses de Gábor Klaniczay, confirmées par les recherches de Viktória Deák[22]) – tout comme, plus à l'ouest, le margrave Conrad de Thuringe avait cherché à appuyer la cause de feu sa belle-sœur Élisabeth au siècle précédent. Dans les deux cas, les Mendiants semblent arriver après-coup, alors que la lutte pour la reconnaissance des deux princesses arpadiennes était déjà bien engagée.

Hors du groupe des puissants, les plus ardents défenseurs des saints mendiants centre-européens se rencontrent, sans surprise, parmi les membres de l'Ordre. Ce sont des Prêcheurs qui consignèrent les premiers témoignages sur la vie et les miracles de Marguerite de Hongrie ainsi que sur ceux d'Hyacinthe de Cracovie (A. Zajchowska) ; ils rédigèrent leurs légendes et leurs offices propres ; ils commanditèrent leur représentation dans leurs églises. Point de cloison étanche, d'ailleurs, entre les ordres mendiants sur ce plan. Les Franciscains de Transylvanie exaltaient Pierre de Vérone sur les murs de leurs églises (C. Florea). La *vita* la plus prolixe et la plus diffusée d'Élisabeth de Hongrie naquit vers 1290 – à une période où elle était déjà considérée comme « franciscaine » – sous la plume d'un Dominicain, Thierry d'Apolda[23].

Curieusement, la promotion en haut lieu des saints mendiants natifs de Hongrie semble résulter de l'implication de frères italiens, français ou

---

[21] Jean Népomucène n'accéda à la gloire des autels qu'au XVIIe siècle, mais les signes de son culte en Bohême remontent au tournant des XIVe et XVe siècles. P. Lerou, « Le culte de saint Jean Népomucène », *Mélanges de l'École française de Rome. Moyen Âge*, 103 (1991), p. 273-295.
[22] V. H. Deák, *La légende d'Avignon, op. cit.*
[23] Le trait n'est pas propre à l'Europe centrale puisque, rappelons-le, dans la *Légende dorée*, Jacques de Voragine fait la part belle aux saints franciscains ou perçus comme tels (dont Élisabeth de Hongrie).

allemands, et non des religieux natifs de la région. C'est un Auxerrois proche de la cour pontificale avignonnaise, Garin de Gy-l'Évêque, qui a écrit la légende la plus développée de Marguerite de Hongrie, reprise ensuite par les chroniqueurs italiens de l'ordre. De même, c'est en Italie qu'apparaissent dès 1340 les portraits puis les textes rapportant la stigmatisation de Marguerite de Hongrie (selon la communication de Gábor Klaniczay). Ce sont des hagiographes proches du centre des *ordines mendicantes* qui dotèrent Élisabeth de Hongrie de traits mendiants[24]. Les indices de « franciscanisation » d'Élisabeth en Europe centrale sont exogènes, minces et tardifs – aussi bien dans l'iconographie (d'après les travaux d'Ivan Gerát et de Laura Pacindová[25]) que dans les textes. Que disent d'Élisabeth les sermonnaires rédigés par le Dominicain silésien Pérégrin d'Opole et par le Franciscain observant hongrois Pelbart de Temesvár aux XIVe et XVe siècles ? Ils soulignent son ascendance royale (hongroise) et vantent sa pratique de la charité comme de l'abaissement volontaire, dans les mêmes termes que ceux qu'ils appliquent à des saintes de sang princier mais non mendiantes (Hedwige de Silésie)[26].

Ce phénomène de promotion-appropriation des *beati* mendiants hongrois « de l'extérieur » vaut également pour les groupes anonymes. La description des hauts faits et des supplices endurés par les martyrs dominicains des missions organisées jusqu'en 1259 à partir de la Hongrie a d'abord été forgée et véhiculée par la tradition centrale dominicaine avant de réinvestir la tradition hongroise, qui plaça alors à la tête du groupe de martyrs Paul de Hongrie, fondateur présumé de la première province dominicaine de Hongrie (A. TALLON). Par un mouvement analogue, les miracles survenus sur la tombe de Maurice de Csák après sa mort au couvent dominicain de Győr en 1336 ne sont rapportés que dans les années 1490 (!) au chapitre général de Ferrare. Ils prennent la forme d'une légende, ajoutée par Borselli à l'*appendix* de sa fameuse chronique des maîtres généraux. Reproduite dans celle du Milanais Ambrogio Taeggio, elle ne revint au pays qu'au XVIIe siècle, lorsque Sigismondo Ferrari l'intégra à son histoire de la province dominicaine de Hongrie vers 1635[27].

---

[24] O. GECSER, *Árpád-házi Szent Erzsébet kultusza a középkori Európában*, Budapest, 2007.
[25] L. PACINDOVÁ, *Le culte de sainte Élisabeth en Slovaquie médiévale (XIIIe-XVIe siècle). Textes, images, lieux*, Thèse pour le Doctorat, Université Pierre-Mendès-France (Grenoble), 2013.
[26] H. MARTIN, *Pérégrin d'Opole. Un prédicateur dominicain à l'apogée de la chrétienté médiévale*, Rennes, 2008, p. 137-138, 187-188.
[27] E. MADAS, « Boldog Csáki Móric », dans *A domonkos rend, op. cit.*, p. 27. On reviendra plus loin sur les enjeux stratégiques que recouvrent ces interventions extérieures.

A contrario, les Franciscains observants hongrois semblent presque réticents à exalter la sainteté des frères issus de leurs rangs. Cinq profès de la vicairie de Bosnie (noyau de l'observance franciscaine hongroise) auraient été assassinés à Vidin, en Bulgarie, au moment de la reprise de la ville par un tsar bulgare ennemi du roi Louis Ier en 1369. Leur *passio* occupe plusieurs folios de la Chronique observante bosno-hongroise[28]. Aucun culte ne paraît pourtant leur avoir été rendu avant l'époque moderne – alors que les Franciscains observants jouèrent un rôle décisif dans la diffusion du culte de Jean de Capistran au lendemain de sa mort, par la consignation de ses miracles[29] et l'exemple qu'ils donnaient de départs en pèlerinages sur sa tombe à Ilok[30].

Pour que la réputation de sainteté d'un frère ou d'une sœur sorte des murs de son couvent ou des limites de sa province, il fallait bien pourtant que ceux qui l'avaient côtoyé(e) la divulguent. Autrement dit, il y avait toujours, au départ, promotion locale. Elle est attestée pour Marguerite de Hongrie, dont les miracles ont été enregistrés sur place et dont la *legenda vetus*, perdue, aurait été écrite par son confesseur, Marcel, avant d'inspirer sa légende la plus connue, celle de Garin de Gy-l'Évêque. La *vita* de Maurice de Csák due à Borselli comporte des motifs possiblement hongrois[31]. Le récit des tribulations des martyrs dominicains hongrois s'appuie sur l'énigmatique Svipert de « Porroch », vraisemblablement originaire de Sárospatak. Pourquoi faut-il attendre la réécriture de leur vie par les membres italiens ou français de leur ordre pour que les saints mendiants de Hongrie accèdent à une large notoriété, dans leur famille régulière et hors de celle-ci? Auraient-ils été seulement victimes de leur éloignement par rapport à Rome, Assise ou Bologne, en d'autres termes de leur position de périphérie de la Chrétienté? Ces difficultés pourraient découler des critères de sainteté valorisés sur leur terre natale.

Dans toute l'Europe centrale, le premier critère semble avoir été l'aptitude à produire des miracles. On rappelle que, une fois surmontées les réticences des premiers Dominicains et Franciscains – qui privilégiaient la *conversatio*

---

[28] *C[h]ronica seu Origo fratrum minorum de Observantia in Provincia Boznae et Hungariae...*, éd. F. TOLDY: *Analecta monumentorum Hungariae historicorum litterariorum maximum inedita*, t. I, Pest, 1862 (reprint: Budapest, 1986), p. 235-236.
[29] S. ANDRIĆ, *The Miracles, op. cit.*, p. 311-326.
[30] M.-M. de CEVINS, *Les Franciscains observants hongrois de l'expansion à la débâcle (vers 1450 – vers 1540)*, Rome, 2008, p. 256-257.
[31] La vision qu'eut sa mère avant sa naissance, parallèle possible avec saint Dominique mais aussi avec Étienne de Hongrie, et surtout la mention de saint Alexis, très vénéré en Europe centrale au XIVe siècle. E. MADAS, « Boldog Csáki Móric », *art. cit.*, p. 28-29. Sur le culte de saint Alexis, voir les articles de: *In Stolis Repromissionis. Светци и святост в Централна и Източна Европа*, éd. A. ANGUSCHEVA-TIHANOVA, M. DIMITROVA, R. KOSTOVA, R. MALCHEV, Sofia, 2012 – en particulier celui de G. KLANICZAY, « The fate of the legend of St Alexius: Christian antiquity in medieval Hungary », p. 29-46.

sur les événements prodigieux –, les miracles avaient retrouvé un poids décisif au second XIIIe siècle (dans les procès de canonisation en particulier), avant de reculer à nouveau à partir de la fin du XIVe siècle – du moins pour les miracles *in vita*, en particulier thaumaturgiques : la papauté se méfiait alors des guérisseurs érigés en saints par les foules. Les expériences mystiques et ascétiques s'en trouvèrent valorisées : c'est par leurs vertus éclatantes et leurs charismes extraordinaires que brillaient désormais les candidats à la sainteté[32]. En Europe centrale, et tout spécialement en Hongrie, cette inflexion semble avoir été lente et timorée.

Pour démontrer la sainteté de l'évêque Stanislas vers 1250, le Dominicain cracovien Vincent de Kielcza invoque en premier lieu les miracles qu'il avait suscités (St. KUZMOVÁ). Pérégrin d'Opole poursuit sur cette lancée vers 1300, à propos de Stanislas comme du duc Venceslas et de bien d'autres personnages, mendiants ou non. On note que la part reconnue aux prodiges dans la sainteté d'un individu n'est pas moins grande lorsqu'il s'agit de frères mendiants. La liste des miracles attribués à Hyacinthe s'est même étoffée au XVe siècle (A. ZAJCHOWSKA). Dans les dernières décennies du XVe siècle, les prodiges survenus auprès de la tombe de Jean de Capistran occupent l'essentiel de son dossier de canonisation[33]. Des *beati* ayant vécu au couvent d'Esztergom entre la fin du XIIIe siècle et le milieu du XIVe, la tradition franciscaine hongroise forgée autour de 1490 au plus tard ne retient finalement que les exploits surnaturels[34].

Par une sorte de mise en abîme, les saints mendiants d'Europe centrale fournissent eux-mêmes l'exemple de ce rapport privilégié aux miracles. C'est parce qu'il avait été témoin à Rome d'un prodige attribué à l'intervention de saint Dominique que Hyacinthe serait entré chez les Prêcheurs. Deux siècles plus tard, son compatriote Simon de Lipnica vécut une expérience similaire : le spectacle de la *translatio* des reliques de Bernardin de Sienne en 1472 l'aurait conforté dans sa vocation. Critiqué par les siens pour avoir choisi d'entrer chez les Prêcheurs, Maurice de Csák décida de quitter son couvent de l'Île aux Lièvres (actuelle Île Marguerite, à Budapest) pour se retirer dans

---

[32] A. VAUCHEZ, « L'influence des modèles hagiographiques sur les représentations de la sainteté, dans les procès de canonisation (XIIIe-XVe siècle) », dans *Hagiographie, cultures et sociétés (IVe-XIIe siècles)*, éd. E. PATLAGEAN et P. RICHÉ, Paris, 1981, p. 584-590 ; *Id.*, « Saints admirables et saints imitables », dans *Saints, prophètes et visionnaires, op. cit.*, p. 56-66.

[33] Certes, la plupart des miracles sont décrits comme étant survenus au moment du vœu de pèlerinage, et non par contact physique avec les reliques comme aux siècles précédents (dans la Légende majeure de Marguerite, par exemple). On est loin malgré tout de la « théologie des miracles » d'un Thomas d'Aquin, pour qui les événements prodigieux confirmaient une sainteté déjà amplement prouvée par la *conversatio*.

[34] J. KARÁCSONYI, *Szent Ferencz, op. cit.*, p. 163-165.

celui de Bologne, au plus près de la dépouille de saint Dominique. Il y demeura trois ans. Point de miracles dans ce cas précis, mais la recherche d'une proximité physique avec les reliques du fondateur de l'ordre. En 1530, alors que la conquête ottomane rendait leur voyage périlleux, deux frères mineurs observants de Hongrie obtenaient de leur provincial l'autorisation de partir à Assise[35].

Or, cet attachement aux miracles, et tout spécialement aux miracles *post mortem* – dont André Vauchez avait remarqué qu'ils caractérisaient l'Europe « froide » – était perçu comme archaïque aux yeux des frères issus du berceau des ordres mendiants et proches de la cour pontificale, où se décidaient les canonisations. Il paraît significatif que, dans sa légende sur Maurice de Csák, Borselli résume en quelques lignes les « innombrables » miracles attestés autour de sa tombe, tandis qu'il rapporte avec précision ceux produits de son vivant – et même avant sa naissance[36]. Garin de Gy-l'Évêque met également en avant les prodiges réalisés par Marguerite de Hongrie au cours de son existence. En Hongrie au contraire, les miracles *in vita* étaient manifestement tenus pour suspects jusqu'à la fin du XVe siècle. C'est après leur mort que les Franciscains observants hongrois ont vanté les mérites de deux membres de leur province et ceux de Jean de Capistran[37]. Les stigmates – miracle *in vivo* par excellence et formidable instrument de promotion a priori puisqu'ils identifiaient le *beatus* au Christ lui-même – ne font pas exception. Si les Dominicains hongrois ont déclaré en 1409 qu'Hélène de Hongrie, personnage inventé à cet effet, avait reçu les stigmates, c'était pour en dépouiller Marguerite, d'après Gábor Klaniczay. Il faut attendre le tournant des XVe et XVIe siècle pour que se diffuse, en positif cette fois, le thème de la stigmatisation de François d'Assise dans les écrits religieux en langue vernaculaire (E. KONRÁD).

Certes, les miracles ne faisaient pas tout. Sur quelles vertus, sur quels actes et pratiques mémorables reposait la gloire posthume des candidats mendiants à la sainteté originaires d'Europe centrale ? Ceux-ci n'ont malheureusement laissé aucun écrit autographe ou autobiographique : même les lettres d'Agnès de Prague à Claire d'Assise ont disparu. En bons hagiographes, les Mendiants ne s'embarrassaient pas de vérité historique, l'important étant moins de savoir ce qu'avait dit, fait ou pensé leur héros que de le charger des valeurs spirituelles prisées à l'époque. Dans la vague montante du mysticisme tardo-médiéval, Marguerite de Hongrie se vit créditée, dans la « Légende

---

[35] M.-M. de CEVINS, *Les franciscains observants hongrois, op. cit.*, p. 257.
[36] E. MADAS, « Boldog Csáki Móric », *art. cit.*, p. 29-30.
[37] J. KARÁCSONYI, *Szent Ferencz, op. cit.*, p. 163-165.

majeure », d'expériences de lévitation que Gy-l'Évêque présente comme le couronnement de son parcours spirituel – alors que les témoignages recueillis immédiatement après sa mort n'en soufflent pas mot. Le Bernardin Ladislas de Gielniów doit sa célébrité posthume à ses lévitations spectaculaires les bras en croix, en particulier le Vendredi Saint précédant sa mort ; elles ponctuaient une existence dominée par la mortification extrême et le désir de subir le martyre, selon l'auteur de sa *vita*.

Une demi-douzaine de motifs traverse la littérature et l'iconographie décrivant la vie terrestre des saints et bienheureux mendiants centre-européens. Le thème de la conversion, assorti du refus du pouvoir et des richesses matérielles, est illustré par le renoncement à leur rang des princesses du XIIIe siècle (à côté d'Élisabeth, Agnès, Marguerite) ; il est plus discret chez les hommes, en dehors de Maurice de Csák. La pauvreté absolue, fortement soulignée jusqu'à la fin du XIIIe siècle (dans les premières *Vitae* d'Agnès comme d'Élisabeth, dans une logique d'humiliation volontaire), s'édulcore ensuite (à propos de Marguerite chez Gy-l'Évêque, dans les années 1330-1340). Elle revient à l'honneur au temps de l'Observance franciscaine mais elle est alors subordonnée à l'humilité et à la mortification corporelle. Au début du XVIe siècle, le *beatus* polonais Raphaël de Proszowice commençait sa journée en nettoyant les latrines de son couvent[38]. Le zèle pastoral est fortement souligné dans les « vies » dominicaines de Stanislas, et plus encore dans les sermons de Pérégrin d'Opole et de ses émules de la fin du XIVe siècle et du début du XVe siècle, dans le cadre de la relance de la réforme de l'Église et de ses ministres. L'activité prédicante constitue l'un des *leitmotive* des *vitae* des quatre Bernardins polonais qui firent l'objet d'un culte local à la fin du XVe siècle[39]. À toutes époques, on l'a dit, l'ardeur à obtenir des conversions (des hérétiques, des « Schismatiques », des païens) a assuré la promotion de saints missionnaires, de Hyacinthe (chez les Dominicains) à Jacques Strepa (chez les Franciscains), sans oublier Jean de Capistran.

Le modèle de sainteté mendiante que dessine cette liste de vertus et de pratiques exemplaires n'a somme toute rien de très original, si ce n'est l'insistance sur l'activité apostolique et évangélisatrice. Elle tendit à revaloriser la figure du martyr, sur ce front toujours actif de la *christianitas*. Par ailleurs, en dépit de tendances régionales communes – importance des miracles *post mortem* au détriment des stigmates, idéaux de pauvreté et d'humilité, zèle

---

[38] K. KANTAK, « Les données historiques sur les bienheureux Bernardins (Observants) polonais du XVe siècle », *Archivum Franciscanum Historicum*, 22 (1929), p. 436 et 461.
[39] *Hagiografia polska*, Poznań, 1971-1972, 2 vol. ; J. KŁOCZOWSKI, « L'Observance en Europe centro-orientale au XVe siècle », dans *Il rinnovamento del francescanesimo. L'Osservanza*, Assise, 1985, p. 190 ; K. KANTAK, « Les données historiques », *art. cit.*

pastoral ou missionnaire –, le rapport des Mendiants à la sainteté n'a pas été partout le même. Pourquoi tant de *beati* dans la province franciscaine observante de Pologne et aucun dans celle de Hongrie ? Cela tient sans doute à la genèse de la réforme franciscaine dans ces deux pays. En Pologne, la corrélation est manifeste entre la « Grande Mission » de Capistran, le choix des Franciscains réformés polonais de s'appeler « Bernardins » et l'éclosion de plusieurs *beati* dans la province polonaise à la fin du XVe siècle et au début du suivant – des *beati* dont la vie était marquée par l'ascétisme, le mysticisme et la prédication aux accents prophétiques, sur le modèle de Bernardin de Sienne (L. Viallet). À l'inverse, insérés depuis le début du XVe siècle dans le tissu nobiliaire et hostiles à l'hégémonie cismontaine, les Mineurs observants de Hongrie se méfiaient des formes radicales de spiritualité. Cela peut expliquer l'absence de *beati* hongrois dans la province observante de Hongrie[40] – alors qu'il s'en trouve chez les Conventuels, plus « modernes » en cela que leurs détracteurs observants[41]. La Bohême illustre un cas encore différent par la tâche d'extirpation du hussitisme assignée d'emblée aux Mineurs observants.

Au total, le terrain centre-européen révèle qu'emprise (institutionnelle, démographique, politique, spirituelle) des Mendiants et actualisation du sanctoral n'allaient pas nécessairement de pair au Moyen Âge. Les fondateurs d'ordre ou de famille régulière (Dominique, François puis Bernardin de Sienne) ont bénéficié dans cet espace d'un culte nourri et prolongé. Producteurs de l'essentiel des textes hagiographiques (en incluant dans cet ensemble la littérature homilétique, relativement délaissée) à partir de la seconde moitié du XIIIe siècle, les frères mendiants ont été les propagateurs efficaces dans toute la Chrétienté, Europe centrale incluse, des critères de sainteté à l'honneur dans les foyers avignonnais, romains ou italiens. Cependant, en Hongrie surtout, le décalage persistant entre les critères de sainteté en vigueur parmi les frères autochtones et ceux qui prévalaient à Rome ou dans les

---

[40] Avant même la naissance officielle de la vicairie (puis province) franciscaine observante de Hongrie en 1448, et avec une vigilance redoublée à partir de 1510, les Mineurs réformés hongrois cherchèrent à se démarquer du modèle diffusé par les leaders (italiens) de l'Observance. Jean de Capistran fut peu entendu en Hongrie de son vivant en tant que réformateur régulier. Les sermons et exhortations des dirigeants franciscains destinés aux frères de la province de Hongrie se réfèrent inlassablement aux « pères fondateurs », François mais aussi Bernard de Clairvaux ou encore Thomas d'Aquin. M.-M. de Cevins, *Les franciscains observants hongrois, op. cit.*, p. 75-80 et 287-295.

[41] Le frère cuisinier Gilles, *beatus* qui aurait vécu au couvent d'Esztergom dans les années 1350, passait des heures entières à prier, en lévitation, selon une compilation franciscaine du début du XVIe siècle. J. Karácsonyi, *Szent Ferencz rendjének, op. cit.*, t. I, p. 164-165 ; source : S. Borovszky (éd.), « A ferencziek történetéhez », *Történelmi Tár* 1895, p. 749-755, ici p. 750.

centres italiens de chaque ordre mendiant a visiblement ralenti la promotion universelle des candidats mendiants locaux.

Nous avons choisi en troisième lieu d'aborder de front le paradigme qui sous-tend la géographie de la sainteté proposée par André Vauchez, à savoir l'enclavement supposé de l'Europe centrale, et plus précisément de scruter le flux à double sens des saints « entrants » et « sortants ». Comment départager ceux-ci ? Non pas seulement selon le critère du lieu de naissance ou de formation, ou de l'appartenance ethnique – que privilégiait Aleksander Gieysztor en 1979 pour distinguer « saints d'implantation » (ou extérieurs) et « saints de souche »[42] –, mais en tenant également compte (comme Olivier Marin l'a proposé en introduction) des relations qu'ils avaient nouées de leur vivant avec l'Europe centrale[43].

De nombreux « saints d'implantation » ont en effet été adoptés par les fidèles centre-européens au point de cesser d'être perçus par eux comme étrangers. « Adopter » un saint ne consiste pas uniquement à le choisir comme patron céleste d'un sanctuaire ou d'une confrérie, à acquérir ses reliques et à créditer celles-ci de miracles, à lui faire une place dans les calendriers liturgiques, à lui consacrer des biographies (en latin et en langue vernaculaire) et des sermons, à commander des représentations iconographiques à son effigie, à porter son nom ou à le donner à sa progéniture. Le processus nécessite une véritable appropriation du personnage. Elle passe souvent par un *reshaping*, une reconstruction qui ne se contente pas d'occulter l'extranéité de ce dernier (ou son universalité, le cas échéant), mais travaille à lui conférer – par différents artifices (symboliques, littéraires, esthétiques) – l'ancrage local qui lui fait défaut. Ces transformations ne sont pas propres à l'Europe centrale : que l'on songe à la « francisation » de saint Michel dans la France capétienne ou, en Orient, à la « bulgarisation » de sainte Sophie. La question est donc de savoir : *primo*, si le palmarès des saints « adoptés » ou « naturalisés » par les fidèles d'Europe centrale s'écartait plus ou moins fortement de celui que l'on rencontre ailleurs à différentes époques (c'est la question du « qui ? ») ; *secundo*, si les procédés d'appropriation de ces figures saintes y présentaient des traits spécifiques (« comment ? ») ; *tertio*, quelles correspondances, enchaînements ou interactions rattachent ces éventuels particularismes au milieu centre-européen (« pourquoi ? »).

---

[42] A. Gieysztor, « Saints d'implantation, saints de souche dans les pays évangélisés de l'Europe du centre-est », dans *Hagiographie, op. cit.*, p. 573-584.
[43] Voir Introduction.

Les contributions réunies dans ce volume ne permettent pas de répondre à l'ensemble de ces interrogations. Elles ont néanmoins posé de précieux jalons pour des recherches futures. Les travaux menés par Aleksander Gieysztor montrent que, même en laissant de côté la Vierge Marie, les saints « importés » en Europe centrale appartiennent, sans surprise, au fonds commun de la Chrétienté, « ancien ». Ils reflètent la provenance et les pérégrinations des premiers clercs ayant accompli ou orchestré l'évangélisation des peuples slaves et hongrois, en apportant avec eux leurs dévotions (ou celles de leur église, diocèse ou abbaye) et leurs manuscrits liturgiques. Prenons le cas de saint Gilles, abordé en introduction. Derrière les événements conjoncturels et personnels, généralement princiers, sur lesquels les chroniqueurs insistent à plaisir (les prières adressées à saint Gilles par le couple ducal Vladislas-Hermann et Judith vers 1085 pour vaincre leur stérilité) se cachent des tendances de fond (les circuits de pèlerinage) ainsi que des ramifications ou déterminants politiques (les liens entre le duc Vladislas et l'empereur germanique). La combinaison de ces facteurs explique que des dizaines d'églises polonaises se soient placées sous la protection céleste de saint Gilles au cours du XIIe siècle[44].

Dans l'éventail des « saints d'implantation » évoqués dans ce livre, deux ou trois figures retiennent particulièrement l'attention. Éloi illustre la conjonction de deux moteurs de circulation des dévotions : l'*Ostbewegung* et la politique royale. C'est la présence à Prague depuis les années 1250 d'associations d'orfèvres venus des pays allemands qui, renforcée plus tard par la « fringale de reliques » de Charles IV et par l'attachement du Luxembourg au mythe des origines franques de l'Empire, explique la vénération à Prague de l'évêque de Noyon depuis la fin du XIIIe siècle (H. PATKOVÁ). Elle est attestée simultanément à Timişoara (Temesvár), carrefour des voies du commerce entre Hongrie centrale et provinces orientales[45]. La propagation du culte de Sébastien et de Roch en Hongrie plus de cent ans après la France ou l'Italie pourrait tenir à la moindre virulence de la peste noire dans le bassin carpatique au milieu du XIVe siècle, jusqu'aux « retours pesteux » du tournant des XVe et XVIe siècles. S'est surimposé à la fonction apotropaïque de ces saints une dimension anti-ottomane : elle a ainsi transformé les persécuteurs de Sébastien en Turcs (O. GECSER). Elle rejoint la tendance des récits de miracles imputés à Jean de Capistran et à Paul l'Ermite – deux autres saints

---

[44] A. GIEYSZTOR, « Saints d'implantation », *art. cit.*, p. 577.
[45] I. PETROVICS, « A középkori Temesvár egyházi viszonyai », communication présentée au colloque d'histoire religieuse médiévale de Szeged en mémoire de László Koszta (Szeged, 21-22 mars 2016), à paraître.

d'implantation finalement « naturalisés » – à faire du Turc l'ennemi de la Chrétienté (E. Csukovits).

En 1979, Aleksander Gieysztor proposait une lecture de classe de la « naturalisation » des saints exogènes. Les princes voulaient favoriser par ce moyen une union diplomatique opportune (entre la Pologne et le Saint-Siège, en soutenant le culte de l'apôtre Pierre dès le XIe siècle) ou consolider une autorité encore fragile (Adalbert servit à cautionner le pouvoir des premiers Piastes) ; en s'identifiant aux saints guerriers, les nobles légitimaient leur domination sociale ; les humbles recherchaient des protecteurs contre toutes sortes de maux (à commencer par les pandémies, avec Sébastien et Roch). De leur côté, les clercs valorisaient les membres du clergé, et les moines et frères mendiants exaltaient les grandes figures de leur ordre, fondateurs en tête. Cette ventilation sociale n'a rien de proprement centre-européen, on s'en doute. Néanmoins, la promotion de tel saint plutôt que tel autre par les membres de chaque groupe pourrait traduire les particularismes structurels de la région. Aleksander Gieysztor avait noté à cet égard la place privilégiée des saints militaires (Georges, Michel, Martin, Maurice) en Europe centrale, reflet d'une société longtemps guerrière. En Occident, ils étaient convoqués pour valoriser la noblesse et la chevalerie, exalter le prince et promouvoir la réforme dite grégorienne[46]. En Europe centrale aussi, semble-t-il, à cette différence près que, jusqu'au XIIIe siècle inclus, se substitue à la troisième fonction la valorisation de l'expansion du christianisme par la réduction des derniers îlots de paganisme – une tâche dévolue aux souverains, qui obligeait en retour la papauté à renoncer à une partie de ses prétentions « grégoriennes ».

De fait, l'apôtre Pierre a rencontré un beau succès en Pologne : patron de l'église cathédrale de Poznań, qui remonterait au Xe siècle, il compte de nombreuses églises dans tout le pays[47]. Trait plus original, il y a été « militarisé ». Dès la fin du XIe siècle, il est appelé *pugnans Petrus in rudi paganismo*, dans un contexte de poursuite de l'évangélisation – sous la direction du prince. La vogue des saints guerriers s'accompagna dans ce pays de la « militarisation » d'autres saints (Sébastien ou encore Laurent, à qui les Piastes attribuaient la victoire remportée en 1109 sur les Poméraniens)[48]. En Hongrie, Sébastien n'a pas subi cette transformation[49], sans doute à cause de son arrivée tardive dans

---

[46] Comme l'a établi Esther Dehoux dans sa thèse doctorale, à partir de sources écrites et iconographiques françaises : *Saints guerriers. Georges, Guillaume, Maurice et Michel dans la France médiévale (XIe-XIIIe siècle)*, Rennes, 2014.
[47] A. Gieysztor, « Saints d'implantation », *art. cit.*, p. 575.
[48] *Ibid.*, p. 578.
[49] D. Radocsay, *Gótikus festmények Magyarországon*, Budapest, 1963 (notamment n° 22, BE Mester, Csegöld, 1494). Voir aussi la contribution d'Ottó Gecser dans le présent volume.

le pays (vers 1300), autrement dit à une période où l'Arpadien Ladislas tenait déjà le rôle. Mais la diffusion précoce du culte à Georges et à Michel dans le bassin des Carpates, sauf à imaginer qu'elle résulte de la proximité avec le christianisme oriental, confirme cette tendance commune à la militarisation du panthéon céleste.

L'étude diachronique de la dévotion à saint Georges en Hongrie montre que le phénomène se poursuivit au Moyen Âge tardif. C'est au tournant des XIVe et XVe siècles que Georges envahit les églises (pour preuve, les nombreux autels qui lui sont alors dédiés, de même que les retables et les peintures murales qui le représentent), les palais (la célèbre statue équestre en bronze réalisée en 1373, aujourd'hui à Prague, en est l'illustration la plus connue) et jusqu'aux intérieurs princiers, aristocratiques et bourgeois (d'après les nombreux carreaux faïencés qui tapissaient les poêles de Buda au XVe siècle). Il gagna simultanément la tradition folklorique hongroise[50]. Des historiens d'art ont cru repérer des formes d'appropriation nationale dans les représentations locales du martyr cappadocien : tout en reproduisant le schéma de composition transmis à l'Occident par Simone Martini (dans sa version remaniée par les artistes tchèques et autrichiens), les peintres et sculpteurs hongrois auraient ajouté des détails inspirés de l'équipement des cavaliers magyars[51]. Toujours est-il que l'impulsion royale a été décisive dans l'« adoption » et la « naturalisation » de Georges à partir du XIVe siècle. Les Angevins, pour amadouer la noblesse hongroise, n'ont pas seulement exalté l'idéologie chevaleresque par le biais de saint Ladislas. Ils ont aussi mobilisé Georges : Charles-Robert a resserré autour de lui la nouvelle élite du royaume dans l'Ordre de Saint-Georges en 1326 et Sigismond de Luxembourg a fondé en 1408 l'Ordre du Dragon, placé sous la protection du même saint[52]. Rien d'étonnant donc à ce que la figure de Georges terrassant le dragon devant une jeune princesse en prière ait

---

[50] Voir en particulier, en sus des travaux menés dans les années 1970-1980 par Bálint Sándor et Dénes Radocsay, K. MELIS IRÁSNÉ, « Szent György-alakos budai kályhacsempék », dans *Művelődéstörténeti tanulmányok a magyar középkorról*, éd. E. FÜGEDI, Budapest, 1986, p. 254-268.

[51] La forme de la selle, par exemple. K. MELIS, « Szent György-alakos », *op. cit.*, p. 259, 264 et 356, note 13.

[52] Si le motif du dragon pourrait avoir un lien avec la légende de Mélusine, mythe des origines des Luxembourg forgé autour de 1300 (M. NEJEDLÝ, *Středověký mýtus o Meluzíně a rodová pověst Lucemburků*, Prague, 2014), le texte de la charte de fondation de l'Ordre du Dragon, ainsi que l'emblème choisi (un dragon dont la queue s'enroule autour du cou et dont le dos est fendu d'une croix rouge) renvoient explicitement à la figure de saint Georges. P. LŐVEI, « Les ordres de chevalerie princiers au Moyen Âge, en particulier l'Ordre du Dragon de Sigismond », dans *Sigismundus Rex et Imperator. Art et culture à l'époque de Sigismond de Luxembourg 1387-1437*, éd. I. TAKÁCS *et al.*, Luxembourg, 2006, p. 258-259, et notices 4.38 à 4.41, p. 338-341.

fourni l'essentiel des motifs iconographiques utilisés par les artistes hongrois de la fin du Moyen Âge pour représenter l'Arpadien Ladislas Ier.

La littérature hagiographique fournit des exemples encore plus insolites de « naturalisation » de saints exogènes. Honorat, le fondateur de l'abbaye de Lérins, a été « hungarisé » au début du XIVe siècle dans le milieu curial angevin. Le troubadour (puis moine) Raimon Feraut, alors au service de Marie de Hongrie – épouse (1270) puis veuve (1309) du roi de Sicile Charles II – fait d'Honorat l'un des fils du roi de Hongrie *Andrioc*. Un siècle et demi plus tard, Jeanne de Laval, mariée à René d'Anjou depuis 1454, commandita de nouvelles copies de la *Vida* de saint Honorat. L'intention politique ne fait aucun doute : il s'agissait de créer un lien fictionnel entre la seconde maison d'Anjou, la Provence et la Hongrie, par l'intermédiaire de la figure d'Honorat, afin d'appuyer les prétentions du « roi René » sur la Hongrie, en même temps que sur le royaume de Naples. Démarche aussi artificielle qu'éphémère, puisque les origines prétendument hongroises d'Honorat n'étaient (re)connues manifestement qu'à la cour de René[53].

Les revers que subirent les saints exogènes résultaient parfois des fluctuations de la politique extérieure des princes centre-européens. Aux exemples polonais de résistance à la germanisation énumérés par Olivier Marin en introduction, on peut ajouter l'échec du culte de Brunon de Querfurt. Mort peu après Adalbert (1009) et dans des circonstances assez analogues (une mission d'évangélisation des Baltes soutenue par les ducs polonais, ce qui en fait presque un « saint de souche »), il ne fut guère vénéré en Pologne, les princes piastiens s'opposant à l'incorporation des évêchés polonais à l'Église d'Empire[54]. Il existe une autre catégorie de « saints d'implantation » dont la promotion en Europe centrale était vouée à l'échec : ceux dont la vie et l'œuvre ont été spontanément associées à une région ou à une « nation » précises. En 1055, le roi de Hongrie André Ier choisit l'évêque d'Orléans Aignan (*Anianus*, en hongrois *Ányos*) (v. 358-v. 453) pour saint protecteur de l'abbaye royale de Tihany. Deux hypothèses ont été avancées pour expliquer ce vocable. La première invoque les liens matrimoniaux noués entre André Ier et la dynastie capétienne : André avait épousé Anastasia de Kiev, fille de Jaroslav le Sage et sœur d'Anne de Kiev, elle-même mariée au roi de France Henri Ier, auprès

---

[53] Honorat n'a bénéficié d'aucun culte en Hongrie, ni sous les Angevins de la première maison, descendants de Marie de Hongrie, ni dans la seconde moitié du XVe siècle. A.-M. LEGARÉ, « Livres et lectures de la reine Jeanne de Laval », dans *Bretagne : art, création, société. Textes en l'honneur de Denise Delouche*, éd. J.-Y. ANDRIEUX, M. GRIVEL, Rennes, 1997, p. 220-234. Source : *Aventures de Baudouin de Gavre*, Paris, Bibliothèque nationale de France, Ms. Nouv. acq. fr. 1821, fol. 48.
[54] A. GIEYSZTOR, « Saints d'implantation », *art. cit.*, p. 580.

de qui André aurait cherché une alliance de revers pour résister à la pression germanique. Les médiévistes actuels préfèrent y lire l'implication des clercs lotharingiens dans l'évangélisation et la formation de clercs autochtones, concomitante de l'arrivée en Hongrie de manuscrits liturgiques copiés à Saint-Vanne de Verdun[55]. Quoi qu'il en soit, le culte de l'évêque d'Orléans ne fournit en tout et pour tout que deux vocables en Hongrie (Tihany et Marcali). Il faut dire que, comme sainte Geneviève, Aignan souffrait d'une tare majeure aux yeux des Hongrois, celui d'avoir épargné aux habitants d'Orléans leur massacre par les troupes d'Attila – à une période où les Hongrois se posaient en descendants des Huns. Sainte Ursule a cependant été vénérée en Hongrie dès l'époque arpadienne, rapporte le chroniqueur Simon de Kéza. L'échec d'Aignan paraît donc plutôt s'expliquer – outre par la fin de règne pitoyable d'André Ier, brutalement détrôné par son frère Béla en 1060 – par l'ancrage explicitement orléanais du saint. Autre exemple concordant : celui du roi Saint Louis qui, en dépit de son envergure internationale, ne fournit aucun vocable en Hongrie. Il n'est représenté, au mieux, que dans des « brochettes » de saints rois, pour renforcer la sainteté des trois Arpadiens[56]. À l'inverse, une figure apatride comme saint Roch ne rencontra aucune résistance sur le sol hongrois (O. GECSER).

Au bout du compte, il est bien difficile de repérer des processus d'« adoption » ou de « naturalisation » des saints qui seraient propres à l'Europe centrale, tant le faisceau de paramètres (religieux, sociaux, politiques, diplomatiques) à l'origine de leur réussite ou au contraire de leur défaveur ressemble à celui que l'on peut observer en d'autres lieux. De leur côté, les « saints de souche » centre-européens furent, dans l'ensemble, assez médiocrement accueillis dans le reste de la Chrétienté.

Otton III avait pris toutes les précautions nécessaires pour que le culte d'Adalbert de Prague s'enracine dans l'Empire : il avait rapporté de Gniezno un bras du saint et l'avait dispersé entre diverses fondations monastiques étirées d'Aix et Reichenau jusqu'à Rome. Conséquence probable des frustrations

---

[55] P. TÓTH, « Vallon főpapok a magyar egyház újjászervezésében a pogánylázadás után », dans *Tanulmányok a 950. éves tihanyi alapítólevél tiszteletére*, éd. G. ÉRSZEGI, Tihany, 2007, p. 31-36 ; G. KISS, « 11-13. századi magyar főpapok francia kapcsolatai », dans *Francia-magyar kapcsolatok a középkorban*, éd. A. GYÖRKÖS et G. KISS, Debrecen, 2013, p. 341-350.
[56] En particulier sur le retable de l'église collégiale Saint-Martin de Spišská Kapitula, en hongrois Szepeshely, peint dans le dernier quart du XVe siècle. E. MAROSI, « Saints at Home and Abroad. Some Observations on the Creation of Iconographic Types in Hungary in the Fourteenth and Fifteenth Centuries », dans *Promoting the Saints. Cults and Their Contexts from Late Antiquity until the Early Modern Period. Essays in Honor of Gábor Klaniczay for His 60th Birthday*, éd. O. GECSER, J. LASZLOVSKY, B. NAGY, M. SEBŐK, K. SZENDE, Budapest, 2010, p. 205-206.

des archevêques de Magdebourg et d'Augsbourg, qui avaient échoué dans leurs projets d'intégration de l'Est européen à leurs provinces ecclésiastiques, ces efforts furent déployés en vain (G. Bührer-Thierry). De même, les grandes figures dynastiques arpadiennes et přemyslides (Étienne, Émeric et Ladislas pour la Hongrie, Venceslas et sa grand-mère Ludmila en Bohême) ont faiblement rayonné hors des frontières nationales ou régionales. La promotion de la triade arpadienne à Naples ne dura pas plus longtemps que le pouvoir angevin. Et les procédés employés sont éloquents. Dans le légendier composé à l'époque où Charles-Robert d'Anjou rêvait de créer un « empire angevin » enjambant l'Adriatique, comme sur les retables de Slovaquie et de Transylvanie, saint Ladislas est privé d'attributs hongrois (I. Gerát). Tout se passe comme si les promoteurs des saints « de souche » avaient pris soin d'en gommer la couleur locale, de traduire leur parcours dans ce qu'on pourrait appeler le langage hagiographique international – à l'heure du « gothique international » – afin de faciliter leur exportation.

Sans grand succès. Il est vrai qu'objectivement, leur « archaïsme » nuisait à leur attractivité. La *legenda maior* rapporte qu'Étienne de Hongrie faisait crever les yeux et couper les mains des réfractaires[57]. Difficile dans ces conditions d'en faire un modèle de souverain après le XIIe siècle. Les évêques n'échappent pas à cet enfermement. Parmi les saints « nationaux » de Hongrie, seul Gérard (Gérard Sagredo), d'origine vénitienne et mis à mort en 1046 par les révoltés païens sur le mont de Budapest qui porte aujourd'hui son nom, réussit l'exploit d'être vénéré à la fois en Hongrie, dans sa terre natale et dans l'espace germanique. La quasi-totalité des sermons écrits qui vantent les mérites de saint Stanislas viennent d'Europe centrale[58]. Car partout ailleurs, passé le XIIe siècle, l'idéal de l'évêque évangélisateur (ou martyr), même transformé en pasteur accompli – donc transposable aux curés de paroisse –, n'était plus d'actualité. On aurait là, avec la persistance du modèle martyrial déjà signalée à propos des Mendiants et la militarisation des saints universels, une troisième spécificité hagiologique centre-européenne.

Géographiquement parlant, la diffusion du culte des saints autochtones semble avoir suivi un schéma auréolaire. L'analyse des textes liturgiques mentionnant les trois saints « rois » arpadiens (E. Madas) et celle des sources iconographiques qui les représentent (I. Gerát) mettent grossièrement en évidence trois cercles de diffusion. Le noyau central correspond au royaume

---

[57] F. Graus, « La sanctification du souverain dans l'Europe centrale des Xe et XIe siècles », dans *Hagiographie*, p. 563.
[58] St. Kuzmová, *Preaching Saint Stanislaus. Medieval Sermons on Saint Stanislas of Cracow, His Image and Cult*, Varsovie, 2013.

de Hongrie, où le culte des rois arpadiens (notamment Ladislas) et de Gérard fut incontestablement le plus vigoureux. La deuxième auréole se compose des royaumes ou principautés limitrophes, Pologne et Autriche principalement. Elle fait la part belle au fondateur Étienne. Ladislas devint un nom très courant en Pologne à partir de la fin du XIIe siècle, constatait Aleksander Gieysztor – il est vrai que la mère de Ladislas Ier était polonaise. Le troisième cercle, caractérisé par un culte diffus – et parfois lié à des événements précis (comme la fondation par l'empereur Henri II, beau-frère de saint Étienne, de la cathédrale de Bamberg, où sont figurés les trois « saints rois ») –, englobe Allemagne méridionale et Italie. La documentation homilétique sur Stanislas montre une progression similaire en tache d'huile (St. KUZMOVÁ).

Ce sont les frères mendiants qui ont obtenu les meilleurs résultats en matière de diffusion universelle de la renommée des saints centre-européens – du moins de ceux qui se prêtaient aux manœuvres de consolidation de chaque ordre. On s'en souvient, les frères hongrois tombés sous les coups des Tatars, Maurice de Csák ou encore Marguerite de Hongrie, permirent aux Prêcheurs de vanter au XIVe siècle la richesse et la diversité des membres de leur congrégation ; ils soutenaient désormais la comparaison avec les Franciscains, qui lançaient au même moment leur campagne de promotion des martyrs d'Orient et du Maghreb, de Louis d'Anjou – et d'Élisabeth de Hongrie. Les Mendiants « de souche » furent également mobilisés sur les fronts intérieurs de la sainteté mendiante – de la stigmatisation à la définition de modèles féminins –, au même titre que d'autres personnages réputés saints.

Les contributions de ce volume font ressortir en définitive la perméabilité des limites de l'Europe centrale en matière de culte des saints et le déséquilibre de sa balance hagiographique en faveur des « saints d'implantation ». Est-ce à dire que l'hagiologie centre-européenne n'acquit de réelle consistance qu'au temps de la Réforme catholique, dans sa variante habsbourgeoise ? Deux arguments plaident en sens inverse : l'existence d'une figure sainte véritablement centre-européenne en la personne d'Adalbert de Prague ; la fluidité et l'intensité de la circulation des cultes dans toute l'Europe centrale entre X[e] et XVIe siècles.

Par ses origines et son parcours, mais aussi par l'itinéraire de diffusion de son culte, Adalbert de Prague forme un véritable trait d'union entre Bohême, Pologne et Hongrie. Tchèque de naissance, évêque de Prague, parti évangéliser les confins des terres polonaises et mort près des rives de la Baltique, il a été enseveli à Gniezno puis à Prague. Peu vénéré en Germanie et en Italie, il est devenu autour de l'an mille le protecteur des deux églises métropolitaines les plus anciennes de Pologne (Gniezno) et de Hongrie (Esztergom) et il a résisté à plusieurs mesures d'appropriation « nationale » (le vol de ses reliques par le duc de Bohême Bretislas en 1039, sa « réinvention » par les clercs de Gniezno en 1127). Il devint également une sorte de plus petit dénominateur commun du sanctoral centre-européen par le fait que les figures d'évêques, d'évangélisateurs et de martyrs – étendues aux membres des ordres mendiants à partir du XIIIe siècle – restèrent, avec les saints guerriers, entourées d'un prestige exceptionnel dans l'ensemble de la région. Cette constante rappelle la position de frontière de la Chrétienté qu'a occupée l'Europe centrale jusqu'à la fin du Moyen Âge.

Par ailleurs, les conquêtes territoriales, les alliances diplomatiques et dynastiques, conjuguées aux flux migratoires (ceux des « colons occidentaux », des marchands, des clercs, des grands officiers, des artistes) ont facilité la circulation dans l'espace centre-européen des reliques, des images saintes, des manuscrits liturgiques et hagiographiques ou encore des prénoms en vogue[59]. De manière violente parfois (dans le cas des reliques d'Adalbert), pacifique le plus souvent (Wolfgang, saint bavarois adopté par plusieurs confréries de métier en Bohême, a donné un prénom attesté précocement en Hongrie). À la fin du Moyen Âge, l'avènement dans les trois pays de dynasties exogènes soucieuses d'ancrer leur lignée dans les traditions nationales et cumulant plusieurs couronnes centre-européennes (Luxembourg, Anjou puis Jagellons) a accéléré ce processus d'homogénéisation[60].

C'est sur cette base que l'on peut parler de paysage hagiographique centre-européen à propos de l'époque médiévale. Encore faut-il prendre trois précautions, qui témoignent de la complexité de notre objet d'étude. La première consiste à ne pas enfermer l'Europe centrale dans des limites figées et étroites : pour appréhender la totalité du phénomène, il convient d'inclure dans le champ de vision les pays allemands voisins – Autriche, Bavière, Saxe, Brandebourg, qui dessinent la *Germania slavica* (ou *hungarica*) évoquée en introduction – mais également, sur son flanc oriental et méridional, les terres de christianisme mêlé (outre la Transylvanie et la Slavonie, la Galicie, la Lituanie, la Moldavie, la Serbie). Ces dernières expliquent entre autres le succès

---

[59] Ainsi, les intrusions des ducs přemyslides en Petite Pologne à la fin du Xe siècle seraient à l'origine du choix de Venceslas comme saint patron de la cathédrale de Cracovie. Après avoir accueilli le Slavníkide Sobeslas à sa cour, le duc polane Boleslas le Vaillant a placé son pays sous la protection de Venceslas, son grand-oncle maternel. Son nom figure sur les premières monnaies ducales polonaises. Certes, le même Venceslas, érigé en protecteur officiel d'une Bohême devenue ennemie, a subi ensuite une totale désaffection dans le diocèse de Cracovie. A. GIEYSZTOR, « Saints d'implantation », *art. cit.*, p. 575. Voir aussi les travaux de Stanisław Suchodolski cités par Przemysław Wichewski dans N. BEREND, P. URBAŃCZYK, P. WISZEWSKI, *Central Europe in the High Middle Ages : Bohemia, Hungary and Poland, c. 900 – c. 1300*, Cambridge, 2013, p. 144-145.
[60] Voir en particulier G. KLANICZAY, *Holy rulers, op. cit.*

prolongé, aux marges de la Hongrie et de la Pologne, des cultes de Côme et Damien, Démétrius et Alexis[61]. Deuxièmement, on gardera à l'esprit que le foyer privilégié du culte des saints locaux restait local (le diocèse de Cracovie pour Stanislas) ou national (pour les saints dynastiques), plutôt que régional. Enfin, on n'oubliera pas qu'en dépit du travail d'uniformisation mené par les acteurs de la pastorale (curés de paroisse, prédicateurs séculiers et mendiants) depuis le XIIIe siècle, l'attachement des fidèles à tel personnage réputé saint plutôt qu'à tel autre était fonction de leur extraction sociale, de leur environnement culturel et de leur formation intellectuelle, ainsi que de leur degré de proximité avec le pouvoir royal. On nous permettra pour finir d'insister sur la vitalité de l'Europe centrale en matière de « fabrique des saints » au XVe siècle, réalité longtemps ignorée de l'historiographie occidentale. À l'automne du Moyen Âge, le soleil de la sainteté s'est aussi levé à l'Est.

---

[61] S. BÁLINT, *Szeged reneszánszkori műveltsége*, Budapest, 1975 ; *Id.*, *Ünnepi kalendárium*, Budapest, 1977.

Résumés – Abstracts
dans l'ordre alphabétique des auteurs

Geneviève BÜHRER-THIERRY, *Saint national ou saint européen ? Les tribulations d'Adalbert de Prague et de ses reliques dans le temps et dans l'espace (X^e-XIIe siècles)*

Adalbert de Prague († 997) est vénéré en Europe centrale, mais également dans la péninsule italienne et en Rhénanie, dès le début du XIe siècle, autrement dit quelques années seulement après sa mort. La vie d'Adalbert, originaire de Bohême et premier évêque slave de Prague, peut se lire comme une vaste pérégrination à l'échelle de l'Europe, une tribulation qui le conduit au martyre sur les bords de la Baltique. Immédiatement, ses reliques deviennent un enjeu de pouvoir entre l'empereur (ottonien puis germanique) et les princes d'Europe centrale, notamment polonais puis tchèques. Elles jouent un rôle non négligeable dans les reconfigurations de pouvoir qui surviennent dans cette région au XIe siècle, tandis que les tentatives de diffuser son culte à l'échelle de l'ensemble de l'Empire se soldent rapidement par un échec.

Il s'agit dans cette étude de montrer comment la logique de compétition autour des reliques de saint Adalbert aboutit à la construction d'un saint qui ne peut être « national », puisqu'il est revendiqué par plusieurs nations à la fois. Mais il faudra aussi comprendre pourquoi, malgré l'échec de la diffusion de son culte hors d'Europe centrale *stricto sensu*, Adalbert de Prague passe aujourd'hui pour être l'un des tout premiers saints « européens ».

Enikő CSUKOVITS, *Les saints libérateurs des Turcs en Hongrie à la fin du Moyen Âge*

La conquête d'une partie du royaume de Hongrie par les Ottomans à partir des années 1520 est l'achèvement d'une longue suite d'incursions et d'attaques qui causèrent d'énormes pertes humaines et matérielles, ceci pendant plus de cent trente années, soit cinq à six générations. Les premières irruptions, en 1390, affectèrent les régions méridionales du pays : la région de *Szerémség* (Syrmie) au sud du Danube, ainsi que le *Temesköz*, entre le fleuve Temes (Timiş) et le Bas-Danube. Elles furent encore victimes des attaques des décennies suivantes mais elles atteignirent des régions toujours plus étendues. Au début du XVe siècle, les cavaliers ottomans firent irruption en Croatie et en Slavonie, réputées sûres jusqu'alors, puis ce fut le tour de la Transylvanie dans les années 1420. Le royaume de Hongrie fut désormais contraint d'organiser la défense de l'ensemble de sa frontière méridionale (près de 800 kilomètres), de la mer Adriatique jusqu'en *Barcaság (Burzenland)*.

L'objectif principal des envahisseurs était le pillage. Le butin le plus recherché n'était autre que les hommes, faciles à vendre sur les marchés aux esclaves. Dans leur malheur, les captifs ne pouvaient compter que sur leur habileté personnelle pour sortir de leur condition... ou bien sur une assistance spirituelle. Aussi n'est-il pas très surprenant de rencontrer la plupart des récits de libération dans les recueils de miracles rédigés sur les lieux de pèlerinage de la Hongrie médiévale. Parmi les plus importants centres hongrois de pèlerinage du Moyen Âge tardif, seuls deux ont conservé un recueil de miracles: Újlak (Ilok, en Croatie), lieu de sépulture de Jean de Capistran, et Budaszentlőrinc (près de Buda), où l'on vénérait la relique de saint Paul l'Ermite. Le recueil d'Újlak recense des cas survenus entre 1458 et 1461; celui de Budaszentlőrinc, réuni par le prieur Bálint Hadnagy, couvre la période 1422-1505. Parmi les miracles attribués à Jean de Capistran, 4,6 % (23 cas) racontent comment le saint obtint la libération de ceux qui l'avaient imploré; dans le cas de saint Paul l'Ermite en revanche, ce chiffre s'élève à 18 cas, qui représentent 20 % du total des miracles. Les narrations détaillent souvent avec une minutie remarquable les circonstances de chaque enlèvement et les souffrances endurées pendant la captivité mais aussi l'instrument de chaque libération. Elles offrent ainsi un éclairage inédit sur les conséquences des irruptions turques, sur les manifestations de la vie religieuse en Hongrie, ainsi que sur la vision des Turcs (« païens »). Elles révèlent par ailleurs la force du sentiment d'appartenance à la *christianitas* de ces prisonniers évoluant en milieu non chrétien.

Christian-Frederik FELSKAU, *Shaping the Sainthood of a Central European Clarissan Princess. The Development of the Earliest Hagiographic Texts on Agnes of Bohemia and Saint Clare's Epistolary Tradition*

Agnes of Bohemia (1211-1282) was one of the most important proponents of the female Franciscan movement in its era of creation and institutionalization. Since her canonisation in 1989 and recent anniversaries dedicated to that event (2009) or her birth (2011), historians and a broader public have paid increasing attention to her impact on the development of the Poor Clares in East Central Europe, but also on the local politics of the ruling Bohemian dynasty of the Přemyslids. The paper summarizes first the most important steps in Agnes' secular life, during her *vita religiosa*, then the traceable medieval attempts for canonization, carried out with substantial retardation to her death. The second part deals with the canonisation attempts accomplished in the fourteenth century and their relation to the two basic hagiographic branches of Agnes of that time, that is the *Vita Prima* and the legend *Candor lucis eterne* tradition. Following own research and confirming the investigations of Cardinal Beran from the 1970s, the *Legenda*-branch represents a Franciscan *réécriture* of an earlier composed textual witness represented by the *Vita*. The revision of the hagiographic tradition is strengthened by a textual comparison between the requests for canonisation and the hagiographic material, and refers to a complex process of re-writing enacted during the course of the fourteenth century. The third part entails a brief analysis of the miracle recounts as a crucial element for clarifying the intertextual relations. In addition, this approach helps to understand the redactor's working method. The forth part is addressing the reconstruction of Agnes' perception in the Later Middle Ages under the point of view of her affinity to the Order's foundress. Starting with the examination of the two crucial documents, the Rule for San Damiano and the four letters attributes to Agnes as addressee (*EpCl 1-4*). It is demonstrated that the granting of the rule also for the Prague monastery cannot be proven beyond doubt. The remarks on the tradition of Clare's four letters are embedded into a broader analytical frame including all hagiographies, i.e. also the Middle-High translations on Agnes. Based on own research, a contextual analysis of the texts on Clare and the developing standardized set of hagiographic material called *Klarenbuch* paves the way to a deeper understanding of how the written memory on Agnes was formed and shaped. This approach allows some suggestions for a deeper understanding of the origin and impact of this important epistolary corps of the two female Franciscan founding figures. Though the remembrance on the Princess shifted due to the 'loss' of Bohemia as her memorial homeland during Hussitism to neighbouring territories, the basis for the refreshment of memory on Agnes was set already in the fourteenth century in the South German monastery of Nuremberg, most probably promoted by Emperor Charles IV and the local Poor Clares.

Carmen FLOREA, *The Universal Cult of the Virgin Martyrs in Late Medieval Transylvania*

Neither a single process of canonization nor a request for canonization concerned a would-be-saint from late medieval Transylvania. Furthermore, the carrying of saints' relics in processions did not occur in the surviving sources, whereas the pilgrimage places preferred by Transylvanian men and women were those primarily associated with the saints of the early Church. Undoubtedly, Transylvania was a region of archaic sanctity, dominated by long-established cults such as those of the Virgin Mary, the Apostles, the martyrs and confessors.

In 1431, George Lépes, Transylvanian Bishop, forwarded a supplication to the Holy See in order to get approval for the foundation of two altars in Alba Iulia cathedral. These were to be dedicated to St Michael, the patron saint of the Episcopal See and to St Barbara, the Virgin Martyr. At that time, the cult of the Virgin Martyrs was growing in this region and thus the Bishop's pious foundation could be considered not only an integral part of this growth, but also most likely as giving further impulses to the development of the cults of the *Virgines Capitales*. Therefore, the main aim of this study is to decipher the role played by the clerical elite in the promotion of the Virgin Martyrs' cults and their subsequent transformations as a result of this support. Highly informed by recent research on the cults of Sts. Barbara, Catherine and Margaret that argued – in the light of medieval gender studies – the potential of the Virgin Martyrs as powerful cultural symbols, this paper attempts to scrutinize the profile of these cults at both Episcopal and parish levels. Whilst previous research on the Transylvanian development of the cults of the Virgin Martyrs has emphasized the importance of the sufferings and the martyrdom which transformed these beautiful, young women into powerful intercessors, the present study focuses instead on the modalities within which these cults were refashioned in such a way as to reflect the social and political standing of both clerical and lay elites. Textual and visual sources are explored in order to attain this goal, whereas the main analytical framework is provided by taking into account the specificities of late medieval sainthood in one of the border zones of the Latin Christendom.

Ottó GECSER, *Intercession and Specialization. St Sebastian and St Roche as Plague Saints and their Cult in Medieval Hungary*

From the Black Death of 1348-1351 until the eighteenth century the cult of St Sebastian was as one of the main channels of imploring supernatural intervention against pestilence. St Roche had joined him in this capacity from the last third of the fifteenth century onwards. The veneration of St Sebastian in Hungary can be attested since the turn of the thirteenth and fourteenth centuries, although its connection to the plague only appears in the sources much later, at the end of the fifteenth century, roughly at the same time, when the cult of St Roche arrived, in this case quite early, in the 1490s. But it is not only the specificities of diffusion that makes the local cult of these two saints interesting. Sebastian and Roche in the fifteenth and early sixteenth centuries represent a category of association between saints and believers where the former tend to have a largely functional relevance: their intercession is implored to resolve one specific type of problem (plague) as opposed to a territorial-political or kin-based focus of intercession demanded from saints in other cases (dynastic saints, patron saints of cities etc.). Arguably, such a functional specialization of cults, in terms of which – to use the words of Erasmus – "we have appointed certain saints to preside over all the things we fear or desire", had become more salient by the end of the Middle Ages. The cult of the fourteen holy helpers could be another good example. Hungary, like other countries (in the modern sense) of East-Central Europe was poor in indigenous cults, and even those that did exist tended to be national and not regional or urban. As a consequence, functional specialization could play an even bigger role than elsewhere. Apart from tracing the diffusion of the cults of St Sebastian and St Roche in Hungary, this article also tries to assess their veneration in terms of such a functional specialization.

Ivan GERÁT, *Some Structural Comparisons of Pictorial Legends from Medieval Hungary*

The pictorial narratives were mostly constructed from the well-known *topoi* – traditional compositions, which could be associated with more than one saint. The legend of Saint Ladislas, as represented in the so-called Hungarian Angevin Legendary (Cod. Vat. lat. 8541, fol. 80r-85v), was composed of 24 scenes. They have analogies in the pictorial lives of other saints, such as the miraculous feeding, the solitary prayer of the saint or his levitation. Four scenes focusing on an encounter of the saint with the devil during a nightly vigil in the church are similar to exorcisms as well as to solitary fight of hermits against the demons. These compositions (together with the topical image of levitation on the other side of the fighting sequence) were used to integrate into the legend of the holy king the most popular topics of early fourteenth century murals – his fight against a Cumanian abducting a Hungarian girl.

The last sequence focuses on the passing away of the saint, his burial and the cult of his grave. The miracle of a carriage miraculously finding its way to the burial site and the image of the pilgrims gathering around his sarcophagus has analogies in the legends of Saint James of Compostella and the Hungarian bishop-martyr Gerhard.

Very similar images and sequences were used on altar retables – the most important medium of broader public communication in the late medieval period. Interestingly, the main hero of these pictorial narratives is not the holy king of Hungary, but by the saints imported from abroad, e.g. St Georges, St James of Compostella, St Anthony the Hermit, etc. This phenomenon is hardly explainable from traditional nationalist perspectives and leads to some more general questions. These older saints imported from abroad inspired the pictorial legend of the holy king. The patrons of the altarpieces in multi-national towns, frequently merchants with a broad network of business partners at home and abroad were rarely interested in promoting the hagiographic constructions from the centre of the kingdom. Their interests in building smoothly functioning international communication networks were better implemented by focusing the attention on universal saints.

Eszter KONRÁD, *The Oldest Legend of Francis of Assisi and his Stigmatization in Old Hungarian Codex Literature (c. 1440-1530)*

The emergence of the vernacular religious literature in Hungary was strongly related to the Observant reforms in the fifteenth century as well as to the change in the devotional life of women. The heyday of the vernacular literary production was in the early sixteenth century: more than 40 survive from this period, mostly written for and copied by nuns. Francis of Assisi was the saint of the mendicant orders who turned up most often in the old Hungarian codices. This paper proposes to discuss thoroughly the legend of Francis of Assisi and his companions in the Jókai Codex (c. 1440) – which is the earliest surviving codex written entirely in Hungarian –, as well as the most emblematic episode of his hagiographic dossier, the stigmatization, as it is reflected in four codices written in the vernacular, placing it in the context of the evolution of the stigmatization narratives.

The Jókai Codex is a compilation of mainly fourteenth century works originating from the environment of the Spiritual Franciscans. This paper re-examines its sources. It proposes that the 'core' of Jókai Codex was not put together by its Hungarian translator. The latter used an already existing Latin compilation. The detailed presentation of the content of the codex is required for the clarification to what extent it can be associated with the Observant Franciscans and whether it suggests an intended audience. The codices that report the stigmatization or the stigmata of St Francis are of different provenance and were made for different purposes. In addition to the Franciscan Jókai Codex, the paper analyses two stigmatization narratives in the Virginia Codex (before 1529) copied by Dominican nuns and the Lázár Zelma Codex (1525) made for private use for a Clarissan nun that both go back ultimately to a certain *Vita sociorum sancti Francisci*. It shows that the description of the stigmatization of Francis was reshaped in lines with the late medieval affective piety, centred on the Passion. Finally, the paper presents how the Carthusian author of the Érdy Codex (1526/27), a collection of sermons made for public reading for nuns and lay brothers, adapted the Italian Franciscan Roberto Caracciolo's sermon on St Francis to his own goals: he not only emphasized the image of the stigmatized Francis but also reminded his audience that he was not the only saint to whom this divine gift was given.

Petr KUBÍN, *Saints fondateurs contre saints mendiants dans la Bohême médiévale*

Cette contribution s'efforce de répondre, à partir du cas de la Bohême tardo-médiévale, à la question posée par Olivier Marin en ouverture de ce volume, qui est celle de comprendre pourquoi les saints du haut Moyen Âge étaient préférés à ceux des ordres mendiants en Europe centrale, contrairement à l'Europe occidentale. Cela ferait de cette région une « région froide », pour reprendre la classification employée, c'est-à-dire prêtant un intérêt moindre aux nouveaux saints à la fin du Moyen Âge. Les deux protecteurs principaux de Bohême, le prince Venceslas (Václav) († 935) et Adalbert de Prague (Vojtěch) († 997), eurent une signification symbolique fondamentale, véritablement incomparable, pour le pays, et ils ne furent jamais remplacés dans cette fonction. Ils furent seulement rejoints un peu plus tard par saint Procope (Prokop) († 1053) et par Ludmila († 921). Ces saints anciens commencèrent à faire l'objet d'un culte à l'époque ou l'approbation épiscopale tenait lieu de canonisation.

À partir du moment où la décrétale *Liber extra* réserva en 1234 le droit exclusif de canoniser au pape, une longue procédure était devenue nécessaire, sans garantie de succès. Ni la cause de l'ermite bénédictin Gunther (Vintíř) († 1045) ni celle de la supérieure Clarisse Agnès (Anežka) († 1282) n'aboutirent, ce qui cantonna leur culte à des cercles réguliers spécifiques. D'autres, dont le chanoine de Prémontré Hroznata († 1217), la noble dame pieuse Zdislava († 1252), le prédicateur réformateur Jean Milíč de Kroměříž († 1374) ou encore l'archevêque de Prague Jean de Jenštejn († 1400), restèrent à l'écart du processus de canonisation. Un frémissement s'observe tout juste pour l'archevêque de Prague Arnošt de Pardubice († 1364). Mais le seul véritable succès est celui remporté par l'empereur Charles IV lorsqu'il érigea les saints tutélaires anciens Guy et Sigismond en saints protecteurs de la Bohême. Toutefois, l'avènement du hussitisme et la propagation de l'utraquisme changèrent la donne. Les saints utraquistes – les martyrs Jean Hus († 1415) et Jérôme de Prague († 1416) –, qui n'avaient pas besoin de confirmation pontificale, prirent place aux côtés des anciens protecteurs de la Bohême, infléchissant la thèse de la prédominance des cultes anciens en Bohême au Moyen Âge.

Stanislava KUZMOVÁ, *The Old and the New: St Stanislaus and Other Cults in Krakow*

The cult of St Stanislaus of Krakow, a martyr-bishop, started to flourish in the thirteenth century. He was canonized by Pope Innocent IV in 1253. Thus, the local bishop achieved this honour more than 150 years after his death in the conflict with King Boleslas II of Poland, and ultimately became the patron-saint not only of Krakow, but of Poland. The cult of this bishop, who represented a rather traditional type of sainthood, was supported from various sides, besides the bishop and the chapter also by the Dominican and Franciscan orders, who had established themselves in the region a short time ago.

Before that, though, Krakow (and Poland) had looked for a saint elsewhere. The translation of the relics of St Florian, Roman martyr, from Italy did not bring permanent success. When the imported cult was challenged by the emergence of a local, native one, the significance of the former diminished.

Various sources confirm the high importance of the cult of St Stanislaus in the late Middle Ages. This was the period, though (especially in the fifteenth century), when a number of new cult places were emerging in Krakow, related especially to recent figures connected with various religious orders who enjoyed popular devotion. In a way, they both coexisted and competed with the officially established and traditional cult of Stanislaus.

The paper will present the cult of St Stanislaus, as the first Pole to be canonized, with focus on preaching and various forms of devotion, among others building on an analysis of collected manuscript sermons on him. The aim is to investigate the challenges posed by the rise of Stanislaus to the earlier cults (especially that of St Florian), as well as those challenges that he faced from the new late medieval cults.

Edit MADAS, *À la recherche des sources liturgiques et hagiographiques du culte des « saints rois » hongrois en Europe centrale*

Le propos est d'examiner la diffusion du culte de trois saints « nationaux » hongrois, le roi Étienne Ier († 1038), le prince Émeric († 1031) et le roi Ladislas Ier († 1095), ainsi par ailleurs que celui de l'évêque martyr saint Gérard († 1046), ceci à l'aide des missels, bréviaires, légendiers et sermonnaires non hongrois.

Le culte officiel des « saints rois » s'est limité à l'espace de la Hongrie médiévale. La présence des saints hongrois dans les livres liturgiques bohémiens, polonais et autrichiens découle des relations de voisinage – de même que, en sens inverse, la mention des saints polonais et tchèques dans les livres liturgiques en usage en Hongrie. Le culte liturgique de saint Étienne à Bamberg reçoit quant à lui une explication historique : le fondateur de la cathédrale, Henri II, n'était autre que le beau-frère du premier roi de Hongrie, Étienne.

Vingt-quatre *codices* de provenance ou d'utilisation étrangère à la Hongrie mentionnant les légendes des « saints rois » hongrois ont été répertoriés à ce jour. Les exemplaires sont principalement autrichiens et polonais, puis allemands du Sud, tchèques et enfin italiens. Des trois saints arpadiens, c'est de loin Étienne qui revient le plus souvent dans ces manuscrits. Alors que saint Ladislas occupait le devant de la scène en Hongrie même, il n'y a guère qu'à Vienne qu'il reçut un culte individuel, étant le saint protecteur de la « nation » hongroise à l'université. Il n'apparaît pas en revanche dans les livres provenant du royaume de Naples. Arrivé de Venise et mort martyr, l'évêque Gérard appartient à un genre différent. Son culte liturgique à Venise et la réception de sa légende en Allemagne divergent fortement de ceux des saints arpadiens. Ils tiennent à ses origines, vénitiennes, et à son statut d'évêque martyr. Gérard offre ainsi un contrepoint instructif pour appréhender les modalités de la diffusion du culte des saints endogènes et exogènes en Europe centrale.

David MENGEL, *Bohemia's Treasury of Saints. Relics and indulgences in Emperor Charles IV's Prague*

Since late antiquity, the bodies of saints have anchored the practice of Christianity in Europe to the places where they lay. Especially prominent were those sites associated with the cults of saints known for producing miracles. The network of high-medieval pilgrimage routes identifies such holy sites clearly. Not surprisingly, this network was significantly less developed in high-medieval Bohemia and other parts of "younger Europe", not least because some of them adopted Christianity well after the most active period of late-antique relic distribution had come to an end.

The Kingdom of Bohemia in particular was notably relic-poor at the start of the fourteenth century. Emperor Charles IV (1346-1378) dramatically changed this situation with an unusually active program of relic collection across Europe throughout his long reign. As a result, Prague and its new cathedral came to enjoy a large and impressive collection of saints' relics. Historians have rightly characterized this activity as part of a conscious program of political and dynastic presentation, reinforced by art and architecture. Until recently, far fewer have noted the careful establishment in Prague of the conditions for a new miracle-producing cult associated with the newly acquired relic of St Sigismund († 524). For this royal saint, the emperor and his archbishop set the stage for Prague cathedral to become a traditional pilgrimage site, at which a saint's shrine attracted miracle-seeking and miracle-proclaiming visitors from across and beyond the kingdom. Pilgrims did respond, at least in modest numbers. This paper argues, however, that this new, miracle-producing cult of St Sigismund was an exception that points to an important transformation occurring in the late-medieval cult of relics – namely, the rise of indulgences. Charles IV repeatedly and insistently sought increasingly long indulgences to adorn his new relics, to draw visitors to Prague, and support a range of economic and political goals. This paper argues that Charles IV's activities – and, to the extent that it can be determined, the positive lay response – illustrate the more general rise of indulgences in Europe that historians are still working to integrate more fully into our understanding of late-medieval religious culture.

Hana PÁTKOVÁ, *Confréries de métier et culte des saints dans la Bohême médiévale*

Les premières traces documentaires sur les confréries de métier remontent en Bohême à la première moitié du XIVe siècle (1318, pour la confrérie des tailleurs de Prague). Elles sont mentionnées de plus en plus fréquemment du XIVe siècle jusqu'au début du XVIe siècle, ceci dans des sources provenant généralement des municipalités. Bien que celles-ci aient pris davantage de soin à consigner leurs activités professionnelles et économiques que leurs pratiques religieuses, il est possible, en rassemblant les mentions éparses dont on dispose à ce jour, de brosser un tableau du culte des saints dans les associations de métier.

La tradition qui attribue à chaque métier un saint protecteur se fonde en réalité sur la situation des temps modernes (du XVIIe au XIXe siècle). Les sources médiévales de Bohême ne fournissent, elles, aucune liste précise établissant une correspondance entre tel saint et telle profession. De manière générale, on peut distinguer trois types de cultes des saints liés aux métiers. *Primo*, ceux qui affectent un saint précis (Éloi, Luc) à telle spécialité ou famille de métiers – configuration très rare, qui privilégie les saints « importés ». Deuxièmement, les cultes plus aléatoires faisant intervenir des facteurs difficiles à déterminer ou à caractère local (les autels déjà aménagés dans l'église paroissiale, la dévotion personnelle de tel membre pour un saint, etc.). Enfin, les cultes résultant des échanges avec les pays voisins (Wolfgang, saint bavarois dont le culte s'est propagé en Bohême du Sud-Ouest).

Dans l'ensemble, on observe une grande variété de situations. Elle ne fut pas remise en cause par les guerres hussites, que ce soit en contexte utraquiste, autrement dit dans la majorité de la population, ou en milieu catholique. S'y mêlent saints d'implantation – importés des régions voisines ou véritablement « transnationaux » –, saints natifs de Bohême (dont Venceslas), saints rattachés à un métier précis et saints promus localement.

Anne TALLON, *Les martyrs dominicains de Hongrie et leur insertion réussie dans la mémoire hagiographique de l'ordre des Frères prêcheurs*

Quelques décennies seulement après l'institution de l'ordre des Prêcheurs, l'hagiographie dominicaine cesse de se concentrer sur la seule figure du fondateur pour faire toute leur place, à ses côtés, à d'autres figures censées illustrer une sainteté constamment renouvelée au sein de leur famille religieuse. Tel est le but premier de cette nouvelle politique hagiographique. Mais elle est également porteuse d'un véritable effort pour mieux articuler les différents cultes locaux à une hagiographie d'ordre alors en pleine construction et dont la visée principale est identitaire. Dans ce contexte, une attention particulière est portée aux espaces périphériques, parmi lesquels la province dominicaine de Hongrie se distingue précocement comme une grande pourvoyeuse de matériel hagiographique neuf, destiné à s'insérer harmonieusement dans la mémoire collective de l'Ordre.

Or, à bien y réfléchir, une telle fortune n'allait pas de soi, compte tenu du caractère « archaïque » du modèle de sainteté véhiculé par ces cultes venus de la Hongrie dominicaine, modèle faisant une large place au martyre et à la sainteté royale, à l'opposé de la sainteté « moderne » mise en évidence à partir des XIIe au XIIIe siècles par la thèse d'André Vauchez (plus particulièrement, il est vrai, en contexte méditerranéen). Cette contribution s'attache donc à essayer d'éclairer les raisons qui ont permis l'accueil enthousiaste réservé par l'hagiographie dominicaine médiévale à ce matériel hongrois pourtant si éloigné, en apparence du moins, du modèle évangélique incarné par les Prêcheurs comme par l'ensemble des ordres mendiants. Pour ce faire, elle étudie plus particulièrement l'insertion réussie dans la mémoire hagiographique de l'Ordre des dominicains hongrois martyrs des Coumans et surtout de l'invasion tartare de 1241. Elle montre que ce succès résulte sans doute en partie de l'effort de modernisation de l'image du martyre qui accompagna la promotion de ces nouveaux saints.

Ludovic VIALLET, *Sainteté et Observance franciscaine en Europe centrale : Bernardin de Sienne et Jean de Capistran*

Parce qu'elle est intervenue dans le contexte d'une accentuation des tensions au sein de l'Ordre franciscain et d'un raidissement des positions de chaque camp (« Conventuels », i.e. réformateurs *sub ministris* d'un côté, Observants *sub vicariis* de l'autre), mais aussi par la façon dont elle a été menée, la mission de Jean de Capistran en Europe centrale (1451-1456) a joué un rôle essentiel dans la propagation et surtout dans la définition même de la sainteté de Bernardin de Sienne.

Cette contribution s'intéresse aux contours de cette sainteté. Elle examine les modalités de la pastorale mise en œuvre par Capistran, véritable « saint vivant », grâce aux reliques de son maître et ami – une pastorale du miracle qu'il est possible d'appréhender, en particulier, grâce au travail de frères qui ont accompagné le réformateur italien dans son périple et œuvré ensuite à la propagation des mérites de celui-ci. La façon dont Capistran a utilisé la sainteté de Bernardin pour la construction identitaire de l'Observance n'était pas sans ambiguïtés pour sa propre sainteté. Curieusement, les traces de dévotion envers saint Bernardin, y compris en Pologne, sont assez peu nombreuses. En définitive, il faut s'interroger sur la portée de ce qui a peut-être été la principale conséquence de cet usage intensif de la sainteté d'un homme érigé en véritable modèle et en père fondateur : une sorte de « figure totémique » et un nom, celui de « Bernardins ».

Anna ZAJCHOWSKA, *Medieval Hagiography of St Hyacinth*

Medieval hagiography of St Hyacinth (Jacek) († 1257), a disciple of Saint Dominic and the founder of the Polish Province of Dominicans, is surprisingly limited to a few texts only. The most important of them is a fourteenth century De vita et miraculis sancti Hiacynthi written by a Polish Dominican friar named Stanislas. It's the main source for a biography of the Dominican saint and at the same time the only testimony of a lost book of miracles from the thirteenth century. De vita et miraculis is followed by a fifteenth-century list of miracles and a rhymed poem about the saint written by a Renaissance poet, Nicholas Hussoviensis.

All those works are related to various attempts made to bring about the canonisation of Hyacinth, which eventually happened in 1595. It turned out that even though Polish Dominicans were very active in the field of promoting cults of local Polish saints (mainly those coming from Krakow), they were not effective enough in terms of promoting their own candidate for sainthood. The article provides, on the one hand, a summary of hitherto research on the hagiography of St Hyacinth, known to date first of all to Polish researchers, and, on the other hand, it outlines an entire spectrum of various types of sources, with hitherto unknown ones, related to the Polish saint and places them in the context of canonisation efforts.

INDEX

Index nominum

Adalbert, évêque de Prague (saint) : 22-24, 26, 33, 38, 60, 63, 69, 247-260, 276-278, 287, 343, 345-346
Agnès, martyre (sainte) : 41
Agnès de Bohême ou de Prague (sainte) : 16, 19, 36, 38, 125-171, 332-333, 338-339
Agnès d'Assise : 161-162, 169
Agnès de Beřkovic, abbesse : 131
Agnès de Peranda (ou Barcelone) : 161
Aignan (saint) : 25, 345
Alain de Lille : 8
Albert de Sarajevo, évêque : 169
Alexis (saint) : 27, 336, 350
Alexandre IV, pape : 151, 153
Alexandre V, pape : 266-267
Alexandre de *Muschna* : 47
Albert de Šternberk, évêque : 23
Alberzoni, Maria Pia : 227
Ambrogio Taegio, dominicain : 218, 335
André, apôtre (saint) : 39, 322
André, évêque de Transylvanie : 53
André Ier, roi de Hongrie : 345-346
André de Parczow, dominicain polonais : 205
Andrić, Stanko : 235, 239
Andrioc, roi fictif des Hongrois : 345
Ange Clareno : 180
Angevins, dynastie : 24, 175, 288, 344, 349
Anne, mère de Marie (sainte) : 28, 320, 322, 325
Anne, épouse de l'empereur Henri II : 153
Anne de Kiev, reine de Hongrie : 345
Anne, veuve de Jacques Golschmidt : 55-56
Anne, habitante de Sânmartin : 116
Antoine le Grand, ermite : 102, 294, 298, 303, 331
Antoine de Padoue : 189

Antoine, chanoine de Transylvanie : 48-49
Antoine Heem : 50
Antonin (saint) : 28
Antonio Bonfini, historiographe : 112
Apolline (sainte) : 321, 325
Arnobius le Jeune : 79
Arpadiens, dynastie : 49, 96, 249, 281, 288
Athanase, hagiographe : 302
Attila, chef des Huns : 346
Augustin (saint) : 332
Aymeric de Plaisance : 215

Babenberg, dynastie : 126, 285
Bajazet Ier, sultan ottoman : 109
Bánfi, Florio : 284
Barbe (Barbara), martyre (sainte) : 39-45, 47-50, 52, 56, 103, 320-322, 324-325, 331
Barthélemy, apôtre (saint) : 256
Barthélemy, habitant d'Erdővég : 117-118
Barthélemy de Pise, chroniqueur franciscain : 133, 136, 167, 178, 243
Bartolomeo dal Bovo : 88-89
Bartoniek, Emma : 284
Baudouin, archevêque de Trêves : 62
Béatrice d'Aragon, reine d'Hongrie : 106
Behaim : 46-47
Béla Ier, roi de Hongrie : 346
Béla III, roi de Hongrie : 281
Beneš Krabice de Weitmil : 72-73
Benno, évêque de Meissen : 7
Benoît de Nursie (saint) : 252, 254
Benoît XII, pape : 132
Benoît, habitant de la région du Timiş (Temes) : 115
Benoît de Löwenberg, custode : 230
Beran, Josef : 138, 145
Bernard de Clairvaux (saint) : 321

INDEX

Bernardin de Sienne (saint) : 14-15, 227-243, 325, 329, 332, 337, 339
Bernard Gui, inquisiteur : 57, 215
Blaise, martyr (saint) : 97, 295, 321
Blaise Sárkány de Csanád, noble : 118
Blaise de Szentgyörgy : 118
Bok, Václav : 145
Boleslas Ier, duc de Bohême : 32
Boleslas II, duc de Bohême : 32
Boleslas (Bolesław) le Vaillant, duc de Pologne : 22, 251-253, 255, 257-258
Boleslas II, roi de Pologne : 262-263, 272, 330
Boleslas Bouchetorse, duc de Pologne : 259
Boleslas V le Chaste, duc de Cracovie : 274
Boleslav : voir Boleslas
Bolle, Pierre : 88
Bonagrazia Tielci, ministre général : 130, 184
Bonaventure (saint) : 143, 178, 179, 184, 190, 243
Boniface de Ceva, franciscain colétan : 229
Bonmann, Ottokar : 234
Botticelli : 81
Bovo (saint) : 90
Brentano, Robert James : 12
Bretislas Ier, duc de Bohême : 22, 24, 34, 60, 258, 349
Břetislav : voir Bretislas
Brigitte de Suède (sainte) : 333
Brunon de Querfurt : 248, 256, 258, 345

Casimir (saint) : 8
Casimir, duc polonais : 258
Casimir le Juste, duc de Cracovie : 267
Catherine d'Alexandrie, martyre (sainte) : 40-53, 55-56, 102, 321, 325, 331
Catherine Hoffmann, abbesse : 159, 164
Catherine de Sienne (sainte) : 186, 191-193, 205
Cécile, martyre (sainte) : 49
Ceslas (bienheureux) : 16-17, 196-197, 199
de Cevins, Marie-Madeleine : 7
Charlemagne, empereur : 33, 60, 64

Charles le Chauve, empereur : 85
Charles IV, empereur romain germanique : 22, 24, 27, 32, 36, 58-64, 66, 68-76, 132-133, 135, 143, 167-168, 170, 330, 342
Charles IV, roi de France : 60
Charles Ier (Charles-Robert), roi de Hongrie : 334, 344, 347
Charles II, roi de Sicile : 345
Charles le Téméraire, duc de Bourgogne : 85
Chartreux anonyme, chroniqueur : 176, 189-192
Chiffoleau, Jacques : 86
Christian Baumann, prêtre de Cluj : 52, 54
Christophe (saint) : 103
Christophe de Varèse : 236-238
Claire d'Assise (sainte) : 49, 127-128, 134, 143, 150, 155, 161, 166, 168, 170, 181, 189, 233, 338
Clément VI, pape : 68-70, 83
Colette de Corbie (sainte) : 244
Coloman, roi de Hongrie : 285
Côme et Damien (saints) : 39, 103, 350
Conrad, margrave de Thuringe : 334
Conrad de Freystadt : 235, 239
Conrad d'Offida : 180, 185-186
Conrad de Trebensee : 224
Conrad de Waldhausen : 13
Conrad de Worms : 151
Constance, princesse arpadienne : 126, 144
Constantin, empereur : 31
Cosmas de Prague, chroniqueur : 35, 258
Cristoforo da Soldo : 233
Cunégonde de Cracovie ou de Pologne : 16-18, 264, 274
Czesław : voir Ceslas

Daniel, évêque de Prague : 33
Deák, Viktória : 334
Dehoux, Esther : 343
Démétrios ou Démétrius (saint) : 27, 350
Démétrius Kónya, noble hongrois : 113-114, 117, 118
Démétrius Mezesi, évêque d'Oradea : 40

INDEX

Denis, martyr (saint) : 252, 254
Diacetto : 219
Dioclétien, empereur romain : 78, 270-271
Domenico da Vincenza : 88-89, 91-92
Dominique (saint) : 15, 195, 197, 202, 206, 211, 221, 264, 332, 336, 338-339
Domislas de Squorz : 144
Domka de Squorz, religieuse : 144, 147
Dormeier, Heinrich : 91
Dorothée, martyre (sainte) : 40, 42-44, 48, 103
Drahomíra : 31

Eberhard, Winfried : 61
Édouard le Confesseur (saint) : 22
Élémosine, Clarisse italienne : 166
Élie, prophète : 202
Élie de Cortone : 183
Élisabeth, reine de Bohême : 36, 130-131, 147
Élisabeth Piast, reine de Hongrie : 175, 334
Élisabeth de Hongrie (sainte) : 15, 19, 21, 49, 127, 135, 139, 143, 150, 333-334, 339, 348
Élisabeth de Töss : 15
Éloi (saint) : 24, 315-316, 319-320, 342
Émeric (saint) : 26, 49, 103, 281-282, 284-288, 300-301, 347
Émeric Zudar, évêque de Transylvanie : 53
Emmeran (saint) : 33
Entz, Géza : 39
Ermentrude de Bruges : 155
Ernest de Pardubice, évêque de Prague : 10, 37
Esculape : 256
Étienne Ier de Hongrie, roi de Hongrie (saint) : 21, 26, 49, 103, 112, 249, 281-288, 300, 336, 347-348
Étienne V, roi de Hongrie : 334
Étienne, évêque de Transylvanie : 52
Étienne Horvát : 114, 120
Étienne de Salagnac, dominicain : 215, 217
Étienne de Szapolya, comte de Spiš : 103
Eugène II, pape : 80

Fabien (saint) : 92-98, 101-102, 107
Febvre, Lucien : 327

Felix Fabri : 105, 166
Filippo di Neri dell'Antella, prieur : 82
Florent, évêque de Strasbourg : 61
Florian (saint) : 22, 49, 261, 267-269, 276-281, 330
Foulques de Chanac : 82
Francesco Diedo : 88, 89, 92, 105
François d'Assise (saint) : 13-15, 49, 134, 143, 173, 176, 183-194, 241, 244, 321, 323, 332, 338-339
Franz Günthers : 242
Frédéric III de Habsbourg, empereur germanique : 287
Fried, Johannes : 247-248, 255

Gabriele de' Mussi, notaire : 82
Gallus Anonymus : 256, 259, 262
Gallus d'Esztergom : 16
Garin de Gy-l'Évêque : 335, 338-339
Gaudentius-Radim : 26, 251-253, 255
Gédéon (Gedko), évêque de Cracovie : 267, 270
Geffrey Chaucer : 58
Georg Barthold Pontanus de Breitenberg : 136
Georg Kruger, jésuite : 136
Georges, martyr (saint) : 69, 85, 103, 247, 294, 303-304, 322, 328, 331, 344
Georges *Ferus* (Plachý) : 136-137
Georges de Hongrie (*Georgius de Hungaria*) : 111, 120-121
Georges Lépes, évêque de Transylvanie : 39-40, 43, 48-49
Georges Pállócz, évêque de Transylvanie : 43
Gérard Sagredo, évêque de Cenad (saint) : 285, 299, 347
Gérard de Frachet : 212
Gerát, Ivan : 335
Géza, frère de Ladislas Ier de Hongrie : 309
Giacomo Filippo Foresti de Bergame : 106
Gieben, Servus : 243
Gieysztor, Aleksander : 20, 247, 341-342
Gilles (saint) : 24, 69, 342
Gilles li Muisis, chroniqueur : 83

Gilles d'Esztergom: 16
Gilles de Modène, évêque: 270
Giovanni del Biondo: 84
Giovanni Marignolli: 132
Gisèle de Bavière, reine de Hongrie: 283
Gothard (saint): 24-25
Grégoire le Grand, pape (saint): 80-81
Grégoire V, pape: 252
Grégoire IX, pape: 129, 184
Grégoire XIII, pape: 208
Grégoire, tailleur hongrois: 115
Guibert, roi des Lombards: 81
Guiglielma, sœur d'Agnès de Bohème: 126, 146
Guilelma di Chiaravalle: 126
Günther (Vintíř): 20, 35, 38
Guta: voir Judith
Guy, martyr (saint): 22-23, 36, 38, 59, 61, 63, 69, 88
Guy, évêque et dominicain polonais: 199, 275
Guy, prêtre de l'église Saint-Florian de Cracovie: 269

Hammerschmid, Johann Florian: 154
Hartmann Schedel: 106, 206
Hartuic (Hartvik), évêque hagiographe: 285-286
Hedwige d'Anjou: 279
Hedwige d'Andechs (sainte): 103, 126, 143, 203-204, 231, 335
Hedwige de Cieszyn: 103
Héléna (sainte): 235
Hélène (sainte): 31
Hélène de Hongrie, religieuse dominicaine: 15-16, 338
Hélène de Gara: 116
Henri IV, empereur germanique: 309
Henri VII, empereur germanique: 127
Henri II, roi d'Angleterre: 74
Henri Ier, roi de France: 346
Henri Ier l'Oiseleur, roi de Saxe: 22, 59
Henri II, duc de Bavière puis empereur germanique: 153, 250, 257-258, 283, 286, 348
Henri de Heimburg: 129
Herman Niemiec: 197

Hermann Vlkoš, consul de Kutná Hora: 130
Hermogène, sorcier: 302
Hilduin: 80
Hlaváček, Petr: 14, 325
Hofer, Johannes: 234
Hohenstaufen, dynastie: 127
Honorat de Lérins: 345
Hroznata, chanoine prémontré: 35-38
Hugolin, cardinal d'Ostie: 129
Humbert de Romans: 212-213
Hyacinthe, dominicain (saint): 9, 16, 17, 195-209, 275, 279, 329, 333-334, 337

Innocent III, pape: 34, 285
Innocent IV, pape: 35, 151, 267
Innocent VI, pape: 75
Isaïe Boner, ermite augustinien: 16, 18, 280
Iwo Odrowąż, évêque de Cracovie: 197

Jacques, apôtre (saint): 24, 88, 104, 294, 296, 299, 302, 304-306, 322-323, 325, 328
Jacques de Brescia: 236
Jacques Bulkescher: 52, 54
Jacques (Jakub) Joanides Streller, dominicain: 207
Jacques de la Marche (saint): 243
Jacques (de) Strepa: 16, 17, 333, 339
Jacques de Velletri, franciscain: 264
Jacques de Voragine (Varazze): 82, 101, 107, 287, 334
Jagellons, dynastie: 9, 349
Jansen, Philippe: 236
Jaroslav le Sage, prince de Kiev: 345
Jean, apôtre et évangéliste (saint): 328
Jean XXII, pape: 36, 130
Jean Ier de Luxembourg, roi de Bohême: 130-132
Jean l'Aumônier (saint): 9, 112
Jean Baptiste (saint): 39, 247, 328
Jean Canaparius: 247
Jean (de) Capistran: 15, 112-114, 116-120, 228, 230-244, 328-329, 332, 336-337, 339-340, 342
Jean (Jan) Długosz: 204, 276-277
Jean de Dąbrówka: 278
Jean de Dražice: 131

INDEX

Jean de Dukla : 16
Jean Figuera : 233
Jean Gaetanus Orsini : voir Nicolas III
Jean de Gara : 119
Jean Henckel : 305
Jean Hus : 10, 28, 37
Jean de Jenštejn, archevêque de Prague : 10, 37-38, 68
Jean de Kęty (*Cantius*) : 11, 203, 280, 329
Jean de Lazo, archidiacre de Tileagd : 105
Jean (Johannes) Meyer : 217-218
Jean Népomucène : 25, 334
Jean de Nevers : 109
Jean Odrowąż de Szczekocin : 205
Jean Pecham, franciscain anglais : 178
Jean Pilecki : 205
Jean Rokycana : 231
Jean de Schwenkenfeld : 16, 17, 333
Jean de Słupca, prédicateur : 278
Jean Tanner, jésuite : 136
Jean le Teutonique : 17
Jean-Paul II, pape : 17
Jeanne d'Arc (sainte) : 7
Jeanne de Laval : 345
Jérôme (saint) : 27
Jérôme Borselli : 205, 217, 335-336, 338
Jérôme de Prague : 37
Johann Eberlin de Günzburg : 243
Johan Jacob Vogel : 234
Johannes Henckel, prêtre à Levoča : 305
Jourdain, dominicain : 199
Joseph (saint) : 103, 322, 325
Josse Lieferinxe : 83
Judith, personnage biblique : 297
Judith de Bohême, princesse de Pologne : 24, 342
Judith de Habsbourg, reine de Bohême : 147
Jules II, pape : 230

Kinga : voir Cunégonde
Klaniczay, Gábor : 334, 338
Kłoczowski, Jerzy : 13, 240
Körmendy, Kinga : 284
Kowalczyk, Maria : 204
Kubínová, Kateřina : 27
Kwietusza, habitante de Cracovie : 269

Ladislas : voir aussi Vladislas
Ladislas, roi de Hongrie (saint) : 26, 49, 78, 93, 103, 112, 281, 282, 284-288, 293-310, 331, 344-345, 347-348
Ladislas IV, roi de Hongrie : 334
Ladislas de Gielniów : 16, 339
Lambert (saint) : 328
Lanéry, Cécile : 80
Lauf, Judit : 282
Laurent, martyr (saint) : 39, 103, 321, 328, 343
Laurent Pignon, dominicain : 217
Lazare : 62
Léandre Alberti : 205, 219
Léon X : 94, 195
Léon, frère mineur : 186, 188
Léon, grand maître des Croisiers : 169
Léonard (saint) : 320
Léopold VI Babenberg, duc d'Autriche : 127
Lévi-Strauss, Claude : 8
Loenertz, Raymond J. : 196-197, 200
Lothaire III, empereur : 25
Louis IX, roi de France (saint) : 321
Louis Ier le Grand, roi de Hongrie : 283, 336
Louis de Toulouse ou d'Anjou, évêque (saint) : 24, 329, 348
Louis le Pieux, empereur : 80
Louis IX, roi de France : 59, 62, 135, 346
Lubomerczyk, Seweryn : 196
Luc, apôtre et évangéliste (saint) : 316, 319
Lucius III, pape : 270
Ludmila (sainte) : 21, 31-33, 36, 38, 69, 347
Lupa, reine : 306
Luxembourg, dynastie : 349

Magyar, Arnold : 179
Maître Martin : voir Martin, peintre
Maître Vincent : voir Vincent
Marc (saint) : 63
Marc de Bologne, vicaire cismontain : 229
Marcel, confesseur dominicain : 336
Marguerite d'Antioche, martyre (sainte) : 41-42, 103, 331
Marguerite de Cortone : 135

INDEX

Marguerite de Hongrie (sainte) : 16, 23, 186, 329, 331, 335, 338-339, 348
Marianus de Florence, chroniqueur : 171
Marie, mère de Jésus (sainte) : 9, 39, 40, 49, 54, 83, 87, 179, 297, 317, 320-322, 324, 328
Marie : voir Mlada
Marie Madeleine (sainte) : 304-305
Marin, Olivier : 7, 31, 235, 327, 341, 345
Marketa, fille de Judith de Bohême : 149
Martin (saint) : 252, 321, 328, 343
Martin, peintre : 103
Martin V, pape : 7
Martin de Beřkovic : 131
Martin Tinctoris, frère mineur : 244
Martin Schongauer : 104, 304
Maternus, évêque de Transylvanie : 53
Mathias Ier Corvin, roi de Hongrie : 51, 105, 114, 331
Mathieu, habitant de Kő : 117
Matthias Döring, provincial de Saxe : 228, 231
Matthias de Janov : 10
Maur (saint) : 252
Maurice (saint) : 26, 247, 328, 343
Maurice de Csák : 16, 335-338, 348
Maximilien, empereur romain : 78
Mazzili Savini, Maria Teresa : 79
Médard, martyr (saint) : 80
Mengel, David : 22
Menhart, abbé de Břevnov : 35
Michel, archange (saint) : 39, 103, 321, 328, 341, 343-344
Michel de Césène : 132
Michel de Szilágy, régent de Hongrie : 114
Miklós Oláh : 112
Mileszka : 199
Milíč de Kroměříž, prédicateur : 10, 37, 38
Mlada (Marie) : 32
Moïse : 243
Moraw, Peter : 26

Nagy, Emese : voir Sarkadi Nagy
Nagy, László : 285
Nanker, évêque de Cracovie : 202
Nicolas, martyr (saint) : 51, 132, 301, 308, 321
Nicolas III, pape : 142, 266

Nicolas, évêque pragois : 130
Nicolas de Fara : 238
Nicolas Glassberger : 157, 159, 233
Nicolas *Hussoviensis* (Hussowczyk), poète : 195, 207, 208
Nicolas Kamieniecki de Pilawa : 206
Nicolas *Moravus*, provincial franciscain de Bohême : 36, 150
Nicolas Mün, échevin de Cluj : 52, 54
Nicolas d'Osimo, franciscain : 228
Norbert de Xanten : 35-36
Notker (Notger), évêque de Liège : 248, 256

Obertyński, Zdzisław : 196
Odilon de Saint-Médard : 80
Oldřich, duc de Bohême : 34
Opicino de Canistris, chroniqueur : 81
Ó Riain, Diarmuid : 286
Oswald de Lug (Laskó), prédicateur : 174
Ottokar Ier, roi de Bohême : 125-127, 141
Ottokar II, roi de Bohême : 35, 129, 154, 285
Otton II, empereur germanique : 250
Otton III, empereur germanique : 33, 247, 250, 252-255, 257, 260, 346
Otton IV, margrave de Brandebourg : 142

Pacindova, Laura : 335
Palacký, František : 126
Paul, apôtre (saint) : 27, 183, 190, 202, 242, 254, 328
Paul l'Ermite (saint) : 112-116, 119, 342
Paul de Hongrie, dominicain : 219, 335
Paul V, pape : 208
Paul, menuisier hongrois : 115
Paul Diacre : 79, 107
Paul de Zator, prédicateur : 278
Pelbart de Timișoara (Temesvár), prédicateur : 45, 101, 187, 189, 335
Pérégrin d'Opole, prédicateur : 14, 174, 195, 199, 278, 335, 337, 339
Piast(es), dynastie : 202, 249-250, 252, 258, 343
Pie II, pape : 192, 205
Pie XI, pape : 138
Pierre, apôtre (saint) : 27, 39, 70, 79, 247, 320-321, 328, 343

Pierre Clarificator, chanoine : 10
Pierre Imhoff l'Ancien : 91
Pierre de Rosenberg : 70
Pierre de Vérone ou Pierre Martyr (saint) : 15, 17, 199, 211, 213-214, 221-223, 332, 334
Pietro Barrozzi, évêque de Padoue : 90
Pietro Ranzano (Petrus Ranzanus) : 112
Pierre de Zittau (Žitavský) : 130
Pilecki, Mikołaj : 205
Plantagenêt, dynastie : 127
Pomian, Krzysztof : 27
Prandota, évêque de Cracovie : 203, 263, 273, 275, 279, 329
Přemyslides, dynastie : 21, 31, 34, 126, 144, 249, 250, 251, 255, 257-258
Přibík Pulkava de Radenín, chroniqueur : 168
Procope, ermite (saint) : 23, 24, 34-36, 38, 330-331
Pruszcz, Piotr : 239

Racco (Rocco) d'Autun : 88
Radim : voir Gaudentius-Radim
Rainald de Jenne : voir Alexandre IV
Rainald (Reginald, Rinaldo) d'Ostie : voir Alexandre V
Raphaël de Proszowice : 16, 339
Raymond de Capoue : 192
René d'Anjou, roi de Sicile et duc d'Anjou : 345
Richard, habitant de Cracovie : 268
Roberto Caracciolo, franciscain : 189, 191-193
Roch, martyr (saint) : 77, 78, 87-92, 103-108, 342, 343, 346
Rodolphe de Habsbourg, empereur germanique : 129
Ruh, Kurt : 160

Sadoch, dominicain hongrois : 219
Salomé de Galicie (Halicz) ou de Pologne : 16-18, 200, 203, 274
Salomon, roi (fictif) des Hongrois : 309-310

Sarkadi Nagy, Emese : 104
Sébastien, martyr (saint) : 77, 78, 80, 82-87, 91-103, 107, 328, 342-343
Sensi, Mario : 91
Seton, Walter Warren : 138
Séverin de Lubomel : 206
Séverin, évêque de Prague : 258
Sigismond, roi des Burgondes (saint) : 23, 36-38, 64-66, 75, 330
Sigismond de Luxembourg, roi de Hongrie, de Bohême et empereur germanique : 43, 109, 344
Sigismond Ferrari : 335
Sigismond Rosicz, clerc : 232
Simon, chapelain : 137
Simon de Kéza, chroniqueur : 346
Simon de Lipnica : 11, 16-17, 203, 239, 279-280, 329, 337
Simone Martini : 344
Sixte IV, pape : 192
Slavnik, duc : 248
Slavnikides, dynastie : 248, 250-252, 255
Slíz, Mariann : 97
Sobieslas (Sobiěslav) Ier, duc de Bohême : 25, 252
Sophie, reine de Pologne : 204-205
Spież, Jan Andrzej : 196
Stanislas, évêque de Cracovie (saint) : 14, 26, 69, 195, 201, 261-280, 282, 287, 329, 337, 347, 350
Stanislas, *lector* dominicain : 195-196, 198, 201, 204, 208-209
Stanislas, enfant polonais : 273
Stanislas Kazimierczyk, franciscain observant : 11, 279-280
Starnawska, Maria : 201
Starzyński, Marcin : 235, 239
Stejskal, Karel : 298
Šternberk ou Sternberg, lignage noble : 144, 148, 150
Svipert de Porroch (*Porrochia*) : 213-225, 336
Swanson, Robert N. : 58, 74
Sylvestre Ier, pape : 80
Sylvestre II, pape : 33

Théodoric, chapelain du roi de Bohême : 142
Théophano, impératrice : 251
Thierry d'Apolda, hagiographe dominicain : 224, 334
Thietmar, évêque de Prague : 32
Thomas, apôtre (saint) : 82
Thomas d'Aquin (saint) : 200, 202, 206
Thomas Becket (saint) : 330
Thomas (Tamás) Bakócz : 93
Thomas de Bechyně, évêque de Prague : 130
Thomas de Cantimpré : 216-217
Thomas de Celano : 143, 184
Thomas Müntzer : 242
Thomas Štitný, chevalier : 23
Thomas de Sycow : 207
Tobias de Bechyně, évêque de Prague : 130
Tommaso Caffarini : 192

Uhlíř, Zdeněk : 8
Ulric de Paběnic, vicaire de Prague : 139
Urbain Ier, pape : 62
Urbain IV, pape : 153
Ursule, martyre (sainte) : 41-42

Valentin d'Erdőd : 116
Valentin Hadnagy : 112-113
Vauchez, André : 5-10, 209, 220, 240, 266, 327, 329, 331, 341
Végh, János : 103
Venceslas (Wenceslas), duc de Bohême (saint) : 21-23, 26, 28, 31, 33-34, 36, 38, 59-60, 63-65, 259, 267, 276-278, 282, 286-287, 317, 321-322, 324, 325, 330, 337, 347
Venceslas (Wenceslas) Ier, roi de Bohême : 127

Venceslas (Wenceslas) II, roi de Bohême : 147
Venceslas (Wenceslas) IV, roi de Bohême : 133, 317
Véronique, habitante de Cracovie : 277
Victorin (saint) : 23
Vincent, Catherine : 328
Vincent, Nicholas : 76
Vincent (Maître Vincent), chroniqueur polonais : 262, 265-266, 273
Vincent Ferrier (saint) : 205
Vincent d'Izsép : 106
Vincent de Kielcza : 198, 201, 273, 337
Vintíř : voir Günther
Vizkelety, András : 285
Vladislas (Ladislas) Ier Hermann, duc de Pologne : 24, 342
Vojtěch : voir Adalbert de Prague
Vyskočil, Jan Kapistran : 138-139, 142, 145

Wadding, Luke : 155
Wenceslas : voir Venceslas
Willigis, archevêque de Mayence : 251
Williko, prévôt de Prague : 251
Wislaus, évêque de Cracovie : 263
Witkowska, Aleksandra : 11, 196, 203, 280
Wojciech Jastrzębiec, évêque de Cracovie : 279
Wolfgang, martyr (saint) : 49, 103, 320-321, 324, 349
Woroniecki, Jacek : 200, 202

Zavis Rosenberg (Rožmberk) : 285
Zajchowska, Anna : 235, 239
Zbigniew Oleśnicki : 196, 204, 276, 279
Zdislava, femme noble de Bohême : 36, 38

Index locorum

Admont : 286
Afille : 33
Agaune : 22, 64
Aix-en-Provence : 152
Aix-la-Chapelle : 33, 62, 119, 256-257, 283-284, 346
Alba Iulia (Gyulafehérvár, Weissenburg) : 39, 41, 43, 49, 94
Albigeois : 9, 11, 17
Alexandrie : 9, 11
Allemagne : 5, 26, 84, 101, 103-104, 256, 287, 334, 348
Almakerék : voir Mălâncrav
Alsace : 85
Alsóbajon : voir Boian
Andlau : 61
Angera : 92
Angleterre : 5, 6, 12, 127, 334
Aquapendente : 89
Arles : 22
Arnstadt : 235
Arnótfalva : voir Arnutovce
Arnutovce (Arnótfalva) : 103-104
Assise : 146, 151, 167, 171, 184, 267, 273, 338
Augsbourg : 45, 286, 289, 347
Autriche : 271, 279, 285-286, 348-349
Aventin : 251
Avignon : 86, 179

Bădeşti (Bádok) : 42
Bádok : voir Bădeşti
Băgaciu (Szászbogács, Bogeschdorf) : 41
Baltimore : 83
Bamberg : 233, 283, 286, 348
Banská Bystrica (Besztercebánya) : 304-305
Barcelone : 161
Bardejov (Bártfa) : 102, 104
Bari : 308

Bártfa : voir Bardejov
Báta, monastère : 112, 119
Bavière : 20, 250, 349
Beia (Homoródbene, Meerburg) : 41
Belgrade : 112, 114, 117, 118
Benešov-sur-Černa : 321
Bénévent : 256
Berény : voir Beriu
Berethalom : voir Biertan
Beriu : 40
Besztercze : voir Bistriţa
Besztercebánya : voir Banská Bystrica
Biertan (Berethalom, Birthälm) : 41, 46, 103, 104
Birka : 253
Bistriţa (Besztercze, Bistritz) : 40, 50, 51-52, 56, 105
Blatná : 322
Bogeschdorf : voir Băgaciu
Bögöz : voir Mugeni
Bohême : 7-8, 10, 14, 18, 20-21, 23-27, 31, 34-35, 37-38, 57, 59, 65, 129, 144, 171, 247-249, 251, 257, 259, 287, 311-325, 329, 330, 332, 334, 340, 347
Boian (Alsóbajon, Bonnesdorf) : 42
Bologne : 270, 338
Bonnesdorf : voir Boian
Bordeaux, chapitre : 199
Bošilec : 70
Bosnie : 219
Bosnie, vicairie observante : 182, 336
Braller : voir Bruiu
Brandebourg : 349
Braşov (Brassó, Kronstadt) : 41, 53, 110
Bratislava (Pozsony, Presbourg) : 99, 152, 284, 310, 328
Brescia : 233, 235
Breslau : voir Wrocław
Břevnov, monastère : 20, 35

373

Broumov : 323
Bruges : 84
Bruiu (Brulya, Braller) : 104
Brüx : voir Most
Buda : 21, 112, 332, 344
Budaszentlőrinc : 112
Bulgarie : 27

Cagliari : 233
Cahors, chapitre : 184
Campo Verano : 270
Canterbury : 57
Čáslav (Tschaslau), monastère : 131
Césène (Cesena) : 89
České Budějovice : 315, 320, 323-324
Český Krumlov : 70, 169, 320, 322, 324
Cheb : voir Eger
Chilieni (Kilyén) : 42
Cisnădi (Nagydisznód, Heltau) : 104
Cluj (Kolozsvár, Klausenburg) : 42, 50, 52-56, 100, 105
Cluj-Mănăştur (Kolozsmonostor) : 53-54
Cojocna : 40, 48
Cologne : 284
Comtat Venaissin : 86
Constance : 10, 37
Constantinople : 27, 114
Corvey : 22, 249
Cracovie : 9, 11, 106, 195, 196, 200-201, 203, 206, 209, 230, 235, 239-240, 250, 252, 258, 261, 265-272, 273, 275, 279-280, 282, 330, 333, 350
Crossen : voir Krosno Odrzańskie
Cseri : voir Sacoşu Turcesc
Csíkszentimre : voir Sântimbru
Csíkszentlélek : voir Leliceni

Daia (Szászdálya, Denndorf) : 42
Dalmatie : 219
Dantzig : voir Gdańsk
Daróc : voir Drăuşeni
Denndorf : voir Daia
Dömös, prieuré : 97
Dortmund : 257
Doxan : voir Doxany
Doxany (Doxan), monastère : 126

Drass : voir Drăuşeni
Drăuşeni (Daróc, Drass) : 42, 44
Dubenec : 70
Dumitra (Mettersdorf) : 50-51

Eger (Cheb), couvent de Clarisses : 137, 158, 163, 169
Eichstätt : 62
Erdevik (Erdővég) : 117
Erd-Šomljo (Érdsomlyó) : 332
Erstein : 61
Esztergom : 28, 33, 41, 43, 49, 93, 99, 282, 306, 333, 337, 348

Fábiánsebestyén : 99
Felfalu : voir Suşeni
Felsőtatárlaka : voir Tătârlaua
Ferrare : 205, 229, 335
Finlande : 283
Fleury : 252, 254
Florence : 83
Florentia : voir Kleparz
Foligno : 83
France : 5, 19, 24, 60, 328, 334
Friesach, couvent : 197

Galicie : 349
Garamszentbenedek : voir Hronský Beňadik
Gdańsk (Dantzig) : 197, 253-254
Gelence : voir Ghelinta
Ghelinta (Gelence) : 42
Georgenberg : voir Spišská Sobota
Glanfeuil : 252
Glogau : voir Głogów
Głogów (Glogau) : 241
Goldberg : voir Złotoryja
Gniezno : 24, 33-34, 200, 253, 255-259, 267, 330, 346, 348-349
Görlitz : 244
Goslar : 257
Gotzlin : voir Kolín
Graz : 285, 287
Grossprobstdorf : voir Proştea Mare
Gubbio : 182
Gyöngyös : 106
Győr : 99, 335

INDEX

Gyulafehérvár : voir Alba Iulia

Haguenau : 45
Hainaut, monastère Saint-Pierre : 82
Haithabu : 253
Haslach : 61
Heiligenkreuz : 285, 289
Heltau : voir Cisnădi
Hermannsdorf : 40
Hermannstadt : voir Sibiu
Herrieden : 63
Hohenfurth : voir Vyšší Brod
Homoródbene : voir Beia
Homoródszentmárton : voir Mărtiniş
Hongrie : 7, 15, 18, 19, 21, 24, 27, 33, 41, 60, 77, 92, 93, 95, 96-102, 106-108, 109-110, 121, 174, 182, 219, 237, 247, 259, 281, 282, 283, 288, 294, 328, 329, 330, 331, 332, 333, 335, 340, 342, 347, 350
Horšovský Týn : 322
Hradec Králové : 318
Hronský Beňadik (Garamszentbenedek) : 301

Iglau : voir Jihlava
Île aux Lièvres [à Budapest] : 175, 337
Ilok (Újlak) : 15, 112, 116, 118, 119, 332, 336
Imper (Kászonimpér) : 42
Ingelheim : 257
Isola Tiberina : 256
Italie : 5-6, 10, 12, 19, 77, 89, 104, 228, 238, 287, 339, 348

(Sv.) Jakub : 304-306
Janovce (Jánosfalva) : 103
Jérusalem : 57
Jičín : 322
Jihlava (Iglau) : 141
Jimbor (Székelyzsombor, Sommerburg) : 42
Jirkov : 321
Jungfernteinitz : voir Panenský Týnec
Jüterborg : 242

Kadaň : 321, 323, 325
Kájov : 324
Kakaslomnic : voir Veľka Lomnica
Kamenz : 230, 240

Kaplice : 321
Karaszkó : voir Kraskovo
Karlštejn (Karlstein) : 61, 68, 71
Kászonimpér : voir Imper
Kazimierz : 280
Keisd (Százkézd, Saschiz) : 100
Kiev : 197, 208, 250
Kilyén : voir Chilieni
Kisselyk : voir Şeica Mică
Klatovy (Klattau) : 131, 318
Klausenburg : voir Cluj
Kleparz (*Clepardia, Florentia*) : 268
Kłodzko : 37
Kő : 117
Kolín (Gotzlin) : 131, 317
Kolozs : voir Cojocna
Kolozsmonostor : voir Cluj-Mănăştur
Kolozsvár : voir Cluj
Korsendonck : 291
Košice : 99
Kosovo Polje : 110
Kraskovo (Karaszkó) : 298
Krasnik : 291
Kremnica (Körmöcbánya) : 308
Kronstadt : voir Braşov
Krosno Odrzańskie (Crossen) : 241
Krupka : 324
Kutná Hora : 38, 130, 318, 322

L'Aquila : 229
Lammdorf : voir Beriu
Latium : 256
La Verna : 184
Lechfeld, bataille : 249
Leipzig : 232, 234
Leliceni (Csíkszentlélek) : 42
Lérins : 345
Lešan : 144
Levoča (Lőcse) : 102, 104, 305
Libice : 248, 250, 252
Liège : 33, 248, 256
Lilienfeld : 285, 289
Limoges, couvent dominicain : 216
Linz : 271
Litoměřice : 68
Litomyšl : 23
Lituanie : 349

INDEX

Lőcse : voir Levoča
Loket : 324
Lombardie : 90, 108
Lomnice-sur-Lužnice : 321
Longchamp, couvent : 152
Lourdes : 58
Lövöld (Városlőd), prieuré : 189, 287
Łowicz : 207
Lubeck : 283, 304
Luckau : 62
Lucques : 224
Luisberg : 257
Lusace : 230, 241

Macău (Makó) : 115
Magdebourg : 23, 26, 250, 253-254, 257, 347
Maghreb : 348
Makó : voir Macău
Mălâncrav (Almakerék, Malmkrog) : 41-42
Malmkrog : voir Mălâncrav
Mantoue : 162
Marcali : 346
Marchfeld, bataille : 129
Mareit : 304
Maroc : 241
Marosszentkirály : voir Sâncraiul de Mureş
Marseille, église Notre-Dame des Accoules : 83
Mărtiniş (Homoródszentmárton, Sankt Marten) : 42
Martorana : 297
Matejovce : 300
Mayence : 71, 249, 252-253, 290
Meerburg : voir Beia
Melk : 285, 289, 291
Mělnik : 131
Mersebourg : 257
Meschen : voir Moşna
Mettersdorf : voir Dumitra
Milan : 88, 126, 138, 142, 156, 167
Milanais : 211
Moldavie : 349
Mondsee : 290
Mont Cassin : 251, 254, 256, 302
Monteluce, couvent de Clarisses : 152
Monticelli, couvent de Clarisses : 152, 162

Moravie : 14, 144, 149, 231
Moşna (Muzsna, Meschen) : 41, 46-47
Mošovce (Mosóc) : 303, 305
Most (Brüx) : 136, 314-315, 318-319, 321, 325
Mugeni (Bögöz) : 42
Munich : 166
Muzsna : voir Moşna

Nagydisznód : voir Cisnădi
Nagyekemező : voir Proştea Mare
Nagypetri : voir Petrindu
Nagyszeben : voir Sibiu
Nagyvárad : voir Oradea
Naples : 152, 345, 347
Niemesch : voir Nemşa
Neisse : voir Nysa
Nemşa (Szásznemes, Niemesch) : 42
Nikopol (Nicopolis) : 109-110
Nitra (Nyitra) : 93
Norique : 268
Novara : 87
Noyon : 342
Nuremberg : 47, 63, 91, 106, 157, 159, 160, 162, 163, 166, 168, 170, 233, 235, 284
Nyitra : voir Nitra
Nysa (Neisse) : 230

Óbuda, couvent de Clarisses : 175, 180
Olomouc : 144, 149, 150
Oradea (Nagyvárad) : 78, 93, 97, 112, 299, 305

Padoue : 90, 162, 178, 270, 284
Palerme : 297
Panenský Týnec (Jungfernteinitz) : 132
Pannonhalma : 285
Paris : 13, 60, 178, 252
Passau : 271, 282, 284
Pavie : 79, 81, 90
Pays-Bas : 287
Pécs : 93, 99, 328
Peranda : 161
Pereo : 33
Pérouse : 229
Petrindu : 40
Pfullingen : 158
Pise : 70

Plaisance : 89
Plzeň : 313, 321, 323
Pologne : 18, 19, 21-22, 24, 26, 33, 60, 195, 202, 209, 230, 237, 240, 247-248, 261, 266, 272, 329, 333, 340, 342-343, 348, 350
Pologne-Lituanie : 7, 12
Poméranie : 259
Porroch : voir Sárospatak
Portioncule : 179
Poznań : 343
Pozsony : voir Bratislava
Prachatice : 321
Prague : 11, 22, 24, 27-28, 32-36, 59, 60-63, 65, 68, 70, 72-73, 75-76, 127, 130-131, 144, 152-153, 156-157, 167, 170, 197, 249-251, 267, 282, 312-317, 319, 322, 324, 342, 344, 348
Prázsmár : voir Toarcla
Presbourg : voir Bratislava
Prešov : 99, 301
Přeštice : 324
Proştea Mare (Nagyekemező, Grossprobstdorf) : 41-42
Provence : 345
Prusse : 33, 60, 197, 248, 259

Raguse : 114
Rakovník : 322
Ratisbonne : 32-33, 166, 249, 284, 325
Ravenne : 33, 256
Reichenau, abbaye : 33, 257, 346
Reims : 152
Rein : 289
Rokycany : 322
Rome : 6, 8, 27-28, 33, 57, 79, 81, 89, 93, 132, 197, 204, 208, 252, 254-257, 266, 337, 346
Roudnice : 8
Rouge-Cloître : 290
Rožmberk-sur-Vltava : 321
Rupella : voir Skałka
Rus : 197, 208

Sachsendorf : voir Sásová
Sacoşu Turcesc (Cseri) : 115, 118
Şaeş (Segesd, Schass) : 41, 46

Šahy (Ság) : 94
Saint-Jacques-de-Compostelle : 57
Saint-Victor, abbaye : 82
Sainte-Foy : 57
Sajan (Szaján) : 113
Salzburg : voir Cojocna
Salschelk : voir Şeica Mică
Salzbourg : 249
San Damiano : 128, 151, 162
Sankt Florian : 271, 279
Sankt Lambrecht : 290
Sankt Marten : voir Mărtiniş
San Pier Scheraggio, abbaye : 82
San Pietro in Vincoli : 79, 81
San Sebastiano fuori le mura : 78
Sant'Agata dei Goti : 80
Sant'Alberto : 256
Sântimbru (Csíkszentimre) : 42
Sandomierz : 16, 204, 206
Sâncraiul de Mureş (Marosszentkirály, Weichseldorf) : 42, 102
Sânmartin (Szentmárton) : 116
Sárkány : voir Şercaia
Sárospatak : 213, 214
Saschiz : voir Keisd
Sásová (Szászova/Zólyomszászfalu, Sachsendorf) : 302, 306-307
Saxe : 22, 349
Sázava, région de : 34
Scandinavie : 5
Schass : voir Şaeş
Schässburg : voir Sighişoara
Schirkanyen : voir Şercaia
Sedlec (Sedletz) : 131, 318
Segesd : voir Şaeş
Segesvár : voir Sighişoara
Şeica Mică : 40
Sieciechov : 291
Seiden : voir Tătârlaua
Seitz : 193, 287
Serbie : 349
Şercaia : 40
Šiba (Szekcsőalja) : 104-105
Šibenik, couvent franciscain : 131, 155, 169
Sibiu (Nagyszeben, Hermannstadt) : 41, 48-49, 56, 106
Sic (Szék) : 42

Siciu : 40
Sienne : 83, 152
Sieciechov : 291
Sighișoara (Segesvár, Schässburg) : 40
Silésie : 14, 18, 37-38, 126, 230, 237, 240, 241, 250, 349
Skala : 274
Skałka (Rupella) : 272, 276
Slavonie : 349
Slovaquie : 347
Smederevo (Szendrő) : 114, 117
Soběslav : 321
Söflingen (Ulm), couvent de Clarisses : 158
Șoimeni (Sólyomkő) : 100
Soissons : 80, 82
Sólyomkő : voir Șoimeni
Sombor : 99
Somlyószécs : voir Siciu
Sommerburg : voir Jimbor
Sopron : 100, 282
Spišská Sobota (Szepesszombat, Georgenberg) : 302-304
Stará Boleslav : 32
Stary Sącz : 274
Strasbourg : 61, 158, 282
Subiaco : 33, 256
Šumava, massif : 35
Sușeni (Felfalu) : 42, 114
Svätý Jur : 304
Syrmie (Szerémség) : 110
Szabolcs : 93, 328
Saján : voir Sajan
Szászbogács : voir Băgaciu
Szászdálya : voir Daia
Szászkézd : voir Keisd
Szásznemes : voir Nemșa
Szászova : voir Sásová
Szászvolkány : voir Vulcan
Szék : voir Sic
Szekcsőalja : voir Šiba
Székelyzsombor : voir Jimbor
Szendrő : voir Smederevo
Szentgyörgy : voir Svätý Jur
Szentmárton : voir Sânmartin
Szentsebestyén : 99
Szepesszombat : voir Spišská Sobota
Szerémség : voir Syrmie

Tachov : 323
Tarteln : voir Toarcla
Tassow : 144
Tătârlaua (Felsőtatárlaka, Seiden/Taterloch) : 41
Tegernsee : 291
Telegd : voir Tileagd
Temesvár : voir Timișoara
Teplá : 35, 323-324
Terracine : 256
Tetín : 31
Thorenburg : voir Turda
Thuringe : 21, 24, 35, 333
Tihany : 97, 345-346
Tileagd (Telegd) : 105
Timiș, région de (Temesköz) : 110
Timișoara (Temesvár) : 115
Tisza, région de : 98
Toarcla : 40
Tongres : 99
Torda : voir Turda
Toulouse : 57, 216, 235
Tournai : 83
Tours : 252
Transylvanie : 40, 49, 56, 111, 188, 328, 334, 347
Trebnitz : voir Trzebnica
Třeboň : 321
Trente : 127
Trêves : 62, 70, 72
Trhové Sviny : 321
Trieste : 152
Trnava (Tyrnau) : 99, 152
Truso : 253
Trzebnica (Trebnitz), monastère : 126
Tschaslau : voir Čáslav
Turda (Torda, Thorenburg) : 56
Turku : 283
Turnov : 318
Tyrnau : voir Trnava

Újlak : voir Ilok
Ulm : voir Söflingen
Ústí nad Labem : 323-324

Városlőd : voir Lövöld
Veľká Lomnica (Kakaslomnic) : 297

INDEX

Veľky Slavkov : 301
Vénétie : 90
Venise : 85, 90-91, 105-106, 108, 113, 162, 283
Verdun : 346
Vérone : 250
Veselí-sur-Lužnice : 321
Veszprém : 93
Vidin : 336
Vienne : 43, 54-55, 282-283, 287
Voghera : 87, 90, 92, 106, 108
Vulcan : 40
Vyšehrad : 70
Vyšší Brod (Hohenfurth) : 285, 289

Wawel : 276, 278
Weichseldorf : voir Sâncraiul de Mureș
Weissenburg : voir Alba Iulia
Westminster : 74-75
Wilhering : 290
Wilsnack : 319
Wolkendorf : voir Vulcan
Wrocław (Breslau) : 153, 157, 197, 207, 230, 232, 239-240, 252
Würzburg : 85

Ząbkowice Śląskie : 16
Zagreb, couvent dominicain : 219
Zalakomár : 94
Zderaz : 73
Złotoryja (Goldberg) : 241
Znaim : voir Znojmo
Znojmo (Znaim), église franciscaine : 142
Zólyomszászfalu : voir Sásová

Table des matières – Table of Contents

Introduction, par Olivier MARIN.................................5

I
SAINTS ANCIENS ET SAINTS MODERNES : PERMANENCES, RÉINVENTIONS, CONCURRENCES

Petr KUBÍN, *Saints fondateurs et saints modernes dans la Bohême médiévale* 31

Carmen FLOREA, *The Universal Cult of the Virgin Martyrs in Late Medieval Transylvania* 39

David C. MENGEL, *Bohemia's Treasury of Saints: Relics and Indulgences in Emperor Charles IV's Prague* 57

Ottó GECSER, *Intercession and Specialization: St Sebastian and St Roche as Plague Saints and their Cult in Medieval Hungary* 77

Enikő CSUKOVITS, *Les saints libérateurs des Turcs en Hongrie à la fin du Moyen Âge* 109

II
L'EMPRISE DES ORDRES MENDIANTS

Christian-Frederik FELSKAU, *Shaping the Sainthood of a Central European Clarissan Princess. The Development and Fate of the Earliest Hagiographic Texts on Agnes of Bohemia and St Clare's Epistolary Tradition*...125

Eszter KONRÁD, *The Oldest Legend of Francis of Assisi and his Stigmatization in Old Hungarian Codex Literature (c. 1440-1530)* 173

Anna ZAJCHOWSKA, *Medieval Hagiography of St Hyacinth* 195

Anne Reltgen-Tallon, *Les martyrs dominicains de Hongrie et leur insertion réussie dans la mémoire hagiographique de l'Ordre des frères Prêcheurs* 211

Ludovic Viallet, *Sainteté et observance franciscaine en Europe centrale : Bernardin de Sienne et Jean de Capistran* 227

III
SAINTS D'IMPLANTATION ET SAINTS DE SOUCHE

Geneviève Bührer-Thierry, *Saint national ou saint européen ? Les tribulations d'Adalbert de Prague et de ses reliques dans le temps et dans l'espace (X^e-XIIe siècles)* 247

Stanislava Kuzmová, *The Old and the New: St Stanislaus and Other Cults in Krakow* 261

Edit Madas, *À la recherche des sources liturgiques et hagiographiques du culte des « saints rois » hongrois en Europe centrale* 281

Ivan Gerát, *Some Structural Comparisons of Pictorial Legends from Medieval Hungary* 293

Hana Pátková, *Les confréries, les métiers et le culte des saints dans la Bohême médiévale* 311

Conclusions, par Marie-Madeleine de Cevins 327

Résumés – Abstracts 351

INDEX

Index nominum 365

Index locorum 373